Spain FOR DUMMIES®

4TH EDITION

by Neil E. Schlecht

Wiley Publishing, Inc.

Spain For Dummies®, 4th Edition

Published by
Wiley Publishing, Inc.
111 River St.
Hoboken, NJ 07030-5774
www.wiley.com

For general information on our other products and services, please contact our Customer Care Department within the U.S. at 800-762-2974, outside the U.S. at 317-572-3993, or fax 317-572-4002.

For technical support, please visit www.wiley.com/techsupport.

Wiley also publishes its books in a variety of electronic formats. Some content that appears in print may not be available in electronic books.

Library of Congress Control Number: 2007920010

ISBN: 978-0-470-10573-3

Manufactured in the United States of America

10 9 8 7 6 5 4 3 2 1

Spain For Dummies®, 4th Edition

Cheat Sheet

A List of Handy Spanish Words and Phrases

English	*Spanish*	*Spanish Pronunciation*
Thank you	*Gracias*	*grah*-thyahs
Please	*Por favor*	por fah-*bohr*
Yes/No/And	*Sí/No/Y*	see/no/ee
Do you speak English?	*¿Habla usted inglés?*	*ah*-blah oo-*sted* een-*glehs*
I don't understand	*No comprendo*	no cohm-*pren*-doh
I'm sorry	*Lo siento*	lo *syen*-toh
Good day/ Good evening	*Buenos días/ Buenas tardes*	*bweh*-nohs *dee*-ahs/ *bweh*-nahs *tar*-dehs
Excuse me (to get attention)	*Perdóneme*	pehr-*doh*-neh-meh
Excuse me (to get past someone)	*Perdón/Disculpe*	pehr-*dohn*/ dee-*skool*-peh
How much is it?	*¿Cuánto cuesta?*	*kwan*-toh *kweh*-stah
Where is . . . ? . . . the bathroom . . . the train station	*¿Dónde está . . . ? . . . el servicio/el baño/ el lavabo . . . la estación*	*dohn*-deh eh-*stah* el sehr-*bee*-thyoh/el *bah*-nyoh/ el lah-*bah*-boh lah es-tah-thee-*yon*
to the right/ to the left	*a la derecha a la izquierda*	ah lah deh-*reh*-chah/ ah lah ee-*thkyehr*-dah
straight ahead	*siga derecho*	*see*-gah deh-*reh*-choh
ticket	*un billete*	oon bee-*yeh*-teh
first class/ second class	*primera clase/ segunda clase*	pree-*meh*-rah *klah*-seh/ seh-*goon*-dah *klah*-seh
one-way/round trip	*ida/ida y vuelta*	*ee*-dah/*ee*-dah ee *bwehl*-tah
a double room for X nights	*una habitación doble por X noches*	*oo*-nah ah-bee-ta-*thyon doh*-bleh por X *noh*-chehs
1/2/3	*uno/dos/tres*	*oo* noh/dohs/trehs
restaurant	*un restaurante*	oon reh-stow-*rahn*-teh
I would like . . . . . . some of this/that . . . a glass of . . . sparkling water/ still water . . . red wine/white wine . . . beer	*Quisiera . . . . . . algunos de éste/ése . . . un vaso de agua con gas/sin gas vino tinto/vino blanco cerveza*	kee-*syeh*-rah al-*goo*-nos deh *eh*-steh/*eh*-seh oon *bah*-soh deh *ah*-gwah cohn gahs/seen gahs *bee*-noh *teen*-toh/*bee*-noh *blahn*-coh thehr-*beh*-thah
The check, please	*La cuenta, por favor*	lah *kwehn*-tah por fah-*bohr*
Is the tip included?	*¿Está incluido el servicio?*	eh-*stah* een-*clwee*-doh el sehr- *bee*-thyo

Recommended Spanish Wines

I recommend seeking out the following wines while touring Spain.

Reds (Tintos)

- **Rioja:** Viña Ardanza, Allende, Imperial, CVNE, Marqués de Riscal, La Rioja Alta, San Vicente, Castillo de Ygay, López Heredia, Muga, Remírez Ganuza, Roda, Artadi
- **Ribera del Duero Reds:** Condado de Haza, Pago de los Capellanes, Emilio Moro, Pesquera, Hacienda Monasterio, Aalto, Atauta, Alión, Mauro, Leda, Vega Sicilia
- **Toro:** Quinta Quietud, San Román, Dos Victorias, Pintia, Numanthia
- **Priorat:** Cims de Porrera, Clos Martinet, Clos Mogador, Mas Doix, Vall Llach, L'Ermita
- **Jumilla:** Casa Castillo, Finca Sandoval
- **Montsant:** Celler de Capçanes, Joan d'Anguera
- **Others:** Dominio de Valdepusa/Marqués de Griñón (Toledo), Castillo de Perelada (Penedès), Chivite (Navarra), Dominio de Tares (Bierzo), Torres (Penedès)

Whites (Blancos)

- **Albariño** (from Galicia): Lagar de Cervera, Laxa, Martín Codax, Terras Gaudia, Pazo de Señorans
- **Rioja:** Muga, Marqués de Riscal, López-Heredia
- **Rueda:** Dos Victorias José Pariente, MartinSancho, Belondrade y Lurton

Other

- **Cava** (sparkling wine from Catalonia): Agustí Torelló, Avinyó, Gramona, Juvé y Camps, Segura Viudas
- **Sherry:** San León (manzanilla), Tío Pepe (fino), Alvear (Pedro Ximénez)

Recommended Vintages for Rioja and Ribera del Duero Wines

Year	Rioja	Ribera del Duero	Year	Rioja	Ribera del Duero
1990	Good	Excellent	1998	Excellent	Excellent
1991	Average	Average	1999	Excellent	Excellent
1992	Good	Good	2000	Excellent	Excellent
1993	Average	Fair	2001	Outstanding	Outstanding
1994	Outstanding	Excellent	2002	Average	Average
1995	Outstanding	Outstanding	2003	Good	Good
1996	Excellent	Outstanding	2004	Outstanding	Outstanding
1997	Good	Good	2005	Excellent	Very good

Plan your trip with For Dummies

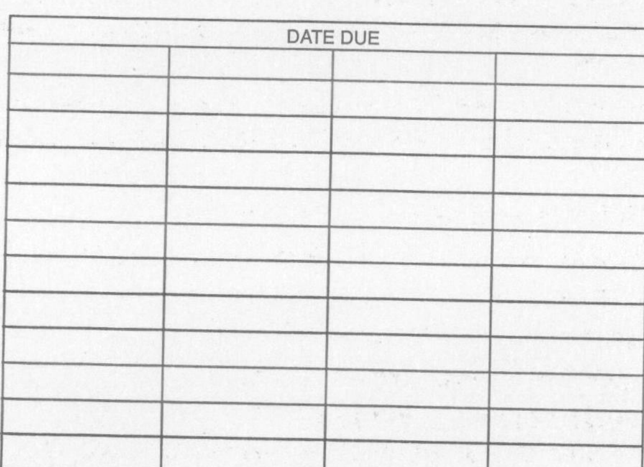

- Share trip photos and stories
- And much more

Frommers.com, rated the
#1 Travel Web Site by PC Magazine

About the Author

A writer and cycling aficionado who has lived in Spain, Brazil, and Ecuador, **Neil E. Schlecht** now resides in Litchfield County, Connecticut. His first exposure to Spain was as a college sophomore teaching English at Col.legi Sant Ignasi in Barcelona. He returned to Barcelona just before the 1992 Summer Olympics and stayed for most of the following decade, working as a consultant on social and economic development projects for the European Union and as a contributing writer for a Spanish art and antiques magazine. The author of a dozen travel guides, as well as articles on art and culture and art catalogue essays, Neil is especially keen on assignments that take him back to Spain.

The author counts among the highlights of his Spanish travels a few treasured road miles cycling in the Navarra countryside alongside Miguel Indurain, Spain's five-time Tour de France champion. Neil's favorite reminder of Spain is his Labrador retriever, who hails from a farm on Ibiza, one of the Balearic Islands. Despite her relocation to the United States, she plays deaf to any commands not in Spanish.

Dedication

To Keny, who immersed me in the ways of Spain, and Solà, whose wine-fueled *charlas* in his art studio helped me interpret them.

And to Sharon, who makes me want to hurry home.

Author's Acknowledgments

A special thanks (and *un abrazo muy fuerte*) to Pilar Vico of the Tourist Office of Spain in New York. Her generosity and good-natured assistance proved essential to the completion of this book.

Publisher's Acknowledgments

We're proud of this book; please send us your comments through our Dummies online registration form located at www.dummies.com/register/.

Some of the people who helped bring this book to market include the following:

Editorial

Editors: Matthew Brown, Development Editor; Suzanna R. Thompson, Production Editor

Copy Editor: Cara Buitron

Cartographer: Roberta Stockwell

Editorial Assistant: Melinda Quintero

Senior Photo Editor: Richard Fox

Cover Photos:

Front: Sierra Nevada and the Alhambra in Andalusia (© John Lawrence/Getty Images)

Back: Girls in traditional costume in Seville's Plaza de España (© Anthony Cassidy/Getty Images)

Cartoons: Rich Tennant (www.the5thwave.com)

Composition Services

Project Coordinator: Patrick Redmond

Layout and Graphics: Claudia Bell, Carl Byers, Julie Trippetti

Special Art: Anniversary Logo Design: Richard Pacifico

Proofreaders: Laura Albert, Jessica Kramer, Sossity R. Smith

Indexer: Aptara

Publishing and Editorial for Consumer Dummies

Diane Graves Steele, Vice President and Publisher, Consumer Dummies

Joyce Pepple, Acquisitions Director, Consumer Dummies

Kristin A. Cocks, Product Development Director, Consumer Dummies

Michael Spring, Vice President and Publisher, Travel

Kelly Regan, Editorial Director, Travel

Publishing for Technology Dummies

Andy Cummings, Vice President and Publisher, Dummies Technology/General User

Composition Services

Gerry Fahey, Vice President of Production Services

Debbie Stailey, Director of Composition Services

Contents at a Glance

Maps at a Glance

Table of Contents

Introduction

For decades Spain has ranked as one of Europe's premier vacation destinations, popular among both Europeans and visitors the world over. If you've been considering a trip to Europe, but haven't been sure which country would best fit your interests and budget, Spain makes a superb choice for just about everyone. It appeals to the art lover, ecotourist, historian, gourmand, pop-culture scholar, backpacker, and unrepentant hedonist. And, although Spain may no longer be the European destination of choice for individuals on a budget — who among us remembers *Europe on Five Dollars a Day*? — bargain hunters can still find enticing deals across the country.

One of Europe's oldest yet most dynamic countries, Spain offers rich travel experiences: architecture dating back to the Romans and Moors, some of Europe's most spectacular art museums, warm and welcoming people, vibrant festivals, fantastic food, and brilliant weather. Its well-rounded roster of attractions makes it ideal for year-round vacationing; you can soak up the good life at outdoor cafes, hit the beaches, and join sports-mad Spaniards in everything from golfing and boating to cycling and skiing. Spain is a nation of many cultures, traditions, and even languages. From the stoic independence of the Basques to the progressive architecture and design of the Catalans and the sultry rhythms and sun-drenched siestas of the Andalusians, you will discover a country that in fact comprises many Spains and many different Spaniards.

Since its incorporation into the European Union, Spain has represented one of the E.U.'s most rapidly modernizing nations. Yet many parts of the country refreshingly hold on to ancient Spanish traditions and mores. It's not yet a place where the young and old speak English as well as they do their native tongue — so you may have to trot out some beginner's Spanish to get by when visiting. Spain is one of the most relaxed and rewarding European countries you can visit, and compared to many northern European nations, it still remains affordable. You shouldn't have to kiss your retirement fund goodbye for a two-week jaunt to Spain.

About This Book

Spain is one of Europe's largest countries, so it's unlikely that you can go everywhere you want — at least not on a single trip. You have to pick and choose carefully, and that's where this book comes in handy. Rather than try and pack the entire country into a tome that's too heavy to carry around, I focus on the best of the best, the top destinations for a first- or second-time traveler to Spain — the places you just have to see, the best spots to stay and eat, and the easiest ways to design efficient regional trips instead of trying desperately to scurry across the country. I also offer you tips for saving money and give you careful selections and recommendations in every crucial category, from small, intimate inns to tantalizing tapas bars (bars that serve Spanish appetizers). Furthermore, I provide detailed insider information on activities such as choosing the best seat at a bullfight. And just as important, I steer you away from the places that really aren't worth your time.

This book differs from other guides. It doesn't just dump the information in your lap and expect you to sort it all out, somehow unearthing the gems in all that rough. I've traveled throughout Spain for nearly two decades now, and in this book, I list the destinations and activities that I recommend to my family and close friends. Spaniards are famously welcoming and helpful, but if you've never been there, arriving in Madrid or Barcelona and just winging it would be pretty daunting. I've done the homework so that you can hit the ground running — or relaxing, if that's more your speed.

I load *Spain For Dummies,* 4th Edition, with easy-to-understand information and advice about Spanish customs, culture, and, of course, language. The best place to start, though, may be with two simple phrases you're likely to hear frequently in Spain: ***Bienvenido*** (Welcome) and ***¡Salud!*** (Cheers!).

Conventions Used in This Book

In this book I use some standard terminology to help you access information quickly and easily. I give all prices in euros, the common European Union currency. The euro has held its strength relative to U.S. dollar, with the rate of exchange at 1:1.20 or even slightly higher. For last-minute updates on the exchange rate, please see one of the currency conversion tables in major newspapers or online (such as at `http://money.cnn.com/markets/currencies`).

I use the Spanish method for providing street addresses. Using this style, the building number comes after the street name, not before. For example, if a hotel has a building number of 22 and is located on Calle Atocha (Atocha Street), the address is written "Calle Atocha 22." Likewise, in many small towns, you often come across an address in which the building has no number. In these cases, the address is written "Calle Atocha, s/n," where s/n stands for *sin número* (without number).

I compile my favorite hotels, restaurants, and attractions across Spain. Especially for the hotels and restaurants, I include abbreviations for commonly accepted credit cards:

AE American Express

DC Diners Club

MC MasterCard

V Visa

In the larger destinations, I divide hotels into two categories: my personal favorites (in a variety of price categories) and those that don't quite make the standout list but are still very much worth a stay. Don't be shy about considering these "runners up" if you're unable to get a room at one of my favorites or if your preferences diverge.

What the Dollar Signs Mean

Cost	*Hotel*	*Restaurant*
$	less than 50€ ($60)	less than 15€ ($18)
$$	50€–100€ ($60–$120)	15€–25€ ($18–$30)
$$$	101€–175€ ($121–$210)	26€–45€ ($31–$54)
$$$$	176€–275€ ($211–$330)	46€–75€ ($55–$90)
$$$$$	more than 275€ ($330)	more than 75€ ($90)

I define price categories as double room (and double occupancy) for hotels; for restaurants, it's the average cost of a three-course, à la carte lunch or dinner (appetizer, main course, dessert, one nonalcoholic drink, tax, and tip) for one person. Where available, a prix-fixe *menú del día* usually is cheaper, and a multicourse *menú de desgustación,* or tasting menu, more expensive.

For those hotels, restaurants, and attractions that are plotted on a map, I provide a page reference in the listing information. If, however, a hotel, restaurant, or attraction is outside the city limits or in an out-of-the-way area, it may not be mapped.

Travel information is subject to change at any time — this is especially true of prices. Therefore, with listings in this book, I suggest that you write or call ahead for confirmation when making your travel plans. As much as we've invested in the creation of this travel guide, the author, editors, and publisher can't be held responsible for the experiences of readers while traveling. Your safety is important to us, however, so above all, we encourage you to stay alert and pay attention to your surroundings. Keep a close eye on cameras, purses, and wallets — all favorite targets of thieves and pickpockets.

Foolish Assumptions

When writing this book, I make a few assumptions about you and what your needs may be as a traveler:

- You're an inexperienced traveler looking for guidance when determining whether to take a trip to Spain and how to plan for it.
- You're an experienced traveler, but you don't have much time to devote to trip planning, or you don't have much time to spend in Spain after you arrive. You want expert advice on how to maximize your time and enjoy a hassle-free trip.
- You're not looking for a book that provides every last bit of information available about Spain or one that lists every hotel, restaurant, or attraction available to you. Instead, you're looking for a book that focuses on the places that give you the best or most unique experiences in Spain.

If you fit any of these criteria, rest assured that *Spain For Dummies,* 4th Edition, gives you the information you're looking for!

How This Book Is Organized

Spain For Dummies, 4th Edition, is divided into six major parts. It starts with introductory information about the country and planning advice, and then moves on to the major regional sections, which contain individual destination chapters.

Part I: Introducing Spain

The first part introduces you to the glories of Spain and helps you decide exactly where and when to go. It gives tips on planning your budget and offers tailored tips to travelers with special interests — everything you need to consider before planning a trip to Spain.

Part II: Planning Your Trip to Spain

The second part helps you with all the nitty-gritty stuff — everything from deciding what documents you need to bring with you to searching the Web for more information. It helps you choose and book the best airfare and hotel (or package tour); understand how to get around Spain and how to budget and pay for your trip; and figure out exactly what you need to pack.

Part III: Northern Spain: Barcelona, the Costa Brava, and the Basque Country

In Parts III through V, you can find a chapter on each major destination in the region. Each chapter includes all you need to know about getting there and getting around; information on the top hotels and restaurants; recommendations of the best attractions and what to do, including shopping and nightlife; and details about easy day trips in the area.

Part III covers the best of Northeastern Spain, including Barcelona, the Costa Brava, and the Basque Country.

Part IV: Central Spain: Madrid and Castile

This part covers central Spain, which includes Madrid — Spain's capital — and the best of the surrounding region of Castile — Segovia, Salamanca, and Toledo. These destinations are all easy day trips from the capital.

Part V: Southern Spain: Andalusia

This part is all about the region of Andalusia: Seville and Córdoba; Ronda, the so-called *pueblos blancos* (white villages), and the sunny coasts; and Granada.

Part VI: The Part of Tens

With a nod to my habit of making and keeping lists, the final part is a couple of Top 10 lists — a compendium of both my personal faves and curious tidbits about Spain.

Appendix: Quick Concierge

I also include an appendix, the "Quick Concierge," which contains handy information that you may need when traveling in Spain, such as phone numbers and addresses for emergency personnel or area hospitals and pharmacies, contact information for babysitters, lists of local newspapers and magazines, protocol for sending mail or finding taxis, and more. Check out this appendix when searching for answers to the many little questions that may come up as you travel.

Icons Used in This Book

Keep your eyes peeled for these icons, which appear in the margins:

This icon provides you tips on pinching euros and cutting corners to make your trip more affordable, as well as activities that are, in my opinion, great deals.

Best of the Best highlights the best the destination has to offer in all categories — hotels, restaurants, attractions, activities, shopping, and nightlife.

Watch for the Heads Up icon to identify annoying or potentially dangerous situations such as tourist traps, unsafe neighborhoods, budgetary rip-offs, and other things to beware. On occasion, Heads Up icons also indicate words to the wise aimed to make you look and feel less like a *guiri* (foreigner).

Find out useful advice on what to do and ways to schedule your time when you see the Tip icon.

Look to the Kid Friendly icon for attractions, hotels, restaurants, and activities that are particularly hospitable to children or people traveling with kids.

This symbol designates authentic doses of Spanish culture and España at its most real, from customs to food and drink.

Where to Go from Here

Spain for Dummies, 4th Edition, is designed for use as a reference text. You don't have to plow through all the chapters like a novel from front to back; the chapters function independently of each other, allowing you to pick up any planning section or city or regional chapter without worrying about losing out on information placed elsewhere in the book.

At this point, you're ready to dive into Spain and design the trip that best suits you. You don't need to get all stressed out about finding time to brush up on your Spanish, visit travel agents, research Spain, and plan your trip at the same time. Relax. Planning your trip doesn't have to be a hassle, and daydreaming about all the cool stuff you'll see and do can actually be fun.

Part I
Introducing Spain

"And how shall I book your flight to Spain -First Class, Coach, or Medieval?"

In this part . . .

I highlight my choices for the best of Spain and give you a concise overview of the country, including its people, art and architecture, history, cuisine, and some of its biggest attractions region by region.

Use the information in this part to help you decide where and when to go to Spain.

Chapter 1

Discovering the Best of Spain

In This Chapter

- Enjoying Spain's unique travel experiences
- Admiring ancient and modern architecture
- Staying at the coolest hotels
- Tempting your taste buds
- Appreciating great art at Spain's finest museums

It's easy to rhapsodize about many things in Spain, so vast is its history and culture and so delightful are its people, cuisine, and wines. You'll literally trip over your own contenders for the best restaurants, hotels, architecture, and museums, no matter where you go. Surely you'll return from a trip to Spain having compiled your own "best travel experiences."

The following are places and experiences that rank among the best I've encountered in a couple of decades of travel in Spain. I consider many to be "must-sees" that I'd recommend to any friend going to Spain. In others, you might just as well treat them as suggestions and jumping-off points. The idea, though, isn't for you to just check off my list of what I think is best, but to plunge into Spain and discover for yourself all that it has to offer.

The Best Travel Experiences

- **Strolling Barcelona's La Rambla.** Much more than just a pretty mile-long pedestrian boulevard, La Rambla is a vibrant street parade and the epicenter of life in the Catalan capital. Lined with newspaper kiosks, fresh-flower stands, bird sellers, human statues in elaborate costumes and face paint, and historic buildings, it's where locals come day after day to practice the art of the *paseo* (stroll). Stop for tapas, dip into the redolent Boquería food market, and continue your rambles in the Gothic Quarter — the city's oldest section and a maze of palaces, squares, antiques shops, and surprises. See Chapter 10.

- **Racing with beasts at the Running of the Bulls.** If you're nuts enough to run, you'll be running from, not with, the bulls. Every July, Pamplona hosts the festival of San Fermín and the *encierro,* a mad, exhilarating rush in which throngs of locals and tourists high-tail it through narrow cobbled streets with one-ton beasts nipping at their heels. To live it up, you don't have to run; the 24/7 festival ranks as one of Europe's great party scenes, with nonstop drinking and dancing (and sleeping) in the streets. Whether you run or just watch safely behind barriers, you're unlikely to forget the mayhem. See Chapter 12.
- **Tripping along on a tavern and tapas crawl.** The most inescapable element of Spanish cooking is tapas, small snacks now popular the world over. A *tapeo* is the food equivalent of an Irish pub crawl — a bar-to-bar treasure hunt, searching for and wolfing down finger foods that range from the endearingly simple, such as a wedge of tortilla omelet, to the piled-high *pintxos* in the Basque Country. You'll see Spaniards at their most festive and famished when they're out grazing. Traipse along the streets of medieval **Madrid,** the Triana neighborhood across the river in **Seville,** San Sebastián's **Parte Vieja,** the old town of **Bilbao,** or the Gothic Quarter in **Barcelona** — or any small town in Spain, for that matter. Pop into a tavern, knock back a drink and a couple of snacks, and hit the road, onto your next stop. See Chapters 10, 12, 13, and 15.
- **Getting lost in a tangle of time.** Spain overflows with fine museums, excellent repositories of Spanish art and history, but Spaniards live with their history on a daily basis. As a visitor, wandering the crooked streets in a lively old quarter makes for an exceptionally enjoyable history lesson.

  The streets of **Toledo** may be impossible to make sense of, but they teem with synagogues, mosques, and palaces — centuries of Jewish, Moorish, and Christian history. Cordoba's **Judería** and Girona's **El Call,** two of Spain's best-preserved old Jewish quarters, are appealing mazes of white-washed streets, while Barcelona's **Barri Gòtic** (Gothic Quarter) is a slightly spooky but vibrant warren of alleyways that once formed the core of a walled-in city. **Salamanca's old quarter** around the stunning Plaza Mayor is the place to relive the academic life and extracurricular activities of university students. Other great places to wander, get lost, and absorb a dose of history are Granada's **Albaycín** district, San Sebastián's **Parte Vieja,** Bilbao's **Casco Viejo,** and Seville's enchanting **Barrio de Santa Cruz.** See Chapters 10, 12, 13, 14, 15, and 17.
- **Joining the faithful at Andalusia's fiestas.** There's nothing quite like the stately pageantry of springtime festivals in southern Spain. The biggies are **Semana Santa** (Holy Week) and **Feria de Abril,** the April Fair that erupts two weeks after Easter in Seville. The galas

transform Seville into the most festive and colorful place in Spain. For Easter, the mood is deadly serious: Long processions parade throughout the city carrying religious floats, accompanied by penitents in long robes and pointy hoods, dirge music, and candles. The Feria de Abril is the purging after Easter, when the city erupts with a festival of flamenco and *sevillana* dancing, drinking, horse parades, and gorgeously bedecked Andalusian women in polka-dotted flamenco dresses. At the end of May, the **El Rocío pilgrimage** in Huelva is perhaps the rowdiest religious festival you'll witness. Attending one of the big festivals can mean extra headaches in terms of hotel rooms, crowds, and expense, but that's the cost of cultural immersion. See Chapter 15.

- **Appreciating art for art's sake.** Name the greatest artists of all time, and you'll count a significant, perhaps even disproportionate, number of Spaniards among them. You can view many of the masterpieces at some of the finest art museums in Europe. Madrid's **Prado,** endowed by kings, has monumental works by Velázquez, El Greco, and Goya (as well as great Italian and Flemish works). Pablo Picasso's impassioned *Guernica* is on view down the street at the **Reina Sofía**, as are the works of many other modern masters. Barcelona boasts an impressive collection of Picasso's early works, single-artist museums dedicated to native sons Joan Miró and Antoni Tàpies, and a splendid collection of Romanesque and Gothic religious art at the **Museu Nacional d'Art de Catalunya.** Salvador Dalí's tortured genius holds surreal court at several museums in Spain, but the best place to get a taste of his unique gifts is his museum-theater in Figueres (Catalonia) and the home-museums he left behind in the Catalan countryside. See Chapter 10, 11, 13, and 15.
- **Meandering through Andalusia's *pueblos blancos.*** Dotting the rolling hills and earthy olive groves of southern Spain is a collection of tiny, picturesque whitewashed villages, some dramatically perched atop 1,524m (5,000-ft.) limestone slopes. Onetime defensive strongholds under the Moors, the perfect white towns are tiny mazes of medieval alleyways. The two largest *pueblos blancos* are **Ronda** and **Arcos de la Frontera;** from a base at either, you can easily take a driving tour of the many villages that lie between. See Chapter 16.

The Best Architectural Landmarks

- **Barcelona's *moderniste* madness.** The Catalan Art Nouveau movement, known locally as *modernisme,* was spearheaded by the austere aesthete Antoni Gaudí, the stunningly imaginative architect behind the futuristic (but still unfinished) cathedral **La Sagrada Familia** and the wondrously wavy **La Pedrera** (Casa Milà). But Gaudí was just one of several *moderniste* masters who left their imprints on Barcelona. Follow the city's **Ruta del Modernisme** and visit some of the other standouts, such as the apartment houses on Paseo de Gracia's Manzana de la Discordia (Block of Discord). See Chapter 10.

- **Museo Guggenheim Bilbao.** Frank Gehry's rapturous titanium sculpture on the banks of the River Nervión not only single-handedly revitalized industrial Bilbao, it revolutionized the way the public sees art museums, setting off a competition among cities across the globe to get their own Gehry (or something nearly as distinct and attention-grabbing). Critics have called it the greatest building of the modern era. Even if the structure were devoid of art inside, droves would come to experience its sensual curves and soaring presence. See Chapter 12.
- **Segovia's Roman Aqueduct.** Going on 2,000 years, the graceful Roman Aqueduct is one of the greatest examples of Roman engineering — in Spain or anywhere. Constructed of massive blocks of granite, in A.D. 90, without the aid of mortar or clamps, the 1km-long (⅔ of a mile) aqueduct is 29m (95 ft.) high and has 166 perfectly designed arches. Whether appreciated as a feat of engineering or for the incredible beauty with which it stretches across the city, it's one of Spain's most memorable sights, especially when illuminated at night. See Chapter 14.
- **Avila's city walls.** The imposing city walls *(murallas)* that enclose the small but surprisingly plain city of Avila are perhaps the finest in Europe. Built in 1090, Spain's very own great wall is 2.4km (1½ miles) long, 11m (36 ft.) high, and 3m (9 ft.) thick. If you're an architecture buff, get up close for a view of how remarkably unscathed the walls remain, and then retreat to see them framed against the horizon, from Cuatro Postes (Four Pillars), an old shrine just beyond the river. See Chapter 14.
- **Salamanca's stunning Old Quarter.** A university town and a living museum of early Spanish Renaissance architecture, Salamanca is a stately assembly of unique architecture built around Spain's loveliest Plaza Mayor. Salamanca's architecture is renowned for ornate Plateresque details — masterful Baroque carving — on stately facades. See Chapter 14.
- **Cordoba's Mezquita.** After the Alhambra, the great mosque stands as the pre-eminent architectural achievement of the Moorish dynasty that ruled Spain for 700 years. Unlike any mosque you've ever seen, the eighth-century structure dazzles visitors with a magical forest of candy cane–striped arches, consisting of more than 850 columns constructed of granite, jasper, and marble. See Chapter 15.
- **Granada's Alhambra.** The supreme achievement of the Moors, and one of the greatest pieces of architecture anywhere in Europe, is the spectacular fortress and palace complex La Alhambra, a place of magic, mystery, and legend. Built by the Nasrid dynasty in the

13th and 14th centuries, it's a stunning, sprawling, and serene compound of palaces, residences, mosques, gardens, reflecting pools, patios, and a royal summer estate. It truly is as the Moors' intended — an earthly paradise. See Chapter 17.

The Best Luxury Hotels

- **Hotel Arts** (Barcelona; ☎ **800-241-3333** or 93-221-10-00). This waterfront high-rise overlooks Barcelona's beaches and is within easy reach of the Gothic Quarter and Las Ramblas. It's a model of modern, high-tech sophistication. Rooms are spacious and airy, with dazzling views of the Mediterranean Sea and the city creeping up into the hills. See Chapter 10.
- **Hotel Claris** (Barcelona; ☎ **800-888-4747** in the United States, or 93-487-62-62). The Catalan capital's other great top-of-the-line hotel is wonderfully eclectic: Its chic contemporary design coexists easily with a 19th-century palace facade and a private museum of Egyptian art. This hotel draws a stylish crowd. See Chapter 10.
- **Gran Hotel Domine Bilbao** (Bilbao; ☎ **94-425-33-00**). A luxury hotel with hipster design cred and abundant style, its primary calling card is its unrivaled location: Across the street looms the titanium juggernaut that has the world beelining to Bilbao, the Guggenheim Museum. Rooms are sleek, and the lounge resounds with retro charm. See Chapter 12.
- **Hotel María Cristina** (San Sebastián; ☎ **888-625-5144** in the United States, or 943-43-76-00 in Spain). A stately, Belle Epoque hotel where stars hunker down for the San Sebastián Film Festival, this place has formal grace and unrestrained Old World opulence. It can't be beat in northern Spain. See Chapter 12.
- **AC Palacio del Retiro** (Madrid; ☎ **902-29-22-93**). Overlooking the serene expanse of Retiro Park and within walking distance of the Prado, this handsome upscale hotel, in a beautiful early-20th-century palace, adds a perfect dose of modern style and creature comforts to a historic structure. See Chapter 13.
- **AC Ciudad de Toledo** (Toledo; ☎ **902-29-22-93** or 925-28-51-25). With spectacular views across the river to Toledo, pretty nearly as El Greco painted it, this stylish, modern, midsize hotel with cheerfully decorated rooms is the top choice in this tourist magnet south of Madrid. See Chapter 14.
- **AC Palacio de San Esteban** (Salamanca; ☎ **923-26-22-96**). Tasteful contemporary design complements the historic shell of a 16th-century convent in the heart of Salamanca's monumental quarter. Though chic and minimalist, the building's beautiful bones, including stone walls, arched ceilings, and an interior courtyard, have been lovingly preserved. See Chapter 14.

- **Hotel Alfonso XIII** (Seville; ☎ **800-325-3535** in the United States, or 95-491-70-00). One of Spain's most famous hotels, this historic place is a favorite of royalty and others with noble means. At the edge of lush María Luisa park, it is elegance incarnate, with marble floors, carved wooden ceilings, and Moorish arches and tiles. It has plenty of attitude to go with its exalted status. See Chapter 15.
- **Hacienda Benazuza** (Sanlúcar la Mayor/Seville ☎ **95-570-33-44**). In the countryside about 16km (10 miles) outside Seville, this lovely farmhouse estate, an Arab country house dating to the tenth century, seems far too extravagant to be a hotel. It pampers guests in rustic Andalusian luxury, and the restaurant, overseen by the famed chef of El Bulli in Catalonia, ranks as one of the most exclusive in Spain. See Chapter 15.
- **Casa de Carmona** (Carmona; ☎ **95-419-10-00**). In a pretty small town 32km (20 miles) east of Seville, this magnificent property gracefully inhabits a distinguished Renaissance palace. The small hotel evokes a feeling of aristocratic luxury and privilege, with chess and billiard rooms and a richly styled library. See Chapter 15.
- **AC Palacio de Santa Paula** (Granada; ☎ **902-29-22-93**). A beautifully converted convent is home to Granada's plushest accommodations. Though its location can't compete with the Parador de San Francisco (within the grounds of the Alhambra), it has style to burn, a winning mix of contemporary and historic design. See Chapter 17.

The Best Unique and Boutique Hotels

- **Prestige Paseo de Gracia** (Barcelona; ☎ **902-20-04-14**). Surrounded by the city's most upscale shops and quintessential *moderniste* buildings, this new boutique hotel is a quiet, Zen-like retreat bathed in soothing style. Confident and restrained, it does design as well as any hotel in the city, but never shouts its cutting edge. See Chapter 10.
- **Relais d'Orsà** (Barcelona; ☎ **93-406-94-11**). High on a hill with a bird's-eye view of Barcelona and the sea is this handsome secret of an inn laid out in a palace dating to 1900. Refined and oh so relaxing, it exudes a fresh air that's not really a part of the city, though getting down to Gaudí and the Ramblas is easy enough if you can tear yourself away. See Chapter 10.
- **La Plaça de Madremanya** (Baix Empordà; ☎ **972-49-04-87**). Part fine-dining establishment and part relaxed country hotel, this delightful little place, converted from a 15th-century farmhouse, has an abundance of chic style. Terraces overlook gardens, an architectural pool, and green rolling hills. The restaurant, La Plaça, is among the best north of Barcelona. See Chapter 11.

- **Castell de'Empordà** (Baix Empordà; ☎ **972-64-62-54**). This winning rural inn exhibits a comfort and elegance that belie the fact that it's in a 700-year-old castle. Although rooms in the castle, tower, or more modern annex are all inviting, you'll be drawn outdoors to the handsome pool, gardens, and terrace with serene views of the plains and rolling hills of the Baix Empordà. See Chapter 11.
- **Miróhotel** (Bilbao; ☎ **94-66118-80**). One of Spain's hippest fashion designers, Antonio Miró, created this chic, modern boutique hotel just down the street from the Guggenheim Museum. The high-tech hotel is like Miró's clothes: clean, cool, artful, and quietly luxurious. See Chapter 12.
- **Posada Mayor de Migueloa** (Laguardia; ☎ **945-62-11-75**). In a tiny, hilltop medieval town in the heart of the Rioja wine region, this charming and friendly family-run inn is a place for wine aficionados and gourmands. Rooms are cozy, the restaurant is first-rate, and the cavernous wine cellars deep beneath the inn have been storing wine since the early 17th century. See Chapter 12.
- **Villa Soro** (San Sebastián; ☎ **943-29-79-70**). An exquisite small hotel in a late-19th-century villa nestled in a residential neighborhood of San Sebastián, Villa Soro combines the services of an upscale hotel with the intimacy (and more accessible prices) of an inn. Quiet and elegant, it's a perfect discreet retreat — and it's just down the street from one of Spain's finest restaurants, Arzak. See Chapter 12.
- **Parador Príncipe de Viana** (Olite; ☎ **948-74-00-00**). This fine *parador,* or state-owned hotel, has bones no other hotel can match. In Olite, one of the oldest towns in the Navarrese kingdom, just south of Pamplona, it's ensconced within one section of the fairytale medieval Palacio Real de Olite, the royal palace and castle topped by cone-shaped turrets. See Chapter 12.
- **Casa de Madrid** (Madrid; ☎ **91-559-57-91**). Bed and breakfasts aren't exactly common in Spain, and although technically a B&B, this swank little place is more like a small 18th-century palace. Perfectly located near an actual palace, the Palacio Real, the seven rooms are superbly decorated with antiques and rich fabrics. A few rooms have kitchenettes, ideal for longer stays. See Chapter 13.
- **Hotel Residencia Rector** (Salamanca; ☎ **923-21-84-82**). This fine small hotel, in a distinguished mansion at the edge of Salamanca's monumental historic district, is an oasis of refined calm. It gets all the details exactly right, and the friendly, unobtrusive service is unequaled in hotels of this size. You'll think you've stepped into a five-star luxury hotel, only the prices are much friendlier. See Chapter 14.
- **Casa de los Azulejos** (Córdoba; ☎ **957-47-00-00**). Finally, a small hotel worthy of the gorgeous Mezquita and old Jewish quarter in Córdoba. The 17th-century colonial house features a central patio

overflowing with plants and just eight character-filled, colorful rooms — which don't lack for the Andalusian tile floors of the inn's name. See Chapter 15.

- **Hotel Las Casas de la Judería** (Seville; ☎ **95-441-51-50**). Tucked into a tiny street at the edge of the Santa Cruz neighborhood, this midsize hotel, part of a small chain, nailed an unbeatable formula — stylish inns housed in historic mansions — and begat a wave of imitators across Seville and the rest of Andalusia. In a 17th-century palace that once belonged to the patron of Cervantes, it wears its colorful history with a dose of good cheer. See Chapter 15.
- **Hotel San Gabriel** (Ronda; ☎ **95-219-03-92**). This folksy and family-operated inn aims to be more personal even than most boutique hotels. The friendly owners and their children put their heart and soul into this lovely 1736 mansion, and San Gabriel is as cozy as staying at your favorite aunt's house — if she lived in a beautiful, historical part of charming Ronda. A bargain. See Chapter 16.
- **Hotel Casa Morisca** (Granada; ☎ **958-22-11-00**). This is a romantic and magical place to stay after you've visited the Alhambra, which itself is romantic and magical and then some. This small inn, in a 15th-century villa in the Arab quarter, is similar in style to the nearby, equally atmospheric **Palacio de Santa Inés** and **Carmen de Santa Inés.** See Chapter 17.

The Best Fine Dining Restaurants

- **Àbac** (Barcelona; ☎ **93-319-66-00**). A pioneer in El Born, the hippest dining scene in Barcelona, still-trendy Àbac continues to stand out for its confident and stylish presentation of Catalan haute cuisine. Details clearly matter here, and this chic restaurant competes with the best in Spain. See Chapter 10.
- **Comerç 24** (Barcelona; ☎ **93-319-21-02**). A creative and chic take on tapas by one of Barcelona's hottest young chefs, this Born district spot is cool enough to be a nightclub. And the suitably theatrical tapas are tiny works of art. See Chapter 10.
- **El Celler de Can Roca** (Girona; ☎ **972-22-21-57**). Just outside of Girona is this modern but relaxed restaurant that showcases the individual talents of three brothers. One is the chef, another the wine master, and the youngest the dessert wizard. Dining here is a culinary treat of the imagination, with flavors and presentation that are cutting edge but not self conscious. See Chapter 11.
- **El Bulli** (Roses/Catalonia; ☎ **972-15-04-57**). North of Cadaqués on the Costa Brava is one of the most famous and innovative restaurants in Europe. Foodies from around the world fight for reservations at Ferrán Adrià's legendarily experimental and influential dining palace, which is open just six months a year. If you think you've had

inventive cuisine, you'll reassess all that's come before — if you can get in. See Chapter 11.

- **Zortziko** (Bilbao; ☎ **94-423-97-43**). Basques are famous for their cooking, and Bilbao's top restaurant is right up there with San Sebastián's finest. The elegant and formal dining room allows patrons to appreciate Daniel García's memorable menu of both innovative dishes and traditional Basque dishes. The wine cellar is one of the most impressive in the region. See Chapter 12.
- **Akelarre** (San Sebastián; ☎ **943-31-12-09**). Pedro Subijana's distinguished restaurant, on a hill above the Bay of La Concha, is a major destination for gourmands. A perennial, amicable rival of the other San Sebastián gurus, Arzak and Martín Berasategui, Subijana is perhaps the most classic of the three, but that's not to say he's not a creative artist in the kitchen. See Chapter 12.
- **Arzak** (San Sebastián; ☎ **943-27-84-65**). The standard-bearer of new Basque haute cuisine, Juan Mari Arzak refuses to rest on well-earned laurels. In a house that's been in his family for more than 100 years, Arzak and his daughter Elena run surely the friendliest gastronomic temple in Spain. Elegant but inviting, this is one place not to miss in Spain if you're serious about eating. See Chapter 12.
- **Martín Berasategui** (San Sebastián; ☎ **943-36-64-71**). How can one city have so many exquisite restaurants? The youngest of San Sebastián's top-ranked fine-dining establishments continues in the esteemed tradition of Arzak and Subijana, though the determined and creative Berasategui isn't one to be content. He's now involved with several restaurants, including the one at the Guggenheim Bilbao, but it's clear why this one carries his name. See Chapter 12.
- **Santceloni** (Madrid; ☎ **91-530-88-40**). Until recently, Madrid's top restaurants were formal and largely traditional. However, creative fine dining has arrived in a big way, and leading the pack is this chic and starkly modern place connected to the upscale Hespería hotel. Santi Santamaría, who has a thing for truffles and foie gras, has brought some of the flair and creativity of legendary El Bulli to the capital. See Chapter 13.
- **El Pecado** (Salamanca; ☎ **923-26-65-58**). Salamanca may be a dignified, ancient university town, but it gets an unexpected dose of Almodovarian flair at this campy but excellent restaurant not far from the Plaza Mayor. Outfitted with a wink-wink religious theme and named for wrongdoing, the kitchen makes few missteps in its creative, modern approach to Spanish cooking. See Chapter 14.
- **La Ermita** (Toledo; ☎ **925-25-31-93**). This sleek new restaurant is all picture windows looking across the river to Toledo on the hill. If you can distract yourself from the unrivalled view, you'll find a well-executed and refined contemporary menu, which adds a modern touch to traditional Castilian dishes. See Chapter 14.

- **Almudaina** (Córdoba; ☎ **957-47-43-42**). This elegant and inviting restaurant in a 16th-century mansion, with six dining rooms and a vine-covered patio, is Cordoba's most sophisticated. The market-based menu includes regional Andalusian as well as French dishes. See Chapter 15.
- **Egaña Oriza** (Seville; ☎ **95-422-72-11**). In Seville, land of fried finger foods, is this top-notch restaurant specializing in Basque cuisine. Elegantly located in a restored mansion just off the Murillo Gardens and near Parque María Luisa, it's the place to go in town for a unique dining experience. See Chapter 15.
- **Tragabuches** (Ronda; ☎ **95-219-02-91**). Quiet, charming Ronda, one of the south's "white villages," seems almost too easygoing to have a wildly inventive restaurant. With a young chef at the helm, unapologetically modern Tragabuches creates audacious interpretations of classic Andalusian dishes. See Chapter 16.

The Best Museums

- **Museu Picasso** (Barcelona; ☎ **93-319-63-10**). Before moving to Paris and making his mark as the greatest artist of the 20th century, Pablo Picasso spent much of early creative career in Barcelona. His museum in the Catalan capital, in a dazzling, sprawling palace in the Gothic Quarter, is the largest collection of his works in Spain. It's not comprehensive, but it's a great place to get a handle on Picasso's forming genius. Also of interest, in Picasso's native city in southern Spain, is the new Museo Picasso Málaga. See Chapters 10 and 16.
- **Museu Nacional d'Art de Catalunya** (**MNAC;** Barcelona; ☎ **93-622-03-76**). The foremost museum of Catalan medieval art, one of the best of its kind in the world, is a surprisingly lively and engrossing collection of Romanesque and Gothic. Especially cool is how the museum displays altarpieces, icons, and frescoes in apses, just as they were in the country churches in which they were found. See Chapter 10.
- **Teatre Museu Dalí** (Figueres; ☎ **972-67-75-00**). Salvador Dalí was one of the most famous artists of the 20th century, and the Catalan surrealist painter designed this funky theater-museum as his legacy. Oddball, idiosyncratic, and amusing, it's as much funhouse as it is museum. See Chapter 11.
- **Museo Chillida-Leku** (San Sebastián; ☎ **943-33-60-06**). On the outskirts of San Sebastián is the open-air museum of the city's favorite son and one of the greatest sculptors of the 20th century, Eduardo Chillida. Scattered around the pastoral grounds surrounding a 500-year-old farmhouse are a couple dozen of his monumental abstract sculptures in stone and iron. It makes for a lovely, relaxed outing, and it's great for families. See Chapter 12.

- **Museo del Prado** (Madrid; ☎ **91-330-28-00**). The granddaddy of Spanish museums and one of the very finest and most extensive classical art collections in the world, the Prado is a place art aficionados could get lost in for weeks. Even casual fans should thrill at the opportunity to see so many Old Masters and masterpieces by Velázquez, Goya, El Greco, Titian, Raphael, Botticelli, and Rubens. Velázquez's stunning masterpiece, *Las Meninas,* is the showstopper. See Chapter 13.
- **Museo Nacional Centro de Arte Reina Sofía** (Madrid; ☎ **91-467-50-62**). Madrid isn't only about Old Masters. The Reina Sofía is all about contemporary art, and you can't find a greater modern work than Picasso's *Guernica,* a massive statement about war that still sends shivers up the spine. The museum also possesses a wonderful collection of works by Miró, Dalí, and the top painters and sculptors of abstract expressionism, pop art, and minimalism. See Chapter 13.
- **Museo Thyssen-Bornemisza** (Madrid; ☎ **91-369-01-51**). A private collection purchased by the Spanish government, this major art museum contains more than 800 works that span the range of Western Art, from primitives and medieval art to 20th-century Avant Garde and Pop Art. It may not be the Prado (which is literally across the street), but it's the next best thing. See Chapter 13.

Chapter 2

Digging Deeper into Spain

In This Chapter

- Introducing Spain
- Reviewing Spanish history
- Eating in Spain: What you need to know
- The King's *Castellano:* Getting by in Spanish
- Understanding the basics of Spanish art and architecture
- Enjoying shopping, bullfighting, music, art, and film

As the old refrain goes, it never rains in Spain, but this southern European country of 40 million people definitely reigns on the pop-culture radar. Think about it: the legends of Don Quixote and Don Juan; death-defying bullfights (chronicled by Hemingway in *Death in the Afternoon*) and Pamplona's crazed Running of the Bulls; and Pablo Picasso and Salvador Dalí, towering figures as inimitable as their groundbreaking art. Sultry Spanish actors, such as Antonio Banderas and Penélope Cruz, have become stars in Hollywood, making Spain even sexier in the world's eyes.

Of course there's much more: the fiery rhythms of gypsy flamenco, miles of sun-drenched beaches, lazy midafternoon siestas, costumed religious festivals, and raucous bars flowing with wine and tantalizing tapas (small plates of appetizers). In the language of travel brochures, Spain has become easy shorthand for sun, fun, and passion.

Although the tourism industry has figured out how to trade quite handsomely on that reputation, Spain is much more than a Mediterranean cliché. The third-largest country in Europe — but a little smaller than Texas — Spain is a stunningly varied nation with five indigenous languages, regions and peoples defined by their own unique cultures and histories, and an astounding geographical diversity. The Spanish landscape ranges from 3,300m (11,000-ft.) peaks to misty green hills that look more like Ireland than the stereotypical Spain and the parched plains in which Carmen, the opera heroine, once strutted her stuff. Wherever you touch down, Spain is a fascinating country, a place to plunge into, absorb, and return to again and again.

Welcome to España

Spain has been on the international tourism radar since the 1960s, but it really exploded in the 1980s and 1990s, following the demise of the long-ruling dictator Francisco Franco, Spain's return to democracy, and its integration into the European Union. Today, incredibly, Spain's annual visitors outnumber its citizens. The 1992 Summer Olympics splashed cutting-edge, design-crazy Barcelona across TV screens, and, more recently, Frank Gehry's gleaming Guggenheim Museum in Bilbao piqued the interest of art and architecture lovers around the globe. Hedonist Spain draws not only topless sun worshippers but also night owls intent on keeping up with Spaniards' unparalleled ability to forego sleep, not to mention thrill-seekers with a hankering to run for their lives while 900kg (2,000-lb.) bulls chase them down narrow cobblestone streets. Others, meanwhile, come to experience the traditional, gentle attractions of Spain — the great castles and cathedrals, grand plazas, Moorish monuments, art masterpieces at the Prado, and slow-paced "white villages" of the south.

At the apex of its golden age, in the 16th and 17th centuries, Spain was the most powerful nation in the world, ruling an empire that stretched from the Americas east to the Pacific. Modern Spain is forward-looking and dynamic, but it's also starkly traditional, with reminders of its illustrious history at every turn. It's a place where ultramodern design, cutting-edge cuisine, and a robust economy coexist easily with medieval villages seemingly untouched by the passing of centuries.

Ancient Spain was inhabited by waves of successive cultures, including the Romans, Visigoths, Celts, and Moors (the Muslims who crossed into Spain from North Africa and lived in and ruled Spain for more than 700 years). Today, Spain continues to be a nation of disparate cultures fashioned together as one people. In fact, what is perhaps most remarkable about modern Spain is its hard-won regionalism. Under Franco, regional languages and cultures were suppressed in the service of a centralized state, but today those same cultures thrive as part of 17 separate *autonomías,* or autonomous regions, each with its own government.

For example, the Catalans in the northeast corner have a long history independent of the rest of Spain, and for the most part they speak Spanish as a second language, after Catalan. Up north, the Basques are an ancient people who have preserved an inscrutable language that boggles linguists, and many Basques continue to argue for political independence from Spain. Gallegos, the people of Galicia, a region in the extreme northwest of Spain, descended from the Celts; their language is a melding of Portuguese and Spanish. The Spaniards of central and southern Spain speak the national language, but their regional ties are just as strong as those felt by the Basques and Catalans. Despite these distinct cultures and unique points of view, which occasionally have degenerated into outbreaks of separatist violence, Spain seems wholly unlikely to disintegrate into small factions of independent states. (To get an idea of where these regions are located, see the "Spain" map in Chapter 3.)

Spain is a historic, complex European nation, as well as a Mediterranean vacation wonderland, the second-most toured destination in the world. Northern Europeans flock to the far south for its vastly superior year-round weather. Enticed by 300 sunny days a year, they crowd the beaches along Spain's east and south coasts, as well as on the islands. You can go boating, golfing, hiking, cycling, or take part in virtually any outdoor activity — including skiing. Although Spain's two major mountain ranges may not quite rank with the Alps, the Pyrenees in the north and the Sierra Nevada down south are both excellent spots to hit the slopes in winter.

Spanish History 101: The Main Events

Spain, one of the oldest inhabited places on Earth, has a long and complicated history of conquerors and cultures. Cave dwellers and hunter-gatherers — perhaps the forefathers of the Basque people — arrived on the Iberian Peninsula around 800,000 B.C. The prehistoric cave paintings of animals in **Altamira,** in the north of Spain, date from at least 13,000 B.C. and are possibly the world's oldest.

Some 5,000 years ago, at the beginning of recorded history, a people known as Iberians occupied parts of Spain. By 1100 B.C., a series of Mediterranean invaders began a pattern of conquests. First came the Phoenicians, followed by the Greeks and Carthaginians. The Romans conquered Iberia around 200 B.C., and it remained part of their massive empire until A.D. 414, when they ceded the Peninsula to the Visigoths, who stayed in Spain some 300 years.

The next group of invaders had a huge and lasting impact on Spanish culture, language, and architecture. The **Moors** crossed the Strait of Gibraltar from North Africa in 711. In 756, they founded an independent Muslim emirate in Córdoba, Europe's most advanced city during the ninth and tenth centuries. The Moorish occupation of Iberia — which endured for nearly eight centuries — extended all the way to the Basque Country in the north of Spain and resulted in a prosperous civilization, **al-Andalus** (today's Andalusia).

By the 11th century, though, Muslim dominance weakened, and Christian kingdoms ruled the north of Spain in Navarra, León, Castile, Aragón, and Barcelona. About this time, pilgrims began to make their way from all over Europe along the St. James trail across northern Spain to **Santiago de Compostela,** in Galicia. Factions developed in the Moorish Caliphate and eroded the emirate's power and influence. The Moors suffered losses to the Christians in many parts of Spain, and the sphere of Moorish control shrank to the Nazarid kingdom in **Granada,** site of the spectacular Alhambra palace. Los Reyes Católicos, the Catholic Monarchs Ferdinand and Isabel, captured Granada in 1492, capping the **Reconquest** campaign to rid Spain of the Moors. The year was the beginning of perhaps the most important — certainly the best documented — phase in Spanish history.

The **Spanish Inquisition,** a campaign of religious fervor and severe repression of Jews, Moors, and Protestants, was instituted several years before the end of the Reconquest. After their victory, the Spanish Monarchs, los Reyes Católicos, declared Catholicism the national religion of Spain. All Jews were expelled in 1492, and Moors were given the choice to convert to Christianity or suffer the same fate. Also that year, Italian-born Cristóbal Colón — Christopher Columbus — was credited with discovering the Americas. Under the Catholic monarchs, Spain entered a period of glory during the 16th century. Carlos, a Habsburg and the son of Queen Juana (called Juana the Mad) and King Philip (called Philip the Fair), became king and was named Carlos V, Holy Roman Emperor, in 1519. Riches flowed back to Spain from the unabashed pillaging of the New World. Under Carlos (Charles) V and Felipe (Philip) II, Spain flourished, extending its colonies throughout the Americas and, to the east, as far as the Pacific. Madrid became the capital of Spain in 1561, but an economic crisis of inflation and debt rocked the country, the result of a succession of wars against France and other European countries.

By the end of the 16th century, political and economic decline beset Spain, even as it entered its greatest artistic period. The 17th century is known as Spain's Golden Age, because the art patronage of the Habsburgs gave rise to brilliant painters, such as Velázquez, El Greco, Zurbarán, Ribera, and Murillo. Felipe V and the Bourbon dynasty assumed the throne in the 1700s, but additional wars and unenlightened leadership further weakened the country. Another artistic genius, the wildly talented court painter Francisco de Goya, emerged. Napoleon invaded Spain in the early 19th century, and Spain lost its American colonies to wars of independence. In Barcelona and then Paris, Pablo Picasso became an art-world star, basically defining 20th-century modern art.

Spain was neutral during the First World War (1914–1919), but political instability reigned. By the 1920s, Spain found itself under a military dictatorship (though the king remained on the throne); in 1931, a revolution led to the formation of a republic, forcing King Alfonso XIII to flee the country. In 1936, the army ended the five-year-old Second Republic, and civil war broke out. Ultraconservative Nationalist troops led by General Francisco Franco stormed the country and fought Republican and Anarchist factions for three years, defeating them in horrific battles that drew volunteers to the Republican side from England and the United States. Franco emerged as the military victor. He ruled as a repressive dictator for almost 40 years.

After the end of World War II, Franco was the only remaining fascist head of state in Europe, and he isolated Spain from the rest of the continent, severely impeding economic development. After his death in 1975, Juan Carlos, the handpicked successor to Franco, became king of Spain, and democracy was restored. Spain's budding democracy suffered a grave threat on February 23, 1981, when the military launched a coup, even firing shots in Parliament. But King Juan Carlos interceded, putting the military in its place and preserving Spain's post-Franco democracy.

Spain entered the European Economic Community (now called the European Union) in 1986 and announced its growing international presence with the celebration of the Summer Olympics in Barcelona and the World Expo in Seville, both in 1992. The Socialist Prime Minister Felipe González failed to get elected for a third term, and the center-right Partido Popular (Popular Party) candidate José María Aznar was elected in 1996. Aznar positioned himself as a committed ally to the United States and backed the war efforts in Afghanistan and Iraq.

Terrorists linked to Islamist groups attacked Madrid's commuter rail lines on March 11, 2004, just days before a national election, killing nearly 200 and injuring more than 1,400. The worst terrorist attack in the history of modern Europe, the date in Spain is referred to as "3-11." Aznar's administration initially (and erroneously) linked the bombings to ETA, the Basque terrorist group, and the Partido Popular lost the national elections to the Socialist Party's José Luís Rodríguez Zapatero, who made good on a campaign promise to withdraw Spanish troops from Iraq. Zapatero has also followed through with plans to negotiate a ceasefire with ETA and to give the independent-minded region of Catalonia greater autonomy.

Tourism, one of the country's most important industries since the late 1960s, has continued to grow exponentially, and by the beginning of the 21st century, Spain had catapulted to second place among the most visited countries in the world. Today, with the consolidation of the European Union and full implementation of the euro, Spain is more integrated in Europe than at any point in its history.

The Legacy: Spanish Art and Architecture

From religious art of the Middle Ages to the latest revelations of the contemporary art scene, Spain has produced more great artists than virtually any other country. Several — Veláquez, Goya, El Greco, and Picasso — are among the finest artists the world has ever seen. Spain abounds with Romanesque and Gothic masterpieces, but the masterworks of Spain's Golden Age, the 17th century, and the 20th century are what most visitors come to see. Don't miss the Prado, Thyssen-Bornemisza, and Reina Sofía museums in Madrid (see Chapter 13); the Museu d'Art de Catalunya, Museo Picasso, and Fundació Miró in Barcelona (see Chapter 10); the Theatre-Museu Dalí in Figueres (Catalonia) (see Chapter 11); and the Museo de Bellas Artes in Seville (see Chapter 15). Those museums are the biggest and finest, but I also highlight other eminently worthwhile repositories of Spanish art throughout the country in individual destination chapters.

The wealth of architectural styles on display throughout Spain is astounding; the country is like a survey of architecture from the fifth century B.C. to the present. With relatively little effort, your trip to Spain can encompass everything from **Roman** and **Romanesque** to **Moorish** and ***Mudéjar,*** **Gothic** and **Renaissance** to **baroque** and Catalonia's unique ***moderniste*** architecture, not to mention the latest in avant-garde design and works by some of the finest contemporary international architects, including Frank Gehry's famed Guggenheim Museum in Bilbao.

Taste of Spain: Local Cuisine

Spain has earned a reputation as one of Europe's most sensual countries, and nowhere is this reputation more evident than in the abundant pleasure that Spaniards take in eating and drinking. One of the greatest attractions of a visit to Spain is the chance to follow suit, with all the gusto of the locals. Spain's predominantly Mediterranean diet is rich in olive oil, garlic, tomatoes, and peppers. The Moors introduced Middle Eastern elements, such as rice and saffron, to Spanish cooking. You've probably heard of, and maybe even have tried, signature dishes like paella (the huge rice-based seafood dish), gazpacho (cold vegetable soup), and tapas. (See the box "Talking tapas," later in this chapter.)

If you're expecting to find only the heavy, medieval-style cooking of classic Castilian dishes, such as roast suckling pig, or if you assume Spanish cooks crank out spicy Latino dishes, you're in for a big surprise. Beyond tapas, gazpacho, and the ubiquitous *tortilla española* (a potato-and-onion omelet, served hot or cold), speaking of a national Spanish cuisine is nearly impossible. Instead, Spain takes pride in a number of unique regional cuisines. With Catalonia's rich Mediterranean diet — both sophisticated and rustic — the Basque Country's delicate preparations, Central Spain's roasted meats and game, the north coast's fresh seafood, and Andalusia's revered cured hams, fried fish, and refreshing cold vegetable soups, you'll find a culinary variety in Spain that's hard to match anywhere else in the world. In addition to the almost endless regional bounty, a number of young Spanish chefs, especially in places such as Barcelona and San Sebastián, have revitalized Spanish cooking with edgy, modern flair and catapulted Spain into a European gastronomic temple. Indeed, many gastronomes and critics now cite Spain, rather than France, as the European leader in culinary achievement.

Spain is surrounded on almost all sides by water, and fresh seafood is a fundamental part of the Spanish diet. But meat is equally important. Spaniards especially love pork and cured ham. In fact, *jamón serrano* (cured ham) is one of Spain's true delicacies. Spaniards also eat plenty of salads, fresh fruits, and vegetables. Spain may not be the easiest place for vegetarians (and it's harder still for vegans), because good vegetarian restaurants are few and far between. But nearly every restaurant has a good selection of salads, nonmeat soups, and vegetables.

Spanish cooking has really started to make its mark around the world, with tapas bars sprouting like mushrooms in the United States, Canada, and the United Kingdom. At some places abroad, tapas are just an excuse to serve a tiny bit of food for a big price, but that's not the case in Spain. Tapas, which cover everything from free little snacks, such as

Talking tapas

The hunt for tapas is called a *tapeo.* The term tapas covers all types of snacking, but there's actually an entire vocabulary that goes along with finger foods. A *ración* (rah-*thyohn*) is a full serving, a plate to be shared with one or more *amigos.* You may, however, consume a *media-ración* (half-ration) solo. A tapa, strictly speaking, is a tiny morsel served free along with your beverage, or a slightly more substantial single serving, also called a *pincho* (*peen*-choh).

The word tapa means *lid,* and tapas, the snacks, emerged from a tradition of placing scraps of food on top of wine jugs in taverns. Patrons drank the wine and then downed the contents of the lid, too. Pretty soon, tavern owners started setting snack-filled saucers on top of drinks. The *tapeo,* the often boisterous bar-to-bar snack cruising, has its own curious origin. After church, men would gather at the tavern while the women went home to prepare the Sunday meal. The men would stroll from tavern to tavern, meeting up with friends and scarfing down finger foods and wine until it was time to go home for dinner.

olives, chips, slices of spicy chorizo sausage, and cubes of cheese, to haute-cuisine minimeals, are a longtime Spanish tradition. Joining a jubilant *tapeo,* or tapas crawl, is one of the finest eating experiences in Spain. People refer to tapas bars by a variety of names — *tascas, mesones, bodegas,* and *tabernas* — but they all serve small amounts of food and free-flowing beer and wine. Like ravenous Spaniards, you can saunter from bar to bar, nibbling on an amazing array of snack foods laid out before you and then wash it all down with a sherry, *un tinto o vino blanco* (red or white wine), or *cerveza* (beer).

Knowing what to expect when you're eating out

Spaniards are passionate about many things, eating chief among them. Dining — whether at home, at a tavern, or at an elegant restaurant — is an important social affair, a time to relax, and an event to prepare for, savor, and talk about afterwards. Lunch is the main meal of the day, and savoring a fine meal is always cheaper at this time than it is at night. Look for the fixed-price *menú del día* (menu of the day), which usually includes an appetizer, main course, dessert, bread, and wine or water for a reasonable price (often around 15€, or $18). Be warned, though, that for most North Americans and northern Europeans, Spain's dinner hours are absurdly late (see "Chow time: Knowing when and what to eat," later in the chapter).

One of the highlights of eating in Spain is sampling regional specialties — *suquet de peix* (seafood stew) in Catalonia; *cordero asado* (roast baby lamb) in Castile; *bacalao al pil-pil* (salt cod in garlic sauce) in the Basque Country; *gambas al ajillo* (garlic-soaked shrimp) in Andalusia; and many more. In each dining section, I highlight some of the typical regional dishes. Look for the sections titled "Eating Like a . . ." and try what I recommend.

You'll find a whole range of restaurants in Spain, from informal taverns and family-owned joints to elegant European dining rooms. In the cities, finding a wide variety of cuisines won't present a problem — French and Italian are common, and more diverse ethnic choices, such as Vietnamese, Mexican, and Indian, are also beginning to take hold. In this book, however, I focus largely on the best Spanish restaurants and regional Spanish cooking.

Keeping the price right

You can keep your costs down and eat wonderfully for much less than you may spend in most other parts of Europe. However, if you eat like most Spaniards — four-course meals twice daily with a bottle of wine each time — you may find your food budget becoming as tight as your belt. At lunch, a cheap *menú del día* costs 1€ to 15€ ($12–$18) or less; at a mid-range restaurant, expect to pay from 15€ to 20€ ($18–$24); and an upscale-restaurant meal costs from 20€ to 30€ ($24–$36). At lunch, paying much more than that is rare. You generally spend more at dinner, when the *menú del día* is much less common. Dinner is almost always à la carte (menu items priced separately). An inexpensive restaurant often costs from 15€ to 20€ ($18–$24) for a full dinner; at the moderate range, from 20€ to 35€ ($24–$42); and at upscale restaurants, dinner starts around 35€ ($42) per person and goes up from there. At even the finest Spanish restaurants in top dining cities, though, you're unlikely to spend

Still smoking — but not as much

Spain — among the E.U.'s biggest consumers of tobacco — has long been one of those European nations, like France and Italy, where it seems as if smoking is, simply, a national characteristic. In fact, the number of adult smokers has dropped steadily, and only about one-third of the population continues to smoke. That doesn't necessarily mean you won't see groups of 11-year-old girls in Catholic-school uniforms lighting up on the way to their first class (despite the fact that the legal age for purchasing tobacco has been raised from 16 to 18). Still, a new law banning smoking in public places, including on public transportation and in offices, hospitals, and some bars and restaurants, was enacted in early 2006 (similar to laws already in effect in Ireland, Norway, and Italy). The law allows bars and restaurants smaller than 100 square meters to choose whether or not they will be smoke-free; larger establishments must demarcate nonsmoking areas. In addition, the current ban on tobacco advertising on TV will be extended to billboards. Though 70 percent of the population in a government survey supported the ban, Spain is still adjusting to the new law (after all, this is a country where it is legal to smoke small amounts of marijuana and hashish). Though smoking is not as prevalent as it was only a few years ago, in practice, many Spaniards simply disregard the smoking ban. To sit in a nonsmoking section, ask for *no fumar.*

much more than 75€ ($90) a head — a figure that's almost ridiculously easy to reach in London, Paris, or New York. One exception is the multiple-course tasting menus at the Michelin-starred restaurants in San Sebastián, known to be the best and most expensive dining scene in Spain, where the dinner of your life will run you more than 100€ ($120) a head.

Chow time: Knowing when and what to eat

Spaniards eat late — often very late — and meals are leisurely. You may want to try and adopt the rhythm of later mealtimes before you go, even if that requires snacking and/or napping. Only a handful of restaurants outside of the tourist areas adapt to foreigners who want to eat lunch at noon and dinner at 6 p.m.

Breakfast (desayuno)

For *desayuno* (breakfast), most Spaniards eat little — perhaps just a *café con leche* (coffee with milk) and a few *tostadas* (toast with jam, cheese, or sometimes, ham and olive oil) or *churros* (fritters) on their way to work. They more commonly get to the office and then, around 10 a.m., drop down to the local bar or cafe for a croissant and coffee, or even a beer, sherry, or a shot of a stronger drink.

Lunch (almuerzo; comida)

Membership in the European Union is slowly but surely changing Spaniards' daily routines and eroding some long-held traditions. Today, fewer and fewer people return home from the office for the midday meal and quick *siesta.* Sandwich shops are making inroads, and many bars and cafes sell *bocadillos* (cheese, ham, tortilla, and chorizo sandwiches). However, *almuerzo* (lunch — known as *comida,* too) remains the centerpiece of the day, and many offices close from 1:30 or 2 p.m. to 4 p.m. Most restaurants open for lunch at 1 p.m., but many only begin to see crowds just after 2 p.m. (Sneaking in before the 2 p.m. rush is wise.)

The midday fixed-priced menu, which has all but disappeared in most of Europe, remains one of Spain's best deals. A set price of about 12€ to 15€ ($15–$18) buys a three-course meal, often including a bottle of house wine. (Spaniards not only share a bottle of wine over lunch, even

Taking a *siesta!*

The *siesta,* a post-lunch nap, used to be one of the defining customs of Spain. Yet only 20 percent of Spaniards, according to a study by Barcelona's Dexeus Institute, continue to find time for daily siestas. But, although businesses and shops have slowly conformed to American and European work schedules, many continue to close between 1:30 or 2 p.m. and 4 p.m.

during the week, but they may very well have a cocktail before or cognac after the meal, too.)

Dinner (cena)

In Spain, the *tarde* (afternoon) lasts until about 8 p.m., so if you sit down to supper at 6 or 7 p.m., you'll be eating dinner in the afternoon, a most peculiar concept. People in Spain eat dinner uncommonly late, usually beginning no earlier than 9 p.m. and often starting as late as 11 p.m. or even past midnight.

You don't have to eat quite as late as locals, however. Restaurants generally open for dinner at 8 p.m., though you can expect to be one of the few people ordering dinner at that hour. Everybody else is enjoying tapas and cocktails in the bar. The best plan is to down some tapas at your normal dinnertime to pace yourself for the late hours.

Tasting Spanish wines

A lot of visitors are surprised to discover that Spain grows more wine grapes than any other country. Although Spain still ranks behind France and Italy in terms of wine production and reputation, Spanish wines are definitely on the rise, and some of the most exciting wines to emerge in the last few years have come from previously little-known wine-producing regions and small vineyards in Spain. Spanish wines enjoy a long and illustrious history, and many excellent Spanish wine producers are finally earning the worldwide acclaim that they deserve, with their wines sitting alongside great Bordeauxs and Brunellos in the cellars of the most celebrated restaurants. For their level of sophistication, though, Spain's fine wines are remarkably affordable, even in restaurants. Red wines remain the country's standouts for fine dining, while light whites and dry rosés are prized casual wines. The fortified wines from the south make particularly good aperitifs and dessert wines.

Among Spain's most celebrated *vinos tintos* (rich reds, made predominantly from tempranillo and garnacha grapes) are those from wineries in the most traditional regions: **La Rioja, Ribera del Duero,** and **Navarra** (north of Madrid). Riojas are by far Spain's best-known wines, and in general still the most traditional, though Riberas are now every bit their equal. Other regions producing quality reds are **Penedès** (south of Barcelona) and the two newest stars, **Priorat** (southwest of Barcelona) and **Toro** (northwest of Madrid), both of which turn out sophisticated and powerful wines that have garnered plenty of international attention. Several regions still largely unfamiliar to many wine drinkers outside Spain — **Yecla, Jumilla,** and **La Mancha,** all southeast of Madrid, and **Bierzo,** in Galicia — in the last few years have begun to market very good reds that are excellent values both home and abroad. Many regions, including **Penedès, Rueda,** and **Rioja,** produce refreshing *vinos blancos* (white wines). The young, light, and fruity whites of **Galicia, Albariños,** and **Ribeiros** are excellent with shellfish and seafood. To top it off, there's ***jerez*** (or ***fino***), classic sherry from Andalusia, and the world's best-selling bubbly, ***cava*** — the sparkling wine of Catalonia.

The coffee buzz

Spaniards love coffee, and stopping for *café* is a several-times-a-day ritual. For the most part, people stand or sit in a cafe to have a coffee rather than get it in a paper or Styrofoam to-go cup. If you order *un café* in Spain, you get a small cup of rich, strong, and delicious espresso. *Un cortado* is an espresso with a dash of creme. If you aren't an espresso drinker, ask for a *café con leche* (coffee with milk, which is half milk) or a *café americano* (weaker coffee diluted with water). Because few Spaniards opt for an *americano,* yes, they're sort of making fun of gringos.

Individuals who already know Spanish wines will be delighted to discover lengthy *cartas de vino* (wine lists) that offer many wines unavailable outside Spain. If you're not really much of a wine connoisseur, you usually can't go wrong with the *vino de la casa,* the house wine. (In small restaurants the house wine is a carafe or bottle of regional wine, while in fine restaurants it may be a bottle selected by the sommelier or a wine made especially for the restaurant.) *Vino de mesa* refers to the most basic category of standard, young table wines.

The following are terms to look for if you want to taste Spain's best table wines (note, however, that some modern winemakers are moving away from these designations to allow themselves greater aging flexibility). They're generally used with red wines, and all indicate wood-matured (predominantly red) wines that have spent from one to five years aging in *barricas* (oak casks) and bottles:

- A **crianza** is the youngest of wood-matured wines; it has spent at least one year in a cask and several months in a bottle aging and can't be sold until its third year.
- **Reservas** wines are so designated from a particularly good vintage and spend at least three years aging, with at least one year in a cask. Reservas aren't released until the fourth year after harvest.
- **Gran reservas,** culled from vintage years judged to be outstanding, spend at least two years in a cask and another three years in a bottle; they aren't released until six years after harvest. *Cosecha* (which literally means "harvest") is the term for vintage year.

For recommended vintages and specific wines to look for when dining out in Spain (or shopping at Duty Free at the airport), see the yellow "tear-out" charts at the beginning of this book.

You've probably had sangria, and many tourists who go to Spain sit down to a fruity pitcher of it at nearly every stop. But most sangria is a tourist concoction, little more than wine-based Kool-Aid. Many restaurant owners know foreigners want it, so they trot out their cheapest wine, dilute it, and toss in a handful of thin orange slices. Voilà! Sangria. Maybe you'll be lucky, though, and enjoy splendid, fruity sangria that actually tastes like wine at a small tavern or restaurant. However, I don't recommend ordering it at one of those obviously touristy places with menus in six languages displayed on sandwich boards. You're usually much better off ordering an inexpensive bottle of *tinto, blanco,* or *cava.*

Word to the Wise: The Local Lingo for Gringos

Until recently, Spaniards mostly studied French and spoke little English. That all changed with the country's 1986 introduction into the European Union and with the increasing linguistic globalization brought on by MTV, CNN, and the Internet. English is now the foreign language of choice, and even if relatively few people older than 40 speak it fluently, most young people have at least a basic grasp of English. And, of course, major hotels have staff fluent in English and other languages.

However, Spain remains thankfully resistant to some elements of global homogenization. Only in primarily tourist areas and in tourist restaurants is English flung around with impressive ease. Knowing (or remembering from high school or college) some *español* can help you on your trip. You can talk to more people and get clearer directions, and you may not be quite as surprised when plates are set down in front of you.

If conjugating verbs is way beyond you and all you want is the ability to utter a few basic pleasantries and ask a few questions, you probably won't have too much trouble. The most important words and phrases to learn are: ***por favor*** (pohr fah-*vohr;* please), ***gracias*** (*grah*-thyahs; thank you), and ***¿Habla inglés?*** (*ah*-blah een-*glehs;* Do you speak English?). Never automatically assume that someone speaks your language. You win big points by asking politely if she does.

The art of the *paseo:* The stroll *español*

In towns small and large, Spaniards seem to be in constant motion, walking to and fro. They don't necessarily seem to be walking with particular purpose, however. Where are they going? Often, nowhere in particular. They're strolling. The stroll *español*—the *paseo*—is a time-honored tradition, an inescapable component of Spanish social life. There's the lovers' stroll, the family *paseo,* and the takin'-care-of-business stroll. Not only good exercise, they're also expressions of Spanish life at full tilt. The *paseo* is usually timed around meals, coming before or after lunch or coinciding with prime tapas hour at the end of the work day. People meet up with old friends, stop at a cafe, have a drink and a few tapas, and move on. Join the *paseo,* or pull up at a sidewalk cafe and watch Spanish life lazily roll on by.

In the ring: The raging bull

To many, if not most, Spaniards, bullfighting is an art — a cultural tradition suffused with high drama and delicate choreography. *Los toros* (the bulls), as it's called colloquially, is a time-honored ritual with all the solemnity of midnight Mass — anything but a sport. I have attended a number of bullfights and had Spanish friends explain it and heard them praise its virtues with great passion, but, much as I try to see the appeal, it remains a tough sell — as it does for many foreigners. No matter how you spin it, I can't get past the fact that at its most basic level it celebrates the cruel slaughter of innocent and magnificent creatures. Despite those who became fans of the sport — most famously, Ernest Hemingway and Orson Welles — most foreigners probably need Spanish blood coursing through their veins to really appreciate the drama of life-and-death struggle. Everyone else is more likely to see it only as a life-and-death struggle for the bull.

Even though you're unlikely to fully grasp and appreciate its complex nature, a *corrida* — bullfight — in Madrid, Seville, or Ronda remains a quintessential Spanish experience and a sight to see once in your life (but not if you're squeamish). While Spanish opposition to the sport has grown, Spaniards still spend over $1 billion annually at bullfights, of which there are some 17,000 every year. The season runs from March to October and is especially popular in Madrid and Andalusia (Seville and Ronda are two of the best spots to see a *corrida*). The bullfight revels in pageantry, bravery, and risking death for one's art, which underlines the Spanish obsession with mortality and a fascination with violence and blood. Practiced since the Middle Ages and once unleashed in town squares, bullfighting, formerly on the wane, is again enjoying renewed popularity in Spain. Top *matadores* are national celebrities whose spotlights eclipse even matinee idols. The current king of Spanish cinema, Pedro Almodóvar, has prominently featured bullfighters in at least two of his films, even calling one of them *Matador.*

Each bullfight has three basic chapters.

- In the first, the *matador* appraises his opponent and entices the fighting bull with a large pink cape. *Picadores* (horsemen) use long lances to weaken the 1,000-pound bull's brute shoulders (so his head will drop and allow the *matador* to kill him eventually).
- In the second stage, *bandilleros* (assistants on horseback) plunge colorful pairs of darts into the bull, further weakening him for the *matador.* (You begin to grasp what a "fair" fight this really is.)
- In the final stage, the *matador,* in his brilliant *traje de luces* (suit of lights, so named for its vivid colors that seem to glow in the sun), orchestrates showy passes at the bull with his *muleta* (red cape) while choruses of *¡olé!* resound throughout the ring. It's all dramatic buildup to the kill — the moment of truth in which the *matador* plunges (in theory, precisely) his sword between the bull's shoulders. If the lance drives straight to the heart, the bull drops in a heap, dead.

Bullfights go through six bulls; a spectacular kill earns the matador the doomed bull's ear or tail. For more detailed information about bullfighting in Spain, visit `www.mundotaurino.org`.

In regions such as Catalonia and the Basque Country, which have their own indigenous languages that are used in preference to Castilian Spanish, trying a few words of the native tongue is a very polite gesture — though no one expects you to be able to speak it.

Speaking Spanish in Spain

Two features distinguish Iberian Spanish (the type of Spanish spoken in Spain) from Latin American Spanish. One is the lisp-heavy pronunciation of the letters *c* and *z*. Thus, in Spain, *cerveza* (beer) is pronounced thehr-*beh*-thah. And the second is that the native population uses the third-person *vosotros* (you) form, rather than the *ustedes* form common throughout Latin America. So in Spain, "What are you doing?" becomes *"¿Qué hacéis?"* (keh ah-*thays*) rather than "*¿Qué hacen?*" (keh *ah*-thehn).

Beyond these minor differences, Spanish is one of the rare languages that's perfectly phonetic, so don't worry about lisping and give it your best shot. Spaniards aren't at all like the notoriously snooty French (okay, Parisians), who sometimes look down on foreigners mangling their language. Locals amply appreciate any effort to speak Spanish, and you'll receive a warm response. Check out the handy Cheat Sheet in the front of this book for some more phrases and important menu terms. Also, check out *Spanish For Dummies,* by Susana Wald (Wiley), if you're interested in broadening your foreign-language abilities.

Sounding like a Spaniard

Spaniards are wonderfully expressive. Their voices are deep — most Spanish women sound as though they're speaking straight from the sternum. If you know some Spanish, and especially if you know the kind they never taught you in high school, you'll marvel at how widely everyone swears. A foreigner prone to parroting the locals can run into difficulties. Don't repeat anyone unless you know what he or she is saying — and you mean to say the same.

A couple of key, indigenous phrases will give you a head start on understanding the locals. ***¡Hombre!*** (*ohm*-breh; meaning "Man!") is a common exclamation with a zillion applications and intonations. You'll see men and women say it with great satisfaction when they cut into a great steak, see an old friend, or when they don't believe a word that the old friend says. ***Vale*** (*bah*-leh) is uttered about as often as most people say, "Um." It means roughly, "Okay, yeah, right, I'll do it, yep, okay, no problem, I said okay, all right?" Spaniards are capable of using *vale* about eight times in a single sentence.

Chapter 3

Deciding Where and When to Go

In This Chapter

- Looking at Spain, region by region
- Determining what times to go and what times to avoid
- Building your trip around special events, festivals, and holidays

Your options in this complex, delightfully varied, and scenically rich country are virtually endless. And almost any kind of trip is possible: You can storm the Prado and every other art museum in a country that has produced a disproportionate number of masters, including Velázquez, El Greco, Goya, Picasso, and Dalí. Indulge in seafood paella (a rice and seafood casserole) and red wines from Rioja. Attend a bullfight or one of the many colorful festivals. Relive Spain's past in great palaces, castles, and cathedrals. Savor cosmopolitan cities or soak up small villages where time seems to stand still. Hit nightclubs where the action doesn't start until the wee hours and pulses until dawn. Or bask in the beach culture that has made Spain a magnet for sun-starved northern Europeans. One of the hardest things about planning a trip to Spain is that it offers so much variety and so many possibilities. But I'm here to help you figure it all out.

In this chapter, I review the different regions of Spain and cover the best times to enjoy Spain's great weather and the special festivals that you may want to be a part of, such as Semana Santa (Easter) or the San Fermín (the Running of the Bulls). And, if you prefer traveling off-season to avoid crowds and high prices, I have you covered there, too.

Going Where You Want to Go

A first-time traveler to Spain could be forgiven for believing the stereotype: that all of Spain is sunny and hot; dotted with castles, cathedrals, and windmills; overwhelmingly flat; and lined with long beaches. But, in fact, Spain is one of Western Europe's most diverse nations, with wildly distinct regions, cultures, cuisines, and even languages. Spanish is obviously the national language, but the locals in three regions of the country speak a primary language — Catalan, Euskera (Basque), and Gallego — in addition to Spanish (*castellano,* or Castilian Spanish).

Of course, much of Spain *is* as advertised: hot and sunny, flat, and lined with sparkling beaches. However, visitors can just as easily see a Spain that is quite the opposite: one of rich green mountains, winding rivers, and misty skies. The good news is that no matter where you are in the country, a dramatically different region is usually just a short flight away.

Which Spain do you want to visit? Many visitors, whether on their first trip or fifth, find it better to concentrate on a single region and see some of the diversity within it. Others have more wanderlust and time and want to experience two or more regions of Spain. Either way, you're in for a treat.

When planning a trip to a big country, you not only choose where to go, but you also choose where *not* to go. So that you can start narrowing down your own choices, the sections below break down Spain's regions, following the order in which I discuss them in greater detail in later chapters. To see where these regions are located in the country, refer to the "Spain" map in this chapter.

Northeastern Spain: Barcelona, the Costa Brava, and the Basque Country

The region of Catalonia may not be familiar to you, but I'm sure Barcelona is. The site of the 1992 Summer Olympic Games, **Barcelona** (bar-theh-*loh*-nah) is a 2,000-year-old city that was founded by the Romans. It's a thoroughly modern place with rich architectural and artistic legacies, including those of Antoni Gaudí, Pablo Picasso, and Joan Mirò. Barcelona is the capital of **Catalonia,** a region of 6 million people whose first language is Catalan (though almost everybody also speaks Spanish, even if it takes a little prodding). Catalonia (Catalunya in Catalan) is Spain's most prosperous region, and many fiercely independent Catalans choose to think of their homeland as a separate nation within Spain. It borders France in the north and traces the long Mediterranean coastline, including the rocky **Costa Brava** north of Barcelona. Catalonia's interior is a largely agricultural region of beautiful, fertile plains and small medieval villages. It seems sedate and pastoral, until you realize that this region gave birth to Salvador Dalí's surreal genius.

An independent streak doesn't come any stronger than in the unique País Vasco (pah-*ees bahs*-koh; the **Basque Country**), which begins just west of the French border and the Pyrenees, hugging the northern coastline and inhabiting the remote interior above the River Ebro. (For simplicity's sake, I lump Navarra in with the Basque Country, though strictly speaking it's no longer Basque. My apologies to geographical purists.) The Basque Country is primarily agricultural, hilly, and full of emerald meadows, quiet villages, and rustic farmhouses.

Spain

Rio Altas
Costa Verde
La Coruña
Ribadeo
Gijón
Santander
Oviedo
CANTABRIA
Santiago de Compostela
Lugo
C. Finisterre
Reinosa
GALICIA
Cantabrian Mts.
Rio Bajas
Miño
ASTURIAS
León
Pontevedra
Vigo
Orense
Burgos
Túy
Benavente
Palencia
ATLANTIC OCEAN
Valladolid
Aranda de Duero
Zamora
CASTILLA-LEÓN
Porto
Douro
See Chapter 14: Castile
Salamanca
Segovia
Ávila
Guadalajara
San Lorenzo de El Escorial
Ciudad Rodrigo
Coimbra
MADRID
Chinchón
Talavera de la Reina
PORTUGAL
Plasencia
Coria
Aranjuez
Tagus
Toledo
Guadalupe
Cáceres
Valencia de Alcántara
Trujillo
See Chapter 13: Madrid
EXTREMADURA
LISBON
Badajoz
Mérida
Ciudad Real
CASTILLA-LA MANCHA
Guadiana
Zafra
Peñarroya-Pueblonuevo
Sierra Morena
Linares
See Chapter 15: Seville & Córdoba
Córdoba
Ubeda
Jaén
Guadalquivir
See Chapter 17: Granada
Seville
Genil
Ayamonte
Huelva
Guadix
Cape St. Vincent
Faro
ANDALUCÍA
Costa de la Luz
Antequera
Granadá
Gulf of Cádiz
Jerez de la Frontera
Málaga
Motril
Marbella
Cádiz
Costa del Sol
Estepona
See Chapter 16: The Pueblos Blancos
Algeciras
Gibraltar (U.K.)
Strait of Gibraltar
MOROCCO
Ceuta (Spain)

Bay of Biscay
FRANCE
Toulouse
Montpellier
Gulf of Lions
Bilbao (Bilbo)
San Sebastián (Donostia)
See Chapter 12: The Basque Country & Navarra
BASQUE COUNTRY
Pamplona (Iruñea)
Vitoria
ANDORRA
Andorra la Vella
Pyrenees
See Chapter 11: Girona & the Costa Brava
Logroño
NAVARRA
Figueres
LA RIOJA
Huesca
CATALONIA
Gerona (Girona)
Tudela
Ebro
Lérida (Lleida)
Tàrrega
Costa Brava
Soria
Zaragoza
See Chapter 10: Barcelona
BARCELONA
Duero
Calatayud
Tarragona
Costa Dorada
ARAGON
Tortosa
Monreal del Campo
C. de Tortosa
Tagus
Vinaròs
Teruel
Balearic Sea
Menorca
Castellón de la Plana
Costa del Azahar
Balearic Islands
Mahón
Cuenca
Tarancón
Inca
Artá
Palma de Mallorca
Valencia
Mallorca
Mota del Cuervo
Júcar
Gulf of Valencia
Ibiza
Cabrera
Ciudad de Ibiza
Albacete
Formentera
Benidorm
Segura
Alicante
Elche
Costa Blanca
Villacarrillo
Torrevieja
MURCIA
Murcia
Lorca
Cartagena
MEDITERRANEAN SEA
Costa Cálida
Almería
ALGERIA
Alborán (Spain)
0 100 mi
0 100 km
N

Spain's sixth-largest city, **Bilbao,** was, for most of the 20th century, a grimy industrial metropolis. That all changed with the arrival of Frank Gehry's stunning Guggenheim Museum, which has suddenly transformed the city into one of Spain's top tourist attractions. **San Sebastián** (called Donostia in Basque) is a splendid summer resort and one of Spain's prettiest cities, with serene beaches framing a perfect shell-shaped bay. It's also Spain's acclaimed dining capital.

Navarra (sometimes spelled Navarre in English) is an ancient region that was once an independent kingdom. People in some parts of the province still speak the Basque language. Navarra is a mountainous region, dominated by the Pyrenees, and, like most of the north, is agricultural. The capital, **Pamplona,** is a conservative place that rockets to life once a year, during its famous summer festival, **San Fermín** — the Running of the Bulls. You can drink especially well in Navarra; besides its own reds and rosés, the famous red-wine region, La Rioja, is just a few kilometers southwest.

The main attractions in this region are

- Barcelona's medieval **Gothic Quarter,** mind-altering early-20th-century architecture (including Gaudí's Sagrada Familia), and sparkling urban beaches.
- Barcelona's dynamic restaurant and bar scene.
- **Girona,** a quiet medieval city on a hill with a Jewish past, ancient Empordà villages, and the **Dalí Triangle** — three towns touched by surreal Salvador.
- The beaches, piney coves, and icy blue waters of the **Costa Brava.**
- Bilbao's mind-blowing **Guggenheim Museum,** universally acclaimed as one of the standout buildings of the 20th century.
- **San Sebastián,** a leisurely small city perched on a perfect bay — with Spain's greatest concentration of haute cuisine restaurants.
- **Pamplona,** a reserved city where hysteria reigns once a year when one-ton bulls rule the streets.
- **Basque cuisine** — Spain's most sophisticated and inventive. In other places, eating is a complementary activity; in the Basque Country, everything else takes a back seat.

But keep in mind . . .

- Barcelona is especially popular now with tourists, and its hotels and restaurants do a good job helping you part with your euros.
- In the verdant Basque Country, rain often rules the day. If you only get mist while in the area, it's the equivalent of brilliant sunshine anywhere else.

- Pamplona, during the Running of the Bulls, is an expensive nightmare if you don't have reservations, and though the festival is a blast, it's also a messy, raucous, and smelly affair.

Central Spain: Madrid and Castile

When most people think of Spain, they probably picture the central and southern parts of the country. The flat, arid plains of Central Spain are punctuated by dozens of castles and palaces marking ancient kingdoms and conflicts.

Madrid is the largest city in Spain. In addition to occupying the geographic middle, Madrid is the core of the Spanish cultural world: It claims several of the finest art museums in Europe, with the world-famous Prado leading the way.

The previous Spanish capital was **Toledo,** just south of Madrid. Toledo's fascinating juxtaposition of Arab, Christian, and Jewish cultures has made it one of Spain's top draws for decades. Toledo, along with **Segovia** and **Salamanca,** are the top day trips (or better yet, "couple-of-days" trips) from Madrid. Their proximity to the capital makes it extremely easy to design a Central Spain visit.

The main attractions in this region are

- Madrid and its many parts: Viejo Madrid (Old Madrid), Habsburg Madrid, and Bourbon Madrid. Across the board, the capital is lively, full of world-class art, and the most frenetically paced nightlife scene in Spain.
- Right on the outskirts of town: the somber — but still eye-popping — palace **El Escorial** and **Aranjuez,** the regal garden retreat of royals.
- **Segovia,** a town molded like a medieval dreamscape, with a 2,000-year-old Roman aqueduct and a picture-book castle on a hill.
- **Salamanca,** one of Spain's most architecturally inviting cities — a classic university town, much the same as Oxford in England.
- **Toledo,** the labyrinthine city on a hill where the artist El Greco thrived, as well as Romans, Visigoths, Christians, Jews, and Moors.

But keep in mind . . .

- An arid, flat plain like the *meseta* is unforgivably hot in summer and brutally cold in winter.
- Much of Central Spain, especially Toledo, is a tourist magnet; it's tough to visit the cities of Old and New Castile and not get trampled by boisterous bus groups.

Southern Spain: Andalusia

Andalusia, or **Andalucía** (ahn-dah-loo-*thee*-ah), is the sultry, passionate Spain touted on posters: flamenco-dancing gypsies, bloody bullfights, blistering sun, and scorching *señoritas.* Clumps of olive groves sprawl across unending acres of khaki-colored earth, producing golden extra-virgin olive oil for much of the world.

Andalusia (called al-Andalus by the Arabs who once inhabited this region) is the part of Spain that the Moors influenced most distinctly. They ruled Spain for seven centuries, and their dominance and sophistication are evident in the alluring Alhambra palace in **Granada,** the magnificent Great Mosque in **Córdoba,** and the arresting Alcázar, or palace-fortress, in **Seville.** The south of Spain is also home to some of the country's most colorful and traditional local festivals, such as Semana Santa (Holy Week) and the Feria de Abril (April Fair) in Seville. You also see a distinctive Moorish presence in the white villages, or *pueblos blancos,* perched in the Andalusian Mountains.

Spain's southern coast is an international playground for the rich, famous, and often tacky. The glitzy **Costa del Sol** has been Spain's jet-setting beach getaway for decades, but you can find better, less crowded, and less expensive beaches — on the **Costa de la Luz,** for example.

The main attractions in this region are

- Seville, Córdoba, and Granada — the three pillars of Moorish Andalusia — and their great monuments: Seville's **cathedral,** the world's largest Gothic building; the awe-inspiring **Great Mosque** in Córdoba; and Granada's **Alhambra,** a miracle palace of light and legend.
- Andalusia's famous spring festivals: Seville's **Holy Week** and **April Fair,** Cordoba's decorated patios and **May Festivals,** and the **pilgrimage to Rocío.**
- The delicious art of the tapas crawl, invented by Andalusians, who still practice it with unequaled flair (see Chapter 1).
- The ***pueblos blancos,*** medieval whitewashed villages perched on the peaks of the southern mountain ranges.
- The leisurely, hedonistic south: Andalusia's famed coasts.

But keep in mind . . .

- In summer (and to a lesser extent year-round), few places on earth are hotter.
- Those great spring festivals draw crowds from around the world and push prices through the roof.
- To see much of the south, you have little choice but to rent a car.

Scheduling Your Time

If you've never been to Spain and think of it as a smallish European country, you may believe that you can cover Barcelona, the Basque Country, Madrid, the castles of Castile, and all of Andalusia in a couple of weeks. Although doing so is theoretically possible (and easier than ever with faster trains and cheaper flights), you'd have to endure a lightning-fast tour across Spain, and quantity rarely equals quality when you're traveling.

Many travelers today instead focus on one particular region, concentrating on the big and small attractions of that area and (I think) getting a better overall flavor of the country. I encourage you to do that as well, and not get too manic about seeing *every*thing. The hassles of transportation can eat into your vacation; if you spend more time getting to places than experiencing them after you're there, you may return from your trip feeling that you need a vacation to recover from the one you just had. Especially if you think you may return to Spain some day, I advise that you plan a regional-based trip.

Because you can get a huge dose of Spanish flavor in any region, I always tell friends to start with a list of what they absolutely must see or experience, and then build an itinerary around that. If you're a certified art head and you can't step foot in Spain without seeing the great Spanish masters at the Prado, plan a couple of days in Madrid and then decide on day trips to Castile or a visit to southern Spain. If you're dying to see Barcelona's famed *moderniste* architecture, focus on the Catalan capital and add the Costa Brava, perhaps. Food junkies may want to take a seat at the splendid tables of San Sebastián and Bilbao and then walk it off touring northern Spain.

Spain is fairly easy to get around, whether by public transportation or rental car — though distances can be significant, and you have to factor

Dealing with the daily tourist grind

When planning your trip, be sure to build some time into your schedule to get into the rhythm of Spanish life. Taking time to relax and absorb your stay in Spain — listening to the exuberant Castilian Spanish all around you, checking out the fashions, and so on — is, for most people, more important than seeing that one last cathedral or museum.

The easiest way to dive into the culture is to get off your feet and plunk yourself down at an outdoor cafe. Cafes are a Spanish institution and a daily ritual for most Spaniards. Not only can you reflect on what you've seen so far, but you can also watch Spanish life all around you. In smaller towns, take time to stroll the central promenade — also a time-honored element of Spanish life — and hit the local tapas joints.

in travel time. You can't just zip effortlessly from Barcelona to Madrid to Seville to Bilbao unless you fly. Some Spanish trains still aren't up to par with those in northern Europe, but between major destinations the trains are generally excellent. The best of the lot is the fantastic high-speed rail (abbreviated in Spanish as AVE) between Madrid and Córdoba and Seville in Andalusia. Unfortunately, the long-awaited high-speed line between Barcelona and Madrid still isn't a reality; trains between these two cities are pretty slow, and the best option is to fly.

Revealing the Secret of the Seasons

Almost any time of year is the right time to go to Spain, which has some of the best year-round weather in Europe. Though Spain is renowned and revered for its sun, avoid some sunny areas in the deadly hot summer. Fortunately, no matter when you go, you can find a part of Spain tailor-made for the time of year you're visiting.

Even in winter you can find the warmth of the Spanish sun. Spring and fall are overall the most pleasant seasons, when you can enjoy festivals, fewer crowds than in summer, and a respite from scorching summer heat. If you visit Spain in summer, you may want to do as Spaniards themselves do and head north.

Spring

Spring (especially late spring, from mid-April to mid-May) is ideal for Central Spain, Andalusia, the Mediterranean coast, and the Balearic Islands. The sun hasn't cranked up to its full potential yet (many regions only get up to between 15°C and 25°C (60°F–75°F), flowers are in dazzling bloom, and Spaniards, who love to be outside, fill sidewalk cafes. In addition, some of the best festivals take place in spring.

But keep in mind that the north can be pretty rainy, and the spring festivals in Andalusia put hotel accommodations at a premium.

Summer

Summer is an excellent time to hit northern "green" Spain, which is usually rainy in winter and spring. From the Basque Country to Galicia, the temperatures are the peninsula's coolest, averaging around 21°C (70°F).

Keep the heat and crowds in mind, however. Madrid and Andalusia are extremely hot and dry, like an overheated brick oven. Temperatures routinely soar to the near 38°C (100°F) or worse. Barcelona's pretty humid, so even though temperatures may only be around 29°C (85°F), you can feel sticky and uncomfortable. During summer, Europeans pour into Spain, especially the coastal regions. In August, 90 percent of Spaniards are on vacation, so much of the country (inland, at least) closes up for the month. During the last week of July and first week of August, highways crisscrossing Spain clog with expatriate Moroccans returning home from northern Europe for the summer holidays.

Fall

Fall may be the best time to visit Spain as a whole, with sunny days, clear skies, comfortable temperatures, and fewer crowds than in summer. Temperatures range from lows of 4°C (40°F) to highs in the low to mid-20s (mid-70s or low 80s) in the south.

Although fall offers great weather for traveling, the Atlantic coast gets a good bit of rain, and the summer heat may still linger in central and southern Spain.

Winter

Winter is a good time to travel to the southern Mediterranean and the mountains in both the north and south for snow sports. Crowds are non-existent, and prices drop for hotels and airfares.

But consider that some coastal resorts, especially on the Costa Brava, virtually shut down during this slow season. And in Central Spain, where extremes rule, winter can be as cold (with temperatures dipping into the single digits Celsius/30s Fahrenheit) as summer is hot.

Getting a handle on crowds and prices

Spain is one of the world's top tourist destinations; it gets more visitors every year than it has citizens. During much of the year, parts of Spain are quite crowded with tourists and expensive. You can find the best bargains during the shoulder seasons (late fall and early spring) and off-seasons. Prices are lower at hotels, and getting a reservation and doing just about everything else — going to a restaurant, visiting a museum or cathedral, traveling by train or on the highway, and so on — is much less difficult. The shoulder seasons are cheaper than summer (if not rock-bottom).

Prices in Spain are usually lowest in November through February and highest in July and August. If a bargain trip is high on your list, keep this pricing information in mind when making your reservation.

Besides July and August, prices are also highest during Easter week. Avoid these times if you don't want rushes of Spanish and European tourists sweeping you away. Traditionally, Europeans, en masse, take off the month of August and try to beat each other to the beaches (as it happens, they end up clogging highways leading to the beaches and then squeezing in next to each other on the sand). Most Europeans don't yet have the vacation flexibility that many North Americans enjoy (that said, though, most Europeans get a full month or more of vacation!). So take advantage of your greater flexibility if you can visit Spain in fall, winter, or early spring.

Knowing when not to go

You've probably already figured out that Spain in August can be miserable. The sun bakes the heck out of everything in sight, major cities become ghost towns as wise Spaniards flee to the coasts, and the most desirable places where water or cooler temperatures are within reach are packed with Spanish and European tourists. If you're not on the coast, you may find the short hours and closings frustrating, and few restaurants are even open.

Christmas and Easter holidays can be great times to visit Spain as long as you know what you're getting into: religious holidays, during which a number of museums and businesses are closed for business. But that's the trade-off to see Spain at its religious and folkloric best. Many Spaniards have the entire Holy Week (Easter) off, so coasts and popular Easter cities such as Seville and Málaga fill up not only with Spaniards but also with people from the rest of the planet.

Prices follow the law of supply and demand and go through the roof when everybody wants to visit a particular place. That's April and May, during the celebrated festivals of Seville and Córdoba, and summer (July and August) in the Balearics, Northern Spain, and along the Mediterranean coasts. If you don't want to run with the bulls or watch other people perform that original extreme sport, stay away from Pamplona in early July (July 6–14).

Perusing a Calendar of Events

Spain's special fiestas are what make it unique. No other European country has maintained the variety of vibrant expressions of culture and color like Spain has. However, if you want to plan your vacation around them, keep in mind two important words: *Plan ahead.* Several of the festivals are extremely popular with national as well as international travelers, and unless you're partial to sleeping on the street, they require reservations way in advance.

Every city and town in Spain also celebrates a patron saint's feast day. These days are impossible to keep track of, so understand that you may arrive in a place and discover that it's a holiday, even though I don't list it with the rest of Spain's major holidays in the "Spain's national holidays" box in this chapter. Having some cash on you at all times is a good idea in case banks are closed. For a more comprehensive list of the patron saints' feast days, consult the Web site for the **Spain Institute of Tourism,** www.tourspain.es.

Note that with most of these events, exact dates change from year to year, according to the calendar. Therefore, confirm the dates with the National Tourist Office of Spain (see the Appendix) if you want to make sure that you're in town for a specific event.

Spain's national holidays

National holidays celebrated in Spain include January 1 (New Year's Day), January 6 (Feast of the Epiphany), March 19 (Feast of St. Joseph), Good Friday, Easter Monday, May 1 (May Day), June 10 (Corpus Christi), June 29 (Feast of St. Peter and St. Paul), July 25 (Feast of St. James), August 15 (Feast of the Assumption), October 12 (Spain's National Day), November 1 (All Saints' Day), December 8 (Immaculate Conception), and December 25 (Christmas).

January

Spain has traditionally celebrated the gift-giving of Christmas on **Día de los Reyes (Three Kings Day),** although Santa Claus, also known as Papá Noel, is starting to visit Spanish kids. In most cities, elaborately dressed kings and their entourages parade through the city. January 6.

February/March

Cádiz's **Carnaval** — Spain's best and most flamboyant carnival celebration — is also the oldest. It's the closest Spain comes to Venice or Rio at carnival time, but with a flavor all its own. Get more information online at `www.cadiznet.com/carnaval` and `www.andalucia.com/festival/carnival-cadiz.htm`. Late February or early March, depending on the dates of Easter.

April

Spain's most revered religious celebration is Easter, and nobody celebrates it like the residents of Seville. Dead-serious processions run round the clock during **Semana Santa (Holy Week),** from Palm Sunday until Easter Sunday. Brotherhoods of men carry *pasos* (floats) of Christ or one of the pantheons of traditionally honored Virgenes (Virgins) and shuffle through the streets to the eerie wail of the *saeta,* a religious funeral hymn. Make hotel reservations three months to a year in advance. To find out this year's dates for Semana Santa, visit the Web sites `www.andalucia.org` and `www.sevilla.org`. Mid-April.

Sevillanos pull out all the stops for **Feria de Abril (April Fair),** which follows the solemn Easter celebrations. Women dazzle in brightly colored, polka-dotted flamenco dresses; men play the part of country *caballeros* (gentlemen). Coaches are decked out with so many flowers they look like floats in the Rose Bowl parade, and the streets rock with all-night flamenco dancing, bullfights, and horseback riding. Feria de Abril fills Seville to the rafters. For more information visit the Web sites `www.andalucia.org` and `www.sevilla.org`. Third week of April.

May

Cordobeses, known for the beauty of their whitewashed patios and courtyards, go all out every May during **Festival de los Patios (Patio Festival),** daring their neighbors to better their flower-bedecked displays. For more information, visit the Web site www.andalucia.org. First two weeks in May.

San Isidro is the patron saint of Madrid, and locals throw a ten-day celebration to honor him during **Fiesta de San Isidro.** You can enjoy daily bullfights at Las Ventas, food fairs, folklore, parades, parties, concerts, and plenty of food and drink. Make hotel reservations early. For more information, visit www.descubremadrid.com/en. Mid-May.

You must see **Romería del Rocío (Pilgrimage of the Virgin of the Dew;** also called simply El Rocío), Spain's most famous religious procession, to believe it. A million people go south to see a large group of men carry the statue of the Virgin 16km (10 miles) to Almonte, through the marshes of Coto Doñana, for consecration. Massive crowds do their best to touch the Virgin and feel her healing power. For more information, visit the Web site www.andalucia.com/festival/rocio.htm. Mid- to late May.

June

For 50 years, Granada has put on the **International Music and Dance Festival,** a notable program of dance and music at incredible venues: the Alhambra and Generalife palaces, among others. This festival is a great way to see those places enlivened by top-notch talent. Reserve at least a couple of months in advance. Visit the Web site, www.granadafestival.org, for more information, tickets, and reservations. June 21 through July 7.

Vino becomes ammo during the **Battle of Wine Festival** in Haro (La Rioja) as people douse each other with 70,000 liters of red wine — then they stumble around a lot. For more information, visit www.haro.org/ingles/turismo.htm. June 29.

July

Spanish classical and flamenco guitar fuels the rhythms of everyday life in Andalusia, and Córdoba gets some of the finest national and international guitar heroes to town for its **Festival de la Guitarra (Guitar Festival),** a series of concerts. For more information, visit www.guitarracordoba.com. First two weeks of July.

Popularized by Hemingway, the **Fiesta de San Fermín (Running of the Bulls)** involves massive beasts racing through the streets of Pamplona, while joyful and crazy humans try to outrun them. People who choose not to run get swept up in the revelry just the same. Reserve months or, at some hotels, years in advance. For more information visit www.sanfermin.com. July 6 through 14.

Spain's oldest and most prestigious jazz party, Jazzaldia, the **San Sebastián Jazz Festival,** unites some of the international biggies for smooth jazz and soulful bebop every July. Enjoy big-ticket shows (Wynton Marsalis and Pat Metheny were recent performers), as well as some freebies. Visit `www.jazzaldia.com` for more information. Last two weeks in July.

September

The site of Spain's oldest bullfighting arena and the home of a legendary matador, Ronda dips back in time every September for **Feria de Pedro Romero (Pedro Romero Fair).** Its *corrida goyesca* re-creates the atmosphere of an 18th-century bullfight from the era of Spain's great painter, Francisco Goya. Men and women decked out in fancy dress ride through the streets on horse carriages, and bullfighting aficionados come from all over the world to see classical exhibitions. For more information, visit `www.turismoderonda.es`. First week of September.

The **International Film Festival,** Spain's top film festival, shakes up the beautiful resort city of San Sebastián. You can find nearly as many screenings and stars here as at the Cannes Film Festival in France. For more information, visit `www.sansebastianfestival.com`. Second half of September (dates vary).

Head to Logroño (and throughout La Rioja) for the **Fiestas de la Vendimia Riojana (Wine Harvest Festival)** to celebrate the great grape with dancing, bullfighting, music, and parades. Oh yeah, and drinking, too. For information, visit `www.larioja.org/turismo`. Third week of September.

During **La Mercé** Barcelona rolls out the *cabezudos* — big papier mâché heads — that roam the streets, fascinating (or frightening) kids and honoring Our Lady of Mercy. For more information, visit `www.barcelonaturisme.com`. September 24.

October/November

Spanish and international artists participate in Madrid's **Festival de Otoño (Autumn Festival),** a program of opera, ballet, dance, music, and theater. Make hotel reservations early; information about schedules and tickets is at `www.madrid.org/clas_artes/fo06/index.html`. Late October to late November.

December

Noche Vieja (New Year's Eve) revelers throughout Spain stuff grapes into their mouths, one at the sound of each of 12 chimes at midnight, to ring in the New Year. In Madrid, people crowd into the Puerta del Sol plaza and cheer on the clock tower. December 31.

Part II

Planning Your Trip to Spain

The 5th Wave — By Rich Tennant

In this part . . .

Use the information in this section to get down to the nitty-gritty and start planning. To have a successful trip, you need all the facts at hand so you can tackle issues such as planning your budget, handling money, and deciding on (or against) package tours. The biggest questions you probably have at this point, though, are the following: What's the best way to get to Spain? How do I get around after I've landed? And where the heck am I going to stay?

In addition to addressing those questions, I offer some suggestions for keeping costs down and provide specific advice for families, seniors, gays and lesbians, and other travelers with individual needs. This section lays the best resources on the line (including many that are online). I also explain preliminary matters you need to consider, such as passports and visas, Customs, travel insurance, staying connected by cellphone and e-mail, and airline security.

Chapter 4

Managing Your Money

In This Chapter

- Developing a realistic budget
- Looking out for hidden expenses
- Keeping costs down
- Checking out sample budgets for one- and two-week tours
- Finding out what things cost in Spain

You're probably at least curious — if not yet clutching a calculator — to know approximately how much a vacation to Spain will set you back. Of course, that amount depends on what kind of trip you're taking — an anniversary or honeymoon blowout, or a more economical taste-of-Spain trip. Although Spain was once the European destination of choice for budget-minded travelers, that's no longer the case. And the euro has risen to an uncomfortable exchange rate against the dollar, so now more than ever before, budgeting accurately for a trip to Spain is important.

Although Spain isn't the bargain it once was, on the whole it remains relatively affordable compared with other popular destinations such as England, France, Germany, and Italy. You may find that some items in Spain are cheaper than they are in your home country. Dining out can be a remarkably good value, with excellent wines — thought of as a staple and thus not overtaxed in restaurants — surprisingly accessible. Renting a car isn't cheap, and, as in all of Europe, gas is very expensive, but public transportation is a good deal. And many smaller inns and hotels are affordably priced. Not surprisingly, the big cities (especially Madrid and Barcelona), nicer hotels, and top-tier restaurants are still expensive (though cheaper than in many other parts of Europe).

Planning Your Budget

Budgeting a trip to Spain depends on where you go, how long you plan to stay, and what you plan to do while you're there. Your major expenditures are airfare and accommodations. You can find reasonably priced dining, but if you want to sample the best in big cities, expect to pay for the privilege. Where and when you go greatly affects your budget. A room in Barcelona or Madrid costs a lot more than a room in a smaller city; and accommodations in Pamplona during the Running of the Bulls, or in Seville during Easter or April Fair, cost considerably more than during the shoulder or off-seasons. This same principle of expecting to pay more in cities also applies to all other expenses (meals and so on).

Table 4-1 gives you a sampling of what things cost in a large Spanish city. (Smaller cities and towns are less expensive, especially for hotels and restaurants.) Check out Table 4-2 for a sampling of transportation costs, along with other common travel-related expenses.

Table 4-1 Sample Per-Person Budgets: Average One- and Two-Week Tours

Expense	*Cost for One Week*	*Cost for Two Weeks*
Airfare (round-trip New York City to Madrid)	$900	$900
Individual rail tickets (based on train trips of average length, $60 each)	$120 for two trips	$300 for five trips
A tank of gas ($60)	$70	$140
Overnight in hotels ($90 per person per night)	$630	$1,260
Meals per person (assuming breakfasts at $7, lunches at $18, and dinners at $50)	$525	$1,050
Sightseeing admission ($25 per day)	$175	$350
City transportation ($15 per day)	$75	$150
Souvenirs, postcards, miscellaneous ($12 per day)	$84	$168
Total	$2,599	$4,318

Transportation

Airfare is one of your biggest expenses, even after you apply all the cost-cutting tips that I give you later in this chapter. Airfares fluctuate year-round, with airlines offering special deals during low travel season and hiking up prices for holidays. Of course, fares vary widely depending on your point of origin and your destination. For example, from the New York area, with the shorter distance to Europe and the greater frequency of flights, you may pay anywhere from $700 to $1,000 for a round-trip coach ticket to Madrid or Barcelona. Prices from the rest of the United States are usually at the upper end of that range, or even slightly higher. If you're flying from London, you're in especially good luck, because you can take advantage of plenty of special flight deals and charters. If you're flying from another country, check out Chapter 5 for airline information.

Most transportation costs on the ground are reasonable — even surprisingly affordable — in Spain. Within major cities (such as Barcelona, Bilbao, and Madrid), the *metro,* or subway, is efficient and a great deal, especially if you purchase a multitrip ticket. Buses are just as affordable, and even taxis won't bust too many budgets (most in-town trips cost less than 8€/$9.60).

As for transportation in a specific region or around Spain, your primary choices are air, rail, or rental car (though particularly in the Basque Country in the north, buses are a better bet, because the highways are superb and the buses much faster than trains). Unless you're in a real hurry, or you need to cover a lot of ground (say, Barcelona to Seville or Madrid to Bilbao), you probably don't need to fly. Flights within Spain aren't overly expensive; the Barcelona-Madrid shuttle flight — once prohibitively costly — is now very affordable (around 100€/$120, though certain flights are as low as 50€/$60) and a worthwhile alternative to the slower trains and buses. As a whole, Spanish trains are punctual and attractively priced.

The most costly option is renting a car. At 40€ ($48) and up per day, only consider renting under certain circumstances; a rental is great for traveling in areas where good public transportation options don't exist, where you need to cover a lot of ground in a short period of time, or where the flexibility of your own car really adds to the trip (the *pueblos blancos* in Andalusia is a good example). In each region's chapter, I discuss whether a rental car is a good idea.

Petrol (gasoline) is one of the major expenses in European countries, and this holds true in Spain. At this writing, unleaded gasoline *(sin plomo)* costs .94€ per liter, or about $4.25 per gallon — although very expensive by North American standards, believe it or not Spain has one of the cheapest prices in Europe for gas! Diesel is cheaper, at .91€ per liter (about $4.15 a gallon). One U.S. gallon equals 3.79 liters. (For the latest costs, consult `www.aaroadwatch.ie/eupetrolprices`.) Though not low-priced in Spain, renting a car isn't quite as costly as it is in many other European countries.

Table 4-2 What Things Cost in Barcelona

Item	*Cost*
Taxi from airport to downtown	20€ ($24)
One metro or bus ride (not discount ticket)	1.20€ ($1.44)
Coffee	1€ ($1.20)

(continued)

Table 4-2 *(continued)*

Item	*Cost*
Beer at tapas bar	2€ ($2.40)
Scotch at nightclub	10€–12€ ($12–$14)
Local phone call	.30€ (36¢)
Double room at Duquesa de Cardona	185€ ($222)
Ticket to concert at Palau de la Música	30€ ($36)
Movie ticket (*versión original,* in English)	7€ ($8.40)
Admission to the Picasso Museum	6€ ($7.20)
Dinner for two with wine at Cal Pep	100€ ($120)
Lunch for two with wine at Restaurant 7 Portes	60€ ($72)
Cover charge and one drink at Tablao Flamenco Cordobés	30€ ($36)

Lodging

Unless you book a package that combines the costs of airfare and accommodations (see Chapter 5 for details), lodging vies with (or may exceed) the cost of flying. You can find a budget hotel for about 50€ ($60) a night, though in some popular destinations, such as Barcelona or Seville, finding a good and clean place for that price is becoming increasingly tough. An economy hotel runs 50€ ($60) to 100€ ($120) per night for a double room. A moderately priced hotel costs from 100€ ($120) and 195€ ($234). Expensive hotels run 195€ ($234) and up to 300€ ($360). For the most part, only the famous palacelike hotels and ultraluxe designer hotels in Spain (such as Hotel Arts in Barcelona, the Ritz in Madrid, and Alfonso XIII in Seville; see Chapters 10, 13, and 15) cost upwards of 300€ ($360) a night. Many hotels include buffet breakfast but not the 7 percent IVA tax in their rates; make sure you inquire about both items. (See "Taking Taxes into Account" later in this chapter for more about the IVA.)

Dining

You can subsist on cheap tapas and fast food, or break the bank with fancy, multicourse dinners at restaurants specializing in seafood or Basque Country cuisine. Sensible tapas munching (heck, sometimes you can put a small meal together with the free snacks you get with glasses of wine and beer) and fixed-price *menús del día* (daily menus that are usually available for lunch) can really keep down your costs. Indeed, eating out in most of Spain is considerably less expensive than it is in much of Europe. So what does an average Spanish dining experience

Is there no such thing as a free munch?

All tapas aren't created equal. You can enjoy the free variety — small snacks that you get to nibble along with a *vinito* (glass of wine) or *cerveza* (beer) — or the slightly larger tapas and *raciones* (full portions) that you must pay for but that are inexpensive (unless you order the king-sized prawns). However, beware of the place that sets down a too-good-to-be-true salad or whopping plate of food next to your glass of wine. It may be none-too-good to your wallet. Ask about any unsolicited food if you're unsure whether additional charges apply.

cost? A typical three-course dinner in a low-key neighborhood restaurant runs about 15€ to 30€ ($18–$36) a head. You can also find restaurants serving satisfying two- (or more) course meals for as little as 12€ to 15€ ($14–$18). Lunch is always cheaper than dinner, so follow the Spaniards and eat a full lunch (when most sights are closed anyway) and go light at dinner.

As a rule, Spaniards don't eat much more than some toast or a croissant and coffee for breakfast. Breakfast buffets at hotels usually aren't included in the cost of your room, and if you blindly stumble into the breakfast room each morning, you may find that you're tacking as much as 20€ ($24) onto your daily lodging bill.

Sightseeing

Entry fees to museums and other sights aren't too expensive in most parts of Spain, but they can quickly add up, especially if you're a museum maniac. (Museum and monument admissions generally range from 1€–8€, or $1.20–$9.60.) Make a list of must-dos to get a ballpark figure of how much money to set aside for sightseeing. Many museums offer free admission on certain days; when applicable, I list good deals along with hours and admission costs in attraction listings throughout this book.

Shopping

Shopping is the most elastic part of your budget, and the part most dependent on your own tendencies, because you can buy nothing at all or enough to fill a dozen suitcases. Spain isn't exactly Mexico — a haven for inexpensive crafts — and although the steady rise of the euro has made things considerably more expensive, you may still well want to bring home Spanish fashions, crafts, or ceramics. Steering clear of most items you can buy at home is a good idea. Although the clerk won't add on a tax to your purchase price, you can rest assured that it's built in. If you live outside the European Union, you may be able to reclaim a healthy portion of the 16 percent value-added sales tax (VAT, or *IVA* in Spanish), but only if you meet certain requirements. (See "Taking Taxes into Account" later in this chapter, for information on how to get your IVA refunded.)

Your dollars may go further in Spain than you imagine, even with the recent ascension of the euro, the European Union's common currency. (See "Handling Money" later in this chapter for more about the euro.) Although Europe is now generally more expensive than the United States, you may still find some good deals if you know where to look (barring, of course, a major crash in the dollar or sudden surge of the euro between the writing of this book and your trip).

In Spain, the law actually determines when sales take place, with twice-annual sell-offs of inventory that all begin at the same time: the second week of January and the last week of July (as you'll find in much of Europe). Signs announcing *rebajas* (sales) are plastered over store windows. Prices continue to drop when stores move from first to second *(segundas rebajas)* and, finally, to *últimas rebajas* (like the final clearance sale).

Nightlife and entertainment

The price of your evening entertainment depends on your finances and stamina level. See Table 4-2, earlier in this chapter, for a general idea of what tickets and cover fees cost around town. Although beer and wine are rather affordable, alcoholic drinks in nightclubs and special bars can make even a New Yorker weep. If you're planning on several late nights out, budget big in order to paint the town *rojo* (red).

Keeping a lid on hidden expenses

Unless you plan for hidden costs, you're likely to return from your trip over budget. Among costs that you must consider are

- **Additional rental car costs:** Surcharges such as a 10€ ($12) airport pickup; a value-added tax of 15 percent if you don't prepay for the car; and gasoline costs.
- **Costs of communicating with folks back home:** Either through international phone calls or Internet cafes.
- **Hotel taxes:** Factor in an additional 7 percent of your total hotel bill — including goods and services.
- **Tipping:** Though it's probably less here than you're accustomed to back home (see "Tipping tips," below), you'll still want to factor it in.

You can't avoid some of these costs, of course, but keeping them in mind can certainly inform the decisions you make on your trip to Spain.

Tipping tips

Many Americans over-tip in Spain. The difference is most noticeable in a Spanish restaurant, where a gratuity is officially figured into the bill — but none of it goes to the server. In nice restaurants, adding about 10 percent to the cost of the bill is customary. If you leave a 20 percent tip, you may see your picture hanging on the wall the next time you come back. Don't tip bartenders for each round of drinks; leave a 1€ ($1.20) coin or two at the end of the night to show your appreciation. Give 1€ ($1.20) per bag to bellhops and doormen, and 1€ to 2€ ($1.20–$2.40) per night for a maid. Pay a concierge who has gone out of her way to help you between 5€ and 10€ ($6–$12). Tipping taxi drivers isn't necessary; just pay the meter, or at the most, round up (though a driver who is especially helpful should receive about a 5 to 10 percent tip). Likewise, give ushers who help you to your seat in a theater or bullring a few small coins.

Cutting Costs — but Not the Fun

Throughout this book, Bargain Alert icons highlight money-saving tips and/or great deals. Here are some additional cost-cutting strategies:

- **Go off-season.** If you can travel at nonpeak times (Oct–Mar, for example), hotel prices and flights cost less than during peak months — often saving you anywhere from 20 to 50 percent. Note that major holidays and local festivals are the exceptions to the cheaper off-season rules; on those occasions, you may see hotel prices double.
- **Travel midweek.** If you can travel on a Tuesday, Wednesday, or Thursday, you may find cheaper flights to your destination. When you ask about airfares, see if you can get a cheaper rate by flying on a different day. For more tips on getting a good fare, see Chapter 5.
- **Try a package tour.** For many destinations, you can book airfare, hotel, ground transportation, and even some sightseeing just by making one call to a travel agent or packager, for a price much less than if you put the trip together. (See Chapter 5 for more on package tours.)
- **Reserve a room with a small refrigerator and coffeemaker.** You don't have to slave over a hot stove to cut a few costs. Buying supplies for breakfast can save you money — and probably calories.
- **Always ask for discount rates.** Membership in AAA, frequent-flier plans, trade unions, AARP, or other groups may qualify you for savings on car rentals, plane tickets, hotel rooms, and even meals. Ask about everything; you may be pleasantly surprised.
- **Ask if your kids can stay in the room with you.** A room with two double beds usually doesn't cost any more than one with a queen-size bed. And many hotels won't charge you the additional-person

rate if the additional person is pint-size and related to you. Even if you have to pay 10€ or 15€ ($12–$18) extra for a rollaway bed, not taking two rooms can save you hundreds.

- **Try expensive restaurants at lunch instead of at dinner.** Lunch is the main meal in Spain, and lunch tabs are usually a fraction of what dinner would cost at a top restaurant even though the menu often boasts many of the same specialties. Plan to load up on midday menus — lunchtime fixed-price meals are a Spanish classic — and you can get a full meal for around 12€ to15€ ($14–$18). Also, order house wine, or *vino de la casa.*
- **Get out of town.** In many places, big savings are just a short drive or taxi ride away. Hotels just outside the city, across the river, or located in less-convenient areas are great bargains. Outlying motels often have free parking, with lower rates than downtown hotels offering amenities that you may never use. Sure, at a motel you'll be carrying your own bags, but the rooms are often just as comfortable and a whole lot cheaper. Big cities and resorts are, in general, much more expensive than small towns and the Spanish countryside. See Chapter 7 for more on hotels.
- **Walk a lot.** Spaniards love to stroll, so you'll fit right in if you walk. A good pair of walking shoes can save you money on taxis and other local transportation. As a bonus, you'll get to know your destination more intimately as you explore at a slower pace.
- **Sit in the *sol* and not the *sombra*.** At bullfights, the cheap seats are in the *sol,* or sun. Sitting in the *sombra* (shade) costs more. Similarly, if you're going to see the inside of a hall more than to hear a particular program, choose the nosebleed seats; they're often around 5€ ($6).
- **Skip the souvenirs.** Your photographs and memories are the best mementos of your trip; do without the endless T-shirts, key chains, salt-and-pepper shakers, Mexican *sombreros* (why they sell those in Spain, I don't know), and other trinkets.

Handling Money

You're the best judge of how much cash you feel comfortable carrying or what alternative form of currency is your favorite. That's not going to change much on your vacation. True, you'll probably be moving around more and incurring more expenses than you generally do (unless you happen to eat out every meal when you're at home), and you may let your mind slip into vacation gear and not be as vigilant about your safety as when you're in work mode. But, those factors aside, the only type of payment that won't be quite as available to you away from home is your personal checkbook.

Making sense of the euro

The euro gives the European Union a single common currency, so currency-exchange headaches in member nations — including Spain — are largely a thing of the past. You no longer have to worry about getting your hands on pesetas. But even with currency exchange simplified, you still need to think about some money matters before your trip. What's the best way to deal with money matters while you're traveling in Spain? With traveler's checks? Using local ATMs to withdraw cash, just like at home? Or whipping out plastic across the country? This section answers your questions about dishing out your dough.

The common E.U. currency, introduced January 1, 2002, is the euro (in Spain, it's pronounced *eh*-oo-roh), abbreviated by the symbol €. Coins come in eight denominations: 1, 2, 5, 10, 20, and 50 eurocents, and 1 and 2 euros. Bank notes are issued in seven denominations: 5, 10, 20, 50, 100, 200, and 500 euros.

The euro has held its strength against the U.S. dollar, and the rate of exchange between the two at press time was 1.20:1 (meaning 1€ was roughly equivalent to 83¢).

Look for information about the European Union's common currency on the Web at `www.euro.ecb.int`. For the latest exchange rates, log on to CNN's travel Web site, `www.cnn.com/travel/currency`, which features a convenient conversion tool. Plug in any world currency against the euro and instantly receive the current, official exchange.

Take some time at the beginning of your trip to familiarize yourself with the euro. Bank notes differ in size and design. In color, the euro notes are also distinct; the 5 is gray; the 10 is red; the 20 is blue; the 50 is orange; the 100 is green; the 200 is yellow; and the 500 is purple. Architectural features, from classical to modern, are represented on the bank notes, which are the same across Europe. The front of each bill features landmark windows and gates, and the back features images of landmark European bridges. Coins have one face common to all member countries; the images on the reverse sides are chosen and produced by individual nations.

Exchanging money

You can exchange foreign currency for euros at all banks, open Monday to Saturday from 8:30 a.m. to 2 p.m. (except June–Sept, when they close on Sat), as well as at *casas de cambio* (exchange bureaus) in the main cities. Many hotels and travel agencies also exchange money. Banks (including Banco de España, BBV, and Barclays), even those that charge a 1 percent commission, almost always offer more advantageous rates. When you can avoid exchanging money at *casas de cambio* and hotels, do; their rates are much worse. Likewise, be careful of exchange houses that advertise no commission; their rates are so low that you lose money. Also, don't exchange much money into euros before leaving for your trip. The rates at home are considerably less advantageous than those rates in Spain.

Using Spanish ATMs and carrying cash

The easiest and best way to get cash away from home is from an ATM (automated teller machine). The **Cirrus** (☎ **800-424-7787;** www.mastercard.com) and **PLUS** (☎ **800-843-7587;** www.visa.com) networks span the globe; look at the back of your bank card to see which network you're on, and then call or check online for ATM locations at your destination. Be sure you know your personal identification number (PIN) before you leave home and find out your daily withdrawal limit before you depart.

ATMs are as ubiquitous in Spain as they are in the United States, Canada, and other places. Look for signs advertising *cajero automático* or *cajero 24 horas* (24-hour ATM). As long as your bank card uses a four-digit PIN, you can use your card at ATMs abroad to withdraw money directly from your home bank account. Instead of withdrawing U.S. or Canadian dollars or British pounds like you do on your home turf, you get euros. The exchange rate is usually the best you can get; it's calculated at the current rate, and ATMs (and their affiliated banks) don't usually charge a commission.

Spanish ATMs only accept four-digit PIN codes. If your PIN is more than four digits, make sure you change it before leaving, or you won't be able to withdraw money from any ATM on Spanish soil. Check with your bank to see whether you need to reprogram your PIN code for usage in Spain.

Keep in mind that many banks impose a fee every time your card is used at a different bank's ATM, and that fee can be higher for international transactions (up to $5 or more) than for domestic ones (where they're rarely more than $1.50). In addition, the bank from which you withdraw cash may charge its own fee. Ask your bank for what its international ATM fees are.

Charging ahead with credit cards

Credit cards are invaluable when traveling; they're a safe way to carry money and provide a convenient record of all your travel expenses when you arrive home. You can get cash advances from your credit card at any bank, and you don't even need to go to a teller; you can receive a cash advance at the ATM if you know your PIN (in Spain, ATMs accept only a four-digit PIN). If you've forgotten your PIN or didn't know that you had one, call the phone number on the back of your credit card and ask the bank to send it to you. Receiving your PIN usually takes five to seven business days, though some banks will give you the number over the phone if you tell them your mother's maiden name or follow some other security-clearance procedure.

A hidden expense to contend with when receiving a cash advance from your credit card is that interest rates for cash advances are often significantly higher than rates for credit card purchases. More importantly, you start paying interest on the advance the moment you receive the cash. Likewise, on an airline-affiliated credit card, a cash advance doesn't earn frequent-flier miles.

The most commonly accepted credit cards in Spain (in order of most widely accepted to least widely accepted) are Visa, American Express, Diner's Club, and MasterCard (called Eurocard in Spain). Don't bother taking your Discover Card — it's only good in the United States.

When you use your credit card abroad, the exchange rate you receive is the rate that is in place when the charge actually goes through — as much as a month after the fact. Therefore, you're essentially functioning as a foreign-exchange trader, betting on an exchange rate. If you want to bet on the dollar (or pound, and so on) getting stronger against the euro, use plastic. If you prefer the current exchange rate to a future one, use cash. Don't sweat this decision, though. Unless you're purchasing Picassos, the difference in exchange rates between when you make the purchase and when your transaction goes through is likely to be negligible.

Keep in mind that when you use your credit card abroad, most banks assess a 2 percent fee above the 1 percent fee charged by Visa or MasterCard or American Express for currency conversion on credit charges. But credit cards still may be the smart way to go when you factor in things such as exorbitant ATM fees and higher traveler's check exchange rates (and service fees).

Some credit card companies recommend that you notify them of any impending trip abroad so that they don't become suspicious when the card is used numerous times in a foreign destination and block your charges. Even if you don't call your credit-card company in advance, you can always call the card's toll-free emergency number if a charge is refused — a good reason to carry the phone number with you. But perhaps the most important lesson is to carry more than one card with you on your trip; a card may not work for any number of reasons, so having a backup is the smart way to go.

Toting traveler's checks

Although most Spanish hotels, restaurants, and shops accept traveler's checks, they are less necessary these days because most cities have 24-hour ATMs that allow you to withdraw small amounts of cash as needed. However, keep in mind that you will likely be charged an ATM withdrawal fee if the bank isn't your own, so if you're withdrawing money every day, you may be better off with traveler's checks — provided that you don't mind showing identification every time you want to cash one.

You can get traveler's checks at almost any bank. **American Express** offers denominations of $20, $50, $100, $500, and (for cardholders only) $1,000. You pay a service charge ranging from 1 to 4 percent. You can also get American Express traveler's checks over the phone by calling ☎ **800-221-7282;** Amex gold and platinum cardholders who use this number are exempt from the 1 percent fee.

Visa offers traveler's checks at Citibank locations nationwide, as well as at several other banks. The service charge ranges from 1.5 to 2 percent; checks come in denominations of $20, $50, $100, $500, and $1,000. Call ☎ **800-732-1322** for information. AAA members can obtain Visa checks without a fee at most AAA offices or by calling ☎ **866-339-3378. MasterCard** also offers traveler's checks. Call ☎ **800-223-9920** for a location near you.

If you choose to carry traveler's checks, be sure to keep a record of their serial numbers separate from your checks in the event that they are stolen or lost. You'll get a refund faster if you know the numbers.

Taking Taxes into Account

In Spain, the only thing you need to worry about tax-wise is something called IVA (pronounced *ee*-bah) — Spanish for value-added tax (abbreviated VAT in English). IVA is a tax assessed on virtually everything you purchase, from clothing to hotel rooms to meals.

Europe's value-added tax is hefty — ranging from 6.5 to 25 percent, depending on the item being taxed. The good news for nonresidents of the European Union is that you can get back much of the tax heaped on items you buy — with a few conditions. Spain's IVA on most consumer goods is 16 percent. Hotels and restaurants charge 7 percent IVA, but you can't get that money refunded. To get money back, you have to be vigilant. Global Refund, a company that acts as a third-party agent for IVA refunds, claims that Americans lose an estimated $50 million a year in unclaimed refunds.

When shopping, look for the blue-and-gray TAX FREE SHOPPING or TAX FREE FOR TOURISTS signs in the windows of stores. Such a sign means that the store participates in the IVA Refund Program and, therefore, can provide you with the necessary forms. The required paperwork — filled out at each store and then signed and stamped by Customs officials at the airport on your way out of the country — can be a pain, though, so hold on to all your receipts and forms. (Fortunately, personnel in many stores accustomed to dealing with tourists are well-versed in IVA refund matters, and most can walk you through the steps.)

You're only eligible for a refund if you spend a minimum of 90.15€ ($108) in a single store (you can get multiple refunds as long as you spend that minimum amount in each store). At the departing airport (or border crossing), present the refund request forms at Customs and get them stamped. Afterward, go to the "Cash Refund" office and show the receipt for the purchase and, if requested, the actual items bought, and surrender the stamped tax-free slips and receipts. (You can also mail receipts and slips from your home country; when you get the forms from each store, an envelope is included for doing this.) At the Global Refund airport kiosk, show your stamped receipts, and Global Refund gives immediate cash refunds in the local currency or in the currencies used for the purchases. It can also issue a credit to a major credit card (your refund amount is converted to your home currency). Global Refund claims a fee of approximately 3 percent, and if you want your refund in dollars, you must pay another fee. In the end, your refund is slightly less than the 16 percent VAT — 13.8 percent.

Be sure to leave a little extra time to complete the necessary bureaucratic steps at the airport if you want a refund. For more information before you go, consult the Global Refund Web page: www.globalrefund.com.

Dealing with a Lost or Stolen Wallet

Be sure to contact all your credit card companies the minute you discover your wallet has been lost or stolen. Most credit card companies have an emergency toll-free number to call if your card is lost or stolen; they may be able to wire you a cash advance immediately or deliver an emergency credit card in a day or two. Call the following emergency numbers in Spain: **American Express, ☎ 917-43-70-00; Diners Club, ☎ 902-40-11-12; MasterCard, ☎ 900-97-12-31; Visa, ☎ 900-99-11-24.**

Odds are that if your wallet is gone, you've seen the last of it, and the police aren't likely to recover it for you. However, after you realize that it's gone and you cancel your credit cards, call to inform the police — either the Policía Municipal (municipal police) or Policía Nacional (national police). Your credit card company or insurer may require a police report number or record of the loss.

If you need emergency cash over the weekend, when banks and American Express offices are closed, you can have money wired to you via **Western Union (☎ 800-325-6000;** www.westernunion.com).

Identity theft and fraud are potential complications of losing your wallet, especially if you've lost your driver's license along with your cash and credit cards. Notify the major credit-reporting bureaus immediately; placing a fraud alert on your records may protect you against liability for criminal activity. The three major U.S. credit-reporting agencies are **Equifax (☎ 800-766-0008;** www.equifax.com), **Experian (☎ 888-397-3742;** www.experian.com), and **TransUnion (☎ 800-680-7289;** www.transunion.com). Finally, if you've lost all forms of photo ID, call your airline and explain the situation; the airline personnel may allow you to board the plane if you have a copy of your passport or birth certificate and a copy of the police report you've filed.

Chapter 5

Getting to Spain

In This Chapter

- Deciding whether to use a travel agent to plan your trip
- Finding out what you need to know about package tours
- Booking special-interest tours

Getting there is supposed to be half the fun, so the saying goes — but researching *how* you're going to get to Spain probably seems much less of a thrill. Nevertheless, before you start packing for your trip, you need to do a little homework. Sort out package and escorted tours and find a good airfare. With all the information now available online, this homework isn't as complicated as it sounds.

Flying to Spain

Logically, most travelers will be flying to Spain. After you arrive in Spain, low-cost airfares across Europe make flying more convenient than taking a train or ferry, even for those travelers arriving from another European country.

Finding out which airlines fly to Spain

Spain is the second most popular destination in the world, and most of the big airlines fly there from North America, the United Kingdom, Australia, and New Zealand. A majority of travelers fly into either Madrid or Barcelona, although several European airlines also fly directly to Málaga as well as several to other Spanish cities (such as Bilbao and Palma de Mallorca).

Flying from North America

Iberia Airlines (☎ **800-772-4642;** `www.iberia.com`), the national carrier of Spain, is the principal carrier with the most routes into and within Spain. It offers daily nonstop flights from New York, Chicago, and Miami to Madrid (with connecting flights to Barcelona and other cities). You can also catch flights from Los Angeles (with a brief stop in Miami). Iberia also offers daily service to Madrid from Montreal.

Air Europa (☎ **888-238-7672;** www.aireuropa.com), another Spanish carrier, offers daily nonstop service from Newark, New Jersey, to Madrid (and on to Barcelona after switching planes). It flies once a week from New York to Málaga.

Air Plus Comet (☎ **877-999-7587;** www.airplususa.com), headquartered in Madrid, flies once a week (Fridays) from New York JFK to Málaga and then on to Madrid.

Many North American airlines also fly to Spain. **American Airlines** (☎ **800-433-7300;** www.aa.com) offers daily nonstop service to Madrid from Miami and New York (sharing routes with Iberia). **Continental Airlines** (☎ **800-231-0856;** www.continental.com) has daily nonstop flights from Newark to Madrid. **Delta** (☎ **800-241-4141;** www.delta.com) maintains daily nonstop service from New York to both Madrid and Barcelona (separate flights) and from Atlanta to Madrid. **US Airways** (☎ **800-428-4322;** www.usair.com) features daily flights to Madrid from Philadelphia.

Among European (non-Spanish) airlines, **British Airways** (☎ **800-AIR-WAYS;** www.britishairways.com) flies from Toronto, Montreal, and Vancouver (as well as from cities in the United States) to Madrid, Barcelona, and Bilbao via London. **TAP Air Portugal** (☎ **800-221-7370;** www.tap-airportugal.pt) flies daily from New York to Madrid and Barcelona via Lisbon. **Lufthansa** (☎ **800-645-3880;** www.lufthansa-usa.com) travels via Frankfurt, Germany, from major U.S. and Canadian cities to the Madrid, Barcelona, Málaga, Bilbao, and Palma de Mallorca.

Flying from the United Kingdom

British Airways (☎ **0870-850-9850** in London; www.britishairways.com) and **Iberia** (☎ **0845-601-2854** in London) are the two major carriers that fly from London's Heathrow and Gatwick airports, as well as from Manchester. British Airways flies to Alicante, Barcelona, Bilbao, Madrid, Málaga, Palma de Mallorca, Seville, Tenerife, and Valencia. Iberia offers daily service to several points in Spain from London and Manchester, including Alicante, Barcelona, Bilbao, La Coruña, Madrid, Oviedo, Málaga, Santiago, Seville, and Valencia. **Air Europa** (☎ **0870-777-7709** in London; www.aireuropa.com) flies from London Gatwick to Madrid and Palma de Mallorca.

A number of low-cost European air carriers, among them **EasyJet** (☎ **087-0600-0000;** www.easyjet.com) and **RyanAir** (☎ **087-1246-0000;** www.bookryanair.com), fly from the United Kingdom to many cities in Spain. For more information, visit www.tourspain.co.uk.

Flying from Ireland

From Ireland, **Aer Lingus** (☎ **1-886-8844** in Ireland, or **0845-084-4444** in London; www.aerlingus.com) flies daily to Barcelona, Bilbao, Madrid, Málaga, Palma de Mallorca, and Tenerife from Dublin. **RyanAir** (☎ **081-830-3030**) flies to several smaller Spanish cities from Dublin.

Flying from Australia and New Zealand

There are no direct flights to Spain from either Australia or New Zealand. Often the cheapest routes are through Asia, on carriers such as **Japan Airlines** (☎ 02-9272-1111 in Australia; ☎ 09-379-9906 in New Zealand; www.japanair.com), **Garuda Indonesia** (☎ 02-9334-9970 in Australia; ☎ 09-366-1862 in New Zealand; www.garuda-indonesia.com), **Singapore Airlines** (☎ 13-10-11 in Australia; ☎ 0800-808-909 in New Zealand; www.singaporeair.com), and **Thai Airways** (☎ 1-300-651-960 in Australia; ☎ 09-377-0268 in New Zealand; www.thaiair.com).

British Airways (☎ **1-300-767-177** in Australia; ☎ **09-966-9777** in New Zealand; www.britishairways.com) flies to a number of Spanish cities via London (see "Flying from the United Kingdom," earlier in the chapter). You can also fly **Qantas** (☎ **13-13-13** in Australia; ☎ **0800-808-767** in New Zealand; www.qantas.com) to London and catch a British Air flight to Spain from there.

Deciding which airport to fly into

Most international flights go to Madrid's **Barajas** or Barcelona's **El Prat** airports (though others, especially European flights, also use Málaga, Palma de Mallorca, and Bilbao). Which airport you fly into depends upon your itinerary in Spain. If you plan to see Catalonia (including Barcelona) or the north of Spain, flying into Barcelona's El Prat is your best bet. For most other parts of Spain, including Castile and Andalusia, you're better off flying into Madrid's Barajas, which offers more direct train and air service to those destinations, or into Málaga. Madrid also has easy connections to the Basque Country and Navarra.

Getting the Best Deal on Your Airfare

Competition among the major U.S. airlines is unlike that of any other industry. Every airline offers virtually the same product (a coach seat is a coach seat is a . . .), yet prices can vary by hundreds of dollars.

Business travelers who need the flexibility to buy their tickets at the last minute and change their itineraries at a moment's notice — and who want to get home before the weekend — pay (or at least their companies pay) the premium rate, known as the *full fare.* But if you can book your ticket far in advance, stay over Saturday night, and are willing to travel midweek (Tuesday, Wednesday, or Thursday), you can qualify for the least-expensive price — usually a fraction of the full fare. On most flights, even the shortest hops within the United States, the full fare is close to $1,000 or more, but a 7- or 14-day advance-purchase ticket may cost less than half of that amount. Obviously, planning ahead pays.

The airlines also periodically hold sales, in which they lower the prices on popular routes. These fares have advance-purchase requirements and date-of-travel restrictions, but you can't beat the prices. As you plan your vacation, watch for these sales, which tend to take place in seasons of low travel volume — in Spain, traditionally from October through March. You almost never see a sale around the peak summer vacation months of July and August, or around Thanksgiving or Christmas, when many people fly, regardless of the fare they have to pay.

Consolidators, also known as bucket shops, are great sources for international tickets, although they usually can't beat the Internet on fares within North America. Start by looking in Sunday newspaper travel sections; U.S. travelers should focus on the *New York Times, Los Angeles Times,* and *Miami Herald.* For less-developed destinations, small travel agents who cater to immigrant communities in large cities often have the best deals.

Bucket shop tickets are usually nonrefundable or rigged with stiff cancellation penalties, often as high as 50 to 75 percent of the ticket price, and some put you on charter airlines with questionable safety records.

Several reliable consolidators are worldwide and available on the Net. **STA Travel** (☎ 800-781-4040; www.statravel.com), the world's leader in student travel, offers good fares for travelers of all ages. **ELTExpress** (☎ 800-TRAV-800; www.flights.com) started in Europe and has excellent fares worldwide, but particularly to that continent. **Flights.com** also has "local" Web sites in 12 countries. **FlyCheap** (☎ 800-FLY-CHEAP; www.1800flycheap.com) is owned by package-holiday megalith MyTravel and has especially good access to fares for sunny destinations. **AirTicketsDirect** (☎ 800-778-3447; www.airticketsdirect.com) is based in Montreal and leverages the weak Canadian dollar for low fares. **Air Brokers International** (☎ 800-883-3273; www.airbrokers.com) specializes in round-the-world travel, but also offers one-way and business travel tickets to Europe. **Airline Consolidator.com** (☎ 888-468-5385; www.airlineconsolidator.com) is an online travel agency offering discounted fares from more than 50 airlines, as well as Eurail and hotel discounts.

Booking Your Flight Online

The "big three" online travel agencies, **Expedia** (www.expedia.com), **Travelocity** (www.travelocity.com), and **Orbitz** (www.orbitz.com), sell the majority of the air tickets bought on the Internet. (Canadian travelers should try www.expedia.ca and www.travelocity.ca; U.K. residents should check out expedia.co.uk and opodo.co.uk.) Each has different business deals with the airlines and may offer different fares on the same flights, so shopping around is wise. Expedia and Travelocity will also send you an **e-mail notification** when a cheap fare becomes available to your favorite destination. Of the smaller travel agency Web sites, **SideStep** (www.sidestep.com) receives good reviews from users. It's a browser add-on that purports to "search 140 sites at once," but in reality only beats competitors' fares as often as other sites do.

Great **last-minute deals** are available through free weekly e-mail services provided directly by the airlines. Most of these deals are announced on Tuesday or Wednesday and must be purchased online. Most are only valid for travel that weekend, but some can be booked weeks or months in advance. Sign up for weekly e-mail alerts at airline Web sites or check megasites that compile comprehensive lists of last-minute specials, such as **Smarter Living** (smarterliving.com). For last-minute trips, www.site59.com in the U.S. and www.lastminute.com in Europe often have better deals than the major-label sites.

If you're willing to give up some control of your flight details, use an *opaque fare service* like **Priceline** (www.priceline.com) or **Hotwire** (www.hotwire.com). Both offer rock-bottom prices in exchange for travel on a "mystery airline" at a mysterious time of day, often with a mysterious change of planes en route. The mystery airlines are all major, well-known carriers — and the possibility of being sent from Philadelphia to Chicago via Tampa is remote. But your chances of getting a 6 a.m. or 11 p.m. flight are pretty high. Hotwire tells you flight prices before you buy; Priceline usually has better deals than Hotwire, but you have to play their "name our price" game. ***Note:*** In 2004 Priceline added nonopaque service to its roster. You now have the option to pick exact flights, times, and airlines from a list of offers — or opt to bid on opaque fares as before.

Great last-minute deals are also available directly from the airlines themselves through a free e-mail service called *E-savers*. Each week, the airline sends you a list of discounted flights, usually leaving the upcoming Friday or Saturday and returning the following Monday or Tuesday. You can sign up for all the major airlines at one time by logging on to **Smarter Living** (www.smarterliving.com), or you can go to each individual airline's Web site. Airline sites also offer schedules, flight booking, and information on late-breaking bargains.

Arriving by Other Means

By train, the major international routes to Spain are from Lisbon to Madrid, from Paris to Barcelona or Madrid, and from Geneva and Zurich to Barcelona (all on sleeper-car trains). For more information, contact **Rail Europe** (**☎ 800-382-7245;** www.raileurope.com).

Joining an Escorted Tour

You may be one of the many people who love escorted tours. The tour company takes care of all the details, and tells you what to expect at each leg of your journey. You know your costs upfront and, in the case of the tame ones, you don't get many surprises. Escorted tours can take you to the maximum number of sights in the minimum amount of time with the least amount of hassle.

If you decide to go with an escorted tour, I strongly recommend purchasing travel insurance, especially if the tour operator asks to you pay upfront. But don't buy insurance from the tour operator! If the tour operator doesn't fulfill its obligation to provide you with the vacation you paid for, there's no reason to think that they'll fulfill their insurance obligations either. Get travel insurance through an independent agency. (I tell you more about the ins and outs of travel insurance in Chapter 9.)

When choosing an escorted tour, along with finding out whether you have to put down a deposit and when final payment is due, ask a few simple questions before you buy:

- **What is the cancellation policy?** Can the tour operators cancel the trip if they don't get enough people? How late can you cancel if you're unable to go? Do you get a refund if you cancel? If they cancel?
- **How jam-packed is the schedule?** Does the tour schedule try to fit 25 hours into a 24-hour day, or does it give you ample time to relax by the pool or shop? If getting up at 7 a.m. every day and not returning to your hotel until 6 or 7 p.m. sounds like a grind, certain escorted tours may not be for you.
- **How large is the group?** The smaller the group, the less time you spend waiting for people to get on and off the bus. Tour operators may be evasive about this, because they may not know the exact size of the group until everybody has made reservations, but they should be able to give you a rough estimate.
- **Is there a minimum group size?** Some tours have a minimum group size, and may cancel the tour if they don't book enough people. If a quota exists, find out what it is and how close they are to reaching it. Again, tour operators may be evasive in their answers, but the information may help you select a tour that's sure to happen.
- **What exactly is included?** Don't assume anything. You may have to pay to get yourself to and from the airport. A box lunch may be included in an excursion but drinks may be extra. Beer may be included but not wine. How much flexibility do you have? Can you opt out of certain activities, or does the bus leave once a day, no exceptions? Are all meals planned in advance? Can you choose your entree at dinner, or is it the same chicken cutlet for everyone?

Depending on your recreational passions, I recommend one of the following tour companies:

- **Petrabax Tours (☎ 800-634-1188;** `http://petrabax.com`) has organized, escorted motorcoach tours of Spain for nearly three decades. Its long list of tours include bus tours, locally hosted city packages, and fly/drive packages combining stays at different *paradores* (a government-run chain of hotels; see Chapter 7). The company offers four different *parador* routes through major cities. Combinations with trips to Portugal or France are also available.

- **Trafalgar Tours** (☎ **866-554-4434;** www.trafalgartours.com) is the world's biggest-selling escorted tour operator, which translates into attractive prices. Tours to Spain include a ten-day **Spanish Discovery** trip that visits Madrid, Toledo, and the highlights of Andalusia. Prices begin at $775 per person.

Choosing a Package Tour

For the most popular, tourist-oriented destinations in Spain, such as Costa del Sol or Madrid, package tours are a smart way to save money. In many cases, a package tour that includes airfare, hotel, and transportation to and from the airport costs less than the hotel alone on a tour you book yourself. That's because packages are sold in bulk to tour operators who resell them to the public. It's kind of like buying your vacation at a buy-in-bulk store — except the tour operator is the one who buys the 1,000-count box of garbage bags and resells them ten at a time at a cost that undercuts the local supermarket.

You can buy a package at any time of the year, but the best deals usually coincide with low travel season — October through March — when room rates and airfares plunge. You may find your flight dates are more limited during this time, because airlines cut back on their schedules during the slow season, but if you're flexible and don't mind a little rain or chilly weather, you can get some great bargains.

To find package tours, check out the travel section of your local Sunday newspaper or the ads in the back of national travel magazines. **Liberty Travel** (call ☎ **888-271-1584** to find the store nearest you; www.libertytravel.com) is one of the biggest packagers in the Northeast, and usually boasts a full-page ad in Sunday papers.

Another good source of package deals is the airlines themselves. Most major airlines offer air/land packages, including **American Airlines Vacations** (☎ 800-321-2121; www.aavacations.com), **Delta Vacations** (☎ 800-221-6666; www.deltavacations.com), **Continental Airlines Vacations** (☎ 800-301-3800; www.covacations.com), and **United Vacations** (☎ 888-854-3899; www.unitedvacations.com). Several big **online travel agencies** — Expedia, Travelocity, Orbitz, Site59, and Lastminute.com — also do a brisk business in packages. If you're unsure about the pedigree of a smaller packager, check with the Better Business Bureau in the city where the company is based, or go online at www.bbb.org. If a packager won't tell you where it's based, don't fly with it.

Most European airlines also offer competitive packages (see the appendix for their Web sites and toll-free numbers). Likewise, the biggest hotel chains, casinos, and resorts offer packages. If you already know where you want to stay, call the hotel or resort and ask if it offers land/air packages (airfare, hotel room, and sometimes car rental, depending on the deal).

Sometimes penny-pinching packages pop up right before your trip. To get the latest on last-minute package deals, log on to the Frommer's Web site (www.frommers.com) and check out deals for Spain. You may find a $299 round-trip airfare or a $599 hotel and air package.

General-interest package tours

When considering a trip to Spain, you have hundreds of packagers to choose from. (For a thorough, if still not exhaustive list, visit www.okspain.org, which features more than 220 tour operators.) Spain specialists organizing general-interest package tours include

- **Abreu Tours (☎ 800-223-1580;** www.abreu-tours.com), a Portuguese agency that claims to be the world's oldest and, with offices in New York and the United Kingdom, has an extensive roster of package, escorted, and self-drive tours to Spain (and Portugal). They also offer cruise, city combo, and rail travel options at competitive prices.
- **Solar Tours (☎ 800-388-7652;** www.solartours.com), a wholesaler, offers many standard packages. The company also conducts themed tours like "Castles of Spain," "Horses and Wine," "White Villages," and "Jewish Heritage," as well as self-drive packages through Andalusia and Northern Spain. The service is only available through U.S. travel agents.
- **Spanish Heritage Tours (☎ 800-456-5050;** www.shtours.com) specializes in low-cost airfares to Spain and arranges custom tours of Barcelona, Madrid, Costa del Sol, the Balearic and Canary Islands, as well as cruises. Packages include round-trip air fare from New York, transfers, three- or six-night hotel accommodations (starting at just $229 per person), and daily buffet breakfast.

Special-interest tours

Dozens — if not hundreds — of tour companies cater to travelers with specific active or cultural interests. The following list is just a tiny sample of good organized trips targeting special interests:

- **AtlanticGolf (☎ 800-542-6224;** www.atlanticgolf.com) has been organizing golf tours of England and Scotland since 1987 and now also offers golfing vacations along the Costa del Sol in southern Spain, with opportunities to play eight of Spain's finest courses.
- **Art Horizons International (☎ 212-969-9410;** www.art-horizons.com) organizes specialized, in-depth art and architecture tours, many of them designed for museum staffers. Its sole Spanish tour is "From Gaudí to Gehry."
- **Cellar Tours (☎ 34-91-521-39-39** in Spain; visit www.cellartours.com to call toll free via Skype), based in Madrid, targets wine enthusiasts, offering high-end food and wine tours of Spain and Portugal. Most itineraries include stays at luxury hotels and inns and dining

at some of Spain's most celebrated restaurants. In addition to hitting the standard-bearers of the Spanish wine industry, the tour also exposes travelers to wine secrets, such as Mallorca and the cork forests of southern Portugal.

- **Heritage Tours (☎ 800-378-4555;** www.heritagetoursonline.com) creates "specialty travel" custom itineraries and unique private experiences for sophisticated travelers, with an emphasis on luxury and culture. Tours feature private cars and drivers, off-the-beaten path destinations, and accommodations and meals in the best hotels and restaurants, including private homes.
- **Saranjan Tours (☎ 800-858-9594;** www.saranjan.com), based in Washington state, offers all-inclusive, upscale tours in Spain and Portugal including regional walking, wine, and cooking itineraries. Some trips are truly unconventional, such as the "Art, History & Guitar Shops" tour for guitar aficionados.
- **Spain Adventures (☎ 877-71-SPAIN;** http://spainadventures.com) is a Florida-based agency with an interesting lineup of programs focusing only on Spain. From active travel such as skiing/snowboarding and biking to more relaxed, hedonistic pursuits such as spas, wine and gastronomy, and golf tours, these trips are for folks who don't want to sit on a tour bus.
- **Tenedor Tours (☎ 34-943-313-929;** www.tenedortours.com), based in San Sebastián, Spain, features gastronomic tours of Spain's exalted land of haute cuisine, the Basque Country, as well as wine trips to Rioja.
- **Vintage Spain (☎ 34-699-246-534;** www.vintagespain.com) is based in Spain and specializes in "Rutas de Vino" (wine routes) to Rioja, Ribera del Duero, and La Mancha. In visits to bodegas, the emphasis is on luxury and wine tastings, though with a good bit of art, culture, and history mixed in. Trips are generally short, from one to three days, and pretty affordably priced.

Chapter 6

Getting Around Spain

In This Chapter

- Jetting across Spain by plane
- Riding the country's rails
- Boarding a bus to select destinations
- Renting a car and saving money while you do it

Spain is easy to navigate with lots of excellent train and air options. It isn't nearly as big as the United States or Canada, but Spain is one of the largest countries in Europe, and distances are deceptively long. If you plan to cover a lot of ground after you arrive in Spain, you'll probably want to travel those long legs of your trip by air. On the other hand, if you're planning more of a regional trip, rail and road are the best ways to get around. In the destination chapters that follow, I give tips on the best way to get to and around given regions.

By Plane

Flying between distant points sometimes makes sense in Spain; doing so is not only efficient but relatively inexpensive. Some airlines advertise domestic routes as inexpensive as 60€ ($72), and most 100€ ($120) or less. The following carriers fly the domestic routes within Spain:

- **Air Europa** (☎ **888-238-7672** in the United States or 902-40-15-01 in Spain; www.aireuropa.com)
- **Iberia** and its smaller cousins, **Aviaco** and **Air Nostrum** (☎ **800-772-4642** in the United States or 902-40-05-00 in Spain; www.iberia.com)
- **Spanair** (☎ **888-545-5757** in the United States or 902-13-14-10 in Spain; www.spanair.com)

By Train

Unless you're traveling in a region where renting a car for a driving tour makes sense (see "By Car," later in this chapter), the most economical — and generally the most enjoyable and relaxing — way to travel in Spain

Save with air passes

The **Iberiabono España** allows you to fly within Spain for 60€ ($72) per flight coupon (minimum two coupons; 160€/$192 in business class). The air pass is good for all of Spain's most popular mainland destinations as well as the Balearic Islands. The air pass is available year round, but you must purchase it prior to departure and in conjunction with a round-trip transatlantic ticket to Spain on Iberia. It's only available to nonresidents of Spain. Additional coupons can't be purchased after international travel has begun; route changes are permitted at a cost of 25€ ($30) per change. Call ☎ **800-772-4642** or visit `www.iberia.com` for more information and conditions.

Spanair offers two different air passes. The **Discover Spanair Pass** is a program that allows passengers to purchase discounted tickets (68€/$87 per flight) to as many as 21 destinations in Spain, with no minimum; you must purchase the tickets outside the country before arrival. Flights to the Canary Islands are 98€ ($125). The **Spain Pass** offers flights within Spain for 55€ ($70) each (110€/$140 for the minimum of two flights). Additional flights are 55€ ($70) each plus tax (flights to the Canary Islands are 102€/$130). Call ☎ **888-545-5757** or, in Spain, 902-13-14-10; or visit `www.spanair.com` for additional information.

The **Europe by Air Flightpass** allows you to create customized flight itineraries within Europe for 78€ ($99) per flight (plus tax). The Europe by Air Pass works with Spanair and other European carriers. For information, call ☎ **888-321-4737,** or visit its Web site at `www.europebyair.com`.

is on the **Spanish State Railroad** (abbreviated RENFE in Spanish). The network of trains crisscrosses Spain, allowing you to travel to all but the smallest towns. RENFE trains now enjoy a 98 percent punctuality rate. Primary long-distance routes are served by night express trains with first- and second-class seats as well as *literas* (bunks). High-speed trains include the TALGO and AVE trains. Although TALGO and AVE trains are slightly more expensive than regular *largo recorrido* (long distance) trains and *regionales* (regional) and *cercanías* (local) trains, they are vastly superior and faster.

Spain's train fares are among the cheapest in Europe, and discounts are available for students and seniors. Purchase tickets at the *estación de tren* (train station) or RENFE *taquilla* (tah-*kee*-yah; ticket office). Many stations are equipped with automated ticket-vending machines. Generally, reservations are only necessary for overnight sleeper berths and the high-speed AVE trains during high season. Make reservations in person at the train station or call the local RENFE office (see specific destination chapters) or the toll-free number (☎ **34-902-24-02-02**). You can find timetables at any train station or travel agent's office in Spain. You can also log on to the RENFE Web site (`www.renfe.es`) to download schedules and fares.

Two superb vintage luxury trains, reminiscent of the Orient Express, operate in Spain. One is **El Transcantábrico,** which runs across the green north of Spain, from San Sebastián to Santiago de Compostela. The other is **Al-Andalus Expreso,** which travels through romantic Andalusia. For more information on El Transcantábrico, visit `www.feve.es`; for additional information about the Al Andalus Expreso, see `www.raileurope.com`. In the United States, for reservations and brochures on Al-Andalus Expreso, contact **EC Tours** (☎ **800-388-0077;** `www.ectours.com`); for El Transcantábrico, contact **Marketing Ahead** (☎ **800-223-1356** or 212-686-0271; `www.marketingahead.com`).

Saving money with rail passes

Rail Europe offers the **Eurail Spain Pass,** which allows any three days of unlimited first- or second-class travel throughout Spain in a two-month period (183€/$234 in first class, 143€/$182 in second). A **Eurail Spain-Portugal Pass,** with prices that start at 212€ ($270), permits any three days of travel within a two-month period for first-class train travel in Spain and Portugal — including the high-speed AVE train from Madrid to Seville. You can purchase additional days, up to a maximum of seven, for an additional 29€ ($37) per day. The **Spain Rail 'n Drive** pass combines three days of unlimited first-class train travel and two days in a rental car (prices begin at 226€/$289 for two people in an economy car). On all these rail passes, children under age 4 travel free, and children ages 4 to 11 pay half the adult fare. You can only purchase passes outside Spain, prior to your departure. For more information, consult **Rail Europe** (☎ **800-4-EURAIL** in the United States, or 800-361-RAIL in Canada; `www.raileurope.com/us/rail/passes/spain_portugal_index.htm`).

Knowing the language of el tren

You don't need to know much Spanish to ride the trains in Spain, but a few basic words can help. When reserving your ticket, ask for either *ida* (*ee*-dah; one-way) or *ida y vuelta* (*ee*-dah ee *bwel*-tah; round-trip). Economy class is *turista* (too-*ree*-stah), and first class, *primera clase* (pree-*meh*-rah *klah*-seh).

By Bus

Reserve bus travel mostly for places that you can't get to by train. Though buses are inexpensive and go everywhere, in my opinion they're a less preferable mode of transportation because they can be hot, crowded, and uncomfortable. The biggest exceptions to this rule are the buses to Toledo from Madrid and those around the Basque Country, which are faster and more frequent than trains. For information about bus travel to those and other locations, see the relevant destination chapters later in this book.

By Car

A car gives you the greatest flexibility while traveling in Spain, allowing you to reach small towns, make detours, and stay any amount of time that you want, independent of public transportation. On the other hand, renting an auto is more expensive than riding the train or bus, and you need to worry about the business of driving in Spain — for example, reading maps, extricating yourself from traffic and one-way streets, and following street signs in Spanish (or Catalan) if you wander into a large city.

Generally, I'd save car rentals for the following regions:

- Day trips from Barcelona and around Catalonia, including the Costa Brava
- Side trips from Madrid — to Segovia, Salamanca, and Toledo
- Touring the *pueblos blancos,* or white villages, of Andalusia

Arriving in Spain with vouchers and reservations in place is both more convenient and more economical. Otherwise, you risk not getting a car (or the car of your choice) during the high season in popular areas.

Getting a good deal on your rental

Car-rental rates vary even more than airline fares. The price depends on the size of the car, the length of time you keep it, where and when you pick it up and drop it off, where you take it, and a host of other factors. Asking a few key questions may save you hundreds of dollars. Check into these issues:

- Weekend rates may be lower than weekday rates. If you're keeping the car five or more days, a weekly rate may be cheaper than the daily rate. Ask if the rate is the same for pickup Friday morning as it is for Thursday night.
- Some companies may assess a drop-off charge if you don't return the car to the same rental location.
- Check whether the rate is cheaper if you pick up the car at a location in town rather than at the airport; this is most often the case.
- If you see an advertised price in your local newspaper, be sure to ask for that specific rate; otherwise you may be charged the standard (higher) rate. Don't forget to mention membership in AAA, AARP, and trade unions. These memberships usually entitle you to discounts ranging from 5 to 30 percent.
- Check your frequent-flier accounts. Not only are your favorite (or at least most-used) airlines likely to have sent you discount coupons, but most car rentals add at least 500 miles to your account.

As with other aspects of planning your trip, using the Internet can make comparison-shopping for a car rental much easier. You can check rates at most of the major agencies' Web sites. Plus, all the major travel sites — **Travelocity** (www.travelocity.com), **Expedia** (www.expedia.com), **Orbitz** (www.orbitz.com), and **Smarter Living** (www.smarterliving.com), for example — have search engines that can dig up discounted car-rental rates. You can even make the reservation through any of these sites.

Covering all the charges

In addition to the standard rental prices, other optional charges apply to most car rentals (and some not-so-optional charges, such as taxes). Many credit card companies cover the *Collision Damage Waiver* (CDW), which requires you to pay for damage to the car in a collision. Check with your credit card company before you go so you can avoid paying this hefty fee (as much as $20 a day).

The car-rental companies also offer additional *liability insurance* (if you harm others in an accident), *personal accident insurance* (if you harm yourself or your passengers), and *personal effects insurance* (if your luggage is stolen from your car). Check your insurance policy on your car at home to see whether it covers any of these sorts of overseas incidents. However, if your own insurance doesn't cover you for rentals, or if you don't have auto insurance, definitely consider the additional coverage (ask your car-rental agent for more information). You can probably skip the personal effects insurance, but driving around without liability or personal accident coverage is never a good idea. Even if you're a good driver, other people may not be, and liability claims can be complicated.

If you decline the insurance offered by car-rental companies because your credit card covers it, keep in mind that, according to Spanish law, you're held liable for damage or theft to the car until your credit card covers the charges. This means that *you're held responsible for up to the full value of the car* (in Europe, easily $20,000–$30,000 or more) *until you file a claim with your credit card company and they pay the claim.* Be *very* sure that your credit card does provide coverage. This Spanish law has never stopped me from relying on my credit card's policy of insurance,

Singing the stick-shift blues

In Spain, prepare yourself for small cars, narrow lanes, expensive gas, and standard transmissions. Almost all Spanish cars have stick shifts. If you can find an automatic-transmission car, it will be larger, more luxurious and significantly more expensive. If you don't drive a stick, make your rental reservations well in advance, because most agencies have access to very few automatic cars. If it's been a while since you last drove a four- or five-speed standard transmission, brushing up before arriving on Spanish soil is a good idea. Otherwise you may wind up on a steep, narrow one-way street, nervously absorbing the impatient honks of a stream of drivers behind you.

Gas facts

In Spain, unleaded gasoline is called *sin plomo.* Americans find that gas (*petrol* in Spanish, pronounced *peh*-trol) is very expensive in Spain — nearly twice as much as in the United States. It's also sold by the liter (a little more than a quart). To fill up, tell the attendant (make sure you tip her a few coins): *"lleno, por favor"* (*yeh*-noh por fah-*vohr*). Many Spanish gas stations, especially off highways, are now automated self-service stations, so you don't need to unleash your Spanish.

but I've also never had an accident or a car stolen, so I hesitate to advise you to do the same. Think about the consequences, and ask your credit card company about its coverage (and response time) in such a situation.

Some companies also offer *refueling packages,* in which you pay for your initial full tank of gas upfront and can return the car with an empty gas tank. If you reject this option, you pay only for the gas you use, but you have to return the car with a full tank or face very high surcharges for any shortfall. If you usually run late and a fueling stop may make you miss your plane, you're a perfect candidate for the fuel-purchase option.

Choosing a company

Most of North America's biggest car-rental companies, including Avis, Budget, and Hertz, maintain offices throughout Spain. You can also find Spanish car-rental companies, but you're better off going with a name and company familiar to you.

Auto Europe (☎ 888-223-5555; `www.autoeurope.com`) may not be immediately recognizable to you, but this wholesaler can reserve cars for you in any Spanish city through its agreements with Avis or Europcar. I found this service uniformly excellent and the prices very competitive. Any reservation problems are easily solved by using a toll-free service with English-speaking representatives, even in the smallest of towns.

Even if you prepay after making your reservations, you must still fork over money for local tax and insurance matters at the local rental agency in Spain. Your cost is a 15 percent value-added tax (IVA tax in Spanish) plus any insurance that you decide to take out. If you're pulling out of an airport lot, expect to pay a surcharge of up to 10€ ($12).

Companies require that drivers be at least 18 years of age (some may stipulate 21). To rent a car, you must have a passport and a valid driver's license; you must also have a valid credit card or a prepaid voucher. Your home-country driver's license is sufficient; no international license is necessary.

Understanding the rules of the road

Most traffic signs are international and easy to understand. Spaniards drive on the right side of the road, and they drive fast. When they pass on the left, they often zoom up quite close before darting around the car in front of them. They may also honk their horns as they move to pass you. Unless you're willing to travel as fast as they do, move to the right lane.

Spaniards tend to drive as though the entire country were one big southern European racetrack, but in fact, speed limits do exist. Routinely ignored but in force just the same, speed limits are: 120km/hr (74 mph) on motorways and highways; 100km/hr (62 mph) on main roads; 90km/hr (56 mph) on secondary roads; and 50km/hr (31 mph) in urban areas.

Spain has two types of express highways: *autopistas,* which sometimes charge exorbitant tolls *(peajes),* and *autovías,* which are free. The prefix A- or E- (the latter a European Union designation) precedes *autopista* numbers on road signs. Exits are labeled *salida,* except in Catalonia, where the sign reads *sortida. Carreteras nacionales* are countrywide main roads designated by N- and a Roman numeral. To turn around and go the other direction on a highway, look for the sign that reads CAMBIO DE SENTIDO (change of direction) or shows a U-turn arrow.

Parking your car facing oncoming traffic is illegal. Cities have *zona azul* (blue zone) areas where you can park in a metered spot. The meter is normally just a few paces away; put in a few euro coins for the time desired (rates are generally about 1.50€/$1.80 per hour) and place the printed receipt on the dash inside your car (face up so parking police can see how long you're legally parked). Parking hours are from 8 a.m. to 2 p.m. and from 4 p.m. to 8 p.m., Monday to Saturday. In underground parking areas, collect the ticket and pay upon exiting.

Never leave anything inside your car in full view. Break-ins and theft of rental cars, especially in Madrid and Andalusia, aren't uncommon. What you can't leave in the hotel, lock securely in the trunk.

Breakdown!

In the event of a vehicle breakdown, look for emergency phone boxes on major motorways. On secondary roads, call for help by asking the operator to locate the nearest *Guardia Civil* (police station), which can direct you to a garage or repair shop.

AAA maintains an association with the **Real Automóvil Club de España** (Royal Automobile Club of Spain), José Abascal, 10, Madrid (☎ **91-594-74-00**), which provides helpful information about road conditions and travel data, as well as limited emergency road service. For assistance, call ☎ **91-593-33-33.**

The American Automobile Association (AAA; ☎ **800-222-4357;** www.aaa.com) publishes a regional map of Spain available free to members at most AAA offices in the United States. Also available free to members is *Motoring in Europe,* a 60-page guide that gives helpful information about road signs and speed limits, as well as insurance regulations and other relevant matters. For more information on obtaining maps for your trip to Spain, consult the appendix of this book.

Chapter 7

Booking Your Accommodations

In This Chapter

- Considering your options, from hotels to castles to *paradores*
- Understanding everything you need to know about rack rates
- Looking for deals and making reservations

When I backpacked around the globe as a college student, where I slept was usually the least of my concerns — I camped out in train stations and on the floors of new acquaintances' homes. Those days — I'm mostly relieved to say — are long gone. For obvious reasons, where you stay is a significant logistical detail when planning your trip to Spain. You need a place to stay after long days of sightseeing. But where you stay can also have a significant impact on how you experience the country. In Spain, you have the chance to stay in everything from family-run inns to 16th-century monasteries and palaces.

In this chapter, I focus on the essentials about accommodations, including what you get for your money (and how to get more).

Getting to Know Your Options

If you play your cards right, your accommodations in Spain can be as evocative as the museums, castles, and flamenco shows that you experience. From converted medieval castles and Renaissance palaces to 16th-century and Art Nouveau mansions, Spain has an unrivaled network of atmospheric palaces in which to stay — and many are surprisingly affordable. If those options sound too grandiose, you can also find simpler hotels and guesthouses. A unique hotel can nearly equal the experience of visiting a special museum, though, as well as enhance your appreciation of Spain. On the other hand, don't overestimate the importance of a hotel room: If you can't get into a particular place or your budget won't permit a stay at high-end hotels, don't sweat it; your trip to Spain can exceed your expectations even if you don't stay at your (or my) top choices.

Hotel accommodations are more reasonably priced in Spain than in many other European countries, so I focus on moderate to expensive hotels and the national *paradores* (a chain of state-owned properties that I discuss in "Introducing *paradores:* Spain's historic, government-run hotels," later in this chapter). Most of the small and very inexpensive *pensiones* (pensions), *hostales* (hostels), and *albergues* (guesthouses) have few amenities (such as private bathrooms) and even fewer personnel who speak English, so with a couple of exceptions, I stay away from this category. Instead, I include the best-value hotels in each city and region and make a special effort to include hotels with convenient locations and hotels with special Spanish character or architectural distinction. I also include a few high-priced hotels in several places, because they're simply worth the splurge.

If you're traveling with a small group or your family and are interested in luxury villas and apartments for weeklong stays, have a look at the Spanish offerings through **Doorways Ltd. Villa Vacations** (☎ **800-261-4460;** `www.villavacations.com`). They list a number of unique, gorgeous properties across Spain.

On the whole, most Spanish hotels are a delight. Don't expect them all to have 24-hour room service, coffeemakers, fax machines, e-mail, and other American-style conveniences, however. What you can expect from most hotels is personal service and a willingness to help you with directions, travel advice, and personal recommendations. At the more pricey properties, you can almost universally expect hotel staff to speak fairly fluent English. At smaller hotels, however, you need a little patience, because sometimes employees may not understand you. Spaniards are patient and eager to help, though, and communicating in simple English or with sign language is part of the fun of traveling abroad. Most larger hotels in large cities and resort towns offer nonsmoking rooms. If you're not a smoker, definitely ask your hotel if it has nonsmoking rooms.

Though Spain has gotten more expensive with the ascendancy of the euro, finding affordable accommodations isn't a massive problem in most parts of Spain, though Barcelona and Madrid are considerably more expensive than the rest of the country. Determining how much to budget for a hotel depends not only on your finances but also on how much time you plan to spend in your room. If you're happy with a clean but functionally furnished double hotel room with a private bathroom and cable TV, expect to pay from 50€ to 100€ ($60–$120). This price doesn't get you luxury; it's strictly budget territory. Rooms for this price are no frills where décor is concerned, but have a livable and perfectly inoffensive environment. Occasionally you can get a great location, but doing so is a rarity.

If you're willing to part with 101€ to 175€ ($121–$210), in most cities and towns you can get a room with a good deal of comfort and, often, some Spanish charm. You can also land a desirable, convenient location. Naturally, the more you're willing to spend, the better the service and more luxurious the accommodations. However, be extremely careful about extras such as telephone calls and minibar goodies, for which Spanish hotels, just like their counterparts all over the world, charge highway-robbery prices. (Avoid calling home from your hotel without a calling card at all costs.) Check out Table 7-1 for a key on the dollar signs I use in this book.

Table 7-1 Key to Hotel Dollar Signs

Dollar Signs(s)	*Price Range*	*What to Expect*
$	less than 50€ ($60)	These accommodations are rather simple and inexpensive. Rooms will likely be quite small, and televisions aren't necessarily provided. Parking isn't provided but rather catch-as-catch-can on the street.
$$	50€–100€ ($60–$120)	A step up, these mid-range accommodations offer more room, more extras (such as irons, hairdryers, or minibars) and often a more convenient location than the preceding category.
$$$	101€–175€ ($121–$210)	Higher-class still, these accommodations begin to look pretty plush. Think chocolates on your pillow, a nice restaurant, and underground parking garages, as well as good views.
$$$$	176€–275€ ($211–$330)	These are what most people think of as first-class hotels (or in Spain, five-star accommodations). They usually come with luxury amenities such as in-room CD players, nice pools, and top-rated restaurants.
$$$$$	more than 275€ ($330)	These top-rated accommodations are the crème de la crème, with the finest of everything (in Spain, this category is usually called "Five-star Grand Luxury"). You will find valet parking, on-premise spas, and other amenities, such as at-your-service concierges. At this rate, the hotel is likely to have a unique quality, such as coveted views or location, a restaurant with a star chef, or ultrachic interior design.

Breakfast most often costs extra, and a 7 percent value-added tax (IVA tax in Spain) is added to the price of your room and anything else you consume (including breakfast, telephone calls, laundry, and minibar items). Note that the hotel VAT, or IVA tax, is nonrefundable to non-European residents, unlike taxes on other consumer purchases (see Chapter 4 for additional information).

In general, make your hotel reservations a couple of months in advance (desirable, smaller hotels fill up fast). If you're traveling in high season (Apr–Sept) or to places that are swamped for special events, make your reservations even earlier. Many hotels fill up in Seville during Feria de Abril (April Fair), in Córdoba during May festival, and in both cities during Easter week; for any of these times, I recommend making reservations six months or more in advance. For Pamplona's Running of the Bulls in July, making your reservations even a year in advance still may not find you a place to stay.

Staying at a luxury hotel

The top-flight hotels in Spain are generally less expensive than their counterparts in other parts of Europe, and Spain has some of the finest luxury hotels on the continent, ranging from 16th-century palaces that still welcome royalty to sleek, ultramodern boutique hotels obsessed with hip design. See Chapter 1 for my picks for the top splurges (several of which are surprisingly affordable).

Introducing paradores: Spain's historic, government-run hotels

Foremost among Spain's hotel offerings is the state-owned chain of national *paradores,* which you can find sprinkled throughout Spain. Many are former castles, convents, or palaces restored and furnished with period pieces and modern amenities (though a few are modern and comparatively unattractive). Staying at a couple of the top *paradores* really adds to the flavor of your vacation. The first *parador* opened in 1928, and several of these establishments are among the finest places you can stay anywhere, at prices far below those of most deluxe hotels.

The best *paradores* rank as both great experiences and bargains. Among the stars of the 86-member network is the top-end and always-full **Parador de San Francisco** in Granada. Even if you can't get into that one, you can find others that are nearly as historic and beautiful. *Paradores* aren't uniform in cost, but with just a couple of more expensive exceptions, most are right around 120€ ($144) per night for a double (and a number are cheaper than that). For reservations at any of the *paradores,* contact the **Central de Reservas** (☎ **91-516-66-66;** `www.parador.es`). You can also go through the North American booking agent, **Marketing Ahead** (☎ **800-223-1356** or 212-686-0271; `www.marketingahead.com`).

Getting paramount deals at *paradores*

Spain's *paradores* are pretty good deals to begin with, but a handful of special offers makes them even more attractive. The **Two-Night Stay** (Especial Dos Noches) promotion (available during certain dates at almost any of the *paradores*) offers a 20 percent discount on the official price of the room, the buffet breakfast, and menu of the day for the second meal of your choice (you must stay two or more nights half-board; breakfast and one other meal included). Another great deal is the **Five-Night Discount Book** (Tarjeta Cinco Noches), which contains five vouchers that you can use to stay at any *parador* included in the promotion for 425€ ($431) plus tax, what amounts to 85€ ($102) per night for a double room (certain dates apply). For those who want to plan their entire trip around staying in *paradores,* the **Dream Week** (Pasaporte de Ensueño) allows for six nights stay in *paradores* along preestablished routes (with two nights in each *parador*). Rates are 468€ ($562) plus tax per double room for six nights; a 15 percent discount on lunch at the *parador* is also offered.

Other deals available include a 50 percent discount for children under 12 and half off the price of adult *menú del día* (menu of the day) in *parador* restaurants and a free cot for children up to age 2. Likewise, seniors (60 and older) receive especially good deals (including a 35 percent discount on official rates), called **Golden Days** (Días Dorados), at *paradores.* The **Youthful Escape** (Escapada Joven) program allows travelers ages 20 to 30 to stay at participating *paradores* for 45€ ($54) per person per night, including buffet breakfast. For more information, including current promotions and dates of deals, visit the group's Web site, `www.parador.es`, or contact **Marketing Ahead** (☎ **800-223-1356;** `www.marketingahead.com`).

Enjoying the charm of Spain's smaller hotels

Spain is loaded with small hotels that are big on character and charm. These hotels usually have a dose of regional flavor: They're often converted mansions, old Arab *cármenes* (houses with enclosed orchards and gardens), and rustic farmhouses. Many are excellent deals. Expect to pay from 70€ to 125€ ($84–$144) for a double at these smaller accommodations, though some are cheaper still.

Finding the Best Room at the Best Rate

Room rates are closely tied to seasonal demand in Spain, with clear high, shoulder, and low seasons. High season is essentially from April to the end of September. In the largest cities and certain other parts of the country, however, the height of summer isn't high season, as many Spaniards evacuate for their annual vacations in July and August. Special events, such as local and regional fiestas, Semana Santa (Easter Week), and major draws such as the San Fermín (Running of the Bulls) in Pamplona and Feria de Abril (April Fair) in Seville occupy a special category; at these times, accommodations are much more expensive (sometimes double or more) and harder to come by than during the apex of regular high season. Deals are frequently available in shoulder seasons (for most of Spain, Sept–Oct and Mar–Apr) and in the off-season (Nov–Feb).

Cheaper accommodations are often available through package tours and tour operators. For package-tour information, see Chapter 5.

Finding the best rate

The **rack rate** is the maximum rate a hotel charges for a room. It's the rate you get if you walk in off the street and ask for a room for the night. You sometimes see these rates printed on the fire/emergency exit diagrams posted on the back of your door.

Hotels are happy to charge you the rack rate, but you can almost always do better. Perhaps the best way to avoid paying the rack rate is surprisingly simple: Just ask for a cheaper or discounted rate. You may be pleasantly surprised.

In all but the smallest accommodations, the rate you pay for a room depends on many factors — chief among them being how you make your reservation. A travel agent may be able to negotiate a better price with certain hotels than you can get by yourself. (That's because the hotel often gives the agent a discount in exchange for steering his or her business toward that hotel.)

Reserving a room through the hotel's toll-free number may also result in a lower rate than calling the hotel directly. On the other hand, the central reservations number may not know about discount rates at specific locations. For example, local franchises may offer a special group rate for a wedding or family reunion, but they may neglect to tell the central booking line. Your best bet is to call both the local number and the toll-free number and see which one gives you a better deal.

Room rates (even rack rates) change with the season, as occupancy rates rise and fall. But even within a given season, room prices are subject to change without notice, so the rates quoted in this book may be different from the actual rate you receive when you make your reservation. Be sure to mention membership in AAA, AARP, frequent-flier programs, any other corporate rewards programs you can think of — or your Uncle Joe's Elks lodge in which you're an honorary inductee, for that matter — when you call to book. You never know when the affiliation may be worth a few dollars off your room rate.

Sometimes getting a better deal may mean scoring a few extra amenities instead of a strict price break on the cost of the room. You may ask for breakfast, parking, or other services — such as a room upgrade — to be included at no extra charge.

Racking up the rates come festival time

Occasionally in Spain, you're not only asked to pay the rack rate, but you're also required to pay it twice over or more. Expect this when you make reservations in Pamplona for the Running of the Bulls in early July, and in Seville during Easter and the city's Feria de Abril (April Fair). Don't think they're taking you for a sucker, though — the hotels charge what they legally can and what they know they can get. Even at those rack-rates–plus, you may still have a hard time getting a room during such festivities. (Some hotels are often sold out months, and even years, in advance.)

Reserving the best room

After you make your reservation, asking one or two more pointed questions can go a long way toward making sure you get the best room in the house. Always ask for a corner room, which is usually larger and quieter, with more windows and light than standard rooms. Spanish street life is often active until the wee hours, so if you're sensitive to street noise, ask for a room that doesn't face the street. Also ask if the hotel is renovating; if it is, request a room away from the work. Inquire, too, about the location of the restaurants, bars, and discos in the hotel — all sources of annoying noise. And if you aren't happy with your room when you arrive, talk to the front desk. If they have another room, they should be happy to accommodate you.

Surfing the Web for hotel deals

Shopping online for hotels is generally done one of two ways: by booking through the hotel's own Web site or through an independent booking agency (or a fare-service agency such as Priceline). These Internet hotel agencies have multiplied in mind-boggling numbers of late, competing for the business of millions of consumers surfing for accommodations around the world. This competitiveness can be a boon to consumers who have the patience and time to shop and compare the online sites for good deals — but shop they must, for prices can vary considerably from site to site. And keep in mind that hotels at the top of a site's listing may be there for no other reason than that they paid money to get the placement.

Of the "big three" sites, **Expedia** (`www.expedia.com`) offers a long list of special deals and "virtual tours" or photos of available rooms so you can see what you're paying for (a feature that helps counter the claims that the best rooms are often held back from bargain booking Web sites). **Travelocity** (`www.travelocity.com`) posts unvarnished customer reviews and ranks its properties according to the AAA rating system. Also reliable are **Hotels.com** and **Quikbook.com.** An excellent free program, **TravelAxe** (`www.travelaxe.net`), can help you search multiple hotel sites at once, even ones you may never have heard of — and conveniently lists the total price of the room, including the taxes and service charges. Another booking site, **Travelweb** (www.travelweb.com), is partly owned by the hotels it represents (including the Hilton, Hyatt, and Starwood chains) and is therefore plugged directly into the hotels' reservations systems — unlike independent online agencies, which have to fax or e-mail reservation requests to the hotel, a good portion of which get misplaced in the shuffle. More than once, travelers have arrived at the hotel, only to be told that they have no reservation. It's wise to **get a confirmation number** and **make a printout** of any online booking transaction.

In the opaque Web site category, **Priceline** (www.priceline.com) is even better for hotels than for airfares; you're allowed to pick the neighborhood and quality level of your hotel before offering up your money. Priceline's hotel product covers Europe, though it's best at getting five-star lodging for three-star. On the down side, many hotels stick Priceline guests in their least desirable rooms. Be sure to go to the **BiddingforTravel** Web site (www.biddingfortravel.com) before bidding on a hotel room on Priceline; it features a fairly up-to-date list of hotels that Priceline uses in major cities. For Priceline, you pay up front, and the fee is nonrefundable.

Online hotel brokers with sizeable rosters of discounted Spanish hotels include www.hotelsspainonline.com, www.spain-holiday.com, and www.searchiberia.com/hotels.

Chapter 8

Catering to Special Travel Needs or Interests

In This Chapter

- Traveling tips for families
- Finding special resources for seniors
- Accessing Spain with disabilities
- Getting out and about for gays and lesbians
- Designing a trip around golf or gastronomy

Whether you're retired or a student, traveling with the kids in tow, looking for hotels with special facilities, wanting a gay-friendly vacation, or consumed by an interest in golf or gastronomy, you may have special requirements that need consideration on your trip. In this chapter, I have you covered.

Traveling with the Brood: Advice for Families

If you have enough trouble getting your kids out of the house in the morning, dragging them thousands of miles away may seem like an insurmountable challenge. But family travel can be immensely rewarding, giving you new ways of seeing the world through smaller pairs of eyes.

Spaniards are extremely family oriented, and they dote on children. The biggest problem you may encounter is meeting parents and grandparents of all ages who want to talk to, play with, and spoil your kids.

However, the Spanish love for children doesn't mean that your kids will immediately adapt to all things foreign about Spain. The food and mealtimes are different, the language is strange, and travel is often exhausting, even for adults with long legs.

The kid-friendly icon used throughout the book indicates family-friendly hotels, restaurants, and attractions.

One of your main considerations is feeding your kids. Do they like tapas (yes, kids are welcome in most tapas bars)? If not, finding food that your kids will eat shouldn't be a problem; you can find American-style fast-food restaurants in every Spanish city. However, the extremely late Spanish lunch and dinner hours may cause a problem, and unfortunately, very few restaurants provide anything that remotely resembles a kiddie menu (though most are happy to provide smaller portions).

Many Spanish hotels offer special deals for children — at the least allowing you to put a cot in your room for a nominal fee. Spain's 86 national *paradores* (government-run hotels, usually housed in historic buildings) offer children ages 12 and under staying in parents' room a discount of 50 percent during most of the year (July–Oct, the discount is 25 percent; not valid during Easter Week or Dec 30–31). Children also receive 50 percent off the price of the buffet breakfast and the adult *menú del día* at lunch and dinner.

When traveling with your family, the cost of public transportation is also a major consideration. Most Spanish buses and metro systems are free only for children under 5; many Spaniards encourage their kids to slip beneath turnstiles to get around (or under) this problem — though you may not be willing to teach your kids how to circumvent the law just yet.

When you need a break from watching the kids, arranging day care and babysitting in the larger cities is pretty easy — ask at your hotel or the tourist information offices for recommendations (and see the Appendix for more information on babysitting). Barcelona, for example, has several babysitting agencies, whose services generally cost about 5€ to 10€ ($6–$12) an hour. Many agencies can provide an English-speaking caregiver upon request.

Children of all ages need a valid passport to travel to Spain; for more information on getting a passport, see Chapter 9. You can find good family-oriented vacation advice on the Internet from such sites as the **Family Travel Forum** (`www.familytravelforum.com`), a comprehensive site that offers customized trip planning; **Family Travel Network** (`www.familytravelnetwork.com`), an award-winning site that offers travel features, deals, and tips; **TravelWithYourKids.com,** a comprehensive site that offers customized trip planning; and **Family Travel Files** (`www.thefamilytravelfiles.com`), which offers an online magazine and a directory of off-the-beaten-path tours and tour operators for families.

Making Age Work for You: Tips for Seniors

Spain has long been a favorite of retirees, who love the country's good weather and relaxed pace. And the Spanish respect for family extends to the older generation. Spaniards view grandparents as pillars of the family, and they treat the elderly and not-quite-ready-to-be-called-elderly with dignity and deference.

Being a senior citizen entitles you to some terrific travel bargains (virtually every Spanish museum and attraction offers senior discounts). If a hotel or attraction doesn't explicitly publish a discount for seniors, never hesitate to ask: ***¿Existe un descuento para mayores de edad?*** (Is there a discount for seniors?)

Iberia Airlines' **Senior Plus Program** offers travelers 62 years of age or older a 10 percent discount on most airfares, including some promotional discounts. For more information, contact Iberia Airlines (see the Appendix for a list of airline toll-free numbers and Web sites).

Members of **AARP** (formerly known as the American Association of Retired Persons), 601 E St. NW, Washington, DC 20049 (☎ **888-687-2277** or 202-434-2277; www.aarp.org), get discounts on hotels, airfares, and car rentals. AARP offers members a wide range of benefits, including *AARP: The Magazine* and a monthly newsletter. Anyone older than 50 can join.

Many reliable agencies and organizations target the 50-plus market. **Elderhostel** (☎ **877-426-8056;** www.elderhostel.org) arranges study programs for those ages 55 and older (and a spouse or companion of any age) in the United States and in more than 80 countries around the world. Most courses last five to seven days in the United States (two–four weeks abroad), and many include airfare, accommodations in university dormitories or modest inns, meals, and tuition. **ElderTreks** (☎ **800-741-7956;** www.eldertreks.com) offers small-group tours to off-the-beaten-path or adventure-travel locations, restricted to travelers 50 and older. **INTRAV** (☎ **800-456-8100;** www.intrav.com) is a high-end tour operator that caters to the mature, discerning traveler, not specifically seniors, with trips around the world that include guided safaris, polar expeditions, private-jet adventures, and small-boat cruises down jungle rivers.

Hotel discounts for seniors

Spain's national network of *paradores* (government-run hotels) offers a great deal for seniors. The Días Dorados (Golden Days) program gives a 35 percent discount on accommodations and breakfast for the over-60 set at almost any *parador* in Spain. (If you're a senior, the same discount applies to your roommate, regardless of age.) Certain dates apply (usually Oct–Mar), and the discount isn't valid for the *parador* in Granada, the most popular one in the country. Request the Días Dorados brochure from **Marketing Ahead** (☎ **800-223-1356**) or log on at www.parador.es for a list of hotels and dates that offer the discounts. See Chapter 7 for more information on the *paradores*.

Recommended publications offering travel resources and discounts for seniors include the following: the quarterly magazine ***Travel 50 & Beyond*** (www.travel50andbeyond.com); ***Travel Unlimited: Uncommon Adventures for the Mature Traveler*** (Avalon); ***The 50+ Traveler's Guidebook*** (St. Martin's Press); and ***Unbelievably Good Deals and Great Adventures That You Absolutely Can't Get Unless You're Over 50*** by Joann Rattner Heilman (McGraw-Hill).

Accessing Spain: Advice for Travelers with Disabilities

Most disabilities shouldn't stop anyone from traveling. More options and resources are available than ever before.

In some respects, Spain lagged behind Europe's most developed countries for many decades and is still catching up with regard to facilities that accommodate travelers with disabilities. For example, in subways and trains, you find a glaring lack of ramps and elevators. Many of Spain's ancient towns were constructed a millennium or more before legislation was introduced to create a level public playing field for people with disabilities, so you may find that mobility is a problem, especially in small, hilly towns. Expect uneven streets, unending stairs, and narrow entryways without the standard American facilities that ease access. However, conditions and awareness are steadily improving. (One of Spain's best-known public organizations is **ONCE,** a society for the blind that sponsors a top cycling team and is known throughout Spain.)

If you're a traveler with a disability, look for the newest hotels and restaurants, and perhaps stick to the larger cities, such as Barcelona, Seville, and Madrid. Keep in mind, however, that Spanish hotels claiming to offer facilities and services for disabled visitors may be less well equipped than hotels in the United States or your native country.

Many travel agencies offer customized tours and itineraries for travelers with disabilities. **Flying Wheels Travel** (☎ **507-451-5005;** www.flyingwheelstravel.com) offers escorted tours and cruises that emphasize sports and private tours in minivans with lifts. **Access-Able Travel Source** (☎ **303-232-2979;** www.access-able.com) has extensive access information and advice for traveling around the world with disabilities. **Accessible Journeys** (☎ **800-846-4537** or 610-521-0339) offers tours for wheelchair travelers and their families and friends.

Avis Rent a Car has an "Avis Access" program that offers such services as a dedicated 24-hour toll-free number (☎ **888-879-4273**) for customers with special travel needs; special car features, such as swivel seats, spinner knobs, and hand controls; and accessible bus service.

Organizations that offer assistance to disabled travelers include **MossRehab** (www.mossresourcenet.org), which provides a library of accessible-travel resources online; **SATH (Society for Accessible Travel and Hospitality)** (☎ **212-447-7284;** www.sath.org; annual membership fees: $45 adults, $30 seniors and students), which offers a wealth of travel resources for all types of disabilities and informed recommendations on destinations, access guides, travel agents, tour operators, vehicle rentals, and companion services; and the **American Foundation for the Blind (AFB)** (☎ **800-232-5463;** www.afb.org), a referral resource for the blind or visually impaired that includes information on traveling with Seeing Eye dogs.

For more information specifically targeted to travelers with disabilities, the community Web site **iCan** (www.icanonline.net/channels/travel/index.cfm) has destination guides and several regular columns on accessible travel. Also check out the quarterly magazine ***Emerging Horizons*** ($14.95 per year, $19.95 outside the U.S.; www.emerginghorizons.com); **Twin Peaks Press** (☎ **360-694-2462**), offering travel-related books for travelers with special needs; and ***Open World Magazine,*** published by SATH (subscription: $13 per year, $21 outside the United States).

Following the Rainbow: Advice for Gay and Lesbian Travelers

Relative to several of its European neighbors, Spain, an overwhelmingly Catholic country, has been a bit slow in accepting openly gay expression — even though it legalized homosexuality after the death of the repressive dictator Francisco Franco in 1978. Progressive film director **Pedro Almodóvar** *(Women on the Verge of a Nervous Breakdown, All About My Mother, Talk to Her)* came of cinematic age during La Movida — the artistic renaissance that flourished in Madrid and elsewhere after Franco's death. Almodóvar's outrageously campy (though lately deadly serious) and wildly popular films have gone a long way toward bringing gay relationships into Spain's cultural mainstream.

Public affection by same-sex couples still raises eyebrows in most places, and it may even provoke hostility in small towns. In **Madrid** and **Barcelona,** you can find many gay clubs and bars, though if you're looking for a specifically gay-friendly vacation, you may want to head to **Sitges,** the beach resort just south of Barcelona, or **Ibiza,** the Balearic island in the Mediterranean Sea, where an everything-goes attitude and summertime hedonism reign.

In Madrid, gay nightlife centers in the area around Plaza de Chueca; Cafe Figueroa (Augusto Figueroa 17) is one of the longtime pillars of gay life in the capital. For more information, contact the **Coordinadora Gay de Madrid** (Espíritu Santo 37; ☎ **91-523-00-70**). Look for the free magazines

Shangay Express and *Revista Mensual,* available at kiosks; they both offer information and listings for clubs, restaurants, and other entertainment options.

The Web site www.gayinspain.com boasts an amazingly complete rundown of gay-friendly events, hotels, restaurants, bars and nightclubs, shops, health clubs, bookstores, and information services, all in English. Another good general resource for gay travelers is *Out and About* (www.outandabout.com), which lists gay travel sites, gay tour operators, and gay-friendly hotels and clubs throughout the world. In Spain, it concentrates on Barcelona, Madrid, Sitges, Ibiza, and the Canary Islands. **Pride Holidays** offers gay and lesbian tours to Spain, including city and day tours (☎ **31-36-523-9965**).

The International Gay and Lesbian Travel Association (**IGLTA;** (☎ **800-448-8550** or 954-776-2626; www.iglta.org) is the trade association for the gay and lesbian travel industry, and offers an online directory of gay- and lesbian-friendly travel businesses; go to its Web site and click on "Members."

Many agencies offer tours and travel itineraries specifically for gay and lesbian travelers. **Above and Beyond Tours** (☎ **800-397-2681;** www.abovebeyondtours.com) is the exclusive gay and lesbian tour operator for United Airlines. **Now, Voyager** (☎ **800-255-6951;** www.nowvoyager.com) is a well-known San Francisco–based gay-owned and operated travel service. **Olivia Cruises & Resorts** (☎ **800-631-6277** or 510-655-0364; www.olivia.com) charters entire resorts and ships for exclusive lesbian vacations and offers smaller group experiences for both gay and lesbian travelers. **Dasi Tours** (Calle Fuencarral 60, Suite 3B, Madrid; ☎ **562-430-7997** in the United States), a travel agency in Madrid, is a member of IGLTA and organizes a variety of gay-oriented travel in Spain.

The following travel guides are available at most travel bookstores and gay and lesbian bookstores: ***Out and About*** (☎ **800-929-2268** or 415-644-8044; www.outandabout.com); ***Spartacus International Gay Guide*** (Bruno Gmünder Verlag; www.spartacusworld.com/gayguide) and ***Odysseus,*** both good, annual English-language guidebooks focused on gay men; the ***Damron*** guides (www.damron.com), with separate, annual books for gay men and lesbians; and ***Gay Travel A to Z: The World of Gay & Lesbian Travel Options at Your Fingertips*** by Marianne Ferrari (Ferrari International; Box 35575, Phoenix, AZ 85069), a very good gay and lesbian guidebook series.

Going to Spain as a Student

The best resource for students is **STA Travel** (☎ **800-781-4040;** www.statravel.com), the biggest student travel agency in the world. It can set you up with the student traveler's best friend, the **International Student Identity Card (ISIC).** It's the only officially acceptable form of student identification, good for discounts on rail passes, plane tickets, and other items. For an additional cost, it also provides basic accident and sickness insurance. The card costs $22 per year. If you're no longer a student but are still younger than 26, you can get a **GO 25 card** (from the same company), which entitles you to insurance and some discounts (but not on museum admissions). In Canada, **Travel CUTS** (☎ **800-667-2887** or 416-614-2887; `www.travelcuts.com`) offers similar services.

Spain is a major destination for students traveling across the continent with a Eurail train pass, and it's also one of the biggest study-abroad centers in the world. International students flood Madrid, Seville, and Salamanca — Spain receives more North American students for study-abroad semesters and language courses than any other European country.

Students receive discounts on public transportation and almost all attractions, including museums. Carry your ISIC with you at all times, and never hesitate to ask: ***¿Existe un descuento para estudiantes?*** (Is there a student discount?) The relative affordability of Spain is especially gratifying for students. You can easily sleep, eat, and, yes, drink while pinching pennies. Low-cost hotels (in Spain, chiefly *hostales* and *pensiones*) and affordable restaurants abound.

Paradores, the national roster of historic hotels and inns run by the Spanish government, has introduced a program of discounts for young people 20 to 30 years old: Called "Escapada Joven" (Youthful Getaway), it offers lodging (including buffet breakfast) in a standard double room at any *parador* for just 45€ ($54) plus tax, per person, per night. And better yet, even if the person accompanying the qualifying youngster isn't similarly blessed with youth, he or she qualifies for the discounted rate while occupying the same room.

Exploring Your Special Interests

Spain has so much to offer that it's the perfect place to indulge yourself in a special passion, whether your particular interest is architecture and design, history, bullfighting, or flamenco dancing. I choose to detail just two possible pursuits — golf and gastronomy — both of which have attracted immense interest in the last few years. See also Chapter 5 for more on special-interest package tours.

Golf

Spaniards are huge golfing enthusiasts. British mining engineers introduced the sport to Spain in the 19th century, and today Spain boasts numerous top golfers, including José María Olazabal and Sergio García. Some of the finest courses in Europe grace the southern coast of Andalusia along the Costa del Sol, while you can find other great courses in Catalonia and across Spain. Golfing vacations in Spain are on the rise;

for tour packagers, see Chapter 5. Other sources of information to consult while planning a golfing holiday, or even a day or two playing golf in Spain, include the following:

- **Golf Spain** (☎ **34-902-20-00-52;** www.golfspain.com) features information on golf courses and clubs, golf schools and associations, greens fees and online booking, and golf travel, including special offers.
- **Golf in Spain** (☎ **34-952-47-48-48;** www.golfinspain.com/eng) has a nice Web site with course reviews, online booking, golf packages, and special offers.

Wine and gastronomy

Spain is in the midst of a gastronomic explosion, with creative chefs, especially in the Basque Country and Catalonia, rivaling the best France and Italy have to offer. Traveling to Spain for the express purpose of indulging in its suddenly chic cuisine and increasingly popular wines is an excellent way to learn about the country's culture and people. Whether you seek out the hottest restaurants or winery tastings, food and wine travel in Spain is an unforgettable treat. For background and practical information on creating your own gastronomic trip, check out these Web sites:

- **Cellar Tastings** (www.cellartastings.com/en/travel-spain.html) offers a gourmet and wine guide to Spain, with good overviews of Spanish cuisine and wines by region (including individual winemakers), recipes, and links to gourmet tours offered by Cellar Tours and Tenedor Tours (see Chapter 5 for more on package tours).
- **Food and Wine** (www.foodandwine.com/travel/destinations/spain.cfm), the gourmet magazine's online presence, has a very good overview of Spanish cuisine, wines, and gastronomic travel, with excellent articles on everything from tapas crawls to revolutionary chefs and a cakewalk through Barcelona, plus great menu ideas for recreating Spanish delights at home.

Penelope Casas has published several excellent books on Spanish cuisine, including ***Delicioso! The Regional Cooking of Spain*** (Knopf), and ***La Cocina de Mamá: The Great Home Cooking of Spain*** (Broadway).

Chapter 9

Taking Care of the Remaining Details

In This Chapter

- Securing your passport and getting into Spain
- Getting the skinny on travel and health insurance
- Communicating via cellphones and the Internet
- Making your way through airline security
- Reserving event and attraction tickets before your travel
- Packing for your trip

With only a few, but very important, details remaining in your trip preparation, you're almost ready to go. You can probably already taste the tapas and, like Don Quixote, envision windmills on the plains. Spain's sights, sounds, and tastes are just a flight away, but before you start to pack your bags, take the time to review this chapter and consider a few odds and ends — passports and Customs, insurance, health questions, safety, making advance reservations, and especially, what to pack.

Getting into Spain

Traveling to Spain is simple. Citizens (adults and children) of the United States, United Kingdom, Canada, Australia, and New Zealand need only a valid passport to enter Spain (for a stay of up to 90 days). As members of the European Union, British citizens have it especially easy: They don't need to get their passports stamped (though they still need to carry one).

Citizens of South Africa, however, need a visa in order to visit Spain. Contact the Spanish Embassy or consulate in the city closest to you. The **Spanish Embassy** is located in Pretoria (169 Pine St., Arcadia-Pretoria 0083; ☎ **27-12-344-38-75**). **The Spanish Consulate** is in Cape Town (37 Shortmarket St., Cape Town 8001; ☎ **27-21-22-24-15**), and you can find an **Honorary Spanish Consulate** in Johannesburg (7 Coronation Rd., Sandhurst, Sandton-Johannesburg 2196; ☎ **27-11-783-20-46**).

Getting a Passport

A valid passport is the only legal form of identification accepted around the world. You can't cross an international border without it. Getting a passport is easy, but the process takes some time. For an up-to-date country-by-country listing of passport requirements around the world, go to the "Foreign Entry Requirement" Web page of the **U.S. Department of State** at `http://travel.state.gov/foreignentryreqs.html`.

Applying for a U.S. passport

If you're applying for a first-time passport, follow these steps:

1. **Complete a passport application in person at a U.S. passport office; a federal, state, or probate court; or a major post office.**

   To find your regional passport office, either check the **U.S. Department of State**'s Web site, `http://travel.state.gov/passport/passport_1738.html`, or call the **National Passport Information Center** (☎ **877-487-2778**) for automated information.

2. **Present a certified birth certificate as proof of citizenship.**

   Bringing along your driver's license, state or military ID, or social security card is also a good idea.

3. **Submit two identical passport-sized photos, measuring 2×2 inches in size.**

   You often find businesses that take these photos near a passport office. ***Note:*** You can't use a strip from a photo-vending machine because the pictures aren't identical.

4. **Pay a fee.**

   For people 16 and older, a passport is valid for ten years and costs $85. For those 15 and younger, a passport is valid for five years and costs $70.

Allow plenty of time — at least two months before your trip, preferably longer — to apply for a passport; processing takes four weeks on average but can run longer in busy periods (especially spring). However, if you've waited too long and you're willing to shell out the money, you can pay extra for an expedited issuance. To expedite your passport — and get it in five business days — visit an agency directly (or go through the court or post office and have them submit your application by overnight mail) and pay an additional $35 fee. For more information, consult the Department of State's Web site or call the **National Passport Information Center** toll-free number (☎ **877-487-2778**).

If you have a passport in your current name that was issued within the past 15 years (and you were older than 16 when it was issued), you can renew the passport by mail for $55. Whether you're applying in person or by mail, you can download passport applications from the **U.S. Department of State**'s Web site at `http://travel.state.gov/passport/passport_1738.html`. For general information, call the **National Passport Agency** (☎ **202-647-0518**). To find your regional passport office, either check the U.S. Department of State's Web site or call the **National Passport Information Center.**

Applying for other passports

The following list offers more information for citizens of Australia, Canada, Ireland, New Zealand, and the United Kingdom.

- **Australians** can visit a local post office or passport office. Call the **Department of Foreign Affairs and Trade** (☎ **131-232** toll-free from Australia), or log on to `www.passports.gov.au` for details on how and where to apply.
- **Canadians** can pick up applications at post offices, passport offices throughout Canada, or from the central **Passport Office, Department of Foreign Affairs and International Trade,** Ottawa, ON K1A 0G3 (☎ **800-567-6868;** `www.ppt.gc.ca`). Applications must be accompanied by two identical passport-sized photographs and proof of Canadian citizenship. Processing takes five to ten days if you apply in person, or about three weeks by mail.
- Residents of **Ireland** can apply for a ten-year passport, costing 57€, at the **Passport Office,** Setanta Centre, Molesworth Street, Dublin 2 (☎ **01-671-1633;** `irlgov.ie/iveagh`). Folks younger than age 18 or older than 65 must apply for a three-year passport that costs 12€. You can also apply at 1A South Mall, Cork (☎ **021-272-525**) or at the counter in most main post offices.
- **New Zealanders** can pick up a passport application at any New Zealand Passports Office or download it from the Web site (`www.passports.govt.nz`). Contact the **Passports Office** at ☎ **0800-225-050** in New Zealand.
- **United Kingdom** residents can pick up applications for a standard 10-year passport (5-year passport for children younger than 16) at passport offices, major post offices, or a travel agency. For information, contact the **United Kingdom Passport Service** (☎ **0870-521-0410;** `www.ukpa.gov.uk`).

Keep your passport, or at the very least a photocopy of its principle pages, with you (securely in your money belt) at all times. The only times you need to hand over your passport are at the bank (for them to photocopy when they change your traveler's checks), at borders for the guards to peruse, or to the conductor on overnight train rides. Also, you'll need to show it to any police or military personnel who ask for it, and briefly to the concierge when you check into your hotel.

Hotel front desks in Spain often want to keep your passport overnight. Because the hotel must register you with the police, the front-desk clerk piles up all the passports in a drawer until the evening so he or she can fill out all the guest slips at once. Smile and ask politely whether the clerk can do the paperwork on the spot or at least whether you can come by in an hour or two to retrieve your passport.

If you lose your passport while abroad, go directly to the nearest embassy or consulate. Bring all forms of ID that you have, and they'll start generating you a new passport. However, try to avoid passport hassles at all costs. Keep yours in a safe place — either on your person or in your hotel room safe, if your room has one.

Dealing with Spanish Customs and Immigration

The paperwork starts before you even set foot on Spanish soil. On the plane, you need to fill out a form for Spanish Customs. (See the Appendix for information on what you can bring into Spain.) When you arrive at the airport, you first go through Immigration. Pay attention to the signs; if you're not a member of the E.U. and you get in that line by mistake, count on being turned around at the front and redirected to the end of the proper line. Exiting the baggage area, you pass Customs officials (who in truth don't pay all that much attention to incoming flights of tourists from such places as the United States and the United Kingdom). They're legally allowed to rifle through your bags if they choose, but they seldom do.

Coming back to the United States from Spain, Customs officials often ask a few questions about where you've been. Mostly, they want to know whether you've visited places other than Spain — North Africa, for example. Customs officials ask these questions because people have been known to make hashish detours to Morocco from Spain. In addition to being illegal, taking controlled substances across international borders is extremely foolish.

Technically, you can bring as much loot as you want back into the United States from a trip abroad, but the Customs authority does limit how much you can take back for free (the limits are mainly for taxation purposes, to separate tourists with souvenirs from importers).

U.S. residents can bring home $400 worth of goods duty-free, providing you've been out of the country for at least 48 hours and haven't used the exemption in the past 30 days. The $400 limit includes one liter of an alcoholic beverage (you must, of course, be 21 years old), 200 cigarettes, and 100 cigars. Anything you mail home from abroad is exempt from the $400 limit. You may mail up to $200 worth of goods to yourself (marked "for personal use") and up to $100 to others (marked "unsolicited gift") once each day, as long as the package doesn't include alcohol or tobacco products. You must pay an import duty on anything over these limits. Art purchases are exempt from U.S. Customs and tax considerations, so if you're thinking about snapping up that long dreamt-about Dalí or perfect Picasso, go for it.

If you're a U.S. citizen, note that buying items at a duty-free shop before flying home *does* count toward your Customs limits (monetary or otherwise). The duty that you avoid in those shops is the local tax on the item (such as state sales tax in the United States), not any import duty that the U.S. Customs office may assess.

For additional information, or for a list of specific items that you can't bring into your home country, contact your Customs office. In the United States, look in the phone book (under U.S. Government, Department of the Treasury, U.S. Customs Service) or check out the **U.S. Customs and Border Protection** Web site at `www.customs.ustreas.gov/xp/cgov/travel`.

Playing It Safe with Travel and Medical Insurance

Three kinds of travel insurance are available: trip-cancellation insurance, medical insurance, and lost luggage insurance. The cost of travel insurance varies widely, depending on the cost and length of your trip, your age and health, and the type of trip you're taking, but expect to pay between 5 and 8 percent of the vacation itself. Here is my advice on all three.

- **Trip-cancellation insurance** helps you get your money back if you have to back out of a trip, if you have to go home early, or if your travel supplier goes bankrupt. Allowed reasons for cancellation can range from sickness to natural disasters to the State Department declaring your destination unsafe for travel. (Insurers usually won't cover vague fears, though, as many travelers discovered who tried to cancel their trips in October 2001 because they were wary of flying.)

  A good resource is **"Travel Guard Alerts,"** a list of companies considered high-risk by Travel Guard International (`www.travelguard.com`). Protect yourself further by paying for the insurance with a credit card. By law, consumers can get their money back on goods and services not received if they report the loss within 60 days after the charge is listed on their credit card statement.

  Note: Many tour operators, particularly those offering trips to remote or high-risk areas, include insurance in the cost of the trip or can arrange insurance policies through a partnering provider — a convenient and often cost-effective way for the traveler to obtain insurance. Make sure the tour company is a reputable one, however, and that means doing your homework and having insurance against trip cancellation or other problems. In general, I think purchasing insurance from a "third party" insurer is better rather than getting insurance from the very same tour or cruise company you're traveling with.

Most health plans (including Medicare and Medicaid) don't provide **medical insurance** coverage for travel overseas, and the ones that do often require you to pay for services upfront and reimburse you only after you return home. Even if your plan does cover overseas treatment, most out-of-country hospitals make you pay your bills upfront, and send you a refund only after you've returned home and filed the necessary paperwork with your insurance company. As a safety net, you may want to buy travel medical insurance. If you require additional medical insurance, try **MEDEX Assistance** (☎ **410-453-6300;** `www.medexassist.com`) or **Travel Assistance International** (☎ **800-821-2828;** `www.travelassistance.com`; for general information on services, call the company's Worldwide Assistance Services, Inc., at ☎ **800-777-8710**).

- **Lost luggage insurance** isn't necessary for most travelers. On international flights (including U.S. portions of international trips), baggage coverage is limited at approximately $9.07 per pound, up to approximately $635 per checked bag. If you plan to check items more valuable than the standard liability, see if your valuables are covered by your homeowner's policy, get baggage insurance as part of your comprehensive travel-insurance package, or buy Travel Guard's "BagTrak" product. Don't buy insurance at the airport, because it's usually overpriced. Be sure to take any valuables or irreplaceable items with you in your carry-on luggage, because many valuables (including books, money, and electronics) aren't covered by airline policies.

  If your luggage is lost, immediately file a lost-luggage claim at the airport, detailing the luggage contents. For most airlines, you must report delayed, damaged, or lost baggage within four hours of arrival. The airlines are required to deliver luggage, once found, directly to your house or destination free of charge.

For more information, contact one of the following recommended insurers:

- **Access America** (☎ **866-807-3982;** `www.accessamerica.com`)
- **Travelex Insurance Services** (☎ **888-457-4602;** `www.travelex-insurance.com`)
- **Travel Guard International** (☎ **800-826-4919;** `www.travelguard.com`)
- **Travel Insured International** (☎ **800-243-3174;** `www.travelinsured.com`)

Staying Healthy when You Travel

Talk to your doctor before leaving on a trip if you have a serious and/or chronic illness. For conditions such as epilepsy, diabetes, or heart problems, wear a **MedicAlert identification tag (☎ 888-633-4298;** www.medicalert.org), which immediately alerts doctors to your condition and gives them access to your records through MedicAlert's 24-hour hot line. Contact the **International Association for Medical Assistance to Travelers (IAMAT; ☎ 716-754-4883** or, in Canada, 416-652-0137; www.iamat.org) for tips on travel and health concerns in the countries you're visiting, and lists of local, English-speaking doctors. The United States **Centers for Disease Control and Prevention (☎ 800-311-3435;** www.cdc.gov) provides up-to-date information on health hazards by region or country and offers tips on food safety.

For travel abroad, you may have to pay all medical costs upfront and be reimbursed later. For information on purchasing additional medical insurance for your trip, see the previous section.

Staying Connected by Cellphone or E-Mail

Staying connected to home (or, heaven forbid, the office!) is easier than ever with technologies that have made the world a smaller place. You can now pick up cellphones to call home and, of course, log on to the Internet to access e-mail either at your hotel or any number of cybercafes across Spain.

Using a cellphone outside the United States

The three letters that define much of the world's **wireless capabilities** are GSM (Global System for Mobiles), a big, seamless network that makes for easy cross-border cellphone use throughout Europe and dozens of other countries worldwide. In the United States, T-Mobile and Cingular use this quasi-universal system; in Canada, Microcell and some Rogers customers are GSM, and all Europeans and most Australians use GSM.

If your cellphone is on a GSM system, and you have a world-capable multiband phone, such as many Sony Ericsson, Motorola, or Samsung models, you can make and receive calls across more developed areas on much of the globe, from Andorra to Uganda. Just call your wireless operator and ask for "international roaming" to be activated on your account. Unfortunately, per-minute charges can be high — usually $1 to $1.50 in Western Europe.

Many cellphone operators sell "locked" phones that restrict you from using any other removable computer memory phone chip (called a **SIM card**) card other than the ones they supply. However, if you have an "unlocked" world phone, you can install a cheap, prepaid SIM card (found at a local retailer) in your destination country. (Show your phone to the salesperson; not all phones work on all networks.) You'll get a local phone number — and much, much lower calling rates. Getting an already locked phone unlocked can be a complicated process, but it can be done; just call your cellular operator and say you'll be going abroad for several months and want to use the phone with a local provider.

For many, **renting** a phone is a good idea. You're much better off arranging to rent a cellphone and a prepaid SIM card before arriving in Spain. That way you can give loved ones and business associates your new number, make sure the phone works, and take the phone wherever you go — especially helpful for overseas trips through several countries, where local phone-rental agencies often bill in local currency and may not let you take the phone to another country. However, if you decide to rent a cellphone (*teléfono móvil,* or simply *móvil*) after you arrive in Spain, I suggest you inquire at the local tourism office, as I don't have any experience with local cellphone rental agents and am hesitant to recommend one. At this point, no such agents are stationed at either the Madrid or Barcelona airport.

CellularAbroad (☎ 800-287-3020; `www.cellularabroad.com/spainRcell.html`) rents Ericsson R520 or a Motorola Timeport tri-band cellphone for use in Spain. Rates are 24€ to 41€ ($29–$49) for one week, 41€ to 58€ ($49–$69) for two weeks, and 58€ to 74€ ($69–$89) for a month. You'll also need a Spain SIM card, which costs 66€ ($79) and is yours to keep. Domestic rates are as low as approximately .1 eurocents (12¢) per minute, and calls back to the United States and Canada are approximately 60¢ per minute. Included is initial airtime worth 18€ ($22), or 48 minutes of outgoing calls back to the United States (off-peak), or 40 to 200 minutes of local dialing within Spain (depending on time of calls).

Accessing the Internet away from home

Most Spaniards still don't have computers and modem connections in their homes, so Internet cafes, usually called *cibercafés* (thee-behr-cah-*fehs*), are common, even in rural Spain. Although no definitive directory for cybercafes exists, two places to start looking are at **`www.cybercaptive.com`** and **`www.cybercafe.com`**. However, finding one is usually as simple as strolling the main street — or asking at the local tourism information office. In general, Spanish *cibercafés* charge around 2€ to 3€ ($2.40–$3.60) an hour (though in a small town where someone has a monopoly on the service, you may have to pay double that).

Wi-Fi (wireless fidelity) is available in selected cities in Spain, with the national telecommunications company **Telefónica** rolling out service and some hotels and cafes offering wireless service, though it's not nearly as common as it is in North America. For information about prepaid Wi-Fi cards, see `www.telefonicaonline.com/on/es/wifi/index_venta.htm` (Spanish only). If you're unable to connect via Wi-Fi, most business-class hotels in Spain offer dataports for laptop modems, and many hotels now offer high-speed Internet access using an Ethernet network cable.

Wherever you go with your laptop, bring a **connection kit** of the right power (220v in Spain) and phone adapters, a spare phone cord, and a spare Ethernet network cable — or find out whether your hotel supplies them to guests. Spain uses the North American RJ11 phone jack. Try `www.walkabouttravelgear.com/c_spain.htm` for any adapters you may need.

Keeping Up with Airline Security

Generally, you'll be fine if you arrive at the airport **one hour** before a domestic flight and **two hours** before an international flight; if you show up late, tell an airline employee and she'll probably whisk you to the front of the line.

When traveling to Spain, you need to bring a passport. Bringing another **current, government-issued photo ID** such as a driver's license is also a good idea to help with security in any U.S. airport. Keep your ID ready to show at check-in, the security checkpoint, and sometimes even the gate. (Children younger than 18 don't need an ID for check-in and the security checkpoint as long as they're with a parent or guardian. However, children younger than 18 do need a passport for flights to Spain. See the "Applying for a U.S. passport" section earlier in this chapter for more information.)

In 2003, the Transportation Security Administration (TSA) phased out **gate check-in** at all U.S. airports. Although **E-tickets** have largely made paper tickets obsolete for domestic flights, when flying abroad you still need to check in at the counter and show your valid passport.

Security checkpoint lines are getting shorter, but some doozies remain. If you have trouble standing for long periods of time, tell an airline employee; the airline will provide a wheelchair. Speed up security by **not wearing metal objects** such as big belt buckles. If you have metallic body parts, a note from your doctor is helpful. Keep in mind that only **ticketed passengers** are allowed past security, except for those escorting disabled passengers or children.

Federalization has stabilized **what you can carry on** and **what you can't.** The general rule is that sharp things are out, nail clippers are okay, and food and beverages must be passed through the X-ray machine — but security screeners can't make you drink from your coffee cup. Bring food in your carry-on rather than checking it, as explosive-detection machines used on checked luggage have been known to mistake food (especially chocolate, for some reason) for bombs. The TSA has issued a list of restricted items; check its Web site (`www.tsa.gov/public/index.jsp`) for details.

Airlines limit you to a single carry-on for crowded flights and impose size restrictions on the bags that you bring on board. The dimensions vary, but the strictest airlines say that carry-ons must measure no more than 22×14×9 inches, including wheels and handles, and weigh no more than 40 pounds. On international flights from North America to Spain, passengers can carry two pieces of checked luggage, not to exceed 70 pounds each. The third bag must be a carry-on, but weight limits vary according to the airline, from 20 pounds to 70 pounds (though no one ever checks; size is more important).

Airport screeners may decide that your checked luggage needs to be searched by hand. You can now purchase luggage locks that allow screeners to open and relock a checked bag if hand-searching is necessary. Look for Travel Sentry certified locks at luggage or travel shops and Brookstone stores. These locks, approved by the TSA, can be opened by luggage inspectors with a special code or key. For more information on the locks, visit www.travelsentry.org. If you use something other than TSA-approved locks, your lock will be cut off your suitcase if a TSA agent needs to hand-search your luggage.

Making Reservations and Getting Tickets in Advance

For most activities, events, and dining, you don't need to make advance reservations — at least not from home before you set out for Spain. You can usually pick up last-minute tickets to music and theater performances.

To find out what's showing during your visit, check out the two Web sites of the leading cultural guide in Spain, ***Guía del Ocio.*** It offers both Madrid (www.guiadelocio.com/madrid) and Barcelona (www.guiadelocio.com/barcolona) editions; the sites (in Spanish) cover music, art, theater, cinema, and so on. In a similar vein is **LaNetro Madrid** (http://madrid.lanetro.com), also in Spanish. English-language stops on the Web include www.timeout.com/barcelona and www.timeout.com/madrid. See the Appendix for a list of other informational Web sites.

If you're traveling in high season, checking into advance tickets to visit the **Alhambra** in Granada is a good idea. (Banco Bilbao Vizcaya handles advance sales up to a year in advance at www.alhambratickets.com or in Spain by calling ☎ **902-22-44-60.**) Big-ticket entertainment shows for which I advise getting advance tickets include the **opera houses** in Madrid (www.teatro-real.com) and Barcelona (www.liceubarcelona.com), the **Palau de la Música** concert hall (www.palaumusica.org) in Barcelona, and the popular **Summer Music Festival** in Perelada (www.festivalperalada.com). You also need to order in advance if you want tickets for the most popular soccer games. For Barcelona's popular *fútbol* (soccer) squad, **FC Barcelona,** log on to www.fcbarcelona.com for information and schedules (call ☎ **93-496-36-00** for tickets).

Madrid's top team, **Real Madrid,** also has a Web page (www.realmadrid.es), or call **Caja Madrid** (☎ **902-488-488**) for tickets.

If you're a jazz fan, catch one of Northern Spain's excellent summer jazz festivals. You can get a schedule and reserve tickets in advance for the festivals in **Bilbao** (☎ **944-91-40-80;** www.getxo.net), **San Sebastián** (☎ **943-48-11-79;** www.jazzaldia.com), and **Vitoria** (☎ **945-14-19-19;** www.jazzvitoria.com).

Serviticket (www.lacaixa.es) handles online ticket sales in Barcelona and Catalonia. In Madrid, **Caja Madrid** (www.cajamadrid.es) lists a wide series of events, including bullfights, *fútbol,* music, theater, opera, dance, and more. At press time, however, you can reserve and purchase tickets only by telephone (☎ **902-488-488**).

Usually only the top Spanish restaurants require a reservation in order to get in. (However, if a restaurant particularly interests you, and especially if you hope to dine late on a Friday or Saturday night, call for a reservation as soon as you hit town.) Be sure to make reservations at the most highly sought-after restaurants in Madrid, Barcelona, and the Basque Country. In Bilbao, dining at Martín Berasategui's **Restaurante Guggenheim Bilbao** (☎ **94-423-93-33**), within the museum, usually requires a reservation at least two weeks in advance. If you have your heart set on a blowout dinner in San Sebastián at either **Arzak** (☎ **943-27-84-65;** www.arzak.es) or **Akelaré** (☎ **943-21-20-52**) in high season (July and Aug), make the reservation from home to make sure you get in (see Chapter 12 for reviews of all three restaurants). The country's most famous restaurant, **El Bulli** (☎ **972-15-04-57**) on the Costa Brava, is impossible to get in without a (lucky) reservation made far in advance.

Packing for Spain

What are the bare essentials for traveling in Spain? Comfortable walking shoes, a versatile sweater and/or jacket, rain gear, sunscreen and a cap, toiletries and medications (pack these in your carry-on bag so you have them if the airline loses your luggage), and a camera with extra film. You'll almost never need a suit or a fancy dress, though for most travelers, some smart casual wear is essential.

Spaniards are generally very stylish and fashion-conscious, and visitors usually need smart casual clothing to feel like they fit in. Men are expected to wear a jacket in top restaurants. Jeans and sport shirts (and sandals and Bermuda shorts in summer) are acceptable in informal bars and restaurants.

If you head to the north of Spain, don't forget some rain gear — a lightweight, water-resistant jacket or poncho. For the rest of the country, take sunscreen and a cap or hat gear also.

Because lost-luggage rates are at an all-time high, many travelers bring their possessions on board to try to divert disaster. However, planes are also more crowded than ever, and overhead compartment space is at a premium. New security measures have made carrying luggage on board more complicated than ever (see "Keeping Up with Airline Security" earlier in this chapter). Make sure that you consolidate your medications, documents, and valuables into your one carry-on bag. And don't pack your jewelry in your suitcase. In fact, don't pack your jewelry, period.

The standard for electricity in Spain is 220 volts, but some hotels have a voltage of 110 to 120 in bathrooms as a safety precaution. Sockets (outlets) take round, two-pin plugs, so you may need to pack an international adapter plug. North Americans also need a transformer unless they have dual-voltage travel appliances.

Part III

Northern Spain: Barcelona, the Costa Brava, and the Basque Country

"Get your room key ready, Margaret!"

In this part . . .

The north might challenge your preconceptions of Spain. For example, in Catalonia, of which Barcelona is the capital, Spanish isn't the main language (Catalan is). Catalonia, in the extreme northeast corner, has long been considered more continental and faster-paced than the rest of the country, and though this part of Mediterranean Spain is definitely unique, it has just about everything for which you come to Spain: history, culture, unique architecture, incredible landscapes, and spectacular coastlines. From the 2,000-year-old but cutting-edge city of Barcelona to the fertile lands of Girona province and the beach coves of the Costa Brava, Catalonia is very nearly what Catalans say it is: a country unto itself.

The Basque Country and Navarra, on the other hand, are remote and primarily rural areas, isolated by harsh climates and rugged terrain. The people living here today trace their roots to some of the earliest inhabitants of Spain, and they stick to their traditional ways. However, that doesn't mean there aren't exciting things happening up north. The revolutionary Guggenheim Museum has single-handedly revitalized industrial Bilbao. San Sebastián is a gourmet paradise — the finest restaurant scene in Spain. And Pamplona, of course, is that near-mythical place where bulls charge through narrow streets on the heels of thrill-seekers.

Whether you want a relaxing trip to traditional Spain or you're looking for more adventure, you can find it in the cities and the little-known countryside of northern Spain.

Chapter 10

Barcelona

In This Chapter

- Getting to know Spain's capital of architecture and design
- Choosing a hotel, from Art Nouveau palaces to chic designer hotels
- Tasting Barcelona — tapas, country cooking, and Mediterranean haute cuisine
- Day-tripping to a secluded mountain monastery, a stylish beach resort, and Catalan wine country

Barcelona has been around since the Romans dubbed it *Barcino* and built a sturdy stone wall around it 2,000 years ago, but it was the 1992 Summer Olympic Games that really thrust this self-assured and cosmopolitan city onto the world stage. In a flash, Barcelona became one of Europe's hottest destinations. And it hasn't cooled off one bit.

The most dynamic city in Spain, Barcelona is as intoxicating as they come; La Rambla boulevard is a pulsating parade of locals, tourists, and cheery hucksters, and the Gothic Quarter's narrow, dark alleys resonate with romance and history. With its palm trees, sparkling urban beaches, and outdoor cafes, Barcelona has the languid air of a sultry Mediterranean capital, while its industriousness and commitment to eye-popping style, design, and architecture give it the air of a progressive northern European city.

Barcelona has a long tradition of embracing visionary artists like Pablo Picasso, Joan Miró, and Salvador Dalí; its favorite eccentric son is Antoni Gaudí, whose wildly imaginative architecture is an appropriate symbol for this ancient yet cutting-edge city. Though parts of the Roman wall still stand and the Gothic Quarter remains fundamentally unchanged since the Middle Ages, Barcelona has reinvented itself several times in the past century. The Olympic Games sparked a rejuvenation that created lively new neighborhoods, reinvigorated the waterfront, and dramatically cleaned up the city's *moderniste* masterpieces. Barcelona has never looked better.

Barcelona is the capital of the province of the same name as well as the capital of independent-minded Catalonia — an autonomous region in the northeast of Spain. The people of Spain's second-largest city are hard working, pragmatic, and serious about their Catalan identity, with its unique language and strong ties to the countryside. Voters overwhelmingly approved a contentious 2006 referendum, backed by Spanish President José Luis Rodríguez Zapatero, that awarded the region greater control over its political and economic affairs than ever before, going so far as to refer to Catalonia as a "nation."

On weekends, many Barcelona residents rush out to beach apartments and renovated 16th-century country *masías* (farmhouses), or head to the hills in search of wild mushrooms. When visiting Barcelona, imitating the natives is a terrific plan: Spend a few days in this head-turning, cosmopolitan city, as well as a couple in the countryside or on the beaches of the Costa Brava (for more on the Costa Brava, see Chapter 11).

Barcelona offers some of the finest dining in Spain. Some of Europe's most adventurous chefs have established themselves in Barcelona, and the city has become a true gastronomic destination. Whether you sit at a chic table or stand at a bar, you can enjoy fresh seafood and local ingredients with a Mediterranean accent (plenty of olive oil, tomatoes, and fresh vegetables). Wash it all down with local Penedès or Priorat red wines, or *cava,* Spain's excellent sparkling wine.

The guru of *modernisme*

Antoni Gaudí, the eccentric architect of several of Barcelona's most mind-bending masterpieces, was the best-known proponent of *modernisme,* or Catalan Art Nouveau. A pious man with a devil of an imagination, Gaudí was destitute and unrecognizable when run over by a tram in 1926. Yet he remains a celebrated figure, and his stature has grown exponentially as more people are exposed to the unique works he left behind only in northern Spain. Gaudí now has disciples across the globe. Pope John Paul II set him on the road to beatification (an act that pre-figures sainthood in the Catholic Church) in 2000, and 2002 was declared the "International Year of Gaudí," with special exhibits and conferences, as well as a special Ruta Gaudí tour, hosted by his native city.

Barcelona brims with buildings molded like ocean waves, roofs tiled like dragon scales, and chimneys straight out of *Star Wars* — and that's just Gaudí. Around the turn of the 20th century, a whole band of *modernistes* in Barcelona dreamed up the most fanciful buildings their imaginations and rich patrons allowed. Gaudí's creative cohorts were Lluís Domènech i Montaner and Josep Puig i Cadafalch, among many others. You can see their unique take on Art Nouveau in its fantastic forms, decorative flourishes (in wrought iron, metal, colorful tiles, and stained glass), and signature elements such as Gaudí's bizarre chimneys. This group also introduced such convention-defying structural innovations as parabolic arches and spirals. Even a century later, the audacious buildings they left in Barcelona, such as the Sagrada Familia church, La Pedrera apartment house, and the Palau de la Música concert hall, as well as dozens of forward-looking residential buildings, still wow visitors as aesthetic and engineering marvels.

The weather in Barcelona is welcoming — mild and sunny much of the year. In the main summer months, this Mediterranean city is beset by heat and humidity and a crush of international visitors. For my money, Barcelona really thrives in spring, early summer, and fall.

Getting There

Several airlines offer direct international flights to Barcelona from North America and Europe. There are frequent shuttle flights from Madrid as well as flights from virtually every Spanish city that has a passenger airport. However, you can also roll into town on rented wheels or aboard a RENFE train — Spain's national train service.

By air

Airlines that fly into Barcelona from North America include **Delta** and **Iberia.** Barcelona's international airport, **El Prat de Llobregat (☎ 93-478-50-00;** www.aena.es), lies 12km (7 miles) south of the center of the city. The international terminal is Terminal A; Terminals B and C handle domestic and European flights. The airport is currently being expanded to handle Barcelona's ever-increasing traffic. If you've flown in from overseas, you must go through Customs first (you'll see two lines, one for European Union [E.U.] members and another for everyone else), and then go downstairs for your luggage.

Carts are free; grab one, sling your bags onto it, and wheel past the usually uninterested guards (who theoretically are allowed to inspect your bags if they choose, something they almost never do) out to the soaring, glass-enclosed lobby, which even has palm trees growing under the roof. You can find rental-car agencies, an ATM, and **a tourism information booth** (open 9 p.m.–9 a.m. daily) just a few feet from where you emerge from baggage claim. Drop in at the tourism counter to pick up a map and get easy directions to the buses, trains, and taxis going into the city.

If you're flying in from Madrid, shuttle flights run on the hour (and more frequently during prime business-travel hours) on **Iberia (☎ 902-40-05-00;** www.iberia.com), **Air Europa (☎ 902-40-15-01;** www.air-europa.com), and **Spanair (☎ 902-92-91-91;** www.spanair.com).

You have three options for getting from the airport into Barcelona — and for returning to the airport — train, bus, or taxi. All three methods from the airport to downtown take between 30 and 45 minutes. Of course, taxis deposit you at your hotel — an important consideration if you're feeling ragged after a long flight or aren't traveling especially light. If you have transportation questions, call **Airport Information,** at **☎ 93-298-38-38.**

- White **taxis,** lined up outside the terminals, take you to the center of the city for about 20€ ($24; in addition to baggage supplements of .90€/$1 per bag). Taxis don't necessarily get you to the city much quicker than the Aerobús, because traffic in Barcelona can be a real drag (unless you're staying at a hotel near the waterfront, which is — surprisingly — quickly accessed along the Ronda Litoral beltway from the airport).

- The inexpensive **Aerobús** (☎ **010** or 93-412-00-00) is probably your best option from the airport if you're traveling light, especially because most of the hotels I recommend are close to the many stops that it makes. Buses depart every 12 minutes for Plaça Catalunya, passing some principal addresses en route, including Plaça de Espanya, Gran Vía, and Passeig de Gràcia. Buses run Monday through Friday from 6 a.m. to midnight; weekends from 6:30 a.m. to midnight. Aerobús buses return to the airport from Plaça Catalunya, following the same schedule. The price is 3.60€ ($4) one-way or 5.90€ ($7) round-trip.
- **RENFE** (☎ **902-24-02-02;** `www.renfe.es`) runs trains just outside the airport terminal. Trains leave every 25 minutes, stopping at Estació de Sants and Plaça Catalunya (so you'll probably need a taxi to complete your journey), and hours of operation are Monday through Friday, from 6 a.m. to 10 p.m.; cost is 2.60€ ($3). RENFE now features a multiuse T-1 ticket (see the sidebar entitled "Multitrip ticket bargains," later in this chapter) that you can use on the airport train.

By train

Trains are one of the best ways to get around Spain, even if they don't have the same reputation for punctuality as Swiss or German trains. **RENFE** (☎ **902-24-02-02;** `www.renfe.es`) is the Spanish national train service. Most national and international trains arrive at **Estació Sants,** Plaça dels Països Catalans, s/n (☎ **93-495-62-15;** Metro: Sants). Trains with international destinations also leave from **Estació de França,** Avinguda Marquès de l'Argentera, s/n (☎ **93-496-34-34;** Metro: Barceloneta). **Ferrocarrils Generalitat de Catalunya,** also known as FGC (☎ **93-205-15-15;** `www.fgc.net`), runs the local trains in Catalonia.

By car

The highways outside of Barcelona are generally excellent — even though everyone drives at warp speed. The A-7 highway leads to Barcelona from France and northern Catalonia — the Costa Brava and Girona. The A-2 leads to Barcelona from Madrid, Zaragoza, and Bilbao. From Valencia or the Costa del Sol, take the E-15 north.

When you get close to the city, look for one of two signs into downtown Barcelona: CENTRE CIUTAT takes you downtown into the Eixample district, and the RONDA LITORAL is a beltway that takes you quickly to the port area.

Autopistas are toll roads, and in Catalonia they're among the best but also the costliest in Spain. If you have more time than euros, look for the local highways (designated by N, as in N-1): not as direct but considerably cheaper. The word you want to stay away from, the one that will make you dig into your pockets, is *peatje* or *peaje* (toll).

By bus

Buses *(autocares)* are generally cheaper than trains, but they're not the most comfortable or relaxing way to travel. You often feel squeezed in your seat.

Several coach operators, including **Enatcar** (☎ 93-245-25-28), **Julià** (☎ 93-490-40-00), and **Sarfa** (☎ 93-265-11-58), offer bus service to Barcelona from cities and towns in Catalonia and farther afield. Most Spanish buses arrive at and depart from **Estació del Nord,** Alí Bei 80 (☎ 902-26-06-06; Metro: Arc de Triomf); international buses use **Estació Sants** (☎ 93-490-40-00; Metro: Sants), next to the Sants train station.

By ferry

With its revitalized port, part of a concerted effort to renew the city's maritime past, Barcelona has become one of Europe's top cruise ports, and shiploads of tourists now stream into the city from across the Mediterranean.

If you're arriving by boat into Barcelona's port (Estació Marítim), you're either steaming in on a huge Mediterranean cruise ship or aboard the ferry that runs to Palma de Mallorca. **Transmediterránea,** Muelle de San Beltrán (☎ **902-45-46-45;** `www.trasmediterranea.com`), operates ferries to the Balearic Islands. Most of the year these ferries take about eight hours to arrive. In summer, Transmediterránea operates an express ferry that takes about four hours to Palma de Mallorca.

Orienting Yourself in Barcelona

A city with a metropolitan population of 4 million, Barcelona doesn't seem nearly that large. It's penned in by natural barriers — the Mediterranean Sea and the low-slung Montjuïc and Tibidabo mountains. However, Barcelona is also among Europe's densest cities; cars and one of the continent's highest concentrations of motor scooters choke the streets.

Barcelona's major neighborhoods tend to overlap (which is why many guidebooks claim the Picasso Museum is in the Gothic Quarter, when it's actually in La Ribera). A focal point of the city is **Plaça de Catalunya,** which neatly divides the Old Quarter from the modern expansion. **Ciutat Vella** loosely encompasses much of the Old City, including the once-walled Barri Gòtic (Gothic Quarter), La Ribera, La Rambla, and El Raval. The elegant shopping avenue Passeig de Gràcia bisects **El Eixample** (the modern city, constructed on a grid). Parallel to Passeig de Gràcia is **Rambla de Catalunya,** a tree-lined extension of the old town's famous boulevard La Rambla. The **waterfront** area comprises a number of smaller areas: Barceloneta, Port Vell, Moll de la Fusta, Port Olímpic, and Vila Olímpica (see "Exploring Barcelona by neighborhood," later in this chapter).

Bar-theh-*loh*-nah: Calling all linguistics majors

In bilingual Barcelona, almost everyone speaks both Spanish and Catalan. The latter, the primary language of Catalonia, isn't a dialect of Spanish but a nasal Latin-derived tongue that sounds — if Catalans will forgive the gross oversimplification — something akin to a cross between French and Castilian Spanish. In Spanish, Barcelona is pronounced with a lisp: Bar-theh-*loh*-nah. In Catalan, the pronunciation has a soft *c,* as it does in English. The region of which Barcelona is the capital is spelled Catalonia in English, Cataluña in Spanish, and Catalunya in Catalan. The back-and-forth between Catalan and Castillian Spanish is ever-present in the Catalan capital; you'll hear both in pretty much equal amounts, and street signs and other communications are in both languages, though predominantly in Catalan.

If you're hoping your high-school Spanish will rescue you, well, you probably didn't learn terms like *carrer* (*calle,* or street); *avinguda* (*avenida,* or avenue); or *passeig* (*paseo,* or boulevard). Still, locals often refer to streets interchangeably by their Catalan and Spanish names. The city's most famous street variously appears as La Rambla, Las Ramblas, or, in Catalan, Les Rambles. The modern gridlike area of downtown is most often called El Eixample (the Extension), though some older Spanish-speakers still call it the Ensanche. Passeig de Gràcia is frequently called Paseo de Gracia in Spanish.

As if that weren't enough, the Catalan language has a number of idiosyncratic features. A period in the middle of a word (Paral.lel) isn't a misprint but a construction used to separate the double letter. The letter *i* (as in *Antoni Gaudí i Cornet*) often separates a person's last name; meaning "and," the letter *i* joins the surnames of both the person's mother and father.

If that sounds confusing, don't worry; you'll get the hang of it. (And if you don't, it won't detract from your enjoyment of the city in the least.)

Much of Barcelona, especially the Gothic Quarter, is a hair-raising maze. How on earth people got their mail back in the 12th century I don't know. Even in the modern city's geometric grid, street numbers can be a confusing mess. Odds and evens don't progress logically or even chronologically on opposite sides of the street; No. 10 may be across from No. 323. When giving addresses, locals often designate *mar o montaña* (sea or mountain side). This designation makes directions easy, because in most parts of the city, all you have to do is look up to see Tibidabo Mountain to orient yourself. To begin, figure out whether an address is above or below Plaça de Catalunya, and then figure out on which side of Passeig de Gràcia or La Rambla it falls. Your next step may be supplementing the maps in this book with a more detailed one from a kiosk.

Introducing the neighborhoods

Check out the sites in the following neighborhoods as you tour Barcelona.

El Eixample

When Barcelona grew beyond its old Roman walls in 1860, the city came up with a hyper-rationalist expansion plan: a major grid of equal-sized blocks. Building took place when industrial and shipping wealth flowed into the city, and the *moderniste* style of architecture took root. **El Eixample** (eye-*shahm*-pluh, occasionally called El Ensanche, in Spanish) is home to fine strolling boulevards, designer shops, and most offices (pinstriped lawyers and bankers have some of the coolest Art Nouveau digs). El Eixample is the best neighborhood for hotels and shopping, but you may also decide to spend much of your sightseeing time here, because most of the *moderniste* buildings are in this neighborhood. The Eixample grid contains the **Plaça de Catalunya,** the geographic heart of the city; the **Passeig de Gràcia,** Barcelona's boulevard of ultrachic shops, Gaudí's masterpiece, the apartment building **La Pedrera** (also called *Casa Milà*), and the **Manzana de la Discórdia,** the "block of discord," a collection of some of the finest *moderniste* buildings in Barcelona; and **La Sagrada Familia,** Gaudí's visionary, still unfinished church, begun in the early 20th century. Expect to find construction crews here midway through this millennium.

Ciutat Vella (Old City)

The Ciutat Vella encompasses a couple of neighborhoods. The **Barri Gòtic** (Gothic Quarter) is where Barcelona was born. Once enclosed by Roman walls, the *barrio* gets its name for its collection of 13th- to 15th-century buildings and medieval atmosphere — it's the true heart of the city. **La Ribera** and its vibrant adjunct **El Born,** site of innumerable bars, restaurants, art galleries, and chic shops, are next to the Gothic Quarter. The **Barri Xinés** (officially know as the **Raval**), a historically seedy neighborhood of prostitutes, beggars, and thieves, is to the west of La Rambla. Though much improved and an area of large regentrification projects led by the MACBA Museum, it remains a ramshackle neighborhood characterized by populations of newly arrived immigrants. The Ciutat Vella vies with the Eixample for the highest concentration of attractions, but the Old Quarter offers even more restaurants and nightlife options. Here you'll find the **Catedral,** a Gothic landmark and heart of the neighborhood; the **Palau de la Música,** a surreal concert hall designed by a Gaudí contemporary, Domènech i Montaner; **Carrer Montcada,** a handsome street of Gothic palaces (one of which is the **Museu Picasso**); and **Santa María del Mar,** an elegant church that's the supreme example of the Catalan Gothic style.

La Rambla

Technically part of the Ciutat Vella and one of the world's most famous streets, La Rambla (also referred to in the plural, Las Ramblas) overflows with people, newsstands, bird and flower sellers, and mimes dressed up like Don Quixote or Greek statues. This boulevard is a great place to stroll without a care in the world, occasionally ducking into a bar or restaurant along the way — just like the locals.

La Rambla — especially around Cafe Zurich, where the boulevard begins — is the best place in the city for people watching. Most visitors to Barcelona storm La Rambla as soon as they set down their bags. Though hotels (and loads of knickknack stores) line the street, I don't think it's the best place to stay — it's noisy and a little rough-and-tumble in the wee hours.

On or near the Rambla are the **Gran Teatre del Liceu,** Barcelona's great opera house, recently rebuilt after a horrific fire; the **Mercat de la Boquería,** one of Europe's liveliest food markets; and the **Monument à Colom,** the statue of Columbus pointing out to sea, at the end of La Rambla.

Waterfront

In 1992, Barcelona remembered it was a port city and reoriented itself back toward the Mediterranean Sea. The city rebuilt the unsightly and dangerous port. It developed a scenic marina and cleaned up its urban beaches. Today, the waterfront is one of the prime places to live and party. You can find most of the city's new restaurants here, but only one major hotel. As a base, the area isn't the most convenient, but it's great for shopping and entertaining kids. The beaches are so convenient that you can spend the morning sightseeing in the Gothic Quarter and the afternoon swimming in the Mediterranean Sea. Here you'll find the **Vila Olímpica,** a planned neighborhood inaugurated by Olympic athletes in 1992; **Port Olímpic,** a popular port area with even more bars and restaurants than boats; **Platja de Barcelona,** the city's most fashionable beaches; and **Port Vell,** the old port transformed into a swank mall, with restaurants, shops, an aquarium, and an IMAX theater.

Montjuïc

Montjuïc, a mountain whose name means "Hill of the Jews," offers amazing views of the city. Olympic TV cameras couldn't get enough shots of divers doing half-gainers from high platforms on the hill, the city forming the backdrop for their twisting, arching bodies. Montjuïc has two top art museums, the Olympic installations, nice gardens, and an amusement park for kids, but no hotels or restaurants to speak of. Montjuïc is home to the **Museu d'Art de Catalunya,** one of the world's top collections of Romanesque art; **Estadi Olìmpic,** the Olympic stadium; and **Fundació Joan Miró,** a museum housing native son Joan Miró's surrealist works.

Tibidabo

Barcelona's other mountain provides perhaps even more spectacular views of the city than Montjuïc — that is, when the smog lifts. You can take a tram up the mountain to bars and restaurants and look at the sea and the block formation of the modern city. A visit here is best for the panoramic views at sundown. On the hilltop are the **Parc d'Atraccions,** a retro amusement park with great views of the city, and **Carretera de les Aigues,** a dirt path that winds along the mountain for several miles — a great place to stroll, jog, ride bikes, or walk the dog.

Barrios Altos

Barcelona's upper neighborhoods — **Sarrià, Pedralbes,** and **Gràcia** — were once isolated villages where people had summer homes. Today, they're residential areas. By far the biggest attraction is **Parc Güell:** Gaudí's fantastic park city, bathed in mosaics and perfectly integrated with nature, and one of Barcelona's must-sees.

Finding information after you arrive

The extremely helpful **Turisme de Barcelona,** Plaça de Catalunya 17, underground (☎ **93-285-38-34**), is open daily from 9 a.m. to 9 p.m. Other city information bureaus are located on Plaça Sant Jaume, at the airport, and at the Sants train station. **Informació Turística de Catalunya,** which provides information on both the city and the entire autonomous region, is in Palau Robert, Passeig de Gràcia 107 (☎ **93-238-40-03**). You can also find tourism information offices at Estació Sants train station and the airport. Call ☎ **010** for general visitor information (operators speak English and other languages) or the tourist information hot line, ☎ **906-30-12-82** (these are both toll numbers). For hotel information, call ☎ **93-285-38-33.** Keep an eye out for roving red-jacketed tourist information officers in the Gothic Quarter, Passeig de Gràcia, and La Rambla.

Getting Around Barcelona

Hemmed in by mountains and sea, Barcelona is compact and easy to manage. You can do most everything by Metro (subway) and on foot, with a few taxis thrown in for convenience, out-of-the-way sights, and late nights (the Metro stops running right about the time that Barcelona's nightlife cranks up). **El Eixample** is constructed on an easy-to-negotiate grid system, and the **Ciutat Vella** is exactly the opposite, a maze of tiny streets and alleyways.

On foot

Compact Barcelona is ideal for walking. Strolling, especially along the wide pedestrian sidewalk that runs down the middle of La Rambla, and the elegant boulevard Passeig de Gràcia, is a pastime ingrained in the local culture. Barri Gòtic is not only a great place to walk and make discoveries — just don't panic if you get turned around! — but it's also so labyrinthine it's really only accessible on foot. If you have trouble finding your way, ask someone to direct you to La Rambla or La Catedral (the cathedral). From there, you can find your way. To get back and forth between the Ciutat Vella or the waterfront and the newer part of town, the Eixample, you'll want to take public transportation or a taxi.

Look out for people zipping through red lights on motor scooters. Despite what the law says, pedestrians definitely don't have the right of way in Spain. Even on sidewalks you may find yourself dodging annoying *motos* (scooters).

By Metro

The **Metro** (☎ **010** or 93-298-70-00; www.tmb.net) is Barcelona's excellent, modern, and clean subway. Its five lines are by far the fastest and easiest way to navigate the city. (The Metro has begun implementing trilingual directions and audio — in Spanish, Catalan, and English.) Red diamond symbols mark stations. (You can find good pocket-size maps at all Metro stations.) Single-ticket fares are 1.20€ ($2), although you can get a T1 pass (good for ten trips) for 6.65€ ($8) — close to half price (see the "Multitrip transport bargains" sidebar in this chapter for more info). A one-day Metro and bus pass costs 5€ ($6), and a three-day is 13€ ($16). You can also get free rides on all public transport with purchase of the Barcelona Card (see "Exploring Barcelona," later in this chapter).

The Metro runs Monday to Thursday from 5 a.m. to 11 p.m.; Friday and Saturday from 5 a.m. to 2 a.m.; holidays from 6 a.m. to 11 p.m.; and Sunday from 6 a.m. to midnight. However, if you want to keep up with the locals at night, you can't rely on the Metro. It goes to bed long before they do.

Besides the Metro, you can also ride something called **FGC Trains** (☎ **93-205-15-15**). Run by the provincial government, not the city, these subway trains share some terminals (it costs the same as the Metro, and you can pay for it using the same Metro multitrip tickets). Two different FGC lines connect the city center to the upper neighborhoods and suburbs, including Sarrià, Vallvidrera, Tibidado, and Gràcia. The only real problem you encounter is when you want to switch between an FGC train and a regular Metro train. To do so, you have to exit the first and reenter the second — paying separately for each line.

By bus

About 70 bus lines crisscross Barcelona. Though lines and hours are clearly marked, using the bus isn't the best option for first-timers. You may have trouble figuring out where you are, and few bus drivers speak English. With the subway, you can at least clearly identify your stop. Buses run Sunday to Thursday from 5 a.m. to 11 p.m. and Friday and Saturday from 5 a.m. to 2 a.m. (fare is 1.20€, or $1.44). If you don't have exact change, by far the best idea is to get a multiticket (T-10) card at the Metro, which also works on city buses (see the "Multitrip transport bargains" sidebar in this chapter for more info). Special night buses run much less frequently (believe me!) from 10:30 p.m. to 5 a.m. For route information, call ☎ **010.**

Multitrip transport bargains

Your best value options for traveling around Barcelona are bargain-basement multi-tickets for the Metro and buses. You can purchase these *tarjetas* (tickets) in automated Metro ticket offices, *estancos* (tobacco shops on the street), newspaper kiosks, and branches of the La Caixa and Caixa de Catalunya banks. The best deal is the **T-10,** good for ten trips on all Metros and the bus (6.65€/$8); several passengers can share the same ticket. Travel cards (for one–five days) are also available for unlimited travel for one person on Metro, FGC, and buses: a one-day pass is 5€ ($6); a three-day is 13€ ($17).

Multiday passes only make sense if you're spending several days zigzagging around the city on public transport. Besides, much of what you want to see in Barcelona is best done on foot. Call ☎ **010** or 93-298-70-00 for further information or visit the Web site at www.tmb.net.

By taxi

Black-and-yellow taxis are affordable and everywhere. Few journeys cost more than 6€ ($7). During the day, however, taxis aren't usually your best option because traffic is very heavy in the city — you can end up paying for the pleasure of watching the meter tick. At night, though, especially if you've dined in the Ciutat Vella, taxis are the best way to return to your hotel or continue with the night (have the restaurant call a taxi if you don't feel comfortable waiting for one on the street). You can either hail a cab in the street (the little green light on the roof means you can hop in) or get one where they're lined up (usually outside hotels). Fares begin at 1.30€ ($1.55; 1.40€/$1.70 at night). Reliable taxi companies include **Servi Taxi** (☎ **93-330-03-00**), **Barna Taxi** (☎ **93-357-77-55**), and **Radio Taxi 033** (☎ **93-303-30-33**).

By car

Trying to negotiate Barcelona's unfamiliar, traffic-clogged streets can put a definite damper on your vacation. Even the calmest drivers lose their nerve driving in Barcelona, and parking is an expensive nightmare. However, a car is useful if you plan to head out on day trips to Sitges, Montserrat, or the Penedès wine country (see "Branching Out from Barcelona," later in this chapter), or to travel to the Costa Brava and Girona (see Chapter 11).

By funicular

Funiculars (cable cars) run up some of the hills around the city, such as Montjuïc; other slopes are fitted with outdoor escalators to ease your way. The Montjuïc cable car remained closed in 2006 for repairs.

The Catalan *país*

Catalans have long referred to their native Catalonia (Catalunya), one of the autonomous regions of Spain, as *un país* — literally, a nation — sometimes leading to confusion among visitors who know little about this fiercely independent and prosperous region and its occasionally testy relationship with the rest of Spain. Voters approved a referendum in 2006 that granted Catalans much greater autonomy than any other region over their political, judicial, and economic affairs; the adopted text also crucially (to both proponents and detractors) refers to Catalonia as a "nation." Some opponents of the measure, supported by Spanish President José Luis Rodgíguez Zapatero, fear that it may lead to a "Balkanization" of Spain. Catalans contend that their homeland has always been more European — by that they mean more *Continental* — than the rest of Spain. You'll likely notice a different temperament, pace, and attitude—as well as language—in Barcelona and the region. Although you can find bullfights and the occasional tourist-oriented flamenco show, Barcelona really isn't the place for such quintessentially *Spanish* arts. The city stubbornly takes pride in its unique cultural identity. You may see T-shirts being sold on La Rambla that proclaim "Catalonia is not Spain," and hear shopkeepers responding to Spanish-speakers only in Catalan. Although some residents might prefer that Barcelona were the capital of an independent, Catalan-speaking nation, mostly these hard-working people have long been frustrated that so much of the region's wealth is rerouted to Madrid and less prosperous parts of Spain.

Staying in Style

Barcelona went nuts building and refurbishing hotels in time for the 1992 Olympics, and more than a decade later new hotels are still sprouting up all over the city to meet the city's ever-growing demand. You can find an amazing assortment of hotels, ranging from ones in historic *moderniste* buildings to others showing off the latest in the cutting-edge design for which the city is known. Across the board, you have to shell out more money for accommodations in Barcelona than you do in most parts of Spain, though a few very good value hotels have recently been inaugurated. I hesitate to recommend some of the cheaper places, because they're mostly located in areas that — even if pretty safe on the whole — may seem a little scary to you if you're unfamiliar with the city. For an explanation on the price breakdowns that I use in this book, see the Introduction.

Most of Barcelona's top attractions, restaurants, and nightlife are concentrated in El Eixample, around La Rambla, and in the Ciutat Vella, so that's probably where you want to stay. Although many visitors choose to stay on or near the Rambla, it can prove to be a very noisy choice. Most mid- to upscale-level hotels are either along La Rambla or in El Eixample.

Barcelona doesn't really have a high and low travel season; hotel rates remain relatively constant throughout the year, though some hotels offer slightly lower prices when Barcelonans escape the city in droves (during Easter, the month of August, and Christmas).

Turisme de Barcelona operates a hotel-booking service online and at its office in Plaça de Catalunya (☎ **93-285-38-34;** www.hotelsbcn.com). The service concentrates on last-minute (same-day) bookings.

The top hotels

Duquesa de Cardona
$$$$ Cituat Vella (Barri Gòtic)

At the edge of the Gothic Quarter and just across the street from the waterfront, this handsome, sedate, small hotel (44 rooms) is, along with the Prestige Paseo de Gracia (see review later in this section), my favorite new place to stay in Barcelona. The location is perfect for walks along the Moll de la Fusta promenade and is within walking distance from restaurants in the port and Las Ramblas. Housed in a lovingly restored 19th-century palace, it's elegant and intimate, but also supremely relaxed. It boasts a bonus feature that few hotels can lay claim to: a large rooftop solarium terrace with an attractive little pool and commanding views of the waterfront and port. It also has a very nice full restaurant, another surprise for a small hotel. Accommodations are luxurious and warm, chic but not coldly "drunk on design" as many aspiring design hotels are in Barcelona. Rooms with sea views are more expensive, but interior rooms are quieter. Check online for packages and special deals (including doubles as low as 135€/$162).

See map p. 124. Passeig Colom 12. ☎ ***93-268-90-90.*** *Fax: 93-268-29-31.* www.hduquesadecardona.com. *Metro: Drassanes. Nearby parking: 20€ ($24). Rack rates: 185€–220€ ($222–$264) double. AE, DC, MC, V.*

Eurostar Grand Marina Hotel
$$$$–$$$$$ Waterfront (Port Vell)

Looming out in the Barcelona port like a giant cruise ship, this large, stylish luxury hotel occupies part of the massive World Trade Center, at the end of a long walkway parallel to the new Ramblas bridge leading to the Port Vell. The views from many rooms, looking back across the water at the city as it climbs into the hills, are nothing short of incredible, and something no other hotel can offer. Popular with business travelers and vacationers on luxury cruises, it's the perfect place to take advantage of Barcelona's waterfront, with the lower Ramblas and Gothic Quarter both within easy walking distance. Rooms are elegant, with a chic modern design and top-shelf bathrooms. Public areas show off an excellent collection of works by Catalan painters and sculptors. On the rooftop terrace, a small pool, gym, and Jacuzzi remain a well-kept secret, though the incredible buffet breakfast seems to escape no one's attention. An added bonus

Barcelona Accommodations, Dining, and Attractions

ACCOMMODATIONS ■
- AC Diplomatic **49**
- Duquesa de Cardona **21**
- Eurostar Gran Marina **5**
- H10 Montcada **31**
- H10 Racó del Pi **36**
- Hostal Gat Xino **24**
- Hotel Arts **9**
- Hotel Astoria **60**
- Hotel Banys Orientals **19**
- Hotel Claris **53**
- Hotel Colón **34**
- Hotel Condes de Barcelona **55**
- Hotel Constanza **46**
- Hotel España **25**
- Hotel Granvía **48**
- Hotel Jardí **37**
- Hotel Majestic **54**
- Hotel Palace Barcelona **47**
- Prestige Paseo de Gracia **52**
- Relais d'Orsà **1**

DINING ◆
- Àbac **14**
- Agua **8**
- Agut **20**
- Agut d'Avignon **29**
- Botafumeiro **62**
- Cal Pep **12**
- Can Culleretes **27**
- Casa Calvet **43**
- Comerç 24 **15**
- Espai Sucre **16**
- Estevet **42**
- Hisop **61**
- La Dentellière **22**
- Les Quinze Nits **28**
- Principal **56**
- Restaurante 7 Portes **11**
- Senyor Parellada **18**
- Talaia Mar **10**

ATTRACTIONS ●
- Casa de la Caritat **41**
- Casa de les Punxes **59**
- Catedral de Barcelona **33**
- Estadi Olímpic (Olympic Ring) **3**
- Fundació Joan Miró **4**
- Fundació Antoni Tàpies **51**
- Gran Teatre del Liceu **26**
- Hospital Sant Pau **64**
- La Boquería **39**
- La Pedrera (Casa Milà) **57**
- La Rambla **43**
- La Sagrada Família **65**
- Manzana de la Discórdia **50**
- Maremagnum Mall **7**
- Monument à Colom **6**
- Museu d'Art Contemporani de Barcelona **40**
- Museu d'Historia de la Ciutat **44**
- Museu de la Música **58**
- Museu Nacional d'Art de Catalunya **2**
- Museu Picasso **17**
- Palau de la Música **42**
- Palau Güell **23**
- Parc Güell **63**
- Plaça del Pi **38**
- Plaça del Rei **32**
- Plaça de Sant Jaume **30**
- Plaça Sant Felip de Neri **35**
- Santa María del Mar **13**

FRANCE
Barcelona
Madrid
PORTUGAL
SPAIN
Tibidabo, Barrios Altos (Sarria, Pedralbes)
Carrer del Vallespir
Carrer de Berlin
Carrer de Numància
Carrer de la Infanta Carlota Joaquima
Carrer de Còrsega
Carrer de Rosselló
Carrer de Sant Antoni
Carrer de Provença
Avinguda de Roma
Carrer de Sants de la Creu Coberta
Carrer de Tarragona
PARC JOAN MIRÓ
Carrer d'Entrença
Carrer de Rocafort
Carrer de Calabria
Carrer de Viladomat
Carretera de la Bordeta
Plaça de Espanya
Carrer de Sant Fructuós
Gran Vía de les Corts Catalanes
Carrer de Sepulveda
Av. de Marqués de Comillas
Av. de la Reina Maria Cristina
Avinguda de Paral-lel
Carrer de Floridablanca
Carrer de Tamarit
Carrer de Manso
Carrer del Parlament
Avinguda de l'Estadi
Estadi Olímpic
PARC DE MONTJUÏC
Avinguda de Miramar
PARC D'ATRACCIONS DE MONTJUÏC
Passeig de Josep Carner

Information
Railway
0 1/4 mi
0 0.25 km
Plaça de Francesc Macia
Travessara de Gràcia
Carrer de Buenos Aires
Carrer de Londres
Carrer de Paris
Avinguda Diagonal
Gran de Gràcia
Av. de Sant Antoni Maria Claret
Carrer de la Industria
Carrer de Còrsega
EIXAMPLE
Carrer de Rosselló
Carrer de Provença
Carrer Enric Granados
Carrer de Balmes
Rambla de Catalunya
Passeig de Gràcia
Carrer de Pau Claris
Carrer de Mallorca
Carrer de València
Carrer d'Aragó
Carrer de Roger de Flor
Plaça de la Sagrada Família
Passeig de Sant Joan
Carrer de Comte Borrell
Carrer del Comte d'Urgell
Carrer de Villarroel
Carrer de Casanova
Carrer de Muntaner
Carrer d'Aribau
Carrer del Consell de Cent
Carrer de la Diputació
Carrer de R. de Llúria
Carrer del Bruc
Carrer de Girona
Carrer de Bailèn
Carrer de Napols
Carrer de Sicilia
Plaça de la Universitat
Gran Vía de les Corts Catalanes
Ronda Universitat
Carrer de Pelai
Plaça de Tetuan
Ronda de Sant Antoni
Plaça Catalunya
Plaça Urquinaona
Carrer de Casp
Carrer d'Ausias Marc
Carrer d'Ali Bei
Ronda de Sant Pere
Carrer de Ribes
Carrer de Sardenya
RAVAL
Ronda Sant Pau
Carrer de Hospital
Av. Portal de l'Angel
La Rambla
Via Laietana
Passeig de Lluís Companys
Carrer de la Marina
BARRI GÒTIC
Carrer de Sant Pau
C. de Ferran
C. de la Princesa
Carrer del Comerç
Passeig de Pujades
Carrer Nou de la Rambla
Avda. de les Drassanes
LA RIBERA
Passeig de Picasso
PARC DE LA CIUTADELLA
Carrer de Wellington
Carrer Ample
Pg. Isabel II
Passeig de Colom
Moll de la Fusta
Plaça Portal de la Pau
Villa Olímpica
PARC ZOOLOGIC
Avinguda d'Icaria
Moll d'Espanya
Port Vell
BARCELONETA
Passeig Marítim

of staying here is the ease with which you can get to the airport, avoiding the worst city traffic.

See map p. 124. Moll de Barcelona, s/n. ☎ ***93-603-90-00.*** *Fax: 93-603-90-90.* www.grandmarinahotel.com. *Metro: Drassanes. Parking: 20€ ($25). Rack rates: 230€–350€ ($276–$420) double. AE, DC, MC, V.*

H10 Racó del Pi

$$$ Cituat Vella (Barri Gòtic)

One of the best developments on the Spanish hotel scene in recent years is the appearance of this small, Barcelona-based hotel chain, which has installed several handsome and stylish — and, most important, very reasonably priced — small and midsize hotels in the Catalan capital and a handful of spots across the country. By far, the best thing about this intimate hotel (just 37 rooms) is its prized location. It occupies a historic building on one of the most atmospheric streets in the Gothic Quarter, near the emblematic Plaça del Pi and a short walk from the cathedral. The rooms are reasonably sized and feature the cleanly stylish look that seems de rigueur in Barcelona. Check online for offers (as low as 90€, or $108) for certain dates.

See map p. 124. Carrer del Pi 7. ☎ ***902-10-09-06*** *or 93-342-61-90. Fax: 93-342-61-91.* www.h10.es. *Metro: Sant Jaume. Parking nearby: 20€ ($24). Rack rates: 195€ ($234) double. AE, DC, MC, V.*

Hotel Arts

$$$$$ Waterfront (Vila Olímpica)

Barcelona has only two legitimate skyscrapers, and this high-tech, high-rise structure is one of them. Built for the 1992 Olympics but not opened until 1994 (oops!), the Arts is on the beach in the heart of the Vila Olímpica (Olympic Village). Don't expect to find any old-world flavor here, but rather the ultimate in sophistication and privacy. The pastel-colored rooms are light and airy with incredible views of the Mediterranean Sea and the city. The luxurious bathrooms, with sit-down showers and family-size tubs, are larger than most compact cars. Of course, to live like a king you need royal pockets. A Ritz-Carlton hotel, this is the hands-down favorite of most Americans.

See map p. 124. Carrer de la Marina 19–21. ☎ ***800-241-3333*** *in North America, or 93-221-10-00. Fax: 93-221-10-70.* www.ritzcarlton.com/hotels/barcelona. *Metro: Ciutadella–Vila Olímpica. Parking: 22€ ($26). Rack rates: 375€–570€ ($450–$684) double. Weekend rates and family packages available. AE, DC, MC, V.*

Hotel Banys Orientals

$$ Ciutat Vella (La Ribera)

An exciting option in a lively location, near the Born and Santa María del Mar — and not so far from the waterfront — is this inexpensive but hugely hip little hotel. Managed by the same people who run the excellent Senyor

Parellada restaurant next door, this place is perfect for people with tons of style but not a huge budget. Rooms are small but very cool with a chic monochromatic design. Though it's convenient for sightseeing and dining, it's not ideal for anyone who's averse to crowds and a bit of noise; particularly on weekend nights, this area is overrun with revelers spilling out of bars and restaurants.

See map p. 124. Argenteria 37. ☎ ***93-268-84-60.*** *Fax: 93-268-84-61.* `www.hotelbanysorientals.com`. *Metro: Sant Jaume. Nearby parking: 18€ ($22). Rack rates: 95€ ($114) double. AE, DC, MC, V.*

Hotel Claris

$$$$–$$$$$ Eixample

Behind the 19th-century palace facade and the for-guests-only museum of Egyptian art is a surprise: one of the most modern, design-oriented hotels in Spain. High-tech elevators cruise to the rooms overlooking an interior foyer. Rooms, many of which are split-level and even two-story, are a mix of cool chic and warm sophistication: They have parquet floors, bold color schemes (for example, royal purple), rich fabrics, and furnishings that combine antiques and Catalan design. Each room has original artwork, often a beautiful Nepalese, Indian, or Egyptian piece. The top-floor terrace, which has a small pool, offers sweet views of the surrounding Eixample neighborhood. Although some newcomers have challenged it in the hip-design category, the Claris remains very popular with fashionistas, film and TV people, and architects.

See map p. 124. Pau Claris 150. ☎ ***800-888-4747*** *in North America, or 93-487-62-62. Fax: 93-215-79-70.* `www.derbyhotels.es`. *Metro: Passeig de Gràcia. Parking: 18€ ($22). Rack rates: 220€–350€ ($264–$420) double. AE, DC, MC, V.*

Hotel Constanza

$$$ Eixample

If you're looking for a dose of Barcelona's legendary style but at an affordable price, this boutique hotel may be the answer. It has just 20 rooms; although they're not huge, they're fashionably sleek and very comfortable, with leather trim, plush pillows, and sparkling bathrooms, and the hotel's very nicely located (short walking distance of Plaça de Catalunya) for the bargain rates. In essence, it's like the excellent Prestige Paseo de Gracia (see below), but on a much tighter budget.

See map p. 124. Bruc 33. ☎ ***93-270-19-10.*** *Fax: 93-317-40-24.* `www.hotelconstanza.com`. *Metro: Urquinaona. Parking nearby: 20€ ($24). Rack rates: 120€ ($144) double. AE, DC, MC, V.*

Hotel Palace Barcelona

$$$$$ Eixample

Long known as the Ritz, this 1919 hotel, a member of Leading Hotels of the World, is still one of the toniest addresses in Barcelona, a splendid tree-lined avenue in El Eixample. If you're Old Money (or just want to pretend that you are), come to this hotel for white-glove treatment. Spacious public rooms are grand, aristocratic, and richly decorated, and the guest rooms are large and formal. Some rooms have marble fireplaces, and, befitting an emperor, a select few offer Roman-style baths with rich mosaics. Check for online deals.

*See map p. 124. Gran Vía de les Corts Catalanes 668. ☎ **93-510-11-30.** Fax: 93-318-01-48.* www.hotelpalacebarcelona.com. *Metro: Passeig de Gràcia. Parking: 20€ ($24). Rack rates: 380€–505€ ($475–$631) double. Contact hotel for special offers. AE, DC, MC, V.*

Prestige Paseo de Gracia

$$$$ Eixample

An exquisite new small hotel (45 rooms) smack on Barcelona's swankest boulevard, Paseo de Gracia, this chic place exudes cool. The minimalist rooms have a Zen-like tranquillity, and some have their own quiet and beautiful bamboo garden terraces. The hotel plays the chic, minimalist design card, which is by now de rigueur in Barcelona. It has soothing bathrooms and a well-thought-out, detail-oriented layout — including everything from flowers to intelligent lighting. Extras include a hip "Zeroom" lounge for listening to music and reading, and Bang & Olufsen TVs. For this level of style and comfort, the hotel is a good value, especially given its pricey location.

*See map p. 124. Paseo de Gracia 62. ☎ **902-20-04-14.** Fax: 97-225-21-01.* www.prestigepaseodegracia.com. *Metro: Passeig de Gràcia. Parking: 22€ ($26). Rack rates: 210€–270€ ($252–$324) double. AE, DC, MC, V.*

Relais d'Orsà

$$$$ Barrios Altos (Tibidabo)

Barcelona's most unique hotel is this stunning and tiny inn (just four rooms) inhabiting a perfectly restored 1900 seigniorial palace — once a summer residence of a wealthy city-dweller — perched on Tibidabo, the hill high above Barcelona. In the mid-'90s I used to live up in this neighborhood, called Vallvidrera, and I never tired of the unparalleled views that extend all the way to the sea. If you're looking for a bit of romance during your stay in Barcelona, you won't find a better place to stay. Every room in the house looks as if it has been ripped from the pages of a chic design magazine. More luxurious than any of the city's top-dollar luxury hotels, including the Arts and Claris, it certainly isn't inexpensive, but it qualifies as a relative bargain. The marvelous views and cool air come at a price, however; although you can ride the charming public transportation in the form of an old train that climbs the hill, the Relais d'Orsà is rather inconvenient for dining and sightseeing, and no restaurant is on the premises (though a breakfast fit for a king and queen is served overlooking the pool, with the whole of Barcelona at your feet). However, if tranquillity and a privileged location above the fray are what you seek, you can do no better.

Early reservations are a must; ask for one of the two front rooms with small terraces and drop-dead views.

See map p. 124. Mont d'Orsà 35 (Vallvidrera). ☎ ***93-406-94-11.*** *Fax: 93-406-94-71.* www.relaisdorsa.com. *Metro: FGC train, Vallvidrera. Free parking. Rack rates: $215€ ($258) double. AE, DC, MC, V.*

Runner-up hotels

AC Diplomatic

$$$$–$$$$$ **Eixample** A swank hotel from the small Spanish AC chain that has developed some of the finest properties in the country over the last few years, this elegant place lies in the heart of the Eixample, surrounded by *moderniste* apartment buildings and an abundance of chic shopping opportunities. Rooms adopt a sophisticated and sleek aesthetic, with parquet floors and soothing neutral colors. Service is very efficient, a mark of the chain. *See map p. 124. Pau Claris 122.* ☎ ***902-292-293*** *or 93-272-38-10.* www.ac-hoteles.com.

H10 Montcada

$$$ **Ciutat Vella** In a classic Old Town building, this centrally located, midsize hotel — part of the growing H10 chain of fairly priced and very smart hotels — is right across from Plaça de l'Angel, within walking distance of the Ramblas, port, Gothic Quarter, and *moderniste* buildings of the Eixample. Rooms feature very warm tones and wood and are extremely comfortable for the price. If this hotel's full, check the other H10 Barcelona properties. *See map p. 124. Vía Laeitana 24.* ☎ ***902-10-09-06*** *or 93-268-85-70.* www.h10.es.

Hostal Gat Xino

$$ **Raval** This place has bargain design for travelers with a sense of style and adventure but not deep pockets. A young, upstart minichain, now with two popular locations on the seedier side of the Rambla, Hostal Gat Xino caters to ex-backpackers and young families. Rooms are spare, with a bright green, white, and black aesthetic, and there are hip photographs and flat-screen TVs. Also noteworthy is the surprisingly bountiful breakfast. The open-air deck is a good spot to soak up some sun and meet up with fellow travelers from around the globe and trade info on hotspots. The other location, Gat Raval, is a bit more basic and slightly cheaper still. *See map p. 124. Carrer Hospital 155.* ☎ ***93-324-88-33.*** www.gataccommodation.com.

Hotel Astoria

$$$ **Eixample** Around since the '50s, the Astoria is more elegant than ever, without being at all stuffy. This classy, quiet hotel is where I used to put up friends and family when my apartment in Barcelona got too small for guests. It's a good value, and it's definitely one of the best three-star hotels in Barcelona. Although other hotels in the Eixample are better located, it's just a few blocks from the top of Rambla de Catalunya and

minutes from prime shopping territory on Diagonal. The sound-proofed rooms are modern and elegant, done mostly in creams and blacks, and some have small sitting rooms (perfect for a kid's cot) or garden terraces. *See map p. 124. París 203.* ☎ ***93-209-83-11.*** `www.derbyhotels.es`.

Hotel Condes de Barcelona

$$$$ Eixample Occupying two grand former palaces on opposite corners of elegant Passeig de Gràcia, this is yet another Barcelona hotel in love with current design (this is why it's a favorite with architects and designers). The hotel — which rates as a pretty good value among luxury hotels with such a prestigious address — is in the middle of the Quadrat d'Or, the section of town famed for its singular *moderniste* houses, and is just a block from Gaudí's La Pedrera apartment building. Rooms are modern, large, and elegant, decorated in bright but tasteful colors. *See map p. 124. Passeig de Gràcia 73–75.* ☎ ***93-445-00-00.*** *Fax: 93-445-32-32.* `www.condesdebarcelona.com`.

Hotel España

$$ **Ciutat Vella (Ramblas)** Anything but homogenous, the Hotel España, off the lower part of La Rambla, was decorated by one of *modernisme*'s star architects, Domènech i Montaner. His colorful stamp in the terrific public rooms is what makes this place special. Guest rooms, on the other hand, are simple but attractive enough. They're clean and large, but the neighborhood may give some visitors pause. *See map p. 124. Sant Pau 9–11.* ☎ ***93-318-17-58.*** `www.hotelespanya.com`.

Hotel GranVía

$$$ **Eixample** Located in a 19th-century palace on one of Barcelona's main thoroughfares, this relatively inexpensive, midsize choice has clean and rather charming rooms outfitted with nice antiques. *See map p. 124. Gran Vía de les Corts Catalanes 642.* ☎ ***93-318-19-00.*** `www.nnhotels.es`.

Hotel Jardí

$$ **Cituat Vella (Barri Gòtic)** A small hotel with a great location, overlooking two of the prettiest plazas in old Barcelona; rooms are basic but nicer than you'd expect for the cheap price. *See map p. 124. Plaça Sant Josep Oriol 1.* ☎ ***93-301-59-00.*** `sgs1losa comix.es`.

Hotel Majestic

$$$$$ **Eixample** With a great location on Passeig de Gràcia, the Majestic has large rooms, done in bright colors and patterns, but it's big with tour groups and a tad impersonal. Check online for special Internet and "3×2" offers. The restaurant Drolma is one of the chicest in Barcelona but over-the-top-expensive. *See map p. 124. Passeig de Gràcia 68.* ☎ ***93-488-17-17.*** `www.hotelmajestic.es`.

Dining Out

Catalans love to eat and love to eat out, and they enjoy one of the best and most imaginative cuisines in all of Spain. Barcelona's stature as a dining capital has really exploded in the past few years, as a number of highly creative young chefs have made it perhaps second only to San Sebastián for fine dining. What you'll find across the city are market-fresh ingredients and Mediterranean dishes with a flourish. In addition to haute cuisine *(cocina de autor),* you'll also find the traditional rustic dishes that have nourished Catalans for centuries. Most restaurants are in the Ciutat Vella and Eixample, though the most popular new dining area is along the waterfront and in the new port.

Eating and drinking like a Catalan

Basic Catalan cooking is equal parts Mediterranean and mountain — well prepared but with little stuffiness. So expect fresh seafood, *all i oli* (garlic and virgin olive oil), produce from the countryside, and *setas* (wild mushrooms) — an object of obsession for people all over Catalonia. The basis of rustic Catalan food is *pa amb tomàquet,* literally, bread and tomato. But I'm not talking bread, mayo, and beefsteak tomatoes. *Pa amb tomàquet* are long slices of rustic bread rubbed with halves of beautiful fresh tomatoes, doused with virgin olive oil, and sprinkled with salt. Another typical Catalan dish is *espinacs a la catalana,* which is spinach prepared with pine nuts, raisins, bacon, oil, and garlic. Others you may run across include *escudella* (Catalan stew); *suquet de peix* (fish and shellfish soup); *butifarra* (white Catalan sausage, often with white beans) and *fuet* (long, dry sausage); *fideus* (long, thin noodles with pork, sausage, and red pepper); *escalivada* (grilled peppers, eggplant, tomato, and onion); and *amanida* (salad with meat, fish, shellfish, and cheese). For dessert, try *crema catalana,* an egg custard with a crisp layer of grilled sugar on top.

Catalunya is best known, perhaps, for its sparkling wines, called *cava.* You may have heard of **Freixenet** and **Codorníu,** the two top-selling *cavas* (sparkling wines) in the world. Both are from Penedès, just a half-hour from Barcelona. *Cava* is a perfect accompaniment to the seafood and lighter fare that you can enjoy in Barcelona. Big, expensive boutique red wines from Priorat have become very trendy; though pricey, **Clos Mogador, Vall Llach,** and **L'Ermita** are among the best wines being produced in Spain. But several other regions in the province, such as Penedès, Empordà, Costers del Segre, and Montsant, also produce excellent red and white wines that are worthy rivals to better-known Riojas and Riberas. Be on the lookout for such producers as **Torres, Jean León, Castell de Perelada,** and **Capçanes.**

For more on Spanish dining customs, including mealtimes, costs, and tipping, see Chapter 2.

Language primer: Catalan menu basics

Refer to the following list when translating a Catalan menu.

English	Catalan	English	Catalan
bread	*pa*	salmon	*salmó*
cheese	*formatge*	shellfish	*marisc*
chicken	*pollastre*	soup	*sopa*
dessert	*postre*	steak	*carn*
eggs	*ous*	sugar	*sucre*
fish	*peix*	toast	*torrada*
fruit	*fruita*	veal	*vedella*
hake	*lluç*	beer	*cervesa*
ham	*pernil*	coffee	*café*
ice cream	*gelat*	juice	*suc*
mussels	*musclos*	milk	*llet*
oil	*oli*	tea	*te*
omelet	*truita*	water	*aigua*
rice	*àrros*	wine	*vin*
salad	*amanida*		

Because Barcelona is only 145km (90 miles) from the French border, plenty of restaurants specialize in French cuisine; regional Spanish cuisines, such as Basque, are also popular. (Basque tapas bars pop up like the wild mushrooms that Catalans love so much; for more on Basque culinary arts, see Chapter 12.) About the only difficulty you may have eating your way across Barcelona is ordering at the handful of restaurants that feature menus printed only in Catalan.

Although Barcelona natives aren't quite as addicted to tapas as their brethren in the Basque Country and Madrid, you should spend at least one evening doing a *tapeo,* or tapas-bar crawl, in the Old City, washing down your finger foods with glasses of *cava* (sparkling wine) or local Penedés or Priorat wines.

For more on Spanish dining customs, including mealtimes, taxes, costs, and tipping, see Chapter 2. For a description of the price categories, see the Introduction.

Barcelona's top restaurants

Àbac

$$$$$ Cituat Vella (Barri Gòtic) CATALAN HAUTE CUISINE

A centerpiece of the happening Born restaurant scene, Àbac has quickly become one of the top dining experiences in Barcelona, and the chef, Xavier Pellicer, one of the best-known in the city. Slick and self-assured, with generous space between the few tables and more waiters than diners, this place takes haute cuisine *(cocina de autor)* and high design seriously. From baby squid in dried-fruit sauce to an unbelievable tuna Provençal, everything is delightful and exceedingly well prepared. Details are important: Service is impeccable, and the wine list is sophisticated and extensive. The restaurant boasts both cheese and cigar carts.

See map p. 124. Rec 79. ☎ ***93-319-66-00.*** *Reservations required. Metro: Jaume I. Main courses: 23€–38€ ($28–$46). Tasting menu: 81€ ($97). AE, DC, MC, V. Open: Lunch and dinner Tues–Sat, Mon dinner only. Closed: Second week in Jan, last three weeks in Aug.*

Agua

$$ Waterfront (Port Marítim) MEDITERRANEAN

A bright and informally hip place overlooking the beach, Agua is appropriately named. It's an excellent (and very popular) spot for simply prepared and inexpensive fresh fish and shellfish, as well as rice dishes (such as risottos) and vegetarian preparations. It has a great outdoor terrace with ocean views that are perfect for people-watching. Easygoing and often boisterous — not to mention right on the beach — it's a great spot to take the kids.

See map p. 124. Passeig Marítim de la Barceloneta 30. ☎ ***93-225-12-72.*** *Reservations recommended. Metro: Ciutadella. Main courses: 7€–19€ ($9–$11). MC, V. Open: Lunch and dinner daily without interruption. Closed: Last three weeks in Aug.*

Agut d'Avignon

$$$$ Cituat Vella (Barri Gòtic) CATALAN

A revered classic that's been around for years and never wavered from its commitment to fine, traditional Catalan cooking, this warmly rustic restaurant imparts a bit of the countryside into the capital city. A quiet spot down a tiny alleyway in the medieval maze of the Gothic Quarter, Agut d'Avignon is one of the finest places in the city to sample the fresh and down-to-earth ingredients of *cuina catalana.*

See map p. 124. Trinitat 3 (alley off Avinyó 8). ☎ ***93-302-60-34.*** *Reservations recommended. Metro: Jaume I. Main courses: 19€–44€ ($23–$53). MC, V. Open: Lunch and dinner daily without interruption. Closed: Last three weeks in Aug.*

Botafumeiro

$$$$$ Eixample SEAFOOD

One of the king of Spain's favorite restaurants (his preferred table is on the second floor), this longtime classic is still the place for perfectly prepared seafood. In direct contrast to the influx of chic, minimalist, and cutting-edge restaurants, it's large, informal, and often a little rambunctious. Much of the incredibly fresh seafood is flown in daily from Galicia, the owner's hometown. The shellfish are amazing, and the long seafood bar has repeatedly been named the best in Spain (you can make a great meal of seafood tapas here, and even keep costs down if you're conscientious). Because Botafumeiro doesn't close after lunch, go at off hours — 1 p.m. for lunch and 7:30 p.m. for dinner. It's the only time you'll be able to walk in and get a table — or even a seat at the bar — if you haven't reserved a table well in advance.

See map p. 124. Gran de Gràcia 81. ☎ ***93-218-42-30.*** *Reservations recommended (not necessary at bar). Metro: Fontana or Diagonal. Main courses: 21€–60€ ($26–$75). AE, DC, MC, V. Open: Lunch and dinner daily without interruption. Closed: Last three weeks in Aug.*

Cal Pep

$$$–$$$$ Barri Gòtic/Waterfront SEAFOOD

I try never to miss a visit to Barcelona without dining at least once at Cal Pep, a tiny, bustling, and magical seafood restaurant that serves the freshest specials of the day anywhere. The restaurant has no menu, and virtually no tables (just four in back); everyone sits at the long bar and waits for Pep, the gravelly voiced owner with the funky eyeglasses, to recommend whatever's fresh off the boats and out of the markets. Wait patiently for a table and let Pep guide you (something he's eminently capable of, even if shared language amounts to hand signals). Though you may be in for a long wait—the place just gets more and more popular—you won't be sorry, and prices are pretty reasonable given the phenomenal quality. A classic Barcelona experience.

See map p. 124. Plaça de les Olles 8. ☎ ***93-310-79-61.*** *Reservations not accepted. Metro: Barceloneta. Main courses: 13€–27€ ($16–$32). AE, DC, MC, V. Open: Lunch and dinner Tues–Sat, Mon dinner only. Closed: August.*

Casa Calvet

$$$–$$$$ Eixample CATALAN

Housed on the first floor of one of Antoni Gaudí's earliest but still emblematic apartment buildings (with the oldest elevator in Barcelona), this restaurant's sumptuous white-brick and stained-glass *moderniste* décor alone is enough to recommend a visit. The welcome surprise is that it's an excellent and fairly priced restaurant serving creative contemporary Catalan cuisine. Give the Galician oyster raviolis in champagne a whirl. Dining at Casa Calvet is a great, nontouristy way to get up close and personal with a *moderniste* classic and dine exceedingly well at the same time.

> ## Toasting your trip with *cava*
>
> Tapas bars are everywhere in Spain, but a Catalan specialty is the champagne bar, called a *xampanyería.* These bars serve *cava* (sparkling wine) as well as tapas. Penedès, an area half an hour from Barcelona, is the world's largest producer of sparkling wine. A few good bars serving local wines and plenty of Catalan *cava* are the down-to-earth **El Xampanyet,** Montcada 22 (☎ 93-319-70-03; Metro: Jaume I), **La Vinya del Senyor,** Plaza Santa María del Mar 5 (☎ 93-310-33-79; Metro: Jaume I), the classic *cava* bar **Casablanca Xampanyería,** Bonavista 6 (☎ 93-237-63-99; Metro: Passeig de Gràcia), and **Xampú Xampany,** at Gran Vía 702, at the corner of Bailén (☎ 93-265-04-83; Metro: Girona). Of course, any respectable bar and restaurant in Barcelona features a host of clean, crisp *cavas* on the wine list.

*See map p. 124. Casp 48. ☎ **93-412-40-12.** Reservations recommended. Metro: Jaume 1. Main courses: 19€–32€ ($23–$38). AE, MC, V. Open: Lunch and dinner Mon–Sat. Closed: Holidays and last two weeks in Aug.*

Comerç 24

$$$$ Cituat Vella (Barri Gòtic) CREATIVE CATALAN/TAPAS

The Born district has exploded with trendy restaurants and bars, but this spot, which puts creativity and elegance into that Spanish staple, tapas, continues to be one of the city's coolest places to dine. The kitchen is the work of Carles Abellán, who has quickly become one of Barcelona's hottest young chefs. Here he's essentially created *tapas de autor,* and there's a great bit of theater in his preparations. The bold colors and chic stylings of the restaurant, which feels like an industrial-flavored club (it's in an old salting house), lend the perfect backdrop. The theater begins with a series of "snacks" served in sardine tins. Everything I've tasted here is worthy of recommendation; some dishes are more playful, others more traditional. On my last visit, a companion and I ordered seven plates between the two of us, which was plenty, but I couldn't resist finishing with the thin slices of entrecote served with cippolino onions and tiny mushrooms. It was one of the most straightforward dishes we tried, but probably the best.

*See map p. 124. Carrer Comerç 24. ☎ **93-319-21-02.** Reservations required. Metro: Jaume I. Main courses: 9€–18€ ($11–$22). Tasting menus: 48€ ($58) and 68€ ($82). AE, DC, MC, V. Open: Lunch and dinner Tues–Sat.*

Espai Sucre

$$$ Cituat Vella (Barri Gòtic) CREATIVE CATALAN/DESSERT

Here's something novel and sinfully delicious for the Willy Wonka in you: "Sugar Space" is a tiny, minimalist restaurant that exclusively serves dessert. Though that may sound like a recipe for sugar overload and diabetic coma, the tasting menus of three or five dessert courses are conceived of as balanced dinner menus. The desserts are terrific, and several are quite audacious, covering a surprising taste spectrum. Anyone unsure of constructing a meal from desserts only can add a savory dish, such as magret of duck or ginger couscous to one of the dessert menus. Combining wines with desserts can be a little tricky; Catalan *cava* (sparkling wine) is a brilliant choice.

See map p. 124. Princesa 53. ☎ ***93-268-16-30.*** *Reservations required. Metro: Jaume I. Main courses: 10€–12€ ($12–$14). Tasting menus: 25€–33€ ($30–$40). MC, V. Open: Dinner Tues–Sat. Closed: Last two weeks of Aug and Christmas week.*

Hisop

$$$$ Eixample CONTEMPORARY CATALAN

Barcelona's new fascination with restaurants featuring *cocina de autor* (creative haute cuisine) is at its most accessible at this small and inviting, informal restaurant run by a young team. On a tiny side street just north of the Diagonal shopping drag, it's a slender, predominantly white dining room colored with splashes of red, like the single roses on the wall. Hisop has creative and even trendy impulses — seen in such items as palate-cleansing sorbets of goat cheese and green pepper corn — but it's never haughty. Main courses such as a lovely hake and superb beef tenderloin with mushrooms, and a terrific selection of cheeses for dessert, bring things back to earth. The tasting menu is excellent and very fairly priced (and the chef even allows substitutions!).

See map p. 124. Ptge. Marimon 9. ☎ ***93-241-32-33.*** *Reservations recommended. Metro (FGC): Gràcia. Main courses: 20€–28€ ($24–$34). Tasting menu: 45€ ($54). DC, MC, V. Open: Lunch and dinner Tues–Sat.*

Principal

$$$–$$$$ Eixample CATALAN/MEDITERRANEAN

One of the best spots to see how Barcelona's design craze has taken over new restaurants is this gorgeous, airy, and warmly minimalist space, serving familiar but sophisticated Catalan and Mediterranean dishes, with innovative touches, artfully prepared to go with the surroundings. I have to plug my good friend Manel Solà's cool sculptures, the first two things you see in the restaurant.

See map p. 124. Provença 286. ☎ ***93-272-08-45.*** *Reservations recommended. Metro: Passeig de Gràcia. Main courses: 12€–27€ ($14–$32). MC, V. Open: Lunch and dinner daily.*

Restaurante 7 Portes

$$$ Waterfront (Port Vell) CATALAN/SEAFOOD

This Barcelona institution and national monument, which has seven doors facing the street (hence the name), has been hosting large dining parties since 1836. (It was the first place in Barcelona with running water.) Barcelonans drop in to celebrate special occasions. *Sete Portes,* as it's also known, is famous for its rice dishes; my favorite is the black rice with squid in its own ink. All the paellas are tremendous. Portions are huge and very reasonably priced. The dining rooms — some semiprivate — are classically elegant, with beamed ceilings, checkerboard marble floors, antique mirrors and posters, and plenty of room between tables. The place is hugely popular with families (those small dining rooms are great if your kids tend to get rambunctious at dinnertime) and young people on dates.

See map p. 124. Passeig d'Isabel II 14. ☎ ***93-319-30-33.*** *Reservations recommended. Metro: Drassanes. Main courses:18€–32€ ($22–$38). AE, DC, MC, V. Open: Lunch and dinner daily, without interruption.*

Talaia Mar

$$$–$$$$ **Waterfront (Port Marítim) INNOVATIVE MEDITERRANEAN**

The new (Olympic) port is swimming with restaurants and bars targeting tourists and locals on date night. Talaia Mar, the best of the port restaurants, is anything but. The chef, a disciple of the famed chef Ferran Adrià (of El Bulli; see review in Chapter 11), creates an innovative, seafood-dominated menu, perfectly in tune with Barcelona's fascination with avant-garde design and cutting-edge cooking. Fresh grilled fish of the day is succulent, but what truly distinguishes this restaurant are the daring dishes, full of surprises for the senses: a deconstructed potato tortilla, green beans with squid "noodles" and mint, barnacles with a sea water sorbet. The tasting menu is a terrific way to sample the chef's repertoire. The dining room — a glass-enclosed circular room that mimics a watchtower — has a sweeping bay window overlooking the harbor.

See map p. 124. Marina 16. ☎ ***93-221-90-90.*** *Reservations required. Metro: Ciutadella/ Vila Olímpica. Main courses: 15€–27€ ($18–$32). AE, DC, MC, V. Open: Lunch and dinner Tues–Sat.*

Bargain dining in Barcelona

Barcelona has become a dining destination, and many of its top restaurants threaten to bust most people's budgets. If you're looking for something a little less fancy, here are a few dependable longtime favorites that are downright bargains (and don't miss the tapas bars below, another great source of informal, inexpensive meals).

Agut

$ **Ciutat Vella (Barri Gòtic)** This 75-year-old, bohemian-flavored restaurant, tucked away on a small street in the Gothic Quarter, is a real find — great looking (in a homey way) and dripping with local flavor. Best of all, it's a bargain. The crowd is a cool mix of artists and suited professionals; you won't find any tour groups here. You can't go wrong with the daily specials, whether they're homemade *canelones* (cannelloni), fish, or game. The excellent rice dishes are giant — order them only if you want to share.
See map p. 124. Gignàs 16. ☎ ***93-315-17-09.*** *Closed: August.*

Can Culleretes

$ **Ciutat Vella (Barri Gòtic)** The oldest restaurant in Barcelona (open since 1786), Can Culleretes continues to serve traditional, filling Catalan food. This spot, a Catalan down-home, old-school classic, is the place to try such standards as *espinacas a la catalana* (spinach with pine nuts and raisins) and *butifarra* (white sausage). You can choose from fixed-price menus both day and night during the week. *See map p. 124. Quintana 5.* ☎ ***93-317-64-85.*** *Closed: Sun night, Mon and August.*

Estevet

$$ **Ciutat Vella (Ramblas/Raval)** A busy, crowded, and thoroughly neighborhood restaurant, this little charmer near the University and Museu d'Art Contemporaneo, not far from Plaça de Catalunya, has a very good midday menu and good, inexpensive Catalan standards. *See map p. 124. Valldonzella 46* ☎ ***93-302-41-86.*** *Closed: Sun.*

La Dentellière

$–$$ **Gothic Quarter** Back at its charming, Gothic Quarter location — where I used to take my dog every day for lunch — this rustic French restaurant has understated, easygoing charm. It's the kind of place you'd expect to find in a small French village. The entire menu is well conceived and prepared — and very affordable. The inexpensive three-course meal with homemade desserts is a terrific deal, just 13€ ($16). *See map p. 124. Ample 26.* ☎ ***93-319-68-21.*** *Closed Sun–Mon.*

Les Quinze Nits

$ **Ciutat Vella (Ramblas/Barri Gòtic)** This place often has long lines of folks hungering to pay fast-food prices for surprisingly well-prepared Catalan and Mediterranean dishes. To beat the crowds, do the gringo-thing and come early. The inexpensive and varied dishes may be perfect for the kids, though the wait for a table may not. A nearby sister restaurant, **La Fonda** (on Carrer dels Escudellers 10; ☎ **93-301-75-15**), offers nearly the same menu and decor. *See map p. 124. Plaça Reial 6.* ☎ ***93-317-30-75.***

Senyor Parellada

$$ **Cituat Vella (Barri Gòtic)** This stylish and laid-back two-story restaurant, just up the street from Santa María del Mar, feels like someone's cool old house, full of antiques, lamps on the tables, and contemporary art that enlivens the lemon-yellow and deep-red walls. It's hugely popular among both locals and visitors for nicely executed, fresh preparations of authentic Catalan fare at downright bargain prices. *See map p. 124. Argentaria 37.* ☎ ***93-310-50-94.***

Grazing on tapas

Here's a brief sampling of some of the best tapas joints in the Catalan capital.

- **Bar Pinotxo,** Stand No. 66–68 (no phone), may look like a nondescript bar, but it's a legend, right in the heart of the sensational La Boquería food market on La Rambla (see "Strolling La Rambla," later in this chapter). Grab a bar stool and point to whatever looks good (the fish is as fresh as it is anywhere in the city).
- **Bar Turó,** Tenor Viñas 1 (Parc Turó; ☎ **93-200-69-53**), a neighborhood joint in a chic Barrios Altos residential area north of downtown, serves tapas that are famed the city over. You can also choose from a good-value midday menu for about 12€ ($14).
- **Cuines Santa Caterina,** Av. Francesc Cambó 16 (Barri Gòtic; ☎ **93-268-99-18**), is tucked inside the brand-new, wildly colorful and cool Mercat Santa Caterina, a produce, flowers, and fresh fish-and-meat market. It's a large, open spot offering a wide variety of cuisines, from Asian and vegetarian to Mediterranean, all at very fair prices. It's great for a full meal, early breakfast, or late snacks.
- **Inopia,** Tamarit 104 (Eixample Esquerra; ☎ **93-424-52-31**), is a new, hip tapas joint, but it calls itself a "classic bar." Indeed, that's the vibe of this brightly lit, frenetic place, the brainchild of the brother of famed experimental chef Ferran Adrià (of El Bulli; see Chapter 11 for a complete review). But little bro does something much more traditional with his classic, winning Spanish and Catalan tapas. The *patatas bravas* (spicy fried potatoes) and *croquetas caseras de jamón ibérico* (croquettes stuffed with Spanish ham) are on most tapas menus, but are rarely this tasty. It's a bit off the main Eixample grid (west of Av. Paral.lel), but worth the short taxi ride.
- **Irati,** Casanyes 17 (Barri Gòtic; ☎ **93-302-30-84**), a bustling Basque tapas tavern just off La Rambla, is always at standing-room-only capacity. The tapas (or *pintxos,* in the Basque language) are set out on the bar, and they keep coming. Keep track of how many you eat (by the number of toothpicks you collect) and pay when you're done.
- **La Bodegueta,** Rambla de Catalunya 100 (Eixample; ☎ **93-215-48-94**), is a classic wine tavern from the 1940s; though easy to miss (it's a simple step-down bar next to the chic clothing store Groc), it's ideal for a small snack and a glass of wine or *cava.*
- **Tapaç 24,** Diputació 269 (Eixample; ☎ **93-488-09-77**), is the informal spin-off of the stylish Comerç 24, one of the hippest restaurants in Barcelona (see review above). This below-street-level bar near La Pedrera mimics a seafood shack, and the tapas are every bit as fresh and delectable as they'd be at a beachside spot with Carles Abellán behind the grill. The little plates here are zesty and fun, with just the right touch of creativity. I'm still dreaming about the *bikini de espárragos al pesto* (sandwich of fresh green asparagus in pesto) that I had there recently.

Exploring Barcelona

Barcelona has a greater diversity of things to see and do than any other city in Spain (something folks from Madrid may be loath to admit). When visiting, concentrate your time on distinct neighborhoods, which is how I lay out the attractions in this section. The works of Gaudí and his imaginative *moderniste* cohorts and the lively Rambla Boulevard are perhaps the city's most obvious highlights, but the rich medieval Gothic Quarter, with its Picasso Museum and enticing little corners, and the newly dynamic waterfront are also huge draws. Apart from those sites, Barcelona ranks among Europe's great strolling cities, with secluded plazas, open-air cafes, tree-lined boulevards, and an inexhaustible supply of nooks where you can stop and have coffee, a beer, or tapas during your meanderings.

If you're planning to wear out your shoes sightseeing in Barcelona, you may want to get a discount card offered by the city tourism office. Available in versions of one to five days, the ***Barcelona Card*** offers free public transportation and discounts of up to 50 percent at 100 sites in the city, including museums, bars, shops, and restaurants. The Museu Picasso, La Pedrera, La Sagrada Familia, Museu Nacional d'Art de Catalunya (MNAC), and Fundació Joan Miró are all included, as well as the Aerobus to the airport. The 24-hour card includes a free ten-journey travel card for the Metro and bus, and the 48- and 72-hour cards include a pass offering unlimited travel on the Metro and bus. Cards cost 23€ ($28) for two days and 28€ ($34) for three days. Rates for children between ages 4 and 12 are 4€ ($4.80) less at each level. You can purchase the Barcelona Card at **Turisme de Barcelona** information offices in Plaça de Catalunya, Plaça de Sant Jaume, Estació de Sants (Sants Railway Station), Corte Inglés stores, Casa Battló, and the Barcelona Nord bus station, as well as online (which nets you a 10 percent discount). For more information, call ☎ **93-285-38-32.**

The top attractions

Manzana de la Discórdia
Eixample

The so-called Block of Discord, a single block of the chic shopping boulevard Passeig de Gràcia 35–43 (between Aragó and Consell de Cent), is the best place for a crash course on *moderniste* architecture. At No. 35 is **Casa Lleó Morera,** a gorgeously ornate corner house built in 1906 by Lluís Domènech i Montaner, a serious rival to Gaudí. The house, which features an upscale leather-goods purveyor on the ground floor, has suffered more ill-conceived alterations over the years than almost any other *moderniste* work. Domènech i Montaner also built the acclaimed Palau de la Música Catalana and Hospital de Sant Pau, among many other notable buildings in Barcelona, and many critics judge him to be the greatest of all *moderniste* architects. Up the block, on the same side of the street (No. 41), is the brilliant **Casa Amatller** (1900), a creation of the architect Puig i Cadafalch. The

Museum deals and freebies

Museum hounds should pick up the **ArTicket,** which allows for single-price (20€, or $24) entry into six of Barcelona's top art museums, including La Pedrera (Casa Milà), Fundació Joan Miró, Fundació Tàpies, and Museu Nacional d'Art de Catalunya (MNAC). For tickets and more information, call ☎ **93-285-38-32;** you can also purchase tickets at any of the participating museums or offices of Turisme de Barcelona.

Several Barcelona museums feature free admission on certain days of the month, including the Museu Picasso (first Sun of the month), Museu d'Història, and Museu Marítim (first Sat of the month), as well as MNAC (first Thurs of the month). Tourist information offices have a complete list of museum freebies.

medieval-looking facade, topped by a distinctive Flemish-style roof, displays beautiful carved stone and ironwork of themes related to the chocolate business and other pursuits of the original owners. Children have a ball identifying all the figures. Unfortunately, the interior of the house can't be visited.

Next door, at No. 43, is the extraordinary **Casa Batlló** (1906), a true crowd-pleaser among Gaudí buildings (though Gaudí in fact only remodeled the existing structure, reshaping its interior with fanciful and ingenious signature elements and adding a fantastic face-lift to the exterior). The facade glimmers with fragments of colorful ceramics, the roof curves like the blue-green scales of a dragon's back, and the balconies evoke either *carnaval*-esque masks or menacing monster jaws. Casa Batlló is now owned by the company that produces Chupa Chups, Spain's famous lollipops, and it often rents the house out for corporate dinners and even weddings. The house's interior is now open to the public for tours with audioguides (☎ **93-216-03-06;** daily 9 a.m.–8 p.m.; 16€/$19).

For a *moderniste* bonus, look around the corner (Aragó 225) at the **Fundació Antoni Tàpies** (☎ **93-487-03-15;** `www.fundaciotapies.org`; Tues–Sun 10 a.m.–8 p.m.; 4.20€, or $5; also part of ArTicket joint admission; see the "Museum deals and freebies" sidebar in this chapter), a museum dedicated to the works of the contemporary Catalan painter Antoni Tàpies. The building, a former publishing headquarters, is another splendid example of *moderniste* architecture by Domènech i Montaner. The giant tangle of steel on the roof is a once-controversial sculpture (it has now been accepted by most Barcelonans) called *Cloud and Chair* by Tàpies. Allow about an hour (more if you're a fan of contemporary art and want to visit the Tàpies museum and library in depth).

Palau de la Música
Eixample

Domènech i Montaner's magnificent music hall (1908) is so over-the-top ornate that it may take you some time to appreciate it. After my first visit,

I was shocked; after attending my second concert, I had begun to like it; by my third, I was in love with the place and attended shows I wasn't even that interested in just to have another chance to bask in its splendor. It's surely the trippiest music hall you'll ever see. Apartment buildings hem in the Palau tightly (though a nondescript church next door was demolished to give the hall greater breathing space), and the relatively sedate exterior does little to prepare you for what's inside. The interior is a wild fantasy of ceramics, colored glass, and carved pumice and is crowned by an enormous yellow, blue, and green stained-glass dome that looks like a swollen raindrop. The Palau, a UNESCO World Heritage Site, is indisputably one of Barcelona's *moderniste* masterpieces. If you can't manage to see a performance, you can take a guided tour, which I highly recommend. The tour lasts about an hour.

See map p. 124. Sant Francesc de Paula 2. ☎ ***902-44-28-82*** *or 93-295-72-00.* `http://home.palaumusica.org`. *Metro: Urquinaona. Admission: 8€ ($10) adults, 7€ ($8.40) seniors and students. Open: Guided visits daily 10 a.m.–3:30 p.m.; on the half-hour in Spanish and Catalan, on the half-hour and hour in English.*

Parc Güell

Barrios Altos (Upper Barcelona)

This whimsical open-air park, another of Gaudí's signature creations, is removed from El Eixample but still relatively easy to reach (you can take the bus, but visiting by taxi is easiest and quickest). Envisioned as a housing development for Gaudí's faithful patron, Eusebi Güell, the garden city

A *moderniste* treasure hunt

Barcelona is so littered with Catalan Art Nouveau sights that keeping track of them all can prove difficult. The city's **Ruta del Modernisme** (Modernist Route) gives you a hand and a wealth of information about more than 100 landmarks. For 12€ ($14) you receive a guidebook with a map of sites and up to 50 percent admission discounts, good at the *moderniste* buildings that allow visits (including La Sagrada Familia, Palau de la Música Catalana, Fundació Tàpies, La Pedrera, Palau Güell, the Casa-Museu Gaudí at Parc Güell, and Museu de la Música). You tour on your own, though guided visits are mandatory if you visit Casa Lleó Morera, Palau de la Música, Palau Güell, or Museu d'Art Modern. The complete tour would probably take a full week or more, but even if you only hit the highlights, the pass pays for itself after just a few stops. The route includes all of Barcelona's celebrated landmarks as well as the landmarks you may otherwise overlook. Since trying to see the entire collection would be pretty overwhelming, check out my suggestions on a handful of other *moderniste* sights — a second tier, if you will — in "Finding more cool things to see and do," in this chapter.

Ruta del Modernisme guidebooks and additional information are available at the Centre del Modernisme booth within **Turisme de Barcelona,** Plaça de Catalunya 17, underground (☎ **93-285-38-34**). Also see www.rutadelmodernisme.com.

was never fully realized. Gaudí originally planned to design every detail of the 60 houses; however, only one was finished, in which Gaudí lived as he struggled to complete the project (it now houses the small **Casa-Museu Gaudí**). The parts that Gaudí did finish — in fact, his talented disciple, Josep María Jujol, executed most of what you see — resemble an idiosyncratic theme park, with a mosaic-covered lizard fountain, Hansel and Gretel pagodas, and magically undulating park benches swathed in broken pieces of ceramics, called *trencadis.* Gaudí was so intent on the community's total integration into nature that he inserted part of it into a hill, constructing a forest of columns that look remarkably like tree trunks. On clear days, you can see much of Barcelona, making out the spires of Gaudí's La Sagrada Familia and the twin towers on the beach. Although the park doesn't include much required sightseeing to check off a list, you can easily linger for hours on end, especially if you have children in tow. Allow at least one hour to take in the full flavor of the park.

See map p. 124. Ctra. del Carmel 23. ☎ ***93-219-38-11.*** *Metro: Lesseps (and 6-block walk uphill following the signs). Bus: 24 or 28. Admission: Casa-Museu Gaudí 4€ ($4.80), the park is free. Open: Casa-Museu daily 10 a.m.–6 p.m.; park May–Sept daily 10 a.m.–7 p.m., Oct–Apr daily 10 a.m.–6 p.m.*

La Pedrera (Casa Milà)
Eixample

Gaudí's unfinished church, La Sagrada Familia, leaves jaws agape, but the architect's most fascinating and inspired civic work — and perhaps the crowning glory of *modernisme* — is Casa Milà, named after the patrons who allowed him to carry through with such an avant-garde apartment building back in 1910. The masterpiece is known to almost all as La Pedrera, which means "stone quarry" — a reference to its immense limestone facade.

The massive exterior undulates like ocean waves on Passeig de Gràcia and around the corner onto Provença street; on the roof is a set of chimneys that look like the inspiration for Darth Vader. On the first floor (near the entrance on Provença) is a great exhibition space for temporary art shows. The building received a head-to-toe face-lift in the mid-1990s. The apartments inside had suffered unspeakable horrors, and Gaudí's beautiful arched attics had been sealed up, but the painstaking restoration has revealed its author's genius in new ways. The attic floor is now a high-tech Gaudí museum (Espai Gaudí), with cool interactive exhibits, terrific slide shows, and access to the roof, where you can hang out with the warrior chimneys (which, according to some, represent Christians and Moors battling for Spanish turf). Both the kid-friendly, fast-paced museum and the rooftop will be unqualified hits with children.

One of the original Gaudí apartments — all with odd shapes, handcrafted doorknobs, and idiosyncratic details — has now been opened to the public. The apartment, called El Pis in Catalan, is meticulously outfitted with period furniture, including many pieces of Gaudí's design. For the entire visit, which includes museum, apartment, and rooftop, allow a minimum of two hours (though visitors have hung out, mesmerized, on the roof until they're kicked out!).

Be sure to check out the art exhibits held in another part of La Pedrera, the Centro Cultural Caixa Catalunya. The handsome exhibit space hosts shows by major international contemporary artists, such as Isamu Noguchi and Anthony Caro.

An added bonus at La Pedrera is the scheduled flamenco, opera, and jazz concerts (called *La Pedrera de Nit*) on the fantastic roof Friday and Saturday nights from July to the end of September. A combined ticket (12€/$15, with a drink included) allows access to the three building attractions and the concert, and includes a complimentary glass of Catalan *cava.* It's a splendid way to experience this *moderniste* landmark.

See map p. 124. Passeig de Gràcia 92 (at Provença 261–265). ☎ ***902-40-09-73.*** *Metro: Diagonal or Provença. Admission: 8€ ($10) adults, 4.50€ ($5.40) students; also part of ArTicket joint admission (see the "Museum deals and freebies" sidebar earlier in this chapter). Open: Daily 10 a.m.–8 p.m. Closed: Dec 25–26 and Jan 1–6. Tours available in English, Spanish, and Catalan.*

La Sagrada Familia
Eixample

Barcelona's landmark is Antoni Gaudí's unfinished legacy and testament to his singular vision, the art of the impossible. Hordes of people come to gawk at this mind-altering creation, and it's not anywhere near completion. Begun in 1884 after Gaudí took over from another architect — who was making an ordinary Gothic cathedral — the father of *modernisme* transformed the project with his fertile imagination. Even though Gaudí abandoned all other works to devote his life to this cathedral, which would be the world's largest if completed, he knew he could never finish it in his lifetime. Although he surely intended for future generations to add their signatures (he left only general plans), he probably didn't plan on resigning from the project when he did: Gaudí was run over by a tram in 1926.

The eight bejeweled spires (plans called for 12, one for each of Jesus's disciples) drip like melting candlesticks. Virtually every square inch of the surface explodes with intricate spiritual symbols. Love it or hate it, you can't deny that the church is the work of a unique visionary. A private foundation works furiously to finish the church, and although construction recently reached the halfway point, at present it remains only a facade (though indisputably, it's one wonderful, otherworldly facade). Completion is projected for 2035, though protests continue from many who believe it should be left unfinished, as a memorial to Gaudí. The Barcelona sculptor Josep Maria Subirachs's additions on the west side depicting the life of Christ have been derided as disastrous kitsch, but even the staunchest detractors have little choice now but to live with the notion of a Sagrada Familia considerably changed.

The best stuff at La Sagrada Familia is what you see on the outside. If you're on a budget or pressed for time, your trip to Barcelona won't be too much the poorer if you skip going in and save your 8€; the inside is hollowed out. What you miss if you don't go in is an elevator to the top for the (admittedly excellent) views and a fairly skimpy museum, which pales in comparison to the one at Gaudí's other masterpiece, La Pedrera apartment building. Of course, your money does contribute to the continued construction of the church, so you may want to stake out your position on its proposed completion. If you only want to see the outside, you can do so in 20 minutes; otherwise, allow about an hour.

La Sagrada Familia is prime turf for thieves relieving tourists of their belongings, because most visitors are too busy looking bug-eyed at the sky. Someone offering you a carnation may have an accomplice eyeing your camera or wallet. See tips on safety in the appendix.

See map p. 124. Mallorca 401. ☎ ***93-207-30-31.*** `www.sagradafamilia.org`. *Metro: Sagrada Familia. Admission: 8€ ($10). Open: Jan–Mar and Oct–Dec, daily 9 a.m.–6 p.m.; Apr–Sept daily 9 a.m.–8 p.m.*

Strolling La Rambla

Victor Hugo extolled Barcelona's La Rambla as "the most beautiful street in the world," and the Spanish poet Federico García Lorca said it was the "only street he wished would never end." La Rambla (also referred to as "Las Ramblas") is much more than an attractive street; it's an interminable street parade. With its variety of people, vendors, markets, and historic buildings, La Rambla is the perfect introduction to the city, an intriguing and occasionally uplifting expression of life in Barcelona. Many locals practice the fine art of the *paseo* (stroll) every day of their lives along this mile-long pedestrian avenue.

La Rambla is a feast of sounds, smells, and activity. Subdivided into five separate *ramblas,* each of different character and attractions, are a succession of newspaper kiosks, fresh flower stands, bird sellers, and mimes (or human statues) in elaborately conceived costumes and face paint hoping for a few stray euros. La Rambla may turn out to be the

Baby Jesus, wise men, and . . . who's that?

Barcelona's flair for the unusual and whimsical is more than apparent in its avant-garde *moderniste* architecture. But nothing seems odder than the *caganer,* a figure who creeps into most nativity scenes at Christmas time. The little guy, outfitted with a traditional red Catalan peasant's cap, appears squatting down in the straw and . . . defecating. He's not meant to cause offense; locals explain that he's a symbol of the fertile earth. Despite the figure's serious roots, today you can find the *caganer* marketed in all kinds of variations (priests, nuns, Bart Simpson — all assuming the position).

highlight of your trip to Barcelona (to ensure that it is, keep a keen eye on your bag and camera). You can walk the length of La Rambla in a half-hour, but allow a couple of hours if you want to make pit stops for refreshments, shopping, and exploring along the way.

Begin your stroll at the very top of La Rambla, near Plaça de Catalunya, where you can find a number of chairs that are usually filled with older men talking about *fútbol* and Spanish politics. To sit in a chair, you have to part with a few coins — they're for rent. The water gurgling from the **Calanetes Fountain** that's on the upper Rambla is safe to drink *and* is said to confer instant "native of Barcelona" status to its drinkers.

Farther down La Rambla is a noisy bird market. Continuing toward the water, you come upon bustling flower stalls. Keep an eye out for a gorgeous *moderniste* bakery, **Escribà,** at Antiga Casa Figeras, Rambla 83, on the right side. Another notable *moderniste* building to look for is the **Farmacia Genové** at Rambla 77. Nearby is one of the highlights of La Rambla, **La Boquería** food market. If you aren't already suffering from sensory overload, take a detour in here to see and smell an amazingly lively scene: the selling, slicing, and dicing of fresh fish, meats, produce, and just about everything your tummy wants. If you begin to feel intense hunger pains, hunt down tiny, legendary **Bar Pinotxo** inside the market for excellent tapas.

If you have a taste for the unusual, drop into the **Museu de l'Eròtica,** at La Rambla 96 bis 9, across from the Boquería (☎ **93-318-98-65;** `www.erotica-museum.com`; daily June–Sept 10 a.m.–midnight, Oct–May 10 a.m.–9 p.m.; 7.50€, or $9), a museum dedicated to the expressions, instruments, and whims of human sexuality.

Back on La Rambla is **Gran Theatre del Liceu,** La Rambla 51–59 (☎ **93-485-99-14**), Barcelona's great opera house that went up in flames in 1994 and reopened five years later (it's now a marvel of modern technology, though the city went to great lengths to preserve the seductive look and feel of the original). The international opera stars José Carreras and Montserrat Caballé, both from Barcelona, paid their dues at the Liceu (lee-*seh*-oo), which was founded in 1874. Full guided tours, including visits to the private Cercle del Liceu, are available daily at 10 a.m. (8.50€, or $10 for adults, free for children younger than 10); "quick visits" (that don't include entry to the Cercle del Liceu) are held daily at 11:30 a.m., noon, and 1 p.m. (3.50€, or $4.20, for adults, free for children younger than 10).

Gracing the middle of La Rambla is a large mosaic by Joan Miró, and across the street is a great 19th-century cafe-bar, **Café de la Opera,** La Rambla 74, long a gathering spot for opera-goers and literary types and now a hangout for students, gays, tourists, and old-timers. A little farther down La Rambla, off the left side as you face the sea, is the **Plaça Reial,** a grand plaza with palm trees, arcades, and lampposts designed by none other than Antoni Gaudí. In the past, the Plaça Reial was a drug dealer's hangout and a place you definitely wanted to avoid. However, the square has been drastically cleaned up, and it's now full of cafes and bars dealing in legal stimulants.

The character of the strip changes again in the last section of La Rambla, near the water. At night, the area feels pretty seedy, but by day it's perfectly safe. Look for an artisans' fair on your way to the **Monument à Colom** (Columbus Monument), which stands at the bottom of La Rambla at the harbor, punctuating the end of this preeminent stroller's avenue. (Columbus, ostensibly pointing to the Americas, is in fact turned in the wrong direction. He's pointing out at the Mediterranean, which isn't exactly the way to get to Florida.) Visitors can take the elevator up to Columbus's head for good views of the waterfront.

Nearby are the Drassanes, fantastic, vaulted medieval shipyards that now house the **Museu Marítim,** Av. Drassanes 1 (☎ **93-342-99-20;** 6€, or $7.50), a seafaring museum that includes a handsome replica of a massive 16th-century ship, the Galería Reial. It's open daily from 10 a.m. to 8 p.m.

The lower end of La Rambla and the side streets that lead from it to the Gothic Quarter, hugely popular with tourists, are areas that thieves tend to trawl. Keep a firm grip on your handbag and camera, and keep your wallet in your front pocket. See tips on safety in the Appendix.

Exploring the Old City and the Gothic Quarter

Barcelona's Barri Gòtic (or Barrio Gótico, Gothic Quarter) — below Plaça de Catalunya and between La Rambla and Vía Laietana — is the oldest part of the city. Segments of the original Roman walls that once contained the whole of the city still survive. The district today is an intricate maze of palaces and treasures from the 11th through 15th centuries. Although some late weeknights and quiet Sunday mornings it may seem as though you've been transported back in time, the Gothic Quarter is hardly a time-forgotten museum. People live and work — and especially go to restaurants and bars — here. You can find a number of monuments in the area, but don't forget to take a sightseeing time-out and enjoy one of Barcelona's greatest pleasures: an idle wander among the Quarter's narrow streets, along alleys filled with hanging laundry and shouting neighbors, past shops of antiques dealers, and onto stunning little squares.

The cathedral and Picasso Museum (covered later in this section) are the district's major sights, but also worth a visit is the noble **Plaça del Rei,** the courtyard of the 14th-century palace of the kings of Aragón (the Catholic monarchs received Columbus here after his successful voyage to the Americas). Inside the palace are the **Saló del Tinell,** the main hall, and **Capella de Santa Àgata** (Chapel of St. Agatha), both part of the **Conjunt Monumental de la Plaça del Rei** (for hours and admission, see the next paragraph). Climb the lookout tower of King Martin for unrivaled views of the neighborhood and waterfront.

Just off the Plaça del Rei is the **Museu d'Història de la Ciutat** (City History Museum; Plaça del Rei, s/n; ☎ **93-315-11-11;** `www.museuhistoria.bcn.es`). The chief attraction lies in the surprising basement, where excavations have uncovered the foundations — including sculptures, walls, a bathing pool, and cemeteries — of the ancient city of the Romans and Visigoths. You can also view a multimedia show that brings Barcelona's unique history to life. The museum is open October through May, Tuesday through Saturday from 10 a.m. to 2 p.m. and 4 to 8 p.m., and Sunday and holidays from 10 a.m. to 3 p.m.; June through September, Tuesday through Saturday from 10 a.m. to 8 p.m., and Sunday and holidays from 10 a.m. to 3 p.m.; admission, which also grants access to the Saló del Tinell, Capella de Santa Àgata, and Museu Monestir de Pedralbes, is 4€ ($4.80) for adults, 2.50€ ($3) for students and seniors (free 4 p.m.–8 p.m. the first Sat of every month).

On your strolls through the Gothic Quarter, don't miss the **Roman walls** at **Plaça Nova; Plaça de Sant Jaume,** the heart of the Roman city and today the site of the municipal and regional governments; **Plaça del Pi,** the district's liveliest square, teeming with outdoor cafes and a weekend art market; peaceful **Plaça Sant Felip de Neri** (though walls ravaged by Spanish Civil War shrapnel indicate it wasn't always so quiet); and the lovely winding streets **Carrer de la Palla** and **Carrer Banys Nous,** known for their antiques dealers.

Allow at least a full morning or afternoon — more if you have it — to take in the Gothic Quarter and its myriad highlights.

Contrary to what someone who visited Barcelona a decade ago may tell you, walking around the Gothic Quarter is for the most part safe (and not a haven for hoodlums and drug dealers, though you may stumble across small numbers of both). The area has been cleaned up considerably, but of course you need to exercise caution, especially at night. Purse-snatchers and pickpockets wait for unwary tourists, so make sure you put your wallet in your front pocket, and don't carry either a camera or a bag. If you're going to a restaurant or bar in the area late at night, call a taxi to take you to your hotel.

Catedral de Barcelona
Barri Gòtic

This Catalonian Gothic cathedral, the focal point of the Old City, is actually a mix of architectural styles. Though construction began in 1298, most of the structure dates from the 14th and 15th centuries. The facade was added in the 19th century. Even with that lengthy birth process, the cathedral is a splendid example of Gothic architecture. Inside, check out the handsome carved choir and surprisingly lush cloister. With its magnolias, palm trees, pond, and white geese, the cathedral is a lovely oasis in the midst of the Medieval Quarter. (In the Middle Ages, geese functioned as guard dogs, their squawks alerting priests to intruders.) Try to visit at least

Catalan culture classics

On Sundays at noon, people perform that quintessential (and, to foreign eyes, quaint) expression of the Catalan spirit, the *sardana,* in front of the cathedral. The disarmingly simple dance looks and feels medieval. People place their bags in the middle of an ever-widening circle, join hands, and hop and skip to the music. Feel free to throw your backpack in and give it a whirl.

The *castellers* offer another great Catalan spectacle. Groups of men in white pants, sashes, and matching shirts climb each other's backs and stand on each other's shoulders to form successive levels that create a cylindrical pyramid; each ascending level is composed of fewer and smaller members. The crowning moment is when the eighth or ninth level is formed by a small child who races to the top and raises his hand before scrambling back down. Look for *castellers* performing their gravity-defying stunt in main squares on any important Catalan or Barcelona holiday, such as Sant Jordi (Apr 23), Diada Nacional de Catalunya (Sept 11), or La Mercè (Sept 24).

Spaniards are rabid *fútbol* (soccer) fans, and Barcelona is a legendary club in Europe. The team is known as Barça (*bar*-sa), or Fútbol Club Barcelona (`www.fcbarcelona.com`). For tickets to a game at the 120,000-capacity stadium, **Camp Nou** (Avenida del Papa Joan XXIII; Metro: María Cristina/Palau Reial), visit the ticket office at Carrer Aristides Maillol 12–18 or call ☎ **93-496-36-00.** You can also visit the **Museu del Fútbol Club Barcelona** (Camp Nou's Barça Soccer Museum), at Carrer Aristides Maillol 7–9 (☎ **93-496-36-08**), which (believe it or not) ranks as one of the most-visited museums in Spain. Admission for adults is 5.30€ ($6.35) and for children 2.80€ ($3.35).

once at night, when the cathedral is illuminated and birds soar in the floodlights. A half-hour or an hour is sufficient to see the cathedral.

See map p. 124. Plaça de la Seu, s/n. ☎ ***93-342-82-60.*** *Metro: Jaume I. Admission: Cathedral free; cloister museum 1€ ($1.20). Open: Cathedral Mon–Fri 8 a.m.–1 p.m. and 4–7:30 p.m., Sat–Sun 8 a.m.–1:30 p.m. and 5–7:30 p.m.; rooftop Mon–Fri 9:30 a.m.–12:30 p.m. and 4–7:30 p.m., Sat 9:30 a.m.–12:30 p.m.; museum daily 10 a.m.–12:15 p.m and 5:15 p.m.–7 p.m.*

Museu Picasso
Ciutat Vella

Pablo Picasso, though born in Málaga in southern Spain, spent much of his youth and early creative years in Barcelona before making the requisite artistic pilgrimage to Paris, where he soon became the most famous artist of the 20th century. Barcelona's Picasso museum, the second most-visited museum in Spain (after the Prado in Madrid), can't compete with the superior collection in Paris, but it's the largest collection of his works in his native country. Picasso (1881–1973) donated 2,500 paintings and sculptures to the museum, many of them early (and more traditional figurative) pieces, including several from his blue period. If you're already a fan, you're likely to love the museum, even though few works are considered among Picasso's masterpieces — and individuals looking for a comprehensive career-spanning collection may be disappointed. The artist's loopy series based on Velázquez's renowned painting *Las Meninas* is unusual but evidence of Picasso's playful genius. The Picasso museum currently occupies several exquisite 15th-century palaces on a pedestrian-only street lined with medieval mansions. It's one of the city's loveliest streets, and the museum's administrators are continuing their expansionist craze, with plans to take over yet more buildings along Carrer Montcada in the next several years. Even if you're convinced you despise Picasso, visit to the museum just to see the distinguished palace's interior and patios — you may change your mind, at least about his early work. At minimum, plan on spending a couple of hours here.

See map p. 124. Montcada 15–23 (Ribera). ☎ ***93-319-63-10.*** `www.museupicasso.bcn.es`. *Metro: Jaume I. Admission: 6€ ($7.20); free for children 12 and under and first Sun of month. Open: Tues–Sun 10 a.m.–8 p.m.*

Santa María del Mar
Barri Gòtic

I'm wowed every time I duck into this 14th-century Catalan Gothic church, and I am powerless to pass by without at least peeking my head in. It's not opulent or jewel-encrusted, and it doesn't boast amazing cloisters or a fabulous art collection — it's a simple and solemn, but wholly inspired, space. Architects understandably wax poetic about Santa María del Mar. The church is gorgeously conceived, with perfect proportions in its three soaring naves, wide-spaced columns, and handsome stained-glass windows. The cathedral, which took only five years to complete, once sat on the Barcelona waterfront, and sailors and fishermen (and their wives) prayed for safe returns. You can take a ten-minute spin through, though even the nonreligious tend to linger in this supremely serene space. It's an unforgettable experience to attend one of the music concerts occasionally held here.

See map p. 124. Plaça de Santa María (Ribera). ☎ ***93-215-74-11.*** *Metro: Jaume I. Admission: Free. Open: Mon–Sat 9 a.m.–1:30 p.m. and 4:30–8 p.m., Sun 9 a.m.–2 p.m. and 5–8:30 p.m.*

Visiting Montjuïc: More than Olympics

Montjuïc, the hill overlooking Barcelona from the south, is best known to most visitors as the place where the big-draw Olympic venues (including the attention-getting stadiums and the dramatic platform diving) held some of the highest-profile events of the 1992 Summer Games. But there's much more to this historic hill.

If a taxi or subway is too boring for you, you can take a *teleférico* (aerial cable car) or funicular to the top of Montjuïc, the hill south of El Eixample. That is, once it reopens. In 2006, the *teleférico* — which glides above the port — remained closed for renovation and modifications. Climb aboard in Barceloneta or Port Vell (4.80€/$5.75 round-trip, 3.40€/4.10 one-way). The funicular, now integrated into the city Metro, or subway, system, leaves Avenida Paral.lel. Call ☎ **010** for more information. Otherwise, the Plaça d'Espanya Metro is the easiest way to get to the bottom of Montjuïc. While visiting Montjuïc, check out the following sights:

- Leading to the Palau Nacional is the terrace of the **Font Màgica** — the Magic Fountain. On Friday and Saturday evenings, from 8 p.m. to midnight May through October (7–9 p.m. Mar–Apr), the fountains perform a tricky ballet of rising and falling jets bathed in a mist of changing colors — all programmed to music.
- Barcelona is loaded with flamboyant Catalan *modernisme,* but fans of modernist architecture need to check out the ultraminimalist design of the **Pavelló Mies van der Rohe,** a pavilion created by the German architect for the 1929 International Exhibition in Barcelona. The small dark onyx-and-glass structure, rebuilt in the 1980s, is something of a pilgrimage spot for architecture and design freaks (van der Rohe's famous Barcelona chair was designed expressly for the pavilion). It's on Avenida Marqués de Comillas, near the Montjuïc fountains (☎ **93-215-10-11;** `www.miesbcn.com`; open daily 10 a.m.–8 p.m.; admission 3.50€, or $4.20).

Museu Nacional d'Art de Catalunya (MNAC)

If you want to get a sense of Catalonia's unique history, this splendid medieval art museum — one of the world's finest, and Barcelona's preeminent art collection — is a vital stop (though many rushed visitors unjustly overlook it). At the top of the stairs and fountains leading up to Montjuïc, housed in the domed **Palau Nacional** (National Palace), the museum is anything but a stale repository of religious art. The collection of Romanesque works, salvaged from churches all over Catalonia, is unequaled. Here you can view superb altarpieces, polychromatic icons, and treasured frescoes displayed in apses, just as they were in the country churches in which they were found. The museum also holds paintings by some of Spain's most celebrated artists, including Velázquez, Ribera, and Zurbarán. Plan on spending a couple of hours at the MNAC.

See map p. 124. Mirador del Palau 6 (Palau Nacional, Parc de Montjuïc). ☎ ***93-622-03-76.*** `www.mnac.es`. *Metro: Espanya. Admission: 8.50€ ($10); free for children 7 and under and first Thurs of month (also part of ArTicket joint admission; see the "Museum deals and freebies" sidebar in this chapter). Open: Tues–Sat 10 a.m.–7 p.m., Sun 10 a.m.–2:30 p.m.*

Fundació Joan Miró

The Catalan surrealist painter and sculptor Joan Miró was one of the 20th century's most celebrated artists. Though his work may look like colorful doodles to the uninitiated, Miró was one of the rare artists successful in creating his own artistic language. The museum displays more than 200 of his canvases, as well as a wealth of drawings, graphics, and sculptures. Likewise, it has a real knack for landing some of the city's most interesting temporary exhibitions. Be sure to check local listings in the *Guía del Ocio* (the local arts and entertainment guide) to see what's on when you're in town. Seeing the full museum requires a couple of hours, but if you find Miró's work a series of incomprehensible squiggles, you may jog through it in a quarter of that time.

See map p. 124. Av. Miramar 71/Plaça de Neptú (Parc de Montjuïc). ☎ ***93-443-94-70.*** `www.bcn.fjmiro.es`*. Metro: Espanya (then take the escalator from Palau Nacional); alternatively, take bus No. 50. Admission: 7.50€ ($9), free for children 14 and under (also part of ArTicket joint admission; see the "Museum deals and freebies" sidebar in this chapter). Open: Oct–June Tues–Wed and Sat 10 a.m.–7 p.m., July–Sept Tues–Wed, and Sat 10 a.m.–8 p.m., and year-round Thurs 10 a.m.–9:30 p.m., Sun 10 a.m.–2:30 p.m.*

Estadi Olímpic

The Estadi Olímpic (Olympic Stadium) that served as the setting for much of the 1992 Summer Olympics is on Montjuïc Hill. You can take a peek at the track-and-field stadium, originally built in 1929 for the World's Fair, and see Arata Isozaki's sleek Palau d'Esports Sant Jordi, the indoor stadium that hosted the gymnastics and volleyball events. Both stadiums are significant pieces of architecture, bookending international events that brought Barcelona to the world's attention. If you remember watching the Olympics and want to see the installations, a quick visit here is worth the time, which shouldn't take longer than half an hour. But unless something's going on at the stadiums, a visit entails seeing their exteriors only.

See map p. 124. Av. del Estadi, s/n (Parc de Montjuïc). Metro: Espanya (then take the escalator from Palau Nacional), alternatively, take bus No. 50.

More cool things to see and do

In case you still have a few days to spend in Barcelona and you've hit the main areas that I've already covered in this chapter, you may want to try out these fun activities.

Hanging out at the waterfront

In 1992, using the upcoming Olympics — and incoming government funds — as an excuse to remake the city, Barcelona completely revamped its port, which was unsightly and dangerous. The formerly polluted urban beaches are now quite clean — though the water may not be — and the waterfront is now one of the hottest places to live and party. Check out **Vila Olímpica,** an award-winning neighborhood and medley of conceptual architecture, where swimmers, baseball players, weightlifters, and other Olympic athletes were the first to inhabit the apartments, which were later sold and rented to the public. The two towers on the beach, Barcelona's only skyscrapers (one is the chic Hotel Arts, the other an office complex), were initially very controversial, but Barcelonans now accept them as another component of their forward-looking city. **Port Olímpic,** the new harbor, swims with bars and restaurants, and **Port Vell** (the old port) is a hyper-developed entertainment and shopping area, with such attractions as the IMAX Port Vell cinema, Maremágnum mall, and L'Aquarium. Near the Estació de França train station, **Barceloneta,** a former shambles of a neighborhood with great seafood-shack restaurants propped right on the beach, has been given a makeover, but it's still home to several good restaurants serving fresh fish, paella, and shellfish. The pedestrian boulevard along the old harbor, called the **Moll de la Fusta,** makes for a very enjoyable *paseo,* or stroll; it stretches from the Columbus statue at the bottom of La Rambla to a giant Liechtenstein sculpture. (See map p. 124. Metro: Drassanes, Barceloneta, or Ciutadella–Vila Olímpica.)

Trekking up Tibidabo

Climb Tibidado Mountain (well, you don't have to actually climb; you can take the tram, taxi, or funicular) for marvelous views of the city below. Locals swear that they've seen the island of Mallorca on a clear day. The view is so stunning that you may also believe you can see the Balearic Islands. The tram takes you to an overlook with bars and restaurants with enviable panoramic views of the city and the ocean. A bit farther up the mountain is **Carretera de les Aigües,** a long and winding exercise path popular on weekends. On top of Tibidabo, you find the odd juxtaposition of a neo-Gothic church and a 1950s-style amusement park, **Parc d'Atraccions** (the gentle swing ride is spectacular; it seems to suspend you over the city).

Tibidabo is a storied and strangely poetic name. It comes from Latin, meaning "I will give you" — as the saying goes, words the devil used to tempt Jesus Christ when he took him up on a mountain and showed him the glory below.

To get there: By Blue Tram and Funicular: Take the historic Tramvia Blau (Blue Tram) — the only existing tram in Barcelona — to Mirablau on the way to Tibidabo (3.30€/$3.95 round-trip, 2.20€/$2.65 one-way). From Plaza Kennedy (Metro: Tibidabo), the tram connects with the Funicular Tibidabo, a cable car that completes the trek to the top of the mountain (mid-Sept to the end of Apr, weekends only); (3€/$3.60, round-trip, 2€/$2.40 one-way). Call ☎ **010** for more information.

Tracking down even more modernisme

If your first peeks at Gaudí piqued your interest, look around Barcelona for much more *modernisme.* The easiest way to organize additional architecture visits is with the *Ruta del Modernisme* guidebook and discount pass (see the "A *moderniste* treasure hunt" box, later in this chapter). You're unlikely to have time to see the full roster of sights, but here's the best of the second-tier group.

- **Hospital Sant Pau,** Cartagena at Sant Antoni Maria Claret, Domènech's incredible hospital city and a UNESCO World Heritage Site is down Avinguda Gaudí from **La Sagrada Familia** church. See map p. 124.
- **Palau Güell,** Nou de la Rambla 3–5, one of Gaudí's earliest works; its roof is a surprising forest of tiled chimneys. See map p. 124.

- **Museu de la Música,** Avinguda Diagonal 373, a cool music museum in a wonderful palace. See map p. 124.
- The fairy tale–like **Casa de les Punxes** is at Avinguda Diagonal 416. See map p. 124.
- **Colònia Güell,** considered by some to be Gaudí's secret masterpiece, is also known as **La Cripta** (the crypt). True Gaudí aficionados make the trek beyond Barcelona to his 1915 crypt (and now tiny church), envisioned as part of a much larger but unfinished church built for a worker's cooperative of *moderniste* buildings, Santa Coloma de Cervelló. The Colònia, 13km/7 miles outside of Barcelona, is a wonder of ingeniously inclined columns, brick arches, and stained glass. To get there, take the FGC train from Plaça d'Espanya to the Santa Coloma de Cervelló/Colonia Güell station; call ☎ **93-630-58-07** for more information. The ticket office is a short walk from the entrance to the *cripta,* on Carrer Claudi Güell s/n, in Santa Coloma de Cervelló.

Barcelona from a kid's point of view

Kids and parents have plenty to do in Barcelona.

- Besides beaches, the Port Vell waterfront has the second-largest aquarium in Europe: **L'Aquàrium de Barcelona,** Moll d'Espanya (☎ **93-221-74-74;** `www.aquariumbcn.com`). The aquarium is open daily September through June from 9:30 a.m. to 9 p.m. and July through August from 9:30 a.m. to 11 p.m. Admission is 15€ ($18) for adults, 12€ ($14) for seniors, 10€ ($12) for children 4 through 12, and free for children younger than 4.
- You can also find an **IMAX theater,** Moll d'Espanya (☎ **93-225-11-11**), and lots of diversions in the **Maremàgnum Mall;** just crossing the funky Rambla del Mar drawbridge to get there is fun.
- Near the Columbus statue at the end of La Rambla is the **Museu Marítim** (Maritime Museum; ☎ **93-301-18-71**), an old shipyard with replicas of huge royal ships.
- In the Parc de la Ciutadella, the **Zoo de Barcelona (Parc Zoològic de Barcelona),** Passeig de Picasso (☎ **93-225-67-80**), has the world's only albino gorilla in captivity, named Copito de Nieve (Snowflake). The zoo is open November through February daily from 10 a.m. to 5:30 p.m.; March and October daily from 10 a.m. to 6 p.m.; April and September daily from 10 a.m. to 7 p.m.; and May through August daily from 9:30 a.m. to 7:30 p.m. Admission is 15€ ($17) for adults, 7.70€ ($9.25) for seniors, 8.75€ ($10) for children under 12, and free for children younger than 3.
- **Poble Espanyol** (Avinguda del Marqués de Comillas; ☎ **93-508-63-00**), in Montjuïc Park, is a re-creation of a Spanish village with architectural styles from all over Spain. You may find it a little cheesy, but it's a nice place for families to visit. It's open Monday

from 9 a.m. to 8 p.m., Tuesday through Thursday from 9 a.m. to 2 a.m., Friday and Saturday from 9 a.m. to 4 a.m., and Sunday from 9 a.m. to noon. Admission is 7.50€ ($9) for adults, 4€ ($4.80) for children 7 through 14, and free for children younger than 7; a family ticket for two adults and two children is 15€ ($18).

- If Poble Espanyol isn't enough to wear out your kids, check out the **amusement parks** on both Montjuïc and Tibidabo.
- Children also enjoy attending some of the kid-friendly and fireworks-heavy **festivals** in Barcelona, such as **La Mercé, Festa Major da Gràcia,** and **Sant Joan** (see Chapter 3).
- Don't forget **Parc Güell,** which Gaudí built with the uninhibited imagination of a child (reviewed in the section titled "The top attractions," earlier in this chapter).

Trolling the other side of La Rambla

If you're eager to see Barcelona in transition, and the slightly seedy side of life doesn't make you nervous, check out the Raval neighborhood (to the right of La Rambla if you're facing the sea), also called the Barri Xinés, or Barrio Chino. For decades a mostly underclass and immigrant neighborhood, Raval was also home to clusters of starving artists, down-and-out hookers, and junkies. Today the barrio is a curious mix of rough-around-the-edges and avant-garde design. In the last couple years, the city razed buildings, installed plazas and pedestrian streets (one new boulevard a local resident referred to as "La Rambla de Pakistan," a reference to the burgeoning population of Indians and Pakistanis), and commissioned big projects in an effort to revitalize the district. See one of Gaudí's first private residences, the **Palau Güell,** Nou de la Rambla 3–5, and Richard Meier's glistening white **Museu d'Art Contemporani de Barcelona** (MACBA, or Museum of Contemporary Art), on Plaça dels Angels 1 (☎ **93-412-08-10;** `www.macba.es`; Mon and Wed–Fri 11 a.m.–8 p.m., Sat 10 a.m.–8 p.m., and Sun 10 a.m.–3 p.m; admission: 7.50€, or $9). The **Casa de la Caritat,** an old hospital behind MACBA, has been intriguingly revamped as a city museum.

Although the Raval area (Metro: Liceu or Plaça de Catalunya) is definitely on its way up, you need to be careful and mindful of your belongings, and the area is best avoided at night.

Guided tours

If you don't have a lot of time, the best way to see as much as possible may be on an organized tour. Here are some of my picks.

Bus tours

Hop aboard one of **Barcelona Bus Turístic**'s buses for a tour of 27 city sights. You can take either or both of the Red and Blue routes, and get on and off as you please. Both depart from Plaça de Catalunya at 9:30 a.m.

daily; all stops have full timetables. Complete journey time is about three-and-a-half hours. The bus runs daily throughout the year, except December 25 and January 1. Price is 18€ ($22) for an adult, one-day ticket, 11€ ($13) for children 4 through 12. A two-day adult ticket costs 22€ ($26) and 14€ ($16) for children. Purchase tickets onboard or in advance at **Turisme de Barcelona,** Plaça de Catalunya 17 (☎ **93-285-38-32**).

Walking tours

You can join English-speaking, guided tours of the Gothic Quarter as well as *moderniste,* Picasso, or gourmet routes year-round with **Barcelona Walking Tours.** Walks (90 min.–2 hr.) begin at **Turisme de Barcelona,** Plaça de Catalunya 17. For information call ☎ **93-285-38-32.** Prices are 9€ to 11€ ($11–$13) and 3€ to 5€ ($3.60–$6) for children ages 4 through 12.

Walking tours of El Eixample are perhaps best left to weekends to avoid the overbearing traffic congestion and noise that overtake the area during the workweek. Nighttime is also a good time for a walking tour, because many of the star *moderniste* monuments, including La Pedrera and Casa Battló, are stunningly illuminated. (The area around Passeig de Gràcia is safe at night.)

Bike tours

Two associated groups, **Biketours Barcelona** and **Un Cotxe Menys,** Esparteria 3 (the name means "one fewer car" in Catalan), offer daily guided three-hour bike tours (22€, or $26, including bike rental, guide, and drink) in English and meet at Plaça Sant Jaume. (Tours leave Mon, Wed, and Fri at 11 a.m. and 4:30 p.m.; Tues, Thurs, and Sat at 11 a.m. and 7:30 p.m.; and Sun at 11 a.m.) Call ☎ **93-268-21-05** or visit www.biketoursbarcelona.com. They offer bike rentals by the hour, day, and week, as does **Bike Rental Barcelona** (which will deliver and pick up bikes); call ☎ **666-057-655** or visit www.bikerentalbarcelona.com.

Suggested itineraries

This section offers some tips for building your own itineraries. Two full days will give you a good taste of what the city has to offer.

If you have one day

Begin early in the morning at the only grand cathedral of Europe still in the midst of being built, Gaudí's **Sagrada Familia.** Take an hour or so to clamber around its spires and admire the whimsical sculpture adorning its odd hidden corners. Then take the Metro to Diagonal for more *moderniste* masterpieces in Gaudí's **Casa Milà** and the famed **Manzana de la Discòrdia** along Passeig de Gràcia.

Hop back on the Metro at the Passeig de Gràcia stop and get off at the Jaume I stop so that, after grabbing some lunch on the go, you can pop into the **Museu Picasso,** a museum honoring Barcelona's other artistic giant of the 20th century. Backtrack along Carrer de la Princesa and cross Vía Laietana to the square in front of Barcelona's massive Gothic **Catedral.**

As evening draws near, make your way over to the grand promenade of **La Rambla** to watch the street performers, locals out for their *paseo* (evening walk), and to simply stroll one of the greatest pedestrian boulevards in Europe. Cut out by 6 p.m. or so for the evening *tapeo,* or tapas-bar crawl, then head back to your hotel to rest up from your full day before a 10 p.m. dinner at **Restaurant 7 Portes** or **Los Caracoles** in the Old Quarter.

If you have two days

Begin day one seeing perhaps Barcelona's greatest sight: **La Rambla,** the long, wide, pedestrian boulevard that glides right through the heart of the Old Quarter, from Plaça de Catalunya to the port. Start at the port end, at the Drassanes Metro stop. Stop into **La Boquería** market. Pause at the twittering, tweeting cages of the tiny portable bird market; toss coins to the performers who pose as statues and only move when a clink of change hits their plates. Follow La Rambla all the way to Carrer de Portaferrisa and turn right until you get to the **Catedral.**

After lunch, work your way south through the back streets of the medieval Barri Gòtic and head over to the **Museu Picasso** and then stroll the atmospheric neighborhoods of **La Ribera** and **El Born,** a great place to stop for a glass of wine or *cava.*

Day two is the day for *modernisme.* Start it off by proceeding to **Sagrada Familia** and the Art Nouveau wonderland of **Passeig de Gràcia,** where you'll find the **Manzana de la Discòrdia.** Don't miss a chance to see Antoni Gaudí's masterpice, **Casa Milà.**

Now, because the last day-and-a-half have been pretty packed (and you've done lots of walking), take the afternoon to relax while still sightseeing. Either head up (by taxi) to the Gaudí-designed **Park Güell,** a wonderful place full of whimsical architectural accents, or take the Metro down to the **waterfront,** new port, and revitalized beaches.

Shopping the Local Stores

Barcelona's fascination with design makes it a great place to load up on unique art objects and home furnishings. Likewise, Barcelona is noted for its fashion and jewelry. Although the city has added a couple of megamalls in recent years, small, often family-owned stores still dominate the shopping scene. Window-shopping along the city's picturesque boulevards is an art and a beloved pastime here.

Barcelona's best shopping areas

Tour these shopping areas to find the best that Barcelona has to offer (listed in order of interest):

- **Passeig de Gràcia** and **Rambla de Catalunya.** You can find some of Barcelona's finest boutiques on these two chic streets above Plaça de Catalunya. For fashion, jewelry, and home design, these streets are great for window-shopping — as are nearby Mallorca, Valencia, and Provença.
- **Avinguda Diagonal.** This avenue, which cuts across Barcelona, has some of the finest and most expensive stores in Barcelona. Check it out if your tastes run to Armani and other designers.
- **Plaça de Catalunya.** The entrance to the Old Quarter is the jumping-off point for some of its principal shopping streets: Avinguda Portal de l'Angel and Carrer Portaferrisa always swarm with shoppers.
- **Gothic Quarter.** Deep in the oldest part of town is one of the best spots for antiques and art galleries. Check out the streets Banys Nous, Carrer de la Palla, and Petritxol.
- **La Rambla.** Many of the shops on this street focus on tourist trinkets, but you can still find amazing little pastry and jewelry shops.
- **Old Port.** Barcelona's newest shopping mecca is Maremagnum, a mall teeming with restaurants and all kinds of shops. It's open every day of the year until 11 p.m.

What to look for and where to find it

From antiques to chic fashion and design, Barcelona — Spain's finest shopping city — has it all.

Antiques

The atmospheric streets Carrer de la Palla and Banys Nous in the Gothic Quarter are home to innumerable antiques dealers; many of the shops are as interesting as their wares. **Bulevar dels Antiquaris,** Passeig de Gràcia 57 (Metro: Passeig de Gràcia), is a storefront that hides a maze of at least 70 antiques dealers, but keep in mind that dealers sometimes randomly disappear for long breaks — and not just at siesta time.

L'Arca de L'Àvia, Banys Nous 20 (☎ **93-302-15-98;** Metro: Jaume I), a friendly and inviting little shop that specializes in antique clothing and lace, is reportedly the shop where the costume designer for *Titanic* found the clothes on which that movie's costumes were based. On a recent trip, my wife and I found gorgeous antique lace *mantillas* and an embroidered 20-foot *moderniste* curtain from the 1920s.

Art

Two areas worth exploring are Consell de Cent, in El Eixample, and Passeig del Born, which is a hot gallery area. In particular, keep an eye out for **Sala Parés,** Carrer Petritxol 5 (☎ **93-318-70-20;** Metro: Liceu), Barcelona's oldest art gallery, specializing in traditional art, and **Galería Maeght,** Carrer Montcada 25 (☎ **93-310-42-45;** Metro: Jaume I), a huge and prestigious contemporary gallery down the street from the Picasso Museum.

Books

Barcelona is the headquarters of Spain's publishing industry. You'll find the largest selection of English-language books at the suggestively named **Come In,** Provença 203 (☎ **93-453-12-04;** Metro: Diagonal). Look for art books, books on Spanish culture, cookbooks, and lots of discounted titles — many in English — at **Happy Books,** Passeig de Gràcia 77 and Carrer de Pelai 20 (☎ **93-487-95-71;** Metro: Plaça de Catalunya). **Casa del Llibre,** Passeig de Gràcia 62 (☎ **93-272-34-80;** Metro: Passeig de Gràcia) is a very complete bookstore, with many titles in English. **Llibrería Francesa,** on Passeig de Gràcia 91 (☎ **93-215-14-17;** Metro: Passeig de Gràcia), has many books in English, particularly travel titles and, as the name implies, French titles. The excellent **Crisol** chain, with branches on Rambla Catalunya 81 (Metro: Passeig de Gràcia), and Consell de Cent 341 (Metro: Passeig de Gràcia), is also very well stocked, as is the huge French department store FNAC, on Plaça Catalunya 4, part of the large shopping mall called Triangle (☎ **93-444-59-00;** Metro: Plaça de Catalunya).

Department stores

El Corte Inglés, Plaça de Catalunya 14 (☎ **93-306-38-00;** Metro: Plaça de Catalunya), is the monolith of Spanish department stores. If crowds make you nervous, stay away. Other large and equally crowded branches are located at the corner of Avinguda Portal de l'Angel and Carrer Santa Ana, just southeast of the main store, and at Av. Diagonal 471 and 617.

Design

Vinçon, Passeig de Gràcia 96 (☎ **93-215-60-50;** Metro: Passeig de Gràcia), is Barcelona's premiere design store, with everything that is, in the estimation of founder Fernando Amat, well designed — including lamps, watches, furniture, kitchen utensils, toys, writing instruments, and so on. The display windows are whimsically avant-garde and worth checking out even if you don't have time for shopping. The shop occupies the former house of the great Catalan painter Ramón Casas (this was the first building in Barcelona built with a car garage). **BD Ediciones de Diseño,** Carrer Mallorca 291–293 (☎ **93-458-69-09;** Metro: Diagonal), housed in a marvelous *moderniste* house, sells the high end of Catalan design, including reproductions of Gaudí and Dalí furniture. Check out this store if you've got style and euros to burn.

Fashion

One of the foremost Catalan designers, **Antonio Miró** makes fashions for men and women that are exquisite, but they're for people with a serious interest in fashion. The actor John Malkovich has been known to wear Miró's stuff, but so do regular folks like me. Miró's signature shop is at Consell de Cent 349 (☎ **93-487-06-07;** Metro: Passeig de Gràcia). Look for his other store, **Groc,** on Rambla de Catalunya; it also features chic fashions by such designers as Dolce & Gabbana, Helmut Lang, and Jil Sander. **Adolfo Domínguez,** from Galicia (northwest Spain), has taken his sophisticated, mainstream fashions across Spain. Besides the store at Passeig de Gràcia 32 (☎ **93-487-41-70;** Metro: Plaça de Catalunya), you can also shop at Av. Diagonal 570, and at Passeig de Graci 89. A Galician fashion phenomenon, **Zara** has affordable but stylish clothes for men, women, and children. The stores have sprouted like the European Gap; look for branches on Rambla de Catalunya at Aragó and on Avenida Portal de l'Angel. **Camper** shoes have become hot worldwide, recognized for their downtown edge and reasonable prices; get them in Barcelona before they've made it to your local mall, at the shops on Rambla Catalunya 122, and Valencia 249.

Flea market

If you're a junk-hound, check out **Els Encants,** Barcelona's biggest and best flea market. Vendors hawk their goods and your finds all day every Monday, Wednesday, Friday, and Saturday at Plaça de les Glóries Catalanes (Metro: Glóries).

Foodstuffs

Colmado Quílez offers packaged goods, fine wines, cheeses, and imported beer in an atmospheric shop. After you place an order, the attendant gives you a ticket, you go pay, and then you return to the counter to collect your items. Find it at Rambla de Catalunya 63 (☎ **93-215-87-85;** Metro: Passeig de Gràcia). **Escribà,** Rambla de les Flors 83 (☎ **93-487-06-07;** Metro: Liceu), is a mouth-watering pastry-and-chocolates shop in a lovely *moderniste* little storefront on a corner along La Rambla. Eyeball the window; I defy you to resist stepping inside. **Caelum** means "heaven" in Latin; accordingly, what you find here are all sorts of products, such as Trappist-monk beer, candles, cheeses, and honey, made by monasteries and religious orders. Downstairs is a cave-like tearoom in what were 14th-century baths. Find it on Carrer de la Palla 8 (☎ **93-302-69-93;** Metro: Jaume I). Foodies should pay a visit to **E&A Gispert,** a 150-year-old, terrific little shop, known for its roasted nuts, dried fruits, coffee, and spices, near Santa María del Mar, Sobrerers 23 (☎ **93-319-75-35**). An excellent cheese shop in the Born district is **Tot Formatge,** Passeig del Born 13 (☎ **93-319-53-75;** Metro: Jaume I). **Ol,** Palla 8 (☎ **93-302-29-80**), is entirely dedicated to olive oils — or, as they call them, "liquid gold" — from across Spain.

Gifts

You can find ceramics and handcrafts at **Art Escudellers,** Carrer Escudellers 23–25 (☎ **93-412-68-01;** Metro: Drassanes or Jaume I). Likewise, **BCN Original** offers a very nice selection of gifts, such as T-shirts, paper products, and much more, with the Barcelona stamp — all conveniently located next to the Tourism Information Office at Plaça de Catalunya 17 (Metro: Plaça de Catalunya). If you're looking for Lladró china figurines, **Mils** (Passeig de Gràcia; ☎ **93-412-17-94;** Metro: Passeig de Gràcia) is one of many places to find them. The gift shop at **La Pedrera,** Provença 261–265, offers Gaudí souvenirs and knock-offs, including coasters and chocolates designed to look like the octagonal tiles that form the sidewalk on Passeig de Gràcia.

Keeping Up with Barcelona's Nightlife

Barcelona really buzzes after dark, and though the city doesn't have quite the crazed reputation that Madrid does, Barcelonans are only too happy to stay up all night. To get a grip on what's hip, what's hot, and what's happening, pick up a copy of the weekly *Guía del Ocio,* a guide to all entertainment in Barcelona (available at newsstands, written in Spanish but pretty comprehensible even to non-Spanish speakers). Tickets for many events are available through `www.telentrada.com` (☎ **902-10-12-12**), `ticktackticket.com` (☎ **902-15-00-25**), and `www.servicaixa.com` (☎ **902-33-22-11**).

Opera and classical music

If you're into music, be sure to check out the following venues while touring Barcelona.

- **Gran Teatre del Liceu,** La Rambla 51–59 (☎ **93-485-99-00;** `www.liceubarcelona.com`; Metro: Liceu). Barcelona's grand opera house was completely gutted by fire in January, 1994, but the city raced to rebuild it, and it reopened in October, 1999.
- **L'Auditori (Barcelona Auditorium),** Lepant 150 (☎ **93-247-93-00;** `www.auditori.com`; Metro: Marina or Glóries). This splendid new addition to the music scene, the work of the famed Spanish architect Rafael Moneo, features two halls for classical music concerts. It's high tech all the way. Get tickets at the box office, which is open Monday through Saturday from 10 a.m. to 9 p.m., or by calling ☎ **902-10-12-12,** or 93-247-93-00 from abroad.
- BEST OF THE BEST **Palau de la Música,** Sant Francesc de Paula 2 (☎ **902-44-28-82;** `http://home.palaumusica.org`; Metro: Urquinaona). For a truly singular experience, don't pass up the opportunity to attend a concert in this *moderniste* wonderland. It's really loosened up in recent years; besides classical music, I've seen concerts by Lou Reed, Tindersticks, and David Byrne here.

Flamenco shows

Barcelona can't compare with Madrid or Andalusia for *tablaos* (tah-*blah*-ose) — live flamenco performances — but the city does offer a few decent shows (but, to my mind, rather touristy compared with the most authentic performances in Madrid and Andalusia). One is **Tablao Flamenco Cordobés,** Las Ramblas 35 (☎ **93-317-57-11;** `www.tablaocordobes.com`; Metro: Liceu), which has been around more than 30 years. The show costs between 28€ and 30€ ($36–$38). **El Patio Andaluz,** Aribau 242 (☎ **93-209-33-78;** Metro: Gràcia), puts on flamenco shows as well as *sevillanas* (seh-vee-*yah*-nahs), which showcase more traditional southern-style singing and dancing, and is open until sunrise. At the Poble Espanyol on Montjuïc, **Tablao de Carmen** (☎ **93-325-68-95;** Metro: Espanya) offers flamenco dinner shows Tuesday through Sunday nights starting at 8 p.m. (29€, or $35). **Game-B,** Carrer Atlantida 57 (☎ **93-225-50-87;** Metro: Barceloneta), a club near the waterfront, also puts on flamenco shows every Sunday at 8 p.m. for 6€ ($7.20).

Cafes and bars

Two swank places to drink in the local atmosphere are the gorgeous **Café de la Opera,** La Rambla 74 (☎ **93-302-41-80;** Metro: Liceu), and somewhat more sedate **Els Quatre Gats,** Montsió 3 (☎ **93-302-41-40;** Metro: Urquinaona). Another, which looks unearthed from 1940s Havana, is sleek **Boadas,** Taller 1 (☎ **93-318-88-26;** Metro: Plaça de Catalunya), on the Raval side of the Rambla. **Schilling,** Ferran 23 (☎ **93-317-67-87;** Metro: Jaume I), is a hipster hangout frequented by Barcelona's — and the world's — beautiful people. In the heart of the Gothic Quarter, tiny **Mesón del Café,** Llibreteria 16 (☎ **93-315-07-54;** Metro: Jaume I), is just a tiny nook, but it gets my vote for coolest cafe and the best coffee in the world. For spectacular views along with your cocktails, check out the sleek bar **Mirablau,** Plaza Dr. Andreu, s/n (☎ **93-418-58-79**), high up on Tibidabo. The views of Barcelona beneath your feet are enough to make you dizzy.

El Born, the area near Santa María del Mar and the Mercat del Born, and the **Olympic Port,** near the Hotel Arts, are the two hottest nightlife areas (the latter is more touristy, the former more hipster). You can't walk three feet without stumbling into a bar, and most of them are hopping until very late (or early, depending on your bedtime). Another enjoyable spot, where the rowdy outdoor bars have angered neighbors, is **Plaça del Pi,** near the Catedral in the Gothic Quarter.

Casino

Casino Barcelona, on the port at Marina 19–21 (☎ **93-225-78-78**; `www.casino-barcelona.com`; Metro: Citutadella/Vila Olímpica; 11 a.m.–5 a.m. daily; admission 4.50€/$5.40), features a disco, restaurant, and plenty of gaming opportunities. Be sure to take your passport, because the law requires an official ID for folks who want to gamble.

Good Grec: Barcelona's summer festival

If you find yourself in the Catalan capital in the heat of summer, check out the listings for **Grec,** an annual festival of international dance, music, and theater. For six weeks, from the last week of June to the end of the first week in August, Grec showcases everything from American blues to Brazilian samba and avant-garde Belgian dance. Call ☎ **93-301-77-75** or check the Web site www.barcelonafestival.com for a schedule of events and ticket information.

Live music

El Molino, Vila i Vila 99 (☎ **93-329-88-54;** Metro: Paral.lel), is another legendary place — one of the city's oldest cabarets. **Los Tarantos,** Plaça Reial 17 (☎ **93-318-30-67;** Metro: Liceu), frequently has flamenco or pop-flamenco shows, as well as Latin-flavored dancing. One of the top jazz clubs in Europe, going strong since the 1960s, is **Jamboree,** Plaça Reial 17 (☎ **93-319-17-89;** Metro: Liceu). Some of the most legendary names in jazz have played here, including Duke Ellington, Ella Fitzgerald, and Chet Baker. Cover is generally 8€ ($10). **Harlem Jazz Club,** Comtessa de Sobradiel 8 (☎ **93-310-07-55;** Metro: Jaume I), a tiny affair tucked away in the Gothic Quarter, is another hugely popular jazz club. A discotheque with regular live music is the historic **Sala Apolo,** Nou de la Rambla 113 (☎ **93-441-40-01;** Metro: Paral.lel).

Dancing

Several of the old stalwarts are still going strong. **Antilla BCN Latin Club,** Aragon 141 (☎ **93-451-21-51**), bills itself as a *salsateca* (salsa club). The venerable Latin-flavored nightclub **Nick Havanna,** Rosselló 208 (☎ **93-215-65-91;** Metro: Diagonal), was one of Barcelona's first sleek design-oriented bars. **Luz de Gas,** Muntaner 246 (☎ **93-209-77-11;** Metro: Muntaner), and **Otto Zutz,** Lincoln 15, a stylish warehouse in the Gràcia district (☎ **93-238-07-22;** Metro: Gràcia), remain, as they have for years, among the hottest late-night dance places; both also feature live music. **Torres de Avila,** Marqués de Comillas 25 (☎ **93-424-93-09;** Metro: Espanya), a design fantasy in the Poble Espanyol, is worth a peek if only for the over-the-top look of the place — but a few drinks will really set you back.

Newer clubs, especially popular with a younger set, are mostly in and around the Barri Gòtic and the waterfront. The largest dance club in the Gothic Quarter is **New York,** Escudellers 5 (☎ **93-318-87-30;** Metro: Drassanes), just off La Rambla. It doesn't get going until well after 3 a.m. **Baja Beach Club,** Pg. Marítim 34 (☎ **93-225-91-00;** Metro: Drassanes), is the place to go to see people dressed in little more than they would be if sunning themselves at the beach — and that includes the staff.

One of the most popular gay dance clubs continues to be **Arena,** Balmes 32 (☎ **93-487-49-48;** Metro: Plaça de Catalunya). Its sister club, popular with lesbians, is **Aire,** Valencia 236 (☎ **93-487-49-48;** Metro: Passeig de Gràcia). The *Gay T Dance* sessions at **Sala Apolo,** Nou de la Rambla 113 (☎ **93-441-40-01;** Metro: Paral.lel), on Sunday nights are extremely animated house and disco romps to top off the weekend.

Going Beyond Barcelona: Three Day Trips

If you have some extra time in Barcelona, the following easy side-trips are well worthwhile; all can be done as a half- or full-day trip. If you're an architecture and Antoni Gaudí buff, or a recent convert, don't miss the opportunity to see Gaudí's small, unfinished church, **Colònia Güell** (which many believe to be the most innovative work of his career), just outside the city in Santa Coloma de Cervelló (see "More cool things to see and do" earlier in this chapter). If you have time to explore Catalunya, see the next chapter, "Girona and the Costa Brava."

Montserrat: The holy jagged mountain

Montserrat, home to the Black Madonna — the patron saint of Catalonia — is Barcelona's peculiarly formed and sacred mountain. Montserrat, which means saw-tooth mountain, cuts a dramatic, jagged line across the Catalan sky.

Getting there

Montserrat is 50km (30 miles) northwest of Barcelona. You can go by car, bus, or rail, but the most dramatic approach to Montserrat is via train and a cable car that ascends to the top (though the cycling club I used to belong to regularly biked to the mountain, and that wasn't bad, either). The Ferrocarrils de la Generalitat de Catalunya (FGC) train (see "Arriving by train," earlier in this chapter) connects to an aerial cable car (Montserrat Aeri). FGC offers the **Tot Montserrat** ticket (35€, or $42, including trains, entry into the Montserrat museum, funiculars, and lunch at the Montserrat restaurant; and the **TransMontserrat** ticket, which covers the train and funiculars, for 21€, or $25). The trip leaves from Barcelona's Plaça d'Espanya station (☎ **93-205-15-15;** `www.fgc.net`). **Autocares Juliá** (☎ **93-490-40-00**) offers a complete bus tour leaving direct from Barcelona, departing daily at 9:30 a.m. and returning at 2:30 p.m. (45€/$54 round-trip).

The only other way to visit the mountain is by car, especially if you want to combine the journey with a visit to the Penedès Wineries (see "Penedès: Spain's cava country," later in this chapter). You can easily do both in a single day if you're driving. By car, take the A-2 out of Barcelona toward Tarragona and Martorell, or the Barcelona-Terrassa highway via the Túneles de Vallvidrera. The signs to Montserrat are clearly marked. The **Tourist Information Office** is on Plaça de la Creu, s/n (☎ **93-877-77-77**).

Seeing the sights

Montserrat is no ordinary 1,219m (4,000-ft.) mountain, either in appearance or symbolism. The setting for Wagner's opera *Parsifal,* Montserrat is home to an 11th-century **Benedictine monastery,** which is spectacularly tucked into its ridges. In the 16th-century basilica is a shrine to the famous icon and patron saint of Catalonia, the Black Madonna (Montserrat). Pilgrims come from all over to worship her, and you'll see her reproduced image everywhere in Barcelona. Next door to the basilica, the **Museu de Montserrat,** Plaça de Santa María (☎ **93-877-77-77;** admission 6.50€, or $8.10), contains minor paintings by such celebrated artists as Caravaggio, Degas, Monet, and El Greco, as well as an early Picasso and Dalí.

After you've seen the basilica and museum, take the short funicular (near the cable-car station) to the **Sant Joan** peak, where there's a small hermitage and excellent panoramic views of the coast and Pyrenees foothills. You'll have to hoof it another 45 minutes up to the **Sant Jeroni** hermitage and summit. Another funicular takes you to **Santa Cova,** a 17th-century chapel built in the shape of a cross, where it is alleged that the Black Madonna was discovered. A combined funicular ticket costs 7.30€ ($8.75) round-trip, though you won't need it if you purchased either the Tot Montserrat or TransMontserrat ticket. Or, if you're up for it, you can walk to these sites and other caves and chapels on the mountain.

Besides visiting the monastery and museum, and appreciating the incredible views of the Catalan countryside, time your visit to see the **Esolanía,** one of the oldest boys' choirs in Europe (dating to the 13th century). The choir performs daily at 1 p.m. and 6:45 p.m. On Sundays and holidays, you can hear them at morning Mass (11 a.m.).

Avoid making your pilgrimage to Montserrat on April 27 or September 8. Those holy days draw pilgrims from all over Spain, and the place is a zoo.

Sitges: A stylin' beach resort

The pretty beach town of Sitges is the definite standout along the so-called Costa Daurada (Golden Coast), south of Barcelona. Sitges is anything but laid-back; it's one of Spain's most prominent gay resort areas. During holiday periods it draws thousands of Europeans and Spaniards, so it can get pretty rowdy.

Getting there

Sitges is 35km (21 miles) southwest of Barcelona. The trip (3.80€/$4.55) is 40 minutes by train, with frequent departures from Barcelona's Sants station. For more information, contact RENFE, the Spanish national train service, at ☎ **902-24-02-02** or `www.renfe.es`. By car, take C-246. However, on weekends, opt for toll highway A-7 to avoid traffic. (Allow 45 minutes to an hour.) The **Tourist Information Office** (☎ **93-894-50-04;** `www.sitgestour.com`) is at Sínia Morera 1.

Seeing the sights

Tiny Sitges has long been a cultural center, drawing the painters Santiago Rusiñol and Salvador Dalí, as well as the poet Federico García Lorca to its enclave. A good deal is a combined ticket to all Sitges museums for 5.40€ ($6.48); otherwise admission to any single museum is 3€ ($3.60), free for children under 16. **Museu Cau Ferrat** on Carrer del Fonollar, s/n, was the home of Rusiñol (who converted two 16th-century fishermen's houses), and it is today as it was in his lifetime — chock-full of *moderniste*-period paintings, other artworks by the likes of El Greco, and personal knickknacks. You can also browse through nice collections of ceramics and wrought iron (☎ **93-894-03-64**). It's open Tuesday to Sunday from 10 a.m. to 2 p.m. and 5 to 9 p.m. The other museum of note is **Museu Maricel del Mar,** Carrer del Fonollar s/n, a handsome palace displaying Gothic and Romantic artworks (☎ **93-894-03-64**). The museum is open from 10 a.m. to 1 p.m. and 4 to 6 p.m.

The lazy lifestyle of beaches and seaside restaurants are Sitges's main draw. The beach in town is lovely, and beaches farther west draw some less inhibited behavior. Unless you want an eyeful (of skin and more), stick to the beaches in or near town. When night falls, the best plan is to check out the constant beachfront stream of humanity along the promenade. Otherwise, the Sant Bonaventura section in the town center sizzles with gay party spots. One of Spain's more flamboyant parties is **Carnaval** in Sitges, celebrated the week before Lent.

Where to stay and dine

You can find a number of good restaurants on Paseo de la Ribera. For example, try **El Velero de Sitges,** at No. 38 (☎ **93-894-20-51**), or Mare Nostrum, at No. 60 (☎ **93-894-33-93**). If you want to hang out for a couple of days in Sitges, I suggest checking into either **Hotel Romàntic de Sitges,** Carrer de Sant Isidre 33 (☎ **93-894-83-75;** `www.hotelromantic.com`), which comprises three art-filled 19th-century townhouses, or El Xalet, Isla de Cuba 33–35 (☎ **93-811-00-70**), a good-value *moderniste* house with many original furnishings in the center of town and walking distance from the beach.

Penedès: Spain's cava country

Catalonia's sparkling wine, called *cava,* comes from Penedès, a pretty region just outside of Barcelona.

Getting there

Villafranca del Penedès, the epicenter of the Penedès wine region, is 40km (25 miles) from Barcelona. By car (40 minutes), take A-2 in the direction of Tarragona/Lleida; exit 27 is Sant Sadurní del Noia, and Cordoniu is clearly marked. If you want to get on a bus, **Autocares La Hispano Llacunense** (☎ **93-891-25-61**) makes the trip, leaving from the corner of Avenida de Sarrià and Urgell. Eight buses per day go to Sant Sadurní Monday through Friday, and just two per day on Saturday and Sunday.

Seeing the sights

Several wineries are in the main town, Sant Sadurní del Noia. Best for visits is **Codorníu,** which, though still family-owned, is Spain's largest *cava* producer. It's also one of the oldest wineries in Spain, dating to the mid-16th century. The winery makes an excellent addition to the *modernista* architecture you may have already seen in Barcelona. The main buildings on the Codorníu campus, the work of the esteemed Gaudí contemporary Puig i Cadafalch, are a National Artistic and Historic Monument. The highlight of a visit is a theme park–like cart ride through 26km (16 miles) of underground cellars. Guided visits at the Codorníu cellars and winemaking museum, Av. Jaume Codorníu s/n, are held Monday through Friday from 9 a.m. to 5 p.m. and weekends 9 a.m. to 1 p.m. Visits should be prearranged. Call ☎ **93-891-33-42** or visit www.codorniu.es.

Fast Facts: Barcelona

Area Code

The country code is **34.** The Barcelona city code of **93** is incorporated into the full number, which means you must always dial it. To call Barcelona from the United States, dial ☎ **011-34** followed by the number.

Currency

In 2002, the euro replaced the peseta in Spain. The exchange rate used to calculate the dollar values given in this chapter is 1€ = $1.20. Amounts greater than $10 are rounded to the nearest dollar.

Exchange currency either at banks or *casas de cambio* (exchange houses). You can also find currency exchange offices at the Sants rail stations and El Prat airport. Spanish banks include La Caixa, Caixa de Catalunya, BBV, and Central Hispano. Branches of these are located near Plaça Catalunya. Most banks offer 24-hour ATMs. Currency-exchange houses include BCN World and BCN Change & Transfer.

Doctors/Dentists

Dial ☎ **061** to find a doctor. The U.S. Consulate has a list of English-speaking physicians. For a dentist, call ☎ 93-415-9922.

Embassies/Consulates

The U.S. Consulate is located at Paseo Reina Elisenda 23, in Sarrià (☎ 93-280-22-27); the Canadian Consulate is at Paseo de Gracia 77 (☎ 93-215-07-04); the U.K. Consulate is at Av. Diagonal 477 (☎ 93-419-90-44); the Australian Consulate is at Gran Vía Carles III 94 (☎ 93-90-90-13); and the New Zealand Consulate is at Travessera de Gràcia 64 (☎ 93-209-03-99).

Emergencies

For general emergencies, call ☎ **112.** Medical emergencies, dial ☎ **061.** The National Police emergency number (in and outside Barcelona) is ☎ **091.** For local police, call ☎ **092.** Call ☎ **93-300-20-20** to request an ambulance. For fire, call ☎ **080.**

Hospitals

To locate a hospital, dial ☎ **93-427-20-20.** Barcelona Centro Médico (Av. Diagonal 612; ☎ 93-414-06-43) dispenses information about hospitals and medical specialists to foreigners. The Hospital Clínic is at Villarroel 170 (☎ 93-227-54-00).

Information

Call ☎ **010** for general visitor information. Turisme de Barcelona, Plaça de Catalunya 17 (underground), ☎ 93-285-38-34, is open daily from 9 a.m. to 9 p.m. Informació Turística de Catalunya has information on Barcelona and the entire region; it's located in Palau Robert, Passeig de Gràcia 107 (☎ 93-238-40-03). Tourism information offices are also at Sants train station and the airport. For transit information (Metro, bus, and so on), call ☎ **010** or 93-298-70-00; `www.tmb.net`.

Internet Access and Cybercafes

The Internet Gallery Cafe is down the street from the Picasso Museum, Barra de Ferro 3 (☎ 93-268-15-07). Another excellent center is EasyEverything, La Rambla dels Caputxins 29 (☎ 93-318-2435, Metro: Liceu or Drassenes), open daily 7 a.m. to 2 a.m.

Acoma Cafe-Bar, Boquería 21, offers free Internet access (☎ 93-301-75-97; Metro: Liceu). Open from 10 a.m. to 12 p.m. Monday through Saturday.

Maps

Get free maps at Turisme de Barcelona, Plaça de Catalunya 17 (underground), or purchase maps at any kiosk along La Rambla.

Newspapers/Magazines

News kiosks along La Rambla are open virtually around the clock. The most useful weekly guide *Guía del Ocio,* available for 1€ ($1.20), which includes an English-language section; there are also lots of English-language freebies lying around in every shop, restaurant, and bar. The monthly *Metropolitan* provides a local's-eye-view of Barcelona.

Pharmacies

Pharmacies *(farmàcies)* operate during normal business hours and one in every district remains open all night and on holidays. The location and phone number of this *farmàcia de guàrdia* is posted on the door of all the other pharmacies. A central pharmacy is open 24/7, Farmàcia Alvarez, at Passeig de Gràcia 26 (☎ 93-302-1124). You can also call ☎ **010** or 93-481-00-60 to contact all-night pharmacies.

Police

For municipal police, dial ☎ **092;** for national police, ☎ **091.** The main police station is at Vía Laietana 43 (☎ 932-903-000). The Tourist Police are located at Rambla 43 (☎ 933-019-060).

Post Office

The Central Post Office is at Plaça de Antoni López, s/n, at the end of Vía Laietana (☎ 902-19-71-97). It's open Monday through Saturday from 8:30 a.m. to 9:30 p.m. The yellow sign CORREOS identifies branches of the post office. Those at Aragó 282, and Ronda Universitat 23, are open from 8:30 a.m. to 8:30 p.m.

Safety

The street crime for which Barcelona once drew unwanted attention has largely diminished. Still, be careful around major tourist sights, especially: La Rambla (in particular, the section closest to the sea), Barri Gòtic, El Raval; and La Sagrada Familia. You shouldn't walk alone at night in Barri Gòtic or El Raval. Your primary danger is from pickpockets and purse snatchers.

Turisme Atenció (Tourist Attention Service), La Rambla 43 (☎ 93-256-24-30; Metro: Liceu), has English-speaking attendants who can aid crime victims in reporting losses and obtaining new documents. The office is open 24/7.

Taxes

The government sales tax, known as IVA (value-added tax), is levied nationwide on all goods and services, and ranges from 7 to 33 percent.

Telephone

For national telephone information, dial ☎ **1003.** For international telephone information, dial ☎ **025.**

Phone cards worth 12€ ($14) are good for 150 minutes. Use them to make international calls from booths identified with the word INTERNACIONAL.

To make an international call, dial ☎ **00,** wait for the tone, and dial the country code, area code, and number.

Chapter 11

Girona and the Costa Brava

In This Chapter

- Getting to and around northern Catalonia
- Wandering the walled city of Girona
- Following the strange footsteps of Salvador Dalí
- Exploring the Empordà plains, hilltop villages, and Costa Brava beach towns

Sandwiched between Barcelona and the Pyrenees Mountains that divide Spain from France, and extending from interior farmland to the Mediterranean Sea, the province of Girona (jee-*roh*-nah) is a historic and delightful area, replete with charming old towns and gorgeous scenery. Except for the heavily visited beaches of the Costa Brava — one of the pioneering regions of sand-and-sun tourism in Spain — the region sees relatively few international travelers. Adding a few days of exploration onto a visit to Barcelona, which is only an hour or two from most of the places that I describe in this chapter, makes for a terrific and varied regional trip to Catalonia.

Seductive and surprising, Girona is one of Spain's most ancient towns (the Romans first stepped foot on the Iberian Peninsula here), and it's just beginning to get the attention it deserves. Its Casco Viejo (Old Quarter), which includes the ancient Jewish district called El Call, is perhaps the loveliest in Spain. Within easy reach of Girona is the Costa Brava, the "untamed coast," a stretch of rocky coves and small beaches, with intensely blue Mediterranean waters and whitewashed fishing villages. Steer away from overdeveloped areas where mass-market tourism mars the coastline's natural beauty (for some pointers on that, see "The Costa Brava: Resorts and Rugged Beauty," later in this chapter). And inland from the coast, in the region of plains and rolling green hills called L'Empordà, are movie-set medieval villages with tiny parish churches and ancient stone houses, many of which are weekend and summer homes owned by affluent Barcelonans.

One of the highlights of the region is following the trail of Spain's famous madman, the surrealist painter Salvador Dalí. Dalí hailed from these rural parts, and although his art and antics earned him fame in New York and Paris, he lived much of his life in the Costa Brava. You can visit the three points that form the so-called Dalí Triangle, tracing the artist's life from his birthplace and legendary Costa Brava homes to the agreeably

Girona and the Costa Brava

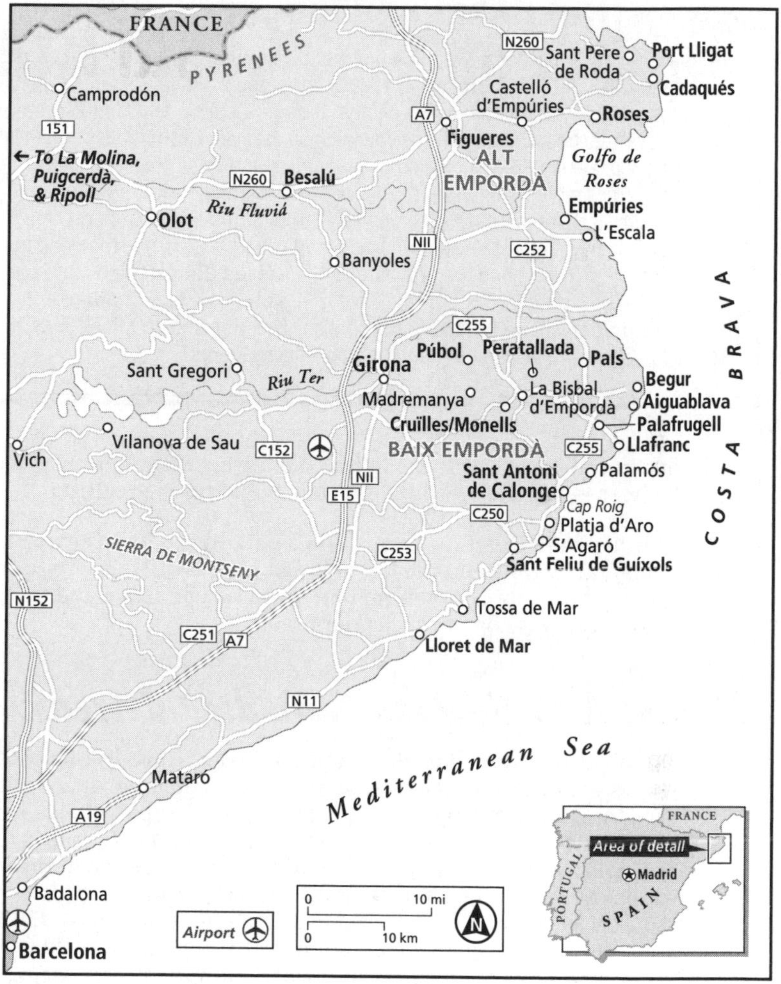

loony museum he designed as his legacy. These visits are a must-see for anyone with an interest in Dalí and contemporary art — and a barrel of fun for anyone with a sense of humor and an appreciation for the absurd.

The climate in the region is blissfully temperate most of the year, although winter can be quite chilly. You can visit year-round, but the Costa Brava closes up shop in mid-winter, as do some of the hotels in the Empordà region (seasonal closings are noted in hotel listing descriptions). In summer — especially July and August — Northern Europeans

The name and language game

Catalan — not a dialect of Spanish but a Latin-derived language that sounds to an untrained ear a bit like a cross between French and Castilian Spanish — is the primary language of Catalonia. In Barcelona, though, Catalan and Spanish are used on an almost equal basis. Especially as you move north from Barcelona, Catalan becomes much more prevalent (although almost everyone in tourist areas also speaks Spanish). As a rule, the smaller the town, the more likely it is that Catalan is the language of choice. Although most name spellings and street signs are in Catalan, you may also come across their Spanish counterparts. *Girona* (jee-*roh*-nah) — referring to both the capital of the province and the province itself — is the Catalan name. In Spanish, it is spelled *Gerona* (heh-*roh*-nah). The larger region is called *Catalunya* in Catalan, *Cataluña* in Spanish, and *Catalonia* in English. The plains area inland from the Costa Brava is *L'Empordà* in Catalan and *El Ampurdán* in Spanish.

overrun the area. At these times, and during Easter, hotel prices are highest — and the need for advance bookings is greatest.

Unless you're Dutch or German on a blitz to the beach, you're probably coming to Girona and the Costa Brava from Barcelona. You can easily access the entire region from Barcelona by car, train, and bus, but a car is the best way to maximize your time.

Girona: A Little-Known Medieval Treasure

Girona, dwarfed by Barcelona and the Costa Brava, is one of the unsung jewels of not only Catalonia but Spain. Its beauty surprises many visitors, who wonder why they hadn't heard of Girona before — especially because it's only 100km (60 miles) from Barcelona. Girona is one of Spain's most historic cities. The **Old Quarter,** steeped in the layered histories of the Romans, Moors, and Jews, is a compact jumble of narrow stone streets, dark alleyways, and the medieval arches of **El Call** — the ancient Jewish neighborhood. Along with Salamanca's Old Quarter (see Chapter 14), it's the most beautiful and complete *casco viejo* in Spain.

Girona is perched on a hill, beckoning athletic climbers with wonderful views of the surrounding countryside. The modern section of town lies across the Onyar River, where multicolored laundry flaps in the breeze from the balconies of yellow and orange sun-drenched apartment houses. In one long day, you can see most of the historic city, but Girona really turns up her charm as night falls, when the town empties of shoppers and tourists, and its silent streets exude an enticing medieval atmosphere. This dignified city became seasonal training home in the last few years to a couple of dozen professional cyclists (the majority of whom are American), including the seven-time Tour de France champion

Lance Armstrong and now disgraced champions Floyd Landis and Tyler Hamilton.

Girona has a reputation as a provincial, emphatically Catalan city and province. The Catalan language dominates here — and in the Girona countryside, you may find that people choose to speak very little Spanish. When people do speak Spanish, they often do so with the rather nasal tone of a heavy Catalan accent. (See the "The name and language game" sidebar in this chapter for more information.)

Getting there

Most people still choose to visit Girona as a day trip from Barcelona or the Costa Brava, so the bus, train, and car directions that I give in this section reflect that supposition.

By bus

Many buses, such as those run by **Sarfa,** leave daily for Girona (and the Costa Brava) from Barcelona's Estació Nord. From Girona, buses leave for Figueres (the Dalí birthplace and home of Teatre Museu Dalí; see "The Dalí Triangle: Connecting the Dots," later in the chapter) and many stops along the Costa Brava (see "The Costa Brava: Resorts and Rugged Beauty" section later in the chapter). Call ☎ **902-30-20-25** or visit `www.sarfa.com` for more information. Tickets are available at Barcelona's Estació Nord and the Tourist Information Office on Plaça de Catalunya.

By car

From Barcelona, take the *ronda* (beltway) in the direction of France and then the A-7 to Girona. The 97km (60-mile) journey takes about an hour, unless you set out during morning or evening rush hour. Figueres is about two hours north of Barcelona (on A-7) and a half-hour north of Girona (on N-II). C-255 and C-252 go along the coast and to principal towns in the Empordà.

By train

Frequent RENFE (Spain's national trains) service connects Girona, Figueres, Port Bou, and Barcelona. You can choose from two dozen daily trains (including the **Catalan Talgo, Catalunya Express,** and **Regional**). Trains leave from Barcelona's Estació Sants between 6 a.m. and 9:30 p.m., and arrive at Girona's Plaça Espanya. For train information, call ☎ **902-24-02-02** (`www.renfe.es`; 5.45€–6.25€, or $6.80–$7.80). Trains take about 90 minutes or less, depending on the service.

From Girona, you can take trains (2.95€, or $3.70) to the Costa Brava towns of **Llança, Blanes,** and **Colera** (the last, a town whose name presents a serious public-relations problem!). For more, see "The Costa Brava: Resorts and Rugged Beauty," later in this chapter.

By air

Girona has a small international airport 12km (7 miles) from the city, which increasingly services flights arriving from the United Kingdom, Germany, and several other European cities. If you're coming in from a European country, contact the airport at ☎ **972-18-66-00.** Taking a taxi (18€/$23) to the city is your best bet, though a shuttle-bus service (☎ **902-36-15-50;** www.sagales.com; 1.95€/$2.40) also exists. If you're flying in from North America, you will most likely travel through Barcelona first.

Getting around

You need only your feet as transportation after you arrive in the historic part of Girona, although you may require an occasional taxi to take you to a restaurant or hotel that's outside the center of the Old Quarter. If you've rented a car and are staying at a hotel removed from the center, drive to the Old Quarter and park.

By car

If you plan on visiting more than just the city of Girona or Figueres, a car is very helpful, if not downright essential. Distances are short, but you can't rely on train and bus service because it's too spotty. With a car, you can easily see a bit of everything — medieval villages, beaches, and Dalí's haunts — in a few short days. You're probably best off renting a car in Barcelona (see Chapter 6 for car-renting tips), though you can also rent through Avis (☎ **972-47-43-33**), Hertz (☎ **972-18-66-19**), and Europcar (☎ **972-18-66-19**) at the Girona train station.

By bus

Sarfa (☎ **972-20-17-96;** www.sarfa.com) buses, leaving from Plaça d'Espanya, s/n, operate throughout the Costa Brava, traveling to Girona, Figueres, and Cadaqués. Call ☎ **902-30-20-25** for bus service throughout the region. However, except for major destinations in the region, bus travel is a little too spotty, and I recommend using a car.

By train

Trains connect Girona to Llança, Blanes, and Colera on the Costa Brava, with increased service in summer. The RENFE station is on Plaça d'Espanya, s/n (☎ **902-24-02-02;** www.renfe.es). Again, trains only service a handful of destinations in the region, so if you're interested in really getting around, you should rent a car.

By taxi

For taxi service — which you'll need mostly to get to the train or bus station, or perhaps to a restaurant on the outskirts of town — call **Taxi Girona** (☎ **972-22-23-23**) or **Girotaxi** (☎ **972-41-90-92**).

Finding information after you arrive

The helpful **Oficina de Turisme** is right on the pedestrian-only main drag, Rambla de la Llibertat 1 (☎ **972-22-65-75**). Another, smaller office is located at the **Punt de Benvinguda** (meeting point) on Berenguer Carnicer 3 (☎ **972-21-16-78**), near the river and the Sant Feliu bridge.

Spending the night

Although I wholly recommend spending a night or two in Girona — it's a good base for exploring the area, and staying overnight allows you to wander the silent Old Quarter at night — the city draws mostly day-trippers from Barcelona and the Costa Brava. Consequently, it's not overflowing with hotels and *pensiones* (boardinghouses). The **Tourism Information Office,** Rambla de la Llibertat 1 (☎ **972-22-65-75**), can help with accommodations if you arrive without a reservation.

Bellmirall
$$

This tiny, charming guesthouse in the heart of the Old Quarter just around the corner from the Cathedral is perfect for individuals wanting to absorb some of old Girona's ancient flavor. In a restored 14th-century stone mansion, it has a slightly bohemian feel and the warmth of a family-owned inn. Its seven rooms, which are perennially booked, are simple but very comfortable, and the downstairs patio and living rooms are great spots to hang out with fellow travelers. Breakfasts are surprisingly ample.

Bellmirall 3 (Old Quarter). ☎ ***972-20-40-09.*** `www.grn.es/bellmirall`. *Free parking. Rack rates: 60€–70€ ($72–$84) double. No credit cards. Closed Jan–Feb.*

Hotel Carlemany
$$$

The second-best option in Girona (behind the Hotel Citutat de Girona), this large (90-room), modern, and mirrored new hotel is a ten-minute walk across the Onyar River from the Old Quarter, and provides easy access to both the train and bus station in the new part of town. Rooms are handsomely appointed, spacious, and very comfortable, and the staff is friendly and efficient. The restaurant, El Pati Verd, is one of the better places to dine in Girona, another reason virtually all business travelers camp here. Check the Web site for special offers.

Plaza Miquel Santaló (3 blocks west of Estació Renfe). ☎ ***972-21-12-12.*** *Fax: 972-21-49-94.* `www.carlemany.es`. *Parking: 15€ ($18). Rack rates: 116€ ($139) double. AE, MC, V.*

Hotel Citutat de Girona
$$$

My favorite place to stay in Girona is this ultrahip, perfectly located mid-size hotel. Friendly and design-conscious, it's just a block from the famed

Pont de Ferro (iron bridge) that leads over the Onyar River to the Old Quarter, and around the corner from one of Girona's best shopping streets, Santa Clara. Rooms are stylishly functional, with excellent beds, nicely equipped bathrooms, and such extras as a free minibar, CD player, and DSL Internet connection — and free laptop for use (upon request). For this kind of comfort, style, and service, Ciutat de Girona is an excellent value. In addition, the hotel is connected to a very cool, popular, and excellent-value restaurant, Blanc.

Nord 2 (2 blocks from Pont de Ferro). ☎ ***972-48-30-38.*** *Fax: 972-48-30-26.* www.hotel-ciutatdegirona.com. *Parking: 15€ ($18). Rack rates: 116€–143€ ($139–$172) double. AE, MC, V.*

Hotel Historic
$$–$$$

In the heart of the Old Quarter, just across from the Hostal Bellmirall and steps from the Cathedral, this handsome and surprising property consists of a tiny hotel (just six rooms) and a series of apartments — perfect for families or longer stays — in the same building. Rooms are modern and well appointed, with nice tiled bathrooms and exposed stone walls. Five ample apartments (all with sitting rooms and full kitchens) have two double rooms, while the other two each have a double room. There's even a restaurant on the premises.

Bellmirall 3 (Old Quarter). ☎ ***972-22-35-83.*** *Fax: 972-20-09-32.* www.hotelhistoric.com. *Free parking. Rack rates: 114€–150€ ($137–$180) double (hotel); 90€–150€ ($108–$180) apartments. AE, MC, V.*

Dining locally

Some of Girona's most celebrated restaurants are clustered along the Costa Brava or in the countryside. But the restaurant scene continues to improve in the city, where you can find several good places to sample authentic Catalan cooking. You can find all the restaurants listed in this section in the Old Quarter. Another option is **El Pati Verd,** within the Hotel Carlemany (see the description in the preceding section). For more on Spanish dining customs, including mealtimes, costs, and tipping, see Chapter 2.

Blanc
$ **CATALAN**

This chic and understandably very popular restaurant, connected to the stylish Hotel Ciutat de Girona (see the listing earlier in the chapter), is part of a successful collection of attractive and very affordable restaurants in Barcelona and several other spots in Catalonia. With white leather banquettes, dashes of color, and label-less wine bottles posing as art, it is surprisingly hip given its family-friendly prices. Blanc (meaning "white") serves Catalan and Mediterranean specialties such as lasagna baked with Iberic ham, onions, and *ceps* (wild mushrooms).

Eating and drinking like a Gironès

The cuisine in the Girona region is ancient, Mediterranean, and based equally on the sea and the region's rolling farmlands. A Catalan staple is *pa amb tomàquet* — bread raked with fresh tomatoes and doused with virgin olive oil. Likewise, native people talk about hunting for wild mushrooms with the same passion usually reserved for soccer. On menus, you find lots of *ali-oli* (olive oil and crushed garlic sauce), *fuet* (long, thin, dried sausage), and *butifarra* (Catalan white sausage). *Escalivada* is a great country dish made with baked eggplant, onions, and sweet peppers. For dessert, don't miss out on *crema catalana* (crème caramel with a burnt-sugar top).

Catalans are almost as wild about leeks as they are about wild mushrooms. During the month of March, *calçotada* madness arrives. *Calçots* are specially grown leeks that are grilled and served with romesco sauce and broiled meat. It's a dish as messy as it is tasty. That's why when you pass a roadside restaurant advertising *calçots* or a *calçotada* (essentially an onion barbecue), most of the diners are decked out in bibs while slurping on long and tasty leeks.

Good wines come from Peralada and the Penedès region just to the south. If you didn't have any crisp *cava* (Catalan sparkling wine) in Barcelona, try some in Girona; it tastes great with tapas.

Nord 2 (connected to Hotel Ciutat de Girona). ☎ ***972-41-56-37.*** *Reservations not accepted. Main courses: 5€–11€ ($6.25–$13). MC, V. Open: Lunch and dinner Tues–Sat, lunch only Sun.*

Cal Ros

$$ CATALAN

Under the arches of a pretty little square — Voltes d'en Roses — in the heart of the Old Quarter, this historic hangout is a favorite with locals who appreciate a good value. The kitchen prepares classic Catalan cooking, with simple, local ingredients. Try the *arroz a la cazuela con sepia, mejillones, y coliflor frita* (rice casserole with squid, mussels, and fried cauliflower).

Cort Reial 9 (Old Quarter). ☎ ***972-21-73-79.*** *Reservations recommended. Main courses: 7€–25€ ($8.40–$30). MC, V. Open: Lunch and dinner Tues–Sat, lunch only Sun.*

Café Le Bistrot

$ MEDITERRANEAN/PIZZA

With a smattering of candlelit tables cascading up the steps of a picturesque *casco viejo* alleyway, this informal, impossibly cool restaurant screams romance. At least it does at the very coveted outdoor tables. Indoors, the restaurant is surprisingly noisy and cavernous, spreading over several dining rooms. By all means, try to snag a table on the steps (which are so popular you'll need to arrive early and get on the list) and enjoy some excellent pizza on rustic *pagès* bread with interesting toppings (spinach, green asparagus), fresh, tasty salads, and pastas. For dessert, try one of the yummy homemade crepes.

Pujada de Sant Domènec 4 (Old Quarter). ☎ ***972-21-88-03.*** *Reservations recommended. Main courses: 4.50€–8€ ($5.40–$10). MC, V. Open: Lunch and dinner Tues–Sat.*

El Celler de Can Roca

$$$$–$$$$$ CATALAN

One of the finest dining spots in Catalonia — in fact, in all of Spain — is this elegant but relaxed modern restaurant run by three brothers (the Rocas of the restaurant's name), on the outskirts of Girona (about a 15-minute drive). Joan is the master chef in the kitchen; he creates carefully executed, imaginative dishes such as *lubina* (sea bass) with a sauce of hazelnuts and lemon peel in cabernet sauvignon vinaigrette or red mullet with orange and cauliflower. The wine list (overseen by Josep) is award winning and voluminous: Its three thick volumes are wheeled to your table on its own lectern.

The menu continues to be consistently innovative, featuring both greatest hits from over the years (listed along with their date of introduction) and new evolutions. By far the best strategy is to choose one of three fixed-price menus: a "surprise" menu left up to the market and whims of Josep, a tasting menu, and a seasonal menu. Desserts, the work of Jordi, the youngest brother, are exquisite flights of fancy; many of them are inspired by perfumes and designed to play off scented strips that accompany them. Less pricey than other restaurants of similar renown, Can Roca is the one restaurant north of Barcelona — besides El Bulli, which is nearly impossible to get in (see the review in the "Where to stay and dine on the Costa Brava" section later in the chapter) — that you don't want to miss. I'd even venture to say it alone is worth a trip to Girona.

Carretera de Taialá 40 (direction of Les Planes, northeast of the Old Quarter). ☎ ***972-22-21-57.*** *Reservations required. Main courses: 19€–36€ ($23–$43). Tasting menus: 40€–75€ ($48–$90). AE, DC, MC, V. Open: Lunch and dinner Tues–Sat.*

L'A9

$$ CATALAN

Decorated with a brilliant and playful color scheme filled with modern art, this funky little restaurant stands out against the stately surroundings of the Old Quarter. It's on a quiet little street across from the tiny Romanesque church of Sant Nicolau and the Museu Arqueològic housed in the church of Sant Pere de Galligants. The menu features creative *cuina d'autor* (innovative cuisine) with fresh local ingredients and many interesting twists on Catalan standards. The 15€ midday menu is a superb deal.

Plaça Santa Llúcia 4 (Old Quarter). ☎ ***972-20-96-54.*** *Reservations recommended. Main courses: 9€–19€ ($11–$23). MC, V. Open: Lunch and dinner Mon–Sat.*

Exploring Girona

Girona may be small, but it's filled with sights to see — most of them in the heart of the Casco Antiguo, or Old Quarter. The **Tourist Information Office** offers guided visits (in English as well as Spanish and Catalan) to the Old Quarter year-round. Daily two-hour walking tours begin at the Punt de Venvinguda (meeting point) at 10:30 a.m. (10€/$12). For more information, call ☎ **972-21-16-78.**

The top attractions

Girona's splendid **Old Quarter,** a harmonious, orderly, and compact center of cobble-stoned streets and stone mansions and churches, is the focus of any visit to the city. As long as you're not trailing a tour group, it's also delightfully peaceful. The city was built on an old Roman settlement surrounded by four rivers, and the original Roman walls date to the first century A.D. One can still walk along a 5km (3 mile) portion of the wall, from where you can enjoy extraordinary views of the Old City and the historic Roman tower. The entire *zona monumental* (historic district) practically begs for a little desultory wandering.

Of particular interest is the **Jewish Quarter,** or El Call (see the review later in this section). The main street in the Call, Carrer La Força, is the old roman Vía Augusta. Girona, which had a Jewish presence for some six centuries, is one of several cities in Spain with strong Jewish ties; others, perhaps better known, are Toledo, Segovia, and Córdoba. For additional information on Jewish heritage in Spain and a network of Jewish sites, including tourist routes, across the country, visit `www.redjuderias.org` (the Web site's name translates as "Routes of Sepharad").

Els Banys Àrabs de Girona (Arab Baths)

The Moors made their presence known in Girona; however, the Arab Baths are one of the only reminders of that important community. Constructed in the 12th century, the Romanesque baths are among the best-preserved in Spain, having been restored in the 1920s when the government took over their administration. Light streams in from the central dome, and you can easily imagine the central role the baths must have played in the Middle Ages. If you're lucky, you may catch a cool underground art exhibit or film here. Allow a half-hour for your visit here.

Carrer Ferran el Católic, s/n. ☎ ***972-21-32-62.*** `www.banysarabs.org`. *Admission: 1.60€ ($2) adults, .80€ ($1) seniors and students. Open: Apr–Sept Mon–Sat 10 a.m.–7 p.m. and Sun 10 a.m.–2 p.m., Oct–Mar daily 10 a.m.–2 p.m.*

Cases de l'Onyar

Cases are houses, and the ones along the Onyar River are a magical sight. They shimmer in the water's reflection, and laundry flutters in the breeze. Despite the picturesque Mediterranean colors, many of the houses date to the Middle Ages — they were then outside the original walls of the Old

Museum discounts

A **Gironamuseus** card, given to you with full-price admission at any participating museum in the city, entitles you to a 50 percent discount on admission at any of the other museums. Participating museums include the Museu d'Historia dels Jueus, Museu d'Arqueologia de Catalunya-Girona, Museu d'Art, Museu del Cinema, and Museu d'Història de la Ciutat.

City. Take a sunset stroll along the river and walk across the Pont de Ferro, the iron bridge built by the Eiffel Company in 1877, 12 years before the Eiffel Tower. A visit here requires little more than a quick drive-by.

Along the Onyar River, at edge of the Old Quarter.

Catedral

Girona's dazzling cathedral, atop the fortresslike hill overlooking the city, is a can't-miss sight in the Old Quarter. Seeing the Baroque stairs — all 90 of them — may tempt you to look for a less challenging visit, but don't shy away. The cathedral, a work-in-progress for seven centuries, is worth the effort. The cloister and tower are the only surviving elements of the original, early-11th-century Romanesque building. The single nave — the cathedral has no aisles — is the widest Gothic nave in the world (and the second widest of any style, after St. Peter's in the Vatican). Don't miss the cathedral's treasury, which houses a magnificent collection of religious art. Of special interest is the gorgeous copy of the *Beatus,* St. John's eighth-century treatise on the Apocalypse. The curiously shaped 12th-century *claustros* (cloisters) contain fine columns with beautifully etched *friezes* (a series of decorations forming an ornamental band around a room). You can climb the 11th-century bell tower named for Charlemagne, but only if you can find someone manning the tower and willing to take you up — not always an easy task. Anticipate spending a half-hour or so here, more if you climb the tower. Afterward, don't miss the lovely, tranquil gardens tucked behind the cathedral and just below the city wall: Jardines de la Francesa (French Woman's Gardens) and Jardines de los Alemanes (German Gardens).

Plaça de la Catedral. ☎ ***972-21-44-26.*** *Admission to cloister and museum: 3.50€ ($4). Oct–Feb Tues–Sat 10 a.m.–2 p.m. and 4 p.m.–6 p.m., Mar–June Tues–Sat 10 a.m.–2 p.m. and 4 p.m.–7 p.m., July–Sept Tues–Sat 10 a.m.–8 p.m.*

El Call and Museu d'Història dels Jueus

Girona was home to a prosperous Jewish community for more than six centuries, until its members were expelled in 1492. Girona's Jewish ghetto, "El Call" in Catalan, is said to be the best-preserved ghetto in Western Europe. It's a tangle of narrow, dark, atmospheric streets tucked within the

Old Quarter. The first Jews arrived in A.D. 895 and constructed the first synagogue just to the right of the cathedral. The principal street in the Jewish Quarter is Carrer de la Força, where buildings date from the 13th to 15th centuries. Don't miss the ever-evolving, handsomely designed **Museu d'Historia dels Jueus,** or Jewish History Museum, in the Centre Bonastruc Ça Porta, a history center that documents the Jewish population of Girona. The fascinating story it tells of how the Jewish community lived in Girona is a little-known piece of Spanish history. The last known synagogue in the city, built in the 15th century, is part of the center. Allow an hour to visit the museum and another hour or two to walk around the old Jewish Quarter.

Guided visits of El Call ("Les Portes de la Memòria," or Portals of Memory) are held on Thursdays (in Spanish) at 6 p.m., Fridays (in Catalan) at 8 p.m., and Saturdays at 11:30 a.m. (in English) and 8 p.m. (in Spanish and Catalan). Inquire at the Museu d'Historia dels Jueus. Tours are in Hebrew, Spanish, English, and French. For reservations (15€/$18 for adults, free for children under 16), call ☎ **972-21-67-61.**

Carrer de la Força 8. ☎ ***972-21-67-61.*** www.ajuntament.gi/call. *Admission to museum: 2€ ($2) adults, 1.50€ ($1.80) students and seniors over 65. Open: May–Oct Mon–Sat 10 a.m.–8 p.m. and Sun 10 a.m.–3 p.m., Nov–Apr Mon–Sat 10 a.m.–6 p.m. and Sun 10 a.m.–3 p.m.*

Museu d'Art

Housed in a former Episcopal palace, Girona's Art Museum, one of the most important in Catalonia, covers almost 1,000 years of history and art. It features excellent Catalan Romanesque and Gothic paintings, as well as a significant collection of contemporary art. Among the highlights is a 15th-century altarpiece, *Sant Miquel de Cruïlles,* one of the finest works of Catalan Gothic art anywhere. If you missed Barcelona's Museum of Romanesque and Gothic Art, the Museu d' Art is the next best thing. Plan on spending at least an hour here.

Pujada de la Catedral 12. ☎ ***972-20-38-34.*** www.museuart.com. *Admission: 2€ ($2.40) adults, 1.50€ ($1.80) students and seniors over 65, free for children under 16. Open: Mar–Sept Tues–Sat 10 a.m.–7 p.m., Oct–Feb Tues–Sat 10 a.m.–6 p.m. and Sun 10 a.m.–2 p.m.*

More cool things to see and do

If you still have a few hours or even an extra day to spend in Girona, check out these fun activities.

- **Roaming La Rambla.** Girona's lively La Rambla de la Llibertat is shorter and less grand than Barcelona's, but it plays just as central a function in the city. The tree-lined pedestrian street in the Old Quarter is packed with chic shops and cafes, many tucked under the ancient arches. (The Rambla was the central marketplace in medieval Girona.) La Rambla begins near the Tourist Information Office, Carrer Nou, at the Onyar River.

- **Checking out Girona's other churches (and the archaeology museum). The Monestir de Sant Pere de Galligants,** Plaça de Santa Llúcia, s/n (☎ **972-20-26-32**), is a handsome 12th-century Benedictine monastery and superb example of Catalan Gothic architecture. It was once a fortress, its bell tower serving as a watchtower. The church houses the city archaeology museum **(Museu d'Arqueologia de Catalunya-Girona),** with several items culled from the Roman ruins at nearby Empúries and a stunning Roman sculpture. Incredibly, the museum dates to the mid-19th century, when it was installed in the church. Admission is 2€ ($2.50); hours are Tuesday through Saturday from 10:30 a.m. to 1:30 p.m. and 4 to 7 p.m., and Sunday from 10 a.m. to 2 p.m.; October through June, closing time is 6 p.m. The tiny **Capella de Sant Nicolau,** Plaça de Santa Llúcia, s/n, across from Sant Pere de Galligants, is a tiny Romanesque chapel that is only open when it holds contemporary and avant-garde art exhibits. If it's open in the afternoon (Tues–Sat), it's well worth a peek. **Església de Sant Feliu,** just outside the original Roman walls on Pujada de Sant Feliu (☎ **972-20-14-07**), includes an imposing bell tower, important *retablos* (altarpieces), the tomb of Saint Narciso, the patron saint of Girona, and eight splendid Paleo-Christian sarcophagi, hand-crafted in Rome from the second to the fourth centuries. It's one of the most important collections of its kind in Iberia. Admission is free; hours are daily from 9 to 10:30 a.m., 11:30 a.m. to 1 p.m., and 4 to 6:30 p.m., and holidays from 4 to 6:30 p.m.
- **Stepping into the celluloid past.** Girona recently inaugurated Spain's only cinema museum, the **Museu del Cinema,** Sèquia 1 (☎ **972-41-27-77;** `www.museudelcinema.org`), which houses the extensive private collection (more than 1,500 objects exhibited, including nine films) of Tomàs Mallol. Film buffs dig seeing the original camera of the Lumière brothers, and kids can enjoy plenty of cool interactive exhibits. Admission is 4€ ($4.80) for adults, 2€ ($2.40) for students and seniors; the museum is open May through September, Tuesday through Sunday from 10 a.m. to 8 p.m.; October through April, Tuesday through Friday from 10 a.m. to 6 p.m., Saturday from 10 a.m. to 8 p.m., and Sunday from 11 a.m. to 3 p.m. Allow about an hour for a visit.

KID FRIENDLY

Shopping for local treasures

One of the wealthiest towns in Spain, Girona has a surprising number of chic design, clothing, and home-furnishings shops sandwiched near El Call. The Rambla de la Llibertat, Carrer Argenteria, and Carrer Santa Clara (the latter across the Pont de Ferro from the Old Quarter) are the top shopping streets. One design store you shouldn't miss, if only for how coolly it's installed in a mansion in the Old Quarter, is **Pabordia,** Catedral 4 (☎ **972-20-17-04**). An attractive antiques store is **La Cononja Vella,** at the end of Plaçeta de L'Institut Vell, next to the Cathedral. A cool, tiny jewelry shop with original designs is **Majoral,** Carrer de la Forca 17. For some of the best chocolates this side of Belgium and funky chocolate drinks infused with fruit, check out **Cacao Sampaka** (which also does a respectable lunch menu), Santa Clara 45. The nearby town of **La Bispal** is famous for its ceramics; in Girona, you can find a good selection of what you'd find in La Bispal (at slightly lower prices) at **Vila Clara,** Vallesteries 40 (☎ **972-22-37-78**).

Living it up after dark

Girona was once written off as a deadly quiet town that forced all the local college-age kids to drive to Barcelona for some weekend action. No more. The Old Quarter has a number of interesting bars along La Rambla de la Llibertat (such as **L'Arcada** at no. 38; no phone) and back toward the Jewish ghetto, along Carrer de la Força. Plaza de la Independencia and Zona La Dehesa are both popular areas lined with cafes, bars, and discos. Bar/pubs worth checking out are **La Taverna de l'Abat,** in the old Bishop's quarters of the Sant Pere de Galligants monastery on Plaça de Santa Llùcia (☎ **972-21-97-04**); **Aleshores,** Plaça Independencia 4 (☎ **972-22-06-06**), with a crowded dance floor and plenty of young people; and **Sidharta,** Pedret 116 (☎ **972-22-04-20**). A cool, dark little jazz club with live music (including good touring combos) on weekends is **Sunset Jazz Club,** just beyond the Old Quarter and near the river on Jaume Pons i Marti 12 (☎ **972-08-01-45**). **Lola Café,** Carrer de la Força 7 (☎ **972-22-88-24**), is a hip spot on the most atmospheric street in the Jewish Quarter; it features occasional live music and DJs in the evening.

Beyond Girona: A Day trip to Besalú

Although the logical thing to do after experiencing medieval Girona might be to move on to follow the Dalí Triangle, hit the beaches along the Costa Brava or visit the medieval towns of the Empordá (all of which I detail later in this chapter), the province of Girona has a couple of other highlights northwest of the capital. If you can spare an extra day or two, a visit to Besalú, a wonderful little medieval town with a spectacular assembly of churches and an 11th-century bridge. By far your best bet is to travel by car; Besalú is 32km (19 miles) north of Girona along N-II.

Besalú

Besalú is a charming small town that's a study in stone. It served as a fortress of an independent principality of a large territory in the 10th and 11th centuries, and its several splendid churches and postcard-perfect medieval bridge stand as testament to the town's illustrious history. The **Oficinal Municipal de Turisme,** on arcaded Plaça Llibertat, at Major (☎ **972-59-12-40**), offers guided 75-minute tours of Besalú's historical monuments. The office distributes a nice map of town. In July and August, guides in medieval costume give night tours of the monuments, and during the first weekend in September the entire town seems to turn out in robes and swords for the **Besalú Medieval Festival.**

The **Monestir de Sant Pere,** Plaça Prat de Sant Pere, begun in 977, was originally part of a Benedictine convent. In both form and size, the church is very atypical for a Romanesque church. Surprisingly large, it is suffused with natural light, and the capitals behind the altar are beautifully carved. You can visit it by guided tour only. Around back, behind the apse, is a 12th-century Gothic portico that belonged to the **Sant Julia Hospital,** which tended to religious pilgrims. The **Església de Sant Vicenç,** also begun in 977, but, as its Gothic details suggest, finished much later, holds the tomb of Pere de Rovira and an image of the patron saint of Besalú, Dolores, meaning "the sufferings." In the Middle Ages, from the 12th to the 15th centuries, Besalú had a pretty sizeable Jewish community living in the walled El Call district. Uncovered only in the mid-1960s was a **Miqvé,** or Jewish purification baths, that dates to the 1100s. They're the only such surviving baths on the Iberian Peninsula (and one of ten in Europe). The baths are located down below Carrera Pont Vell and are next to ruins of the old synagogue. Admission is 1.05€ ($1.25), and guided visits, arranged at the tourist office, are daily at 10:30 a.m., noon, 1:30, 4:30, and 6 p.m. Nearby are two of the most attractive streets in El Call, **Comte Tallaferro** and **Rocafort.** The fortified **Pont Fortificat,** or fortified bridge, though, is the emblematic image of Besalú. Curiously angled and beautifully illuminated at night, it's one of the most spectacular Romanesque bridges in Spain. Walk across it and back through town.

If you want to spend the night in Besalú, the **Hotel Comte Tallaferro,** Ganganell 2 (☎ 972-59-16-09), is an attractive, simple hotel in a historic building. You can dine in several good restaurants in town, including the high-end **Els Fogons de Can Llaudes,** in an old chapel, Plaça Prat de Sant Pere 6 (☎ 972-59-08-58); **Can Quei,** Plaça Sant Vincenç 4 (☎ 972-59-00-85), which serves simple Catalan home cooking; **Cúria Real,** Plaça Llibertat 15 (☎ 972-59-02-63), and **Pont Vell,** Ponte Vell 28 (☎ 972-59-10-27), with gorgeous views over the medieval bridge. The last two are closed on Tuesdays.

The Dalí Triangle: Connecting the Dots

North of Girona, forming a triangle across L'Empordà and the Costa Brava, you can trace the artistic, kooky, and ultimately permanent stamp Salvador Dalí left on his native Catalonia. The so-called **Dalí Triangle** includes his self-designed legacy, the agreeably bizarre Museum-Theater in **Figueres;** the funky home he shared with his controversial and equally flamboyant wife, Gala, in **Port Lligat,** near the beautiful Costa Brava fishing village of **Cadaqués;** and the eccentric 900-year-old castle he bought Gala in **Púbol** and transformed into Dalí-land. Following Dalí's trail is an excellent way to get to know this beautiful and intensely individualistic region of Spain. By car, you can easily see these sights in a day or two, using as a base Girona, a beach town along the Costa Brava, or an inland site in the Baix Empordà (see the sections on the Baix Empordà and the Costa Brava later in this chapter).

Figueres: Dalí's Museum-Theater

Figueres, just 50km (31 miles) north of Girona, is on the tourist map for one reason: Dalí's Museum-Theater in Figueres is the third-most visited museum in Spain. Dalí's eccentric genius and personality infiltrated pop culture throughout North America and Europe, and his legacy draws hordes of the curious and the faithful. His surrealist paintings of melting watches and dreamscapes continue to exert a strong, strange hold on artists and novices alike. Likewise, the museum Dalí himself designed (and wanted to be buried in) is part theater, part amusement park.

Unassuming Figueres (Figueras in Spanish) was once a historically important town, but now it's mostly about Dalí. The artist was born here, and he was determined to build his unique museum here. Crowds flock to the museum and then quickly depart for more appealing destinations in Catalonia.

Honestly, Figueres isn't worth exploring a whole lot. It's one of the few places where I'd advise you to follow the crowds and do like the tour buses: Lose yourself in the Dalí Museum for a couple of hours, perhaps stop for lunch or an early dinner, and then get out of town.

Getting there

Figueres is about two hours north of Barcelona (on A-7) and a half-hour north of Girona (on N-II). Frequent RENFE trains run from Barcelona's Sants Station to Figueres (Barcelona–Port Bou line); the Dalí museum is approximately a ten-minute walk from the train station (on Plaça de

Hello Dalí: Egghead or *señor* dollars?

Few art figures have been as controversial — adored, puzzled over, and reviled — as Salvador Dalí. Was he a genius with a special insight into human psychology or a self-promoting fake?

The artist claimed that recurrent motifs in his work, such as melting watches and rubbery eggs, sprang from the subconscious, which is why giant white *huevos* (eggs) top both the museum in Figueres and his house in Port Lligat. Dalí maintained that he remembered being an embryo inside his mother's womb, and his interest in eggs (and soft-boiled wrist watches) served as a metaphor for his fetal experience. Whatever their artistic merit (many art scholars assert that Dalí was a trailblazing master), the surreal images certainly grab your attention.

When Dalí split from the surrealist movement and became, in the eyes of many, a blatant publicity hound with an unerring commercial streak, he was branded "Avida Dollars" by the surrealist poet André Breton. The cruelly on-target nickname, an anagram, stuck — at least among Dalí's detractors.

l'Estació, s/n; ☎ **902-24-02-02;** www.renfe.com). **Sarfa** buses (☎ **902-30-20-25;** www.sarfa.com) serve Figueres, Girona, the Costa Brava, and Barcelona. The bus station in Figueres is on Plaça de l'Estació 7 (☎ **972-67-33-54**).

Visit the **Figueres Oficina de Turisme** on Plaça del Sol, s/n (☎ **972-50-31-55**). You can also check out a small tourism kiosk at the bus station.

Dining in Figueres

Even though few visitors stick around long enough for a real meal, Figueres has a reputation as a great restaurant town (though two of its best restaurants are actually in hotels). If you stay for lunch or dinner, you can certainly eat well. **Empordà,** Antigua Centra a Francia, s/n (☎ **972-50-05-62**), is one of the best restaurants in Catalonia. As the name suggests, the restaurant focuses on the creative cooking and ingredients of the surrounding Empordà countryside. Dalí was a regular here. The tasting menu (50€, or $60) is superb. Another standout restaurant is **Durán** (Lasauca 5; ☎ **972-50-12-50**), in the hotel of the same name in the center of Figueres. It offers a very good-value fixed-price menu for about 10€ ($12).

If you're lucky enough to score a reservation and you have the deep pockets to experience what's considered to be the most-cutting edge restaurant in Europe, famed **El Bulli** is only a half-hour drive from Figures, in the town of Roses along the coast. (See the listing later in this chapter.)

Exploring Figueres

The primary attraction of Figueres is the legacy of the man who was born here and went on to become an international art superstar, as renowned for his surrealist paintings as for his idiosyncratic lifestyle: Salvador Dalí. His Teatre Museu is the reason everyone comes to Figueres, but his home along the northern Costa Brava, near Cadaqués, is every bit as good an insight into the eccentric world of Dalí.

Teatre Museu Dalí

To some, Dalí was a genius; to others, he was a freak. I'd assert that he was probably both. One of the world's most famously eccentric artists certainly left a museum befitting the stature he earned as an international art celebrity. The museum, now 25 years old, is uncompromisingly idiosyncratic, maddening, and gently witty. If you think of museums as dry, dusty places that make your lower back ache, this one may change your notion altogether. Dalí's own notion — he designed the museum himself — was closer to theater.

As an artist, Dalí was famous for surreal and highly charged imagery; as a personality, he was famous for his eccentricity and exhibitionism. The museum, like Dalí himself, means to provoke and please. It presents a variety of Dalí's works and installations, many of which feature his flamboyant,

Music and wine in Peralada

Northeast of Figueres, in the Alt Empordà (Upper Plains), the tiny hamlet of **Peralada** is famous for its 14th-century castle (site of a popular casino and the excellent Museu del Castell), esteemed Castillo de Perelada wines, and especially its summer concert series (Festival Internacional de Música Castell de Peralada). Some of the world's most prestigious opera singers, symphonies, and dance troupes come here every summer to perform under the stars outside the castle. The setting, under a canopy of stars in the castle's gardens, makes for a magical evening. Call the festival organizers at ☎ **972-53-81-25** or 93-503-86-46 or visit `www.festivalperalada.com` for further information and directions. The luxurious **Hotel Golf Peralada,** Carrer Rocabertí (☎ **972-53-88-30;** `www.golfperalada.com`) boasts a wine spa and is definitely the place to stay if you can swing it.

outrageous Russian wife, Gala. The red building, topped by giant white eggs and a recently rebuilt glass dome, and decorated with glazed ceramic loaves of bread, is every bit as understated as the pieces displayed inside — which is to say not at all. Within you find a salon that uses furniture to teasingly recreate Mae West's face (with a sofa fashioned like soft red lips), as well as a circular central patio that displays an attention-getting work he presented in New York called *Rainy Taxi* — a long black Cadillac with sprinklers inside. (They go off if you drop a coin in the box — Dalí's untethered commercialism is alive even in death.) Dalí himself is buried in a crypt here, next to a series of gold cobra statues. A new permanent exhibit, "Dalí-Joies," in an adjacent building renovated by the locally famous architect Oscar Tusquets, displays a typically oddball collection of jewels of Dalí's design.

Given the crowds and theatrical peculiarities of the museum, expect to spend the better part of a morning or afternoon here.

Plaça de Gala-Salvador Dalí 5. ☎ ***972-67-75-00.*** `www.salvador-dali.org`. *Admission: 10€ ($12) adults, 7€ ($8.40) students and seniors over 65, free for children under 9; Dalí-Joies exhibit only, 6€ ($7.20) adults, 4€ ($4.80) students and adults over 65, free for children under 9. Open: Oct–June Tues–Sun 10:30 a.m.–6 p.m., July–Sept daily 9 a.m.–8 p.m.*

Museu del Joguet de Catalunya (Toy Museum of Catalonia)

Paling in comparison with favorite son Dalí, but fun for kids and kids at heart, is Spain's largest and oldest toy museum. The museum just reopened after years of extensive renovations and an expansion of its original site, the old Hotel Paris (a 1767 home of a baron). Here you can find some 4,000 toys, mostly from the 19th and early 20th centuries, including miniature theater sets, toys belonging to the Catalan artist Joan Miró, and Dalí's childhood teddy bear (also displayed are letters the poet Garcia Lorca, a close acquaintance of Dalí, wrote to the toy bear, named Don Osito Marquina).

Carrer Sant Pere 1 (in Hotel París). ☎ ***972-50-45-85.*** www.mjc.cat. *Admission: 4.50€ ($5.40) adults, 2.70€ ($3.20) children 5–11, free for children under 5. Open: June–Sept Mon–Sat 10 a.m.–1 p.m. and 4–7 p.m., Sun 11 a.m.–1:30 p.m. and 5–7:30 p.m.*

Cadaqués and Port Lligat: Dalí's stamping grounds

Even after he became an international superstar, Dalí continued mixing with the wizened fishermen in Cadaqués. The town gained international fame when Dalí groupies sought out the artist here and next door at Port Lligat. Cadaqués certainly looks the part of the perfect seaside Mediterranean village. Even when bands of playboys and would-be artists decided to set up camp (and swim in Dalí's pool), the town didn't change all that much. In summer, the area attracts chichi Catalans in fancy cars, but Cadaqués remains small and cozy, a function of its isolation.

Access to the town is via a very long and winding (by that I mean tortuous) road, so development hasn't spoiled Cadaqués, as it has some areas farther down the coast. It's still a scenic little town — a sun-dappled cluster of whitewashed houses tucked into the hills with a pretty waterfront. (The beaches, though, are unspectacular by Costa Brava standards.) Cadaqués is ideal for a day trip combined with a visit to Port Lligat — or an even longer stay. (I've met Europeans who came on vacation 20 years ago, determined to follow the path of Dalí, and have yet to leave.) Cadaqués remains a working fishing village; you can watch the fishermen take the day's catch right to the restaurant kitchens.

Getting there

Take C-260 from Figueres, and then a twisting, maddening road down to Cadaqués (38km/23 miles). The **Cadaqués tourism office** is located on Cotxe 2-A (☎ **972-25-83-15**). Port Lligat, the tiny harbor where Dalí's home is located, is a short drive (or 20-minute walk) north of Cadaqués.

Spending the night

Cadaqués doesn't offer a whole lot in terms of hotels — just a few standard places that, although unexciting, are agreeable enough if you don't want to drive the twisting road out of town just yet. Two hotels you might try are **Playa Sol** (Platja Pianc 3; ☎ **972-25-81-00;** www.playasol.com), with nice views of the Cadaqués Bay and the town, and **Port Lligat** (Playa de Port Lligat; ☎ **972-25-81-62**), a small, isolated hotel less than a mile outside of Cadaqués proper.

Dining locally

Cap de Creus
$$$ CATALAN/INDIAN

On the easternmost point of Iberia — a rocky promontory jutting out into the Mediterranean Sea — Chris Little created a very agreeable restaurant within the stone walls of the administration building of an old lighthouse.

The kitchen turns out an interesting array of native Emporda specialties as well as, curiously enough, authentic Indian dishes. You can't go wrong with the *arroz de mariscos* (shellfish rice) or *suquet de pescado* (fish stew). The open terrace overlooking the sea provides amazing, distant views, and makes for an ideal spot for a drink. Cap de Creus also offers occasional evening jazz concerts and three rooms for rent.

*Cap de Creus, s/n. ☎ **972-19-90-05.** Reservations recommended. Main courses: 10€–18€ ($12–$22). AE, MC, V. Open: Daily lunch and dinner. Closed: Nov.*

La Galiota

$$$ CATALAN/FRENCH

A sister-run establishment and the best restaurant in town, La Galiota has been here since Dalí was the star attraction — some 30 years now. Pictures of the artist on the walls attest to his patronage. Located near the cathedral, La Galiota operates a straightforward, quality-driven kitchen. Good choices include the marinated salmon *al sueco* (Swedish style) and beef tenderloin in Port wine sauce.

*Carrer Narcís Monturiol 9. ☎ **972-25-81-87.** Reservations required. Main courses: 12€–22€ ($14–$26). AE, DC, MC, V. Open: Daily lunch and dinner. Closed: Mon–Fri Nov–May.*

Exploring Cadaqués and Port Lligat

Dalí's house in Port Lligat, a tiny fisher's village on a secluded cove along the Costa Brava (1.6km/1 mile north of Cadaqués), is the top attraction in the area, but **Cadaqués** is its rival. Taking in the relaxed and extraordinarily pretty town and its lovely views is the prime activity — if you can call that an activity. If you're moved to do more, visit the cathedral, the 17th-century **Església de Santa Maria,** and the **Museu Muncipal de Arte Contemporáneo** (Municipal Contemporary Art Museum, on Carrer Narcís Monturiol) for works by Dalí and Picasso. The museum is open Monday through Saturday from 11 a.m. to 1 p.m. and 4 to 9 p.m.

Casa-Museu Salvador Dalí

Dalí built his first home with Gala, his equally eccentric Russian-born wife, in Port Lligat. The bay views are still as gorgeous as those that seduced Dalí early in his career, and the village remains isolated — except for the nearby, wildly incongruous Club Med (where Dalí and his followers would no doubt be regulars if he were still living).

Dalí's house in Port Lligat, which climbs a small hill overlooking the bay, opened to the public in 1997. Dalí and Gala, began to acquire property in the early 1930s, cobbling together several modest fishers' residences. What became their seaside home is rustic, but the decor lives up to Dalíesque standards — living spaces sport stuffed swans, a lip sofa, and Dalí-designed chimneys. Gala's bathroom, filled with photos of the couple and famous people, is worth a look. She died here in 1982.

Having such an eccentric character as Dalí living among them must have been peculiar for villagers in this remote part of northeastern Spain. But apparently the artist forged good relationships with the people of Port Lligat and Cadaqués. To this day, local fishers speak of "Señor Dalí," using the Spanish term of respect.

Reservations are required to visit; verify hours when making reservations. Only small groups of eight at a time, with a maximum of 300 people per day, are allowed entry. A visit lasts about an hour.

Port Lligat (Cadaqués). ☎ ***972-25-10-15.*** `www.salvador-dali.org`. *Admission: 8€ ($9.60) adults, 6€ ($7.20) students and seniors over 65, free for children under 9. Open: mid-Mar to mid-June and mid-Sept to Jan 6 Tues–Sun 10:30 a.m.–6 p.m., Mid-June to mid-Sept daily 10:30 a.m.–9 p.m.*

Finding Cadaqués nightlife

In summer you find a very agreeable atmosphere along **Passeig Marítim** (the promenade) at the water's edge. Cadaqués slips out of its quiet skin and gets surprisingly wild at night. A little jazz club on the main drag, **L'Hostal,** has an illustrious history; Dalí once strode in with Mick Jagger on his arm. The club showcases reputable jazz musicians in prime tourist season and often stays open until 5 a.m. For drinks, try **Marítim** (also on the promenade), a bar that's been around since the '50s. Enjoy its nice terrace that overlooks the beach.

Púbol: A castle for Gala

The single reason to visit this tiny, isolated village on the plains of L'Empordà is to experience the medieval castle Dalí bought for his beloved princess, Gala.

Casa-Museu Castell Gala Dalí

Dalí made a gift of this 11th-century castle to his wife, Gala, in the late 1960s. Given the decidedly peculiar marital history of Gala and Dalí, and the fascinating rooms tucked inside the castle's stone walls, the residence is perhaps even more interesting than Port Lligat. During the 1970s, Gala lived here for long stretches of time, while Dalí stayed at the couple's house in Port Lligat. Gala allowed Dalí to visit only when she invited him — which was practically never. The castle, which lords above the town of Púbol, is considerably more austere than anything people associate with Dalí — although a stuffed horse greets visitors in the entrance and other odd Dalíesque touches pop up throughout. In the garden, giant cement elephants (standing awkwardly on spindly giraffe's legs) spray water through their snouts, and a small pool is adorned with an assortment of colorful busts of the composer Wagner. A bit of graffiti reads "Dalí was here."

Dalí wasn't of noble lineage, though he pretended otherwise. The king of Spain did him a bigger favor than he may have known when he decreed Dalí the "Marqués of Púbol." Dalí designed a golden throne for his wife, but he often sat in it to entertain journalists' questions.

Substantiated rumors state that the Púbol castle served as Gala's love palace. Even into her late 60s, she entertained a bevy of considerably younger men, including one young actor/hanger-on whom Gala and Dalí picked up at a performance of the musical *Hair* in New York.

After Gala died, and Dalí no longer needed his wife's permission to come, he lived in the castle for two years. In 1984, a mysterious, dangerous fire erupted in the bedroom where Dalí lay asleep. The enfeebled artist barely escaped with his life, and he never returned to the castle, even though he once hoped to be buried there alongside Gala.

Anticipate spending an hour at the castle, and make sure that you figure in transportation time, depending upon where you're coming from.

Carrer Gala Salvador Dalí, s/n. Púbol is about 25 miles south of Figueres along highway C-252; follow signs to Parlava; it's 10 miles east of Girona along C-255. Drive into town, park below the castle, and walk up. ☎ ***972-48-86-55.*** `www.salvador-dali.org`. *Admission: 6€ ($7.20) adults, 4€ ($4.80) students, free for children under 9. Open: Mid-Mar to mid-June Tues–Sun 10:30 a.m.–6 p.m. (guided visits at noon and 4 p.m., in Catalan and Spanish), mid-June to mid-Sept daily 10:30 a.m.–8 p.m. (guided visits at noon and 5 p.m.), mid-Sept to Nov 1 Tues–Sun 10:30 a.m.–6 p.m.*

L' Empordà: Visiting Medieval Villages

Several small villages of the Baix Empordà, or Lower Plains, are beautifully maintained medieval gems. The plains are dotted with small towns, but I suggest visiting **Monells, Cruïlles, Begur, Pals,** and **Peratallada.** They're all close together, and you don't need much time to see them — only long enough to walk around and have coffee or lunch. The nearby town of **La Bisbal d'Empordà** is renowned for its ceramics, though much of what the shops are churning out is pretty mass-produced these days. The main street is lined with more shops than you can possibly count or stop in. If you have room to lug something back, it's definitely worth a stop. The Baix Empordà is a terrific, relaxed place to spend a few days, and the region has some of the most stylish country hotels in Spain, many of them in ancient Catalan *masias* (farmhouses).

Getting there and getting around

The only reasonable way to see the small villages of the Baix Empordà is by car (public transportation is spotty, and it would take you days to see what you can see in a morning in a rental car). From Barcelona, take highway A-7 to C-253 and C-255; from Girona, hop on C-255. The towns are clearly signposted, but if you blink, you'll miss them, so make sure you pay attention.

For visitor information contact: the tourist offices of **Pals,** Carrer Aniceta Figueres 6 (☎ 972-66-78-57); **Begur,** Av. Onze de Setembre 5 (☎ 972-62-45-20); **Peratallada,** within Peratallada Town Hall, Carrer La Roca, s/n (☎ 972-63-40-05); and for **Cruïlles** and **Monells,** the Tourist Office of La Bisbal d'Empordà, Plaça del Castell s/n (☎ 972-64-25-93).

Where to stay and dine in the Baix Empordà

Many of the rustic hotels in the Baix Empordà have excellent restaurants attached. ***Note:*** Several Costa Brava hotels and restaurants are close enough to be worth considering while you explore this region (see "Where to stay and dine on the Costa Brava," later in this chapter.)

AiguaClara Hotel

$$–$$$ Begur

Right in the midst of pretty Begur, a quiet town that makes a great place to stay, this exquisite, small hotel inhabits the 1866 Colonial-style small palace. Designed and run by a friendly young couple, the eight spacious and sun-filled rooms ooze charm and good taste, with just the right touch of bohemia (seen in old chandeliers, eclectic furnishings, gauzy fabrics, and warm paint tones). Prices are so reasonable that this is the perfect place to splurge on the Aiguaclara junior suite, which is two rooms with a marvelous rooftop terrace. Surprising for such a small hotel, it has a lovely, distinguished, and good-value restaurant on a covered patio.

St. Miquel 2, Begur. ☎ ***972-62-29-05.*** *Fax: 972-62-32-86.* `www.aiguaclara.com`. *Free parking. Rack rates: 87€–140€ ($104–$168) double. AE, DC, MC, V.*

Can Climent i Sa Cuina

$$$–$$$$ Begur INNOVATIVE CATALAN

An adorable little place on the way into town, the elegantly rustic dining room is like the kitchen of an old farmhouse. The young chef-owner, Sergi Climent, who worked in some of the most renowned kitchens in Spain, creates Catalan specialties with innovative twists, using local produce and meats. The midday menu, one of the most carefully and artistically presented inexpensive (13€/$16) menus I've had in Spain, is a steal.

Av. Onze de Setembre, Begur. ☎ ***972-62-20-31.*** *Reservations recommended for dinner. Main courses: 16€–26€ ($19–$31) MC, V. Open: Lunch and dinner Tues–Sat. Closed: Jan–Feb.*

Castell de'Empordà

$$$–$$$$ Castell d'Empordà

A 700-year-old castle magnificently converted into a charming, reasonably priced small hotel (just 27 rooms), this is one of the finest rural hotels in Spain. It is stylish and hip, but respectful of its historic frame. In a quiet corner of the Baix Empordà with a gorgeous large pool, pretty gardens, a lovely terrace, and spectacular views across the plains, this hotel is a place to relax and truly enjoy the setting. Rooms in the ancient castle are large and sumptuously decorated; those in the original tower are smaller, plainer, and cheaper; and the new garden wing is much more contemporary, though no less comfortable, with in-room balconies offering splendid views. Large, brand-new Garden Suites are stunningly chic. I'm hard-pressed to say which I like more, though given a choice, I might opt for the Suite Pere Magrit, the ultimate in decadence. Serving fresh Mediterranean dishes, the excellent restaurant is handsome, but dining outdoors on the candlelit patio is even more appetizing, as is hanging out at the bar in the castle's old wine cellar.

Castell d'Empordà, s/n. Castell d'Empordà (3km/about 2 miles from La Bisbal d'Empordà). ☎ ***972-64-62-54.*** *Fax: 972-64-55-00.* www.castelldemporda.com. *Free parking. Rack rates: 95€–235€ ($114–$282) double. AE, DC, MC, V. Closed: Nov–Mar.*

El Convent

$$$–$$$$ Sa Riera

Tucked between the lovely Sa Riera beach and the handsome hilltop town of Begur, this newly reconditioned convent is a very nice, quiet place to stay, with beautiful gardens and a pool. Rooms are well outfitted, if just a step below deluxe. Although the hotel is cleft into the hillside above the beach, the only room with a view of the water is the very cool (and reasonably priced) suite in the tower, which contains three narrow floors, with a sitting room on the third floor from where you can gaze at the ocean. For longer stays, check out this deal: After the first night, subsequent nights are offered at about a 30 percent discount.

Carrer del Racó 2 (Sa Riera, about 2km/1 mile from Begur). ☎ ***972-62-30-91.*** *Fax: 972-62-31-04.* www.conventbegur.com. *Free parking. Rack rates: 115€–210€ ($138–$252) double. MC, V.*

Hostalet 1701

$$$ Monells

The quiet village of Monells, with its atmospheric stone archways, is one of the Empordà's stunners, so it's a pleasure to find a warm and welcoming little inn right on the main plaza. This place, part antiques shop and part homey, stylish inn, features a half-dozen rooms simply but nicely outfitted with furnishings that guests can purchase if they wish. There's an antiques shop on the ground floor, and given that and the "lived-in" library, dining room, and living room, it's a surprise to find such amenities as a funky indoor pool with a Jacuzzi and cool skylight, as well as a relaxing courtyard solarium with a fountain. Rooms have either a terrace or a chimney, and dinner can be arranged for just 30€.

Plaça Jaume 1, no. 1, Monells. ☎ ***972-63-00-12.*** *Fax 972-63-00-73.* www.hostalet1701.com. *Free parking. Rack rates: 140€–150eu ($168–$180) double. AE, DC, MC, V.*

Hotel El Pati

$$$ Peratallada

In the gorgeously rustic village of Peratallada is this excellent find, a tiny (5-room) inn and restaurant that spills out onto a soothingly verdant patio (hence the name, El Pati). The ambience-filled 18th-century Catalan country house is tucked away on a quiet side street in the heart of the village, in the shadow of the bell tower, and rooms are very romantic, decorated with well-chosen and well-worn antiques. The restaurant is so attractive that it's unlikely you'll want to venture out in search of a meal.

*Hospital 13, Peratallada. ☎ **972-63-40-69.** No fax.* www.hotelelpati.net. *Free parking. Rack rates: 140€ ($168) double. AE, DC, MC, V.*

La Plaça de Madremanya
$$$–$$$$ Madremanya CATALAN

In a tiny, unassuming Catalan village about halfway between Girona and the coast, this absolutely stunning country hotel, converted from a 14th-to-15th-century farmhouse, bursts with more chic style than most urban hotels. The rooms are exquisite, with wonderful, surprising touches. The room my wife and I stayed in, El Xiprer, had a poetic inscription engraved in the wall above the bed in large, romantic letters, a splendid terrace overlooking the gardens, and subtle pool and with distant views of the green rolling Gavarres hills, and a sumptuous stone bathtub large enough for indulgent honeymooners. For this level of style and comfort, the place is unquestioningly a bargain.

Yet the hotel is best known for its handsome restaurant, La Plaça, one of the finest in L'Empordà and a longtime favorite of vacationing Barcelonans. Now under the helm of a young, innovative Catalan chef who spent his childhood in Australia, La Plaça's prix-fixe tasting menu at dinner, just 40€, is about as good a haute-cuisine deal as you'll find in Spain.

*Sant Esteve 17. Madremanya. ☎ **972-49-04-87.** Fax 972-49-05-97.* www.laplacamadremanya.com. *Free parking. Rack rates: 99€–155eu ($119–$186) double. AE, DC, MC, V.*

Mas de Torrent
$$$$$ Torrent CATALAN

If you spring for a splurge, this Relais & Châteaux property is the kind of hotel and restaurant that makes your trip to Spain memorable. A 1751 *masía* (Catalan farmhouse), the hotel is an exercise in rustic elegance. It's charming, peaceful, and geared toward the pleasure-seeker. The gardens and pool are splendid, and the hotel is perfectly placed for car or bicycle explorations of the surrounding Empordà (the medieval towns mentioned in the chapter are just minutes away) and the Costa Brava. Try to get one of the suites in the main house, because they're infinitely more charming than the bungalows in the newer wings; if you're paying to stay here at all, you may as well splurge.

The restaurant is easily one of the region's best, serving fresh fish from the coast (such as *dorada al romero,* or John Dory in romero sauce) and meats from the countryside (try the *solomillo de ternera al foie con salsa de setas* — beef sirloin with foie gras and wild mushroom sauce). The wine cellar contains an outstanding selection of Spanish and French wines.

Get out the clubs: Golfing in Girona, L'Empordà, and the Costa Brava

With nearly a dozen well-kept courses, and offering the possibility to play year-round, Girona is one of the top golfing regions in Spain. Two courses where you're welcome to play are **Club de Golf Costa Brava** (Santa Cristina de Aro, 5km/3 miles from San Feliú de Guíxols, 18 holes; ☎ **972-83-70-55;** www.golfcostabrava.com; greens fee 39€–60€/$47–$72) and **Golf Platja de Pals,** the oldest in the region (Playa de Pals, 7km/4miles from Bagur, 18 holes; ☎ **972-63-60-06;** www.golfplatjadepals.com; greens fee 40€–70€/$48–$84). For additional information on courses and golfing in Girona, L'Empordà, and the Costa Brava, visit www.costabrava.org.

Afueras de Torrent, s/n (Torrent, 6km/about 3 miles from Palafrugell). ☎ ***972-30-32-92.*** *Fax: 972-30-32-93.* www.mastorrent.com. *Free parking. Rack rates: 275€–390€ ($330–$468) double. AE, DC, MC, V. From Jan 15–Feb 15, the restaurant (main courses 24€–50€) is closed to the public, but open to guests.*

Sa Punta

$$$–$$$$ **Platja de Pals**

About a half-mile from the beach, and just outside the perfect medieval ensemble of Pals, this small hotel and restaurant is a great place for lunch if you're touring the Costa Brava beaches or inland villages. If you're staying overnight nearby (or here — it has 25 comfortable rooms, and a huge pool, gym, and sauna), it's also perfect for a romantic dinner. The setting, amid pine trees and tranquil gardens, is lovely. The menu, like most good restaurants in the area, focuses on traditional specialties of the Empordà, such as *Rossejat de arroz con gambas de Palamós* (a baked rice dish with shrimp tails). For dessert, don't miss the *helado de crema catalana* (Catalan custard ice cream).

Urbanización Sa Punta, s/n (Platja de Pals). ☎ ***972-63-64-10.*** *Fax: 972-66-73-15.* www.hotelsapunta.com. *Free parking. Rack rates: 100€–150€ ($120–$180) double. AE, DC, MC, V. Restaurant open daily for lunch and dinner. Main courses: 16€–26€ ($19–$31).*

Exploring the Baix Empordà

You can easily visit all the towns I mention in this section in a single day trip, although you may be tempted to linger and perhaps spend the night in one or more.

Cruïlles and Monells: Unassuming charm

These two quiet villages, connected administratively, are the kind of low-key places to which most people want to retire (but maybe not after seeing the prices for these old stone houses). The villages, handsome and sturdy enclaves of medieval stonework, are completely unassuming. Monells's main feature is a handsome porticoed main square, whilc at the center of Cruïlles, which was once enclosed by walls, is a Romanesque 11th-century monastery.

Begur: A hilltop gem

Gentle, sun-baked Begur occupies a privileged position, with its tile-roof houses sprinkling the sides of a forested hill, at the top of which are ruins of a 13th-century, crenulated castle. Many of the houses have a unique colonial style; in the early 19th century, economic crisis in Begur prompted many locals to set out for Cuba, and having found fortune there, they returned to build their colonial-style dream houses (called *casas indianas*).

After a look around **Plaça de la Villa,** the town square, and its small Gothic church, **Esglèsia Sant Pere** — which has a fascinating series of gray-blue, almost chiaroscuro panels behind and above the altar — climb the antic **Carrer del Castell** and the paved path that winds up the hillside to the castle. There you'll find commanding 360-degree views of the whole of L'Empordà and the Costa Brava, all the way up the coast to Cadaqués (38km/24 miles away). A handy circular map at the top helps you identify all the towns below. Located near excellent beaches (including Aiguablava, Sa Riera, and Sa Tuna) and walking paths, and boasting a couple of terrific small hotels and a superb restaurant (see "Where to stay and dine in the Baix Empordà," earlier in this chapter), Begur makes one of the finest bases from which to explore the region.

Pals: Medieval perfection

A picture-perfect medieval town, Pals sits atop a rise, its silhouette visible from miles around on the plains. Hugely popular with day-trippers, it's a pristine place, meticulously restored and almost too perfect to be real. The tiny alleys and thick stone walls look as though they might be part of a movie set. All kinds of Gothic details, such as windows and wells, adorn Pal's immaculate mansions. Look for the circular Romanesque tower **Torre de les Hores** and the **Church of Sant Pere.** Climb to the lookout point **Mirador del Pedró** for unequaled views of the countryside and coast (on clear days, you can see the Medes Islands).

Peratallada: An unusual castle

Pals (see previous section) is pretty as can be, but I like Peratallada (peh-rah-tah-*ya*-da) even better. More rugged and a bit less slick, it has a history that's readily apparent. An old fortified nucleus, the town grew up around an unusual castle, Castell de Peratallada, which today houses a fine restaurant and a tiny, charming hotel (see "Where to stay and dine in the Baix Empordà," earlier in this chapter). Walking along Peratallada's twisting stone streets, you discover a 14th-century palace, a porticoed main square, and houses rich with Gothic details. The town, a favorite of in-the-know city dwellers from Barcelona, also has a handful of interesting antiques dealers.

The Costa Brava: Resorts and Rugged Beauty

The fabled Costa Brava, the sandy playground of thousands upon thousands of Europeans, stretches for 200km (125 miles), from Blanes, just north of Barcelona, all the way to Cap de Creus and the French border. The coast is an enticing mix of mountains, plains, long sandy stretches, and tiny, gorgeous coves thick with pine trees.

Unless you want to be sorely disappointed, pick and choose carefully when deciding where to stay, and which beaches and coves to visit, on the Costa Brava. In several places — especially the lower half, nearest Barcelona — some of the most overcrowded, overdeveloped, and repugnant tourist ghettoes in Spain have grown up around cheap, mass-market tourism, and have unforgivably wrecked much of the coast's natural beauty. The undisputed megawatt star of the European package tour is **Lloret de Mar,** about 56km (35 miles) north of Barcelona. An overdeveloped and rather crass commercial beach resort, it's the equal of Cancún, or worse. (Other horror spots include Benidorm, near Valencia, and the Costa del Sol in the south.)

Luckily, other places tucked along the coast are well worth exploring for their beauty and seclusion, including charming fishing villages, tiny pine-forested coves, and Empúries, the site of Spain's most impressive Greco-Roman ruins. If you choose not to stay right on the coast, you can easily access these spots from Girona and the medieval towns of the Baix Empordà that I describe earlier in "L'Empordà: Visiting Medieval Villages." In fact, many travelers are discovering that staying at relatively higher-quality inns in the Baix Empordà is preferable to staying at more conventional beach hotels.

Northern Europeans — Germans, Dutch, French, and, increasingly, such newly moneyed Eastern Europeans as Czechs and Russians — overrun parts of the Costa Brava in summer. If you don't want to feel like you've landed unwittingly in a Euro Club Med, stay away from Lloret de Mar, Platja d'Aro, and, to a slightly lesser degree, Tossa de Mar. The cliff-top road that passes these towns, however, makes for a splendidly scenic coastal drive.

Getting there and getting around

Outside of the major destinations, a car remains your best bet for seeing the Costa Brava without waiting for public transportation. Unless you stay at a hotel within walking distance of a beach, a car is particularly important to get to some of the more isolated coves and beaches. For more information after you arrive, contact the tourist information offices in **Palafrugell,** Carrilet 2 (☎ 972-61-18-20); **Sant Feliu de Guixols,** Plaça del Mercat 28 (☎ 972-82-00-51); **Tamariu,** Carrer de la Riera, s/n (☎ 972-62-01-93); or **Llafranc,** Carrer Roger de Llúria, s/n (☎ 972-30-50-08).

Beach watch

The Costa Brava has some beautiful beaches, but many of them suffer from overdeveloped tourism. The following is a list of beaches awarded blue flags (the top rating for best swimming conditions) by the European Union.

Town	Best swimming beach(es)
Begur	Sa Riera, Aiguablava
Palafrugell	Tamariu, Llafranc, Canadell
Palamós	La Fosca
Sant Antoni de Calonge	Torre Valentina, Torretes
Sant Feliu de Guíxols	Platja de Sant Feliu, Sant Pol, Canyerets

By car

The main road, C-255, travels along the lower coast and darts inland; C-252 is the principal road for the northern half of the Costa Brava. From these major thoroughfares, you need to get off onto local, signposted roads, which lead to individual coastal villages and resorts.

By bus

Sarfa (☎ **902-30-20-25;** www.sarfa.com) buses operate throughout the Costa Brava from Girona and Figueres.

By train

Trains leave from Girona's **Plaça d'Espanya** and make their way to several points along the Costa Brava, including Llança, Blanes, and Colera, with increased service in summer. For more information concerning trains along the coast, call ☎ **902-24-02-02** (www.renfe.es).

Where to stay and dine on the Costa Brava

In the high summer months (July and Aug) you may have a hard time finding an available hotel room along the Costa Brava, but in the dead of winter (when the area is actually quite beautiful, and not that cold), you'll have trouble finding hotels and restaurants that are open at all. Much of the coast, including Cadaqués, pretty much boards up the windows. For dining, try **El Bulli,** one of Spain's most celebrated restaurants. It's very expensive and difficult to get to, but a singularly rewarding dining experience for those who make it there. Note that several Baix Empordà hotels and restaurants — especially those near Begur — are close enough to be worth considering while exploring the Costa Brava (see "Where to stay and dine in the Baix Empordà," earlier in this chapter.)

El Bulli

$$$$$ Roses FRENCH/CATALAN

South of Cadaqués and east of Figueres, near Roses, is one of the gastronomic highlights of Spain, if not all Europe: the legendary El Bulli, well worth a road trip for any self-respecting foodie. Ferrán Adrià has become known worldwide as one of the most innovative chefs working today. *Gourmet* magazine called him the "Dalí of the kitchen," and he is one of the few chefs ever to grace the cover of the *New York Times Magazine*. His restaurant, thought by many to be the best in Spain — it surely is the most imaginative — is idiosyncratic and experimental. Adrià spends half the year holed up in a laboratory in Barcelona creating intoxicating new dishes using revolutionary techniques. The menu is ever-changing, and individual courses are almost beyond description: items dominated by air, foam, and liquid, which you have to see and eat to believe just how good they truly are. The wine list and service are appropriately first-rate. True, getting a reservation is next to impossible (I've read that El Bulli receives 30,000 requests a month), and eating here may require a special slush fund, but all that cash will buy you a very memorable meal and the envy of diners worldwide.

Cala Montjoi, Ap. 3D (Roses). ☎ ***972-15-04-57.*** www.elbulli.com. *Main courses: 32€–55€ ($38–$66). Tasting menu: 150€ ($180). AE, DC, MC, V. Open: Dinner only, Apr–June Wed–Sun 8–11 p.m., July–Sept daily 8–11 p.m. Closed: Oct–Mar.*

El Far Hotel Restaurant

$$$$–$$$$$ Platja de Llafranc

The owners of Mas de Torrent (see "Where to stay and dine in the Baix Empordà" section, earlier in this chapter) opened this small hotel with great old bones — the cliff-top property includes a 17th-century hermitage and a 15th-century lighthouse — on a historic site high above the Bay of Llafranc. The hotel is perched on a coastal hill amid thick pine forest and walking trails with just nine charming and colorfully decorated rooms built around a beautiful interior 18th-century patio. From the balconies of several rooms, and the terrace overlooking the ocean, the 180-degree uninterrupted views of the sea and coastline are absolutely unbeatable. El Far is a hugely popular site for weddings, and any other time it makes for a very refined and relaxed stay. Serving seasonal Catalan cuisine, the restaurant is excellent, and both half- and full-board programs are available.

Platja de Llafranc (near Palafrugell). ☎ ***972-30-16-39.*** *Fax: 972-30-43-28.* www.elfar.net. *Free parking. Rack rates: 175€–300€ ($210–$360) double.*

Hostal de la Gavina

$$$$–$$$$$ S'Agaró CATALAN

One of the most famous hotels on the Costa Brava, this classic retreat — which has hosted everyone from Humphrey Bogart to Mick Jagger — is tucked in popular and touristy S'Agaró (between Sant Feliu and Cap Roig).

Swimming in Old World luxury and Mediterranean style, graceful and elegant Hostal de la Gavina has welcomed Spaniards and international guests with perfect service and comfort since 1932. It's clearly not your typical Costa Brava hotel. Rooms are opulent with quality antiques and furnishings, and the hotel features include an Olympic-size salt-water pool graced by statuary and a full spa. Tennis, horseback riding, and massages are also options. The elegant rooms overlooking the gentle curve of S'Agaró Beach are consistently in high demand.

If you can't squeeze in an overnight stay, or prefer to indulge your taste buds, the hotel's restaurant (same phone number) is also one of the finest on the Costa Brava. The elegant dining room serves fine Catalan cuisine, including great fresh seafood, and the more informal terrace offers lighter, but still excellent dishes.

Plaça de la Rosaleda, s/n (S'Agaró). ☎ ***972-32-11-00.*** *Fax: 972-32-15-73.* www.lagavina.com. *Free covered parking. Rack rates: 185€–310€ ($222–$372) double. AE, DC, MC, V. Restaurant closed: Mid-Oct to Easter week. Main courses: 19€–36€ ($23–$43).*

Hotel Aigua Blava

$$$–$$$$ Aiguablava

On Fornells cove, next to the water and surrounded by a remarkable expanse of private gardens, this midsize hotel is one of the better conventional beach hotels along the Costa Brava. In my opinion, it's preferable to the nearby *parador* (government-run hotel) even if it doesn't have the latter's dramatic cliff-top location. Rooms are large and airy, the service personal and gracious. Enjoy the tennis court, pool, and superb views of the cove from the garden — all elements sure to appeal to the kids. The restaurant (same phone number) serves local Ampurdanés cuisine and is fairly priced.

Platja de Fornells, s/n (Aiguablava). ☎ ***972-62-45-62.*** *Fax: 972-62-21-12.* www.aiguablava.com. *Free parking. Rack rates: 139€–224€ ($167–$267) double. AE, MC, V. Closed: Second week of Nov to mid-Feb.*

Hotel Llevant

$$$–$$$$ Platja de Llafranc

This traditional family-run hotel, right on one of the prettiest coves along the Costa Brava, has been around since 1935. Nicely updated, and with a terrific restaurant that opens right to the beach, it's one of the better small coastal properties, but you pay for the privilege of walking out your door and right onto the sand.

Francesc de blanes 5 (Llafranca). ☎ ***972-30-03-66.*** *Fax: 972-30-03-45.* www.hotel-llevant.com. *Free parking. Rack rates: 70€–192€ ($84–$230) double. MC, V.*

La Xicra

$$$–$$$$ Palafrugell CATALAN

For fine local Catalan cooking in the heart of the Empordà region, La Xicra (*shee*-kra) is well worth a stop. The kitchen continually comes up with creative dishes that bring in both regulars and tourists. From fish soup to *calçats* (long green leeks, a Catalan specialty) and *merluza al cava* (hake — a white fish — in Catalan sparkling wine), choosing an unsatisfying dish here is nearly impossible.

Estret 17 (Palafrugell, near Llafranc). ☎ ***972-030-56-30.*** *Main courses: 12€–24€ ($14–$29). MC, V. Open: Lunch and dinner Thurs–Mon, lunch only Tues. Closed: Nov.*

Parador de Aiguablava

$$$ Aiguablava CATALAN

With an enviable perch among the pine trees on a tiny peninsula above a beautiful cove and the Mediterranean Sea, this modern white box of a hotel is a favorite with many travelers, even if it diverges from the more standard offerings of the generally excellent *parador* chain (see Chapter 7 for more information on *paradores*). The views are astonishing, and the pool quite nice, but it's a little hard not to find it a blight on the surrounding cliffs and forest. If you can get past that, this well positioned hotel, with contemporary, well-kept rooms, is the best place to discover that Spanish *paradores* don't always occupy castles and palaces.

The restaurant (same phone number) serves local Ampurdanés cuisine, and is very fairly priced. Its young chef, Lluis Ferrés, is quickly gaining a reputation for his creative local dishes (18€–32€/$23–$41), like *suquet de rape* (monkfish stew). The wine cellar is one of the better ones on the coast.

Platja de Aiguablava, s/n (Aiguablava). ☎ ***972-62-21-62.*** *Fax: 972-62-21-66.* `www.parador.es`. *Free parking. Rack rates: 130€–140€ ($156–$168) double. AE, DC, MC, V.*

Exploring the Costa Brava

Sant Feliu de Guixols is the beginning of the "good" Costa Brava. A historic, easygoing town with a tenth-century church and a lovely 18th-century chapel high on a hill overlooking the rugged coastline, Sant Feliu de Guixols is now mostly submerged under the primary industries of tourism and second-home ownership. Kids of all ages may get a kick out of the **Museu D'Història de la Joguina** (Toy Museum), Rambla Vidal 48. **Palamós,** an attractive old fishing village, with boats bobbing in two bays, is an interesting study of a Costa Brava town caught between tradition, centered on fishing, and modern development, focused on tourism. Its Old Quarter is mostly dwarfed by new construction, though it hides a few traditional restaurants.

Some of the most attractive coves and beach spots along the entire coast are near Palafrugell. **Calella de Palafrugell, Llafranc,** and **Tamariu** — the latter, lined with the tamarind trees that give the town its name — are all small, gentle protected spots with good swimming and excellent paths for walking up into the pine-forested hills. Tiny, predominantly whitewashed villages, many of them old fishing villages, are tucked in among the rocks, trees, and white sands, with clusters of family-run hotels and restaurants, perfect for leisurely beach stays.

High up on **Cap Roig,** a peninsula near Calella de Palafrugell, is an incredible estate that once belonged to a Russian army general (referred to simply as "El Ruso"). It is now a botanical garden (☎ **972-61-45-82**) with extraordinary Mediterranean gardens and super views of the coast. In July and August, the garden hosts the **Festival Jardins de Cap Roig,** featuring jazz, flamenco, and world music, as well as theater productions. Also worth a visit, for the stunning coastal views alone, is **El Far de Sant Sebastià,** a 19th-century lighthouse high above Platja de Llafranc. It's now a luxury hotel and restaurant, El Far Hotel Restaurant (see "Where to stay and dine on the Costa Brava" earlier in this chapter).

Farther north along the coast, near the town of **Begur** (see "Exploring the Baix Empordà" earlier in this chapter) are gorgeous coves, including **Aiguablava, Sa Tuna, Sa Riera,** and **El Racó.**

Taking a side trip to the Greco-Roman ruins of Empúries

Near the summer resort town of L'Escala, along the coast, are the extensive ruins of a Greco-Roman city, **Museu d'Empúries,** or the Museu d'Arqueologia de Catalunya (☎ **972-77-02-08;** `www.mac.es`), one of the most fascinating archaeological finds in Spain. Three different civilizations settled on the coast here between the seventh and third centuries B.C.: the Indigetes, the Greeks, and the Romans. (Empúries is the only place in Spain with incarnations as a Greek village, an Iberian settlement, and a Roman town.) The sea wall is an important engineering achievement, and the Roman mosaic floors are equally impressive.

To visit Museu d'Empúries, take N-II north and make the turn-off toward the coast and L'Escala (signs indicate the Museu d'Empúries). Getting there by bus is a little complicated. You have to take the **Sarfa Girona–L'Escala** bus and ask the driver to let you off at Empúries, which is a ten-minute walk from the main road. Admission is 2.50€ ($3) adults, 2€ ($2.40) seniors and students 16 to 18, and free for children under 16. Hours are June 1 to September 30, daily from 10 a.m. to 8 p.m., October 1 to May 31, daily from 10 a.m. to 6 p.m.

Fast Facts: Girona and the Costa Brava

Area Code

The area code for telephone numbers throughout the province of Girona is **972.** Because the prefix is three digits, only six numbers follow — making a total of nine digits, as throughout Spain. You must dial them all, even when making local calls.

Currency Exchange

Downtown Girona, near the tourist information office, has a number of banks and *casas de cambio* (exchange houses). Stop by the office at Rambla de la Llibertat 2, along the river, or call the tourism office at ☎ 972-22-65-75, for specific locations. All the towns of any size along the Costa Brava and in L'Empordà have banks with ATMs.

Emergencies

Dial ☎ **091** or ☎ **112.** For medical emergencies, call ☎ **061.**

Hospitals

Girona: Hospital de Girona Dr. Trueta (☎ 972-94-02-00); Figueres: Hospital de Figueres (☎ 972-50-14-00); Blanes: Hospital Comarcal de la Selva (☎ 972-35-32-64); Lloret de Mar: Hospital Lloret de Mar (☎ 972-36-47-36).

Information

Girona has three Turisme (tourism information) offices: at the train station, at Rambla de la Llibertat 1 (☎ 972-22-65-75), and at Punt de Venvinguda, Berenguer Carnicer 3 (☎ 972-21-16-78). They're open weekdays from 8 a.m. to 8 p.m., Saturdays from 8 a.m. to 2 p.m. and 4 to 8 p.m., and Sundays from 9 a.m. to 2 p.m. For broader provincial information, contact Patronat de Turisme Costa Brava/Girona (☎ 972-20-84-01; `www.costabrava.org`).

The Figueres tourism office is on Plaça del Sol, s/n (☎ 972-50-31-55).

The Cadaqués tourism office is on Cotxe 2-A (☎ 972-25-83-15).

Police

Dial ☎ **092** in most towns; in Girona, the police station is on Av. Jaume I 18 (☎ 972-20-50-50). In Figueres, contact the Policía Municipal at ☎ 972-51-01-11.

Post Office

The Central Post Office in Girona is on Av. d'En Ramon Folch (☎ 972-20-16-87). It's open Monday to Friday from 8:30 a.m. to 9 p.m. and Saturday from 8 a.m. to 8 p.m.

Chapter 12

The Basque Country and Navarra

In This Chapter

- Getting to and around the Basque Country and Navarra
- "Basque"-ing in art at the Guggenheim Museum in Bilbao
- Wine tasting in La Rioja Alavesa
- Dining and relaxing in San Sebastián
- Sampling Basque food
- Joining the stampede in Pamplona

Spain's great, green north — España Verde — begins in the Basque Country and Navarra, just west of the French border. These historic regions, wedged between the Pyrenees Mountains and the Cantabrian Sea, are characterized by rugged terrain and a famously reserved, independent-minded people. Yet the regions are also famous for star attractions with all the quiet and reserve of a Hollywood Oscar bash: Bilbao's gleaming Guggenheim Museum, San Sebastián's sparkling bay, prized beaches, and a world-class dining scene, and Pamplona's daredevil Running of the Bulls.

Bilbao, San Sebastián, and Pamplona are all within two hours of each other by road or rail. The wine country of La Rioja is also only a couple of hours south from any of these cities. Not called España Verde for nothing, the north is characterized by frequent mist and rain, though brilliant sunshine is also delightfully common, and the region is spectacularly green year-round. Spring, summer, and fall are terrific seasons to visit northern Spain, though in July and August, San Sebastián is full of vacationing Spaniards and French, and Bilbao's Guggenheim is packed with tour groups. The Running of the Bulls in Pamplona is the second week in July, when coming up with a hotel room is pretty well impossible.

If you were to come to Spain for the sole pleasure of eating — not at all an absurd notion — the Basque Country is where you'd want to head first. So elevated and varied are the culinary arts in this part of the country that a gastronomic tour could begin and end in the Basque Country.

The Basque Country (País Vasco) and Navarra

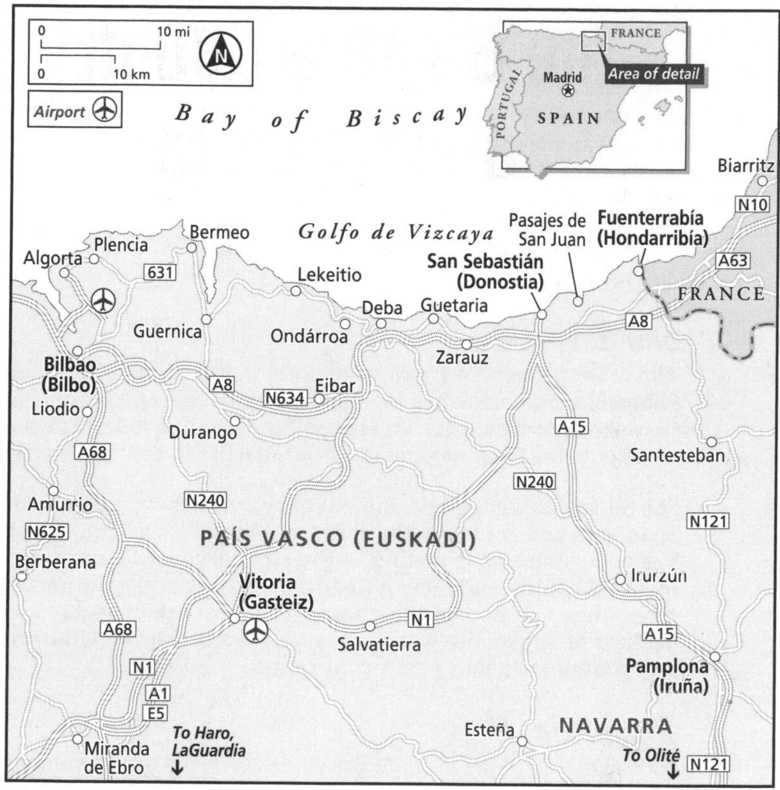

Fine dining is an inalienable fixture of Basque culture. At private gastro nomic societies, members get together to cook for each other, eat, and philosophize about food. Basques talk about food even more than they talk about politics. From tantalizing tapas — works of art called *pintxos* (*peen*-chohs) in these parts — to nine-course tasting menus at Michelin three-star restaurants, exalted dining is an everyday affair.

Major Attractions in the Basque Country and Navarra

Thanks in large part to the Guggenheim Museum's popularity, travelers are discovering a region that has been a secret kept by a select few: brawny green hills, a rocky coastline, and an imaginative cuisine that many consider the finest in all Spain.

Bilbao

The gateway to the Basque Country, **Bilbao** is Spain's biggest commercial port and the political capital of the Basque Country, an inhospitable region that repelled both the Romans and the Moors. The city stretches more than 16km (10 miles) along the River Nervión. Once known only for its shipping and steelworks prowess, it's now experiencing an architectural and cultural renaissance. Indeed, Bilbao seems to be challenging Barcelona for cutting-edge design, and swank new hotels, shops, and restaurants have mushroomed in the past five years. Here you find the **Guggenheim Bilbao,** Frank Gehry's modern masterpiece; the **Casco Viejo,** or Old Quarter, the lively heart of the city; and superb Basque dining and ***pintxos*** (tapas or Spanish appetizers).

San Sebastián

The other prominent Basque city, one that delights visitors, is **San Sebastián,** one of Spain's loveliest and most elegant cities. Capital of Guipuzcoa province, it's an easygoing, sparkling resort town on Spain's northern coast, just downwind from Biarritz in southwestern France.

San Sebastián's aesthetic and culinary delights have held vacationing Spaniards and French in thrall for more than a century. The small city has an incomparable setting — the city curves deliciously around a half-moon bay, and hills frame it at either end — perfect for panoramic pictures. Here you find **La Concha,** Spain's best urban beaches and esplanade, the mouth-watering tapas bars of the **Old Quarter,** and **gourmet dining** at Spain's best restaurants.

Pamplona

Although Pamplona (and its province Navarra) isn't technically part of the Basque Country, it shares ancient roots with the Basque people. In

The name game

As in Catalonia, street signs can get a little confusing up north in the Basque Country. Since the Basques were granted regional autonomy, the area has seen a resurgence of Euskera, the impenetrable and mysterious Basque language (though Spanish is still the primary language for most). Although not as widely spoken as Catalan, Euskera is officially represented almost anywhere you go, and knowing at least the names of cities can help. The Basque Country is called País Vasco in Spanish but Euskadi in Euskera. In Euskera, Bilbao is written Bilbo, San Sebastián is Donostia, Pamplona is Iruña, and Navarra is Nafarroa. *Sanfermines* (san-fehr-*mee*-nehs) is the summer festival with the Running of the Bulls; the actual sprint is called an *encierro* (en-*thyeh*-roh). And, most important, tapas are called *pintxos* (*peen*-chohs) up north. See "Basque-ing in obscurity: Language and politics," later in this chapter, for more on Euskera.

Basque-ing in obscurity: Language and politics

The Basques are one of the most ancient peoples in Europe. Some theorists believe that they're indigenous Iberian peoples descended from the Cro-Magnon man. Others propose, somewhat less convincingly, that the Basques are the living link to the lost city of Atlantis. Modern Basques don't feel the least rootless, however; they revel in their unknown origins, a distinction that sets them apart from the rest of Spain.

The Basque language, called Euskera, completely baffles linguists and ethnologists. Wholly unrelated to any living language, Euskera, scholars believe, pre-dates all Indo-European tongues. Look at the preponderance of letters *k, t, x,* and *y,* and the language is sure to mystify you as well. Although only a third of the population actively speaks it (but it is growing in popularity), schools teach Euskera, and local TV and radio programming broadcast in the language. Unlike with Catalan or Gallego, a knowledge of Spanish will get you nowhere. Basque is insanely difficult to pronounce and master. Knowing an obscure language such as Hungarian or Finnish would likely provide you with a better warm-up!

Not only can no one identify the origins of Euskera, but the language contains no swear words. Basques must dip into Spanish when they want to curse — a case for bilingualism if ever there was one.

Although Basques take their language and unique culture very seriously, Basque politics is an even more complicated matter. Within Spain and the rest of Europe, the Basque Country is at least partially, and unfortunately, known for a secretive terrorist group, known by its Basque-language acronym ETA. For decades, ETA (which stands for Basque Nation and Liberty) has demanded independence from Spain and the establishment of a Basque nation. The sinister organization has pursued this goal with extreme, though highly targeted, violence; hundreds of police, military personnel, and politicians have been assassinated on behalf of the cause over the years. The group's terrorist actions have provoked wide-scale public repudiation across Spain.

As a tourist, you're extremely unlikely to see any signs of the shadowy group. Few of the terrorist acts are committed on home turf, and ETA almost always refrains from indiscriminate mass killing and usually immediately claims responsibility. The previous Aznar administration — which got a lot of political mileage out of its hard-line policy against ETA — sought to place the blame for the 2004 Madrid train bombings on Basque terrorists, and the government's deception led to its electoral defeat later that year.

A true breakthrough in the decades-long conflict appeared to occur when ETA announced a "permanent cease-fire" in March 2006, and Spain's Socialist-led government said it would enter into talks with ETA to ensure a lasting peace after 40 years of violence. However, just five months later the terrorist group warned of an impasse, citing its disenchantment with the government's continued pursuit and arrests of Basque citizens and politicians, and ETA issued a statement that said the peace process was in crisis.

certain parts, locals still speak Euskera. The ninth-century fortified capital of the Kingdom of Navarra, Pamplona is a modest, provincial city with relatively few big attractions. However, it gets the attention of Spain and much of the world during its annual July eruption of daring — practiced locals and crazed visitors running through the streets with harried bulls at their heels. Here you find **San Fermín and the Running of the Bulls,** Europe's liveliest and most dangerous street party. You'll also find the **Cathedral,** a Gothic landmark, and the impressive **Navarra Museum,** near the city's medieval walls, and the new **Oteiza Museum,** dedicated to the sculptor Jorge Oteiza.

Bilbao: A City Rejuvenated

Bilbao, just 16km (10 miles) from the Cantabrian Sea, is split down the middle by the Nervión estuary — what locals call the *ría.* Founded in 1300, the city's atmospheric **Casco Viejo (Old Quarter)** sits on the right bank, connected by four bridges (including one by the other architect of the moment, Santiago Calatrava) to the much larger modern section (Abando, or New City) on the left bank. Between the Casco Viejo and the river is a wide promenade, the Arenal. The main commercial street, Gran Vía, bisects the modern part of the city, a grid called the Ensanche (the Enlargement). The new Guggenheim Museum hugs the riverbank on the northern side of modern section, while across the river is the district known as **Uribarri.**

The city's industrial image has given way to a remarkable transformation spurred on by the Guggenheim. New chic hotels, restaurants, and shops now populate the city, and local government is in the process of completing a thorough redesign of the riverfront, adding dramatic landscaping and public spaces. The finished project will represent one of the most significant urban revitalization programs in Europe.

Getting there

For information on quick trips to Bilbao from either Madrid or Barcelona, see the sidebar entitled "To Bilbao and back in a day."

By plane

Bilbao's spectacular airport, **Aeropuerto Internacional de Bilbao-Sondica (☎ 94-453-23-06)**, designed by the renowned Santiago Calatrava, lies 10km (6 miles) north of the city. It's the only international airport in the Basque Country and the one with the most flights to Madrid and Barcelona. **Iberia, Spanair,** and **Air Europa** all fly to Bilbao from other Spanish cities, and major international carriers, such as British Air, Alitalia, and Lufthansa, arrive from European cities. The airport is easy to get around. Check out the very helpful tourism office (open 7:30 a.m.–1 p.m.) right after you pick up your bags and visit the car-rental agencies, if you want to get wheels for exploring the Basque Country (País Vasco).

Bilbao

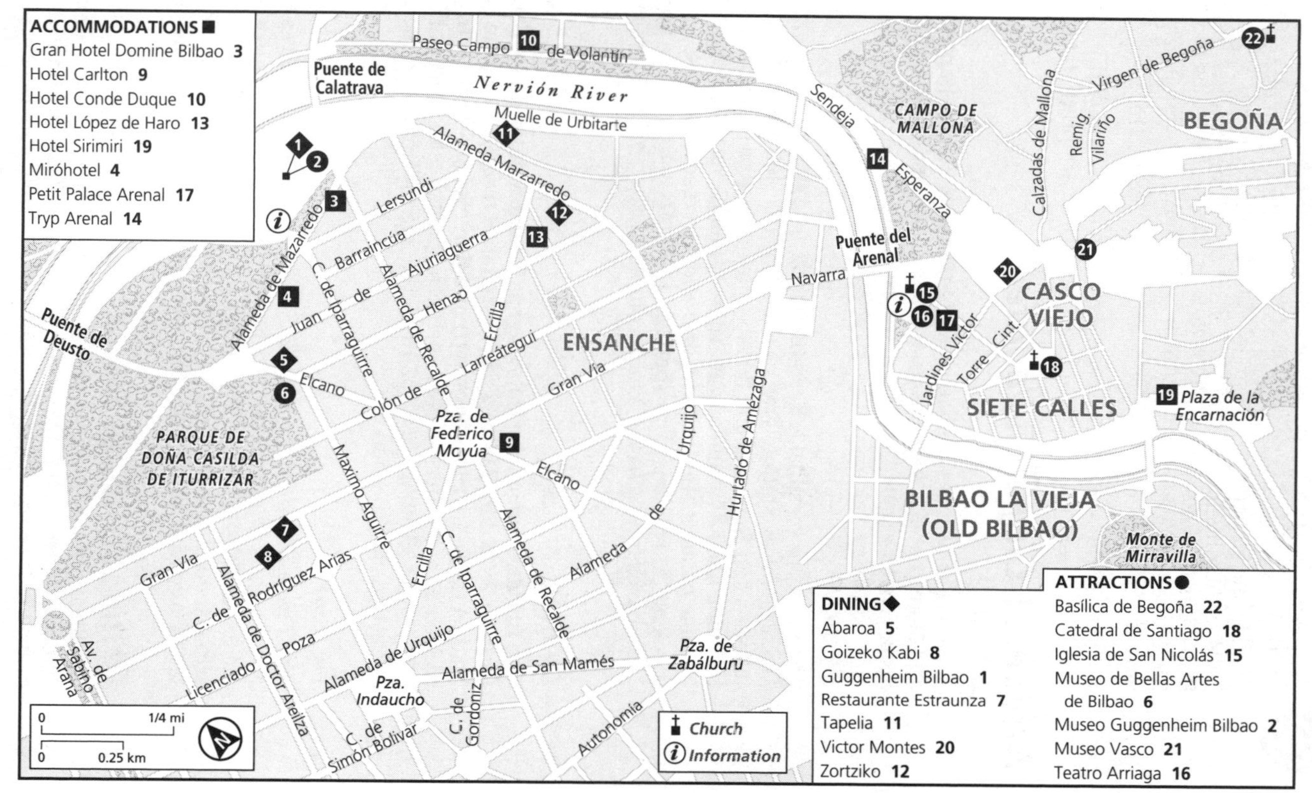
ACCOMMODATIONS ■
Gran Hotel Domine Bilbao 3
Hotel Carlton 9
Hotel Conde Duque 10
Hotel López de Haro 13
Hotel Sirimiri 19
Miróhotel 4
Petit Palace Arenal 17
Tryp Arenal 14
DINING ◆
Abaroa 5
Goizeko Kabi 8
Guggenheim Bilbao 1
Restaurante Estraunza 7
Tapelia 11
Victor Montes 20
Zortziko 12
ATTRACTIONS ●
Basílica de Begoña 22
Catedral de Santiago 18
Iglesia de San Nicolás 15
Museo de Bellas Artes de Bilbao 6
Museo Guggenheim Bilbao 2
Museo Vasco 21
Teatro Arriaga 16
Church
Information
0 1/4 mi
0 0.25 km
BEGOÑA
CAMPO DE MALLONA
CASCO VIEJO
SIETE CALLES
BILBAO LA VIEJA (OLD BILBAO)
ENSANCHE
PARQUE DE DOÑA CASILDA DE ITURRIZAR
Nervión River
Puente de Calatrava
Puente del Arenal
Puente de Deusto
Plaza de la Encarnación
Monte de Mirravilla
Pza. de Zabálburu
Pza. de Federico Moyúa
Pza. Indaucho
Paseo Campo de Volantín
Muelle de Urbitarte
Alameda Marzarredo
Alameda de Mazarredo
Alameda de Recalde
Alameda de Urquijo
Alameda de San Mamés
Alameda de Doctor Areilza
Av. de Sabino Arana
Gran Vía
C. de Iparraguirre
Ercilla
Elcano
Colón de Larreátegui
Juan de Ajuriaguerra
C. Barraincúa
Lersundi
Henao
Maximo Aguirre
C. de Rodríguez Arias
Poza
Licenciado
C. de Simón Bolívar
C. de Gordoniz
Autonomía
Hurtado de Amézaga
Urquijo
Alameda
Navarra
Sendeja
Esperanza
Jardines Victor
Torre
Cint.
Calzadas de Mallona
Remig. Vilariño
Virgen de Begoña

The **airport bus** (☎ **94-448-40-80**), just out in front of the airport, takes you along the river to the city in about 30 minutes for only 1.20€ ($1.44). (Note, though, that even if a bus is waiting to depart, surly drivers may not let you board until they're good and ready to go.) The bus drops you off next to the river, at the open-air bus station across from the Ayuntamiento (City Hall). The yellow urban bus returning to the airport from Plaza Moyua in the new town is the Bizkaibus, No. A3247, marked "Bilbao-Aeropuerto." It leaves every 30 minutes starting at 6:15 a.m.

A taxi from the airport to downtown costs about 18€ ($22). Taxis line up out front where you catch the bus (most taxis are pretty fancy rigs in northern Spain — Mercedes and Audis).

By car

You can easily access Bilbao by national highway from Barcelona (A-2) and Madrid (A-1), as well as from France (A-8) and Pamplona (the N-240). From San Sebastián, Bilbao is due west along A-8.

By bus

The main bus terminal is **Terminbús** (☎ **94-439-50-77**), next to the San Mamés subway station. Transportes Pesa (☎ **902-10-12-10**) buses travel between San Sebastián and Bilbao (one-and-a-quarter hours); Autobuses La Unión and La Burundesa arrive from Pamplona (two hours). The ANSA bus line connects Bilbao to Madrid and Barcelona. See `www.bilbao.net` (click on "Movilidad y Transportes," then "Accesos a Bilbao," and then "Autobuses Interurbanos") for a complete listing of bus companies, origins, and destinations.

By train

The **RENFE** train station is located at **Estación de Abando,** Plaza Circular 2 (☎ **902-24-02-02**). Long-distance trains come from and go to Madrid (a six- to seven-hour trip) and Barcelona (a 12-hour trip), as well as Málaga and other cities in northern Spain. Eusko Tren, Calle Atxuri 6 (☎ **94-433-95-00** or 902-54-32-10) is the line for travel to and from San Sebastián and Guernika.

By boat

The ***Pride of Bilbao* ferry** (P&O European Ferries) travels to Bilbao twice a week from Portsmouth, England (`www.poportsmouth.com`; ☎ **08705-980-333** in the United Kingdom; ☎ 902-02-04-61 in Spain). The trip lasts between 30 and 33 hours — not something to be taken lightly, especially with all the frequent, low-cost European flights available.

Getting around Bilbao

In Bilbao, you can cover almost all points of interest on foot or on the new, efficient Metro (subway) or even newer EuskoTran, the tram. If you're traveling to other city destinations in the region, you don't necessarily need a car (buses are considerably cheaper and easier to ride to both San Sebastián and Pamplona). For most rural destinations, though, a car is nearly essential.

On foot

If you stick to the New City (Abando) district and waterfront near the Guggenheim, walking is the best way to get around Bilbao. Though it's a very long walk from there to the Old Quarter (Casco Viejo), after you're in the old section, the atmospheric streets are perfect for walking (and in fact the only way to get around).

By car

To explore the countryside around Bilbao (and perhaps visit the Basque part of La Rioja; see the "Taking side trips from Bilbao" section later in the chapter), a car is your best option. The roads are among the best in Spain, though highway tolls are high. You can find major rental companies at the Bilbao airport, including

- **Avis (☎ 94-427-57-69)**
- **Europcar (☎ 94-423-93-90)**
- **Hertz (☎ 94-415-36-77)**

By Metro

The new **Metro Bilbao (☎ 94-425-40-25;** `www.metrobilbao.net`), designed by Pritzker Architecture Prize winner Sir Norman Foster, is exceedingly clean and efficient. You can't miss the unmistakable entryways, which are fanciful Plexiglas domes. Trains run from 6 a.m. to 11 p.m. Monday through Thursday, from 6 a.m. to 1 a.m. Friday, from 6 a.m. to 5 a.m. Saturday, and from 6 a.m. to 11 p.m. Sunday. A single ticket costs 1.20€ ($1.50); a ten-journey "BonoPlus" ticket — a much better deal — is 2.50€ ($3), while a single-day pass costs 3€ ($3.60).

By tram

The convenient, bright-green EuskoTran (**☎ 900-15-12-06;** `www.EuskoTran.es`) is a brand-new tram *(tranvía)* that runs along the riverfront through the Ensanche to the Casco Viejo, with stops at the Guggenheim Museum and Arriaga Theater. Trains, which connect with the Metro, RENFE, and bus stations, run every five to ten minutes from 6:30 a.m. to 11 p.m. Monday through Friday, 7:30 a.m. to 11:45 p.m. weekends. A single ticket costs 1€ ($1.20), while a day pass is 3€ ($3.60).

By taxi

Bilbao's **taxis** are plusher than in other parts of Spain, but they're also more expensive — so don't hail a cab for very short journeys if you can walk. Recommended operators include **Radio Taxi Bilbao (☎ 94-444-88-88)**, **Radio Taxi Nervion (☎ 94-426-90-26)**, or **Tele Taxi (☎ 94-410-21-21)**.

Spending the night

Until the Guggenheim Museum landed like a shiny spaceship on the Nervión River, business travelers were Bilbao's most frequent visitors. Today, the construction of new hotels is catching up with tourists' sudden interest in the city.

Because Bilbao is still a business capital with continual convention and fair visitors during the week, you can get excellent weekend deals at many hotels. A tourist service called **Bilbao Reservas** (☎ **902-877-298**) can help make reservations at any level of hotel.

Gran Hotel Domine Bilbao

$$$$–$$$$$ New City (Abando)

If you're lucky enough to score a room facing the Guggenheim Museum just across the street, you'll wake up with a picture window full of glittering titanium courtesy of Frank Gehry. This new, ultramodern hotel is designed to reflect — literally, because it's covered in mirrors — some of the glamor, grace, and attention associated with the Guggenheim. Like the museum, it's ultrahip and reeks of mod style, with bold furnishings, cool lighting, a tall flooded atrium (which contains a massive totem stone sculpture and funky dish-plate waterfall by the hotel's designer, Javier Mariscal), and a futuristic cocktail lounge. The rooms are chic, decked out in light woods and sleek furnishings; executive rooms sport spectacular bathrooms with platform tubs that allow bathers to peek through smoked glass at the Guggenheim. The rooftop terrace, where breakfast is served, overlooks the museum from a privileged bird's-eye perspective. If you're a design freak who has come to Bilbao primarily to experience one of the world's great new architectural landmarks, this large hotel occupies an unparalleled location — and is, along with the Miróhotel down the street, the place to stay.

See map p. 209. Alameda Mazarredo 61. ☎ ***94-425-33-00*** *or central reservations, 902-36-36-00. Fax: 94-425-33-01.* `www.hoteles-silken.com/ghdb`. *Metro: Moyúa. Parking: 15€ ($18). Rack rates: 160€–260€ ($192–$312) double. Weekend rates: 155€–170€ ($186–$204). AE, DC, MC, V.*

Hotel Carlton

$$$–$$$$ New City (Abando)

Over the years, the Carlton has been occupied by the glamorous and powerful: Orson Welles, Ava Gardner, and the Republican Basque government during the Spanish Civil War (I imagine the latter group got a great discount). A grand, gleaming building right on handsome Plaza Moyúa, the Carlton is the city's most prestigious hotel. Constructed in 1925 in the Belle Epoque style (an elegant architectural style popular around World War I), and recently refurbished from head-to-toe, the hotel has continental-style rooms that are elegant and spacious with boldly patterned drapes and bedspreads. It's the kind of refined, Old World décor that will please individuals who aren't fans of the stripped-down modern luxury that now dominates the upper end of Bilbao hotels. The Carlton's preeminence among top-tier hotels has been seriously challenged by the Domine and Mirόhotel, both of which are right across from the Guggenheim, but for this kind and level of luxury, this traditional hotel remains an excellent choice as well as a good value. And the Guggenheim is only a ten-minute stroll away.

See map p. 209. Plaza Federico Moyúa 2. ☎ ***94-416-22-00.*** *Fax: 94-416-46-28.* `www.hotelcarlton.es`. *Metro: Moyúa. Parking: 12€ ($14). Rack rates: 110€–220€ ($132–$264) double. Weekend rates: 100€ ($120). AE, DC, MC, V.*

Hotel Conde Duque

$$$ Along the river (Uribarri)

Facing the space-age Calatrava Bridge, and walking distance downriver from the Guggenheim, this comfortable, midsize hotel is very well located. The top-floor rooms used to have great views of the "Guggy," until a sprawling modern building was erected next door. But some rooms still have good views of the river. Accommodations, overhauled in 2002, are often whimsically decorated in bright colors, comfortable but not what I'd call luxurious, and vary greatly in size (some are huge, some are tiny; ask to see a few upon arrival). The bathrooms, however, are uniformly large. The Conde Duque's standard rack rate is overpriced, but significant discounts are frequently available.

See map p. 209. Paseo Campo de Volantín 22. ☎ ***94-445-60-00.*** *Fax: 94-445-60-66.* `www.hotelcondeduque.com`. *Metro: Abando. Parking: 10€ ($12). Rack rates: 56€–120€ ($67–$144) double. Weekend rates (two-night minimum, includes breakfast): 89€ ($107). AE, MC, V.*

Hotel López de Haro

$$$$ New City (Abando)

For discreet, traditional elegance, this refined midsize hotel is the place to be in Bilbao. Tucked away on a quiet street in the modern section of town near the river, the López de Haro opened in 1990 and has been robbing the city's other top hotels of clients ever since. It's intimate and handsome, with a clubby feel. The rooms and bathrooms are five-star elegance all the way, and the restaurant, Club Nautico, is excellent.

See map p. 209. Obispo Orueta 2–4. ☎ ***94-423-55-00.*** *Fax: 94-423-45-00.* `www.hotellopezdeharo.com`. *Metro: Moyúa. Parking: 15€ ($18). Rack rates: 133€–210€ ($160–$252). Weekend rates (includes breakfast buffet and admission to Guggenheim and Museo de Bellas Artes): 69€ ($83). AE, DC, MC, V.*

Hotel Sirimiri

$$ Old Quarter

This small hotel in the Casco Viejo (Old Quarter) is rather poetically named: *Sirimiri* means "fine mist," which is the kind of weather you're almost certain to find in Bilbao — though I can't say that it accurately describes this functional, clean, and very good-value small hotel. Rooms are good-sized with yellow walls; bathrooms are sparkling, with pearly gray tile. With a dry sauna, hydromassage, and a small gym, the hotel features some surprising extras. And with its personal service, it's a pretty good deal — though a long hike from the Guggenheim.

See map p. 209. Plaza de la Encarnación 3. ☎ ***94-433-07-59.*** *Fax: 94-433-08-75.* `www.hotelsirimiri.com`*. Metro: Casco Viejo. Parking: 10€ ($12) Rack rates: 70€–90€ ($84–$108) double. MC, V.*

Miróhotel

$$$–$$$$ New City (Abando)

This sedately stylish boutique hotel is the first such project for the celebrated Barcelona fashion designer Antonio Miró. The hotel is a perfect reflection of his clothing: clean lines, tranquil colors, meticulous attention to detail, and understated luxury. It's modern and high-tech, but not in your face about its hipness. Just a block down the street from the Guggenheim, and around the corner from Bilbao's other great museum, the Museo de Bellas Artes, Miróhotel is perfectly located for artheads. And for a bit of extra pampering, unusual for a hotel of this size, it has a cool gym and spa downstairs, with excellent massages available, as well as a funky cocktail bar and a superb breakfast buffet. Rooms facing the river have superb views, although some construction is still ongoing along the riverfront promenade.

See map p. 209. Alameda Mazarredo 77. ☎ ***94-66118-80,*** *or central reservations 902-11-77-77. Fax: 902-117-755.* `www.mirohotelbilbao.com`*. Metro: Moyúa. Parking: 15€ ($18). Rack rates: 117€–185€ ($140–$222) double. AE, DC, MC, V.*

Petit Palace Arenal

$$–$$$ Old Quarter (near the Arenal promenade)

At the gate to the Old Quarter, next to the Teatro Arriaga, this modern, midsize hotel, which prides itself on having the latest in high-tech facilities, is a good bet with a good location, especially if you're interested in exploring the Casco Viejo and its *pintxos*-haunts and bars. The hotel inhabits a mid-19th-century building that was once home to the old Hostal Arana. Rooms aren't overly large or luxurious, though they are nicely decorated with a sleek, clean aesthetic. Free high-speed Internet access is available in all rooms.

See map p. 209. Bidebarrieta 2 (corner of Arenal). ☎ ***94-415-64-11.*** *Fax: 94-416-12-05.* `www.hthoteles.com`*. Metro: Abando. Parking: 15€ ($18). Rack rates: 60€–175€ double ($72–$210). AE, DC, MC, V.*

Dining in Bilbao

Gastronomes delight in Basque cooking, the most accomplished in Spain. Basque cuisine means fresh seafood, delicate sauces, and *pintxos,* the stacked tapas of the Basque Country. Top things off with *txakoli,* a young, fresh, fruity white wine that's slightly fizzy and a perfect accompaniment for seafood and light dishes.

The art and ritual of the *pintxo*

Tapas are found across Spain, but nowhere are they the art form that they are in the Basque Country. In fact, calling them mere tapas is to do them a serious disservice. Tapas in Euskadi are so elaborate that they are named for the toothpicks — *pintxos* — that you use to spear the small stacks of smoked salmon, marinated squid, tortilla, salt cod, and pastries stuffed with chicken and capers. They are quite often minimeals, artistically presented to delight both the eye and the taste buds.

Throughout the Basque Country, but especially in Bilbao and San Sebastián, countertops are lined twice a day with a smorgasbord of delectable *pintxos.* The ritual is easy: Muscle up to the bar of any place with plenty of noise and hungry mouths inside, and grab the tastiest morsel within your reach. Ask for a *vino tinto* (glass of red wine), *cerveza* (beer), or *txakolí* (fizzy Basque white wine, pronounced cha-koh-*lee*) and keep track of how many drinks and *pintxos* you have. This informal style of snacking or dining operates strictly on the honor system. Finger counting and pointing does fine when you need to calculate the bill.

At one or two euros ($1.20–$2.40) a pop, *pintxos* may seem like a cheap way to eat. And they can be, if you exercise restraint, but they're so good that doing so is a tall order. It's nearly impossible to resist reaching for one more . . . then one more . . . and still another "last one." Pretty soon, your meal of snacks turns into a full meal, cost included. (In fact, a lunch of *pintxos* may be more expensive than a fixed-price *menú del día,* but it's also more fun.) Be careful if you're watching your wallet — or your weight!

You can find the bulk of the top-notch *pintxos* bars in Bilbao's Casco Viejo (and the enchanting area called *Siete Calles,* or Seven Streets). Among those worth seeking out are **Victor Montes,** Plaza Nueva 8 (see full review later in this section); **Bar Irrintzi,** Santa María 8 (☎ 94-416-76-16), one of the hippest spots, with artistic *pintxos* (and little flags describing what they are); **Berton,** Jardines 11 (☎ 94-416-70-35), which specializes in Iberian hams and traditional *pintxos;* **Café Bar Bilbao,** Plaza Nueva 6 (☎ 94-415-16-71); and Gatz, Santa María 10 (☎ 94-415-48-61). Tiny **Taberna Taurina,** Ledesma 5 (no phone), at the edge of the Abando district, is loaded with bullfighting photos and paraphernalia.

Bilbao ranks second only to San Sebastián for the number of great Basque restaurants — which means that it's one of top places to eat in Spain. Although it's not cheap to dine at the more celebrated Basque restaurants — in fact, it's downright pricey — you can eat very well focusing solely on delectable *pintxos,* or tapas (see "The art and ritual of the *pintxo*" in this chapter).

The Basque Country is lodged between the Bay of Biscay and the rugged Pyrenees, so it's only appropriate that the cuisine is inspired in equal parts by the mountains and the sea. Basques delight in succulent lamb and game, but they adore the day's catch: *bacalao* (salt cod), grilled clams, squid, tuna, and baby eels. The Basque's love of sauces is second perhaps only to the French; their passion for food, however, is second to none.

Bilbao has a few classic old cafes, good places to get a jolt of espresso or a *cerveza* and talk about the Guggenheim (or take a breather from a tapas crawl). **Café Boulevard,** Arenal 3 (☎ **94-415-31-28**), on the perimeter of the Casco Viejo, and just down the street from the Teatro Arriaga, is the oldest cafe in Bilbao. Since 1871, literary types have come to this Art Deco place, which, in addition to a full lineup of caffeine and drinks, has a pretty good assortment of *pintxos* and cheap *platos combinados* (combination platters), ideal for a quick lunch. **Café Iruña,** Berasetegui 5 (☎ **94-423-70-21**), full of Moorish-looking, colorful tiles, dates to 1903. Finally, **Café La Granja,** Plaza Circular 3 (☎ **94-423-18-13**), around since the 1920s, is one of the old-time, simple coffee shops frequented for *merienda,* the term for a late-afternoon snack.

For more on Spanish dining customs, including mealtimes, costs, and tipping, see Chapter 2.

Abaroa

$$ New City (Abando) COUNTRY BASQUE

Ideally positioned between the Museo de Bellas Artes and the Guggenheim, this relaxed, rustic restaurant is perfect if you're looking for a lunch spot between cultural visits. It serves Basque home cooking, as opposed to the *alta cocina,* or haute cusine, found at high-end restaurants in the city. The place looks a bit like a farmhouse's interior, with wooden tables, and the menu serves up very good, and inexpensive, items you'd expect to find in the countryside: *croquetas* (ham croquettes), stuffed red peppers, massive steaks, and simple fresh fish. It's the perfect place to wash your meal down with a bottle of *txacolí* (fizzy white wine) or *sidra,* the cider that's so popular in the countryside.

See map p. 209. Plaza de Museo 3. ☎ ***94-424-91-07.*** *Reservations recommended on weekends. Metro: Abando. Main courses: 8€–16€ ($9.60–$19). Menú del dia: 17€ ($20). AE, MC, V. Open: Lunch and dinner daily.*

Goizeko Kabi

$$$$ New City (Abando) BASQUE

One of the best-known restaurants in Bilbao, this rustic chalet looks like a gussied-up ski lodge. It's a place to snuggle up and try tremendous traditional Basque dishes — especially if you're unfamiliar with Basque cooking. The chef, Fernando Canales, performs what amounts to a daily primer of the food of his hometown. For starters, try homemade *chorizo* (a spicy Spanish pork sausage) or wild *perrichico* mushrooms. Main courses include *entrecote* (a boned rib steak) with foie gras (goose-liver pâté), langoustines (prawns) with oyster ravioli, and sea bass with tomato vinaigrette and artichoke. A specialty that makes Bilbao natives weep is *kokotxas al pil-pil* (fresh cod filets from the "chins" of the fish, cooked in a bubbling and salty green sauce). Desserts are every bit as elaborate and wonderful as main dishes.

*See map p. 209. Particular de Estraunza 4–6 (New City). ☎ **94-442-11-29.** Reservations required. Metro: Moyúa (1 short block south of Gran Vía). Main courses: 14€–32€ ($17–$38). Tasting menu: 40€ ($48). AE, MC, V. Open: Lunch and dinner Mon–Sat. Closed: First two weeks of Aug.*

Guggenheim Bilbao

$$$$ New City (Abando) BASQUE

Dining at the Guggenheim Museum reveals, appropriately, the art of Basque cooking. Carved out of the museum's peculiarly shaped interior, with furniture designed by none other than Frank Gehry, is an excellent restaurant that long ago opened to glowing reviews and has been jam-packed every night since. The menu, the work of star Basque chef Martín Berasategui (and carried out by his protégé, Josean Alija), has as much flair as the playful dining room. Choose from items *del mar* (from the sea) or *del campo* (from the countryside). You can't go wrong on the menu, but you may start with the large and chunky lobster salad, perhaps followed by duck cannelloni. The dessert sampler is heaven for those with a sweet tooth. Although the restaurant isn't cheap, it is certainly high-value, and the lunch deal is a definite bargain.

The restaurant within the Guggenheim is so popular that you may need to call ahead of your visit to Bilbao; in the past, the wait has been two weeks or more. For the fixed-price lunch (for which no reservations are taken) arrive as early as possible, because it's usually totally booked by about 1:30 p.m. (You can also try the more accessible lunch cafeteria, which has an affordable *menú del día.*)

*See map p. 209. Abandoibarra Etorbidea 2 (within Guggenheim Museum, New City). ☎ **94-423-93-33.** Reservations required. Metro: Moyúa. Main courses: 24€–31€ ($29–$37). Menú del día: 17€ ($20). Tasting menu: 47€–58€ ($56–$70). AE, MC, V. Open: Lunch and dinner Wed–Sat, Sun–Tues lunch only.*

Tapelia

$$ New City (Abando) MEDITERRANEAN/RICE DISHES

A casual place, popular with young couples and families, this quality, good-value restaurant specializes in Valencian-style rice dishes and paellas — quite a change from the more intricate cooking and sauces of the north. The menu offers nicely prepared fish and meat dishes, such as beef sirloin in garlic oil, but nearly everyone orders one of the multitude of *arroces,* or rice dishes, which are brought to the table on elevated paella pans. The wine list is quite affordable, although none of the wait staff seems to know much about the wines on offer.

*See map p. 209. Uribitarte 24. ☎ **94-423-08-20.** Reservations recommended. Metro: Abando. Main courses: 10€–21€ ($12–$25). MC, V. Open: Lunch and dinner daily.*

Victor Montes

$$–$$$ Old Quarter BASQUE/TAPAS

Planted on Plaza Nueva in the Casco Viejo, Victor Montes is a classic Basque restaurant and *pintxos* bar. Basque tourism officials could set up cameras during tapas hour and film a winning ad for Bilbao here. Lined with wine bottles, the restaurant is like a cross between an Art Nouveau pharmacy and a wine cellar. It has a cool bistrolike dining room downstairs that opens onto the bar and a lovely, more intimate room upstairs (as well as covered tables in the plaza). The real action is at the bar, however, where amazing specialty *pintxos* (of cod, squid, and spinach tortilla — you name it) are piled high. They fly off the bar into the hands of impatient but good-natured regulars. The easygoing atmosphere, not to mention the delicious tapas, appeals to kids.

See map p. 209. Plaza Nueva 8. ☎ ***94-415-70-67.*** *Reservations recommended. Metro: Casco Viejo. Main courses: 9€–24€ ($11–$29). Menú del día: 35€ ($42). AE, MC, V. Open: Lunch and dinner Mon–Sat, Sun lunch only. Closed: Easter week and Aug 1–15.*

Zortziko

$$$$ New City (Abando) BASQUE

Around the corner from the Guggenheim, in a chic neighborhood, Zortziko has been the pinnacle of *alta cocina* dining in Bilbao for several years. The sophisticated kitchen combines innovative dishes and traditional Basque items. Choose from sea bass roasted in Rioja red wine, prawns with mushroom risotto, or rare pigeon breast in a sweet red wine sauce. Daniel García's tasting menu isn't cheap, but it's a memorable smorgasbord, which is a good move if everyone at your table is willing (and able — it's a ton of food) to go that route. Zortziko is elegant and more formal than most other restaurants in Bilbao, so you may want to dress up a bit. The wine cellar is one of the most extensive in the Basque Country with more than 600 wines. If you want a wine from 1889 or one that goes for 3,000€ ($3,600), Zortziko is the place (but you can also get bottles for as little as 12€/$14). Less formal and less expensive, but very nearly as highly recommended, is the sister restaurant **El Viejo Zortzi,** Licienciado Poza 54 (☎ **94-441-92-49**). Decorated in bold colors and with a funky, easygoing style, it also serves excellent Basque cuisine and changes its highly selective wines every two weeks.

See map p. 209. Alameda Marzarredo 17. ☎ ***94-423-97-43.*** *Reservations required. Metro: Abando. Main courses: 18€–30€ ($23–$38). Menú del día: 52€ ($65). Tasting menu: 70€. AE, MC, V. Open: Lunch and dinner Tues–Sat, Mon lunch only. Closed: Last week in Aug and first two weeks in Sept.*

Exploring Bilbao

No question about it: Everything in Bilbao now plays second fiddle to the Guggenheim Museum. By all means, beeline to the wondrous museum, which meets and beats expectations, but don't miss out on exploring Bilbao's other attractions, including its atmospheric Casco

Viejo (Old Quarter) and its other very worthwhile museum, the fine Museo de Bellas Artes.

The Bilbao Tourism Office offers guided, 90-minute **"Panoramic and Monumental Bilbao"** walking tours, leaving every Saturday and Sunday at 10 a.m. from the BIT office at the Teatro Arriaga (3€, or $3.75, adults). The language of the tour depends upon the linguistic leanings of the group assembled. Contact **Bilbao Iniciativas Turísticas,** Plaza Arriaga 1 (☎ **94-479-57-60**); EuskoTran: Arriaga.

Bus Visión Bilbao at Calle Marqués del Puerto 9, offers 90-minute bus tours of the city (passengers can get on and off at any of nine stops throughout the day). Daily departures are at 10 a.m., and 12, 4, and 6 p.m. at the Plaza del Sagrado Corazón; stops at the Guggenheim, technically the last stop of the tour, are 90 minutes later at each interval (☎ **94-410-40-04;** `www.bisertur.com`). Commentary is in Spanish and English, as well as in Euskera and French. Adult price is 6€ ($7.50), and for children younger than 12, it's 3€ ($3.75). It's also possible to get a combined ticket good for a Casco Viejo walking tour and the tour bus, good for 48 hours; adult price is 12€ ($15), students and seniors 10€ ($13) and for children ages 6 to12, 6€ ($7.50).

For a bird's-eye view of Bilbao, or to entertain the kids, take the elevator near the Ayuntamiento (City Hall) by the river — at Calle Esperanza 6 — to the upper town. You can reach the massive Gothic church Basílica de Begoña from there by foot. Aim your camera downriver for the space-age Calatrava Bridge and Guggenheim Museum.

The **BilbaoCard** is a discount card that provides access to local transportation, including the Metro and EuskoTran, and discounts between 10 and 50 percent at museums, shops, and selected restaurants. The BilbaoCard is available at any BIT (tourism) office and costs 6€ ($7.50) for a single day, 10€ ($12) for two days, and 12€ ($15) for three days.

Casco Viejo
Old Quarter

Just east of the Nervión River is Bilbao's Old Quarter. Though Bilbao dates to the Middle Ages, it isn't rich in medieval buildings and monuments. However, the small Casco Viejo, or Old Town, designated a "national historical and artistic monument," dates from the city's founding in 1300 and remains a great and lively part of the city. One atmospheric section is known as Siete Calles, named for the seven parallel streets that begin at the river. They're packed with restaurants and bars, and any day of the week after work, large groups spill noisily into the streets as they pursue a Basque ritual dear to their hearts and stomachs: the *poteo,* or tapas crawl.

Wander the Old Quarter as the mood strikes, stopping here and there for small glasses of wine or beer and assorted *pintxos.* At the edge of the barrio are the impressive **Teatro Arriaga,** a 19th-century theater, and the neighborhood's most important church, **Iglesia de San Nicolás.** Don't miss

Plaza Nueva (on Plaza Arenal), the spiritual heart of old Bilbao, which has 64 arches and only slightly fewer tapas bars. Also nearby is the **Catedral de Santiago,** originally constructed in the 14th century, and then restored in the 16th century after a fire.

You can take a good walk around the district in under two hours.

See map p. 209. East of the River Nervión, bounded by Puente del Arenal on the north side and calle Zabalbide on the south. Metro: Casco Viejo; EuskoTran: Ribera. Or walk across the Arenal bridge from Gran Vía.

Museo Guggenheim Bilbao
New City (along River Nervión)

Frank Gehry's critically lauded, much-photographed museum was called the "greatest building of our time" by Philip Johnson, himself a legendary New York architect. Imagining a more exciting art and architecture experience than the one Gehry crafted on the banks of the River Nervión in Bilbao is impossible. When the Guggenheim Foundation announced its plans to build another European branch in this rough-and-tumble industrial city in Spain, the art world was shocked. What's more shocking is the commanding success of the museum's design and execution. It's as if Gehry took a look at the magnificent Frank Lloyd Wright–designed Guggenheim in New York and said "I'll raise you one." The Bilbao museum is just about perfect: daring, inspired, and conceptual. It is a sculpture on a monumental scale.

As revolutionary as it is, its detractors are few — if any exist. Locals affectionately call it "Guggy" (pronounced *goo*-ghee) or "El Guggen," and it has single-handedly brought new life to Bilbao. The building is sheathed in 30,000 thin titanium panels, which are like the scales of a gigantic fish. Sadly, the panels are already beginning to show signs of deterioration, but they still shimmer in the sun. The structure's sensual curves give it the sensation of motion, as does the soaring atrium; when you wind your way through the structure, you keep returning to the building's heart. Except for Richard Serra's stunning sculpture, *Snake* (perfectly in tune with the long "fish gallery"), the museum is almost wholly given over to itinerant exhibitions and works on loan from the other Guggenheims — but, frankly, it could be empty and still be a spectacular art experience. The giant, cuddly sculpture that sits guard at the street is Jeff Koons's *Puppy;* covered in fresh flowers, it was to have been merely a temporary presence at the museum. Locals and museum-goers were so fond of it, though, that the Guggenheim was persuaded to make it a permanent watch dog.

Bilbao's Guggenheim is wildly popular, drawing about two million people a year, but it rarely feels too crowded to appreciate. Allow at least two hours to see the museum, and more if the temporary exhibits interest you (in that case, expect to spend the better part of a full morning or afternoon). See the sidebar "Getting the most out of the Guggenheim" for advice on tours and discounted admission.

Getting the most out of the Guggenheim

To get the most our of your Guggenheim experience, keep these tips in mind.

Listen up: Try the excellent hand-held audio tours (included in the admission cost), which offer an analysis of the building's revolutionary architecture and commentary from the architect, Frank Gehry. The go-at-your-own-pace tour also leads you through the current exhibitions.

Guided tours: The Guggenheim offers excellent free guided visits in English, Tuesday through Sunday at 11 a.m., and 12:30, 4:30, and 6:30 p.m. A special family tour — at this writing, in Spanish only — is Sunday at noon. Guided tours focus on current temporary exhibitions and the museum's architecture and permanent collection. To reserve a guided tour, call ☎ **94-435-90-90.**

Art bargain: Combined entrance to the Guggenheim Museum and the next-door Bilbao Museum of Fine Arts is just 12€ ($15) with the "Bono Artean" Joint Voucher, which you can purchase at the box office of either museum (just 1.50€, or $1.90, more than entrance to the Guggenheim only).

Go when everyone's having lunch: To have the Guggenheim virtually to yourself, eat an early lunch and go to the museum from 1 to 4 p.m. — when Spaniards and many European visitors clear out. In summer and on weekends, though, you have a harder time buying yourself this lunchtime peace and quiet.

See map p. 209. Av. Abandobiarra 2. ☎ ***94-435-90-80.*** `www.guggenheim-bilbao.es`. *Metro: Moyúa; EuskoTran: Guggenheim. Admission: 11€ ($13), students and seniors 6.50€ ($8.10), free for children under 12; special exhibits 13€ ($16) adults, 7.50€ ($9.40) students and seniors. Combined entrance with Museo de Bellas Artes (Bono Artean Voucher) 12€ ($15). Advance tickets available through the Web site; guarantee with a credit card, tickets held at the front desk. Open: Tues–Sun 10 a.m.–8 p.m., July–Aug daily 10 a.m.–8 p.m.*

Museo de Bellas Artes de Bilbao

New City

The Guggenheim's not the only art show in town, though it does unfortunately overshadow the excellent Fine Arts Museum, founded in 1908. The latter's rich and varied collections include paintings by the Old Masters El Greco, Zurbarán, and Goya; contemporary artists such as Francis Bacon and Antoni Tàpies; and a survey of 19th- and 20th-century Basque artists. Eduardo Chillida's large-scale *Monument to Iron* is a good introduction to the work of this tremendous Basque sculptor. The museum, exempt from the crowds across the way at the Guggenheim, is nicely quiet most of the time. Art fans may need a couple of hours here; those with only moderate interest can make do with an hour.

See map p. 209. Plaza del Museo 2 (Doña Casilda Iturriza Park). ☎ ***94-439-60-60;*** *guided tours* ☎ *94-439-61-37.* `www.museobilbao.com`. *Metro: Moyúa; EuskoTran:*

Guggenheim. Admission: 5€ ($6.25) adults, 3.50€ ($4.40) students and seniors, children under 12 free; free Wed. Combined entrance with Guggenheim (Bono Artean Voucher) 12€ ($15). Open: Tues–Sat 10 a.m.–8 p.m. and Sun 10 a.m.–2 p.m.

Museo Vasco
Old Quarter

This interesting museum of Basque archaeology and ethnography occupies a handsome Jesuit *colegio* (high school) and its beautiful cloisters in the Old Quarter. Well-designed exhibits address the ancient history of the Basque people, including carved stonework, prehistoric utensils, furniture, and ceramics. Allow an hour, at least.

See map p. 209. Plaza Miguel de Unamuno 4. ☎ ***94-415-54-23.*** `www.euskal-museoa.org`*. Metro: Casco Viejo; EuskoTran: Ribera. Admission: 3€ ($3.75) adults, 1.50€ ($1.90) students, children under 10 and seniors free. Open: Tues–Sat 11 a.m.–5 p.m., Sun 11 a.m.–2 p.m.*

Shopping for local treasures

Bilbao's best shopping areas are the Old Quarter and, in the modern section of town, along Gran Vía — the long, elegant main drag — and Calle Ercilla. Fine clothing shops abound, and cutting-edge fashion has flourished in the wake of the Guggenheim's arrival. For chic women's fashions, check out **Corso XXI,** Heros 21 (☎ **94-423-23-36**) and **Stock Options,** Elcano 11 (☎ **94-416-72-71**).

One of the most emblematic things you can buy in Bilbao is an authentic Basque *boina* (beret). The oldest hat shop in town, run by seven brothers who are fourth-generation hat makers, is **Sombreros Gorostiaga,** Victor 9, in the Old Quarter (☎ **94-416-12-76**). If the talkative brother, Emilio, is working, he can tell you more than you ever wanted to know about berets, including how to prop one on your head like a Basque. A good beret, durable enough for daily wear in Bilbao's constant mist, runs about 20€ ($24) or so.

The Basques make a fashion statement with their berets; few men of a certain age dare leave the house without their favorite *boinas* artfully perched atop their heads. Emilio Gorostiaga says that *abuelos* (old timers) buy a new beret and stick it under the mattress for a year, until they deem it wearable. The lesson? Never fold your beret; you must store it perfectly flat. And never, ever buy a *boina* that's not 100 percent wool. Such a beginner's mistake is considered sacrilege in these parts.

For a good selection of wines from La Rioja, Ribera del Duero, and other regions in Spain, visit **D'Vinno La Tienda,** Ibañez de Bilbao 6, or the **Club de Gourmet** at the Corte Inglés department store, Gran Vía 7–9 (☎ **90-222-44-11**). **Basandere,** Iparraguirre 4 (☎ **94-423-63-86**), near the Guggenheim, has cool T-shirts and other gift items from the Basque Country.

Gettin' jazzed

Be-boppers dig the Basque Country in summer, when three major jazz festivals play the north of Spain, all in the span of three weeks. The **Bilbao Getxo Jazz Festival,** which started in 1976, hits the stage the first week of July with performers such as Bill Bruford and Phil Wood. **Jazzaldia,** the San Sebastián Jazz Festival, has grown steadily since the mid-'60s. Hosting a wide range of musicians, such as James Brown, Keith Jarrett, and Van Morrison, it draws music fans the last week in July. A short drive from either of those cities is Vitoria, which hosts a highly touted festival in mid-July. In past summers, Pat Metheny, Chick Corea, Paco de Lucía, and Wynton Marsalis have all dropped in on the **Vitoria-Gasteiz Festival de Jazz.**

You can obtain schedules and ticket information for the Basque Country Jazz Festivals at the following numbers and Internet addresses: in **Bilbao (☎ 94-491-40-80;** `www.getxo.net`), in **San Sebastián (☎ 943-44-00-34;** `www.jazzaldia.com`), and in **Vitoria (☎ 945-14-19-19;** `www.jazzvitoria.com`).

Hitting the tapas bars and more: Bilbao's nightlife

Bilbao's best early-evening scene is the one spilling out of the *pintxos* bars in the Casco Viejo. Basques are enthusiastic about food, and all that excited noise you hear is probably people talking about what they've just eaten. Crammed in the Siete Calles district of the Old Quarter are more bars than you can ever visit; stick your head in any that seem appealing, order a beer or a glass of wine, and snatch some snacks off the bar. Join the flow as it rolls on to the next spot and repeat steps one through three. On weekend nights, Siete Calles becomes a boisterous affair, with crowds of jovial bar-goers spilling out into the streets. The most easygoing scene in the Casco Viejo is the Plaza Nueva, where several bars operate terraces with outdoor tables, perfect for a relaxed drink.

Perhaps it's because of the frequent mist and green hills of the Basque Country that so many Irish pubs populate Bilbao. If you're looking for a pint of Guinness, Bilbao will almost seem like Dublin or Galway. **The Dubliners,** Plaza Moyúa 6 (**☎ 94-423-03-20**); **Molly Malone,** Particular Estraunza 8 (**☎ 94-427-11-47**); and, perhaps the best of the lot, **The Wicklow Arms Irish House,** Rodríguez Arias 30 (**☎ 94-442-51-48**), are but three of a couple dozen Irish pubs in the city.

Hot dance clubs include **Congreso,** Uribitarte 8 (**☎ 94-424-73-82**), which has been around a decade but is still stylish, with good house and electronic music, go-go dancers, and audiovisual effects; and **The Image,** Sabino Arana 56 (**☎ 94-668-28-66**), a large and flashy club with house and alternative music in one section and more classic R&B and funk in another.

Several hopping gay bars populate **Calle Barrencalle** in the Old Quarter. **The High Club,** Calle Naja, is one of the most popular, and active, gay dance clubs, with porn films and a secret "dark room." **Badulake,** Hernani 10, is a cabaret-type bar with a good indie soundtrack and drag shows Thursday through Saturday at 11 p.m.

If you've had your fill of *pintxos,* check out the **Teatro Arriaga,** Bilbao's handsome monument to high culture. Opera, dance, theater productions, and a wide variety of concerts play at the theater, a 19th-century gem renovated and reopened in 1986. Call ☎ **94-479-20-36** for program information. Opera performances and concerts by the Basque Symphony Orchestra are also staged at the **Palacio Euskalduna,** Abandoibarra 4 (☎ **94-431-03-10;** EuskoTran: Abandoibarra). Gamblers and night owls won't want to miss Bilbao's **Gran Casino Nervión,** Calle Navarra 1 (☎ **94-424-00-07**), open daily from 5 p.m. to 5 a.m. (entrance 3€, or $3.75).

Bilborock, Muelle de la Merced (☎ **94-415-13-06**) is housed in an old church, but plays host to gods of rock most nights. Eclectic and often adventurous live acts play at **Kafé Antxokia,** San Vicente 2 (☎ **94-424-46-25**). For additional listings of live rock and pop music, check out the local newspaper *El Correo.*

The **Cotton Club,** Gregorio de la Revilla 25 (entrance on Simón Bolívar; ☎ **94-410-49-51**), where Antonio Flores and other well-known national and international performers have appeared, is a stalwart of the live pop, blues, and rock scene.

Taking side trips to La Rioja Alavesa: Wine and gastronomy

Spain's oldest and most traditional wine region is La Rioja, the fertile province immediately south of the Basque Country and Navarra. The Ebro River runs through a valley of lush vineyards and ancient towns in the shadows of the stony Sierra Cantabria peaks. Many of Rioja's finest wineries are in fact clustered in the Basque province of Alava, on the north bank of the Ebro; the wine region there is known as La Rioja Alavesa.

Haro, an hour-and-a-half south of Bilbao, is the winemaking capital of La Rioja Alta (Upper Rioja). The spectacularly located and marvelously preserved walled medieval village of **Laguardia** (about 20 minutes east of Haro), rising on an outcropping in the midst of vineyards all around, is one of the highlights of a trip to the region, as are visits to wineries *(bodegas),* both modern and starkly traditional. Haro and Laguardia make excellent bases for exploring the region.

In recent years, other winemaking regions, such as Priorat, Toro, and Rioja's perennial rival Ribera del Duero, have succeeded in stealing some of the thunder from Rioja, but in the last few years, many Rioja winemakers have adapted and modernized and are again producing some of the country's finest wines — many of which are considerably bigger and denser than the typical past Riojas. (See Chapter 2 and the Cheat Sheet at the beginning of this book for more information on

Spain's wine regions and vintages.) Just as notable is the sudden impact of wine and gastronomy tourism, which has resulted not only in more wineries opening their doors to the public, but also in the importation of such superstar architects as Frank Gehry, Santiago Calatrava, and Rafael Moneo, who have built bodegas and luxury hotels in the midst of the vineyards in the Upper Rioja.

Although the area is accessible by bus from Bilbao as well as from Pamplona, a car is necessary if you want to explore the region beyond the main towns. And although you could theoretically see a winery or two and either Haro or Laguardia in a rushed day trip, whether or not you're a wine aficionado, I'd strongly advise spending a night or two in the area to get to know this pretty and historic region. In addition to great wines and great food, you can choose from several terrific country hotels.

Haro

Approximately 110km (68 miles) south of Bilbao, Haro (*ah*-roh), at the edge of the Río Ebro, is the capital of La Rioja Alta. Driving south from Bilbao, take A-68, the national highway, past N-622 (the turnoff to Vitoria) to Haro. If you don't have a car, you can get to Haro but getting to the wineries will be more difficult. From Bilbao, you can take **Autobuses La Unión Alavesa** (☎ **944-27-11-11**). **La Estellesa** (☎ **948-22-22-23;** `www.laestellesa.com`) runs daily buses from Pamplona to Haro.

You'll quickly see evidence of the local importance of the wine industry, as a disproportionate number of *vinotecas* (wine shops) and taverns populate the small town. Haro's lovely, tranquil Casco Viejo, or Old Quarter, is full of stone churches and aristocratic mansions with glass balconies. Worth a look are the Renaissance church **Parroquia de Santo Tomás,** a National Monument with a sculpted portal on Plaza de la Iglesia, and the (naturally peaceful) **Plaza de la Paz.**

Rather less atmospheric is the dry and didactic **Museo del Vino de la Rioja,** or Rioja Wine Museum (Av. Bretón de los Herreros 4 (☎ **941-31-05-47;** 2€/$2.50; Mon–Sat 10 a.m–2 p.m. and 4–8 p.m. and Sun 10 a.m.–2 p.m.) in the modern section of town. It offers three floors of background on the winemaking process and history of grape cultivation in La Rioja, information that is routinely passed on (in a much more engaging manner) in most winery visits.

Haro is at its finest during the last week of June, when the **fiestas of San Juan, San Felices,** and **San Pedro** converge and wine flows even more freely than usual in town. On June 29, the feast day of San Pedro, the annual **Batalla del Vino** (Wine Battle) rages in Haro; echoing a medieval conflict between neighboring communities. The event features participants climbing the Riscos de Bilibio, a nearby hill, and dousing each other with red wine. **Haro's fiesta day,** September 7, is also a great deal of fun.

The wines of La Rioja

The La Rioja province is synonymous with winemaking in Spain, but in fact Rioja's vineyards extend into the Basque Country and Navarra. Rioja was the first wine region in Spain to receive the Denominación de Origen (Designation of Origin, or D.O.), in 1926, although documentation of efforts to safeguard the quality of local wines dates back as far as 1650. In 1102, though, the King of Navarra had already issued a legal recognition of Rioja wines. Today Rioja is one of 56 designated wine regions in Spain, and its largest, with more than 1,300 registered bodegas and winegrowers. However, it is the only region so far to be designated Denominación de Origen Calificada, or D.O.C., which denotes wines of superior quality. The predominant varietal in red Rioja wines — for which the region is best known — is Tempranillo, although Garnacha, Marzuelo, and Graciano are also used. Rioja's whites are made from Viura, Malvasia, and Garnacha Blanca grapes.

To find out more about the categories of aged wines (crianzas, reservas, and gran reservas), see Chapter 2. For additional information on Rioja wine history, vintage ratings, and more, see `www.riojawine.com`.

Visiting the bodegas

Many of the wineries that you can visit in and around Haro have been producing wine since the late 19th century. Many of the oldest bodegas in Rioja — where you'll see oak casks and deep cellars rather than stainless steel vats and modern technology — are just a short drive from town, in the Barrio de las Bodegas across the Río Tirón. Haro's tourist information office, Plaza Monseñor Florentino Rodgríguez, s/n (☎ **948-30-33-66**), has maps of the bodegas as well as helpful information about the Ruta del Vino (Wine Route) and winery tours. Some 17 wineries are in the immediate area of Haro, with at least nine offering regularly scheduled tours (some require appointments in advance). A few charge for visits, while others don't (though almost all include tastings at the end of tours). Among the best for visitors (in the order of my preference) are

- **Bodegas Muga:** Av. de Vizcaya, s/n (☎ **941-31-18-25;** `www.bodegasmuga.com`; 75-minute tours Mon–Fri 10 a.m. in English, 11 a.m and noon in Spanish; 5€, or $6.25). Founded in 1932, Muga is one of the best-known Rioja wineries, producing excellent reds such as Torre Muga and Aro. The tour is one of the best and most popular, taking visitors down to see the massive, picturesque oak wine vats, which are hand-crafted on-site. You don't need to make an appointment for winery visits.
- **Bodegas C.V.N.E.:** Av. de Vizcaya, s/n (☎ **941-30-48-09;** `www.cvne.com`; free tours Mon–Fri 10 a.m. and 1 p.m. in Spanish, 11 a.m. in English; Mon–Thurs 4 p.m. in English). This family-owned winery, the makers of Imperial and Viña Real wines, began in 1879 and nicely combines traditional Rioja winemaking with innovative

technology; the bodega still largely consists of the original 19th-century buildings that are set around a courtyard. A prior appointment is necessary.

- **Bodegas Bilbaínas:** Av. de Vizcaya, s/n (☎ **941-48-69-99;** free tours Tues–Sun 9:30 a.m. and 2:30 p.m. in either English or Spanish). This historic winery, founded in 1901 and the makers of Viña Pomal, was recently acquired by the Codorníu (makers of *cava*) family, but it continues to adhere to traditional methods. A prior appointment is necessary.
- **Bodegas Ramón Bilbao:** Av. Santo Domingo 34 (☎ **941-31-02-95;** `www.bodegasramonbilbao.es`). This 75-year-old winery and classic Rioja producer on the outskirts of Haro, offers tours (in Spanish and English) of its traditional bodega (3€/$3.75) Wednesday to Saturday from 9 a.m. to 1 p.m. and 4 to 6 p.m. and Sunday 9 a.m. to 1 p.m. A prior appointment isn't necessary, but the winery recommends calling in advance to make sure tours will be held on the day in question.

The **Beronia Association,** Plaza Monseñor Florentino Rodgríguez, s/n (☎ **914-30-33-66;** `www.beronia.org`) conducts organized, instructional wine tastings in English, Spanish, and French.

If you're shopping for wine to lug home, check out **Vinícola Jarrera,** Calle Castilla 3, and Calle Santo Tomás 17 (☎ **941-31-14-25**), or **Rodríguez Alonso,** Conde de Haro 7 (☎ **941-30-32-72**), both of which have excellent rosters of Rioja wines.

Where to stay and eat in Haro

If you're looking to stay the night in Haro, check out the elegant **Los Agustinos,** a 14th-century convent handsomely converted into a hotel, Calle San Augustín 2, Haro (☎ **941-31-13-08;** `www.aranzazu-hoteles.com`. Rack rates: 97€/$121 double). Rooms are very comfortable, if not overly luxurious, and there's a nice restaurant on-site. The hotel is at the edge of the Old Quarter, across the street from the Tourism Office.

The finest restaurant in town — and one of the best in the entire region — is the new and elegantly understated **Las Duelas** (Plaza Monseñor Florentino Rodgríguez, s/n; ☎ **941-30-44-63**). Although quite upscale, it's the place for fine Rioja cuisine and fine wines from local producers — a winemaker or two is likely to be at the next table — in Haro. The wine list is definitely impressive with a number of bottles that are very hard to get elsewhere. **Casa Terete,** Lucrecia Arana 17 (☎ **941-31-00-23**), a 19th-century inn near the Plaza de la Iglesia in the Old Quarter, is another good choice. It specializes in lamb roasts.

Laguardia

Approximately 150km (93 miles) south of Bilbao and east of Haro, but across the provincial border in the Basque Rioja Alavesa, is the charming 12th-century village of Laguardia. Enclosed by thick medieval walls and rising proudly above the surrounding vineyards in the Ebro Valley, against a backdrop of the Sierra Cantabria mountains, it is one of the loveliest small towns in northern Spain. Its narrow, cobbled, and largely pedestrian-only streets are lined with noble stone mansions from the 16th to 18th centuries, and tucked within the walls are tiny, quiet plazas and churches. Beneath the town are its famous *cuevas,* or bodegas, several hundred deep catacomblike cellars that once served as hideouts and provisions-storage when the town was called La Guardia de Navarra, a strategically important military fortress. Today its importance, however, is due almost entirely to the wine industry and wine tourism.

Worth visiting as well is the Gothic **Iglesia de Santa María de los Reyes,** begun in the 12th century in the Romanesque style and completed 300 years later, with a spectacularly carved Gothic portal. Its bell tower, Torre Abacial, functioned as a military tower in the 13th century. To visit Santa María, you have to ask for the keys at the tourism office (☎ **945-60-08-45**) in the **Casa Palacio de Samaniego,** on Plazuela de San Juan. The Renaissance Samaniego palace is itself one of the most beautiful buildings in town. The oldest example of civil architecture in Laguardia is the **Casa de la Primicia,** on Calle Páganos, constructed at the end of the 14th century.

Visiting the bodegas

The bodegas for the past 150 years have served as private wine cellars. Guests staying at the Posada Mayor de Migueloa (see the next section, "Where to stay and eat in and around Laguardia") can visit its deep cellars and taste wines still produced by that family-owned winery (and hotel and restaurant).

Your best chance to see what lies beneath Laguardia's streets is at **Bodegas El Fabulista,** next to the Casa de Samaniego and the tourism office, which offers regular visits for the general public and is one of the most charming wineries you're likely to visit. It dates to the 15th century and produces only a few thousand bottles of wine a year, including about 32,000 liters by the traditional *maceración,* or grape-stomping, method. On the ground floor are the two lagars, where the stomping is done, along with a wine press from 1903. The maze of cellars that descend 7m (23 ft.) below the street, where you can taste wines, contain stone- and brick-vaulted ceilings and date to the eighth century. Call ☎ **945-62-11-92** for an appointment, or stop by; tours (5€, or $6.25) are generally scheduled Monday to Saturday at 11:30 a.m., and 1, 5, and 7 p.m. (Sun 11:30 a.m. and 1 p.m. only). If you're lucky, Fernando will be your guide, and perhaps Eusebi, the winemaker, will be on hand to comment on his wines. The winery has gotten so popular recently, with so many international group bookings, that it may be necessary to reserve your place in advance online at `www.bodegaelfabulista.com`. Among the artisanal wines produced here in limited production are El Fabulista and Fábula.

On the outskirts of Laguardia is **Bodegas Palacio,** a large-scale producer that's been making wines since 1894 and now operates an excellent inn and restaurant in its old bodegas (see below). It offers tours (3€, or $3.75) Tuesday through Friday at 1 p.m. and Saturday at 12:30 and 1:30 p.m.; prior appointment by telephone is necessary. The winery, an interesting mix of traditional and modern winemaking (and wine architecture) is located on the Carretera a Elciego (☎ **945-62-11-95**). Its notable wines include Cosme Palacio y Hermanos and Glorioso.

Bodegas Ysios, owned by a large winemaking group with properties in several regions, has turned the quaint bodega tradition on its head. Its stunning winery is the work of the famed architect Santiago Calatrava (designer of the Athens Olympic Stadium, the Milwaukee Museum of Art, and the forthcoming Port Authority train station in New York City). His interpretation resulted in what appears to be a modern cathedral of wine with an undulating roofline that resembles the Sierra Cantabia and a grand altar window that frames the village of Laguardia in the distance. Inside, the winery is sparkling and somewhat antiseptic, with stainless vats, and the tour is pretty pro forma — but the Calatrava building is worth the trip. The winery is located 2km (1¼ mile) from Laguardia on the Camino de La Hoya; ☎ **945-60-06-40**). Guided tours (3€, or $3.75) are at 11 a.m., and 1 and 4 p.m. Monday through Friday and at 11 a.m. and 1 p.m. on weekends. Call ahead, although you could probably just show up and be accommodated.

In the tiny village of Elciego, 6km (2 miles) from Laguardia, is the winery most everyone is talking about: **Bodegas Marqués de Riscal,** one of the region's oldest. It was founded in 1860 and has long produced some of the most renowned wines in Spain, but it recently made news by contracting none other than Frank Gehry, the architect of the Guggenheim Bilbao and the Disney Center and countless other modern masterpieces, to build a small luxury hotel, spa, and visitors center on its campus in the middle of 220 hectares (543 acres) of vineyards. **Hotel Marqués de Riscal** — part of a grand "Ciudad del Vino" (City of Wine) project that includes a restaurant and facilities for wine therapy and wine study — finally opened in 2006. It's a swank 43-room hotel that's as idiosyncratic and attention-getting as you'd expect a Gehry-designed property to be, and it is likely to change the face of wine tourism in this laid-back region. Even without the new hotel, the large winery is a fascinating blend of ancient tradition and modern technology, ranging from futuristic computer controls to what the winery calls its "Cathedral of Wine" but what looks more like a Cemetery of Wine. Deep beneath the symmetrical arches of the 19th-century cellars are where 140,000 bottles, representing every vintage since 1862, are stored. They're eerily covered in cobwebs and thick mold. Because of the delicate storage conditions, groups can only peek in the gate. You can arrange visits (Mon–Sat; 6€/$7.50) by calling ☎ **945-60-65-95** or contacting the winery through its Web site, `www.marquesderiscal.com`. To get there from Laguardia, drive south on A-3210.

Another bodega with a fancy, imported-architect makeover is **Viña Real,** Ctra. Logroño a Laguardia, Km 4.8, Laguardia (☎ **945-62-52-10;** www.cvne.com/desarrollo/html/vina_real.html). Owned by the well-known family-operated C.V.N.E., which recently celebrated 125 years of winemaking, this bodega opted for an innovative and sleekly modern (and award-winning) new building, part of which resembles a giant wine vat, designed by the French architect Philippe Mazières and inaugurated in late 2004. For information about visits, call or contact the winery via its Web site.

Where to stay and eat in and around Laguardia

Even without counting the new super-luxury Gehry hotel and spa at Marqués de Riscal (see the previous section), three of the best small country hotels in northern Spain are in and around Laguardia, reason enough to spend a couple of nights in the region and take a more leisurely approach to visiting its small towns and wineries. **Posada Mayor de Migueloa,** Mayor de Migueloa 20 (☎ **945-62-11-75;** www.mayordemigueloa.com; Rack rates: 93€/$116 double) is an absolute charmer, an upscale family-run inn and restaurant (and winemaker) within the old walled section of Laguardia. Rooms are warm and inviting, with stone walls and wood-beamed ceilings; the swanky restaurant is superb; and beneath the house, open to guests, are wine cellars built in 1619.

Another great location for wine aficionados is just down the hill from Laguardia, the small hotel at Bodegas Palacios, the **Hotel Antigua Bodega de Don Cosme Palacio,** Carretera de Elciego, s/n (☎ **945-62-11-95;** www.habarcelo.es; Rack rates: 68€–74€/$85–$93). True to its name, the inn occupies parts of the old cellars at this winery, built in the late 19th century. Rooms are named for grape varietals, but the handsome Tempranillo Suite is the only one to look out over vineyards. The restaurant, which serves very good Rioja specialties and house wines, is a big draw even for people not staying at the hotel, so reservations are recommended. If you stay but don't take the wine tour, don't miss the chance to walk around the cellars and mural-covered walls beneath the hotel and restaurant.

In the nearby village of Samaniego is another wonderful small hotel and restaurant, **Hotel Palacio de Samaniego,** Calle Constitución 12 (☎ **945-60-91-51;** www.palaciosamaniego.com; Rack rates: 52€–88€/$65–$110 double). Housed in an exquisitely restored 18th-century palace, a stone's throw from the bodegas of Remírez de Ganuza (one of my favorite Spanish wines), this tasteful inn, run by a young couple, is very peaceful and beautifully decorated. It is also an excellent value. Outside of high season, the delightful restaurant, run by the Basque chef Jon Ugalde, who studied under the renowned San Sebastián chef Martín Berasategui, is open only on weekends. It serves a good-value tasting menu for 40€, or $50. Samaniego is west of Laguardia on A-124.

Fast Facts: Bilbao

Area Code

The area code for telephone numbers in Bilbao is **94.** You must dial it with all local numbers.

Currency Exchange

You can exchange currency either at banks downtown, near Gran Vía and Plaza Moyúa, or at *casas de cambio* (exchange houses). The Bilbao airport also has a currency exchange.

Emergencies

For medical emergencies, call ☎ **902-21-21-24** or contact Servicio Vasco Salud (☎ 94-410-00-00). For police emergencies, call ☎ **112.**

Hospitals

Hospital de Basurto is at Av. de Montevideo 18 (☎ 94-441-88-00).

Information

Call ☎ **010** to obtain general visitor information. Bilbao Turismo offices are located at the airport, just outside the Guggenheim Museum, on Av. Abandoibarra 2 (Tues–Fri 11 a.m.–6 p.m., Sat 11 a.m.–7 p.m., Sun 11 a.m.–2 p.m.; in summer, Tues–Fri 10 a.m.–7 p.m. and Sun 11 a.m.–3 p.m.; no phone), at Plaza del Arriaga, s/n (Teatro Arriaga; ☎ 94-479-57-60; Mon–Fri 11 a.m.–2 p.m. and 4–7 p.m., Sat 9 a.m.–2 p.m., and Sun 10 a.m.–2 p.m.), and at Plaza Ensanche 11 (☎ 94-479-57-60; Mon–Fri 9 a.m.–2 p.m. and 4–7:30 p.m.).

Police

For emergencies, call ☎ **112** or 94-444-14-44. The main police station is located at Calle Luís Briñas 14 (☎ 092).

Post Office

The Central Post Office is at Calle Av. Urquijo 19 (☎ 94-422-05-48). It's open Monday through Friday from 8:30 a.m. to 9 p.m. and Saturday from 8 a.m. to 8 p.m.

San Sebastián: Food Capital on the Bay

Elegant, seaside **San Sebastián** (called Donostia in the Basque language) is the capital of the tiny Guipúzcoa province. Sandwiched between two green hills (Monte Urgull and Monte Iguelda) and fronting a beautiful half-moon bay (Bahía de la Concha), the city is one of Spain's most spectacular. Two long beaches, La Concha and Ondarreta, follow the gentle curve of the bay, while the residential neighborhood of Gros faces a third beach, Zurriola, popular with locals. Those beaches, as well as a cool summer climate and the finest dining in all of Spain, are why San Sebastián, a city of just 180,000 residents, swells with Spanish and international vacationers and French weekenders from just across the border.

Once a quiet fishing village, San Sebastián became a fashionable resort for aristocrats and royalty in the late 19th century, after Queen Isabel II headed to this coast in search of a cure for a pesky skin ailment. The royal court, including her son King Alfonxo XII and Queen María Cristina, followed, building the Miramar Palace and transforming the Bahía de la Concha into one of Spain's chicest spots.

The city retains much of its past grandeur, ranging from quiet medieval alleyways to stately Belle Epoque apartment buildings, wrought-iron lampposts, sculpted bridges, and wide boulevards. A handsome promenade, where locals seem to be forever strolling, frames the gentle curve of the main beaches. But perhaps the most interesting section of town is the **Parte Vieja,** the Old Quarter, home to a warren of ancient streets and plazas that hide dozens of *pintxos* bars. San Sebastián also hosts important annual jazz and film festivals, which attract big-name international stars.

Getting there

Despite its huge popularity as a resort for Spanish and French visitors, very few airlines fly into San Sebastián; instead, they go to the main regional airport in Bilbao, just 75 minutes away. You may want to consider that factor when planning a trip to the Basque Country (such as visiting Bilbao first before hopping a bus or driving to San Sebastián).

By air

Relatively few visitors arrive by air, because connections to nearby Bilbao are much more frequent and extensive. The city's airport, **Aeropuerto de San Sebastián,** is 20km (12 miles) from the city in Fuenterrabia (☎ **943-66-85-00**). Frequent **Bizcai Buses** (6 a.m.–10:30 p.m.) travel to San Sebastián from the airport.

By car

You can reach San Sebastián from Bilbao along the main coastal highway, A-8; the trip takes about an hour. From Pamplona, take A-15 followed by N-1. From Barcelona, the fastest route is through Pamplona (A-15), from Madrid, through Bilbao (A-68).

By bus

San Sebastián is well connected with major cities. The routes are especially painless in the Basque Country, where the bus is faster than the train. The city is a one-and-a-quarter-hour bus rise from Bilbao and a little more than one-and-a-half hours from Pamplona (buses leave every half hour). The major bus companies are **Pesa,** for Bilbao and other points in the Basque Country (☎ **902-10-12-10**); **La Roncalesa,** for Pamplona (☎ **943-46-10-64**); and **Vibasa,** for Barcelona (☎ **943-45-75-00;** `www.vibasa.es`). The bus station is at Plaza Pío XII (☎ **902-10-12-10**).

By train

Trains to San Sebastián roll in from Madrid and Barcelona, as well as from Bilbao (though the train from the latter meanders along the coast and takes twice as long as the bus). The train station, **Estación el Norte** (for RENFE trains), is at Av. de Francia, s/n (☎ **902-24-02-02;** `www.renfe.es`).

San Sebastián

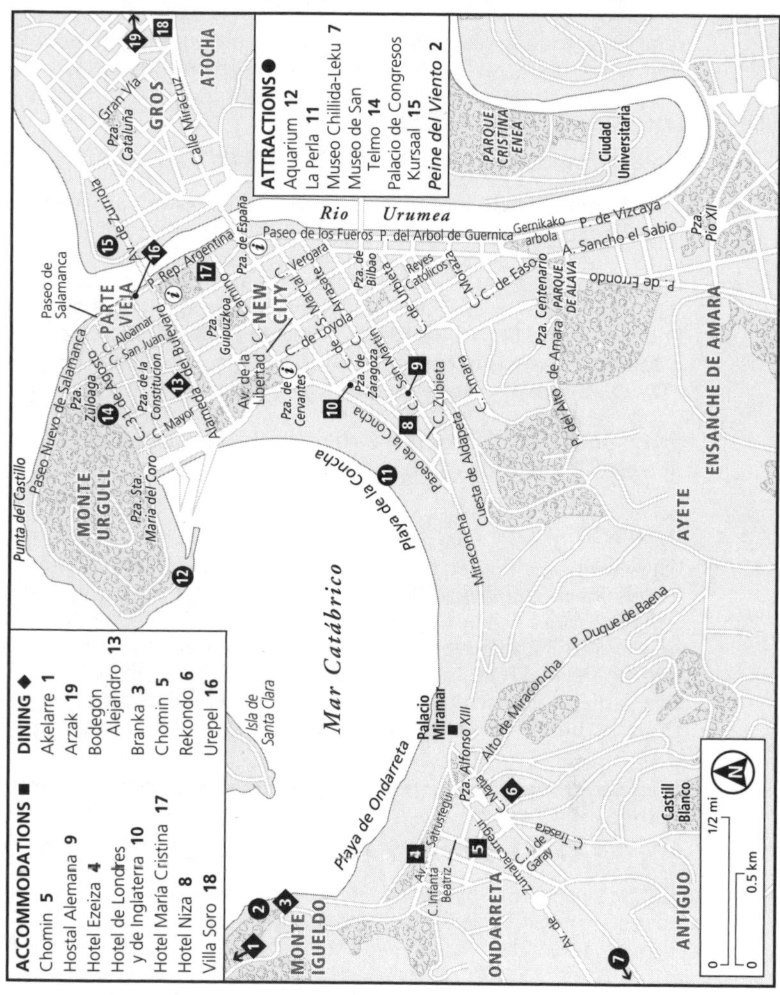

Estación de Amara, for Eusko Tren trains (local Basque Country trains), is at Plaza Easo, s/n (☎ **902-54-32-10;** www.euskotren.es).

Getting around San Sebastián

San Sebastián is compact enough that getting about — especially from beach to beach — makes walking or renting a bicycle attractive options. The cycle lane lining the Paseo de la Concha is very popular, and you can now cycle the entire 8km (5-mile) coastline of the city. Pick up a bike (or scooter) at **Bici Rent Donosti,** Paseo de la Zurriola 22 (☎ **943-29-08-54**), and stop by the CAT Turismo office for "Pedalea por la Ciudad," a brochure with biking itineraries.

A car is a good way to explore the surrounding Basque countryside. Rental-car agencies, at the airport and in town, include

- **Avis:** Triunfo 2 (☎ **943-46-15-27**)
- **Europcar:** Estación de RENFE (☎ **943-32-23-04**)
- **Hertz:** Centro Comercial Garbera, Travesia de Garbera 1 (☎ **943-66-86-26**)

Frequent buses are available to other major cities in the region (see "Getting there," earlier in this chapter); bus service also runs to Fuenterrabia (☎ **943-64-13-02**), Guernica (☎ **94-454-05-44**), and many other small towns in the Basque Country, as do **Eusko Tren trains** (☎ **902-54-32-10**). Buses depart from Plaza Pío II.

If you need to hail a cab, try either **Radio-Taxi Donosti** (☎ **943-46-46-46**) or **Tele-Taxi Vallina** (☎ **943-40-40-40**).

Spending the night

An extremely popular summer destination, San Sebastián has plenty of hotels for its small size (but that doesn't mean they don't fill up in high season). Most hotels are located near **Playa de la Concha,** in the Centro, or **New City,** convenient to almost everything in San Sebastián (including the **Parte Vieja,** or Old Quarter). New City is probably the most desirable area in which to stay. **Ondarreta** is also near the Playa de la Concha, but not close to the Parte Vieja and the main shopping and

San Sabastián's *pensiones*

Especially in summer, San Sebastián can get very crowded with Spanish and French tourists seeking cooler climes. If the hotels listed in this section are full, check out any of the following good-value *pensiones* (guesthouses or inns): **Pensión Aldamar,** Aldamar 2 (☎ 943-43-01-43; www.pensionaldamar.com), a clean and bright inn that opened in 2000; **Hotel Parma,** Paseo Salamanca 10 (☎ 943-42-88-93; www.hotelparma.com), a comfortable small inn near the Kursaal and Zurriola beach; or **Pensíon Kursaal** (☎ 943-43-01-43; www.pensionesconencanto.com), a ten-room inn with good installations and services, also very near the Kursaal Center and Zurriola beach. Larger hotels that may have rooms available include **Hotel Europa,** San Martín 52 (☎ 943-47-08-80; www.hotel-europa.com), a very nice, midsize hotel with classic style in central San Sebastián, near La Concha beach; **Costa Vasca,** Av. Pío Barroja 15 (☎ 943-31-79-50; www.aranzazu-hoteles.com), in the Antiquo neighborhood near the Parque de Miramar; or **NH Aranzazu,** Av. Vitoria-Gasteiz 1 (☎ 943-21-90-77; www.nh-hoteles.com).

restaurant districts; you'd likely need to take cabs or buses to get back and forth. **Gros** is just across the Río Urumea from the Centro and Parte Vieja, near less-crowded Zurriola beach; this residential neighborhood has a number of stately apartment buildings and many *pintxos* bars.

If you can, avoid San Sebastián in July and August, when hotels fill to capacity and charge special supplements (if you do come during this time, make reservations far in advance).

Chomin
$$ Ondarreta (beachfront)

With just eight rooms in a quiet residential neighborhood, a stay here is like crashing at a friend's house — if you had a friend lucky enough to live in a chalet a short walk from San Sebastián's perfect beach. Rooms are simple but charming and very comfortable, and the restaurant of the same name is an excellent value (it takes precedence, in fact; the rooms are merely a bonus). Breakfast, however, is not served here. (So make do with a croissant on the street, head to the beach, and then come back for a shower and lunch.) It's so comfortable that you may want to stick around for dinner, too (see the listing in the "Dining in San Sebastián" section later in the chapter).

See map p. 233. Av. Infanta Beatriz 16. ☎ ***943-31-73-12.*** *Fax: 943-21-14-01.* www.restaurantechomin.com. *Parking: Free on the street. Rack rates: 62€–82€ ($78–$103) double. MC, V.*

Hostal Alemana
$$ Playa de La Concha

One flight up in a handsome downtown building, this friendly little hotel with large rooms is perfect for kids. It's one of San Sebastián's better bargains if you're looking for something simple and straightforward, and rooms are surprisingly large for the price (room 203 is downright huge). And they're sparkling, as are the bathrooms.

See map p. 233. San Martín 53 (first floor). ☎ ***943-46-25-44.*** *Fax: 943-46-17-71.* www.hostalalemana.com. *Nearby parking: 12€ ($15). Rack rates: 63€–93€ ($79–$116) double. AE, DC, MC, V.*

Hotel de Londres y de Inglaterra
$$$–$$$$ Playa de La Concha

The name of this emblematic 19th-century hotel (translated as "Hotel of London and of England") loudly proclaims its English character. Known simply as the Hotel Londres, it has one of San Sebastián's best locations: It faces the bay and La Concha beach, and is a short walk from the Old Quarter. The hotel was recently remodeled, and guest rooms are tasteful, formal, and spacious, with modern marble bathrooms. Rooms with gorgeous views of the bay cost more but are worth it in a place as pretty as San Sebastián.

*See map p. 233. Zubieta 2. ☎ **943-44-07-70** or 900-42-90-00. Fax: 943-44-04-91.* www.hlondres.com. *Nearby parking: 15€ ($19). Rack rates: 144€–222€ ($150–$230) double. AE, DC, MC, V.*

Hotel María Cristina

$$$$$ New City

The city's most famous hotel, this is your place of refuge if you want to live like a queen or a pampered film star. The María Cristina now hosts all the A-list stars during the San Sebastián Film Festival in September, but the Belle Epoque hotel has been the choice of aristocrats and the merely wealthy and famous — such as Charlie Chaplin, Orson Welles, and Johnny Depp — since its opening in 1912. Named for the queen who ruled Spain during the Spanish-American War, the hotel is grand and graceful, with opulent halls and lavish rooms, but to some it may feel overly formal or even snooty in a town as unfussy as San Sebastián. A Starwood property, it's perched on the banks of the River Urumea, but not right on the bay, as some of the other hotels are.

*See map p. 233. Orquendo 1. ☎ **888-625-5144** in the United States or 943-43-76-00 in Spain. Fax: 943-43-76-76.* www.westin.com. *Parking: 15€ ($19). Rack rates: 275€–370€ ($344–$463) double. AE, DC, MC, V.*

Hotel Niza

$$–$$$ Playa de La Concha

The Niza is the perfect small hotel for San Sebastián. It's intimate, family-run (owned by relatives of the great Basque sculptor Eduardo Chillida), and absolutely charming. A hotel since the 1920s, it's right in the middle of La Concha beach, with incomparable views of the entire bay and opening up onto the promenade. The hotel is warmly decorated, with antiques, bright modern colors, and a cool old elevator. Some rooms are a little cramped, but the whole place is so comfortable and charming, not to mention well located, that I prefer it to several of the fancier hotels in town. Try to snag a room with a sea view (make reservations as far in advance as possible). Breakfast is served in a cafe right on the promenade, part of a cute pizzeria run by the hotel.

*See map p. 233. Zubieta 56. ☎ **943-42-66-63.** Fax: 943-44-12-51.* www.hotelniza.com. *Nearby parking: 12€ ($15). Rack rates: 108€–128€ ($135–$160) double. AE, DC, MC, V.*

Villa Soro

$$$–$$$$ Gros

The most exciting thing to hit the San Sebastián hotel scene, and one of my favorite new hotels in Spain, is the Villa Soro, in the residential Gros neighborhood. It's just a short drive or taxi trip from the main part of town, and only a mile from Playa de la Zurriola and, in the opposite direction, the famed Arzak restaurant. Swank and elegant but unpretentious, the inn occupies a late-19th-century villa, declared a Historical Heritage building in San Sebastián. Accommodations are warm, sedate, and sophisticated, with plush fabrics and handsome furnishings. The majority of the 25 rooms are located in the main house with several more in the carriage house. Breakfast is served outdoors on the terrace in nice weather, and you can relax at a bar or in two elegant sitting rooms downstairs. Villa Soro has many of the services and attention to detail of a much larger hotel, but it's notably quieter and more discreet. And for the style and comfort it offers, it's a relative bargain. Check online for special package deals.

See map p. 233. Av. de Ategorrieta 61. ☎ ***943-29-79-70.*** *Fax: 943-29-79-71.* www.villasoro.com. *Free parking. Rack rates: 160€–250€ ($200–$313) double; weekend 160€–195€ ($200–$244). AE, DC, MC, V.*

Dining in San Sebastián: An unrivaled restaurant scene

Basques, other Spaniards say, live to eat. And San Sebastián is the pinnacle of that culinary universe, the home of *nueva cocina vasca* (nouvelle Basque cuisine). San Sebastián has as many top-rated restaurants as Madrid and Barcelona, although both dwarf this coastal city in size; in fact, San Sebastián is said to have more Michelin stars (representing the most prestigious restaurant ratings in the world) per square meter than any other city. With chef's tasting menus and *pintxos* bars everywhere you look, clearly, this is one city to indulge your appetite and inflate your budget (but hopefully not your waistline!). For more on the art eating of *pintxos,* see the "The art and ritual of the *pintxo*" and "On the *poteo:* San Sebastián's *pintxos* bars," in this chapter.

Eating and drinking like a Basque

You don't have to look hard for local specialties, including: *bacalao al pil-pil* (salt cod in garlic and red pepper sauce), *marmitako* (tuna and potato stew), *besugo* (sea bream), *bacalao a la viscaína* (stewed salt cod in fresh tomatoes), *angulas* (baby eels in garlic), *kokotxas* (hake cheeks — Basques swear they're a delicacy — in green sauce), and *txangurro* (stuffed spider crab).

In other parts of Spain, a tapas crawl is called a *tapeo.* In the Basque Country, where tapas are more commonly called *pintxos,* the crawl goes by another name: *poteo* (poh-*teh*-oh). Whatever you call it, it's a great (and relatively inexpensive) way to assemble a delicious meal while you barhop at the same time. See "On the *poteo:* San Sebastián's *pintxos* bars," later in this chapter, for some tasty recommendations.

The drink of choice up north is *txakolí* (cha-koh-*lee*), a young white wine produced only in the Basque Country and typically poured with dazzling dexterity from high above the barman's head. *Txakolí* goes especially well with *pintxos.* If this fizzy wine doesn't do it for you, choose from among many excellent Rioja and Ribera del Duero red and white wines. *Sidra,* or low-alcohol cider, is also popular with the locals.

Nothing demonstrates what food nuts the locals are more than the private, all-male gastronomic societies that flourish in this small city. Born in San Sebastián in the 19th century, these societies (called *txokos*) number more than 100 today. They still revel in the culinary creativity of the coast, still eat to their hearts' contents, and, alas, still exclude women except for special occasions.

Eating in San Sebastián is considerably more expensive than anywhere else in Spain, but what can I say? It's absolutely worth it. Dining in the Basque Country can rightly be considered a highlight of a trip to Spain; I've had a couple of the finest meals of my life in San Sebastián.

Akelarre

$$$$$ Monte Igueldo (outskirts of San Sebastián) BASQUE

In a chalet perched on Igueldo Hill overlooking the Bay of La Concha and the Cantabrian Sea, this classic restaurant has sweeping views every bit as spectacular as its menu. By most accounts, chef-owner Pedro Subijana is considered one of the leading lights of Basque cooking, along with his rival Arzak (see the following review). Whether you opt for such classic dishes as sea bass with green peppers or more innovative preparations, such as puff pastries stuffed with anchovies, you're sure to find the experience memorable. The in-house pastries are delectable. One of Subijana's seasonal tasting menus is definitely the way to go, though it's certainly not cheap and is quite a bit of food. The restaurant is about 8km (5 miles) west of San Sebastián, in Barrio de Igueldo on Monte Igueldo.

See map p. 233. Paseo del Padre Orcolaga 56. ☎ ***943-31-12-09.*** www.akelarre.net. *Reservations required. By car, drive up Paseo del Faro to Monte Igueldo and continue west for about 6.5km (4 miles). The restaurant is on your right. Main courses: 37€–58€ ($46–$73). Tasting menu: 110€ ($138). AE, DC, MC, V. Open: Lunch Tues–Sun, dinner Tues–Sat. Closed: Feb and Oct 1–15.*

Arzak

$$$$$ Outskirts of Gros BASQUE

Juan Mari Arzak — one of the originators of *nueva cocina vasca* — is an artist as well as San Sebastián's diplomat in a chef's coat. His restaurant, one of the finest in Spain (and one of the best in Europe), is housed in a simple-looking cottage (built by his grandparents in 1897) in the Gros neighborhood on the eastern outskirts of town. It has earned the praises of presidents and queens and the recognition of numerous "Restaurant of the Year" awards in Spain. It is, simply, exquisite in every detail — and though the dining room is quite elegant, decorated in warm yellow tones, it's far from an affair. Diners delight in the experience, and a jovial Arzak comes out and circles the room like everyone's best friend. With the classic dishes on the menu to the creative flourishes Arzak and his daughter, Elena, continually come up with, this is the one place to go if you're going to have only one meal to sample the best of Basque cooking. From *puding de krabarroka* (rockfish terrine) to roasted gamecock and wild boar, choosing among the mouth-watering appetizers and entrees is so difficult that

On the *poteo:* San Sebastián's *pintxos* bars

The Parte Vieja, or Old Quarter, near the waterfront positively swims with appetizing little taverns, each offering bar counters full of the best little meals on a toothpick you've ever seen. Calling these *objets d'art* mere snacks is hardly fair; they beat the pants off cocktail weenies. You can easily construct a fun and varied meal picking off *pintxos* and washing them down with wine or beer, moving from bar to bar like locals on a *poteo,* or *pintxos* crawl. Among the top *pintxos* spots in the Parte Vieja are **Ganbara,** San Jerónimo 21, a small space with an L-shaped bar loaded with a great variety of artistic *pintxos,* including mini croissants stuffed with cod and terrific *txangurro* (crab), which you'll have to ask for rather than just grab off the bar; **Bar Martínez,** 31 de Agosto 13, which has specialized in cold *pintxos* for six decades; **Bar Txepetxa,** Pescadería 5, a rustic spot where the specialty is anchovy *(antxoa)* combination *pintxos;* **La Cuchara de San Telmo,** 31 de Agosto 28 (around back, near San Telmo church), which has tables outside and a chalkboard full of modern, avant-garde *pintxos,* such as risotto de aueso Idiazabal and roast-pork canellones; and **La Viña,** 31 de Agosto 3, known for its grilled squid.

The residential neighborhood of Gros, near Playa de Zurriola, is fast becoming a mandatory stop on the San Sebastián *pintxos* route. Worth seeking out are **Bergara,** General Artetxe 8, known for its cod and duck *pintxos;* **Aloña Berri,** Bermingham 24, offering hot *pintxos* such as oyster gratin; **Restaurante Kursaal,** Zurriola 1, on the ground floor of the Kursaal Center and the work of famed chef Martín Berasategui; and **Patio de Ramuntxu,** Peã y Goñi 10, a recent *pintxos* contest champion and originator of creative dishes such as crispy chicken with caramelized apple.

Note that many *pintxos* bars are closed Sunday or Monday, or both.

the fixed-price tasting menu may be the only way to go. Make reservations as far in advance as possible (online).

See map p. 233. Av. Alcaldo José Elosegui 273 (east of San Sebastián on N-I, en route to Pasajes). ☎ ***943-27-84-65.*** `www.arzak.es`. *Reservations required. Main courses: 36€–60€ ($45–$75). Tasting menu: 110€ ($138). AE, DC, MC, V. Open: Lunch Tues–Sun, dinner Tues–Sat. Closed: Last two weeks of June and last three weeks of Nov.*

Bodegón Alejandro

$$–$$$ Parte Vieja (Old Quarter) BASQUE

Run by one of the celebrated new generation of Basque chefs called the "Berasategui boys" (also see Martín Berasategui's eponymous restaurant in this section, as well as his restaurant at the Guggenheim Museum in Bilbao), this charming restaurant features excellent fixed-price menus. It's easily one of the best bargains in San Sebastián. The menu changes daily and always has a healthy number of mouth-watering choices. You can start with artichokes with clams and follow it up with *bacalao de la Isla de Feroe con pimientos* (salt cod, which the restaurant claims is the "Rolls Royce of cod," in red peppers). For dessert, how about *tarteleta de chocolate con naranja amarga y helado de chocolate* (chocolate cake with orange marmalade and chocolate ice cream)? It's a literal and a linguistic mouthful. Two inviting dining rooms boast bright yellow walls and colorful *azulejos,* or tiles.

*See map p. 233. Fermín Calbetón 4. ☎ **943-42-71-58.** Reservations required. Main courses: 9€–21€ ($11–$25). Menú del día: Weekdays lunch 14€ ($18), evenings and weekends 31€ ($39). AE, MC, V. Open: Lunch Tues–Sun, dinner Tues–Sat. Closed: Last two weeks Dec and first week Jan.*

Branka

$$$$ Ondarreta BASQUE

Quickly becoming a fashionable dining spot for hip Basques, this modern and even funky restaurant, with a lively cafeteria and bar downstairs, has one of the most privileged locations in San Sebastián. Its second-story floor-to-ceiling windows frame panoramic views of the bay from the base of Monte Igueldo, just steps from Eduardo Chillida's famed *Peine del Viento* sculpture. The bright and colorful décor is as much nightclub as restaurant, but the kitchen turns out excellent Basque dishes, including a host of daily specials using very fresh local vegetables and seafood.

*See map p. 233. Paseo Eduardo Chillida 13. ☎ **943-31-70-96.** Reservations recommended. Main courses: 14€–32€ ($18–$40). AE, MC, V. Open: Lunch and dinner Tues–Sun. Closed: Last two weeks in Dec.*

Chomin

$$$ Ondarreta BASQUE

Some top Basque restaurants threaten to burst your vacation budget. Not Chomin. Prices at this comfortable, friendly restaurant on the first floor of a private chalet are extremely reasonable given the quality of the cooking and service. Near Ondarreta Beach in a quiet neighborhood, Chomin is worth seeking out, especially for the midday lunch deal, a real bargain. The *brocheta de rape y langostinos* (kebab of monkfish and prawns) and steak tartare are especially savory. A standard, the *merluza Chomin* (white fish with clams) amounts to comfort food for spoiled locals.

*See map p. 233. Infanta Beatriz 16. ☎ **943-31-73-12.** Reservations required. Main courses: 11€–24€ ($14–$30). Menú del día: 22€ ($28). Tasting menu: 30€ ($38). AE, MC, V. Open: Lunch and dinner Wed–Sun; daily in summer. Closed: Last two weeks in Dec and first week in Jan.*

Martín Berasategui

$$$$$ Lasarte-Oria (outskirts of San Sebastián) BASQUE

This restaurant bears the name of one of the new generation's star chefs, carrying on and updating the traditions of *nueva cocina vasca.* His eponymous eatery sits in a modern *caserío* (country house) just outside San Sebastián on the way to Fuenterrabia. Berasategui, who ranks as one of the Basque Country's most innovative chefs, has amassed a number of restaurants, including the one at the Guggenheim in Bilbao, and even more accolades (including the Euskadi Gastronomy Award for best Basque chef). Try the smoked-eel soup or grilled tuna, served in a crème of artichokes, asparagus, clams, and squid. For a superlative culinary experience, order the nine-course tasting menu — a meal that will make the highlight reel of your trip to Spain.

Loidi Kalea 4 (in Lasarte-Oria, 6.5km/4 miles from San Sebastián). ☎ ***943-36-64-71.*** `www.martinberasategui.com`. *By car, take the N-1 highway south to the small town of Lasarte-Oria and ask anyone for the well-known restaurant (pronounced mahr-teen bear-ah-sah-tay-ghee). Reservations required. Main courses: 27€–48€ ($34–$60). Tasting menu: 135€ ($169). AE, DC, MC, V. Open: Lunch Wed–Sun, dinner Wed–Sat. Closed: Mid-Dec to mid-Jan.*

Rekondo

$$$ Above San Sebastián BASQUE

Just up the hill from San Sebastián proper, beyond the Miramar Palace, Rekondo is the kind of place that draws everyday diners and families and couples celebrating special occasions. It's a longtime, family-run favorite in San Sebastián, around since 1964, and is an oenophile's dream. The menu is brief and focuses on the Basque basics: squid in their own ink, lamb chops, and fish dishes of turbot and sea bream. The kitchen's great, but many savvy diners here are committed wine lovers who come for one of Spain's best wine cellars. It boasts more than 100,000 bottles, including some very rare vintages. It's the kind of place where you can blow a big wad of cash on a special *Gran Reserva* wine from your birthday year.

See map p. 233. Paseo de Igueldo 57. ☎ ***943-21-29-07.*** *Reservations required. Main courses: 16€–32€ ($20–$40). Fixed-price menu: 48€ ($60). AE, DC, MC, V. Open: Lunch and dinner Thurs–Tues Sept–June 15, daily July–August. Closed: Last two weeks in June and first three weeks of Nov.*

Urepel

$$$$ New City BASQUE

Classically decorated, with dark wood and flowered wallpaper, this handsome, intimate restaurant serves some of the best food in San Sebastián. It's great for such classic dishes as grilled sea bass in tomato vinaigrette or roasted venison, but Urepel's team of chefs continues to introduce new, innovative fare. Though a little formal looking, the restaurant draws a diverse crowd — from seniors to hipsters. Its prices are reasonable, at least for the five-star crowd.

See map p. 233. Paseo Salamanca 3. ☎ ***943-42-40-40.*** *Reservations required. Main courses: 15€–34€ ($19–$43). AE, DC, MC, V. Open: Lunch and dinner Wed–Sat, lunch only Tues. Closed: First three weeks in July, last two weeks in Dec, and Easter week.*

Exploring San Sebastián

San Sebastián is a great walking city, but the city recently introduced a tour bus, **Donosti Tour** (Bus Turístico). It offers 23 stops throughout the

The cider house rules

After you have your fill of fancy Basque restaurants, you may need something a little down-n-dirty to bring you back to earth. Soaring in popularity are rustic *sidrerías* (see-dreh-*ree*-ahs), or cider houses, on the slopes of the hills overlooking San Sebastián. From mid-January to the end of March, you can grab a simple meal and as many glasses of fresh, low-alcohol cider as you can drink, served directly from the spigots of giant oak vats. You sit at long wooden picnic tables; the simple fare — a codfish omelet, beef, or *bacalao* (salt cod) with green pepper — is brought out on metal trays and is accompanied by enormous baguettes. The cider is the real star, though its slightly sour taste may not be for everyone. In truth, the meal is mainly an excuse to have something to do between trips back to the vat room to fill up your glass. If it's really crowded, the owner may come around, authorizing tables one at a time to rise and ritualistically collect their cider. Contact the **Tourism Office,** Calle Reina Regente 8 (☎ **943-48-11-66**) for a list of open *sidrerías.* If you're not in town during the height of *sidra* season, don't worry; you can always get a bottle of *sidra* at *pintxos* bars and informal restaurants in the city.

city and allows passengers to get on and off an unlimited number of times during a single day. The route begins twice daily, Tuesday through Sunday, at noon and 2 p.m. The entire route takes just under two hours, and tickets are 12€ ($15) for adults, 10€ ($12) for seniors and students, and 6€ ($7.50) for children. The bus leaves from Teatro Victoria Eugenia, Calle Reina Regente, across from CAT (Centro de Atracción y Turismo, the main Tourism Information Office), though you can purchase tickets on board at any of the stops. For more information, call ☎ **696-28-80-27** or visit `www.busturistikoa.com`.

For gorgeous perspectives of San Sebastián, drive or take the funicular (cable car) up to the top of Monte Igueldo (the hill on the left as you face the bay). The funicular leaves from Plaza del Funicular 4 (☎ **943-21-05-64**). It runs from 10 a.m. to 8 p.m. in summer, and from 11 a.m. to 6 p.m. in winter. You can visit a small theme park (with a turn-of-the-20th-century roller coaster) and a rather bland hotel, but the main draw is the spectacular view of the town and its perfect shell-shaped beach, promenade, leafy avenues, and Belle Epoque buildings. Early evening, when the city lights begin to sparkle, is the best time to take the trip. If you're driving, you may want to consider eating at top-rated Akelarre, farther along the coast. (For a review, see "Dining in San Sebastián: An unrivaled restaurant scene," earlier in this chapter.)

The former summer palace of the royal family, **Palacio Miramar,** and its grounds and gardens, sit on a small hill above the two main beaches. It's a lovely, relaxing spot with pretty views. A leisurely stroll, including a funicular ride, may take two to three hours.

Strolling the Promenade

As much as the Basques of San Sebastián love to eat, it's not surprising that people are always out walking. The **Paseo de la Concha Promenade** (also known as Paseo Nuevo) is one of the most inviting places for a stroll that you're likely to set foot upon. It gracefully bends along the length of La Concha beach, with great views at every step.

In the middle of the shell-shaped Playa de la Concha is the Royal Bathing Hut and former "Pearl of the Ocean" spa (today the La Perla Spa). At some point in your stroll, you'll probably be tempted to take the steps down to the beach and kick off your shoes. People are out at all hours, but particularly before and after mealtimes. An intricate white-iron railing and turn-of-the-20th-century apartment buildings line the walkway. As you near the Parte Vieja, you come upon the gorgeous Ayuntamiento (City Hall) — the former casino during the city's Belle Epoque heyday — and a plaza with an old-time carousel and lovely gardens dominated by tamarind trees.

Another tempting place to stroll is the Zona Romántica, or "Romantic San Sebastián," along the left bank of the **River Urumea,** which stretches from the Old Quarter to the neighborhood of Amara. Begin at the Kursaal Bridge, across from the very distinctly modern Kursaal Congress Palace, and pass the grand, Victorian-looking María Cristina Hotel and Victoria Eugenia Theater. Farther down the river are Santa Catalina Bridge, the oldest in the city, and the ornate María Cristina Bridge, dominated by four sculpted obelisks.

At the western extreme of the Bahía de la Concha — the base of Monte Igueldo and the end of Ondarreta Beach — is a small plaza and one of native son Eduardo Chillida's most famous and evocative sculptures, ***Peine del Viento (The Wind Comb).*** Three rust-colored iron pieces jut out of the rock, just above the crashing surf of the Cantabrian Sea, and appear to sift the winds that come ripping in off the ocean. Chillida claimed that the pieces represented past, present, and future. It's a daring and suggestive work — and a beautiful spot at the edge of the sea. From Ondarreta beach, it's just about a ten-minute walk out to the Chillida sculpture, past the tennis club. Allow a couple of hours for strolling.

Basking at the beaches

Beach-loving Spaniards from the sultry center and south of the country flock to San Sebastián in summer. The city has three beaches right in the middle of the city: **La Concha, Ondarreta,** and **La Zurriola.** La Concha, one of the most splendid urban beaches in Europe, became famous in the mid-19th century when Queen Isabel made pilgrimages there for skin treatments. Ondarreta, at the foot of Monte Igueldo, features aristocratic villas and gardens overlooking sunbathers. In the mid-'90s, San Sebastián inaugurated a new beach, La Zurriola, on the right of the Urumea River (near the striking Palacio de Congresos Kursaal); locals looking to escape the crowds on the two better-known beaches favor La Zurriola.

During summer, if the beaches get too crowded (or the number of bare breasts on display becomes overwhelming), you can hop a boat out to the city's fourth beach, on **Santa Clara Island** in the middle of the bay. It's less crowded and more family-oriented. Inquire along the beach or at the central tourism office for information about ticket prices and times for boats traveling to the island (it's all very informal, with no set schedules).

Prowling the Parte Vieja

Around the curve of the bay, just before Monte Ugull, is the Parte Vieja (Old Quarter), where San Sebastián was born. It's a handsome tangle of small streets and fishermen's houses that really comes alive in the afternoon and evening when people flood the *pintxos* bars. (Don't miss performing your own *pintxo* crawl, or *poteo.*) The heart of the Old Quarter is **Plaza de la Constitución,** a handsome yellow-and-white arcaded square affectionately called "La Consti." The other important old town site is the handsome **Museo de San Telmo,** Plaza Zuloaga 1 (☎ **943-42-49-70;** `www.museosantelmo.com`). Admission is free and it's open Tuesday through Saturday from 10:30 a.m. to 1:30 p.m. and 4 to 7:30 p.m.; and Sunday from 10:30 a.m. to 2 p.m. A museum of Basque culture, it's housed in a 16th-century Dominican convent with beautiful Renaissance cloisters. It features European and Basque art from the 15th to 19th centuries (including works by El Greco, Van Dyck, and Rubens), and occasionally presents very challenging modern art exhibitions on the first floor, where the dialog between convent and collection is often fascinating. Perhaps most notable, however, are the spectacular canvas panels by the Catalan artist José María Sert that decorate the interior of the church. The canvases depict episodes in Basque history.

San Sebastián dates back to the Middle Ages, but over time much of the city has been destroyed by 12 major fires. You can peek around the Old Quarter in less than an hour, unless you get hungry and duck in a few *pintxos* bars.

Chillida Sculpture Museum

Hernani

Eduardo Chillida, born in San Sebastián in 1924, was one of the world's great modern sculptors and arguably Spain's foremost contemporary artist of the late 20th century. In 1998, he received the International Sculpture Center's Lifetime Achievement Award. Chillida and his family saw the inauguration of a private sculpture museum dedicated to his work, the **Museo Chillida-Leku,** come to fruition only a couple of years before the artist's death in August 2002. Zabalaga, a 16th-century *caserío* (farmhouse) that Chillida restored (and which he considered the largest sculpture on the grounds), is a magnificent showcase — as are the bucolic acres of wooded grounds — for his often monumental, abstract sculptures in stone and iron. Inside the house are several smaller pieces, including early works, and the artist's famous works on paper, called *Gravitations.* Although the museum only presents works from the last decade or so of the Chillida's career, it's a superb introduction to a giant among modern artists. Allow a couple of hours, including transportation (the farmhouse is in the suburbs of San Sebastián, about a 20-minute drive from downtown). Before or after visiting the museum, be sure to check out Chillida's *El Peine del Viento,* a large iron work cleaved into the rock of Monte Igueldo at the edge of the Bahía de la Concha.

*See map p. 233. Cacería Zabalaga, Barrio Jauregi 66, Hernani (☎ **943-33-60-06;** `www.eduardo-chillida.com`). Take the bus marked "Hernani" from downtown San Sebastián; the bus stop is just after the Campsa gas station after the turnoff from the highway. Inquire at the Tourism Office, Reina Regente 8 (☎ **943-48-11-66** or 943-27-12-79), for additional transportation information. Admission: 8€ ($10) adults, 6€ ($7.50) students and seniors; 75-minute guided visits in Spanish and English 5€ ($6.25); audioguides 3.50€ ($4.40). Open: Sept–June Mon–Sat 10:30 a.m.–5 p.m.; July–Aug Mon–Sat 10:30 a.m.–8 p.m.; Sun year-round 10:30 a.m.–3 p.m.*

More cool things to see and do

After hitting the beaches and seeing the Old Quarter, parents may want to acknowledge San Sebastián's long history as a resort and go to a relaxing spa, while kids may want to visit the aquarium. Fans of modern architecture will want to have a look at the striking Kursaal building by one of Spain's most famous architects.

Relaxing at a spa

If you're the type who comes back from vacation needing a vacation, then **La Perla,** one of Spain's coolest spas, is a must-visit. La Perla's ample facilities, including the soothing water-therapy circuit, sit smack in the middle of the Paseo de la Concha area. Try the amazingly restorative treatments and the series of pool stations that isolate parts of your tired body against water jets; relax on waterbeds or beneath waterfalls; and massage your aching feet in thick-grained, sand-bottom pools. The direct beach access means you can dart out for a swim in the bay and come back for more therapy. Day visits are welcomed (and if you just can't tear yourself away, La Perla also has a gym and cafe-restaurant overlooking the bay). Single visits range from 19€ ($23) for a one-and-three-quarter-hour session to 24€ ($30) for a three-hour session — a real deal. The spa is open daily from 8 a.m. to 10 p.m.; reservations for spa treatments beyond the water-therapy pools are essential. **The Perla Café-Restaurant** overlooking the bay is also a good stop for lunch (☎ **943-45-88-56;** `www.la-perla.net`). See the "San Sebastián" map, earlier in this chapter, for more information.

Getting a fish-eye view

San Sebastián's recently revamped **Aquarium,** with an underwater walkway that provides a 360-degree view of marine life swimming around you, is a good spot for kids. It's not the biggest or best aquarium you'll ever see, but I'd give kids at least an hour here. It's in the port, near the Parte Vieja, Paseo del Muelle 34/Plaza Carlos Blasco de Imaz, s/n (☎ **943-44-00-99;** `www.aquariumss.com`). It's open mid-September through mid-June, Monday through Friday from 10 a.m. to 7 p.m., and Saturday and Sunday from 11 a.m. to 8 p.m.; July and August daily from 10 a.m. to 9 p.m. Admission for adults is 10€ ($12), for seniors and students 8€ ($10), for children ages 3 to 11 it's 6€ ($7.50), and children under 3 enter for free.

Giving kudos to Los Cubos

Those attention-getting angled white boxes on the Zurriola Beach and the banks of the Urumea River constitute the **Palacio de Congresos Kursaal,** San Sebastián's convention center and auditorium. Affectionately, or perhaps quizzically, known to locals as Los Cubos (The Cubes), the building is the work of the renowned prizewinning Navarran architect Rafael Moneo. When illuminated from within, the building looks like a glowing spaceship. Home to concerts, conferences, and the San Sebastián Film Festival, it has aroused such interest that it offers free guided tours on weekdays at 1:30 p.m and at noon and 1:30 p.m. on weekends. Call ☎ **943-00-30-00** for more information. The Kursaal is a great place to drop in for lunch: The restaurant and cafeteria in the building are the work of the renowned Basque chef Martín Berasategui.

Shopping for local treasures

As a destination for summering Spaniards and across-the-border weekenders, San Sebastián has plenty of chic shops all along the bay and throughout the new city. The most stylish shops are located along the Alameda del Boulevard, which divides the Parte Vieja from the Centro, and the elegant streets that lead south from there, to Avenida de la Libertad, another main shopping drag. A shopping mall with lots of clothing and jewelry boutiques is located on Alameda del Boulevard, just down the street from the CAT Tourism Information Office at Reina Regente 3, and another concentration of clothing and foodstuffs shops is gathered at the ground floor of the Kursaal Palacio de Congresos on Avenida de la Zurriola. Yet your best bet may be to pick up something authentically Basque, like the classic berets worn by older men. Pick up a *boina* (beret) at **Casa Ponsol,** the oldest hat shop in San Sebastián, founded in 1838. It's at the corner of Narrica and Plaza de Sarriegui (no phone). For a good selection of coffee-table books and tomes on Spanish and Basque cooking, visit **Hontza,** at Okendo Kalea 4 (☎ **943-42-82-89**).

San Sebastián's nightlife

Hands down the best evening activity in San Sebastián is joining the rowdy, famished natives on a *poteo* (tapas crawl) in the Parte Vieja. Locals say that San Sebastián's Parte Vieja holds the world record for most bars per square meter. (It's a wonder no U.S. party schools offer study-abroad programs in San Sebastián.) Most are clustered in the small streets around Plaza de la Constitución; see "On the *Poteo:* San Sebastián's *pintxos* bars," earlier in this chapter, for names and addresses of some of the best *pintxos* bars. More traditional bars include **Pub Wimbledon,** Paseo Eduardo Chilida 9 (☎ 943-31-41-18), near the Chillida sculpture *Peine del Viento,* at

Lights, camera, actors!

Ever since the reign of Queen Isabel II, San Sebastián has courted royalty. Now it's royalty of a different sort that hits the Cantabrian coast. Although not as well known as the film festivals held in Cannes, Berlin, or Venice, the annual **San Sebastián International Film Festival,** held at the Kursaal Palacio de Congresos, is one of the most important in Europe. Every September, the silver screen's firmament descends on this small Basque city — past guests have included Bette Davis, Johnny Depp, and Martin Scorsese. If you're here in mid-September, join the paparazzi party at the María Cristina Hotel.

the end of Ondarreta beach, an English pub next to (what else?) a tennis club; **Museo del Whisky,** Boulevard 5 (☎ 943-42-64-78), a piano bar with a large selection of whiskey. There's live jazz on Thursday nights at the subterranean **Altxerri Jazz Bar,** Reina Regente 2 (☎ 943-42-29-31), and at **Branka Jazz,** Paseo Eduardo Chillida 13 (☎ 943-31-70-96), on the ground floor of the restaurant Branka. **Be Bop Bar,** Paseo de Salamanca 3 (☎ 943-42-98-69), has weekly DJ sessions on Sunday nights. Starting to feel like all you do in Spain (and especially in San Sebastián) is eat, eat, eat? You can lose a couple pounds sweating it out at a disco — check out **Discoteca La Kabutzia,** on Paseo Muelle, s/n (☎ 943-42-97-85), a sleek disco housed in an old ship in the Parte Vieja by the harbor— or just watch your wallet get thinner at the **Casino Kursaal,** Mayor 1 (at the corner of Alameda del Boulevard, at the edge of the Parte Vieja; ☎ 943-42-92-14), or **Casino de San Sebastián,** in the swank Hotel de Londres y Inglaterra, Zubieta 2 (☎ 943-42-92-15), which has been around since the turn of the 20th century.

Taking side trips from San Sebastián

In addition to the trips in this section, see the section "La Rioja Alavesa: Wine and gastronomy" for a discussion of visiting the towns and wineries of the Upper Rioja and Rioja Alavesa region, which are easily accessible from San Sebastián as well as from Bilbao and Pamplona. If you're looking for a small package tour to explore some of the Basque Country or sample the great outdoors, **Green Services Tours** organizes a bundle of visits throughout the Basque Country. Their guided tours and excursions include the Guggenheim in Bilbao, Fuenterrabia, and horseback and hot-air-balloon rides. Contact them through **Viajes Olatz,** Calle Fermín Calbetón 44 (☎ **943-26-05-98;** `www.gsincoming.com`).

Pasajes de San Juan

Visiting this fishing village (called Pasaia Donibane in Euskera) doesn't actually get you too far out of town — it's only 10km (6 miles) from San Sebastián. But it's a very popular, charming spot to spend half a day and eat lunch at one of the famous fish restaurants. From the neighboring village of Pasajes de San Pedro you can walk or take a little blue boat across the harbor to the town. Pasajes de San Juan is a pretty (if touristy in summer) collection of balconied houses along one main street — where Victor Hugo lived in the mid-1800s. Two family seafood restaurants worth checking out are **Casa Cámara,** San Juan 7 (☎ **943-52-36-99**), a historic place where the lobster and crab pots are hoisted up through the floor of the dining room, and **Txulotxo,** San Juan 82 (☎ **943-52-39-52**), an attractive stone restaurant overlooking the harbor.

To get there, take a Herribus (☎ **943-49-18-01**) bus marked "Pasaje de San Pedro" or "Pasaia Donibane" from Plaza Pío II in San Sebastián; although, given the short distance, a taxi would be preferable. Even if you have a car, travel by bus or taxi because the area is a bottleneck waiting to fill up.

Fuenterrabia

About 24km (15 miles) along the coast on the way to France — through spectacular mountain countryside — is this historic and pretty seaside resort and fishing port (called Hondarribia in Basque). The town, extremely popular in summer, has thick medieval walls, stone houses with coats of arms and colorful balconies, and a tenth-century castle that today is a *parador.* It also has a nice, long beach and marina.

Interbus buses (☎ **943-64-13-02**) frequently depart Plaza Pío II in San Sebastián for Funeterrabia.

If you want to stay overnight, the elegant **Parador de Hondarribia Carlos V** is one of the very best of the *parador* bunch, on the small, pretty Plaza de Armas 14 (☎ **943-64-55-00;** www.parador.es; Rack rates: 190€/$238 double). Occupying an imposing medieval castle with thick stone walls, it has terrific rooms with period furnishings, a beautiful, plant-filled patio, and a terrace with lovely sea views. Much smaller, but also in an attractive medieval structure, is **Hotel Obispo,** Plaza del Obispo (☎ **943-64-54-00;** www.hotelobispo.com; Rack rates: 96€–162€, or $120–$203, double). A cool, atmospheric little restaurant is **Sebastián,** Mayor 9–11 (☎ **943-64-01-67**), and one of the fanciest places to dine is the excellent **Ramón Roteta,** just outside the city at Irún, Villa Ainara (☎ **943-64-16-93**).

Fast Facts: San Sebastián

Area Code

The area code for telephone numbers within San Sebastián is **943.**

Currency Exchange

Currency exchange houses include Change, Av. de la Libertad 1 (☎ 943-43-14-93); Agencia de Cambio, Easo 35 (☎ 943-45-17-55); and Change Baraca, Ijentea 4 (☎ 943-42-06-90).

Emergencies

Contact SOS Deiak, ☎ **112.**

Hospitals

Hospital Nuestra Señora Aranzazu is at Dr. Begiristain 114 (☎ 943-44-70-00). On the same street is Hospital de Guipuzkoa, Dr. Begiristain 115 (☎ 943-45-40-00).

Information

The main city tourism office is the helpful Centro de Atracción y Turismo (CAT) de San Sebastián, Calle Reina Regente 3 (☎ 943-48-11-66). Open Monday to Saturday from 9 a.m. to 8 p.m., Sunday from 10 a.m. to 2 p.m. and 3:30 to 7 p.m. Oficina de Turismo del Gobierno Vasco, the provincial office, is at Fueros 1 (☎ 943-42-62-82), and is open from 9 a.m. to 1:30 p.m. and 3:30 to 6:30 p.m. Monday to Friday, and from 9 a.m. to 1 p.m. and 3:30 to 6:30 p.m. on Saturday. There's also a small *turismo* kiosk in the Parque de Alderdi-Eder, in front of the Ayuntamiento, or Town Hall, at the eastern edge of the Playa de la Concha.

Internet Access

If you need an e-mail fix, pay a visit to Donosti-NET, Calle Embeltrán 2, and Calle San Jerónimo 8, both in the Parte Vieja (☎ 943-42-94-97). They're both open daily from 9 a.m. to 11 p.m.

Police

For municipal police, dial ☎ **092.** For national police, ☎ **091.** The main municipal police station is located at Easo 41 (☎ 943-45-00-00).

Post Office

The Central Post Office is located at Paseo de Francia, s/n (☎ 902-19-71-97).

Pamplona: The Running of the Bulls

Pamplona is the principal city of the Spanish Pyrenees and the province of Navarra — an ancient territory that shares borders with the Basque Country, Aragón, and France. Pamplona once reigned as the fortified capital of the independent kingdom of Navarra. But what seemingly everybody knows about Pamplona today is that it's the site of the legendary Running of the Bulls, called the *encierro* (ehn-*thyeh*-roh), an adrenaline rush of popular culture that dramatizes Spain's up-close-and-personal relationship with death. Ernest Hemingway wrote enthusiastically about the festival in *The Sun Also Rises,* published in 1926, and, since then, people have flocked to the city every July.

The **Festival of San Fermín** (also called **Sanfermines**), during which the daily *encierros* take place, is the kind of exhilarating experience that stays with you (and you don't have to actually hit the streets ahead of the bulls to live it to the hilt). The oddest thing about one of Europe's great party scenes is that Pamplona, the rest of the year, is one of Spain's more conservative cities. Indeed, outside of the bedlam of Sanfermines (held annually the second week in July), Pamplona hardly ranks as one of Spain's top attractions. When bulls aren't in the streets, it's merely a pleasant northern city, with little to occupy most visitors for more than a couple of days. And when the bulls are stampeding — well, there's no place to sleep. If you're not here for the Running of the Bulls, you probably only want to spend a day or two in Pamplona and then head off to the countryside, or to the more interesting towns of the neighboring Basque Country.

Getting there

Most people roll into Pamplona by road or rail from other parts in the north, or perhaps from Madrid or Barcelona. You can also fly in, if you're only coming for the Sanfermines.

By air

Daily flights from Madrid and Barcelona (Iberia only) arrive at **Aeropuerto de Noáin,** Centra Pamplona-Zaragoza, Km 6.5 (☎ **948-16-87-00**), about 7km/3 miles from Pamplona. You have to take a taxi into town (about 10€/$12). A local bus does exist, but it goes to the town of Noáin, and it has no luggage compartments. You're better off taking a cab.

By car

From San Sebastián, N-240 leads to Pamplona. Take the route through San Sebastián or Vitoria (N-1) from Bilbao.

By bus

The **Estación de Autobuses** (the bus station) — a messy place guaranteed to give you bus-fume headaches — is located at Av. Conde Oliveto 8, at the corner of Yanguas and Miranda (☎ **948-22-38-54**), just beyond the Old Quarter. Buses arrive from most major cities, including Barcelona (**Vibasa:** ☎ **948-22-09-97**), Madrid (**Conda:** ☎ **948-22-10-26**), San Sebastián, and Bilbao, as well as from smaller towns in Navarra and the Basque Country.

By train

The **RENFE** train station is at Plaza de la Estación, s/n (at Avenida San Jorge; ☎ **948-13-02-02** or 902-240-202). Several trains a day steam in from Madrid (four-and-a-half hours) and Barcelona (five-and-a-half hours), as well as from San Sebastián and Bilbao.

Getting around Pamplona

The Old Quarter of Pamplona is so small that you don't need more than your feet to explore it. The heart of the Old City is **Plaza Castillo,** also the hub of Sanfermines when bulls aren't running through the streets or dodging matadors in the bullring. Calle Estafeta is the main street, well known to the hundreds who run in the *encierros* each year. It leads right to the Plaza de Toros, or bullring (well known to the bulls). Parks bound the Old Quarter: Parque de la Media Luna to one side and Parque de La Ciudadela and Parque de La Taconera to the other.

You'll probably only need to call a taxi to get to the bus station or airport. Two cab services are **Teletaxi San Fermín** (☎ **948-23-23-00**) or **Radio Taxi** (☎ **948-22-12-12**). For information on traveling around Navarra and to La Rioja, see "Taking side trips from Pamplona," later in this chapter.

Pamplona

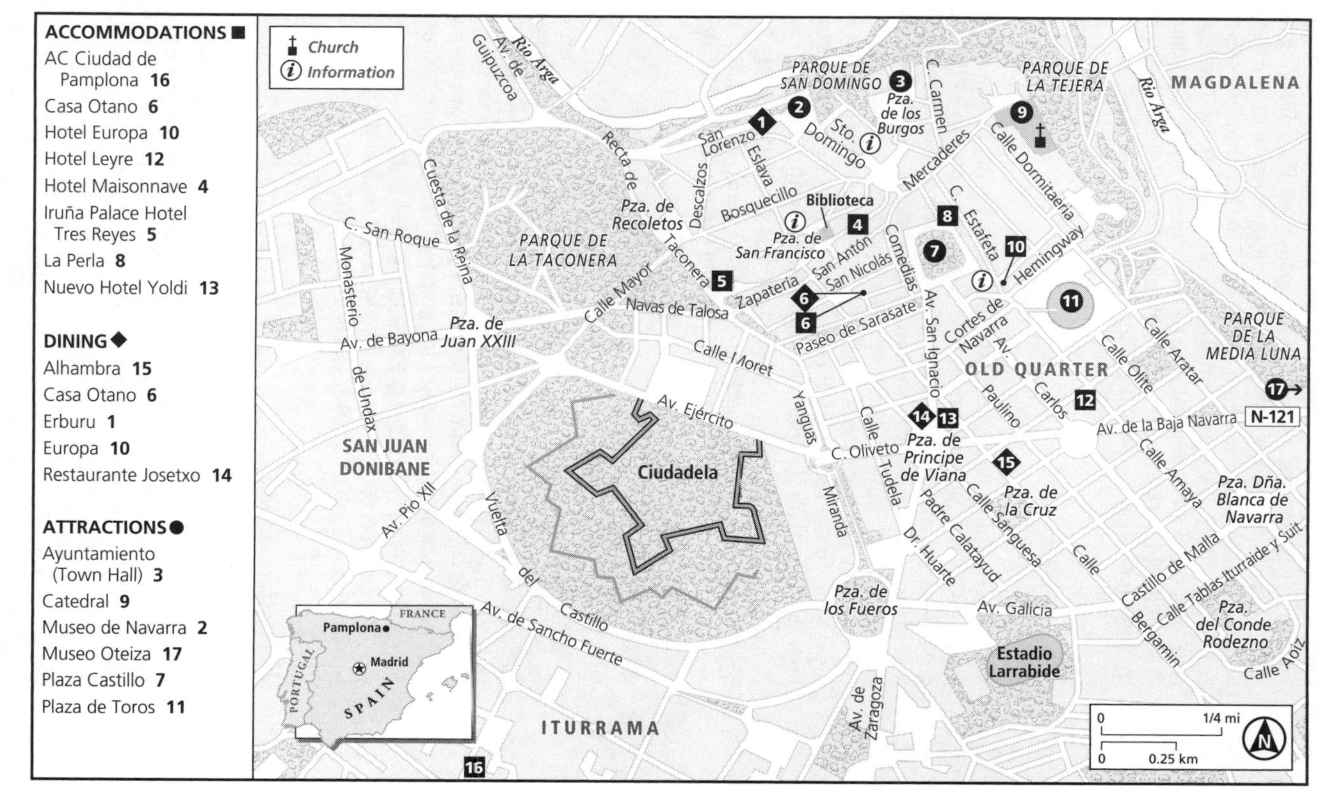
ACCOMMODATIONS
AC Ciudad de Pamplona 16
Casa Otano 6
Hotel Europa 10
Hotel Leyre 12
Hotel Maisonnave 4
Iruña Palace Hotel Tres Reyes 5
La Perla 8
Nuevo Hotel Yoldi 13
DINING
Alhambra 15
Casa Otano 6
Erburu 1
Europa 10
Restaurante Josetxo 14
ATTRACTIONS
Ayuntamiento (Town Hall) 3
Catedral 9
Museo de Navarra 2
Museo Oteiza 17
Plaza Castillo 7
Plaza de Toros 11
Church
Information
MAGDALENA
Rio Arga
PARQUE DE LA TEJERA
PARQUE DE SAN DOMINGO
Pza. de los Burgos
Sto. Domingo
Biblioteca
Pza. de San Francisco
Pza. de Recoletos
PARQUE DE LA TACONERA
Pza. de Juan XXIII
OLD QUARTER
PARQUE DE LA MEDIA LUNA
N-121
Pza. de Principe de Viana
Pza. de la Cruz
Pza. Dña. Blanca de Navarra
Pza. del Conde Rodezno
Pza. de los Fueros
Estadio Larrabide
Ciudadela
SAN JUAN DONIBANE
ITURRAMA
0 1/4 mi
0 0.25 km
FRANCE
Pamplona
Madrid
SPAIN
PORTUGAL

Spending the night

Pamplona has only a tiny fistful of decent hotels, a couple of which have historically been associated with the *encierros.* The following list (with the exception of the runner-up choices that may have beds during San Fermín; see "No bull: No room at the inn," in this chapter) describes hotels all within or very near the old center of the city. The high rate listed is always the special festival rate (often triple or more the regular rack rate). Pamplona has a centralized number for hotel reservations; call ☎ **948-20-65-41** (Fax: 948-20-70-32; central.reservas@navarra.es).

Hotel Europa

$$$ Old Quarter

A small, charming, family-owned hotel — originally built as a private house in the 1930s and now going on five decades as an inn — the Europa has a great location and real intimacy. Twenty-five nicely decorated rooms (in soft pinks and purples) are tucked away upstairs, past the excellent restaurant (even the owners consider their operation a restaurant with rooms on the side). Several rooms overlook Calle Estafeta, which the bulls rumble down during the *encierros.* If one could only get a reservation during the festival. (The truth is you can't. Don't even bother trying.)

See map p. 251. Calle Espoz y Mina 11. ☎ ***948-22-18-00.*** *Fax: 948-22-92-35.* www.hreuropa.com. *Nearby parking: 10€ ($12). Rack rates: 120€ ($150) double. Weekend rates: 69€ ($86) double. During San Fermín: 270€ ($338). AE, MC, V.*

Hotel Leyre

$$$ Old Quarter

A good-looking, midsize option not far from the Plaza de Toros (where the bulls end up after their dash through town), the Leyre is extremely comfortable. Carefully renovated in the mid-1990s, the 55 warm and large rooms have hardwood floors and colorful headboards and curtains. The hotel is associated with two of the better restaurants in town, Europa and Alhambra, and offers a deal at the former for guests. The hotel itself is also a deal.

See map p. 251. Leyre 7. ☎ ***948-22-85-00.*** *Fax: 948-22-83-18.* www.hotel-leyre.com. *Parking 10€ ($12). Rack rates: 120€ ($150) double. Weekend rates: 69€ ($86) double. During San Fermín 260€ ($325). AE, DC, MC, V.*

Hotel Maisonnave

$$ Old Quarter

A large and stylish hotel on a nice street in the Old Quarter, near Plaza de San Francisco, the Maisonnave is a fine place to crash during Sanfermines. Completely renovated in the late '90s, the 140 rooms are a bit small but attractive, decorated in clean beige, white, and black tones. The hotel's calling card says it's "very personal," and for a large place, that's not far from the truth. It's a good value all year, except for that brief and crazy time in early July.

See map p. 251. Nueva 20. ☎ ***948-22-26-00.*** *Fax: 948-22-01-66.* `www.hotelmaisonnave.es`. *Parking: 10€ ($12). Rack rates: 75€–102€ ($94–$128) double. During San Fermín: 330€ ($413). AE, DC, MC, V.*

Iruña Palace Hotel Tres Reyes

$$$$ Parque de la Taconera (edge of Old Quarter)

Large and modern, the Tres Reyes (Three Kings) is a good choice for anyone looking for convenience and comfort. It's downtown Pamplona's biggest and finest hotel. The cement block exterior is a little less than charming; but even if the place doesn't drip with personality, it's a fair value, especially on weekends. Rooms are contemporary and tasteful, and the hotel has a nice swimming pool (a plus for kids), a pretty garden, and an excellent gymnasium, as well as squash courts. It's located just outside the Old Quarter, on the edge of La Taconera Park, but within easy walking distance — an important factor during the all-hours craziness of San Fermín.

See map p. 251. Jardines de la Taconera, s/n. ☎ ***948-22-66-00.*** *Fax: 948-22-29-30.* `www.hotel3reyes.com`. *Parking: 10€ ($12) indoors, free outside. Rack rates: 191€ ($239) double. Weekend rates: 89€ ($111). During San Fermín: 360€–475€ ($450–$594). AE, DC, MC, V.*

La Perla

$$$ Old Quarter

For many decades, La Perla (The Pearl) has stood as an old-fashioned and formerly grand hotel — a kind way to say that it's a little dumpy — but it's still a classic. Finally getting a makeover, La Perla is scheduled to reopen in July 2007. The oldest hotel in town, inaugurated in 1880 on Plaza del Castillo, it overlooks Calle Estafeta. In its glory years it hosted Ernest Hemingway (Room 217) and continues to draw legions of fans of the annual *encierros,* dated and worn furnishings being part of the charm.

See map p. 251. Plaza del Castillo 1. ☎ ***948-22-77-06.*** *Fax: 948-21-15-19.* `www.sanfermin.com/laperla.html`. *No parking available. Rack rates: 138€–144€ ($132–$138). During San Fermín: 247€ ($309). AE, DC, MC, V.*

Nuevo Hotel Yoldi

$$$ Old Quarter

The Yoldi is a simple, quiet, and functional hotel that only comes to life during the San Fermín Festival. Very near the Plaza de Toros, it hosts just about all the best-known bullfighters in attendance for the *corridas* (bullfights). They stay here year after year (they're a superstitious bunch) as do their obsessed followers. The Yoldi ranks, along with La Perla, as *the* San Fermín hotel. Don't even dream of getting a booking during the party, though; it's booked four years in advance.

See map p. 251. Av. San Ignacio 11. ☎ ***948-22-48-00.*** *Fax: 948-21-20-45.* `www.hotelyoldi.com`. *Parking: 8€ ($10). Rack rates: 130€ ($163) double. Weekend rates 67€ ($84) double. During San Fermín: 270€ ($338). AE, DC, MC, V.*

No bull: No room at the inn

Pampolona's Running of the Bulls is one of Spain's greatest hits. But finding a hotel during the festival is a real pain. You either have to make a reservation six months or more in advance and dish up an absurd sum of money, or be carefree enough to try your luck at scoring a *pensión* (guesthouse) when you arrive. A mediocre 70€ ($84) hotel can easily set you back 300€ ($375) during Sanfermines. That's if you're lucky enough to score a reservation. Some better-known hotels in Pamplona are sold out three and four years in advance of the annual San Fermín festival, with rooms occupied by perennial bull aficionados. Even for less popular spots, you need to make reservations six months to a year in advance. Plenty of people just crash in the park, which may be fine for inebriated college kids, but it's akin to trying to sleep on the bathroom floor at a frat house.

Visiting Pamplona during the Running of the Bulls is one of those situations that demands you take a good, realistic look at your budget. If you're dying to attend the weeklong mayhem in July, and you don't have a reservation or a pile of disposable income, check with the Tourism Office for a list of some 50 *pensiones,* where prices are probably double the 25€ to 50€ ($31–$63) they get the rest of the year. Locals looking to make a buck also open up their homes, and you can score a spare bedroom for a price that, compared to what hotels charge, is a bargain. Inquire at the tourist office or look around town for signs posted.

If the hotels listed in "Staying in Pamplona," above, are full, you can try these runners-up (expect to pay top dollar during San Fermín; during the rest of the year rooms go for only a fraction of the festival fare):

AC Ciudad de Pamplona, Iturrama 21 (☎ **948-26-60-11;** `www.ac-hoteles.com`), located in the modern section of town, is popular with business travelers to Pamplona. **Pensión Casa Otano,** San Nicolás 5 (☎ **948-22-70-36;** `www.casaotano.com/pension.htm`), is a slightly chaotic family-run *residencia* (residence) on bar-lined San Nicolás right in the Old Quarter of Pamplona. You have to pay for rooms in advance. Don't expect too much (or any) sleep during the festival. Three miles from Pamplona is **NH El Toro,** Carretera de Guipúzcoa, Km 5 (☎ **948-30-22-11;** `www.nh-hoteles.es`), a reliable entry in the NH hotel chain. **Tryp Burlada,** Calle La Fuente, Burlada (☎ **948-13-13-00;** `www.solmelia.com`), has 53 functional rooms and is located in Burlada, about 3km (2 miles) from Pamplona.

Dining in Pamplona

You can eat well in Pamplona; the haute cuisine of the nearby Basque Country and more rustic dishes from the mountains of Navarra both influence the fine dining.

During Sanfermines, *always* make dinner reservations so that you don't waste time in line or risk not getting into the restaurant of your choice. Fortunately, lots of places are open around the clock. All the restaurants

I recommend in this section are within walking distance of Plaza del Castillo in the Old Quarter.

Alhambra

$$$–$$$$ Old Quarter NAVARRESE/SPANISH

Pamplona is pretty far north for a restaurant named for the Moorish palace in Granada, especially considering that the restaurant in question focuses mainly on regional Navarrese and Basque dishes. No matter. Now owned by the same local company that owns Hotel Leyre and Europa, Alhambra has long been a Pamplona favorite. For an appetizer, try a warm salad of foie gras and duck *confit* (duck cooked and preserved in its own fat). For a main course, the risotto of mushrooms, truffles, and shrimp is a winner. The various *menús* are good values.

*See map p. 251. Calle Bergamín 7. ☎ **948-24-50-07.** Reservations recommended. Main courses: 18€–27€ ($23–$34). Menú del día: 35€–55€ ($44–$69). AE, DC, MC, V. Open: Mon–Sat lunch and dinner. Closed: Last week in July, first week in Aug.*

Casa Otano

$$ Old Quarter NAVARRESE/SPANISH

Going on its seventh decade, Casa Otano is the kind of good-value, unpretentious restaurant that you may find yourself eating at several times during a stay in Pamplona. On the second floor above an informal *pensión,* along one of the city's busiest bar streets, the dining room is surprisingly large and attractive. It's got just the right Spanish feel with exposed brick walls and dark-wood beams. The local Navarrese dishes and grilled meats aren't surprising — just very well done for the reasonable prices. A standard is the *merluza al cantábrico en salsa verde con almejas* (Cantabrian

Eating and drinking like a Navarrese

Several of the dishes you find in the Basque Country are also stars of restaurants in Pamplona. But in general the food in Navarra is simpler, with a greater emphasis on game, lamb, and trout. Dishes to try include *pimientos rellenos* (spicy red pepper stuffed with fish, meat, or shellfish); *trucha a la Navarra* (grilled or fried trout, stuffed with cured ham); and *cochifrito* (lamb stew). When you've got the munchies, get your hands on *queso Roncal* (cured sheep's milk cheese) and *chistorra* (a local variety of chorizo sausage).

Navarra's wines may not be as well known as those from Ribera del Duero or La Rioja, but the region makes some excellent reds as well as whites, and the local dry rosés are among the best in Spain. Good Navarra wines to look for include Artazu, Chivite, Ochoa, and Castillo de Monjardín. Navarra is very close to Rioja, however, and in fact some Rioja wineries are actually in Navarra, so most good restaurants have a healthy representation of Riojas on their wine lists.

hake in green sauce with clams). The midday menu is a good deal. If you need a place to crash, ask about the simple, inexpensive rooms upstairs.

See map p. 251. San Nicolás 5. ☎ ***948-22-50-95.*** *Reservations recommended. Main courses: 7€–28€ ($9–$35). AE, MC, V. Open: Mon–Sat lunch and dinner, Sun lunch only. Closed: Last two weeks of Feb and July.*

Europa

$$$$ Old Quarter SPANISH

This sophisticated restaurant is a stone's throw from the bullring and Plaza del Castillo. The place for perhaps Pamplona's most elegant dining experience, Europa is classic with modern touches. It began as a private house in the 1930s and has several small dining rooms. Also a small hotel, it has 21 rooms (see the Hotel Europa listing earlier in this chapter). The restaurant, though, is the undisputed star. It serves creative regional dishes, such as grilled salmon in olive vinaigrette, roasted lamb with mint *cuajada* (curd), and grilled monkfish with fresh peas and fried green asparagus. Desserts are elaborate; note that several, such as the chocolate soufflé with mint sauce, must be ordered at the beginning of your meal.

See map p. 251. Calle Espoz y Mina 11. ☎ ***948-22-18-00.*** *Reservations recommended. Main courses: 19€–27€ ($24–$34). Menú del día: 39€–58€ ($49–$73). AE, DC, MC, V. Open: Mon–Sat lunch and dinner.*

Restaurante Josetxo

$$$$ Old Quarter BASQUE

Pamplona's self-consciously classiest restaurant, which may strike some as a little fussy and stuffy, Josetxo is where families and dates come for special celebrations. The formal dining room, which opened in 1955, is everything you want in an Old World European restaurant with service to match. As a Basque restaurant, the best dishes are from the sea — the shellfish pastry and lobster salad are terrific, but don't pass up the super goose liver.

See map p. 251. Plaza Príncipe de Viana 1. ☎ ***948-22-20-97.*** *Reservations recommended on weekends. Main courses: 17€–34€ ($21–$43). Tasting menu: 45€ ($56). AE, DC, V. Open: Mon–Sat lunch and dinner. Closed: Aug.*

Exploring Pamplona

Whether you come to sprint with bulls snorting at your heels or to see the historic city of Pamplona (with no one snorting anywhere in your general vicinity), you want to stick to the Old Quarter. Modern Pamplona, although flush with gardens, isn't terribly attractive. For art aficionados, the most exciting development in the city is the museum dedicated to the sculptor Jorge Oteiza. You can easily see the small number of Pamplona's sights in a single day. Guided city tours are available by calling ☎ **948-21-08-27.**

The bull by the horns: To run or not to run?

Should you try to outrun annoyed, 1-ton animals rushing madly through the medieval streets of Pamplona? Even if you're the adventurous sort, this is a no-brainer — at least to me. Every year a number of people get maimed while dashing through the streets, and it's usually the out-of-towners, often young and inebriated. Sure, fatal gorings are rare (15 or 16 in the last 100 years), but one college student from Chicago was killed in the mid-1990s. My advice for most people? Come, drink too much if you must, but climb the barricade and get a good look at the madness from a safe distance.

The *encierro* is regarded as a male-only event (boys and bulls only). Women are still thought of as the fairer, or perhaps slower, sex, and are prohibited from trying to outrun the charging bulls. (Of course, most women are simply too smart to try to outrun bulls, although a few disregard the rules and run anyway.)

You've probably heard people who've done it and say it's a terrific rush. If you're one of those who will never be dissuaded, all I can say is *suerte!* (good luck!).

Here's a tip for the brave souls who do run and survive: If a bull comes anywhere near you, check the photography stores near the Plaza del Castillo. Photographers snap pics to sell as souvenirs. You may just spot your harried self with a bull at your heels — proof for those extreme tales of *machismo* you'll no doubt spin back home.

The Encierro: Running of the bulls

Few international visitors to Pamplona's Fiesta de San Fermín are likely to know or care that Spain's biggest street party is actually religious in origin and dates to at least 1591. The experts who run ahead of the bulls pray to Pamplona's patron saint to keep them out of hooves' way. For most people, Sanfermines is eight days of mayhem highlighted by a daily running of the bulls through the streets.

The party begins at noon on July 6 (and lasts through July 14), when a swarm of people dressed all in white, except for red sashes and kerchiefs, gathers at the Town Hall. With a cry of "Citizens of Pamplona: Viva San Fermín!" a rocket explodes, and so does the city. Each day begins (it's tempting to say ends, because virtually no one goes to bed) with the *diana,* a 6 a.m. marching of bands through the streets, and the 8 a.m. *encierro.*

If you're one of the smart ones, determined to watch the *encierro* from the safety of the barricades along Calle Estafeta, you've got to get up early (or do like everyone else and stay up all night). The crowd stakes out their places at 6 a.m. for the 8 a.m. running.

People crowd balconies and climb the barricades that have been set up along the route. Experts and foolish novices crowd the area near the gates. The most daring actually run *toward* the gates just before the shot

Running of the nudes

Animal-rights activists and anyone against forcing bulls to run through the streets will be pleased to find that People for the Ethical Treatment of Animals (PETA) has organized an alternative to San Fermín. PETA folks do a human version of the run, in the nude, with political messages painted across their bare chests. As a protest to both San Fermín and bullfighting in Spain, it is at once expectedly confrontational and good-natured (er, literally cheeky); as PETA says, their run is full of "babes, not bulls." See www.runningofthenudes.com for more information.

rings out and the gates fly open, releasing the beasts. The mad rush begins, runners inevitably stumble, and the six bulls hurtle over bodies and cobblestones toward the unseen goal: the bullring. If a bull becomes separated from the pack, he is apt to freak out and attempt to run down anything that moves. Minutes later, a second pistol signals that all the bulls have entered the Plaza de Toros. Everyone heads to the Plaza del Castillo for breakfast and excited — and, no doubt, inflated! — tales of near misses.

Late in the afternoon is the day's bullfight, which draws some of Spain's top matadors. If you want to score some first-come, first-served tickets to that afternoon's bullfight, go directly to the ticket office at the Plaza de Toros. Tickets go on sale at 6:30 a.m., but you need divine intervention to get one. They sell out weeks and months in advance, mostly to locals. Try asking your hotel concierge if she knows how to get a ticket, but be prepared to pay the premium scalper's rate.

The party cranks up again afterwards, with marching bands, spontaneous dancing, and parades of costumed figures — literal giants and big heads. And the daily revelry begins anew. The pattern repeats each day until the 14th, when the closing song is a lament: "Poor me, poor me," the Pamploneses sing, "San Fermín is finished." See the "The bull by the horns: To run or not to run?", as well as the official Web site, www.sanfermin.net, for practical information on enjoying the festival.

The top attractions

If you're in Pamplona not to see the Running of the Bulls, check out the following activities and attractions to keep you busy.

Catedral and Museo Diocesano
Old Quarter

The Gothic cathedral, built in the 14th century on the foundations of a former Romanesque church, is the single most important sight in Pamplona. The squat interior houses a marble tomb of Charles III, the last great king of Navarra, and his queen, Leonor. The delicate medieval cloisters, considered among the finest in Spain, feature an intricately carved door with scenes from the Bible. A small museum (the Museo Catedrático y Diocesano) occupies the former refectory and kitchen, and exhibits religious objects, including a series of 13 virgins (er, that's polychrome virgin sculptures). You can conduct a decent visit in under an hour.

See map p. 251. Plaza de la Catedral. ☎ ***948-21-08-27.*** *Admission: (including museum) 4.15€ ($5.20), children and seniors 2.50€ ($3.10). Open: Winter Mon–Fri 10 a.m.–1:30 p.m. and 2–7 p.m.; summer Mon–Fri 10 a.m.–7 p.m.; year-round Sat 10 a.m.–1:30 p.m. Guided visits in Spanish only.*

Museo de Navarra
Old Quarter

Pamplona's other major sight in the Old Quarter, its excellent and well-designed museum, occupies a 16th-century charity hospital. Of great interest are the fourth- and fifth-century Roman mosaics, several in pristine condition, and the Gothic and Romanesque pieces. Look for the unusual French Gothic statue of the Virgin with child. The collection of paintings includes Goya's expressive portrait of the Marqués de San Adrián. Plan on spending a couple of hours here.

See map p. 251. Cuesta de Santa Domingo, s/n. ☎ ***948-42-64-92.*** *Admission: 2€ ($2.50) adults, 1€ ($1.25) students, free for seniors and children under 18. Sat afternoons and Sun free. Open: Tues–Sat 9:30 a.m.–2 p.m. and 5–7 p.m., Sun 11 a.m.–2 p.m.*

Museo Oteiza
Alzuza (outskirts of Pamplona)

This new museum, dedicated to the career of the celebrated Basque abstract sculptor Jorge Oteiza, was inaugurated in 2003 — just a month after Oteiza's death at the age of 95. The museum consists of some 1,600 sculptures, as well as drawings and collages, from the artist's personal collection. Oteiza was considered one of the most important Spanish sculptors of the 20th century, and he was frequently at odds with the other great Basque sculptor of even greater renown, Eduardo Chillida. The museum, a starkly modern and large, earth-red concrete cube, incorporates what was Oteiza's country home since 1975, including his studio. From the roof, which is crowned by several of Oteiza's monumental pieces, you can take in excellent views of the surrounding countryside. The museum is 9km (6 miles) east of Pamplona in the rural community of Alzuza. (Río Irati buses leave from the Pamplona bus station; ☎ **948-22-14-70**). Give yourself a couple of hours here.

See map p. 251. Calle de la Cuesta 7 (in the town of Alzuza). ☎ ***948-33-20-74.*** `www.museooteiza.com`. *Admission: 4€ ($5) adults, 2€ ($2.50) seniors and students; free for children under 12; free on Fri. Open: Summer Tues–Sun 10 a.m.–7 p.m.; rest of the year Tues–Fri 10 a.m.–3 p.m., Sat–Sun 11 a.m.–7 p.m.*

More cool things to see and do

Pamplona is dominated by its annual Running of the Bulls festival. If you're here then, doing anything else other than partying is nearly impossible. If you're here any other time, you'll be able to explore the Old Quarter in peace — or catch a game of jai alai, native to these parts.

- **Exploring the Old Quarter on foot.** A short walk around Pamplona's Old Quarter gives you a good feel for the town. Beyond the cathedral, up cobblestoned Calle Bedin, is a nice view of the city and river below, and the medieval walls that once enclosed Pamplona. Check out the baroque City Hall, where the rocket signaling the beginning of the San Fermín festival, in Plaza de los Burgos, fires. On Calle Ansoleaga 10, is the 13th-century **Cámara de Comptos** (General Accounting Office, the oldest in Spain), a beautiful example of Gothic civic architecture. **Plaza Castillo,** built in 1651, is the heart of Pamplona and a zoo during festival time. Leading from it are several streets famous for their *tascas* (tapas bars). You can take a brief walk around the small *casco histórico* (historic district) in an hour.
- **Taking the no-bull route.** If you're not in Pamplona during the San Fermín festival, you can trace the well-worn *encierro* route. The bulls leave the gates from their corrals just outside the Old Quarter; they proceed along Cuesta de Santo Domingo, race past the Ayuntamiento (Town Hall), and down the long stretch of Calle Estafeta. Then the bulls and staggering runners cross Paseo Hemingway and flood into the Plaza de Toros — the bullring.

  Can you guess which macho American writer is represented by a bust on Pamplona's Paseo Hemingway? Yep, Ernest Hemingway, the author of *The Sun Also Rises,* the novel that brought Sanfermines to a worldwide audience. Papa is depicted in a thick Irish sweater, above an inscription that reads, "A friend of the people of Pamplona and an admirer of their festivals." During San Fermín, he'll almost certainly be wearing a red kerchief around his neck, just like the locals.

- **Catching a game of flying balls.** Pamplona hosted the World Championships of pelota, or jai alai, the wickedly fast-paced sport played in only a few countries in the world. If you want to see a professional game, you can catch one at the **Frontón Euskal Jai Berri** in Huarte, about 6.5km (4 miles) from Pamplona. Games are generally Thursdays, Saturdays, and Sundays. Call ☎ **948-33-11-59** for more information and directions.

Getting adventurous: Navarra outdoors

If you're looking for something different (and running with the bulls just wasn't enough), check out the services of these tour companies, which organize food and wine trips, balloon excursions, and adventure sport outings in beautiful, rural Navarra. See `www.pamplona.net` for additional organizations and tours.

- **Erreka,** Calle Curia 18 (☎ **948-22-15-06;** `www.erreka.net`), offers a wide program of routes through Navarra, including food and wine tours — and guided tours in Pamplona.

- **Nattura,** Calle Marcelo Celayeta 75, Edificio Iwer, B-1 (☎ **948-13-10-44;** www.nattura.com), organizes aquatic and mountain activities in the Pyrenees accompanied by trained guides. Activities include rafting, canoeing, spelunking, cross-country skiing, and snowshoe walks.
- **Novotur**'s mantra is *Unusual Navarra,* which means this tour company offers musical itineraries as well as trips to wine cellars and amateur bullfights. If San Fermín whetted your appetite for more, they can set up tests of bravery with young bulls. Novotur's offices are located at Av. de Bayona 9, second floor, left entrance (☎ **948-23-00-80;** www.bideak-navarraactiva.com/cas/novotur.htm).

Roaming the tascas: Pamplona nightlife

Notwithstanding San Fermín — when the town roars, bars are open 24 hours, and revelers stumble half-crocked from one to the next — Pamplona's usually a conservative and fairly quiet town. At night, wander the streets of the Old Quarter, visiting the *tascas.* The liveliest streets are San Nicolás, San Lorenzo, and Jarauta. The bars in the main square, Plaza del Castillo, are also good watering holes; **Café Iruña** (no. 44) is a legendary Art Deco hangout.

Taking side trips from Pamplona

See the section "Taking side trips to La Rioja Alavesa: Wine and gastronomy," earlier in the chapter, for a discussion of visiting the towns and wineries of the Upper Rioja region.

Getting away from it all

To explore a bit of the province of Navarra and regions nearby a car is the best way to go. Several trains per day run to **Olite;** contact RENFE (☎ **902-24-02-02;** www.renfe.es) for schedules and fares.

The major car-rental agencies in Pamplona are

- **Avis:** Monasterio de la Oliva 29 (☎ **948-17-00-36**)
- **Budget:** Polígono Iturrondo 2 (☎ **948-13-17-00**)
- **Europcar:** Av. Pío XII 43, Hotel Blanca de Navarra (☎ **948-17-60-02,** or 948-31-27-98 at the airport)
- **Hertz:** Av. de Navarra 2 (☎ **948-26-12-56** or 948-31-15-95)

Buses that offer frequent service to major cities include

- **Conda** (☎ **948-22-10-26;** www.conda.es), which travels to Madrid
- **Vibasa** (☎ **948-22-09-97;** www.vibasa.es), which travels to Barcelona

- **La Burundesa** (☎ **948-22-17-66;** www.laburundesa.com), which travels to Bilbao
- **La Roncalesa** (☎ **948-22-20-79;** www.conda.es), which travels to San Sebastián

The government of the province of Navarra pretty much invented the idea of rural home-stays (staying in farmhouses and small rustic *hostales,* or hostels) in Spain. If you want to get away from it all, losing yourself in the intensely green, hilly Navarrese countryside makes for a terrifically restorative and cheap vacation. (I did it one summer near Ochagavia, and wound up in an amazing, quiet old farmhouse — a week there cost me about what two nights in a city hotel cost.) You go on hikes, bike, and, most of all, eat at simple local restaurants, where the food is good and the Rioja wines are even better. For information, contact the **Association of Rural Hotels of Navarra** (☎ **948-17-60-05;** www.hotelesruralesnavarra.es, though online reservations are still not possible) or contact the Centralized Reservations bureau of the **Navarra Tourism Office** (☎ **948-42-47-03;** turismo@navarra.es), which publishes a comprehensive book with photos of rural houses in the region.

Olite, in the nearby countryside, makes an excellent day trip from Pamplona (see the following section). The Rioja wine country is also within easy reach, although far enough away that at least a single overnight stay would greatly enhance your enjoyment of the region; for more information on visiting the towns and wineries of the upper Rioja region (Rioja Alavesa), see "Taking side trips to La Rioja Alavesa: Wine and gastronomy" earlier in this chapter.

Olite: A Gothic town

Just more than 40km (25 miles) south of Pamplona, Olite (oh-*lee*-teh), one of the most ancient towns in the Navarrese kingdom, was a favorite of King Charles III. The town's most notable feature is the spectacular medieval castle and French Gothic **Palacio Real de Olite,** the royal palace with distinctive cone-shaped turrets. Much of the castle is a faithful reconstruction — it was burned in 1813 for fear of its being taken by Napoleon's troops — but it continues to impress and delight visitors. Because the Palacio Viejo (Old Palace) houses a *parador,* public visits are confined to the Palacio Nuevo (New Palace). The palace is open Monday to Friday from 10 a.m. to 2 p.m. and 4 p.m. to 7 p.m. (until 8 p.m. July and Aug); admission is 2.80€ ($3.50) for adults, 1.40€ ($1.75) for students and seniors.

Next door to the castle, the **Santa María la Real,** the former royal chapel, is a lovely example of the Navarra Gothic style.

Though Olite is certainly dominated by its massive castle, its medieval streets possesses several other interesting religious constructions dating from its heyday, such as the Iglesia de San Pedro, Monasterio de San Francisco, and Monasterio de Santa Engracia, as well as an intricate series of 14th-century subterranean galleries that run underneath the town. Those under the main plaza can be visited; they house an exhibit on medieval Olite. The galleries are open Monday to Friday 10 a.m. to 2 p.m. and from 4 p.m. to 7 p.m. (until 8 p.m. July and Aug); admission is 2.50€ ($3.10).

The local **Bodegas Ochoa** winery, Alcalde Maillata 2, offers tours in summer from 8 a.m. to 3 p.m. and in winter from 8 a.m. to 1:30 p.m. and again from 3 to 5 p.m.; call ☎ **948-74-00-06** or e-mail info@bodegasochoa.com for more information.

The **Parador Príncipe de Viana,** one of the most dramatic of the state-owned hotels, occupies three towers of the Palacio Viejo. Rooms are sedate and elegant, with period antiques (☎ **948-74-00-00;** www.parador.es; Rack rates: 110€–120€/$138–150).

To get to Olite by car, take N-121 south. Or, two bus companies run the Pamplona-Olite route: **Conda** (☎ **948-22-10-26;** www.conda.es) and **La Tafallesa** (☎ **948-22-28-86**). Each runs four to five buses a day (3€, or $3.75 each way).

Fast Facts: Pamplona

Area Code

The area code for telephone numbers within Pamplona is **948.**

Emergencies

In case you get gored by the bulls, call S.O.S. Navarra, ☎ **112.** For medical emergencies, call ☎ **061.** To contact after-hours pharmacies, call ☎ 948-22-21-11.

Hospitals

Three hospitals are located on Calle Irunlarrea (all s/n, or unnumbered): Hospital de Navarra (☎ 948-42-21-00); Hospital Virgen del Camino (☎ 948-42-94-00); and Clínica Universitaria (☎ 948-25-59-00).

Information

The main tourism office in Pamplona is located at Calle Eslava 1 (at Plaza San Francisco; ☎ 948-42-04-20; www.navarra.es). Open September through June, Monday through Friday from 10 a.m. to 2 p.m. and 4 to 7 p.m., and Saturday from 10 a.m. to 2 p.m. July through August, the office is open from 10 a.m. to 2 p.m. and also from 4 to 7 p.m. During San Fermín, the office is open daily from 10 a.m. to 5 p.m. For tourist information in Olite, visit the office at Plaza de los Teobaldos 10 (☎ 948-74-17-03).

Internet

Several cybercafes are available, including Iturnet, at Iturrama 1-bajos (☎ 948-25-28-20). Rates are 2.50€ ($3) per hour.

Police

For municipal police, dial ☎ **092.**

Post Office

The Central Post Office is located at Paseo de Sarasate 9 (☎ 948-22-12-63).

Part IV

Central Spain: Madrid and Castile

"*Please* stop yelling 'Ole' everytime the bartender spears an olive for a martini."

In this part . . .

If you've dreamed of legendary castles rising from the plains and of seeing the Old Masters who revolutionized Spanish art, make sure that you spend time dead center in the middle of Spain: Madrid and the star attractions of Castile — Toledo, Segovia, and Salamanca.

Besides being Spain's capital, Madrid is hands-down Spain's cultural epicenter. Few cities in the world can challenge Madrid when it comes to civic art collections with its world-famous Prado and other stellar museums. Though Madrid ranks as a relatively new city — at least when compared to other European capitals — the great art on view is testament to Spain's storied past. But nowhere are the glories and ignominies of Spanish history — from the Middle Ages through the Spanish Inquisition and Golden Era — so present as they are in several towns on the plains just outside Madrid. Toledo is the greatest living example of the harmony that once existed among Christians, Jews, and Moors. Likewise, Castile was the land of kings and conquerors, and it's here that you find cathedrals and citadels, as well as Segovia's mind-boggling, 2,000-year-old Roman Aqueduct and one of the world's earliest and greatest universities, in Salamanca.

Chapter 13

Madrid

In This Chapter

- Choosing the best places to stay
- Dining out: haute cuisine, tantalizing tapas, and more
- Keeping busy in Madrid
- Everything you need to know about Madrid's nonstop nightlife
- Getting out of town to Aranjuez and El Escorial

On a target of Spain, Madrid is the bull's-eye, the country's geographic and political center. With its unparalleled roster of art museums and theaters, Madrid is also Spain's cultural capital and one of Europe's foremost art centers. Though Madrid is the home of Velázquez and the Prado Museum, as well as Picasso's *Guernica,* it's also a city full of other, more down-to-earth images we've come to expect of Spain. Bulls charging after matadors and red capes in the afternoon sun. A rollicking nightlife overflowing with tapas joints, wine taverns, and discos — a place where you may find yourself going to bed at the time when you'd normally get up.

Madrid is mostly a modern creation. The site of a rather insignificant Moorish fortress in the ninth century, Madrid was captured by Alfonso VI, but it remained a small medieval town until the 16th and 17th centuries, Spain's Golden Age of exploration and wealth. In 1561, at the height of the era, Felipe II moved the court from Toledo to Madrid. With less than 500 years under its belt, Madrid is one of Europe's youngest capital cities.

Capital of the province of the same name, Madrid has grown unrelentingly since the 1970s, and especially since Spain became a member of the European Community in the mid-1980s. Some residents and long-time visitors feel that Madrid has lost much of its classic Castilian flavor — but you still don't have to look hard to find it. While sipping a glass of Rioja or sherry and munching a morsel of *tortilla española* (Spanish omelet) in a tapas bar in the heart of the Old City, or stumbling back to your hotel at dawn, you can still discover the Madrid that has inspired legions of artists and writers. This is the hedonistic Madrid that invented *la marcha* — the late-night revelry that roars louder and later here than anywhere else in Spain.

3/11: Terrorism strikes Madrid

Spain, an ally of the United States in its post-9/11 wars in Afghanistan and Iraq, was itself struck by terrorism on March 11, 2004, just days prior to a national general election that pitted the conservative incumbent Partido Popular (Popular Party) against the challenger Socialist party. Terrorists simultaneously exploded deadly bombs on four rush-hour commuter trains on their way into the capital's Atocha station, only blocks from the Prado Museum, and other train stations nearby. Nearly 200 people were killed and 1,400 more injured.

The Spanish government initially claimed that ETA, the home-grown Basque terrorist group, was responsible for the attack, even though the bombings didn't fit the pattern of ETA attacks, and ETA refused to claim responsibility. The president and interior minister both insisted that ETA was responsible even after police uncovered direct links to Islamic terrorists who were members of an Al Qaeda network cell and residents of Madrid. When it was revealed that the administration had manipulated available information to mislead the media and the nation, the Spanish population — which had overwhelmingly refused to back conservative President José Maria Aznar's support of the U.S. war efforts — responded by electing José Luis Rodríguez Zapatero of the Socialist party in a tumultuous and emotionally charged election. After his induction into office, Zapatero immediately upheld his campaign promise to withdraw Spain's 1,300 troops from Iraq. Although Al Qaeda terrorists had certainly sought to influence the election's outcome, and some critics felt that Spain had effectively surrendered to and rewarded the terrorists by toppling the incumbent government, most Spaniards believed that voters had used the election to punish the Aznar government not only for its unpopular support of the war but also for its deceptive, politically motivated response to the terrorist attacks.

You can hit the major museums by day, take a side trip to El Escorial or Aranjuez, embark upon an impromptu tapas crawl, and soak up theater, opera, and flamenco by night. The city's atmospheric *mesones* and *tascas* — cavelike restaurants and taverns — get the night started. When the sun goes down, you find that Madrileños, the people of Madrid, are among the most open and gregarious in Spain.

Though the city's dining scene has been overshadowed in recent years by that of Barcelona and smaller cities in the Basque Country, Madrid still has some of Spain's finest restaurants, and it's a particularly great place to feast on Castilian specialties such as suckling pig, lamb, and pheasant. Madrileños claim that the seafood flown in daily is fresher even than that found on the coasts.

The best times to visit Madrid are spring and fall. The weather reaches extremes: cold in the winter, very hot and dry in the summer. If you must go in summer, avoid August. Not only is it fry-an-egg-on-the-sidewalk hot, but also the city is dead. Most Madrileños take the entire month off and escape to cooler climes. Hotel occupancy and rates are pretty consistent all year, except in August, when no one wants to be in Madrid, and during the San Isidro (mid-May) and Autumn Festivals (late Oct–Nov), when everyone does. If you want to be a part of Madrid at its most festive during these celebrations, book several months in advance.

If you only want a taste of Madrid, you still need at least a couple of days to visit the Prado, see some of Viejo Madrid, and check out the capital's dizzying nightlife.

Getting There: All Roads Lead to Madrid

For many years, Madrid was about the only Spanish city you could fly into from North America and many parts of Europe. And even now, with Barcelona on the way up as an international destination, the majority of overseas flights still touch down in Madrid. All roads and flight paths in Spain lead to Madrid. You can jump on a quick shuttle flight from Barcelona, or catch the high-speed train from Seville.

By air

Most international airlines, including **Iberia, American, Delta,** and others, offer direct flights to Madrid. Madrid's newly expanded international airport, **Barajas** (bah-*rah*-hahs), Carretera de Barcelona, Km 16 (☎ **902-100-107** or 91-305-83-43; `www.aena.es`) is 15km (9 miles) from the city center. Brand-new, high-tech Terminal 4 handles most international flights and is a shuttle bus away from the other terminals. Passing through Customs can involve waiting in a long line, but is otherwise hassle-free. Be sure you don't get in the line that says E.U. (which indicates members of the European Union), unless, of course, you hold a passport from one of the E.U. countries. Look instead for the sign that says OTROS PAISES (other countries) or OTRAS NACIONALIDADES (other nationalities).

Barajas airport is large but simple enough to navigate if you're not shuttling between terminals. You'll find major auto-rental agencies, an ATM machine, and a small **Tourism Information Office** (☎ **91-305-86-56;** daily 8 a.m.–8 p.m.). Carts are available for hauling your luggage, for free. T2 is the terminal that handles domestic flights, while T3 is reserved for Barcelona-Madrid shuttle *(puente aereo)* flights.

Travel time from the airport to downtown is about 30 to 45 minutes. You now have three options for transport to the city (and returning to the airport). **Taxis,** the quickest but most expensive option — and the best if you have more than one piece of luggage and/or are tired from a long flight — are lined up outside the terminals and charge about 20€ ($25) for a trip to the center of Madrid (tipping isn't expected). The yellow **Airport Bus** service, called Bus 89 (☎ **91-431-61-92**), leaves from the curb right outside the terminal every 12 minutes for Plaza Colón, making just a handful of stops on the way; it runs Monday through Friday from 6 a.m. to 11 p.m. and weekends from 6:30 a.m. to 11 p.m. Though convenient and inexpensive, the bus requires that you either catch a taxi or walk (and lug your bags) to get to your hotel, so unless you're staying near Plaza Colón, it may not be the best option — especially after a long international flight. The same bus returns to Barajas from the underground station at Plaza Colón. The price either direction is 2.50€ ($3); pay on board (exact change isn't necessary).

Line 8 (the pink line) of the Madrid **Metro** (subway) runs between Barajas airport (out of T2) and the Nuevos Ministerios station, where it arrives in just 12 minutes. It's another 15 minutes from there to downtown. Stop by the Tourism Information booth for a subway map and determine the closest stop to your hotel (check out the Metro Web site, `www.metromadrid.es`, beforehand and arrive with a plan in hand). The subway (single-ticket fares are 1€/$1.20) is the cheapest way into the city, and if your hotel is near a stop, it can also be quite convenient. However, you have to change lines at least once (and possibly two or three times). If you're weighted down by several pieces of luggage, the subway is far from the easiest option.

Rental cars from the major agencies are available at the airport, but unless you're planning on immediately heading outside of Madrid, I wouldn't recommend navigating the capital's intense traffic right after landing (you won't need a car in Madrid, and parking is both expensive and hard to find).

By car

Spain's major highways (Roman numerals I–VI) radiate outward from Madrid, which is measured as kilometer zero on the national highway system. The N-II highway from Barcelona leads to Madrid, as do N-VI from Santiago and N-IV from Andalusia.

Near the city, look for signs reading CENTRO (center) that take you into downtown Madrid.

By train

RENFE is the Spanish national train service; its main office, open weekdays only, is located at Alcalá 44 (Metro: Banco de España); for all train information, call ☎ **902-24-02-02.** Madrid splits its train service among three stations.

- **Atocha,** Glorieta del Emperador Carlos V, s/n (Metro: Atocha RENFE), is the station for destinations in south and southeast Spain and Portugal. The high-speed **AVE train** (☎ **902-24-02-02**) departs for (and arrives from) Córdoba and Seville at Atocha.
- **Charmartín,** Calle Agustín de Foxá, s/n (Metro: Charmartín), the most modern train station, covers most destinations in north and northeastern Spain, in addition to most European capitals.
- **Estación Príncipe Pío,** also called Estación Norte, Paseo del Norte 30 (Metro: Norte), is the station for trains to and from northwestern Spain, including Salamanca and Galicia.

For several years now, travelers have been surprised to discover that though a high-speed (AVE) train links Madrid and Seville, there isn't one connecting the capital and the second-largest city, Barcelona. Such a train is finally in the works, though frustratingly delayed. The hope is that an AVE high-speed railway eventually will make the trip from Madrid to Barcelona in just two-and-a-half hours (currently, it takes six-and-a-half hours).

By bus

Buses that make the most common trips out of the capital to towns in Castile are on the whole clean and efficient, as well as inexpensive options for getting around the region.

- Madrid's main bus terminal, for national and international departures, is **Estación Sur de Autobuses,** Calle Méndez Alvaro 83 (**☎ 91-468-42-00;** `www.estaciondeautobuses.com`; Metro: Palos de la Frontera or Méndez Alvaro).
- The **La Sepulvedana** line travels between Madrid and Segovia. **Estación de la Sepulvedana,** Paseo de la Florida 11 (**☎ 91-530-48-00** or 91-547-52-61; Metro: Príncipe Pío).
- **Empresa Larrea** goes between Madrid and Avila. Estación Sur (**☎ 91-547-52-61;** Metro: Méndez Alvaro).
- **Empresa Auto Res** buses make the journey between Madrid and Salamanca. **Estación de Auto Res,** Calle Fernández Shaw 1 (**☎ 91-551-72-00**).
- **Galliano Continental** travels back and forth between Madrid and Toledo. Estación Sur (**☎ 91-527-29-61;** Metro: Méndez Alvaro).

Orienting Yourself in Madrid

Madrid doesn't have any natural landmarks useful for getting your bearings, though it does have several major plazas (squares) and splendid boulevards linking them that will help you master the city's layout. Street numbers are frequently confusing; also, as throughout Spain, the numbers of addresses don't often follow logically, and some are labeled *s/n,* or *sin número* (unnumbered). Your best bet is to orient yourself using the Metro (subway) map, because most destinations are close to a Metro stop.

After it was named Spain's capital, Madrid took off in successive waves of growth from the 16th to 19th centuries, expanding east and north from the River Manzanares. But getting a fix on the city and its neighborhoods is easy. You want to spend most of your time in Old Madrid (near the Plaza Mayor) and Bourbon Madrid (including the Prado Museum and Retiro Park). Many hotels, restaurants, and shops are located in the northern and eastern neighborhoods. The periphery, the urban sprawl of Madrid, is beyond the interest of most short-term visitors.

The main arteries of Madrid are Calle Mayor, which runs the length of the old center (and becomes Calle de San Jerónimo in the more modern part of the city); Gran Vía and Alcalá, the main commercial streets that border the newer northern neighborhoods; and Paseo del Prado/Paseo de la Recoleta, which run perpendicular to Gran Vía and Alcalá along Madrid's museum mile (from the Atocha train station past Plaza de Cibeles). Heading north, beyond Plaza de Colón, Paseo del Prado becomes the chic, tree- and cafe-lined Paseo de la Castellana.

Introducing the neighborhoods

Three Madrids exist. The first is **Old Madrid,** the city of the Habsburgs, between the Royal Palace and Plaza Mayor. Second is **Bourbon Madrid,** the area Bourbon monarchs expanded in the 18th century. And the third is **modern Madrid** — an urban sprawl that began with such northern neighborhoods as Barrio Salamanca in the 19th century, and that now radiates out from the center into rather bland and undistinguished suburbs.

Viejo Madrid (Old Madrid)

Viejo Madrid is the heart of the city. The Moors established a fortress near the river, and Madrid grew up there in the 16th and 17th centuries. The Old City, the Madrid of the Habsburg royal family, extends from the Palacio Real (which is actually a much later addition) to Madrid's version of Times Square, Puerta del Sol. The old district is a warren of historic buildings and crooked cobblestone streets. This neighborhood is where to go for *tascas* (tapas bars), restaurants, and historical sightseeing. Here you find the **Royal Palace** and the Old City's historic buildings and churches; bustling **Plaza Mayor** and **Puerta del Sol; Monasterio de las Decalzas Reales,** Madrid's most important convent; and a wealth of atmospheric **taverns** and **tapas bars.**

Bourbon Madrid

No, a bunch of Kentucky distilleries didn't suddenly take up residence in Madrid. East of Viejo Madrid, the expansion overseen by Carlos III of the Bourbon dynasty is an area of grand boulevards, plazas, and fountains, but also thick layers of 18th-century apartment buildings. Bourbon Madrid is home to Madrid's major museums — Spain's Big Three, the **Prado, Thyssen-Bornemisza,** and **Reina Sofía** — and its most popular park, **Retiro,** as well as many of the city's finest hotels and restaurants.

Modern Madrid

Beginning in the 19th century, Madrid expanded yet again, north and south and every which way. Modern Madrid is an ever-expanding succession of residential neighborhoods filled with elegant shops, cinemas, restaurants, banks, and smaller museums. You can find a number of fine hotels in these neighborhoods, and they make for a quieter stay if you don't mind taking the subway to get to Madrid's star attractions. Modern Madrid contains the **Barrio de Salamanca,** a 19th-century neighborhood of elegant, expensive apartments and superchic boutiques; **Chueca,** a bohemian barrio full of restaurants, bars, and funky clothing and design shops; **Paseo de la Castellana,** a wide boulevard lined with trees and cafes; and **Plaza de Toros de las Ventas,** one of Spain's best-known bullfighting arenas.

Finding information after you arrive

Municipal Tourism Offices are located at Plaza Mayor 3 (☎ **91-588-16-36;** www.munimadrid.es), open Monday through Saturday from 10 a.m. to 8 p.m. and Sunday and holidays from 10 a.m. to 3 p.m.; Duque de Medinaceli 2 (☎ **902-10-49-51**), open Monday through Saturday from 9 a.m. to 7 p.m. and Sunday from 9 a.m. to 3 p.m.; Mercado Puerta de Toledo 1 (☎ **902-10-00-07**), open Monday through Saturday from 8 a.m. to 8 p.m. and Sunday from 8 a.m. to 2 p.m.; Barajas Airport at the International Arrivals Terminal (☎ **91-305-86-56**), open daily from 8 a.m. to 8 p.m.; and the Chamartín and Atocha train stations. Call ☎ **902-10-21-12** for additional tourism information or to register a complaint; call ☎ **010** for general information. In addition, in summer months (July–Sept), **yellow tourist information kiosks** operate from 10 a.m. to 8 p.m. daily on Calle de Bailén in front of the Palacio Real, at the Museo del Prado, on the Puerta del Sol, and at El Corte Inglés department store on Plaza Callao.

Getting around Madrid

Madrid is large and sprawling, but the places that interest most visitors are in a fairly compact area. In fact, you can walk much of Madrid, and what you can't is accessible using the Metro system, which is easy to navigate and goes just about everywhere you need.

By subway

The **Metro** (☎ **012** or 91-486-07-52; www.metromadrid.es), marked by red and blue diamond-shaped signs, is Madrid's subway — by far the fastest and easiest way to navigate the city. Stops are almost everywhere you want to go. Single-ticket fares are 1€ ($1.20). Hours are Monday to Sunday from 6 a.m. to 1:30 a.m. You can find handy maps *(plano del metro)* at Metro stations.

A ten-trip ticket **(Metrobus)** is available for 6.15€ ($7.40), a nearly half-price bargain. It pays for itself after six journeys on the Metro and can be used by additional passengers. You'll use it up in no time, and it also works on the bus.

By bus

Taking the bus around town is complicated for first-time visitors. Conductors generally don't speak English, and with all the traffic on the wide avenues and tiny streets, getting a read on the city from the window of a bus is tough. I usually stick to the airport bus on the way in, and go with the subway (Metro) and my own two feet until I catch the bus back to the airport. If you prefer your travel above ground, though, about 150 bus lines (called **EMT;** `www.emtmadrid.es`) cover Madrid. Buses run from 6 a.m. to midnight daily; the fare is 1€ ($1.20); special night buses (called *buhos,* or night owls) run much less frequently, from midnight to 6 a.m. For information, call ☎ **012.**

By taxi

Authorized taxis are white with diagonal red bands. Few taxi rides in town cost more than 8€ ($9.60). You can hail a cab in the street (the little green light on the roof means you can hop in) or get one where they line up (usually outside hotels). A slightly higher night rate is charged from 11 p.m. to 7 a.m. Taxi companies include **Tele-Taxi** (☎ **91-371-21-34**), **Radio Taxi** (☎ **91-405-55-00**), and **Radio Taxi Independiente** (☎ **91-405-12-13**), all of which you can call to make transportation arrangements.

Taxi rates in Madrid are pretty reasonable, and most drivers are honest, but a few try to rip off tourists. I have had several taxi drivers in Madrid (but only in Madrid — not in any other Spanish city) try to jack up the fare on me (one even slyly placed his street guide over the meter in an attempt to claim it wasn't working). Check the fare at the beginning of the journey so that you don't end up paying for the last guy's ride, and ask about any suspicious supplements to your fare.

By car

Don't drive in Madrid unless you're forced to. Trust me on this one — traffic is horrendous, especially during rush hour, and you can't park anywhere. A car is really only useful for getting out of the city. Rental-car companies include **Europcar** (☎ **91-721-12-12**) at the Atocha and Chamartín train stations; **Avis,** Gran Vía 60 (☎ **902-13-55-31**); and **Hertz,** Gran Vía 88 (☎ **91-393-72-28**). You can also find these companies at the airport.

On foot

Madrid isn't the classic walking city that Barcelona is, although people walk everywhere around Viejo Madrid and love to stroll the Paseo del Prado and Paseo la Castellana on summer evenings. But, as sprawling as the city is, you can still cover the areas of greatest interest on foot. Just don't overdo it. Hop on the efficient and inexpensive Metro (subway) to pop around the city. When you do walk, be very careful crossing streets; pedestrians have few rights in Spain as a whole and even fewer in Madrid. Check out "Seeing Madrid by Guided Tour," later in this chapter, for information on walking tours organized by the Tourism Office.

Staying in Style

In addition to its status as a top tourist destination, Madrid is also the top draw in Spain for international business travelers, so the capital is flush with hotel options of every stripe. You have plenty of choices, from a surfeit of inexpensive *pensiones* and *residencias* to some of the finest white-glove palaces in Europe, but hotels in Madrid are among the most expensive in Spain. Don't panic: I include some money-wise tips in this section so you don't have to worry about taking out a loan for your trip to Madrid.

Madrid's classic hotel Reina Victoria hotel, which had been around since the 1920s and had been the accommodations of choice for generations of bullfighters, is no longer. It will be transformed into a Hard Rock Hotel, which to my mind indicates something unfortunate about Madrid's evolution.

Many hotels are scattered along the Gran Vía, which isn't the greatest place to be walking after dark, and near Atocha Station. Old Madrid also has a good selection of accommodations ringing the central Plaza Mayor and Puerta del Sol. These areas attract their share of pickpockets because they're popular travel destinations, but due to their proximity to prime dining and sightseeing, they're also among the most exciting places to be in Madrid.

Most hotel rates don't include breakfast or IVA, the 7 percent value-added tax. To ensure the bill isn't a shock at the end of your stay, make sure you ask about these taxes when booking your room. For more information on booking accommodations in Spain, see Chapter 7.

Many of Madrid's hotels cater to business travelers, so weekend rates and special deals are often available — asking is always a good idea. Unless it's high season and the hotel is near capacity, you can probably get a break (sometimes as much as half off the **rack rate**, the maximum rate a hotel charges for a room).

The top hotels

AC Palacio del Retiro

$$$$$ Bourbon Madrid (near Retiro Park)

One of the newest ventures in Madrid by the dependable, upscale AC Hotels chain (which operates a half-dozen other properties in the capital), this midsize luxury hotel (51 rooms), inaugurated in 2004, has a perfect location and terrific bones. It inhabits a beautiful, early-20th-century palace (a National Heritage–protected structure) overlooking Retiro Park and just a few short blocks from the Prado Museum. The palace contains a gorgeous central staircase, stained-glass windows, and marble columns. Rooms are sleek, respecting the original style of the building but adding

Madrid Accommodations, Dining, and Attractions

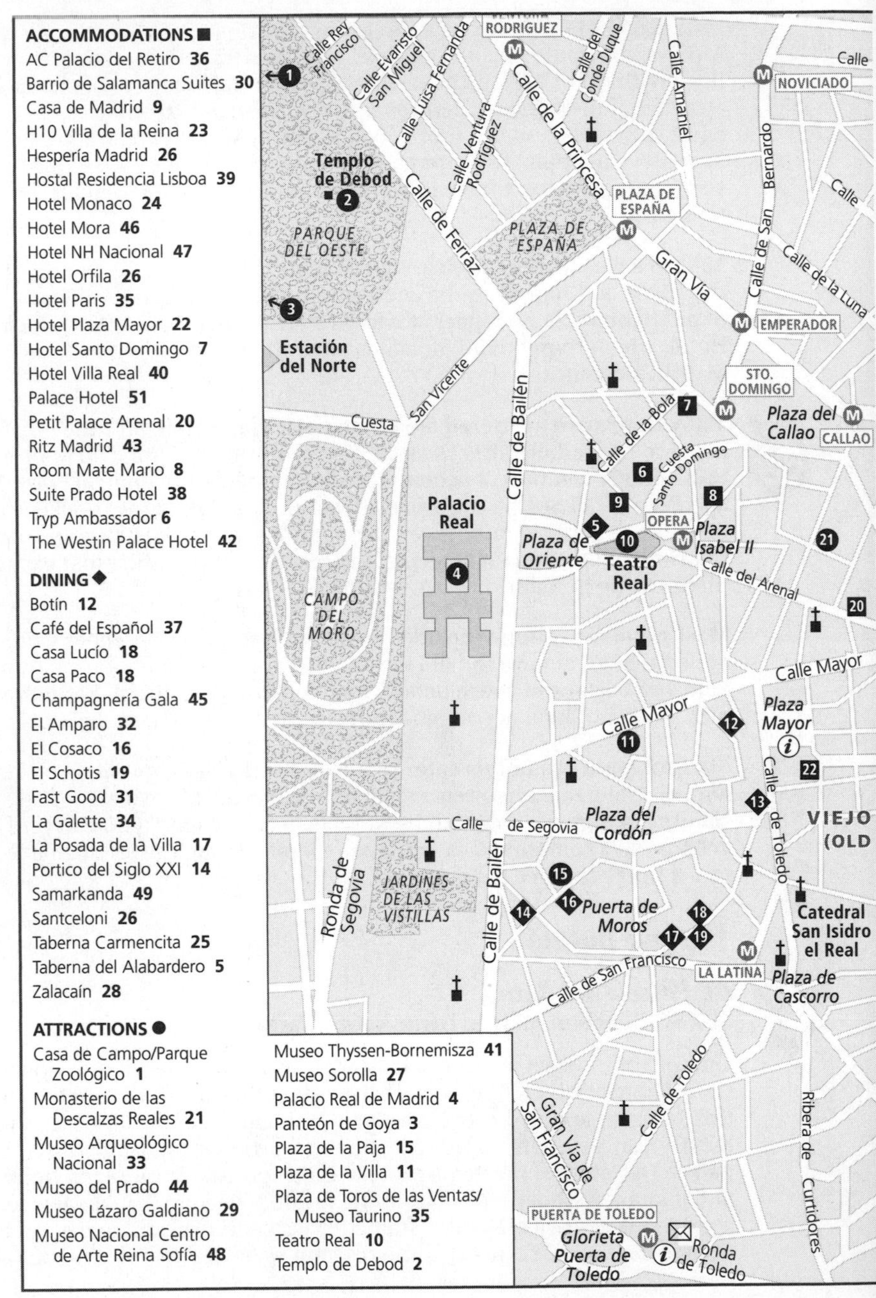

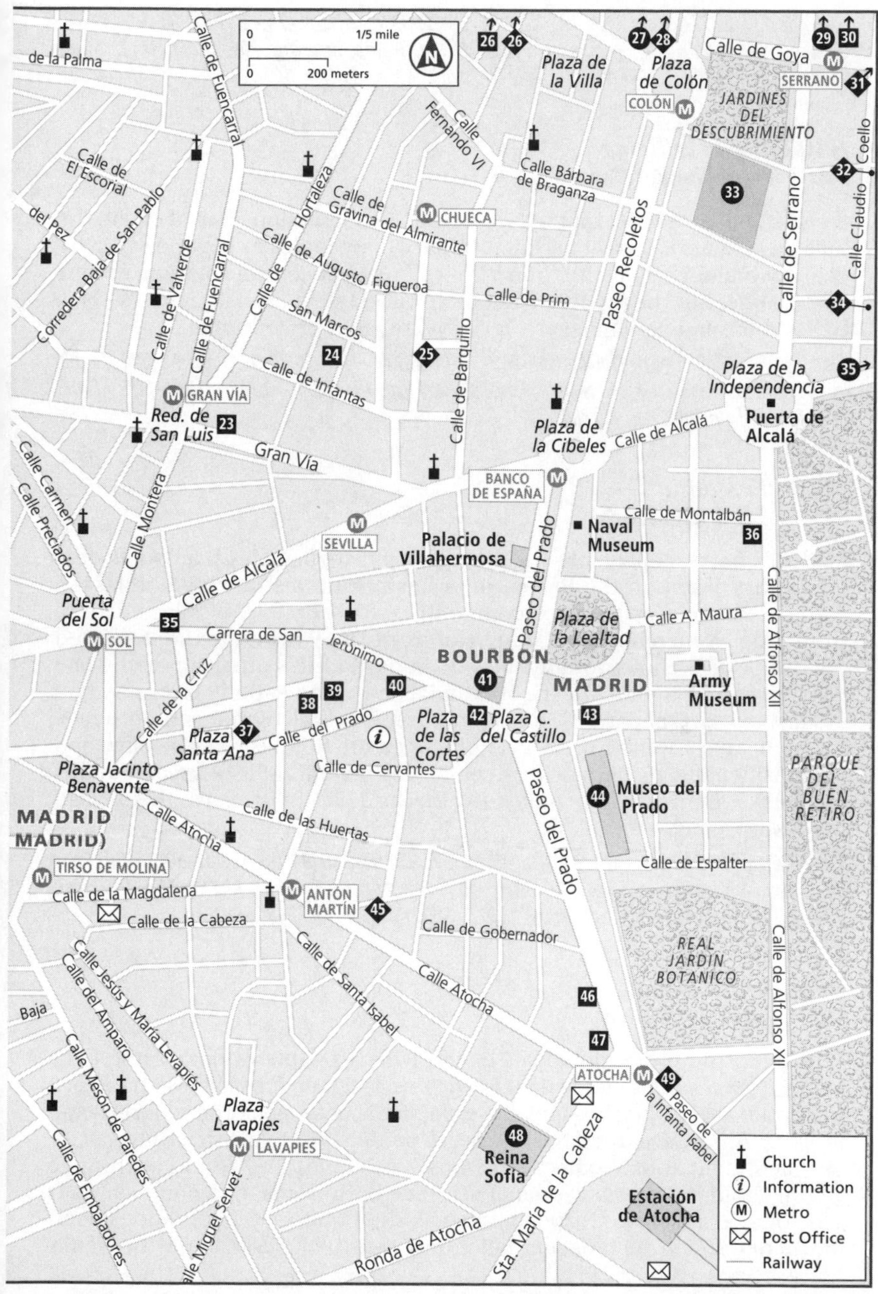

0 1/5 mile
0 200 meters
N
de la Palma
Calle de Fuencarral
Calle Fernando VI
Plaza de la Villa
Plaza de Colón
COLÓN
Calle de Goya
SERRANO
JARDINES DEL DESCUBRIMIENTO
Calle Bárbara de Braganza
Calle Claudio Coello
Calle de El Escorial
Calle de Hortaleza
Calle de Gravina del Almirante
CHUECA
Paseo Recoletos
Calle de Serrano
del Pez
Corredera Baja de San Pablo
Calle de Valverde
Calle de Fuencarral
Calle de Augusto Figueroa
Calle de Prim
San Marcos
Calle de Barquillo
Calle de Infantas
GRAN VÍA
Red. de San Luis
Plaza de la Independencia
Puerta de Alcalá
Plaza de la Cibeles
Calle de Alcalá
Gran Vía
Calle Carmen
Calle Preciados
Calle Montera
BANCO DE ESPAÑA
SEVILLA
Palacio de Villahermosa
Calle de Montalbán
Naval Museum
Paseo del Prado
Calle de Alcalá
Puerta del Sol
SOL
Carrera de San Jerónimo
Plaza de la Lealtad
Calle A. Maura
Calle de Alfonso XII
BOURBON MADRID
Army Museum
Calle de la Cruz
Plaza Santa Ana
Calle del Prado
Plaza de las Cortes
Plaza C. del Castillo
Calle de Cervantes
Plaza Jacinto Benavente
MADRID
MADRID)
Calle Atocha
Calle de las Huertas
Paseo del Prado
Museo del Prado
PARQUE DEL BUEN RETIRO
Calle de Espalter
TIRSO DE MOLINA
Calle de la Magdalena
Calle de la Cabeza
ANTÓN MARTÍN
Calle de Gobernador
REAL JARDIN BOTANICO
Calle de Alfonso XII
Calle de Santa Isabel
Calle Atocha
Calle Jesús y María Levapiés
Calle del Amparo
Baja
Calle Mesón de Paredes
ATOCHA
Paseo de la Infanta Isabel
Plaza Lavapies
LAVAPIES
Calle de Embajadores
Calle Miguel Servet
Reina Sofía
Sta. María de la Cabeza
Ronda de Atocha
Estación de Atocha
Church
Information
Metro
Post Office
Railway
23 24 25 26 27 28 29 30 31 32 33 34 35 36 37 38 39 40 41 42 43 44 45 46 47 48 49

some contemporary flair. The hotel has all the facilities, including a spa, that make it perfect for both business and leisure travelers.

See map p. 276. Alfonso XII 14. ☎ ***902-29-22-93*** *or 91-523-74-60. Fax: 91-308-54-77.* www.ac-hoteles.com. *Metro: Plaza de la Cibeles. Parking: 20€ ($24). Rack rates: 250€–365€ ($300–$433) double. AE, DC, MC, V.*

H10 Villa de la Reina

$$$$ Viejo Madrid/Gran Vía

A smart, midsize hotel that belongs to a small Barcelona-based chain, the Villa de la Reina is a great midrange choice. It occupies a classic early-20th-century building along the Gran Vía — a busy but central location. Rooms aren't huge, but they're finely detailed with stylish furnishings and sleek bathrooms, and personnel are very friendly and professional.

See map p. 276. Gran Vía 22. ☎ ***902-10-09-06*** *or 91-523-91-01. Fax: 91-521-75-22.* www.h10hoteles.com. *Metro: Opera. Parking: 18€ ($22). Rack rates: 120€–140€ ($144–$168) double. AE, DC, MC, V.*

Hespería Madrid

$$$$$ Modern Madrid

Madrid's hottest entry into the ultraluxury category, this handsome contemporary hotel on the Paseo de la Castellana has quickly outclassed many of its more established competitors. It's a couple of miles north of the Prado. A member of Leading Hotels of the World, it exudes refined style. A perfect choice for anyone who finds Madrid's other top-of-the-line hotels, such as the Ritz or the Westin Palace, to be entirely too fussy and old-fashioned. Compared to those, the Hespería is also a bargain, with rack rates cheaper by 100€ or so. As notable as the hotel is its expensive and very fashionable restaurant, Santceloni (see restaurant listings later in this chapter). Offers available online (as low as 139€/$178) make this stylish hotel surprisingly affordable.

See map p. 276. Paseo de la Castellana 57. ☎ ***91-210-88-00*** *or 902-39-73-98. Fax: 91-210-88-99.* www.hesperia-madrid.com. *Metro: Gregorio Marañón. Parking: 20€ ($24). Rack rates: 310€–350€ ($372–$432) double. AE, DC, MC, V.*

Hotel NH Nacional

$$$ Bourbon Madrid

The smoothly professional NH chain, with a couple of dozen hotels in Madrid, leaves nothing to chance. They're designed for business travelers who want things just so, but those demands also make them perfect for tourists. And who cares if NH hotels are predictable, when that only means excellent execution? Expect spacious, well-decorated rooms with light woods, bold colors, and original art, nice bathrooms, and good service. This one, in a historic 1920s building, is right on Paseo del Prado, smack in the middle of the museum mile, between the Thyssen and the Reina

Sofía. Kids younger than 12 stay free in their parents' room (one child per room of two adults).

See map p. 276. Paseo del Prado 48. ☎ ***91-429-66-29.*** *Fax: 91-369-15-64.* www.nh-hoteles.es. *Metro: Atocha. Parking: 18€ ($22). Rack rates: 109€–150€ ($131–$180) double. AE, DC, MC, V.*

Hotel Plaza Mayor

$$$$ Viejo Madrid

This small hotel, situated right off the Plaza Mayor in the heart of Old Madrid, is a bargain hunter's dream. Occupying an old church, the family-run hotel features bright and cheery, smartly outfitted rooms. Most have windows overlooking the street. You can even step it up a notch in the new Suite del Palomar, a large and handsome atticlike space on the top floor with a rooftop terrace.

See map p. 276. Atocha 2. ☎ ***91-360-06-06.*** *Fax: 91-360-06-10.* www.h-plazamayor.com. *Metro: Sol. Parking nearby: 18€ ($22). Rack rates: 79€–90€ ($96–$108) double. AE, DC, MC, V.*

Hotel Villa Real

$$$$ Bourbon Madrid

The less-expensive kid sister of the fancy new Hotel Urban, the Villa Real is a contemporary building designed to look historic (you have to make up your own mind about that; to me it's tasteful kitsch, if such a thing exists). This hotel is much more traditional than the Derby chain's daring, design-oriented hotels (the Urban and Hotel Claris in Barcelona). Richly decorated with dark woods and warm tones and suffused with a quiet elegance, rooms are superior to the functional lobby. Many are split-level with separate sitting areas. Bathrooms are plush with fine linens. Best of all, you can't get a better location, just a short walk from the Prado and Paseo de la Castellana.

See map p. 276. Plaza de las Cortés 10. ☎ ***91-420-37-67.*** *Fax: 91-420-25-47.* www.derbyhotels.es. *Metro: Plaza de la Cibeles. Parking: 18€ ($22). Rack rates: 175€–360€ ($210–$432) double. AE, DC, MC, V.*

Petit Palace Arenal

$$$–$$$$ Viejo Madrid (just north of Plaza Mayor)

This member of an upstart Spanish chain — which in a short time has assembled 18 hotels in the capital city — targets a distinctive niche: sleek, modern hotels with the latest in high-tech facilities. A contemporary mid-size hotel, it's perfect for visitors who want stylish comfort along with convenience and a historic location. Near the Plaza Mayor and Puerta del Sol, this well-run hotel offers free high-speed Internet access in all rooms. Although most rooms aren't especially large, they are a good value; terrific for families are the "Family Rooms" that sleep up to four (however, the hotel's location across a busy street from one of Madrid's most popular

Splurging at Madrid's granddaddy hotels

Madrid has a pair of historic, superluxe hotel options, as well as a couple of boutique hotels that cater to individuals who want pampering and are willing to pay for it. The Ritz and the Palace hotels are storied, famous, and well-located, and they rank among the best hotels in Europe. (The Santo Mauro is right up there, too, and is less fussy; see the listing in the section "The top hotels.")

The turn-of-the-20th-century, recently refurbished **Ritz Madrid** (now owned by Orient Express) is glamor incarnate, but it's also extremely formal (jacket and tie in this heat?). If you want a hotel that exudes Belle Epoque sophistication fit for kings and movie stars — and prices to match — this is it.

See map p. 276. Plaza de la Lealtad 5. ☎ **91-701-67-67.** Fax: 91-701-67-76. www.ritzmadrid.com. Metro: Banco de España. Parking 25€ ($30). Rack rates: 480€–580€ double ($576–$696). Check Web site for special offers that are as low as 195€ ($234) per night. AE, DC, MC, V.

The massive **Westin Palace Hotel,** a Starwood property across the Paseo del Prado, is nearly as stylish and elegant as the Ritz — especially its glitzy public rooms. Madrileña society, well-heeled foreigners, and celebrities are fixtures here. A long-awaited renovation was completed in the late 1990s.

See map p. 276. Plaza de las Cortés 7. ☎ **800-325-3535** in the United States, 800-325-3589 in Canada, or 91-360-80-00. Fax: 91-360-81-00. www.palacemadrid.com. Metro: Banco de España. Parking: 25€ ($30). Rack rates: 389€–498€ ($467–$598) double. AE, DC, MC, V.

If the Ritz and Palace Hotels are too ritzy and regal for your wallet (they certainly are for mine), you can still get a taste of their all-out luxury. Check out the sumptuous lobby of the Palace, with its spectacular glass cupola, or the refined bar of the Ritz — just make sure you're properly dressed. At the Ritz, that means jacket and tie for men, a skirt, dress, or nice pants for women. Stop by on your way to a nice dinner elsewhere in Madrid.

Another first-class option is the newest addition to Madrid's ultraluxury hotels, **Hotel Orfila,** a Relais & Châteaux property set in a gorgeous 1886 townhouse midway between the Plaza de Colón and Plaza Alonso Martínez. With just 32 rooms, it's not an imposing megahotel like the Palace or Ritz, but it offers a similar kind of style and pampering and is a comparative value. The rooms are warm and sumptuously decorated, furnished with lovely period antiques.

See map p. 276. Orfila 7. ☎ **91-702-77-70.** Fax: 91-702-77-72. www.hotelorfila.com. Metro: Alonso Martínez. Parking: 25€ ($30). Rack rates: 380€ ($456) double. AE, DC, MC, V.

late-night discos might give some parents understandable pause). "High Tech" rooms feature flat-screen computers and TVs, as well as stationary bikes. Very good deals are frequently available online. Another, more luxurious Petit Palace hotel, even closer to the Plaza Mayor and Puerta del Sol, is the Posada del Peine, housed in a 1610 building and inaugurated in late 2005.

See map p. 276. Arenal 16. ☎ ***91-564-43-55.*** *Fax: 91-564-43-54.* www.hthoteles.com. *Metro: Sol or Opera. Parking: 15€ ($18). Rack rates: 175€–215€ ($210–$258) double. AE, DC, MC, V.*

Room Mate Mario
$$ Viejo Madrid

A design-oriented hotel that strikes an excellent balance between understated chic and budget inn, this small, 30-room place, very near the Teatro Real, is hip and urban with a gray, black, and cream color scheme (accented by funky, neo-mod patterns). Rooms are good-sized, and bathrooms are cool, with bold black-and-white tiles; the hotel's a definite bargain for anyone looking for style without a hefty price tag. The Room Mate Hoteles group now has other hotels, also given human first names, in central Madrid, including Alicia (Calle Prado 2) and two others on the way, Oscar and Laura—all excellent options for reasonably priced design.

See map p. 276. Campomanes 4. ☎ ***91-548-85-48.*** *Fax: 91-559-12-88.* www.room-matehoteles.com. *Metro: Opera. Parking: 15€ ($18). Rack rates: 90€–100€ ($108–$120) double. AE, DC, MC, V.*

Suite Prado Hotel
$$$ Viejo Madrid/Puerta del Sol

If you think only the super-rich staying at the Ritz and the Palace get to have huge rooms in Madrid, think again. Tucked away on a small street not far from Plaza Santa Ana, this tiny hotel (just 18 rooms) with a pale pink exterior has shockingly large suites, perfect for the whole family. That means unheard-of kitchenettes and comfortable salons for the price of a standard room. Rooms are decorated with contemporary furniture in bright colors. Triples have sofa beds. It's obviously no budget hotel, but the Suite Prado Hotel is still one of the best deals in Madrid, if you can get a room. Call a few weeks in advance.

See map p. 276. Manuel Fernández y González 10 (around the corner from Teatro Español, off Calle de las Huertas). ☎ ***91-420-23-18.*** *Fax: 91-420-05-59.* www.suiteprado.com. *Metro: Banco de España. Nearby parking: 18€ ($22). Rack rates: 156€ ($187) double. AE, DC, MC, V.*

Madrid's runner-up hotels

Barrio de Salamanca Suites

$$–$$$ Modern Madrid/Salamanca These new, very large suites and apartments are stylishly sedate, inexpensive, and well located — an excellent option for families or business travelers who'll be living out of their suitcases for a while. *See map p. 276. Calle General Oraa 17.* ☎ ***91-825-59-00.*** www.greenbarriodesalamanca.com.

Hostal Residencia Lisboa

$ **Viejo Madrid/Puerta Del Sol** Madrid is littered with small, affordable *residencias* (pensions); this is one of the best of the bunch, with decent-sized rooms and spacious bathrooms. It can get a bit noisy, however. *See map p. 276. Ventura de la Vega 17, off Calle Jerónimo.* ☎ ***91-429-46-76.*** www.hostallisboa.com.

Hotel Monaco

$–$$ **Modern Madrid/Chueca** This small and decidedly funky hotel, a former brothel that looks the part, demands a sense of humor and adventure from its guests; it's probably best for young people who want to hang out in the hipster neighborhood. Though kind of run-down, the hotel is a temple of kitsch — all pink marble, ornate columns, neon lights, and faux-Louis XIV furniture. Singles are pretty dismal, and best skipped. Room no. 123 has a giant carved-wood ceiling mirror, and Room no. 127 is an exercise in shocking pink. *See map p. 276. Barbieri 5.* ☎ ***91-522-46-39.***

Hotel Mora

$$ **Bourbon Madrid** This 1930s hotel has simple standard rooms, but it's a bargain given its great location just down the street from the Prado and around the corner from the Reina Sofía museum. *See map p. 276. Paseo del Prado 32.* ☎ ***91-420-15-69.***

Hotel Paris

$$ **Viejo Madrid/Puerta del Sol** Right in the thick of the Puerta del Sol action, and almost bohemian enough to justify the name, this deceptively large place, built in the late 19th century, may seem a little gloomy and dated if you're accustomed to bright and cheery rooms. But it has a nice interior patio and a well-lived-in feel — considering its central location, it's a bargain. *See map p. 276. Alcalá 2.* ☎ ***91-521-64-96.***

Hotel Santo Domingo

$$$–$$$$ **Viejo Madrid/Gran Vía** A short walk from the atmospheric streets of Viejo Madrid — but also from the chaotic rush of Gran Vía — this 1994 hotel seems much smaller and more personal than its 120-room size indicates. The morning-yellow lobby and rooms are classically elegant, with handsome furnishings and fabrics in warm tones. Rooms vary greatly in size. *See map p. 276. Plaza Santo Domingo 13.* ☎ ***900-99-39-00*** *or* ***91-547-98-00.*** www.hotelsantodomingo.com.

Tryp Ambassador

$$$–$$$$ **Viejo Madrid** A large and classy hotel near the Royal Palace, on a quiet, sloping old street, the Ambassador occupies a renovated palace and a converted monastery. Rooms are conservatively elegant, especially in the four floors of the former palace. *See map p. 276. Cuesta Santo Domingo 5–7 (near Palacio Real).* ☎ ***91-541-67-00.*** www.trypambassador.solmelia.com.

Bed-and-breakfasts in Madrid

B&Bs aren't common in Spain like they are in England and Ireland, although a few are worth checking out.

Casa de Madrid (Arrieta 2–2; ☎ **91-559-57-91**; fax 91-540-11-00. www.casademadrid.com) offers a B&B experience of high style in a great location near the Opera House and Royal Palace. On the second floor of a spectacular late-18th-century building, the sprawling apartment has seven rooms that range from 230€ to 260€ ($276–$318) per night. The guest rooms are decorated with exquisite taste, featuring beautiful antiques and themes related to the owner's travels. Note that not all rooms have air-conditioning, and some feature kitchenettes.

A California-based organization, **European B&B,** offers stays at private family residences (and at some unoccupied apartments) in Madrid (as well as in Rome, London, and Paris) that are a nice alternative to the standard hotel scene. Prices are quite reasonable. The Web site has detailed information on the service as well as on each house or apartment, including several photos of all properties. You may find European bedrooms smaller than what you're accustomed to, and not all buildings have elevators. Prices range from 80€ to 145€ ($96–$174) per night based on double occupancy, breakfast and taxes included. Contact European B&B at ☎ **800-872-2632** in the United States and Canada, or 619-531-11-79 in Madrid. Or visit them on the Web at www.madridbandb.com.

Dining Out

For years, dining in Madrid has meant either big, fancy restaurants — where elegant service is king — charming Viejo Madreleño taverns, or *tascas,* in which eating is really an excuse for drinking. With a recently invigorated dining scene, Madrid is trying to catch up to Bilbao, San Sebastián, and Barcelona, where creativity has been more valued. As the capital, of course, Madrid has all the regional specialties, a wide variety of international cuisines, and fresh seafood flown in from the coasts. In many popular places, you can easily imagine macho Hemingway chomping on suckling pig.

The city's *tascas* (tapas restaurants) and *mesones* (cavelike taverns) are ideal places to stop in for a *vinito* (bee-*nee*-toh; small glass of red wine), *jerez* (heh-*reth;* sherry), and a smattering of tapas. Although you can easily put together a good meal from a tapas crawl in Madrid, more than anything else it qualifies as a cultural itinerary. Making the rounds of these bars is one of the highlights of visiting Madrid — a perfect complement to afternoons viewing great paintings in the Prado. For a list of a few worth popping into, see "Living It Up After Dark: Madrid's Nonstop Nightlife," later in this chapter.

Eating like a Madrileño

Because it's the capital (and Madrileños love to eat), you can find any type of cuisine you want in Madrid, from the freshest fish to the most sophisticated Basque preparations. Classic dishes are *cocido* (koh-*thee*-doh, a slow-cooked pork and chickpea soup/stew), *callos* (*kah*-yohs, or tripe with chorizo sausage), and *sopa de ajo* (garlic soup). Carnivores may also want to try *rabo de buey* (oxtail) and *cordero asado* (roast baby lamb). Nothing beats hot chocolate and *churros* (fritters) after a late night — a night that, in all probability, began with rounds of tapas.

Many Madrid restaurants serve *callos* at least once a week for the midday menu. Before you blindly say, "I'll try it" — as I once did and then immediately regretted my decision — you need to know that this classic Madrid dish is tripe and various other innards, which I think are only for the brave.

Texans have their barbecue, New Yorkers have their pizza, and New Englanders have their clam chowder. And Spaniards? Well, Spaniards wax poetic about ham. *Jamón serrano,* cured ham, the entry level of elite hams, is a national obsession. Aficionados of thin Iberian ham — especially *jamón de Jabugo* and *pata negra* — claim it's Spain's greatest delicacy. A *ración* (portion) of dry, razor-thin shavings of the stuff sets you back 20€ ($24) or more, but that matters little to the Spaniards who talk about it the way others rhapsodize about caviar. In Madrid, good places to try some deluxe Iberian ham are **Cinco Jotas,** Serrano 118 (**☎ 91-562 27 10**), **Casa Lucío,** Cava Baja 35 (**☎ 91-365 32 52**), and **Museo del Jamón,** Gran Via 72 (**☎ 91-541-20-23**), which isn't quite (as the name implies) a Ham Museum, but a restaurant-deli dedicated to slicing and serving cured hams from all over Spain. Other branches can be found at Alcalá 155 (**☎ 91-431-72-96**), and Atocha 54 (**☎ 91-369-22-04**).

For more on Spanish dining customs, including mealtimes, costs, and tipping, see Chapter 2.

Madrid's top eats

Botín

$$$ Viejo Madrid CASTILIAN

You want classic Madrid? Botín can serve up the stalwarts of Castilian cooking, roast suckling pig and roast leg of lamb prepared in ancient wood ovens. Prepare to meet your neighbors from back home in this crowded spot, though. Everyone seems to know that Botín has the reputation of being the oldest restaurant in the world (it hasn't closed its doors since 1725). A favorite with families who don't mind the bustle, Botín doubles as a history lesson for kids. How's this for pedigree? Francisco de Goya, the legendary painter, was once a dishwasher at Botín. Not good enough? Okay, how about the fact that Hemingway set a scene in *The Sun Also Rises* in this famed restaurant?

*See map p. 276. Calle de Cuchilleros 17. ☎ **91-366-42-17.** Reservations required. Metro: Opera or Sol. Main courses: 13€–28€ ($16–$34). Fixed-price menu: 28€ ($34). AE, DC, MC, V. Open: Daily lunch and dinner.*

Casa Lucío

$$$ Viejo Madrid CASTILIAN

A historic tavern on one of Madrid's famous night-crawler streets, the Casa Lucío is a favorite spot for locals to take their foreign visitors. With its cinematic, cavelike ambience and hanging forest of cured hams, it's the kind of place that has you considering a sabbatical in Spain before you finish the first bottle of wine. The famous faces and sharp-dressed crowd only add to the buzz. The food is top-quality comfort food — like the house *merluza* (hake, a white fish similar to cod), shrimp in garlic sauce, roasted lamb, and scrambled potatoes and eggs (now there's a dish even a finicky child will love).

*See map p. 276. Cava Baja 35. ☎ **91-365-82-17.** Reservations recommended. Metro: La Latina. Main courses: 14€–24€ ($17–$29). AE, DC, MC, V. Open: Sun–Fri lunch, dinner daily. Closed: Aug.*

El Amparo

$$$$ Modern Madrid BASQUE

Martín Berasategui, the 30-something wunderkind of Basque cooking in San Sebastián, has imported his creative ways to Madrid in the form of this rustically elegant restaurant in the chic Salamanca neighborhood. Many traditional Spanish dishes have interesting touches, such as the roast lamb chops with garlic purée, but the really special ones are innovative nouvelle Basque cuisine items. That can mean sea bass with clams and cauliflower raviolis or tomato-layered salt cod. The restaurant occupies a charming former 19th-century stable with country wooden beams.

*See map p. 276. Callejón de Puígcerdá 8 (at corner of Jorge Juan). ☎ **91-431-64-56.** Reservations required. Metro: Goya. Main courses: 19€–38€ ($23–$46). AE, MC, V. Open: Mon–Fri lunch, dinner Mon–Sat. Closed: The week before Easter and the second week of Aug.*

La Posada de la Villa

$$$ Viejo Madrid SPANISH/STEAK

Here's a way not only to see the Old Madrid but to also feel it in your bones. This inn, founded in 1642 in the heart of the tapas district, is famed for its Castilian roasts. Come for the historic ambience, and while you're at it, dig into the exquisite roast lamb and cured pork.

*See map p. 276. Cava Baja 9. ☎ **91-366-18-60.** Reservations required. Metro: La Latina. Main courses: 11€–36€ ($13–$43). Fixed-price menu: 38€ ($46). Open: Mon–Sat lunch and dinner, Sun lunch only. Closed: Aug.*

Portico del Siglo XXI

$$–$$$ Viejo Madrid BASQUE

A dose of retro-future chic, living up to the name, which means "portal to the 21st century," this ultramod restaurant is all brilliant pastels, with brightly colored plexiglass dish chairs and stripes of neon lighting. It's light years from Madrid's stock of *mesones* and *tascas.* The Basque menu is nicely done and attractively priced. Try the terrific Ensalada Pórtico, a salad wrapped in long slices of zucchini, baby squid with carmelized onions, or braised duck in orange sauce. Even the extras, like tiny palate cleansers, are highly choreographed to go with the stylized look of the place; a small appetizer brought before my meal was a neon green pea soup looking just so perfect in a small martini glass.

*See map p. 276. Calle de la Morería 9. ☎ **91-364-00-33.** Reservations required. Metro: Opera. Main courses: 13€–25€ ($14–$30). AE, DC, MC, V. Open: Tues–Sat dinner only, Sun lunch only.*

Samarkanda

$$–$$$ Bourbon Madrid CREATIVE INTERNATIONAL

Perched like a tree fort in the mini botanical gardens of the Atocha train station, but looking more like an antique railway dining car, this great-looking restaurant serves a reasonably priced, well-prepared, and creative menu. Excellent main courses include beef tenderloin, squid in its ink, and ravioli stuffed with asparagus. The dark rattan chairs, peaked wooden ceiling and fans, long wall of red banquets, and tropical greenery flooding your view evoke a colonial outpost — and may be enough to trick you into believing that the train you're about to board is an old steamer rather than a high-speed rail to Seville.

*See map p. 276. Estación de Atocha (Terminal AVE), Gta. de Carlos V. ☎ **91-530-97-46.** Reservations recommended. Metro: Atocha. Main courses: 11€–20€ ($13–$24). AE, DC, MC, V. Open: Daily lunch and dinner.*

Santceloni

$$$$ Modern Madrid CATALAN/INTERNATIONAL

Attached to the most cooly stylish hotel in Madrid (the Hespería; see above for a review), this is the city's hottest restaurant, where the beautiful and the rich battle to get in. If you're also willing to drop 80€ to 100€ ($96–$120) for one of the most refined dining experiences you're likely to have in Spain, don't hesitate to sample the creative offerings from Santi Santamaría, a disciple of the famed El Bulli restaurant on the Catalan coast. Santamaría specializes in the use of truffles and foie gras; the presentation confidently proclaims the restaurant's importance. The modern and exponentially chic restaurant is a restrained melange of glass and light wood. Service is extremely polished, and the wine list is one of the city's best.

*See map p. 276. Paseo de la Castellana 57. ☎ **91-530-88-40.** Reservations required. Metro: Gregorio Marañón. Main courses: 26€–50€ ($31–$60). AE, DC, MC, V. Open: Mon–Sat lunch and dinner.*

Zalacaín

$$$$ Modern Madrid BASQUE

North of downtown Madrid, this celebrated culinary temple has been one of the top restaurants in Spain for a quarter of a century. It's the place to go if you're in Spain celebrating a special occasion or if you just want to eat like a king. The ambience is elegant without being stuffy. The food, to put it plainly, is the star. The chef is Basque — true of many top kitchens in the capital — and the menu follows traditional Basque and Navarrese lines. Everything is spectacularly presented, and the taste justifies the small loan you may have to take out to eat here. It's a good place to try the six-course *menú de desgustación* (tasting menu), although its sheer quantity may put a damper on your desire to tackle the small volcano of chocolate dessert.

*See map p. 276. Alvarez de Baena 4. ☎ **91-561-48-40.** Reservations required. Metro: Rubén Darío. Main courses: 19€–45€ ($24–$54). AE, DC, MC, V. Open: Mon–Fri lunch and dinner, Sat dinner only. Closed: Week before Easter and Aug.*

Madrid's runner-up eats

Café del Español

$ **Huertas** A new spot at the base of the Teatro Español, this handsome, large restaurant looks like an old-style European cafe and does a very inexpensive and good midday lunch menu, for about 10€ ($12), that changes daily. *See map p. 276. Plaza de Santa Ana, Príncipe 23. ☎ **91-420-17-55.***

Casa Paco

$$$ **Viejo Madrid** A Madrid steak house — a place for Castilian specialities and huge cuts of meat, priced according to weight, seared in oil, and served, usually, very pink; Madrileños like their meat almost mooing. *See map p. 276. Puerta Cerrada 11, in the heart of Viejo Madrid. ☎ **91-366-31-66.** Closed Sunday and August.*

Champagnería Gala

$ **Viejo Madrid** A cheery place specializing in paellas and a long list of other classic rice-and-meat dishes, it's got a great patio in back and is an amazing bargain (but doesn't accept credit cards). *See map p. 276. Calle Moratín 22, in the Huerta district. ☎ **91-429-25-62.***

El Cosaco

$$ **Viejo Madrid** Something different: a fairly priced and romantic Russian restaurant, on one of the city's prettiest and most serene plazas, that has served good Stroganoff Imperial and a long list of vodkas since 1969. *See map p. 276. Plaza de la Paja 2, near La Latina. ☎ **91-365-35-48.***

El Schotis

$$ **Viejo Madrid** An attractive little restaurant in the heart of Viejo Madrid's happening *tasca* (tapas restaurant) scene. Have a few tapas

nearby and come here for *churrasco* (grilled meats) or Basque-style fish dishes. *See map p. 276. Cava Baja 11.* ☎ ***91-365-32-20.*** *Closed Sunday night.*

Fast Good

$$ **Modern Madrid** A Spanish take on fast food that's not tapas, but aims high, created by famed chef of El Bulli, Ferrán Adrià, and the NH hotel chain. It serves inexpensive vegetarian, beef, lamb, tuna, and salmon burgers along with salads, quiches, and pastas in a hip, colorful environment. *See map p. 276. Juan Bravo 3 (corner of Lagasca).* ☎ ***91-365-32-20.***

La Galette

$$ **Modern Madrid** A refuge for vegetarians in meat-mad Madrid; it's not entirely veggie, but the most inventive dishes are. Try the apple croquettes. *See map p. 276. Conde de Aranda 11, in Barrio Salamanca, near Retiro Park.* ☎ ***91-576-06-41.*** *Closed Sunday night.*

Taberna Carmencita

$$–$$$ **Chueca** This classic tavern, which has been around since 1840, was a hangout for the poet García Lorca. The small dining room is charmingly decorated with lace and vivid tiles. A popular spot with locals, it does Castilian and Basque dishes; try the sole in *txakolí* (the Basque wine) or the duck in cognac and prunes. *See map p. 276. Libertad 16.* ☎ ***91-531-66-12.*** *Closed Saturday lunch and Sunday.*

Taberna del Alabardero

$$–$$$ **Viejo Madrid** Just around the corner from the Teatro Real opera house, this tavern is much more than the tapas bar in front implies. The restaurant in back wins raves from locals in the know, serving fresh fish, much of it Basque preparations (such as hake in green sauce with clams), and such delectable meat entrees as *solomillo ibérico* (Iberian pork tenderloin) in three types of peppers. *See map p. 276. Felipe V 6.* ☎ ***91-547-25-77.***

Exploring Madrid

When visiting Madrid, concentrate on two things: gorging on great art and stuffing yourself silly with tapas and small glasses of wine, beer, and sherry. If you're a fan or just curious, attend a sun- and blood-drenched bullfight. Most visitors also have day trips on their mind, but if you have more time in Madrid, take a crack at some smaller museums and graceful parks, and then get to the fantastic shopping and fine dining.

Madrid has the greatest concentration of important museums in Spain — and more first-class works by Spanish masters including El Greco, Velázquez, Goya, and Picasso (among others) than anywhere else. If you can hit only the top two or three, begin with the Prado and the Royal Palace (which is a museum of sorts). Allow a full morning or afternoon for the Prado and a couple of hours for the Royal Palace. The Thyssen and Reina Sofía also require a couple of hours each — more if their enviable collections hook you. Also, allow some extra time to explore the neighborhoods around the museums on foot. In Viejo Madrid, around the Plaza Mayor, spend a couple of hours (preferably in the early evening, when tapas crawlers are out and about) and discover the city's soul in its cinematic *mesones* and *tascas.* Then again, hanging out in tapas bars can easily become an all-night affair.

If you're a serious art lover and are banking on hitting Madrid's Big Three — the Prado, the Thyssen Bornemisza, and the Reina Sofía museums — all within hours of landing, make sure that your visit isn't on a Monday or Tuesday. The first two museums are closed on Monday, and the Reina Sofía collection shuts its doors on Tuesday. None of them closes for lunch, though, and occasionally that's the best time to visit (from 1 p.m. to 4 p.m. or so).

In addition to both the Prado and Reina Sofía museums, many smaller museums throughout the city offer free admission on Saturday afternoons (2 p.m.–closing) and Sunday mornings. However, those times are the most crowded. If you hate crowds, go during the week when the museums are much less crowded. Or, take advantage of the free periods by going Saturday during lunchtime (2–4 p.m.); the museums really clear out then.

The **Madrid Card** Billete Turístico — available in one-, two-, and three-day versions — allows for unlimited travel on the subway (in zone A) as well as free entry to more than 40 museums (including the Prado, Thyssen, Reina Sofía, Palacio Real, Aranjuez and El Escorial) and a host of additional discounts at restaurants and other places of interest. Tickets are 38€ ($48) for the one-day ticket; 48€ ($60) for the two-day; and 58€ ($73) for the three-day. You can purchase them at the Plaza Mayor and Duque de Medinaceli Oficinas de Turismo, as well as at the airport and train stations. For more information, call ☎ **91-524-13-70** or 902-08-89-08, or see `www.madridcard.com` (discounts available for online purchase).

Be extremely careful around the Prado and other museum tourist haunts, where thieves artfully prey upon unsuspecting tourists. If someone offers to clean mustard or some other substance off your clothing, recognize it as a trick and refuse assistance: The thief is the one who put the mustard there, and he or she (or an accomplice) will proceed to rob you after distracting you.

The top attractions

Museo del Prado
Bourbon Madrid

If you were to count the great museums of classical paintings on one hand, the Prado might be, say, your index finger. Many experts consider it to be the second-best art museum in Europe (after the Louvre in Paris). It holds the world's richest and most complete collection of Spanish Old Masters, making the museum one of the top attractions in Spain. Don't miss it — unless the thought of classical painting makes your skin crawl. The museum is finally completing a massive expansion project, overseen by the esteemed Spanish architect Rafael Moneo, that will double its exhibition space and the number of paintings the museum can show from 1,200 to 2,600. The Prado began as the initiative of Spanish kings, great art collectors all, who sought a suitable place to hang the paintings they had amassed. The Prado's 12th- through 19th-century collection of the Spanish school includes masterpieces by Velázquez, Goya, El Greco, Murillo, Ribera, and Zurbarán. The Velázquez and Goya collections are the star draws; so go directly to the galleries featuring their works if your time or interest is limited. Expect crowds there, though; as you approach the room where Velázquez's masterpiece *Las Meninas (The Ladies-in-Waiting)* hangs, you can hear the growing rumble of guides and groups. The Prado also contains extraordinary works by Venetian masters — including Titian, Fra Angélico, Raphael, and Botticelli — and Flemish greats Hieronymous Bosch, Peter Paul Rubens, and Brueghel the Elder.

To try and beat the crowds at the Prado, enter through the Velázquez door (facing Paseo del Prado), and go early (9 a.m.) or during the Spanish lunch hour (2–4 p.m.). If you're an art aficionado, purchasing a room-by-room guide is a good idea.

The Prado is so large, and it possesses so many extraordinary works, that a single visit can only scratch the surface. But don't let that deter you. Head for the highlights first (see "Must-sees: A Prado primer," later in this chapter, for more information) and proceed from there, according to your time and energy. The ground floor features Goya's Black Paintings, the 15th- and 16th-century Flemish School, and El Greco. On the first floor are Velázquez, Goya, 15th- and 16th-century Italian works, and the 17th-century Dutch and Flemish Schools. New galleries dedicated to the work of Velázquez opened in 1999, on the 400th anniversary of the great artist's birth.

You could probably spend several days at the Prado, but because few people have that kind of time or interest, budget at least a half-day to see what will amount to but a small fraction of its immense collection; plan on taking a couple of back-saving breathers at the cafeteria.

See map p. 276. Paseo del Prado. ☎ ***91-330-28-00.*** `http://museoprado.mcu.es`. *Metro: Banco de España or Atocha. Admission: 6€ ($7.20) adults, 3€ ($3.60) students, E.U. seniors free, free for all Sun 9 a.m.–7 p.m. Audioguides: 3€ ($3.60). Open: Tues–Sun 9 a.m.–8 p.m.; Dec 24 and 31 and Jan 6 9 a.m.–2 p.m. Closed: Jan 1, Good Friday, May 1, and Dec 25.*

Monasterio de las Descalzas Reales

Viejo Madrid

A visit to this former royal palace — and splendid example of Renaissance architecture — is a retreat from Madrid's modern madness. Converted into a convent for women in the mid-16th century, it's anything but plain. A grand, fresco-lined staircase takes visitors to an upper cloister gallery with a series of extravagant chapels. The convent's collection of religious art

Must-sees: A Prado primer

Diego Velázquez y Silva's *Las Meninas (The Ladies-in-Waiting)* is the Prado's most popular, and probably its greatest, painting. A masterful achievement of perspective, spatial depth, and lighting, the painting perennially appears near the top on critics' lists of the greatest works in art history. In *Las Meninas,* the Infanta Margarita is depicted in the artist's studio (Velázquez himself, who appears in the lower left corner of the work) along with her maids and two dwarfs. The Infanta's parents, the king, Felipe IV, and his queen are sitting for a portrait; however, they appear only as reflections in a mirror in the background. As you look at the painting, notice how it draws your eyes from the Infanta toward the back of the room, climbing the terraces to the mirrored reflection. In addition to this famed work that draws crowds, check out this partial list of the museum's greatest hits.

From the Spanish School (16th–18th century):

- Diego Velázquez: *Las Meninas; The Spinners; Christ Crucified; Surrender of Breda; The Triumph of Bacchus; The Fable of Arachne*
- Bartolomé Murillo: *Immaculate Conception*
- José Ribera: *The Martyrdom of St. Felipe; The Trinity*
- Francisco de Goya: *The Naked Maja* and *The Clothed Maja;* the "Black Paintings," including *Saturn Devouring His Son; The Second of May; Executions at Moncloa; The Family of Carlos IV*
- El Greco: *Adoration of the Shepherds*
- Zurbarán: *Still Life*

From the Italian School (15th–17th century):

- Titian: *Venus with the Organist; Self-Portrait*
- Fra Angélico: *The Annunciation*
- Sandro Boticelli: *Tale of Nastagio degli Honesti*
- Tintoretto: *The Lavatory*

From the Flemish School (15th–17th century):

- Hieronymous Bosch: *Garden of Earthly Delights; The Hay Cart*
- Pieter Breughel the Elder: *The Triumph of Death*
- Raphael: *The Holy Family with Lamb; Portrait of a Cardinal*
- Peter Paul Rubens: *The Three Graces*

From the German and Dutch Schools (16th–17th century):

- Albrecht Dürers: *Adam and Eve; Self-Portrait*
- Rembrandt: *Artemis*

by the Old Masters is exceptional. The highlights are Breughel's *Adoration of the Magi,* Zurbarán's *Saint Francis,* Titian's *Caesar's Coin,* and a priceless collection of 16th-century tapestries. Visitation hours at the convent, where a small group of cloistered nuns still live, are peculiar and not always adhered to.

This small museum has a past as fascinating as its name (Monastery of the Royal Barefoot Franciscans). The daughter of Emperor Carlos V, Juana of Austria, founded the convent of Poor Clares in a noble palace. The women of noble families that entered the nunnery brought sizable dowries, mostly great works of art. Nobles also squirreled away their young, illegitimate daughters here to be reared by the nuns.

Admission to the convent is by 45-minute guided tour (in Spanish) only; note that hours are rather limited.

See map p. 276. Plaza de las Descalzas 3. ☎ ***91-542-69-47*** *or 91-521-27-79.* `www.patrimonionacional.es`. *Metro: Sol or Opera. Admission: 5€ ($6; joint admission with Real Monasterio de la Encarnación, 6€/$7.20) adults, 2.50€ ($3) students and E.U.-resident seniors, free on Wed for E.U. members. Open: Tues–Thurs and Sat 10:30 a.m.–12:45 p.m. and 4–5:45 p.m., Fri 10:30 a.m.–12:45 p.m., Sun 11 a.m.–1:45 p.m. Closed: Jan 1, Easter week (Wed–Sat), May 1, 2, 11, and 15, Aug 11, Nov 9, and Dec 25.*

Museo Nacional Centro de Arte Reina Sofía
Bourbon Madrid

The third address on Madrid's celebrated Art Avenue — the Paseo del Prado — is this contemporary art museum. It boasts major works from Spain's 20th-century greats, such as Picasso, Miró, Dalí, and Julio González, but it's Pablo Picasso's dramatic *Guernica,* the most famous painting of the 20th century, that dwarfs them all. The massive canvas in gray, black, and white is a moving antiwar protest. (Picasso painted it after the Nationalist bombing of a small Basque town during the Civil War.) Picasso's *Guernica* was housed for many years in New York's Museum of Modern Art, and Picasso stipulated that his most visceral painting not return to his homeland until the dictator Franco died and democracy was restored in Spain. Franco died in 1975, but the work remained in New York until 1981. Ironically, even though Picasso felt that the Prado, his country's greatest museum, was the only logical place for the painting to reside, the painting never made it to the Prado proper. *Guernica* had its own gallery in the Prado annex, Casón del Buen Retiro, before officials moved it to the Museo Nacional Centro de Arte Reina Sofía down the street.

The Reina Sofía is especially strong in early-20th-century works by Spanish artists as well as in abstract art, pop art, and minimalist sculptures and paintings. The museum recently underwent a massive renovation and amplification, adding three new buildings by the French architect Jean Nouvel. If you're a contemporary art lover, you'll want to spend almost as much time here as at the Prado; allow a couple of hours, at a minimum, for your visit

See map p. 276. Calle Santa Isabel 52 (at Paseo del Prado, opposite Atocha train station). ☎ ***91-467-50-62.*** `http://museoreinasofia.mcu.es`*. Metro: Atocha. Admission: 6€ ($7.20) adults, 3€ ($3.60) students, free for seniors and children under 18, free admission Sat 2:30–9 p.m. and Sun 10 a.m.–2:30 p.m. Open: Mon and Wed–Sat 10 a.m.–9 p.m., Sun 10 a.m.–2:30 p.m.*

Museo Thyssen-Bornemisza
Bourbon Madrid

Across the street from the Prado, the museum with a decidedly un-Spanish, tongue-twister of a name has quickly become a premier attraction in Madrid. In 1993, the Spanish government acquired the spectacular private collection amassed by the Baron Thyssen-Bornemisza and his son, two generations of German industrial magnates.

The Spanish government renovated the early-19th-century pink Villahermosa palace to show its new bounty. Begun in the 1920s, the Thyssen collection comprises 800 stylistically diverse works and aims to be no less than a survey of Western art, from primitives and medieval art to 20th-century avant-garde and pop art. Displayed chronologically (starting from the top floor) and heavy on Impressionism and German Expressionism, the collection reads like a roster of the greatest names in classical and modern art: Caravaggio, Rafael, Titian, El Greco, Goya, Rubens, Degas, Gauguin, Cézanne, Manet, Van Gogh, Picasso, Chagall, Miró, and Pollock. Some observers tout it as the greatest private collection ever assembled, while others criticize it as a showy collection of minor works by major artists.

See map p. 276. Paseo del Prado 8 (Palacio de Villahermosa). ☎ ***91-369-01-51.*** `www.museothyssen.org`*. Metro: Banco de España. Admission: 6€ ($7.20) adults, 4€ ($4.80) students and seniors, free for children under 12. Temporary exhibits, 4€ ($4.80) adults, 3€ ($3.60) students and seniors. Open: Tues–Sun 10 a.m.–7 p.m.*

Palacio Real de Madrid
Viejo Madrid

Occupying the site of a ninth-century Moorish *alcázar* (fortress), the Royal Palace built by Spain's Bourbon monarchs makes a grandiose statement about Madrid's place in the world, circa 1750. Each room is an exercise in megawatt wealth, and taste flies out the window. The huge neoclassical palace — it has 2,000 rooms — incorporated the lavish tastes of both Carlos III and Carlos IV. The official residence of the Royal Family until 1931, it's now used only for state functions, because King Juan Carlos and Queen Sofía live in more modest digs, the Zarzuela Palace just beyond Madrid. Allow two to three hours to visit the Palace; guided tours are offered, but not really necessary or particularly worthwhile.

Of special note are the **Throne Room,** with its scarlet wall coverings, Baroque gilded mirrors, and a Tiepolo fresco on the ceiling; the regal **Gala Dining Room,** which shows off a spectacular dining table and jaw-dropping tapestries; and the **Porcelain Room,** covered floor to ceiling in a garish display of green, white, and purple porcelain. Check out the old **Royal Pharmacy** (near the ticket office), which has Talavera pottery jars and old recipe books of medications. In the **Real Armería** is a fine display of arms and armor. Wander to the edge of the large Plaza de la Armería (Royal Armory Square) that faces the palace, and you see how abruptly Madrid ends and the plains begin. Look also for the new temporary exhibits hall, part of what will eventually become the **Museum of Royal Collections** (with a permanent display of carriages, tapestries, paintings, silver, and crystal belonging to Spain's long lines of monarchs).

After your visit to the Royal Palace, step across Calle Bailén to the statue-lined **Plaza de Oriente,** where generations of monarchs and politicos have addressed the masses. The square, a good spot to take a breather, faces the recently remodeled **Teatro Real,** the Royal Opera House.

If you visit the Royal Palace on the first Wednesday of the month, you have a chance to see the ceremonial changing of the guards (at noon for free). And if you're carrying a European Union passport, you can get into the Royal Palace for free on Wednesdays, too.

See map p. 276. Bailén 2. ☎ ***91-542-00-59.*** www.patrimonionacional.es. *Metro: Opera. Admission: 9€ ($11) adults, 3.50€ ($4.20) students and seniors. Open: Summer Mon–Sat 9 a.m.–6 p.m., Sun and holidays 9 a.m.–3 p.m.; winter Mon–Sat 9:30 a.m.–5 p.m., Sun and holidays 9 a.m.–2 p.m.*

Panteón de Goya (Ermita de San Antonio de la Florida)
Parque del Oeste

If you're a fan of Goya, particularly of his dark works, you may want to pay your respects by making a detour out to his pantheon (a bit out of the way beyond the Estación Norte train station). King Carlos IV commissioned Goya, his court painter, to create frescoes for the cupola and vaults of the chapel, *Ermita de San Antonio,* in 1798. Some consider the romantic works among Goya's best. Fittingly, Goya is entombed in the chapel beneath his frescoes of Madrid society, which he was a master of depicting. Goya's remains were exhumed and brought to Madrid in 1908 from the Bordeaux region of France. It's rumored, though, that the artist's head was inexplicably missing.

See map p. 276. Glorieta de San Antonio de la Florida (or Paseo de la Florida) 5. ☎ ***91-542-07-22.*** *Metro: Norte or Príncipe Pío. Admission: 1.80€ ($2.20) adults,.90€ ($1.10) students under 14 and seniors, free on Wed. Open: Tues–Fri 10 a.m.–2 p.m. and 4–8 p.m., Sat–Sun and holidays 10 a.m.–2 p.m.*

Madrid's classic corners

As big and important as the Prado Museum and Palacio Real are, some of Madrid's biggest attractions aren't the museums and palaces the city is so well known for. To get a feel for how Madrileños live and enjoy the capital, be sure to visit the following places and spaces that define modern, yet charmingly traditional, Madrid.

Parque del Buen Retiro
Bourbon Madrid

If your feet and back ache from doing overtime at the museums, peaceful Retiro Park beckons. A pretty expanse of green lawns, lush gardens, fountains, and tree-lined promenades, the park is prime strolling and sunning ground for Madrileños of all ages. Do as they do: Kick off your shoes, smoke lots of cigarettes (just kidding), and take a siesta (but attach your belongings to one of your limbs so you don't wake up without your camera or purse). If you're traveling with children, rent a rowboat and paddle on the small lake in the center of the park. In summer, the park comes alive with ice-cream and handicrafts vendors, musicians, tarot-card readers, and lovers rolling around in the grass. The Palacio de Cristal (Crystal Palace), is a handsome 19th-century iron-and-glass solarium that houses a sculpture garden.

Location: Bordered by streets Alfonso XII and Alcalá, with main entrances on both. If you enter at the corner by Puerta de Alcalá, you can head right down Av. de México to the park lake (Metro: Retiro).

Plaza Mayor
Viejo Madrid

Madrid's Main Square is one of the most famous and attractive plazas in Spain. The early-17th-century arcaded plaza today hosts restaurants, outdoor cafes, shops, and student hangouts, but its past is like a microcosm of Spain itself. The Plaza Mayor was the scene of lively marketplaces and theater festivals, bullfights and coronations of kings, religious processions and public executions, and trials during the Spanish Inquisition. Colorful frescoes above the arcades adorn the Casa de la Panadería (the bakery). Check out an equestrian statue of Felipe III in the plaza's center. Make sure you spend a couple of hours wandering around the neighborhood that spills out from the Plaza Mayor; it's filled with small shops and — guess what? — tapas bars. See "Living It Up After Dark: Madrid's Nonstop Nightlife," later in this chapter, for my recommendations.

Location: Off Calle de Toledo, just south of Calle Mayor (Metro: Sol or Opera).

Plaza de Toros de las Ventas
Barrio Salamanca

Few observers are indifferent to bullfighting. One of Spain's most representative traditions, it has passionate, die-hard fans as well as staunch opponents, who decry it as a barbaric anachronism. If you faint at the sight of blood, don't even consider attending a bullfight. I'm always surprised, though, how many people find themselves transfixed by the spectacle of man and beast squaring off in a ring. To aficionados, bullfighting is more art and ritual than sport. The uninitiated may have a hard time grasping that concept — after all, six bulls are put out to die each afternoon — but if you're up to it, Madrid is one of the top spots in Spain to witness the Spanish fascination with matadors and charging beasts. The Plaza de

Toros de las Ventas isn't the oldest bullring in Spain (that honor goes to Ronda in Andalusia), but it represents, along with Ronda and Seville, the pinnacle of Spanish bullfighting. Built in the 1920s, its tiles and Moorish-style arches are meant to evoke the *mudéjar* architecture so prevalent in southern Spain.

If you can't stomach a *corrida* (bullfight), or if you land in Madrid out of season, you can visit the Museo Taurino (Bullfighting Museum), a modest place with portraits of famous matadors, jewel-encrusted capes and jackets, stuffed bull heads, and Goya etchings. You can see the outfit belonging to Spain's first female bullfighter, Juanita Cruz. Don't miss the bloody *traje de luces,* or suit of lights, that the legendary Manolete was wearing when he was gored to death. If that sounds like fun, you can visit the museum, but you're not allowed inside the actual Plaza de Toros.

To see the bullring, visit during bullfighting season (May–Oct) and choose either a *sol* (sun) or *sombra* (shadows) seat. A word of advice: Spring for the more expensive sombra seat. You can roast like a suckling pig in the *sol.* For tickets to bullfights (which range from 4€–115€, or $4.80–$138), go to the ticket booth at the Plaza de Toros de la Venta, call ☎ **91-356-22-00** for information, or visit `www.las-ventas.com`.

See map p. 276. Museo Taurino, Calle de Alcalá 237. ☎ ***91-725-18-57.*** *Metro: Las Ventas. Admission (museum): Free. Open: Mar–Oct Tues–Fri and Sun 9:30 a.m.–2:30 p.m., Nov–Feb Mon–Fri 9:30 a.m.–2:30 p.m.*

Puerta del Sol

Viejo Madrid

The focal point of Viejo Madrid, this noisy and chaotic square is the heart that pumps shoppers, tourists, and traffic out to the smaller arteries of the city. Although it's not particularly distinguished in appearance, it is an essential feature of Madrid. Originally part of a wall that encased the Old Quarter, the Puerta del Sol (Gateway to the Sun) is Spain's ground zero; a marker indicates the square as the point from which all road distances in Spain are measured. One of the best-known buildings in Madrid is the **Casa de Correos** (the original Post Office), built in 1768 by a French architect. A clock tower that was added in the 19th century tops it. The Puerta del Sol was the scene of many historical events, including an 1808 uprising against Napoleon in the War of Independence, an episode documented in Francisco de Goya's great and harrowing painting, *Dos de Mayo* (which now hangs in the Prado).

To get to the Puerta del Sol, just take any Metro line to the Sol station (yellow, blue, and brown lines all go there); you'll exit the subway in the midst of the large, bustling plaza.

More cool things to see and do

Madrid's collection of smaller and lesser-known, but still excellent, museums and atmospheric strolling grounds are well worth your time if you've got a few extra days in the city.

Sampling some smaller museums

If the crowds at the Prado and Thyssen get you down, sample some of Madrid's smaller museums, great in their own right but just off the prime tourism circuit (literally and figuratively). Not only are these terrific art collections, but they're also your ticket to glorious Madrileño mansions and palaces.

- **Visiting the Museo Lázaro Galdiano.** Serrano 122 (☎ **91-561-60-84;** `www.flg.es/museo/museo.htm`; Metro: Rubén Darío or Núñez de Balboa). This recently renovated museum is a quietly spectacular surprise. One of Madrid's finest museums, though unknown to many, it's housed in an immaculate 19th-century mansion in one of the city's newer northern neighborhoods. The superb private collection includes European Old Masters and applied arts from ancient times to the 19th century. You find lesser-known Goyas (from his black period); works by El Greco, Velázquez, Zurbarán, Ribera, and Murillo; Limoges enamels, and Renaissance jewelry. The museum is open Wednesday to Monday from 10 a.m. to 4:30 p.m., and closed holidays and the month of August; admission is 4€ ($4.80) for adults, 3€ ($3.60) for seniors and students, but it's free on Wednesdays for E.U. citizens. (See the "Madrid Accommodations, Dining, and Attractions" map on p. 276 for more information.)
- **Exploring Museo Sorolla.** General Martínez Campos 37 (☎ **91-310-15-84;** `http://museosorolla.mcu.es`; Metro: Iglesia or Rubén Darío). Check out the former studio and mansion of the celebrated Impressionist Joaquín Sorolla, who lived there in the early 1900s — it looks as if the painter and his family left last week. The home is crammed with objects that the artist collected in his lifetime, as well as a generous selection of his works, including the luminous Mediterranean beach scenes for which he's best known (Sorolla was known as the painter of light). The museum is north of downtown, not far from Paseo de la Castellana. Free guided tours (in Spanish only) are available October through June. The museum, recently renovated, is open Tuesday and Thursday through Saturday from 9:30 a.m. to 3 p.m., Wednesday from 9:30 a.m. to 6 p.m. and Sunday from 10 a.m. to 3 p.m.; admission is 2.40€ ($2.90) for adults, 1.20€ ($1.45) for students, free admission for seniors, and free for everyone on Sunday. (See the "Madrid Accommodations, Dining, and Attractions" map on p. 276 for more information.)

Milling around Viejo Madrid

One of the best ways to absorb the flavor of Madrid is to stroll the atmospheric streets of the Old City, where you uncover remnants of medieval Madrid and the city later built by the Habsburgs. A good place to start is in the **Plaza Mayor** (see "Madrid's classic corners," earlier in this chapter). **Cava de San Miguel,** which you reach through the Arco de Cuchilleros, is a lively strip of *mesones* (cavelike restaurants) and taverns. Along Calle Mayor is **Plaza de la Villa,** Madrid's old town square. The cluster of handsome buildings dates to the 15th and 16th centuries.

The oldest structure is the **Torre de los Lujanes,** a *mudéjar* (Moorish and Christian architectural mix) construction with a tall, minaretlike structure. **Casa de la Villa,** on the opposite side of the plaza, was built in 1640 and once housed both the town hall and city jail. **Casa de Cisneros** is a reconstructed 16th-century palace with a splendid Plateresque facade.

South of the plaza, beyond Calle Segovia, is **Plaza de la Paja,** a pretty and quiet space that was medieval Madrid's commercial center. On this plaza is Madrid's only Gothic building, the **Capilla del Obispo** (Bishop's Chapel). Nearby is the Moorish-looking 14th-century **San Pedro** church. Just east is a jumble of some of Madrid's most animated streets: **Cava Baja, Cava Alta, Almendro,** and **Calle del Nuncio.** Just about every address in this district, called **La Latina,** houses an appealing old tavern or *tasca.* The barrio is one of Madrid's classic, working-class areas. The popular **El Rastro Fleamarket** (see "Shopping in Madrid," later in this chapter) is held every Sunday along the warren of streets near **Calle de Toledo,** a lively thoroughfare that leads back up to the Plaza Mayor.

Getting all turned around in Viejo Madrid is easy, so don't get frustrated. The many taverns along the way make great pit stops for map study. Or, just stop in for a beer, and while you're there, ask the bartender or patrons for some assistance.

Drinking in the best of Bourbon Madrid

Spain's "Art Avenue," **Paseo del Prado,** was the central axis of the Bourbon monarchs' royal expansion plan for the city. It was designed to be the center of arts and sciences (in fact, the Prado was originally scheduled to be a national science museum). Besides connecting Madrid's principal art museums (the Prado, Thyssen-Bornemisza, and Reina Sofía), the leafy promenade, which a fountain of Neptune bisects, hosts beautiful 19th-century palaces and apartment buildings. North of the Prado, at Calle Alcalá, is **Plaza de Cibeles,** crowned by the ornate fountain of the Roman goddess Cybele, one of the city's most famous monuments. When *fútbol* fans get crazy after major wins, they usually wind up in Cybele's lap — and she never seems to mind. Two great buildings frame the Plaza: the **Palacio de Comunicaciones** (Main Post Office) on the Prado side, and **Banco de España** across the way.

Carlos III, continuing his makeover of Madrid, constructed the **Puerta de Alcalá,** gateway to the city. In the 18th century, it marked the eastern border, but of course the city kept growing and growing. Today the massive granite monument's five arches are more like doors in the middle of a living room.

Making the most of Modern Madrid

Upper-crust 19th-century apartment buildings and tonier-than-*tú* shops line Madrid's chicest neighborhood, **Barrio de Salamanca.** It extends from Puerta de Alcalá to Calle Ortega y Gasset and from Serrano to Plaza de Roma. If those euros are burning holes in your pockets, join the elegant *señoras* on their daily rounds of the barrio's antiques shops, fashion boutiques, and art galleries. Calle Serrano is the best street for a stroll.

Digging up some fun

Madrid's massive **Museo Arqueológico Nacional** (National Archaeology Museum), Serrano 13 (☎ **91-557-79-12;** `http://man.mcu.es`), is most notable for its cool replica of Spain's Altamira caves, festooned with prehistoric paintings of bison (a great place to duck in out of the summer sun) and the fourth-century B.C. Iberian bust of *La Dama de Elche.* The museum is open Tuesday through Saturday from 9:30 a.m. to 8:30 p.m. and Sunday from 9:30 a.m. to 2:30 p.m.; admission is 3€ ($3.60), but it's free Saturday starting at 2:30 p.m. and all day Sunday. (See the "Madrid Accommodations, Dining, and Attractions" map on p. 276 for more information.)

Strolling along Paseo de la Castellana

A continuation of Paseo del Prado, this tree-lined promenade stretches from Plaza de Colón way out to Madrid's new northern neighborhoods. A prime strolling ground, Paseo de la Castellana explodes in summer with stylish outdoor terrace cafes and bars. If you want to join the parade, or *paseo,* of beautiful people and Spanish-style "yoopies" (yuppies), grab your cigs and nonchalantly toss a sweater accessory around your neck, but don't dare show up before 11 p.m. Unless you're a real night owl, the *copas* (cocktails) crowd will stay here way past your bedtime.

Missing Madrid's busiest artery, **Gran Vía,** is nearly impossible, if for no other reason than your hotel is likely to be on or near it. Bursting with a dazzling collage of cinemas, shops, hotels, strip shows, and neon and bright lights, the section from Plaza de Callao to **Plaza de España** is Madrid's Broadway. Frenetic and slightly seedy, it offers few if any classic sights, though it's a sight in itself. In the center of Plaza de España is a statue of Cervantes and his beloved characters, Don Quixote and Sancho Panza.

Taking the kids to the parks

North of the Royal Palace, the nicely landscaped **Parque del Oeste** (West Park) extends along the River Manzanares. Young fans of the movie *The Mummy* will enjoy the park's most attention-getting feature, the **Templo de Debod (☎ 91-765-10-08;** `www.munimadrid.es/templodebod`; see the "Madrid Accommodations, Dining, and Attractions" map on p. 276 for more information) a fourth-century B.C. Egyptian temple that once stood next to the Nile. Adults, however, may think it odd to find such a thing marooned in the middle of Madrid. When the Aswan Dam flooded, a group of Spanish engineers rescued the temple; the Egyptian government thanked them by donating the structure to Spain. Admission is free. An aerial cable car connects Parque del Oeste to **Casa de Campo,** a 4,000-acre expanse of green, formerly royal hunting grounds. You can also reach the park by getting off at the Lago or Batán Metro stops (see the "Madrid Accommodations, Dining, and Attractions" map on p. 276 for more information). The park — now christened Parque de Atracciones Madrid — contains a lake (with rowboats), a pretty decent zoo, and theme park. It's a great place to take the kids if they (or you) tire of museums. The theme park (☎ **91-526-80-31;** www.parquedeatracciones.es) is open daily from noon to 10 p.m., and admission is 24€ adults ($30), 14€ ($17) seniors and children. You can also opt to pay 7€ ($8.40) just to enter. The **Zoo-Aquárium de Madrid** (☎ **91-512-37-70;** www.zoomadrid.com) is open daily from 10:30 a.m. to 9 p.m. in summer (though it closes at 6:30 and 7:30 p.m. in other months), and admission is 15€ ($18) for adults, 12€ ($14) for seniors and children under age 8. Kids will especially like taking the *teleférico* (aerial cable car, ☎ **91-541-74-50**) there. The ride is 4.80€ ($5.80) round-trip; catch it at the corner of Pintor Rosales and Marqués de Urquijo (Metro: Argüelles). The cable car runs daily from 11 a.m. to 9 p.m. March through October, and from November through February it runs only on weekends from noon to 9 p.m.

Yet another cultural invasion of Europe that surely has some locals wringing their hands, **Warner Bros. Movie World,** a Hollywood theme park, has landed in Madrid. With Cartoon World, a Tom and Jerry roller coaster, Super Heroes World, and a slice of the Old West, the new park is dreamland for some families, though it may not be what you envisioned for a visit to Spain. Movie World is located outside of Madrid, on N-IV Km 22, in San Martín de la Vega (☎ **902-024-100;** www.warnerbrospark.com). Admission is 32€ ($38) for adults and 24€ ($29) for children younger than 12 and seniors; look for 15-percent-off coupons in tourist publications and in tourist information offices. La Veloz bus no. 416 goes to the park, leaving from Estación Sur de Autobuses.

Guided Tours

Sometimes the most hassle-free way to see a city in a short period of time is on a guided tour. If you don't have much time and want someone else to worry about getting around, the following tours can give you a good overview of the city.

Bus tours

Madrid Visión operates multilanguage city bus tours (with headsets) of "Historic Madrid" and "Modern Madrid." Lasting about 75 minutes, they depart from Gran Vía 32, but you can get on or hop off anywhere along their route. The cost for one day is 15€ ($18) for adults and 8€ ($10), for seniors and children age 7 to 16; two-day tickets are 19€ ($24) for adults and 10€ ($12) for seniors and children ages 7 to 16; admission is free with purchase of the Madrid Card. For more information, call ☎ **91-779-18-88** or visit www.madridvision.es (discounts available for online purchase).

Walking tours

The **Patronato Municipal de Turismo** (City Tourism Office) offers an extensive series of **Descubre Madrid** (Discover Madrid) walks — guided historical and cultural tours of the city — throughout the year, though the schedule is heaviest in summer months. Tours depart from the main tourism office at Plaza Mayor 3. Inquire at any tourism office about the program and scheduled visits or call ☎ **91-588-16-36** or visit `www.descubremadrid.com`. Advance booking (a good idea in summer months) is possible by calling ☎ **902-22-16-22.** Most tours cost 4€ ($4.80) for adults and 3€ ($3.60) for children ages 4 through 12.

Suggested itineraries

If you'd rather organize your own tours, this section offers some tips for building your own Madrid itineraries.

If you have one day

Begin your day exploring the artistic treasures of the **Prado Museum** — which should hold you for several hours, at least until lunchtime. Eat a light lunch at the **Museo del Jamón** on Paseo del Prado before jogging around the corner to pay homage to Picasso's *Guernica* in the **Centro de Arte Reina Sofía.** That and the other modern masters will keep your attention for a couple of hours more, after which it will be time to head back to your hotel for a well-earned siesta.

Make sure you take the time to walk through the **Plaza Mayor** at the heart of town, perhaps just before setting off on your *tapeo* in the early evening. This stroll through the heart of Old Madrid — from tapas bar to tapas bar, nibbling and imbibing along the way — should last from around 6 to 8 p.m. Head back to your hotel to rest up until 9:30 p.m. or so, when you can safely venture out for dinner at **Botín.**

If you have two days

Spend **day one** pretty much as outlined above. Start off **day two** touring the **Palacio Royal.** Afterward, head to the **Thyssen-Bornemisza Museum** to see how serious money and a penchant for art can grow a private collection.

If these two days in Madrid represent the full extent of your time in Spain — and if it's the proper season — try to take in a bullfight at 5 p.m. If it's not bullfighting season, *tapeo* again this evening. Either way, catch a flamenco show in the later evening (after dinner).

If you have three days

Spend **day one** and **day two** as outlined in the preceding sections, then head off on **day three** for a day trip to Toledo, a commanding hilltop town that was once the capital of Spain, home to Christians, Moors, and Jews, and also the adopted city of the Renaissance master El Greco.

Shopping the Local Stores

Madrid is where plenty of Spaniards from around the country go to spend their money (much the way Brits go to London to shop and Americans stock up in New York). As Spain's largest city, Madrid has more of everything, from the chicest designer clothing stores to a healthy supply of all the regional handicrafts you find (usually at cheaper prices) throughout Spain. For my money, though, Barcelona's a more interesting shopping destination, with its design- and fashion-heavy orientation. (See Chapter 10 for more on Barcelona.)

Madrid's best shopping areas

The old center, near **Puerta del Sol,** especially the pedestrian-only streets Preciados and del Carmen, is a dense concentration of shops of all kinds — from little mom-and-pop places to the mega-department stores found in all major cities. Waves of souvenir shops and others selling affordable silver and jewelry surround **Plaza Mayor.** The glamour of **Gran Vía,** once Madrid's most exclusive shopping avenue, has given way to more utilitarian stores, selling fashions, shoes, books, and specialty foods and wines. Just north of Plaza de España, **Calle Princesa** is a main shopping drag with a little bit of everything, but mostly clothing and shoe stores. **Mercado Puerta de Toledo,** south of Plaza Mayor, used to be the old fish market, but it has been recast as a slick shopping center, with a full catch of restaurants, boutiques, and antiques stores. **Barrio Salamanca,** just north of Retiro Park and east of Paseo de la Castellana, ought to have a doorman at the entrance. This elite district is home to Madrid's most upscale boutiques. If you want the latest and chicest in designer wear, jewelry, and home furnishings, and you don't need to ask the price, check out Calles Goya and Serrano and the small streets that feed into them. Calle Claudio de Coello has some of the best art and antiques dealers.

If you're shopping with a mission, you need to plan your attack around Spanish shopping hours, which for the most part continue to respect the midday lunch closing (with a few exceptions, only malls stay open all day). Shop hours are generally Monday through Friday from 9 or (more likely) 10 a.m. to 1:30 or 2 p.m., and 4 or (more likely) 5 to 8 p.m. On Saturdays, they're open from 9:30 a.m. or so to 1:30 p.m. On Sundays, even compulsive shoppers have to take the day off.

What to look for and where to find it

In Spain, the law coordinates sales, with twice-annual sell-offs of inventory that all begin at the same time: the second week of January and the last week of July. Signs announcing *rebajas* (sales or rebates) are plastered over store windows. Prices continue to drop when stores move from first to second and final sales.

From antiques to wine, you'll find no shortage of ways to spend your money in Madrid. The following stores are some of my favorites.

Run to (or from?) El Rastro

Even if you're not a shopper, you probably won't want to miss **El Rastro,** the best-known flea market in Spain, located south of the Plaza Mayor in La Latina district. Every Sunday, the unruly market spills over from the long and narrow Calle Ribera de Curtidores into several adjacent streets. Once mostly an antiques market, today it has fewer rarities and more run-of-the-mill items: clothing, jewelry, art, animals (!), and, of course, monumental piles of junk. A lot of jostling goes on, and pickpockets know it's one of their best chances to target tourists. El Rastro is officially open Sundays from 9 a.m. to 8 p.m., but many sellers take off by midafternoon (you'll also find plenty of activity on Fri and Sat). To get there, take the Metro to the La Latina stop.

Antiques

Check out **El Rastro,** the flea market for odds-and-ends, on Sunday mornings (see the sidebar, "Run to *El Rastro*" for more information). **Calle de las Huertas** is also a good area to conduct your hunt. At **Centro de Arte y Antiguedades,** Serrano 5 (☎ **91-576-96-82;** Metro: Serrano), you find a number of dealers under one roof (of an attractive old building), some with very fine and very unusual items.

Books

Between the Atocha Train Station and the Botanical Gardens, just east of Paseo del Prado, is a weekend open-air book fair, with new, used, and rare books for sale. If you're in Madrid at the end of May or beginning of June, check out the **Feria del Libro de Madrid** (Madrid Book Fair), which virtually takes over Retiro Park.

Crisol is a bookstore chain with numerous outlets across the city; they have a decent selection of books in English. Among their branches: Paseo de la Castellana 90 (☎ **91-344-09-67;** Metro: Colón), and Goya 18 (☎ **91-575-06-40;** Metro: Goya). **VIPS** is an all-purpose chain that often heavily discounts art and architecture books (in both Spanish and English). VIPS stores are seemingly everywhere; one is at Gran Vía 43 (☎ **91-599-66-21;** Metro: Gran Vía); other branches are at Serrano 41; Princesa 5; and Velázquez 136. **Petra's International Bookshop,** Campomanes 13 (☎ **91-541-72-91;** Metro: Santo Domingo), specializes in second-hand books in English and other languages. It will also buy and trade. A great bookstore focusing exclusively on cinematic arts is **8½,** named for Fellini's classic film, at Martín de los Heros 23 (☎ **91-559-06-28**).

Crafts

Artespaña, Hermosilla 14 (☎ **91-435-02-21;** Metro: Serrano) is a government-run store with a large selection of crafts, especially items for the home. **El Arco de los Cuchilleros Artesanía de Hoy,** in the Plaza Mayor, no. 9 (☎ **91-365-26-80;** Metro: Sol), may be a mouthful, but it's also, hands down, the best place to go for crafts from all over Spain. From Spanish fans to embroidered shawls, jewelry, hand-blown glass, and ceramics, you'll find it here — as well as a staff that speaks English. Check out the enormous selection of hand-painted ceramics at **Antigua Casa Talavera,** Isabel la Católica 2 (☎ **91-547-34-17;** Metro: Santo Domingo), including attractive pieces from Valencia and Talavera, and tiles.

Department stores

FNAC, Preciados 28 (☎ **91-595-61-00;** Metro: Santo Domingo), is a French store, specializing in books, music, and magazines, and it offers occasional in-store performances. The granddaddy of Spanish department stores, with an encyclopedic inventory, is **El Corte Inglés,** Preciados 3 (☎ **91-379-80-00;** Metro: Callao or Sol).

Fashion

The ubiquitous **Adolfo Domínguez,** Serrano 18 (☎ **91-577-82-80;** Metro: Serrano), from Galicia, is one of Spain's top designers for both men and women. His stores are elegant, but not ridiculously expensive. **Loewe,** Gran Vía 8, and Serrano 26 (☎ **91-577-60-56;** Metro: Gran Vía and Serrano), a leather heaven since 1846, is the quintessential Spanish luxury clothier with great luggage and handbags.

More adventurous Spanish designers include **Agata Ruiz de la Prada,** Marqués de Riscal 8 (☎ **91-310-44-83;** Metro: Rubén Darío); **Antonio Miró,** Lagasca 65 (☎ **91-426-02-25;** Metro: Velázquez); and **Purificación García,** Serrano 28 (☎ **91-577-83-70;** Metro: Serrano/Colón). Adorable and hip T-shirts, for both adults and kids, are sold at **El Tintero,** Gravina 5 (☎ **91-308-14-18**), near the Plaza in Chueca.

For the budget-minded, **Zara** has hip but surprisingly affordable fashions for both sexes. Look carefully at materials and washing instructions, though, because some pieces aren't so durable. The store boasts two branches, at Hermosilla 16 (☎ **91-575-64-45;** Metro: Serrano) and Gran Vía 32 (☎ **91-522-97-27;** Metro: Gran Vía).

Gifts

If you or your family and friends are fans of Lladró, the famous Spanish porcelain figures, you can pick them up at the source, **Lladró Tienda Madrid,** Serrano 68 (☎ **91-247-71-47;** Metro: Serrano). **Sefarad,** Gran Vía 54 (☎ **91-547-61-42;** Metro: Sevilla), specializes in Lladró and Majorca faux pearls. With an incredible selection of hats (many very imaginative) and souvenir items (such as swords and shields), **Casa Yusta,** Plaza Mayor 30 (☎ **91-366-50-84;** Metro: Sol), has protected heads for more than a century.

Fans, those elegant accessory items that no stylish Spanish woman is without, make great gifts, but if you're in Madrid in summer, buying one for yourself is wise. **Casa de Diego,** Puerta del Sol 12 (☎ **91-522-66-43;** Metro: Sol), has more fans than you've probably ever seen, from cheap to exotic, and a good selection of shawls, too. If you're a really big fan of fans, you can find even more of them at **Almoraima,** Plaza Mayor 12 (☎ **91-365-42-89;** Metro: Sol). Excellent Spanish shawls are available at **Casa Jiménez,** Preciados 42 (☎ **91-548-05-26;** Metro: Sol).

Malls

You find nearly 100 shops, featuring fashions, jewelry, and household items, and a spate of restaurants at **ABC Serrano,** Serrano 61 (☎ **91-577-50-31;** Metro: Serrano), a magnificently restored 19th-century building where the daily newspaper *ABC* was produced.

Serious shoppers should check out the discounts at **Las Rozas Village,** Juan Ramon Jimenez, s/n, in Las Rozas, about 20 minutes outside of Madrid (☎ **91-640-49-00**), on the way to El Escorial and Segovia. The 40-plus stores include Antonio Miro, Camper, Gianfranco Ferre, Levi's, Lottusse, TAG Heuer, and Timberland. The mall is located at Exit 19 off A-6.

Shoes

Try some shoes on for size at **Yanko,** Gran Vía 40 (☎ **91-532-08-20;** Metro: Gran Vía), a top Spanish shoemaker for both sexes. **Calzados Bravo** has a nice selection of shoes for men and women, as well as luggage. Look for branches at Gran Vía 31 and 68; Princesa 58; and Goya 43 (☎ **91-222-73-00;** Metro: Gran Vía or Goya). You can find the latest models of trendy but cool **Camper** shoes, which are made in Spain, at their shop at Preciados 23 (☎ **91-531-78-97**).

Wine and cheese

Palacio de los Quesos, Calle Mayor 53 (☎ **91-548-16-23;** Metro: Sol), has everything you want in Spanish cheeses and wines, as well as *turrón* (a hard candy) and marzipan, which Spaniards are nuts about. **Majorca,** Velázquez 59 (☎ **91-431-99-09;** Metro: Velázquez), is another great gourmet shop, where you can eat as well as pick up Spanish wines for friends back home.

Living It Up After Dark: Madrid's Nonstop Nightlife

Madrid swings like no other city in Spain (or in Europe, for that matter). Madrileños pride themselves on how much they can party and how late they can go — when they sleep is anyone's guess. In the nightlife and cultural capital of Spain, you can find dozens of theaters and concert halls offering classical music, dance, and Spanish *zarzuela* (light comic opera), as well as hundreds of wild discos and the entire spectrum of jazz, rock, alternative, and pop clubs. On top of that, you can enjoy flamenco shows — some about as authentic as you come across in Spain and others targeted strictly at tourists — and everyone's favorite nighttime activity, tapas bar-hopping, which is raised to an art form in Madrid.

The night begins and ends late. In Madrid, the afternoon extends to 8 or 9 p.m., and the language reflects that; when Madrileños greet someone at that hour, they say *buenas tardes* (good afternoon), not *buenas noches* (good evening). Night doesn't really begin until after dinner, and remember that dinner can begin at 11:30 p.m. or midnight on weekends.

For up-to-date listings on what's happening in Madrid, get your hands on the weekly ***Guía del Ocio,*** available at newsstands (it has an English-language section of current events and exhibitions at the back), or the Friday editions of ***El Mundo*** or ***El País.*** For cultural questions of interest to tourists, call ☎ **91-540-40-10.** For information on clubs, discos, and concerts, as well as art exhibits, pick up a free copy of ***In Madrid,*** a monthly digest of happenings in Madrid.

Tickets for some venues are available only at their box offices. For tickets to most other cultural events, including bullfights and soccer matches, contact **Localidades García,** Plaza del Carmen 1 (☎ **91-531-27-32**), or **TEYCI,** Calle Goya 7 (☎ **91-576-45-32**). **Corte Inglés** (☎ **91-432-93-00**) stores around the city also sell tickets to concerts. You can also call **Caja Madrid** (☎ **902-48-84-88**) and **Caixa de Cataluña** (☎ **902-10-12-12**) for theater and movie tickets.

Tavern and tapas crawls

Since the first little wine shacks opened on "Little Taverns" street in medieval Madrid, locals have incorporated tavern hopping into their daily routines. Trolling the old town's innumerable taverns is one of the highpoints of visiting Madrid. *Tavernas* and *mesones* (both names to describe very similar tapas bars) are places to knock back small glasses of red wine, beer, or sherry, mix with boisterous company, and stave off a real meal with an assortment of tapas. Tapas come from the Spanish word *tapar,* meaning to cover.

In most places, you're given small snacks, or *tapitas* — olives, mussels, cheese, spicy potatoes, or *chorizo* (Spanish sausage) — as a bonus with your drink order. You can always order a more substantial tapa or *ración* (full serving). The idea is to pop in, stand at the bar, down a couple of shooters, offer a couple of unsolicited opinions on politics or soccer, and move on to the next place. Your visit can be a pit stop before heading home or on to a restaurant for dinner, or you can make it an all-night, increasingly loud, and loose endeavor.

The best areas are around the **Plaza de Santa Ana, Plaza Mayor,** and the Latina/Lavapies neighborhoods, especially the **Cava Baja** and **Cava Alta** streets. Madrid is swimming with *tascas* and tavernas, so what follows is an abbreviated list of places to check out. So many are available; don't be afraid to pop in wherever folks are drinking and eating.

Tavern and tapas talk

Tapas are small snacks served on saucer plates. The word tapa comes from *tapar,* literally "to cover"; similar saucers were once used to cover the opening of drinks (presumably, to protect them from bacteria and other unfriendly aerial elements); today the term is generic for snack. The art of moving from one bar to another in search of snacks — the art of Spanish grazing — is called a *tapeo.*

All you need to make your way around a tavern or tapas bar is the briefest of Spanish vocabularies — and you may not even need that, because bartenders usually have few problems with the English words for beer and wine. Accompanying your requests with *por favor* (please) goes a long way to getting what you want.

A beer is *una cerveza* (*oo*-nah thehr-*beh*-thah) or *una caña* (*oo*-nah *cah*-nyah), a draft. *Un vino tinto* is a glass of red wine. White wine is *vino blanco.* If you want to try a famous Spanish sherry, ask for *un jerez* (oon heh-*reth*). A dry sherry is simply *un fino.* And when you're ready to move on and want the check, say *¿Me cobra, por favor?* (meh *koh*-brah, pohr fah-*vohr*). You may or may not get a cash-register receipt.

La Latina/Lavapies District (Metro: La Latina)

More than 200 years old, and a classic of bullfighting ambience, **Taberna de Antonio Sánchez,** Mesón de Paredes 13 (☎ **91-539-78-26**), is as authentic as they come. It may be the oldest tavern in Madrid. **Taberna Tempranillo,** Cava Baja 38 (☎ **91-364-15-32**), is a friendly brick bar lined with wine racks (it has an amazing wine list). Located on one of Madrid's most frenetic tapas streets, it looks much more lived in than it is. Nearby, **Almendro 13** (☎ **91-365-42-52**), named for its address on the bend in the road, is hugely popular and a good spot for a cold sherry served from black bottles (but it closes early — at midnight), as is **La Carpanta,** Almendro 22 (☎ **91-366-57-83**). The name **Taberna de Cien Vinos,** Calle del Nuncio 17 (☎ **91-365-47-04**), means tavern of 100 wines, but it offers much more than that, including some great tapas, such as roast beef and salt cod. **Casa Antonio,** Latoneros 10 (☎ **91-429-93-56**), is a Madrid classic with a zinc bar, Moorish tiles, and bright red doors. On nice days, the doors are flung open and people spill out into the pedestrian street.

Santa Ana/Huertas District (Metro: Sol/Antón Martín)

You find an excellent assortment of tapas, such as anchovies and homemade canapés, at the very traditional, tile-lined **Taberna de Dolores,** Plaza Jesús 4 (☎ **91-429-22-43;** Metro: Banco de Sevilla). **España Cañí,** Plaza del Angel 14 (no phone), a funky little tavern just a short distance from Plaza de Santa Ana, is modern, with flamenco on the sound system. Sit at the bar and have a *caña* (small draft beer) and a tapa of *chorizo infierno* (literally, "hell's hot sausage") or *salmorejo,* a gazpacholike cold soup native to Córdoba. **Casa Alberto,** Calle de las Huertas 18 (☎ **91-429-93-56;** Metro: Antón Martín), an 1827 *taberna* with a front tapas bar and charming little restaurant in back, is a classic: Don Quixote's creator, Cervantes, once lived at this address.

Plaza Mayor (Metro: Sol)

The row of cavelike bars built right into the wall along Cava San Miguel outside the Plaza Mayor transport the 18th century to the present (or you back to the 18th century). Though tapas bars are quiet early in the evening, they get steadily more raucous as the night wears on. Most feature a guitar player or two and alcohol-fueled singalongs. The house specialty at **Mesón del Champigñón,** Cava de San Miguel 17 (☎ **91-559-67-90**), is as the name implies: garlicky mushrooms that are stuffed, grilled, salted, you name it. **Mesón de la Guitarra,** Cava de San Miguel 13 (☎ **91-559-95-31;** Metro: Sol), is named for the ever-present Spanish guitar. This tavern is what you expect to find in Madrid; it's almost always hopping with boisterous patrons, and wine and song flow freely.

Chueca District (Metro: Chueca)

This young and hip barrio has plenty of cool places to go out, but my favorite continues to be **Taberna Angel Sierra,** Gravina 11, on the Plaza de Chueca (no phone). With no tables, patrons either saddle up to the fantastic old zinc bar for a glass of *vermut* (vermouth) or spill out onto the street and square. Another good spot, with more than 100 tapas served, is **Santander,** Augusto Figueroa 25 (☎ **91-522-49-10**).

Flamenco music and dancing

Flamenco is as identifiably Spanish as bullfights and the glorious Iberian sun, so it's only natural that most visitors arrive in Madrid determined to see an authentic flamenco show, called a *tablao.* Flamenco may have been born in Andalusia, but some (or most) of its greatest practitioners reside in Madrid. Many shows are firmly directed at tourists, but that doesn't mean they're kitschy productions. The quality of dancing is generally excellent.

Several of Madrid's flamenco shows offer dinner-theater options, but you're better off eating at a real restaurant first and suffering only the cover and drink minimum (generally 23€–32€/$28–$38). Dinner is far from their top priority, but the clubs tend to charge as if they were serving the choicest gourmet meals (around 50€/$60 and up). The shows start late (generally around 11 p.m.), so you can easily get dinner elsewhere first.

Café de Chinitas, Calle Torija 7 (☎ **91-559-51-35;** Metro: Santo Domingo), in an 18th-century palace, is perhaps the best known of the Madrid clubs aimed at tourists, with excellent shows and costumes. It's been around for three decades and drawn such internationally known figures as Lady Di and President Bill Clinton. Shows begin at 10:30 p.m.

every night but Sunday. Reservations are essential. One of the liveliest places in town, and around since 1956, the **Corral de la Morería,** Calle Morería 7 (☎ **91-365-84-46;** Metro: La Latina), schedules good and slick, but not touristy, flamenco troupes and has entertained plenty of bigwigs. It's open every night of the week.

Casa Patas, Cañizares 10 (☎ **91-369-04-96;** Metro: Tirso de Molina), doubles as a tavern and restaurant, with flamenco shows at the back. Shows run Monday to Thursday at 10:30 p.m., and Friday and Saturday at 9 p.m. with another show at midnight (closed Sun). Shows here are less glitzy, more intimate, and more affordable than at most other clubs, but they still have attracted celebs on the order of Johnny Depp and Naomi Campbell.

Candela, Olmo 2 (☎ **91-527-35-94;** Metro: Antón Martín), and **Caracol,** Bernardino Obregón 18 (☎ **91-530-80-55;** Metro: Embajadores), are both popular bars with flamenco music and dance; some of Madrid's finest performers have been known to show up. Equally authentic, and a heck of a lot of fun, is **La Soleá,** Cava Baja 34 (☎ **91-365-33-08;** Metro: La Latina), an informal bar best known for its genuinely participatory nightly shows.

If you can't stop stomping your heels after seeing a flamenco show, you can sign up for a class in flamenco and *sevillanas* (popular folk dances similar to but less formal than flamenco); several spots in Madrid offer flamenco classes for locals and foreigners. Try **Escuela El Tablao,** Santa Polonia 9 (☎ **91-429-22-17**), or check the ads for private tutors in the *Guía del Ocio.* Fans of flamenco who are in Madrid the last week of June and during the month of July also need to check out the **Summer Flamenco Festival,** with major scheduled performances at the Teatro Real and elsewhere. See `www.teatro-real.com` or `www.madrid.org` for more information and a current schedule of events.

Bars and pubs

Two areas thick with back-to-back bars and cafes, many appealing to the young and rowdy, are **Calle de las Huertas** (Metro: Antón Martín), between the Plaza Mayor and Paseo del Prado, and the area around **Plaza Dos de Mayo,** in the Malasaña district (Metro: Tribunal). **Plaza de Santa Ana** (Metro: Sol or Antón Martín) is also extremely lively and flush with barhoppers most nights of the week.

Bar Cock, Calle de la Reina 16 (☎ **91-532-28-26;** Metro: Gran Vía or Banco de España), is a stylishly understated, urbane, and smoky place that features high ceilings and high-priced cocktails. It seems to attract a disproportionate number of models, actors, and public-relations sorts. Another chic hangout is **Teatriz,** Hermosilla 15 (☎ **91-577-53-79;** Metro: Velázquez), a former theater turned restaurant and bar. The attention-demanding decor is the work of design guru Philippe Starck. With a cool 1930s look, **Chicote,** Gran Vía 12 (☎ **91-532-67-37;** Metro: Gran Vía), is one of Madrid's enduring classics, and one of its most famous cocktail bars. Hemingway dug it; he and many other writers and artists drank here often in pre–Spanish Civil War days. The waiters are extraordinarily genteel — and they should be, given the high price of the drinks.

Cervecería Alemana, Plaza de Santa Ana 6 (☎ **91-429-70-33;** Metro: Sol or Antón Martín), is a simple beer hall with a young, cheerful crowd. Elaborately tiled **Los Gabrieles,** Echegaray 17 (☎ **91-429-62-61;** Metro: Tirso de Molina), brings the flavors and sounds of Andalusia to Madrid. In a neighborhood thick with bars, its cellar once housed a *bordello.* An intimate spot just off the Plaza Mayor, specializing in hard-to-find Belgian beers, is **Cafeeke,** Cuchilleros 3 (☎ **91-366-98-42**). Down the street from two of Madrid's most popular *versión original* (original language, or subtitled) cinemas are **El Plaza,** Martín de los Heros 3 (☎ **91-548-84-88**), and **El Café des las Estrellas,** Martín de los Heros 5 (☎ **91-542-16-30**), popular with cinefiles searching out the latest movies. The Metro stop for both is Plaza de España.

Cafes and terrazas

Outdoor cafes and bars are a Spanish specialty and most Madrileños love this opportunity to talk loudly, gesticulate with abandon, and check out the flow of people strutting their stuff. Linger over a *café* or beer and do the same (though you can keep gesticulations to a minimum if you fear spilling your drink). Outdoor cafes are also a good option for nonsmokers, because, despite the recent laws designed to cut down on public smoking, in many Madrid bars you may be the only one who's not lighting up.

Check out Plaza Mayor and Plaza Santa Ana for relaxed, traditional cafes that get going in early evening. In the heat of summer, the *terrazas* (open-air bars) along Paseo de Recoletos and Paseo de la Castellana really sizzle. The famous **Madrileño *marcha,*** the all-night party, begins at terrace cafes and then moves to the clubs and discos. If you want a primer on the latest fashions favored by Madrid's elite, just park yourself at any of the bars under the trees and settle in as the parade begins.

For more relaxed, traditional cafes that get going in early evening, check out Plaza Mayor and Plaza Santa Ana, or either of the following options. **Café Gijón,** Paseo de Recoletos 21 (☎ **91-521-54-25;** Metro: Banco de España), is a revered institution (especially for the literary set) that dates back to the late 19th century. And on historic Plaza de Oriente, near the Royal Palace and Opera House, the **Café de Oriente,** Plaza de Oriente 2 (☎ **91-541-39-74;** Metro: Opera), stands, built on the remains of a 17th-century convent. Sit in the palacelike interior or on the appetizing sidewalk terrace. If those cafes are too genteel for you, check out **Café Acuarela,** Gravina 10 (☎ **91-522-21-43;** Metro: Chueca), a dark and smoky hipster cafe that serves teas from around the world and other drinks amid religious art.

Live rhythms: Jazz, Latino, and rock

Live music in Madrid isn't limited to flamenco. You'll also find a bunch of cool little clubs to hear live jazz and Latin music. Check out the following clubs:

- **Café Central,** an attractive, sophisticated jazz cafe near Plaza de Santa Ana, has nightly piano performances, jazz quartets, and the occasional singer-songwriter. Plaza del Angel 10 (☎ **91-369-41-43;** Metro: Antón Martín).
- **Populart** is always packed and the bar schedules live performances that range from jazz and blues to reggae and samba. Calle de las Huertas 22 (☎ **91-429-84-07;** Metro: Antón Martín).
- For alternative rock shows by Spanish bands, check out **Siroco,** which rocks till 6 a.m. Thursday to Sunday. Calle San Dimas 3 (☎ **91-593-30-70;** Metro: Noviciado).

Disco fever

Discos are alive and well in Madrid, but they're predominantly young (very young), full-throttle affairs. The blinding lights and ear-splitting sound systems don't get cranking until midnight. And you've got to show up (or still be there) at 3 a.m. if you want to see the action in full swing. Most clubs have an admission charge of around $15 or $20, which includes your first drink. Here are a few hot spots: The sleek **Pacha,** the stylish Madrid incarnation of the famous chain that first struck a chord in Ibiza, housed in a 1930s building; open Thursday through Saturday from 2 to 5 a.m. (Barceló 11; ☎ **91-446-01-28;** Metro: Tribunal); the sprawling, anything-goes, cross-cultural **Kapital,** Atocha 125 (☎ **91-420-29-06**); **Palacio Gaviria,** open daily, where you'll find a wildly Baroque 19th-century palace place and everything from over-the-top disco to ballroom dancing and chic, secluded cocktail corners (Arenal 9; ☎ **91-526-60-69;** Metro: Puerta del Sol); and **Joy,** open nightly, a loud and in-your-face kind of place in the historic Teatro Eclava (Arenal 11; ☎ **91-366-37-33;** Metro: Sol).

Late-night munchies

In Madrid, the town that never wants to go to bed, an undying tradition is to top off the night (which is way into morning) with *chocolate con churros. Churros* are deep-fried pieces of dough, served piping hot, accompanied by cups of thick, rich hot chocolate — for dunking, of course. *Churrerías* usually open around 4 a.m., perfect for late-night partiers. A good place to add some much-needed grease and chocolate to your predawn diet is at **Churrería de San Ginés,** on Pasadizo de San Ginés, between Calle Mayor and Arenal.

Opera and classical music

Madrid's performing arts companies — including the Ballet Nacional de España, Orquesta Sinfónica de Madrid, and Orquesta Nacional de España — are among the best not only in Spain but in all of Europe. Look also for the world-famous flamenco troupe of Antonio Canales, Ballet Flamenco Antonio Canales.

Madrid's opera house, **Teatro Real,** Plaza Isabel II, s/n (Metro: Opera), has had a tortured history of delays, interruptions, fires, and even a stint as a gunpowder arsenal. Closed various times, but most recently from 1988 to 1997, it was finally rescued and given a state-of-the-art redesign. You may quibble with the showy, nouveau-antique design — handsome but cheesy faux-wood columns, for example — but you can't argue with the sophisticated stage technology.

Programs, which are extremely popular with Madrileños and visitors to the city, have included biggies such as *Carmen, La Bohème, Tosca, La Traviata,* and *The Barber of Seville.* Ballet (including the National Ballet of Spain) and classical concerts are also held at the Teatro. For information, visit the box office, call ☎ **91-516-06-60,** or visit `www.teatro-real.com`; for tickets, call ☎ **91-516-06-06.** Advance tickets (highly suggested if you really want to see a program during your stay) are available online or by calling ☎ **902-24-48-48.** The box office is open Monday through Saturday from 10 a.m. to 1:30 p.m. and 5:30 to 8 p.m. If there's a performance on Sunday, the box office opens two hours before showtime (generally at 6 p.m.). Guided tours of the sleek opera house (in English if there's a large enough group) are held Tuesday through Friday at 1 p.m. and Saturday and Sunday from 10:30 a.m. to 1:30 p.m. Admission is 3€ ($3.60) for adults or 1.80€ ($2.20) for children 7 to 14.

Opera takes the stage from January to July at the **Auditorio Nacional de Música,** Príncipe de Vergara 146 (☎ **91-337-01-00;** Metro: Cruz de Rayo); they offer excellent classical music concerts from October to June. At **Teatro Calderón,** Calle Atocha 18 (☎ **91-429-58-90;** Metro: Tirso de Molina), you can enjoy such well-known operas as Rossini's *The Barber of Seville.* A visit to **Teatro Lírico Nacional de la Zarzuela,** Jovellanos 4 (☎ **91-524-54-00;** Metro: Banco de España), is a chance to see *zarzuela,* the traditional form of light comic opera indigenous to Madrid. The singing is in Spanish, but you needn't know the language to enjoy the show.

Theater and musicals

Madrid is the *teatro* (theater) capital of Spain, but, logically, nearly all productions are in Spanish. If you don't speak Spanish and wish to see theater, you're best off opting for a performance of *zarzuela* (light comic opera), in which the language doesn't much matter. For other theater productions, you need to be relatively fluent in Spanish.

Teatro Albéniz, Calle Paz 11 (☎ **91-531-83-11;** Metro: Sevilla), has theater as well as dance and an occasional *zarzuela.* The **Teatro Nuevo Apolo,** Plaza de Tirso de Molina 1 (☎ **91-369-06-37;** Metro: Tirso de Molina), often presents popular international musicals, such as *Chicago.* **Teatro Español,** Príncipe 25 (☎ **91-360-14-80;** Metro: Sol), the municipal Spanish theater program, offers a wide variety of Spanish plays.

Film

Madrid has the largest roster of V.O (*versión original,* meaning subtitled) movie houses in the country. Finding an English-language movie isn't that difficult, as long as the Spanish subtitles don't bother you. It's also the best place to get acquainted with what's happening in Spanish cinema — one of the most vital in Europe. The best theaters showing both big-budget and art-house foreign and Spanish films include **Alphaville,** Martín de los Heroes 14 (Metro: Plaza de España); **Cines Ideal Yelmo,** Doctor Cortezo 6 (Metro: Sol); **Princesa,** Princesa 3 (Metro: Plaza de España); and **Renoir Plaza de España,** Martín de los Heroes 12 (Metro: Plaza de España). Foreign films that haven't been dubbed are designated "V.O." Pick up a copy of *Guía del Ocío* for full, current listings.

Going Beyond Madrid: Three Day Trips

One of the highlights of visiting Madrid is getting out of town. That may sound counterintuitive, but just outside the capital are some of Spain's greatest hits, equal in their own way to the drawing power of Madrid. If you're really limited on time and not planning to rent wheels, you can zip in and zip out of **El Escorial,** a beautifully austere 16th-century monastery, or **Aranjuez,** the grand summer palace and gardens of the Bourbon monarchs. Both are in the Madrid province and make easy half-day trips from the capital. More than two dozen trains depart daily from Madrid's Atocha, Nuevos Ministerios, and Chamartin train stations. During the summer, extra coaches are added. For schedules and information, call ☎ **902-24-02-02.**

With just a bit more time, you can do one or more of the Central Spain biggies: **Segovia, Toledo,** and **Salamanca** — three of Spain's most enjoyable, historic spots within a few hours from Madrid. (See Chapter 14 for more information.)

If you don't feel like doing the minimal planning (or driving) yourself, and you don't mind sticking to a group's timetable, you can join one of three major players that operate **no-hassle day trips** to the major sights outside of Madrid (El Escorial, Aranjuez, and the Valley of the Fallen), as well as to Toledo, Avila, and Segovia (see Chapter 14). Prices for day tours range from 30€ to about 70€ ($36–$84), which generally include round-trip transportation, some museum admissions, and a guided tour. Contact **Juliatur,** Gran Vía 68 (☎ **91-559-96-05;** Metro: Plaza de España);

Pullmantur, Plaza de Oriente 8 (☎ **91-541-18-07;** Metro: Opera); or **Trapsatur,** San Bernardo 5 (☎ **91-541-63-20;** Metro: Santo Domingo).

El Escorial: An austere monument to a king

Felipe II was Spain's austere monk-monarch. Known as "The Wise King," he created a Hispanic empire, but he was also a cold tyrant and an unbending religious fanatic. The **Monasterio de San Lorenzo de Escorial,** his legacy and sacred retreat in the foothills of the Sierra de Guadarrama Mountains, is monumental, gray, and spectacularly severe. It was intended as a "city of God," where Mass was heard day and night.

Yet the somber exterior of this mega-monastery, built from 1563 to 1584 and termed the eighth wonder of the world in its day, hides a real treasure trove of artistic wealth. Beyond the fortress exterior of Monasterio de San Lorenzo de Escorial is an art museum displaying the royal Habsburg collection, a marble mausoleum holding the remains of Spanish monarchs, and a royal library containing Felipe's extraordinary collection of manuscripts and tens of thousands of priceless books, arranged beneath a ceiling of brilliant frescoes.

To live like a king at El Escorial — at least during Felipe's reign — didn't mean living large. Although public areas are suitably grand, Felipe's royal living quarters are utterly monastic — quite the opposite of the lavish apartments the Bourbon kings later installed at El Escorial. To get as close as he could to heaven, Felipe requested that his private room, "his humble cell," overlook the massive dome of the basilica.

In the royal pantheon beneath the church's altar almost all of Spain's monarchs are buried, including Felipe II and his father, Carlos V.

The museum holds numerous Titians, as well as paintings by Ribera, Zurbarán, and El Greco. El Greco's *The Martyrdom of St. Maurice* is one of the artist's acknowledged masterpieces. Don't miss two frescoes in the basilica: one of heaven, over the choir, and another by Titian, which depicts the live roasting of San Lorenzo, after whom the monastery is named (the latter being a tidbit for the macabre crowd).

During the summer months, you have little choice but to deal with hordes of tourists streaming out to El Escorial, one of the most popular visits in the Madrid area. Try to go either very early or very late in the day; you may get lucky and run into fewer people. El Escorial (☎ **91-890-59-02** or 91-890-78-19) is open October through March, Tuesday to Sunday from 10 a.m. to 5 p.m. and April through September, Tuesday to Sunday from 10 a.m. to 6 p.m. Admission to the Royal Monastery is 8.50€ ($10) adults and 5€ ($6) for seniors and students. Visits for E.U. members are free on Wednesdays. Additional buildings, such as the outlying lodges **Casita de Abajo** (Casa del Príncipe) and **Casita de Arriba** (Casa del Infante), have separate opening hours and admission fees (the latter is open only Easter Week and July–Sept, while the former is open year-round). For additional information, visit www.patrimonionacional.es/infprac/visitas/escorial.htm.

Guided tours are approximately 90 minutes, but visitors who want a full view of El Escorial may want to budget an entire morning or afternoon to adequately explore the entire complex and its many gardens.

Take either a train or bus to El Escorial, 49km (30 miles) northwest of Madrid. From Madrid's Atocha station, trains leave throughout the day, from 5:48 a.m. to 10:17 p.m. A one-way ticket is 2.50€ ($3), or 5€ ($6) round-trip. The trip takes about an hour. By bus, **Empresa Herranz** (☎ **91-896-90-28**) leaves about every 20 minutes, from 7:15 a.m. to 11:30 p.m. Buses (2.75€/$3.30 one-way, one hour) leave from the Intercambiador de Montcloa Station (Metro: Moncloa) and take about an hour.

Where to dine

Even though El Escorial is an easy half-day trip from Madrid, you may want to eat lunch here before you return to the capital, so try the suitably named **Mesón la Cueva,** San Antón 4 (☎ **91-890-1516;** www.mesonlacueva.com), known for its roasted lamb and suckling pig.

Aranjuez: The royal summer palace

Summer visitors to Madrid beeline to Aranjuez, the Palacio Real (Royal Palace), with the same single-minded purpose that Bourbon monarchs did: They want to escape the heat. In the midst of Central Spain's arid plains, this royal summer palace, near the meeting of the Tagus and Jarama rivers, is a lush oasis with 283-plus hectares (700 acres) of cool, shaded gardens, fountains, sculptures, and leafy trees imported from Spain's former colonies in the Americas.

The immense palace you see, a (relatively) poor man's Versailles, isn't the same as the one favored by Ferdinand and Isabella, the legendary Catholic monarchs. Twice razed by fire, the palace had to be entirely rebuilt in the 1870s. Still, it remains extravagant. The splendid **Porcelain Salon,** bathed in colorful tiles depicting Chinese scenes, may remind you of Madrid's Royal Palace — the tiles are from the same royal pottery factory. However, the standout features at Aranjuez are the serene gardens, particularly the **Jardín de la Isla** (Island Garden) and **Jardín del Príncipe** (Prince's Garden), and romantic parks that inspired one of Spain's most famous pieces of music, Joaquin Rodrigo's *Concierto de Aranjuez.*

In the mile-long **Jardín del Príncipe** (Prince's Garden) at Aranjuez, you find the luxurious, curiously named **Casita del Labrador** — the Worker's Cottage (quite a misnomer: How many blue-collar workers do you know who reside in mini-palaces bursting with Greek busts, marble floors, and brocaded walls?). Queen María Luisa, reputed to be an unrepentant nympho, invited her young lover, Prime Minister Godoy, here for romantic trysts (her husband, King Carlos IV, was nuts, so the cheatin' queen didn't even try to conceal her dalliances).

The Palacio Real (☎ **91-891-03-05** or 91-892-43-42) is open Tuesday through Sunday from 10 a.m. to 6:15 p.m. from April to September, and from 10 a.m. to 5:15 p.m. from October through March. Admission for a guided visit to the Palacio Real is 5€ ($6) and 6€ ($7.20) for visits that include royal bedrooms (4€/$4.80 and 5€/$6, respectively, for seniors and students). Guided visits to the Casa del Labrador, which is currently being restored, are 3€ ($3.60; 2.25€/$2.70 seniors and students) until restoration is completed, after which prices will rise to 5€ ($6; 4€/$5 seniors and students). Visits are free on Wednesday for E.U. residents.

The palace is located 47km (29 miles) south of Madrid. For additional information about Aranjuez and reservations, call ☎ **91-891-0 3-05.** You can easily hop either a bus or a train for Aranjuez.

A couple of dozen **Aisa y Samar** (☎ **902-19-87-88** or 91-468-41-90) buses depart daily from Estación Sur de Autobuses (Metro: Méndez Alvaro). The trip takes an hour and costs 3€ ($3.60) one-way. On Sundays, far fewer buses run. Trains, which take 45 minutes, leave from Atocha station (Metro: Atocha RENFE) every 20 minutes or so; the trip costs 2.50€ ($3) one-way, 5€ ($6) round-trip.

A historic, tourist-oriented old steam train with wooden cars and attendants in period dress, Tren de la Fresa, or the Strawberry Train, travels from Madrid to Aranjeuz, as it first did in 1851 (it was the second rail line in Spain). During the last weekend of April, the months of May, June, and September, and a few selected dates in October, it departs from the Atocha AVE station once daily at 10:05 a.m. (arriving an hour later) and returns at 6 p.m. Adult tickets (which include guided visits to the Palacio Real) cost 24€ ($29); for children ages 2 to 12 the cost is 16€ ($19). Call ☎ **902-22-88-22** or visit `www.museodelferrocarril.org` for more information, or call ☎ **902-24-02-02** for reservations.

Fast Facts: Madrid

American Express

There are branches at Barajas airport and Plaza de las Cortes 2 (☎ 91-743-77-55; Metro: Banco de España); open Monday through Friday from 9 a.m. to 7:30 p.m and Saturday from 9 a.m. to 2 p.m.

Area Code

The area code for telephone numbers within Madrid is **91.** You must always dial the prefix.

ATMs

Automatic teller machines are widely available throughout Madrid; most banks have 24-hour ATMs. You can find such branches along Gran Vía and Calle Serrano in the Salamanca neighborhood and along Gran Vía.

Currency

In 2002, the euro, the European currency, replaced the Spanish peseta. The exchange rate used to calculate the dollar values given in this chapter is 1€ = $1.20. Amounts over $10 are rounded to the nearest dollar.

Currency Exchange

You can find currency exchange offices at the Charmartín rail station and Barajas airport. Major Spanish banks include La Caixa, BBV, and Banco Central Hispano; most have branches on Gran Vía and/or Alcalá.

Doctors

To locate an English-speaking doctor or to report a medical emergency, dial ☎ **112** or ☎ **061** (Insalud, Public Medical Care).

Embassies/Consulates

The U.S. Embassy is located at Calle Serrano 75 (☎ 91-587-22-00; Metro: Núñez de Balboa); Canada's is at Núñez de Balboa 35 (☎ 91-431-43-00; Metro: Velázquez); the United Kingdom's is at Fernando El Santo 16 (☎ 91-700-82-00; Metro: Colón); Ireland's is at Paseo de la Castellana 36 (☎ 91-576-35-00; Metro: Serrano); Australia's is at Plaza Descubridor Diego de Ordás 3 (☎ 91-441-93-00; Metro: Cuzco); and New Zealand's is at Plaza de la Lealtad 2 (☎ 91-523-02-26; Metro: Banco de España).

Emergencies

For general emergencies, dial ☎ **112.** For medical emergencies, call ☎ **061** or visit or call a 24-hour first-aid station: Calle Navas de Tolosa 10 (☎ 91-521-00-25); Avenida Del Paseo de Extremadura 147 (☎ 91-464-76-32); or Gobernador 39 (☎ 91-420-03-56). For a 24-hour pharmacy, call ☎ **098.** For an ambulance, call ☎ 91-588-44-00. For the municipal police, dial ☎ **092.** For a fire, ☎ **080.**

Hospitals

To locate a hospital, dial ☎ **112.** For medical emergencies, visit or call a 24-hour first-aid station: See "Emergencies." For help finding an English-speaking doctor, call the Anglo-American Medical Unit, Calle Conde de Aranda 1 (☎ 91-435-1823). All insurance is recognized, and emergencies will be seen to without bureaucratic red tape.

Information

Municipal Tourism Offices are located at Plaza Mayor 3 (☎ 91-366-54-77), open Monday through Saturday from 10 a.m. to 8 p.m. and Sunday and holidays from 10 a.m. to 3 p.m.; Duque de Medinaceli 2 (☎ 91-429-49-51), open Monday though Saturday from 9 a.m. to 7 p.m. and Sunday from 9 a.m. to 3 p.m.; Puerta de Toledo Market 1 (☎ 91-364-18-76), open Monday through Saturday from 8 a.m. to 8 p.m. and Sunday from 8 a.m. to 2 p.m.; Barajas Airport (International Arrivals Terminal; ☎ 91-305-86-56), open daily from 8 a.m. to 8 p.m. Also look for tourist information offices at the Atocha (☎ 902-100-107), open daily 9 a.m. to 9 p.m., and Chamartín (☎ 91-315-99-76), open Monday through Saturday from 8 a.m. to 8 p.m. and Sunday 8 a.m. to 2 p.m. In summer months, yellow tourist information kiosks are set up near the Prado Museum, the Palacio Real, and Puerta del Sol. You can also call ☎ 902-10-21-12 or 902-10-01-07 to get tourism information by phone, or visit `www.munimadrid.es`. For general information, call ☎ **010.** For bus information, call ☎ 91-530-4800 or 91-468-4200. For train information, call ☎ 90-224-0202 or 90-224-3402 or log on to `www.renfe.es`. For flight information, dial ☎ 91-305-8344.

Internet Access and Cybercafes

If you want to Net surf or need to send an e-mail, try one of the following cafes or computer centers (though it's wise to check with the tourism office, because these tend to come and go with regularity): Interpublic, Carrera de San Jerónimo 18, first floor (☎ 91-523-15-50; Metro: Sol); Brigg, a massive center with 300 terminals at the corner of Alcalá and Virgen de los Peligros (Metro: Gran Vía); easyInternetcafé, Glorieta de Quevedo 5 (Metro: Quevedo; `www.easyeverything.com`), open 24/7; or Cybercafe Lasser, Rosario 21 (☎ 91-365-87-91; Metro: Latina). Prices range from 1.20€ to 3€ ($1.45–$3.60) per hour.

Maps

A free street map covering all of Madrid is available at Tourist Information Offices at the airport, train stations, and in the city. The map is sufficient for virtually all city travel. You should also pick up the pocket-size map of the Metro subway system, available free at any Metro station.

Newspapers/Magazines

Most European newspapers are sold on the day of publication, as are the Paris-based *International Herald Tribune* and European edition of *The Wall Street Journal. USA Today* is also widely available, as well as principal European and American magazines. You can find them at the many kiosks along Gran Vía or near Puerta del Sol. Spanish-speakers should check out entertainment listings in the weekly magazine *Guía del Ocio* (Leisure Guide).

Pharmacies

Pharmacies (*farmacias,* indicated by neon green crosses) operate during normal business hours, but one in every neighborhood remains open all night and on holidays. The location and phone number of this *farmacia de guardia* is posted on the door of all the other pharmacies. You can call ☎ **098** to contact all-night pharmacies.

Police

Call ☎ **112** or **092.**

Post Office

The Central Post Office is located at Palacio de Comunicaciones, Plaza de la Cibeles, s/n (☎ 91-396-24-43). It's open Monday through Friday from 8:30 a.m. to 9 p.m., Saturday from 8 a.m. to 8 p.m and Sundays and holidays from 8:30 a.m. to 2:00 p.m. The yellow sign CORREOS identifies branches of the Post Office. Stamps are also sold at *estancos* (tabacco sellers). An airmail letter or postcard to the United States is .75€ (85¢).

Safety

Madrid has a reputation of having one of the highest crime rates in Spain, though street crime is normally limited to pickpocketing and breaking into cars with items left in the seats. Exercise extra care along Gran Vía, Puerta del Sol, Calle Montera (known as a heavy red-light district), the Rastro flea market, and areas with lots of bars (and rowdy drunks), such as Huertas and Latina. The presence of so many people out at all hours of the night is generally cause for reassurance rather than fear. Also, be especially careful of tourist scams near the art museums on Paseo del Prado.

Taxes

The government sales tax, known as IVA (value-added tax), is levied nationwide on all goods and services, and ranges from 7 to 33 percent.

Taxis

If you need to call a cab, recommended taxi companies include Tele-Taxi (☎ 91-371-21-31), Radio Taxi (☎ 91-447-32-32), and Radio Taxi Independiente (☎ 91-405-12-13).

Telephone

For general telephone information, call ☎ **010.** For national telephone information, dial ☎ **009.** Madrid's area code is **91,** and you must dial it before all numbers. International call centers are located at the main post office, Plaza de la Cibeles, s/n; Gran Vía 30; and Paseo de Recoletos 41 (Plaza de Colón).

Chapter 14

Castile: Around Madrid

In This Chapter

- Setting out on side trips from Madrid
- Visiting Segovia's fairy-tale castle and 2,000-year-old Roman Aqueduct
- Marveling at Avila's massive medieval walls
- Discovering Salamanca, Spain's oldest university town
- Taking in the views at Toledo, El Greco's city on a hill

Castile, the Spain of Roman conquerors and medieval kingdoms, certainly looks the part of the storybook Spain that most first-time travelers expect to find: a place of walled cities rising heroically on the plains, of grand sand-colored castles and cathedrals, and of historic palaces and universities. Segovia, Salamanca, Avila, and Toledo match those expectations and then some, so it's a little surprising that so many people rush by these historic cities in frenzied day trips from Madrid. Sure, they're close together and accessible from the capital, but a very enjoyable Spanish vacation could easily be taken in only these places — all named UNESCO Heritage of Mankind cities. They also make for an excellent leisurely driving tour.

Segovia has a fairy-tale castle and 2,000-year-old Roman Aqueduct, while massive medieval walls that are among the most impressive and best preserved in Europe ring Avila. Stately Salamanca, Spain's oldest university town, is a living museum of early Renaissance architecture with regional flourishes, and Toledo, El Greco's enlightened city on a hill, is where Christian, Muslim, and Jewish cultures all thrived in the days before the Inquisition.

The beauty of these cities is immediately apparent. But to discover the depths of their appeal, you need more than a quick drive-by. These centers of learning, government, and religion — serious cities carved out of stone and wood — are surprisingly pleasant places to spend some time. Consider these great cities of Castile not just as add-on, one-day side trips from Madrid but as unique components of a slower-paced regional trip, similar to possibilities offered by the Basque Country (see Chapter 12), Andalusia's Pueblos Blancos (see Chapter 16), and Girona and the Costa Brava (see Chapter 11). A relaxed pace reveals the towns of Central Spain to be more than handsome museum pieces.

Major Attractions in Castile

Segovia and Salamanca are part of what was once the kingdom of Old Castile (which is now more commonly called Castilla y León), northwest of Madrid in central Spain. Toledo, for all its ancient roots, is part of the region of New Castile, or Castilla y La Mancha, southwest of the capital. Segovia, Salamanca, Avila, and Toledo are all between one and three hours by car, train, or bus from Madrid.

The parched plains of central Spain are especially given to extremes: blisteringly hot in summer, brutally cold in winter. The best times to visit the region are spring and fall; summer brings not only heat waves but oceans of tourists, overrunning some of the quiet beauty of such towns as Segovia and Toledo. The region, though, is popular most of the year; high season is mid-March through the end of October, generally, and low season (with slightly lower hotel rates) is from November through mid-March. (Though in Toledo, December is also high season.)

Regional dining is classic Castilian: This landlocked area goes big for meat and game — suckling pig, oven-roasted lamb, partridge, and sausage and beans. It's the kind of hearty, straightforward cooking that old inns serve in clay bowls.

My advice concerning attractions in Castile is simple: Do as much as you have time for, without blowing through anything. Almost everyone hits the towns of Castile after spending a few days in Madrid, which is the ideal way to organize a trip to central Spain. Although people often try to squeeze in side trips from Madrid on madcap bus tours of only a day or so, Segovia and Toledo each require (at least) full days, and really reward overnight stays. You can best see Salamanca, the farthest from Madrid, in a couple of days. To visit them all by car, you need a minimum of four days, but even that's zooming through in pretty quick fashion.

Some of the big attractions in Castile are the many castles, the military fortresses, and the remains of walled cities. The region was known for its warlike ways — it was fought over by the Visigoths, Moors, and Christians, and spent nearly all of the Middle Ages being attacked and sacked. In fact, even the name of the region relates to war: Castile is a derivative of *castillo,* the Spanish name for castle.

Seeing Segovia

Less touristy than Toledo, but nearly as rich a representative of the golden era of Old Castile, Segovia (seh-*goh*-vyah), 91km (54 miles) northwest of Madrid, is among the most picturesque cities in Spain. The city has one of the more impressive settings in the world: It rises like a mirage upon a limestone elevation from the dry plains. In Segovia, look for the **Roman Aqueduct,** a triumph of superior engineering and a symbol of the city; **El Alcázar,** a castle crowning the city on the hill; and the **Catedral de Segovia,** the last great Gothic cathedral in Spain.

Castile

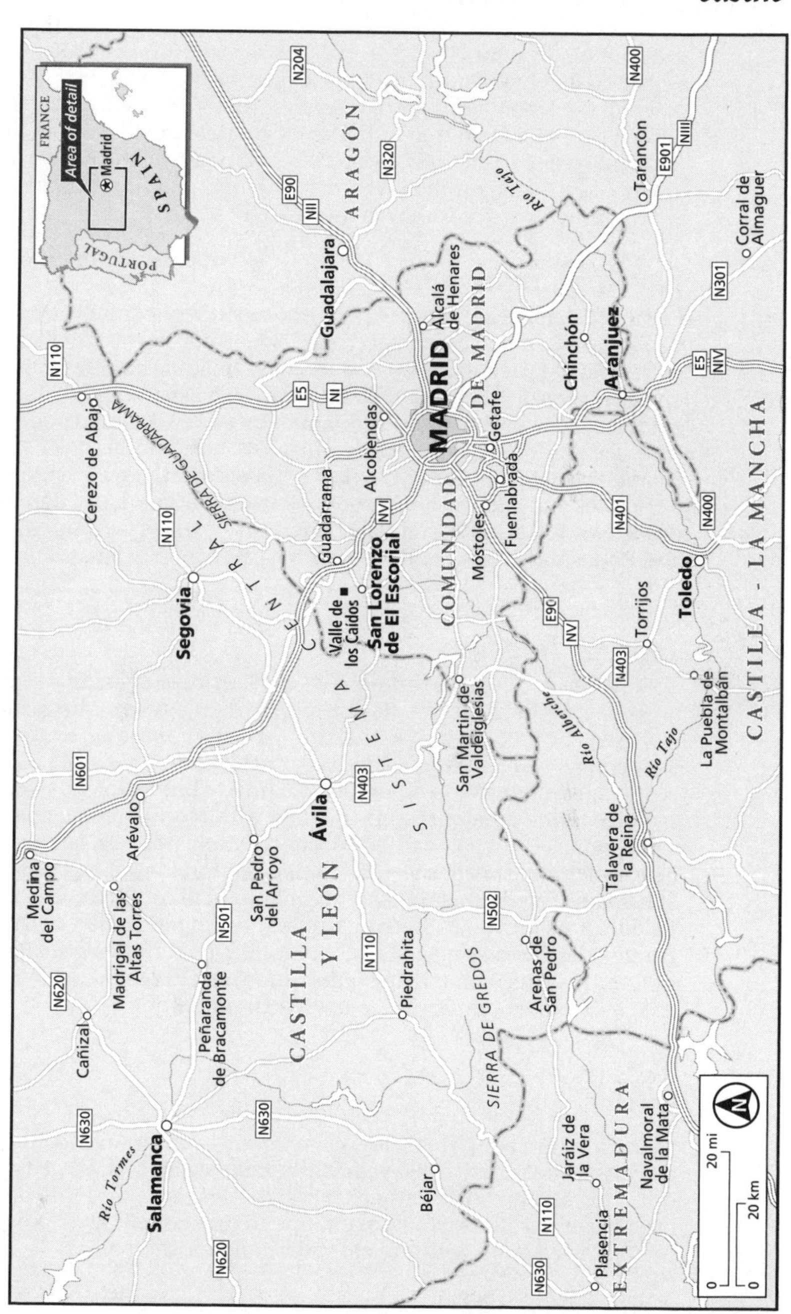

FRANCE
Area of detail
Madrid
SPAIN
PORTUGAL
ARAGÓN
COMUNIDAD DE MADRID
CASTILLA Y LEÓN
CASTILLA - LA MANCHA
EXTREMADURA
SISTEMA CENTRAL
SIERRA DE GUADARRAMA
SIERRA DE GREDOS
Río Tajo
Río Alberche
Río Tormes
MADRID
Guadalajara
Alcalá de Henares
Alcobendas
Getafe
Fuenlabrada
Móstoles
Chinchón
Aranjuez
Tarancón
Corral de Almaguer
Toledo
Torrijos
La Puebla de Montalbán
Talavera de la Reina
Navalmoral de la Mata
Jaráiz de la Vera
Plasencia
Arenas de San Pedro
San Martín de Valdeiglesias
San Lorenzo de El Escorial
Valle de los Caídos
Guadarrama
Segovia
Cerezo de Abajo
Ávila
Arévalo
Medina del Campo
Madrigal de las Altas Torres
San Pedro del Arroyo
Peñaranda de Bracamonte
Cañizal
Salamanca
Piedrahita
Béjar
N204
N320
E90
NII
N110
E5
NI
NVI
N601
N403
N501
N620
N630
N502
N400
E901
NIII
N301
NIV
N401
NV
0
20 mi
20 km

Checking out Avila

Avila, 110km (68 miles) northwest of Madrid, is known for having the greatest medieval walls in Europe. The massive stone fortifications, nearly 40 feet high and 10 feet wide, ring the city. Avila was also the birthplace of the legendary Catholic mystic Saint Teresa. Look for the **convent** named for her, in addition to Europe's greatest medieval **ramparts** and an **Old Quarter** of cathedrals, churches, and convents. However, despite its illustrious history, for most visitors who don't consider themselves true devotees of Saint Teresa, Avila merits only a brief visit.

Savoring Salamanca

Pristine Salamanca, 204km (127 miles) northwest of Madrid, is a great university town, and was Spain's center of learning in the Middle Ages. The entire Old Quarter, made up of university buildings, palaces, monasteries, and convents, is the finest collection of Renaissance and Plateresque golden sandstone buildings in Spain. (For more on Plateresque architecture, see the "Salamanca architecture 101" box, later in this chapter.) In Salamanca, look for the **University of Salamanca,** the alma mater of Cervantes and a draw for students all over the world; **old and new cathedrals,** glowing examples of Gothic and early-Renaissance architecture; and **Plaza Mayor,** a splendid gathering place, one of Spain's most stately public squares.

Touring Toledo

Toledo, 68km (42 miles) southwest of Madrid, is on nearly everyone's must-see list for a reason. Its setting, high on a hill on the plains of central Spain, is incomparable, the subject of a thousand paintings, including favorite son El Greco's. The labyrinthine city looks like a complex castle surrounded by a moat, the Río Tago (Tagus River). Each of its crooked, atmospheric streets, packed with Moorish mosques, Jewish synagogues, Christian cathedrals, and stately palaces, is a rich Spanish history lesson. Before the Spanish Inquisition forced non-Catholics to flee Spain, Toledo was the capital of a tolerant, multicultural Spain. In Toledo, look for the **cathedral,** opulent and spectacular, one of Spain's greatest; **El Greco**'s magisterial painting *The Burial of Count Orgaz,* as well as the artist's house/museum; and the last remaining **synagogues** of the city's influential medieval Jewish community.

Segovia

Segovia is, as the Spanish say, *encantador* — charming. In addition to its top draw, the nearly 2,000-year-old Roman Aqueduct, the city boasts other big sights — the cathedral and El Alcázar — and lots of charming little surprises in its Old Quarter. Spend most, if not all, of your time in the historic center near the cathedral and castle.

Getting there

Driving to Segovia is a breeze, and it's a scenic drive from Madrid, taking about 75 minutes. Take the A-6 northwest from Madrid toward León. The Segovia turnoff (north on N-603) is signposted. If you're only visiting Segovia, though, a car's not necessary to explore the city.

By bus

La Sepulvedana, Paseo de la Florida 11 (☎ **91-559-89-55;** Metro: Príncipe Pio), buses leave Madrid for Segovia (a 90-minute ride) every half-hour Monday through Saturday, beginning at 6:30 a.m. with the last returning at 9:30 p.m. (10:15 p.m. on Sat). On Sunday, service is hourly, with returns every half-hour between 4 and 10:30 p.m. One-way fare is 6€ ($7.20). The **Segovia Bus Station** is at Plaza de la Estación de Autobuses 1 (☎ **921-42-77-07**).

By train

The train takes half an hour longer than the bus, and even though it makes several stops, I find it more comfortable and relaxed. You also have a better view of beautiful mountain terrain as you climb up to Segovia. From Madrid, nine trains a day depart from Atocha station (Metro: Atocha RENFE) between 6 a.m. and 8 p.m. They arrive in Segovia a little more than two hours later. The last train back to Madrid leaves at 8:55 p.m. A one-way trip costs 5.45€ ($6.50). The **train station,** at Plaza del Obispo Quesada, s/n (☎ **921-42-07-74** or 902-24-02-02), leaves you a good ways from the Old Quarter. You either need to take a taxi or bus (no. 3 to Plaza Mayor), or walk about 20 minutes.

Getting around

Segovia's Old Quarter is pretty small. Your own two feet are the best way to get around, unless you stay at the Parador de Segovia, which is a couple of miles out of town and requires a taxi or car. To get a perspective of the city from beyond the walls (writers have long said that it forms a giant ship on the horizon), you either need to put on some long-haul sneakers or hire a cab if you don't have a car.

If you need a taxi, you can either catch one at the stop next to the Roman Aqueduct (pretty hard to miss!) or call **Radio Taxi** (☎ **921-44-50-00**).

Spending the night

Most people drop in on Segovia, rush around, and then bolt back to Madrid or on to their next stop. It's too bad because Segovia's quiet Old Quarter is a special place to stay overnight. With the Roman Aqueduct, the cathedral, and El Alcázar (the storybook castle on the edge of the hill) all brilliantly illuminated at night, the city transmits medieval allure like few others. And for a small place, it's got a fair share of charming hotels. In fact, choosing among the following isn't easy.

Segovia

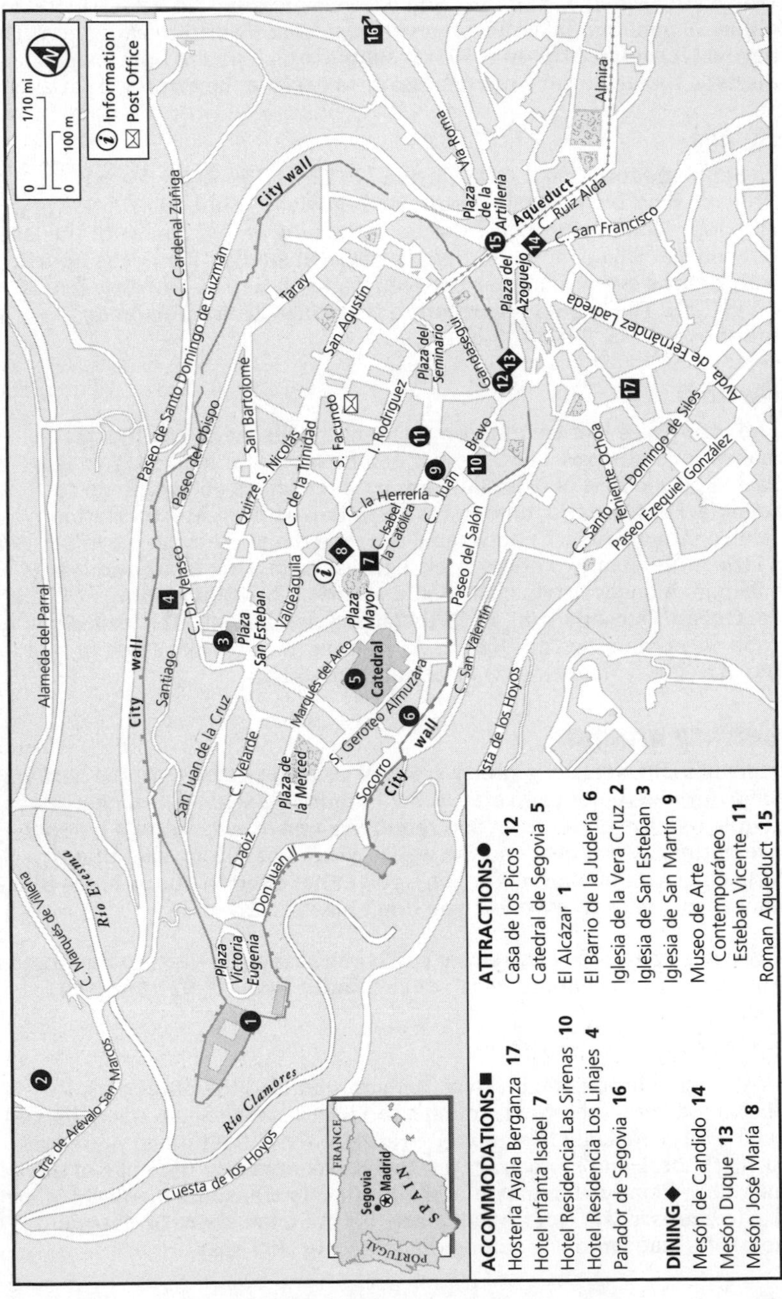

0 1/10 mi
0 100 m
Information
Post Office
ACCOMMODATIONS ■
Hostería Ayala Berganza 17
Hotel Infanta Isabel 7
Hotel Residencia Las Sirenas 10
Hotel Residencia Los Linajes 4
Parador de Segovia 16
DINING ◆
Mesón de Candido 14
Mesón Duque 13
Mesón José María 8
ATTRACTIONS ●
Casa de los Picos 12
Catedral de Segovia 5
El Alcázar 1
El Barrio de la Judería 6
Iglesia de la Vera Cruz 2
Iglesia de San Esteban 3
Iglesia de San Martín 9
Museo de Arte Contemporáneo Esteban Vicente 11
Roman Aqueduct 15
FRANCE
PORTUGAL
SPAIN
Segovia
Madrid
Alameda del Parral
C. Cardenal Zúñiga
Paseo de Santo Domingo de Guzmán
Paseo del Obispo
City wall
Vía Roma
Plaza de la Artillería
Aqueduct
C. Ruiz Alda
C. San Francisco
Almira
Plaza del Azoguejo
Avda. de Fernández Ladreda
Gandesegui
Plaza del Seminario
San Agustín
Taray
San Bartolomé
Quirze S. Nicolás
C. de la Trinidad
S. Facundo
I. Rodríguez
C. la Herrería
C. Isabel la Católica
C. Juan Bravo
Valdeáguila
C. Dr. Velasco
Plaza San Esteban
Plaza Mayor
Catedral
Santiago
San Juan de la Cruz
C. Velarde
Marqués del Arco
Plaza de la Merced
S. Geroteo Almuzara
Socorro
Daoiz
Don Juan II
Plaza Victoria Eugenia
Paseo del Salón
C. San Valentín
Cuesta de los Hoyos
C. Santo Tomás
Teniente Ochoa
Domingo de Silos
Paseo Ezequiel González
Río Eresma
Río Clamores
C. Marqués de Villena
Ctra. de Arévalo San Marcos

Hostería Ayala Berganza

$$$ On outskirts of Old Quarter

The name may not roll off the tongue of most English-speaking visitors, but this small inn (18 rooms) is one of the most comfortable and atmospheric places to stay in Segovia. Located outside the ramparts that encircle the Old Quarter, it's next door to the fine Romanesque church San Millán, and just a short walk south from the Roman Aqueduct. However, it's not easy to locate, and some travelers may not like the neighborhood compared to that of hotels located in the heart of the Old Quarter. Partially inhabiting a 15th-century Castilian palace that was once home to the painter Ignacio Zuloaga, the Ayala Berganza claims a lovely central courtyard with stone columns and spills over to a modern construction. All rooms are uniquely and attractively decorated; some have bathtubs and canopied beds. Try to get one in the original, Gothic-mudéjar palace.

See map p. 324. Calle Carretas 5. ☎ ***921-46-04-48.*** *Fax: 921-46-23-77. E-mail:* `ayalaberanza@partner-hotels.com`. *Parking: Available on street. Rack rates: 114€–137€ ($132–$160). AE, DC, MC, V.*

Hotel Infanta Isabel

$$–$$$ Old Quarter

You can't ask for a better location. This midsize (39-room) 19th-century charmer is right on the central Plaza Mayor. It has attractive Victorian décor, great service, and some very large doubles — some with small terraces and breathtaking views of the plaza and cathedral. With pretty curtains and other elegant touches such as white-painted furniture, the rooms are very reasonably priced — one reason this place is packed in high season. Rooms are priced according to size; you can choose from small, medium, and large, so opt to see a couple before settling on one if several are available. The hotel now features an attractive cafe/restaurant serving lunch and dinner as well as breakfast.

See map p. 324. Calle Isabel la Católica 1 (Plaza Mayor). ☎ ***921-46-13-00.*** *Fax: 921-46-22-17.* `www.hotelinfantaisabel.com`. *Parking: Nearby parking 8€ ($9.60). Rack rates: 78€–114€ ($94–$137). AE, DC, MC, V.*

Hotel Residencia Las Sirenas

$$ Old Quarter

Inexplicably named for mermaids in this land-locked region, this is the best bargain hotel in town (even though its prices have crept up steadily in the last few years). Right in the heart of the Old Quarter, it's a short walk from the Plaza Mayor and cathedral and is across from an animated square, Plaza de San Martín. Enter through a simple door and find a long charcoal-colored marble floor and marble staircase at back. The whole place is well maintained; rooms have a lot of light and are decently furnished for the price. Rooms in the back of the hotel look out over the countryside to the Sierra de Guadarrama.

Calle Juan Bravo 30. ☎ ***921-46-26-63.*** *Fax: 921-46-26-57.* www.hotelsirenas.com. *Parking: Nearby parking 6€ ($7.20). Rack rates: 60€–70€ ($72–$84). AE, DC, MC, V.*

Hotel Residencia Los Linajes

$$–$$$ Old Quarter

This personal, midsize hotel (55 rooms) is probably the best place to experience the charms of old Segovia. On a side street in the San Esteban part of the Old Quarter, the hotel occupies a 17th-century palace that belonged to a noble Segovian family (although much of the hotel is new construction). It's not fancy, but the hotel has a lovely lobby and central patio, and some rooms have priceless panoramic views over the Eresma River and the Parral monastery. (Asking for these rooms is worth it.) The hotel was renovated a couple of years ago; rooms have nice wood furnishings and well-equipped bathrooms. This place is peaceful, making the small disco that the hotel operates down some stairs out back oddly incongruous.

See map p. 324. Calle Dr. Velasco 9 (on the northeast side of town, near the Hospital de Misercordia and Puerta de Santiago). ☎ ***921-46-04-75.*** *Fax: 921-46-04-79.* www.loslinajes.com. *Parking: 10€ ($12). Rack rates: 83€–129€ ($100–$155). AE, DC, MC, V.*

Parador de Segovia

$$$ 3.2km (2 miles) northeast of Segovia

It may not be all that convenient for exploring the Old Quarter of Segovia, but this *parador*'s views are out of this world. This spacious and tranquil government-run hotel, tucked into a hill 3.2km (2 miles) north of the city, has a commanding perspective of Segovia — from the aqueduct to the medieval walls and the cathedral and castle. At night, all are beautifully illuminated, and you have to tear yourself away from admiring the monumental city long enough to get some shut-eye. By day you can hit the pool, which has the same magnificent views as the rooms and is sure to be a big hit with the kids. The place is startlingly modern and very comfortable, if not historic, romantic, and palatial like some *paradores.* Rooms are large, with tiled floors and contemporary furnishings. Most have lovely views of the city down the hill. If you have the time and want to take a leisurely approach to the city, this is a great choice. However, if you're here to see the Old Quarter in a day or so, or you want to walk around the city at night, the inconvenience of having to drive or take a taxi down into town makes the *parador* a less attractive option.

See map p. 324. Carretera de Valladolid, s/n. 3.2km northeast of Segovia along N-601, the Carretera de Valladolid; drive or take a taxi. ☎ ***921-44-37-37.*** *Fax: 921-43-37-62.* www.parador.es. *Free parking. Rack rates: 130€–140€ ($156–$168). Inquire about special discounts for families with children. AE, DC, MC, V.*

Eating and drinking like a Castilian

Central Spain can be a little rough on vegetarians. Everywhere you turn, you see wood ovens fired up with roasted *cochinillo asado* (suckling pig) and *cordero asado* (roast baby lamb). These and other dishes haven't changed much since the Middle Ages; try also *sopa castellana* (a broth with ham, vegetables, eggs, and bread), *cocido castellano* (a chickpea-based stew), and *perdiz* (braised partridge, especially popular in Toledo). If you're looking for a little something to tide you over, try *morcilla* (blood sausage) and *queso Manchego* (sheep's milk cheese that's hard when mature) — both are excellent accompaniments to a glass of red wine.

The region of Old Castile, particularly the Valladolid area around the River Duero, is gaining a reputation for producing some of the finest wines in Spain. Though red wines from Spain's Rioja region are better known (see Chapter 12), in recent years the reds from Ribera del Duero vineyards have been quite literally on everybody's lips. The region produces not only Spain's most expensive wine, Vega Sicilia, but also more affordable, yet also superb, vintages from such wineries as Pesquera and Mauro. They're deeply colored, smooth, and frequently oaky wines. Look for them in restaurants in Castile and throughout Spain. Valdepeñas reds, produced south of Toledo, are also quite good.

Dining locally

Segovia's the place for *cocina castellana* (Castilian cuisine) — roasts, hearty soups, sausages, and beans. The city's Old Quarter has a handful of restaurants that do it right, and that look the part of classic Castilian *mesones* (inns). For more on Spanish dining customs, including mealtimes, costs, and tipping, see Chapter 2.

Mesón de Candido

$$$ Old Quarter CASTILIAN

A meal at Candido's, right beneath the towering Roman Aqueduct, is pretty much an obligatory stop on the Segovia tourist circuit. Salvador Dalí, Ernest Hemingway, and even Tricky Dick Nixon have all dined on suckling pig here. The famous place has been an inn since the 1700s, and five generations of the Candido family have run the place for almost the entire 20th century. The restaurant was declared a national monument in 1941. But that doesn't mean you get a crummy tourist menu. Happily, this restaurant is still one of the best in Segovia. Try to score a window seat on the second floor for dreamlike views of the Aqueduct, illuminated at night — more than enough to keep children entertained. Oh, and the food: Start with a *sopa castellana* or *pimientos de piquillo rellenos de setas* (red peppers stuffed with mushrooms). If you don't have the classic *cochinillo asado* (roasted baby pig), you can always try *jabalí* (wild boar) or fresh grilled salmon.

See map p. 324. Plaza de Azoguejo 5 (right next to the Aqueduct). ☎ ***921-42-81-03.*** *Reservations required. Main courses: 11€–22€ ($13–$26). AE, DC, MC, V. Open: Daily for lunch and dinner.*

Mesón Duque

$$$ Old Quarter CASTILIAN

If you climb the main street from the Roman Aqueduct to the Old Quarter, you pass this classic *mesón* (tavern restaurant) on the left. Loaded with dark wood beams and knickknacks, this must be what grandma's house looks like in the heart of Old Castile. The cozy inn has been serving Segovian specialties since 1895. Start with the *judiones de la Granja con bacalao* (kidney beans with cod) and follow it up with one of the Castilian roasts, which the house cooks about as well as anyone else in town. Wines are a bit pricey.

See map p. 324. Cervantes 12. On road leading from the Aqueduct to the Old Quarter. ☎ ***921-46-24-87.*** *Reservations recommended. Main courses: 11€–22€ ($13–$26). Menú del día: 30€ ($36). AE, DC, MC, V. Open: Daily for lunch and dinner.*

Mesón José María

$$$ Old Quarter CASTILIAN

One of the newer restaurants in town, José María has a hopping tapas bar in front that's usually packed with a mix of animated locals and tourists. The restaurant is in back through an arch. One wall is a model of the Roman Aqueduct, its arches filled with wine bottles — a cute if touristy touch. If you've already had the Segovian roasted lamb or suckling pig at another inn, try something else, because the chef clearly has more than just roasts in mind. The stuffed fish *dorada cantábrico* (golden bream — a type of fish), crammed with garlic and mushrooms, is very tasty. Other appetizing fish dishes are offered, but the leg of lamb stuffed with mushrooms and truffles is tempting.

See map p. 324. Calle Cronista Lecea 11 (just off Plaza Mayor). ☎ ***921-46-60-17.*** *Main courses: 10€–23€ ($12–$28). AE, DC, MC, V. Open: Daily for lunch and dinner.*

Exploring Segovia

No one has any trouble finding Segovia's top tourist attraction, the monumental Roman Aqueduct. The old walled quarter of Segovia rises above it. The cathedral and El Alcázar are the other premier attractions. Old Segovia is also rich in Romanesque churches and monasteries and cool little plazas.

Until the mid-1990s, cars were allowed to pass through the arches of the 2,000-year-old Roman Aqueduct in Segovia. Pollution from auto emissions was causing serious deterioration to the landmark, though, and Segovians finally mustered the political will to prohibit vehicular traffic from passing through — but not around — the Aqueduct. Restoration of the massive structure went on for nearly a decade. Although most locals recognize the value of protecting their city's ancient symbol, that doesn't stop them from complaining about the congestion caused by the rerouting.

The top attractions

Catedral de Segovia
Old Quarter

Called "the grand dame of Spanish cathedrals," this massive but delicately drawn limestone church was Spain's last great Gothic cathedral. Begun in 1525, it rises gracefully on the Plaza Mayor, right across from the spot where Isabella was named Queen of Castile in 1474. It overflows with riches; inside are 23 ornate chapels, including one by José Churriguera, the architect of Salamanca's famed new cathedral (see "Salamanca architecture 101," later in this chapter), a magnificent carved choir, and gorgeous stained-glass windows. The La Concepción chapel is spectacular. The cathedral is actually the second church built on this spot; the cloisters, which you can visit, date from the first church. Allow an hour or so to tour the grounds.

See map p. 324. Plaza Mayor. ☎ ***921-46-22-05.*** *Admission: Free to cathedral; 2€ ($2.40) to cloisters and museum. Open: Summer daily 9 a.m.–6:30 p.m.; winter daily 9 a.m.–5:30 p.m.*

El Alcázar de Segovia
Old Quarter

Finishing off Segovia's trio of great monuments is its fairy-tale, turreted castle, located at the edge of the old town. The ancient fortress, like the aqueduct, may be Roman in origin, but it more likely dates from the 12th century. At any rate, it was wholly reconstructed in the 15th century. It was a favorite residence of the Castilian monarchs during the Middle Ages. In 1862, a great fire destroyed much of the castle, so what you see is largely restoration work. The real highlight is climbing the Tower of John II, once a state prison. The 400 steep, one-way steps leave teenagers huffing and puffing and complaining, but if you're in decent shape, don't miss the amazing 360-degree view from the top of Segovia and the *meseta* (plateau) and mountains beyond. Plan on spending an hour or so at the Alcázar.

See map p. 324. Plaza de la Reina. From the cathedral, walk straight along Marqués del Arco and continue along Daoiz; you run right into the Alcázar. ☎ ***921-46-07-59.*** *Admission: 3.50€ ($4.20) adults, 2.50€ ($3) ages 8–14, children under 6 free, free on Tuesdays for E.U. citizens. Tower access is an additional 1.50€ ($1.80). Open: Summer daily 10 a.m.–7 p.m., winter daily 10 a.m.–6 p.m. Closed: June 16.*

Roman Aqueduct

One of Spain's most sensational sights and the subject of a thousand travel posters, Segovia's aqueduct is one of the greatest surviving examples of Roman engineering. The granite aqueduct, constructed in A.D. 90 (although some contend that it dates to 1 B.C.), has nothing but the force of physics holding its massive blocks together — no mortar, no clamps. Yet it has remained standing for nearly 2,000 years. Designed to carry water from the Ríofrío River in the mountains 16km (10 miles) away, the Aqueduct has 166 perfectly designed arches (35 were destroyed by the Moors in the 11th century), 20,000 blocks, and 120 pillars. The structure reaches a height of 29m (95 ft.; in the Plaza de Azoguejo, where it's easiest to view it) and stretches about 1km (⅔ of a mile). As impressive as it is as a feat of engineering, the Aqueduct is also uncommonly beautiful. The way it frames the city is quite extraordinary. Make sure you check out the sight of it fully illuminated at night against the black Segovian sky. Half an hour is sufficient to walk around and have a good look.

More cool things to see and do

Segovia is a charming town, perfect for leisurely walks and soaking up its Old World Castilian ambience. If you have time to do more than visit the top three showstoppers that draw the busloads of quick-hit tourists, nice walks around the Old Quarter and just outside the city walls will take you past charming Romanesque churches, tiny alleyways, and Renaissance palaces.

- **Traipsing through old town.** The pretty **Plaza Mayor,** a lively place filled with cafes and tapas bars in summer, is the obvious place to start. From there, proceed down Infanta Isabel and over to Canalejas. You come to the 12th-century **Iglesia de San Martín,** one of Segovia's 40 Romanesque churches, notable for its handsome porches and carved portal. Plaza de San Martín is also a very pleasant little square, lined by attractive mansions. Across the way is the elegant house known simply by its Renaissance origins as **Casa del Siglo XV** (15th-century house). The **Museo de Arte Contemporáneo Esteban Vicente (☎ 921-46-20-10)**, back across Plaza de San Martín on Plazuela de las Bellas Artes, is an art museum housing 148 works of the Spanish artist Vicente, best known for his association with the New York School of Abstract Expressionists. The museum is open Tuesday through Saturday from 11 a.m. to 2 p.m. and from 4 to 7 p.m., and Sunday from 11 a.m. to 2 p.m. Admission is 2.40€ ($2.90) for adults, and 1.20€ ($1.45) for students and seniors; free on Thursdays. If you walk down Calle Grabador Espinosa, you come to the **Casa de los Picos,** a Renaissance mansion known for its armored-looking exterior.

  Finally, take Obisbo Gandasequi to San Agustín, turn left, and go straight on La Trinidad. Beyond the Episcopal Palace on Calle Valdeláguila is the handsome Romanesque **Iglesia de San Esteban,** with an impressive tower and a neat side gallery. The little Romanesque **Iglesia de San Miguel** didn't occupy its present spot just off the Plaza Mayor some 500 years ago. Back then it sat right *on* the Plaza Mayor. Though Segovia looks unchanged since the heyday of the Spanish empire, in fact a number of churches and buildings were taken down and reconstructed, stone-by-stone, in other locations in the city. Happily for workers, the massive Roman Aqueduct was not one of the structures that had to be moved.

The small Jewish Quarter, **El Barrio de la Judería,** or Sefarad Segovia, is located behind the cathedral, along the old wall near the castle. In the 13th century, Segovia had a sizeable Jewish community, with at least five synagogues (Toledo originally had ten).

- **Venturing beyond the town walls.** Writers have long described the view of Segovia from outside the Roman walls as that of a giant ship, with the Alcázar at its bow, the cathedral forming the main mast, and the aqueduct representing the helm. A good place to view this city/ship is from the *parador* up on the hill, or the Parque del Alcázar at the crux of the Eresma and Clamores Rivers.

  Just beyond this point is the curious little **Iglesia de la Vera Cruz** (**☎ 923-43-14-75**), one of the most interesting Romanesque churches in Segovia. Though an odd polygon shape on the exterior, it's perfectly round inside. Stand in the middle of the inner temple and test the weird echo your voice produces. The church is said to have been the place of secret rites of the Knights Templar in the 13th century, although some modern historians doubt this claim. The church is open Tuesday through Sunday from 10:30 a.m. to 1:30 p.m. and 3:30 to 6 p.m. It's closed June 24 and in November. Admission is 1.75€ ($2.10).

Shopping for local treasures

Segovia's on the day-trip tour circuit, and the streets around the Plaza Mayor and cathedral are well stocked with shops clamoring for your tourist bucks. Several have good-quality crafts items, including the ironwork, pottery, and embroidery for which Segovia is known.

For a unique shopping experience, visit the **Monjas Dominicas** on Calle Capuchinos Alta 2. It's open from 9 a.m. to 1 p.m. and 4 to 6:30 p.m. daily (**☎ 921-46-00-80**). The Dominican nuns make fine handmade polychrome figures. Prices start at just under 20€ ($24) and go up to more than 3,000€ ($3,600) for a hand-carved and painted altarpiece.

To see the nuns' work, you enter a door and ring the bell; a disembodied voice from behind the wooden turnstile says *"¿Sí?"* (Yes?). A simple *"Hola"* (Hello) will grant you admission into the showroom. The voice will say *"Pase, por favor"* (Come in, please). When inside, you stand alone before a selection of objects on display behind bars. At length, another sister comes out and turns on the lights. Indicate which item you're interested in, and she'll fetch it for you, allowing you to inspect it through the iron gate.

Living it up after dark

Segovia is a pretty quiet town at night. Much of what nightlife it does have centers on the tapas bars and cafes of the Plaza Mayor and Plaza de San Martín. Surprisingly, two good Irish pubs in town pull a decent pint of Guinness: **Canavan's,** a handsome bar on Plaza de la Rubia 2, and **Limerick,** on Escuderos 5. Both are just off the main square. **La Tasquina,** on Vadeláguila 3, also just off the Plaza Mayor, is a cool little corner spot with a good selection of wines and cava by the glass.

Fast Facts: Segovia

Area Code

Segovia's area code is **921,** which you must dial before every number.

Currency Exchange

There are banks and ATMs located around the Plaza Mayor in the Old Quarter and downtown on the main street near the Aqueduct, Avenida Fernández Ladrera, and along Calle Cervantes and Calle Juan Bravo.

Emergencies

For general emergencies, call ☎ **112.** For medical emergencies, call Ambulancias Segovianas, ☎ 921-43-00-28, or the emergency unit of the Red Cross at ☎ 921-44-02-02.

Hospitals

Hospital General de Segovia is on Carretera de Avila, s/n (☎ 921-41-90-65). Hospital Policlínico San Agustín is on San Agustín 13 (☎ 921-41-91-00).

Information

Two main tourism offices serve Segovia. One is right on the Plaza Mayor (no. 10); ☎ 921-46-03-34. Another is next to the Roman Aqueduct, on Plaza del Azoguejo 1 (☎ 921-46-29-06). They're both open daily from 10 a.m. to 8 p.m.

Police

The police station is at Guadarrama 26 (☎ 921-43-12-12).

Post Office

Segovia's main post office is on Plaza del Doctor Laguna 5 (☎ 921-46-16-16).

Avila

One of Spain's most important settlements during the Middle Ages, Avila (*ah*-vee-lah), the country's highest provincial capital, can be seen from miles around. Sitting atop a windswept plateau, its stunning fortresslike exterior — massive medieval ramparts that ring the Old City — ranks as the town's most notable feature. Within those spectacular walls was born the legendary mystic and saint, Teresa, who 500 years later still inspires faithful followers. If you count yourself among the legions of Teresa of Avila devotees, a visit here, to all the places she touched in her lifetime, is obligatory. But for others, Avila will come as a bit of a disappointment. In off-season, it can seem especially bleak. Maybe I'm courting sacrilege in saying this about Saint Teresa's birthplace, but for most, Avila only merits a brief visit.

Avila is en route to Salamanca if you're driving from Madrid or Segovia and you can do a drive-by — taking in the incredible 11th-century walls from the side of the road, stopping for a well-framed photograph — and move on without worrying too much about what you're missing. Especially when viewed alongside the vibrant life and stunning monuments and architecture of Toledo, Salamanca, and Segovia, Avila is comparatively dull within the walls, and even a walk atop the magnificent *murallas* falls short of what you'd imagine it to be.

Getting there

To get to Avila by car, take A-6 northwest from Madrid toward Leon. The Avila turnoff southwest (N-110) is signposted; the drive takes about 90 minutes.

By bus

Empresa Larrea (in Madrid ☎ **91-539-90-05;** Metro: Méndez Alvaro) travels from Madrid's Estación Sur de Autobuses to Avila (90 minutes; 6.25€/$7.50 one-way) many times a day Monday to Friday. On weekends, only three buses travel back and forth. The bus station in Toledo is located at Av. de Madrid 2 (☎ **920-22-01-54**).

By train

From Madrid, many trains depart Atocha station (Metro: Atocha RENFE) daily for Avila; the trip takes between 80 minutes and 2 hours. One-way costs 6.05€ to 16€ ($7.25–$19), depending on the type of train (the fastest and most expensive is the Talgo, which makes the trip in 1 hour, 20 minutes). The train station in Avila, Av. de José Antonio, s/n (☎ **920-24-02-02**), is about 1.6km (1 mile) from the Old City; you can either take a taxi or walk about 20 minutes through a somewhat grungy (but safe) neighborhood.

Spending the night

Because you can see the town in a few short hours, most visitors really don't need to overnight in Avila — unless staying within its ancient walls or near the birthplace of Saint Teresa poses a firm attraction for you. In that case, Avila has an excellent trio of hotels.

Hospedería de Bracamonte
$$ Old Quarter

With just 23 rooms, this inn is a peaceful and appealingly rustic little place within the *murallas*. Simple but charming and very friendly, the 16th-century mansion is decorated with excellent taste. Some rooms upstairs have fireplaces and four-poster beds, while the downstairs salons and dining room feature thick stone walls and heavy wooden beams overhead.

Bracamonte 6. ☎ ***920-25-12-80.*** *Fax: 920-25-38-38.* `www.hospederiadebracamonte.com`. *Parking: Available on street. Rack rates:* ***50€–75€ ($60–$90).*** *MC, V.*

Palacio de los Velada

$$$ Old Quarter

Built around a dramatic interior courtyard, this large, elegant, and splendidly restored 16th-century palace played host to royalty in the Middle Ages and was converted into a hotel in 1995. But it still very convincingly plays the part of medieval palace. It's by far the swankest place in town to stay; situated next to the cathedral within the city walls, it also occupies the best location. The 145 rooms are handsome, modern, and luxurious, with rich wood-beamed ceilings and stone arches and floors. The hotel's pub in the old stables deserves special mention — it's one of the coolest spots in town to take a load off. The restaurant's a winner, too, serving fine lamb and steaks.

Plaza de la Catedral 10. ☎ ***920-25-51-00.*** *Fax 920-25-49-00.* www.veladahoteles.com. *Parking: 14€ ($17). Rack rates: 140€ ($168). Special weekend rate: $100€ ($120). AE, DC, MC, V.*

Parador de Avila (Raimundo de Borgoña)

$$ Old Quarter

A former 16th-century white-stone palace, this is a typical, tasteful *parador* updating of a period house. The lobby and public areas around the central patio have the Castilian look down pat, with heavy leather chairs and dark wood beams. The modern rooms are elegant and nicely appointed, with lively color schemes, stone floors, and good linens. Personnel could stand to be a bit friendlier, but maybe they've been trapped inside the city's walls for too long.

Marqués de Canales de Chozas 2. ☎ ***920-21-13-40.*** www.parador.es. *Parking: 10€ ($12). Rack rates: 110€–120€ ($132–$144). AE, DC, MC, V.*

Dining locally

El Molino de la Losa

$$$ Outside Old Quarter CASTILIAN

This restaurant has a location to die for: a 15th-century mill smack in the middle of the river on the outskirts of Avila. The panoramic views of the city's walls will blow you away. At night, when they're illuminated, imagining a better place for a classic Spanish dinner is impossible. Start with an assortment of goat cheese or quail salad and follow it up with roast suckling pig, cooked in the wood oven you see downstairs, or cuttlefish simmered in garlic and oil. To get there, drive outside the city and across the Adaja bridge, turning right on N-501, toward Cuatro Postes. The restaurant is on your right on an island in the middle of the river.

Bajada de la Losa 12. ☎ ***920-21-11-01.*** *Main courses: 16€–25€ ($19–$30). AE, DC, MC, V. Open: Tues–Sun lunch and dinner.*

Hospedería de Bracamonte

$$ Old Quarter CASTILIAN

This welcoming restaurant is every bit as distinguished as the charming inn it's attached to. The handsome and warm dining room is unexpectedly large (though several smaller dining areas are available) and the *cordero asado al horno de leña* (wood-oven roast baby lamb) is outstanding. If a tour bus beats you here, though, be prepared for a wait.

*Bracamonte 6. ☎ **920-25-12-80.** Main courses: 9€–18€ ($11–$22). MC, V. Open: Lunch and dinner Wed–Mon. Closed: Oct 20–Nov 20.*

Exploring Avila

By far the biggest draw in Avila is the monumental medieval walls that encircle the town, but the churches and convents that serve the cult of Saint Teresa rank a very close second. If you have some extra time in town, the cathedral and San Vicente Basilica are also worth checking out.

The top attraction

Las Murallas de Avila

Avila's dramatic city walls, begun in 1090 and still amazingly intact, are the oldest, most complete, and best preserved in Spain — probably even the finest in Europe. They're a feast of crenellated towers, turrets, and parapets. So solid that it hardly appears to have suffered the effects of nearly a millennium, the great wall of Spain chalks up impressive numbers: It's

Saint Teresa's story

Avila exerts a strange pull on some visitors. Perhaps it's the walls, but more likely it's the legend of St. Teresa, one of Catholicism's most famous saints and Spain's female patron saint. Born to a father of Jewish descent in 1515, Teresa is best known for her mystical visions (in one, an angel pierced her heart with a burning lance, an image that inspired a number of Baroque artists; in others, the devil himself appeared to her). As a young girl, she ventured beyond the walls of Avila intending to become martyred by the infidels, the Moors. As an adult, Teresa was a crusader who took on the excesses of the Catholic Church and reformed the Carmelite Order. She created Las Descalzas, an order of barefoot nuns (actually, they were allowed to wear sandals) given to lives of absolute poverty and piety. In her lifetime she founded 16 convents. She was canonized, or declared a saint, in 1622, and named a "Doctor" of the Catholic Church in the 1970s, placing her in the rarified company of another legendary saint, St. Augustine. Teresa's enduring legend is in part based on her rapturous mystical visions and beliefs among her followers that her severed hand was capable of performing miracles long after her death. The city of Avila plays special tribute to her every year, with the week-long Fiestas de la Santa Teresa that begins October 8. Look for parades, processions, and other religious events that draw plenty of pilgrims.

nearly 2.4km (1½ miles) long, 11m (36 ft.) high, and 2.7m (9 ft.) thick, with 2,500 battlements, 88 cylindrical towers, 6 gates, and a single bell tower. Of the nine gates, the Puerta de Alcázar is by far the most impressive. Don't miss the chance to climb the ramparts and, for a small fee, walk along a section (from the Puerta de Alcázar to Puerta del Rastro); find the tiny ticket booth located just behind the cathedral. Careful, though: The steps are very steep.

Encircling the Old City. ☎ ***920-35-40-13.*** *Admission: 3.50€ ($4.20) adults, 2€ ($2.40) students and seniors, free for children under 8. Open: Summer Tues–Sun 11 a.m.–8 p.m., winter Tues–Sun 10 a.m.–2 p.m. and 4–6 p.m.*

More cool things to see and do

Do you have a few extra hours to spend in Avila? If so, I suggest the following activities.

- **Visiting the Catedral de Avila.** Avila's cathedral is a pretty gloomy affair on the outside, part fortress and part church. Begun in the 12th century in Romanesque style, it was completed as a Gothic cathedral in the 16th century. Thankfully, the interior lightens up; it's dominated by a high Gothic nave and decorated with surprising red and yellow stones. The item of greatest interest is the alabaster tomb of El Tostado, literally "The Toasted One." Don Alonso de Madrigal, the 15th-century Bishop of Avila is buried here. He was a learned man, and apparently also a swarthy one. The cathedral is located at the Plaza de la Catedral 8 (☎ **920-21-16-41**). It is open June through October, Monday to Saturday from 10 a.m. to 8 p.m. and Sunday from noon to 8 p.m.; November through March, Monday to Friday from 10 a.m. to 5 p.m., Saturday from 10 a.m. to 6 p.m., and Sunday from noon to 6 p.m.; April through May, Monday to Saturday from 10 a.m. to 7 p.m. and Sunday from noon to 7 p.m. Admission is 2.50€ ($3).
- **Viewing the walled city.** The best place to view the city is from an old shrine, called **Cuatro Postes** (Four Pillars), just beyond the river. Nothing more than four columns and a cross, it's the spot where the young Teresa of Avila fled with visions of martyrdom already in her head. To get there, exit the city walls and take Avenida de Madrid west. Cross the bridge, Puente Adaja, on the city's western side. Take a right on N-501; the monument is a few hundred yards on your right, above the river.
- **Inspecting the carvings of the Basílica de San Vincente.** This 12th-century church (☎ **920-25-52-30**) is just beyond the city walls on the north side of town. The impeccably carved Romanesque west portal recalls the brilliant carved stone of the cathedral in Santiago de Compostela. The tomb of the martyr St. Vincent, who was tortured and killed on this spot in the fourth century, is a masterful example of limestone carving, and the acts of martyrdom are

depicted in graphic detail. The Basílica is at Plaza de San Vincente. It's open Monday through Saturday from 10 a.m. to 1:30 p.m. and 2 to 6:30 p.m. Admission is 2.50€ ($3).

- **Visiting the Convento de Santa Teresa, the birthplace of Saint Teresa.** In the 17th century, a Baroque church and convent were built on the site where Saint Teresa of Avila, who reformed the Carmelite Order, was born. (See "Saint Teresa's story" in this chapter.) Fittingly, her bedroom has become a chapel. An odd assortment of relics on display includes her finger and the whip she used to flagellate herself. The Convento (☎ **920-21-10-30**) is at Plaza Santa. It's open November through March, Tuesday to Sunday from 9:30 a.m. to 1 p.m. and 3:30 to 6:30 p.m.; April through October, Monday to Saturday from 10 a.m. to 1:30 p.m. and 4 to 6:30 p.m. Admission is 2€ ($2.40).
- **Making a pilgrimage to the Monasterio de la Encarnación.** Built in 1479, this Carmelite monastery is where Saint Teresa entered as a novice in 1535, at the age of 20, and where she lived for 27 years. Of greatest interest to those who come to Avila seeking the Teresa trail is her (reconstructed) cell in the chapel, the **Capilla de Transververación.** A small museum holds items related to Teresa's life, and the Carmelite sisters sell souvenirs. The monastery (Paseo de la Encarnación; ☎ **920-21-12-12**) is just outside the walls on the northern edge of town. It's open daily June through September, 9:30 a.m. to 1 p.m. and 4 to 7 p.m.; October through May, 9:30 a.m. to 1:30 p.m. and 3:30 to 6 p.m. Admission is 1.20€ ($1.45).

Fast Facts: Avila

Area Code

Avila's area code is **920,** which you must dial before every number.

Currency Exchange

You'll find banks and an ATM near the cathedral in the Old Quarter.

Emergencies

For medical emergencies, call Ambulancias Cruz Roja, ☎ 920-22-22-22.

Hospitals

Hospital Provincial is located on Jesús del Gran Poder 42 (☎ 920-35-72-00).

Information

The provincial tourism office is on Plaza de Pedro Dávila 4 (☎ 920-21-13-87). In summer, an additional office is set up in Jardín de San Vicente, s/n. They're open daily from 10 a.m. to 2 p.m. and 5 to 7 p.m., and Saturday from 10 a.m. to 2 p.m. and 5 to 8 p.m.

Police

The police station is at Paseo San Roque 34 (☎ 920-25-10-00). In an emergency, call ☎ **091.**

Post Office

Avila's main post office is on Plaza de la Catedral 2 (☎ 920-21-13-54).

Salamanca

Refined Salamanca (sah-lah-*mahn*-kah) is Spain's City of Enlightenment. If that sounds like an intimidating place for a relaxed visit, don't sweat — this college town is also one of Spain's loveliest and most enjoyable cities. The great Universidad de Salamanca, founded in the early 13th century and one of the world's pillars of learning — still dominates the town and lends it an academic flavor.

The Old Quarter of Salamanca is a stunning assembly of early-Renaissance architecture, with a special emphasis on the ornate style known as Plateresque. Graceful monasteries, convents, palaces, and university buildings carved out of sandstone, known locally as Villamayor — as well as one of Spain's prettiest Plazas de Mayor — dominate a relatively small and largely pedestrian-only *zona monumental* (historic core). It's stacked with architectural sights (see the "Salamanca architecture 101" box in this chapter for more info).

Though Salamanca feels like a small town, it's a provincial capital of nearly 200,000 people — and many more visiting language students. The city's language programs are particularly popular at least in part because Salamanca is said to be the place in Spain where the purest form of *castellano,* or Castilian Spanish, is spoken (surely Salamanca's regal beauty may also be something of a draw for foreigners). Don't be surprised if you hear plenty of English on the streets; Salamanca is a favorite destination among young Americans studying abroad in Spain, and the city has become a gathering place for students from all over the world. As a result, Salamanca has an especially throbbing nightlife.

But Salamanca also features an eclectic range of art exhibits, concerts, and symposia. Since Salamanca was the European City of Culture in 2002, a number of theaters and other cultural centers were inaugurated, and the city now has a better selection of hotels than ever before.

Salamanca is so gracious and beautiful, with so many scheduled events, that it merits — even requires, I'd say — at least an overnight stay. It's too far from Madrid for an easy day trip, and honestly, you need time to fully appreciate its monumental delights and cosmopolitan charms. It's easily the kind of place to hang out in for the better part of a week or more.

Getting there

A car is the easiest way to get to Salamanca. It's about three hours from Madrid, two hours from Segovia, and an hour and a half from Avila. From Avila, which you must pass through whether you're coming from Madrid or Segovia, take N-501 west.

By bus

Seven **Empresa Auto-Res** buses (in Madrid: Calle Fernández Shaw 1; ☎ **91-551-72-00** or 902-02-09-99; Metro: Conde de Casal) leave Madrid for

Salamanca

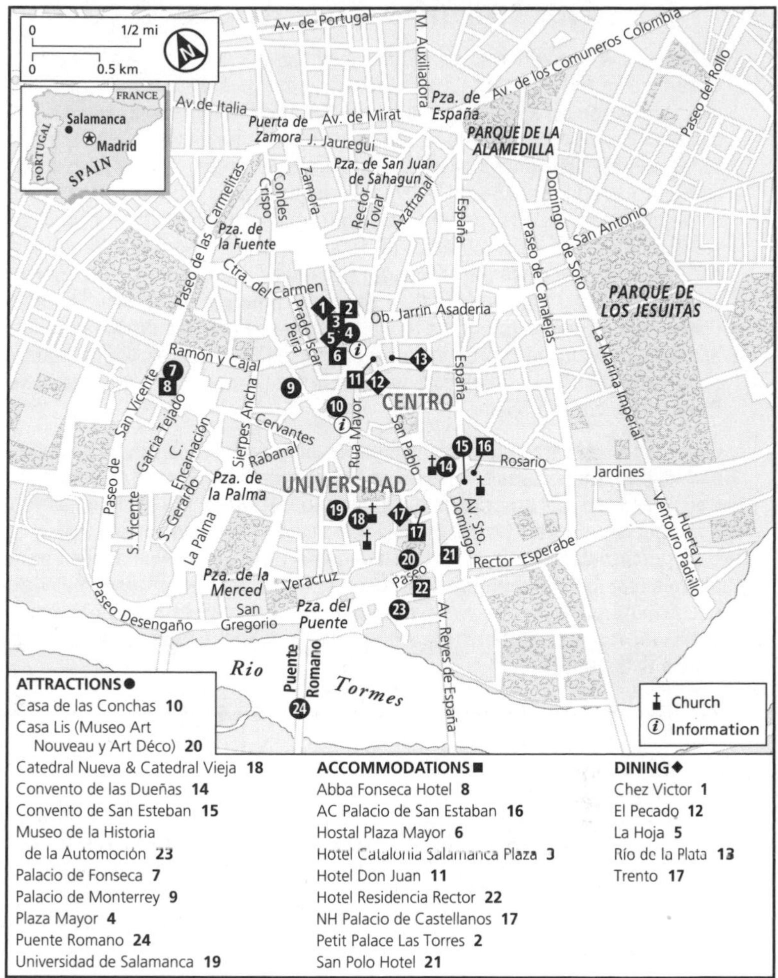

Salamanca daily beginning at 7 a.m., with the last returning at 10 p.m. The trip takes three-and-a-quarter hours and costs 11€ ($13). Returns to Madrid begin at 7:30 a.m., with the last at 5:30 p.m. (7:30 p.m. on Fri and Sun). Express service (16€/$19) takes two-and-a-half hours.

Buses also depart for Salamanca from Segovia. The Salamanca bus station **(Estación de Autobuses)** is located at Av. Filiberto Villalobos 71–85 (☎ **923-23-67-17**).

Salamanca architecture 101

Salamanca is a university town, but one might just as easily call it a living architectural museum. The Old Quarter's lovely convents, churches, palaces, and university buildings form a remarkably harmonious palette of stone on stone, and it's particularly enchanting in the late afternoon, when the fading sun gives Salamanca's sandstone spires and domes a golden glow, and shadows drape across the city's red roofs and stately arcaded Plaza Mayor. Salamanca is the greatest expression of two singular architectural styles, Plateresque and Churrigueresque; nowhere else in Spain was stone molded into such a wealth of ornate detail. Plateresque refers to a form of early–Spanish Renaissance architecture in which rather somber facades are embellished by ornate stone carvings, their fine detail reminiscent of silver filigree. The term Plateresque is itself a reference to the art of silverwork (*platero* means silversmith in Spanish). Elements to look for include sculpted capitals and parapets, medallions, and round arches. The old university facade is perhaps the greatest example of Plateresque work in Spain.

Churrigueresque architecture is named for three architect brothers — Jose, Joaquin, and Alberto Churriguera — natives of Salamanca who worked throughout Spain (as well as Mexico and other parts of Latin America) in the late 17th and early 18th centuries but were especially busy in their hometown. The Churriguera style is like ornate Baroque architecture on speed — it knows no excess. It was applied principally in altarpieces, but Salamanca's handsome Plaza Mayor is also the work of the Churriguera brothers. Everyone seems to get the three brothers confused, though; some works are attributed to the wrong sibling, or, in the absence of identifying traits, merely to the entire clan.

By train

From Madrid, trains leave Chamartín Station (Metro: Chamartín) every couple of hours and take about two-and-a-half hours to arrive. The one-way fare is 15€ ($18). The Salamanca train station, located on Paseo de la Estación (☎ **923-12-02-02**) is northeast of the Old Quarter. Take a taxi from there. The RENFE office in Salamanca is located at Plaza de la Libertad 1 (☎ **923-23-67-17**).

Getting around

Salamanca is yet another thoughtfully designed Spanish city in which visitors are likely to spend all their time in the Old Quarter — called the Casco Antiguo or *zona monumental* (historic center). And, the city is small enough that you only need to depend on your own two feet to get around. All the hotels listed in the following hotel review section are within walking distance of Salamanca's top sights.

Radio Tele-taxi, Don Quijote 1–11 (☎ **923-25-00-00**) and **Radio Taxi,** Paseo Canalejas 49 (☎ **923-27-11-11**) both operate 24 hours a day; pick up a taxi at the train station.

Spending the night

Salamanca has several top-shelf and reasonably priced luxury hotels housed in historic buildings, as well as many excellent medium-range and budget hotels, all within the *zona monumental* (historic center). Because everything of interest is clustered either right in or at the edges of the Old Quarter, try to avoid any hotel that isn't within walking distance of the major monuments and Plaza Mayor (this rules out the *parador* outside the Old Quarter, which is otherwise a fine place to stay; therefore, it's not listed here). In the last few years, hotel developers have gone on a binge, and Salamanca has added several much-needed rooms, but still the city frequently fills up, especially during the month of September, which is jam-packed with local festivals.

Abba Fonseca Hotel
$$$ Old Quarter

Capitalizing on a trend — begun in Salamanca by the exquisite Hotel Residencia Rector (see review later in this chapter) — of erecting stylish hotels within historic buildings, the Abba hotel preserves part of a 16th-century Jesuit construction and inhabits an 18th-century neoclassical mansion next to the Colegio Fonseca. Inside, it has been gutted and refurbished with bold colors and modern furnishings, and outfitted with large rooms. The architecture and design are very contemporary, although not as starkly hip or luxurious as the Palacio de San Esteban. Many rooms have enviable views of the Old City. The hotel is quite a good deal given its location and degree of comfort.

See map p. 339. Plaza San Blas 2. ☎ ***923-01-10-10*** *or 902-15-31-63. Fax: 923-01-10-11.* `www.abbafonsecahotel.com`. *Parking: Nearby 12€ ($14). Rack rates: 120€ ($144); weekend offers as low as 75€ ($90). AE, DC, MC, V.*

AC Palacio de San Esteban
$$$ Old Quarter

Occupying the 16th-century Convento de San Esteban in the heart of the monumental quarter, and catering more to business travelers than other hotels in the city, the AC Palacio opened in 2002 as Salamanca's first five-star luxury hotel. It has spare style in spades; it features handsome modern design juxtaposed against the historic shell of the convent, and is a model of restraint, simplicity, and good taste. The 51 rooms are large and welcoming if you're hip to minimalist luxury, though they retain exposed beams and warm wall colors. Some have spectacular views of old Salamanca, while others overlook a small interior courtyard and gardens. The excellent restaurant El Monje (the Monk) looks the part and is, like the rest of the hotel, sumptuously designed, with beautiful stone walls and arched ceilings. Although I still prefer the smaller and more intimate Rector, this is clearly the best full-service, top-of-the-line hotel in Salamanca.

See map p. 339. Calle Arroyo de Santo Domingo 3. ☎ ***923-26-22-96*** *or 902-29-22-93. Fax: 923-26-88-72.* `www.ac-hoteles.com`. *Parking: 18€ ($22). Rack rates: 120–140€ ($144–$168). AE, DC, MC, V.*

Hostal Plaza Mayor
$$ Old Quarter

Right across from the neat little San Martín church, and a mere stumble home from the tapas bars of the Plaza Mayor, this *hostal* couldn't have a better location, especially at what in Salamanca are bargain prices. Rooms are smallish, but nicely decorated with wooden headboards and attractive curtains. Two of the nineteen rooms have parquet floors. Given the location, noise will be a concern for some guests.

See map p. 339. Plaza del Corrillo 20. Less than 1 block south of the Plaza Mayor. ☎ ***923-26-20-20.*** *Fax: 923-21-75-48. Parking: Nearby 6€ ($7.20). Rack rates: 60€–74€ ($72–$89). AE, MC, V.*

Hotel Don Juan
$$ Old Quarter

A stone's throw from the Plaza Mayor and surrounded by the Old City's monuments, this small and simple family-run budget hotel is unexpectedly attractive. In a 200-year-old building, the comfortable, carpeted, and clean rooms have salmon-colored bedcovers, and hallways aren't the creepy corridors of most budget hotels — here they're done in marble and light wood. The small staff is exceedingly friendly. Top-floor rooms with views are the best. The small cafeteria on the first floor is a good place for a quick bite.

See map p. 339. One block south of Plaza Mayor. ☎ ***923-26-14-73.*** *Fax: 923-26-24-75.* `www.hoteldonjuan-salamanca.com`. *Parking: Nearby 16€ ($19). Rack rates: 60€–75€ ($72–$90). AE, MC, V.*

Hotel Residencia Rector
$$$ Edge of Old Quarter

The stunning stone Renaissance facade — you may think you've stumbled upon a palace from the Salamanca sightseeing circuit — is only a prelude to the elegance within. This quiet and charming small hotel, a private mansion until 1990, is one of the finest I've stayed at in Spain, and certainly my favorite in Salamanca, despite new competition. Details clearly matter here. Everything is perfect, from the elegant, warm-toned décor to the white-gloved breakfast service and friendly attentions of the staff. Service is impeccable. I no sooner checked in than the woman at the desk kindly gave me a packet of information about Salamanca and informed me that the Plaza Mayor was "seven minutes' walking distance down Calle San Pablo." The Rector's 14 enormous rooms are very tastefully decorated; the white marble bathrooms are spacious, the linens and towels plush. Public rooms, including a small bar for guests only, have pretty antiques and stained-glass windows. For the level of comfort, service, and graciousness — five-star in every way — it's an excellent value. I can't wait to go back.

See map p. 339. Calle Rector Esperabé 10. On the edge of the Old Quarter; from Madrid Road, cross first bridge, go left around roundabout; hotel is on left facing Old City wall. ☎ ***923-21-84-82.*** *Fax: 923-21-40-08.* `www.terra.es/personal/hrector`. *Parking: 10€ ($12). Rack rates: 110€–130€ ($132–$156). AE, DC, MC, V.*

NH Palacio de Castellanos

$$$ Old Quarter

This handsome hotel is one of the most luxurious in the Spanish NH chain — known for targeting business travelers. Although decorated with obvious good taste, it isn't quite as refined as the serenely elegant Rector or as sleekly modern as the AC Palacio de San Esteban. A 15th-century palace with a pretty central patio and colorful, modern furnishings in its 62 sleek rooms, it's a good choice for those who find the Rector a little too quiet. The Palacio Castellanos is in the heart of the Old Quarter on a pretty main street that leads directly to the Plaza Mayor. The entrance faces the San Esteban convent.

See map p. 339. Calle San Pablo 58–64. Take Enrique Estevan Bridge and pass Paseo del Rector Esperabé; the hotel is 2 blocks in on the left. ☎ ***923-26-18-18*** *or 91-398-44-00. Fax: 923-26-18-19.* `www.nh-hoteles.es`. *Parking: 16€ ($19). Rack rates: 99€–162€ ($120–$194). AE, DC, MC, V.*

Petit Palace Las Torres

$$$ Old Quarter

High Tech Hoteles, an expanding chain of dependable and affordable Spanish hotels, got this terrifically located property in the heart of the Old Quarter and dramatically renovated the rather dumpy old Las Torres hotel. It's an exciting midsize option (reopened in March 2004) right off of Salamanca's gorgeous Plaza Mayor (some rooms, including the breakfast room, look over the plaza). If you're not one to shy away from the hustle and bustle of all the cafes that spill out into the square, the location simply can't be beat. Housed in a Churrigueresque building, the rooms inside stand in stark contrast to the Spanish Baroque exterior: They're sleekly contemporary, but eminently stylish. If you're one of the high-tech sorts the chain covets, you'll welcome the rooms that come with free wireless Internet connections ("high tech" rooms have computers and even stationary bikes), while families will appreciate the 14 rooms that sleep up to four. Special deals are often available that drop room rates below 100€.

See map p. 339. Plaza Mayor 26 y Concejo 4. ☎ ***923-21-21-00.*** *Fax: 923-21-21-01.* `www.hthoteles.com`. *Parking: Nearby 10€ ($12). Rack rates: 150€–190€ ($180–$228). AE, DC, MC, V.*

San Polo Hotel

$$ Edge of Old Quarter

This small, good-value hotel, tucked just inside the Old Quarter, has a curious conceit: It occupies the site of the ruins of an 11th-century Romanesque church, which have been incorporated into the modern hotel construction. It's a great idea in this ancient city, and if the execution isn't perfect, well, who's to quibble? The 31-room hotel looks as though plans to make it more luxurious were suddenly aborted, but it's still a good, comfortable. midlevel choice. Rooms are a little cold-feeling, but the views of Salamanca's cathedral are inspiring. Ask for a room with a view of the Casco Antiguo.

See map p. 339. Calle Arroyo de Santo Domingo 1–3. At the intersection of Avenida Reyes de España and Paseo del Rector Esperabé, just over the river. ☎*/Fax:* ***923-21-11-77****. Fax 923-21-11-54.* `www.hotelsanpolo.com`. *Parking: Free. Rack rates: 74€–96€ ($89–$115). AE, DC, MC, V.*

Dining locally

You can find all the restaurants in this section in Salamanca's Old Quarter, within walking distances of the hotels I review in the previous section.

Chez Victor

$$$ CONTINENTAL/FRENCH

Salamanca's top restaurant is like the city itself: elegant and refined without being at all stuffy. Chez Victor's owner is from Salamanca, but he trained in France, and his interest in delicate, subtle French preparations shows. The market-fresh vegetables and salads are a nice change in the land of lamb and suckling pig. Among main courses, the turbot (a flounderlike fish) in a hot vinaigrette and medley of peppers and zucchini is wonderful, as is the grilled monkfish on a bed of julienned zucchini. You find a number of terrific meat and game dishes on the hand-written English menu, including *magret de pato,* roasted duck with berries. Save room for the scary part: a separate dessert menu for chocolate lovers. Being one of them, I dived into the delectable *marquise de chocolate* (flourless chocolate cake).

See map p. 339. Calle Espoz y Mina 26. ☎ ***923-21-31-23****. Reservations recommended. Main courses: 15€–29€ ($18–$35). AE, DC, MC, V. Open: Tues–Sat lunch and dinner, Sun lunch only. Closed: Aug.*

El Pecado

$$$ NOUVEAU CASTILIAN

This funky, mod place, with hot pink walls and zebra-striped banquettes upstairs and a campy religious theme throughout, looks more Almodóvar than stately Salamanca, which makes it even cooler. El Pecado ("the sin") has a creative, modern, and very well executed menu, which changes every three months. The daily menu available at lunch or dinner for 20€ is a bargain. Try the lasagna composed of the wonderful local cheese torta del Casar and Bellota Iberian ham and wild mushrooms, or the cod *(bacalao)* cooked three ways. You'll even find unusual items, such as a Thai vegetable wok. El Pecado's sister restaurant, **Grana & Oro,** Plaza del Angel (☎ **923-26-14-05**) is an excellent second choice; it's also contemporary in style but less wild and less expensive — its *menú del día* is just 15€).

See map p. 339. Plaza Poeta Iglesias 12. ☎ ***923-26-65-58****. Reservations recommended. Main courses: 17€–24€ ($21–$29). AE, DC, MC, V. Open: Tues–Sat lunch and dinner, Sun lunch only. Closed: Aug.*

Fast food, Spanish-style

For quickie bites as you tool about Salamanca's Old Quarter, look for **Mesón Cervantes,** Plaza Mayor 15 (☎ **923-21-72-13**), or **El Mesón,** Plaza Poeta Iglesias 10 (☎ **923-21-72-22**), both of which serve good Castilian tavern fare. For tapas, pop in and out of the *tascas* (cavelike restaurants and taverns) on the Plaza Mayor, which is usually hopping with students, and the hotspots **El Patio Chico,** Calle Meléndez 13, and **Casa Paca,** Plaza del Peso 10 (☎ **923-21-89-93**). Also try **La Jamonería de Carmen,** Calle Zamora 57 (☎ **923-60-08-97**), which has a good selection of salads and tapas, with tables on the pedestrian-only street.

La Hoja

$$$ NOUVEAU CASTILIAN

Tucked into a dark and narrow passageway that leads to the Plaza Mayor, this unexpectedly attractive restaurant, lined with modern art, opts to do something more innovative than the standard Castilian menu. The owner and chef, Alberto López, tempts diners with special creations including mushroom risotto and some dishes probably best sampled by adventurous eaters: pig trotters (pigs feet) with apples and prawns, and even partridge cooked in chocolate sauce.

See map p. 339. Pasaje Coliseo 19. ☎ ***923-26-40-28.*** *Reservations recommended. Main courses: 14€–24€ ($17–$29). Menú del día: 28€ ($34). AE, DC, MC, V. Open: Tues–Sat lunch and dinner, Sun lunch only. Closed: Last two weeks of Aug.*

Río de la Plata

$$ CASTILIAN

A charmingly plain little place, with just nine tables and a low ceiling at the back of a bar, Río de la Plata looks like a men's club. Two blocks from Plaza Mayor, it's intimate and cozy, and the white-jacketed waiters seem to know patrons by name. The menu is a long list of well-prepared favorites, such as grilled hake, *solomillo* (beef sirloin), and roasted baby lamb. This basement restaurant with a fireplace (a great place to drop in on a chilly night) has been going strong since the 1950s.

See map p. 339. Plaza del Peso 1. ☎ ***923-21-90-05.*** *Reservations recommended. Main courses: 10€–21€ ($12–$23). Menú del día: 17€ ($20). AE, DC, MC, V. Open: Tues–Sun lunch and dinner. Closed: July.*

Trento

$$$ INTERNATIONAL

Though I don't often recommend hotel restaurants, Trento, on the premises of the Palacio de Castellanos hotel (see review in the hotel section, earlier in this chapter), is a worthy exception. The attractive, modern décor works well in the magnificent 15th-century palace it occupies. The offering of fresh fish, including grilled sole with a medley of fresh vegetables, is good, as is the carefully selected wine list.

See map p. 339. Calle San Pablo 58–64. One block from old and new cathedrals. ☎ ***923-26-18-18.*** *Reservations recommended. Main courses: 12€–24€ ($14–$29). Menú del día: 18€ ($22). AE, DC, MC, V. Open: Daily lunch and dinner.*

Exploring Salamanca

You'll want to spend a full day or so to appreciate this city's beauty and wealth of historic sights. The Old Quarter, with its exquisite Renaissance and Plateresque buildings, is a tangible reminder of Spain's Golden Age in the 15th and 16th centuries. Although the city is bursting with mansions, monasteries, museums, and university buildings to take in, Salamanca's Casco Antiguo, or Old Quarter, is itself the chief sight, and simply wandering around the pedestrian-only area, enjoying tapas and drinks at one of the cafes on the Plaza Mayor, and taking it all in is a highlight. Salamanca is such a thoroughly enjoyable town that lingering for an extra day or two would be an excellent idea.

Guided two-hour walking tours (in English and Spanish) of Salamanca's Casco Antiguo are offered Fridays and Saturdays at 5:30 p.m. and Saturdays and Sundays at 11:30 a.m. They cost 6€ ($7.20) per person. For more information, call ☎ **609-48-65-44.**

The top attractions

Casa Lis (Museo Art Nouveau y Art Déco)
Edge of Old Quarter

If you walk along Calle Rector Esperabé, which borders the historic center to the south, you can't miss this stunning building with its bursts of bold stained glass. An immaculately restored 19th-century private mansion, it now houses the Art Nouveau and Art Deco Museum of Salamanca. The collection, with pieces from the late 1800s to the 1930s, includes porcelain and enamel, Lalique glass, Modernist paintings, jewels, furniture, and dolls. Children may be pleasantly surprised and entertained by some of the pieces. Don't miss the museum shop, not so much for the shopping but for the view of the river and Roman Bridge through that amazing stained glass. Allow one to two hours here.

See map p. 339. Calle El Expolio 14. From Rector Esperabé, walk up the ramp and around the small street to the right. ☎ ***923-12-14-25.*** `www.museocasalis.org/in`*. Admission: 3€ ($3.60), students and seniors 2€ ($2.40), free Thurs mornings until 2 p.m. Open: Apr to mid-Oct Tues–Fri 11 a.m.–2 p.m. and 5–9 p.m., Sat–Sun and holidays 11 a.m.–9 p.m.; mid-Oct to March Tues–Fri 11 a.m.–2 p.m. and 4–7 p.m., Sat–Sun and holidays 11 a.m.–8 p.m.*

Blood simple: Salamanca's graffiti

Everywhere you look in Salamanca, but especially on the university buildings, names are stenciled in scarlet letters, an identifiably Old World academic font. Though today it's a clever marketing ploy, the script dates back to the 15th century, when graduating students proved their mettle by entering the bullring. Students proclaimed their victories (over the bull and, presumably, the university) by taking the bull's blood and painting the word VITOR (victor) on a university building, and signing and dating their work.

Catedrales (Old and New)
Old Quarter

One cathedral just isn't enough for this monumental city. Instead of replacing the old cathedral, Salamanca built a new one next to it. In fact, you enter the old cathedral through the new one. The much larger new cathedral has a dazzling main doorway loaded with Plateresque stone work. (Try to see it in the afternoon sun when it really sparkles.) Work started on the new cathedral in the early 16th century but wasn't finished until 1733. Make sure you check out the ornate choir and Cristo de las Batallas chapel, the work of the Churriguera brothers.

The old cathedral, constructed in the 12th century, is a mix of Romanesque and primitive Gothic. Though the church is literally overshadowed by the new cathedral next door, its rooster tower, the famous Torre del Gallo, gets plenty of attention. Inside, the most spectacular feature is the *retablo* (altarpiece) on the High Altar, a bold work attributed to the 15th-century artist Nicolás Florentino. It consists of 53 different paintings of the life of Christ. Note the elaborate Gothic tombs and chapels around the cloister that feature frescoes and gargoyles.

Don't leave before visiting the Patio Chico, a small courtyard that puts the old cathedral in perspective and provides a gorgeous view of the spires against the Salamanca sky. (You may have to circle around back if the door to the patio at the transept is closed when you visit.) Visiting the two cathedrals probably requires a couple of hours.

*See map p. 339. Calle Pla y Deniel, s/n. ☎ **923-21-74-76.** Admission: New Cathedral free, Old Cathedral 3.50€ ($4.20). Open: New Cathedral daily 9 a.m.–8 p.m., Old Cathedral daily 10 a.m.–7:30 p.m.*

Plaza Mayor
Heart of Old Quarter

I've been lucky enough to see most of Spain's great plazas, and Salamanca's grand main square is one of the finest. To get there, just follow the students and locals, most of whom don't go a day without ducking under its arches. Salamanca's Plaza Mayor is one of the biggest and most animated squares in the country, but what makes it special is the exquisite harmony of its architecture. Mostly designed by the Churriguera brothers, the architects so instrumental in giving Salamanca its renowned Plateresque look, the square was completed in 1733 — though the Baroque Ayuntamiento, or Town Hall, was added about 20 years later. The other important building is the Royal Pavilion, where the royal family used to gather to view events in the square. The arcades' crowning medallions celebrate the lives of such famous Spaniards as Columbus, Cortés, and Cervantes. The Plaza Mayor was once the scene of bullfights (as plazas were throughout Spain), but today it's a place to shop, watch the sun go down, and linger for long hours at one of the outdoor cafes until your espresso buzz finally commands you to move.

Universidad de Salamanca
Old Quarter

In its heyday in the 13th through 16th centuries, Salamanca rivaled Oxford, Paris, and Bologna, the other great European centers of learning. Its university, the oldest in Spain, was founded by King Alfonso IX of León in 1218. It produced some of Spain's great academic figures, including Cervantes, St. John of the Cross, and the philosopher Miguel de Unamuno. The most spectacular building is the *Patio de las Escuelas,* or Old University facade. Erected in 1415, the building gained its glorious Plateresque frontispiece sometime in the 16th century. The figures of Ferdinand and Isabella (called the Catholic Kings) are surrounded by a riot of ornamentation — cherubs, crests, and creatures — that fills virtually every inch of the stone frontispiece. Squint and see if you can find the frog, which features prominently in the minds of students. Legend holds that they must share a moment with it prior to exams if they hope to pass (some claim that finding it on your own means a wedding looms). Go inside and take a look at the famous but plain lecture hall of professor Fray Luis de León, a 16th-century theologian who was imprisoned by the Inquisition for five years because he translated the Biblical *Song of Songs* into Castillian Spanish.

Back outside, cross the Patio de las Escuelas and enter the Escuelas Menores patio, with its beautiful lawn and gorgeous arches. The museum here is known for its planetarium-like *Cielo de Salamanca* (Salamanca Heavens) fresco, painted in 1473. Allot a couple of hours to visit the university.

See map p. 339. Patio de las Escuelas 1. At the intersection of rúa Antigua and Compañía. ☎ ***923-29-44-00.*** *Admission: 4€ ($4.80), 2€ ($2.40) children and seniors, free on Monday mornings and May 18. Open: Mon–Sat 9:30 a.m.–1:30 p.m. and 4–7:30 p.m., Sun and holidays 10 a.m.–1:30 p.m.*

More cool things to see and do

Do you want to try out a few more activities in Salamanca? Consider the following:

- **Oohing and aahing on a house-and-palace tour.** Fine mansions and palaces are wedged in among Salamanca's myriad university buildings, convents, and churches, though only a few are open to the public (as indicated below).
  - **Casa de las Conchas** (House of the Shells, ☎ **923-26-93-17**), on Calle de la Compañía 2 (at Rúa Mayor), is famous, much-photographed, and impossible to miss. The facade of this 16th-century Gothic mansion is decorated with steel grilles and protruding scallop shells — the symbol of the knightly Order of Santiago, a group to which the former owner belonged. The scallop shell is the symbol of the St. James pilgrim's trail, the legendary Camino de Santiago. Don't miss the lovely central patio. A tourism information office and public library are now housed here. Free admission.
  - Massive **Palacio de Monterrey,** also on Calle de la Compañía, is one of Salmanca's most beautiful Renaissance palaces. Had it been completed, it would've been one of the largest private palaces in Spain (what you see is only a quarter of what was planned). Still, the upper deck is a fabulous example of Plateresque ornamentation.
  - **Casa de las Muertes** (House of the Dead), on Calle Bordadores, gets its gruesome name from the tiny skulls that decorate its early-16th-century facade. The owner ordered the skulls to commemorate his uncle, an archbishop.
  - Nearby, at Calle Libreros 25, is **Casa-Museo de Unamuno** (☎ **923-29-44-00**), where the renowned university professor and philosopher Miguel de Unamuno lived and then died in 1936. It's also a museum dedicated to the professor's life. Hours are Tuesday through Friday from 9:30 a.m. to 1:30 p.m. and 4 to 6 p.m.; Saturday and Sunday from 10 a.m. to 1:30 p.m. Admission is 3€ ($3.60).
  - **Palacio de Fonseca,** on Calle de San Pablo, was built in 1538 and has a beautiful interior patio; look for the figures on the second floor with the weight of the world on their shoulders.
  - Check out the **Torre del Clavero,** which isn't a house or a palace, but did once belong to one. It's a turreted octagonal tower that was part of a now-disappeared 15th-century manse. The tower is on Plaza de Colón, just off San Pablo.

- **Bridging the gap.** Just beyond the Old City is Salamanca's oldest surviving monument, the stone Puente Romano, or Roman Bridge, across the Tormes River. Constructed in the first century A.D., it still has 15 of its original 26 arches. Take a walk across, not only for the photo-op view of Salamanca, but also to check out the park below the bridge and alongside the river.
- **Joining the faithful.** After the old and new cathedrals, the two best religious buildings in Salamanca face each other on Plaza del

Concilio de Trento: Convento de San Esteban and Convento de las Dueñas. But you can check out all the following if you love religious architecture.

- **Convento de San Esteban** has a monumental Plateresque doorway, a robust stone canvas of delicate carving. Inside the church are impressive frescoes and a typically ornate José Churriguera altarpiece. Convento de San Esteban (☎ **923-21-50-00**) is open daily from 9 a.m. to 1 p.m. and 4 to 8 p.m. in summer, and from 9 a.m. to 1 p.m. and 4 to 6 p.m. in winter. Admission is 2€ ($2.40).
- **Convento de las Dueñas** is a Gothic construction with a lovely Renaissance cloister — the finest in the city and one of the best examples of the Plateresque style in Spain. Train your zoom lens on the freakish ghouls inhabiting the tops of the upper-story capitals. Convento de las Dueñas (☎ **923-21-54-42**) is open in summer daily from 10:30 a.m. to 1 p.m. and 4:30 to 7 p.m.; in winter Monday through Saturday from 10:30 a.m. to 1 p.m. and 4:30 to 5:30 p.m., and Sunday from 11 a.m. to 1 p.m. and 4:30 to 5:30 p.m. Admission is 1.50€ ($1.80).
- If you can't get enough of the city's splendid religious architecture, check out the **Convento de Las Claras,** Calle Santa Clara 2 (☎ **923-26-96-23**). It features a collection of excellent mural paintings from the 13th through 16th centuries as well as other religious art. It's open Monday to Friday from 9:30 a.m. to 2 p.m. and 4 to 7 p.m., and Saturday and Sunday from 9 a.m. to 3 p.m. Admission is 2€ ($2.40).
- Finally, there's **Convento de las Ursulas,** Calle Ursulas 2 (☎ **923-21-98-77**). It is open daily from 11 a.m. to 1 p.m. and 4 to 6 p.m. (except the last Sunday of each month, when it's closed). Admission is 2€ ($2.40).

Shopping for local treasures

Salamanca isn't exactly what you'd call a shopper's town, but it does have a few unique shops in the Old Quarter. The **Mercadillo de Salamanca (Flea Market),** along Calle Rector Esperable on Sunday mornings, **Gremio de Artesanos (Arts & Crafts Guild),** on Plaza de Sexmeros, and the **Centro de Cultura Tradicional,** on Plaza de Colón, are all worth a look for traditional arts and crafts.

Antiqvaria is a cool little antiques store with interesting books, watches, and silver. It's on Rúa Mayor 43–47 (☎ **923-26-99**). It has a branch called **Antiqvaria Rustic,** on Calle Palominos. Another nice antiques shop, with beautiful jewelry and watches, is **Gal-Art Gaite,** Plaza Poeta Iglesias 18 (☎ **923-21-98-89**). **Mercatus,** on Calle Cardinal Plá y Deniel, is the university shop in this university town. It offers all kinds of gear and paper products with the ubiquitous, quasi-official Salamanca Academic lettering (see

"Blood simple: Salamanca's graffiti," earlier in this chapter). **Tienda de Lis,** the gift shop of the Art Nouveau and Art Deco Museum (Casa Lis; see above), has a good selection of nouveau and deco jewelry, books, and other items.

Living it up after dark

With so many Spanish and international students who crowd discos and pubs on the weekends, Salamanca really buzzes at night. For young people, especially in summer when the foreign students swarm the Old Quarter, Salamanca is a perfect place to hang out and barhop. On warm evenings, the **Plaza Mayor** is in a constant state of motion and is a great spot to begin your evening.

For those who would rather plunge into the night and stretch it out until morning, some caution should be exercised, as nightclubs flow with inebriated students and raging hormones. Women should travel in groups and avoid deserted streets.

A good spot for tapas and drinks, as well as for people watching, is the classic upstairs bar **Mesón Cervantes** (Plaza Mayor 15; ☎ **923-21-72-13**), which overlooks the main square. Although plenty of people start their nights there, just as many seem to end them at Mesón Cervantes before stumbling out into the dawn. Rambunctious students fill **The Irish Rover** (Rua Antigua 11; ☎ **923-28-10-74**), an Irish pub dressed up like a chic theater, which has lively jam sessions on Wednesdays. **Camelot** (Bordadores 3; ☎ **923-21-21-84**) and **El Café Moderno** (Gran Vía 75; ☎ **923-26-01-47**) are two other popular bars (the latter features especially good DJs spinning tunes and occasional live acts).

Discos very popular with young people and students from around the world looking to hook up include **Pachá,** Av. de los Reyes de España 25; **Potemkim,** Consuelo 4; and **Versvs,** Correhuela 11. Young women should keep their wits about them at discos, as overt alcohol-induced sexual come-ons are common.

Latin flavor predominates at **El Savor** (Calle San Justo 28, near Gran Via; ☎ **923-26-85-76**), where you find salsa and other Latin music and sweaty dancing from 10:30 p.m. to very late every night. (You can take Latin dance classes Monday through Friday from 8:15 to 9:30 p.m.)

If sweaty isn't exactly your idea of an ideal evening, classical music concerts and *zarzuelas* (light comic opera) are held at the **Palacio de Congresos y Exposiciones,** Cuesta de Oviedo, s/n. Call ☎ **923-26-51-51,** or visit `www.palaciocongresossalamanca.com`, for more information and a schedule of events. The recently renovated **Teatro Liceo** (☎ **923-27-22-90**), on Plaza de Liceo, s/n, near the Plaza Mayor, is the best venue for theatrical, dance, and concert programs.

Castile, and especially Salamanca, is famed for its *tunas* — the name given to the roving bands of troubadours that stroll the streets, serenading young women with songs of university life and love. Like characters who wandered out of a Velázquez court painting, the *tuneros* keep a great academic and musical tradition alive. With their ruffled collars, black velvet suits, and billowing capes, they look like something plucked from the 17th century — which, in a way, they are. Though they don't hound you like Mexican mariachis do, *tuneros* work for tips. If you enjoy their performance and spectacle (which you're almost certain to), give them a euro or two.

Fast Facts: Salamanca

Area Code

Salamanca's area code is **923,** which you must dial before every number.

Currency Exchange

ATMs are located around the Plaza Mayor in the Old Quarter and ATMs and banks are along Avenida de Portugal and Paseo de Canalejas.

Emergencies

For general emergencies, call ☎ **112.** For medical emergencies, call Ambulancias Cruz Roja, ☎ 923-22-22-22 or 923-26-26-60. For police emergencies, dial ☎ **092.**

Hospitals

Hospital Clínico Universitario is located on Paseo San Vicente 108 (☎ 923-29-11-00). The Cruz Roja (Red Cross) is found on the same street, Plaza de San Vicente 1 (☎ 923-21-68-24 or 923-22-22-22).

Information

The main municipal Tourism Office is on the Plaza Mayor, No. 14 (☎ 923-21-83-42). It's open daily from 10 a.m. to 2 p.m. and 5 to 8 p.m. From June 1 to September 30, an additional office operates at the train station. There's a regional tourism office in the Casa de Conchas (☎ 923-26-85-71), open in summer Monday to Thursday and Sunday, from 9 a.m. to 8 p.m., Friday and Saturday from 9 a.m. to 9 p.m., and in winter daily from 9 a.m. to 2 p.m. and 5 to 8 p.m.

Police

The police station is on Plaza Mayor in the Ayuntamiento (City Hall) building (☎ 923-27-91-38).

Post Office

Salamanca's main post office is on Gran Vía 25–29 (☎ 923-26-06-07). A branch is located at Av. Portugal 75–77 (☎ 923-22-03-91).

Toledo

From a distance, Toledo (toh-*leh*-doh) looks like the set design of a Spanish spaghetti western — one in which Moors on horsebacks storm the citadel on the hill. Rising suddenly from the parched plains of La Mancha from a perch on a granite cluster high above the Río Tago (Tagus River), Toledo's cathedral spires and fortress turrets are visible for miles around. As spectacular as the setting is, the city within the walls is even more extraordinary. The fabled city of the painter El Greco, Toledo was where Spain's ancient cultures met and thrived.

Toledo lives and breathes history. Captured by the Romans and later conquered by the Visigoths, Toledo became the capital of Spain in 1085, as well as a melting pot of Moors, Jews, and Christians in the Middle Ages. For several centuries it was exemplary in its religious and cultural tolerance. Now more than five hundred years after the Moors and Jews were expelled from Spain, Toledo remains a fascinating showcase of their achievements. An intricate jumble of churches, synagogues, mosques, noble houses, and humble residences are virtually unchanged since the 16th century.

The city's past is a rich tale of strategic conquests and interlocking cultures. The Romans captured Toledo in 192 B.C., named it Toletum, and built it into a strategic settlement. The Moors invaded Spain in 711 and headed straight for Toledo, capturing the city in 712. Under Moorish control it remained a rich and cultured city with a thriving Jewish community of 12,000. The legendary general El Cid conquered it in 1085 for Alfonso VI. Toledo became the capital of Spain, but the city fell into a steady decline after the Catholic crusades banished its Jewish and Muslim populations at the end of the 15th century. In 1561, Felipe II chose backwater Madrid as his administrative and political capital, cementing Toledo's second-tier status (but, ironically, probably preserving its medieval appearance).

Toledo ranks as one of Spain's top tourist destinations, and although it hasn't been physically corrupted like the Costa del Sol, it suffers from the impact of massive tourism. It's tiny, hilly, and hemmed in by medieval walls, and in summer, waves of tour groups and mammoth buses overwhelm the city's impossibly narrow streets and small churches, synagogues, and museums. Although Toledo remains an almost obligatory side trip from Madrid (and still one of the most important visits in the entire country), a peak-of-summer visitor who breaks out in hives at the thought of huge crowds and omnipresent tour buses may do well to take a detour to Segovia or Salamanca instead (or, better yet, schedule a fall or spring visit).

If you stay overnight in Toledo, you get to enjoy the city late in the day and evening, when the day-trippers depart, and very early the next morning, before they come barreling in again. I recommend spending a night and a couple of days in Toledo, though surprisingly few visitors actually do this.

Don't plan to visit Toledo on a Monday, when half the sights are closed.

Getting there

Traveling by car to Toledo is simple, but driving within the city walls on the tiny, one-way streets is hair-raising. I suggest going by car only if you're planning to do a tour of other sights in Central Spain, such as Segovia or Salamanca. If you do drive, Toledo is only a quick hour from Madrid on the N-401 south.

Toledo

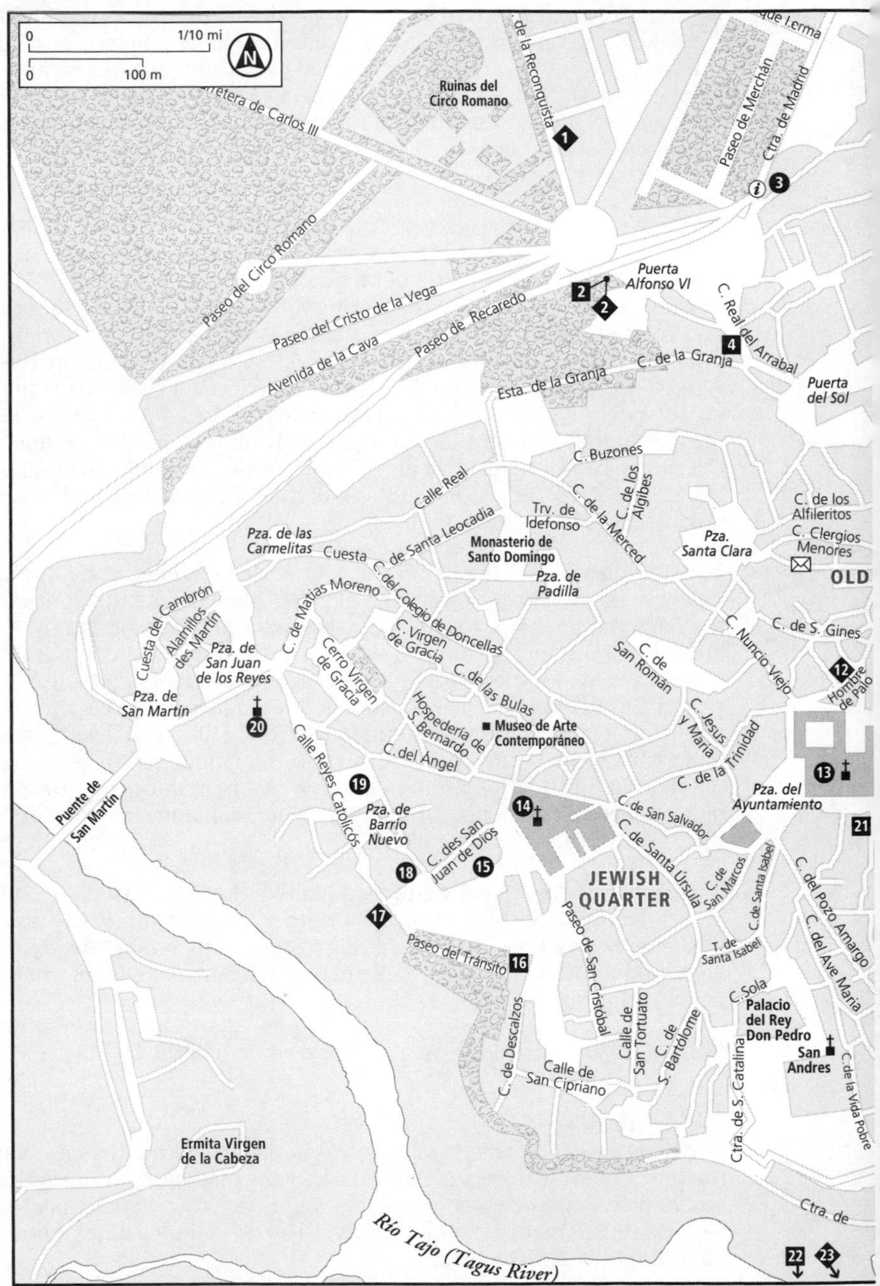
0 1/10 mi
0 100 m
N
Ruinas del Circo Romano
Carretera de Carlos III
C. de la Reconquista
Paseo de Merchán
Ctra. de Madrid
Paseo del Circo Romano
Paseo del Cristo de la Vega
Avenida de la Cava
Paseo de Recaredo
Puerta Alfonso VI
C. Real del Arrabal
Esta. de la Granja
C. de la Granja
Puerta del Sol
C. Buzones
C. de los Algibes
Calle Real
Trv. de Idefonso
C. de la Merced
C. de los Alfileritos
C. Clergios Menores
Pza. Santa Clara
OLD
Pza. de las Carmelitas
Cuesta de Santa Leocadia
Monasterio de Santo Domingo
Pza. de Padilla
C. de Matías Moreno
C. del Colegio de Doncellas
C. Virgen de Gracia
Cerro Virgen de Gracia
Cuesta del Cambrón
Alamillos des Martín
Pza. de San Juan de los Reyes
Pza. de San Martín
C. de las Bulas
C. de San Román
C. Nuncio Viejo
C. de S. Gines
Hombre de Palo
Hospedería de S. Bernardo
Museo de Arte Contemporáneo
C. Jesus y María
C. de la Trinidad
Calle Reyes Católicos
C. del Ángel
Puente de San Martín
Pza. de Barrio Nuevo
C. des San Juan de Dios
C. de San Salvador
C. de Santa Úrsula
Pza. del Ayuntamiento
C. de San Marcos
C. de Santa Isabel
JEWISH QUARTER
C. del Pozo Amargo
C. del Ave María
Paseo del Tránsito
Paseo de San Cristóbal
T. de Santa Isabel
C. Sola
Palacio del Rey Don Pedro
San Andres
C. de la Vida Pobre
C. de Descalzos
Calle de San Tortuato
C. de S. Bartolomé
Calle de San Cipriano
Ctra. de S. Catalina
Ermita Virgen de la Cabeza
Ctra. de
Río Tajo (Tagus River)
Parque Lerma

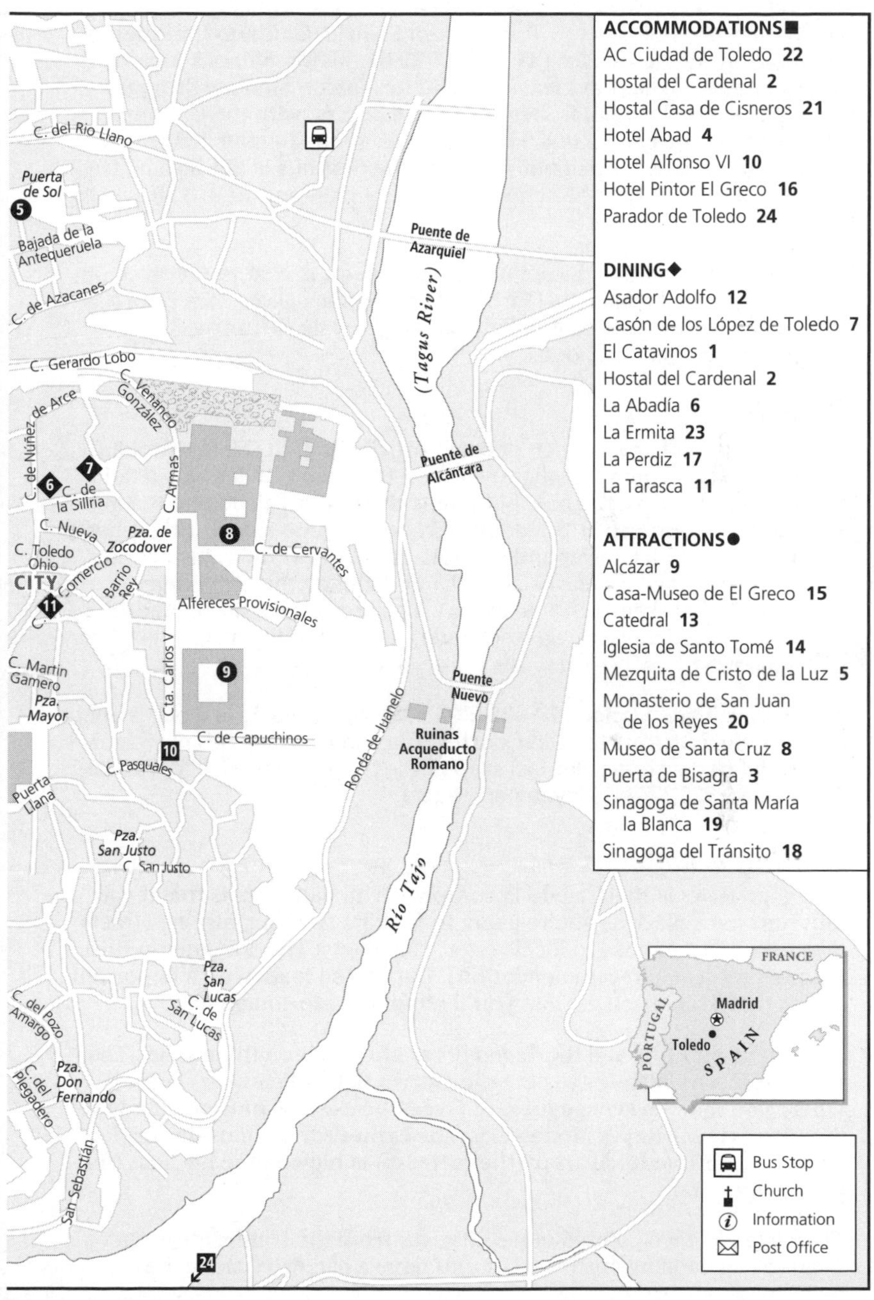
ACCOMMODATIONS
AC Ciudad de Toledo 22
Hostal del Cardenal 2
Hostal Casa de Cisneros 21
Hotel Abad 4
Hotel Alfonso VI 10
Hotel Pintor El Greco 16
Parador de Toledo 24
DINING
Asador Adolfo 12
Casón de los López de Toledo 7
El Catavinos 1
Hostal del Cardenal 2
La Abadía 6
La Ermita 23
La Perdiz 17
La Tarasca 11
ATTRACTIONS
Alcázar 9
Casa-Museo de El Greco 15
Catedral 13
Iglesia de Santo Tomé 14
Mezquita de Cristo de la Luz 5
Monasterio de San Juan de los Reyes 20
Museo de Santa Cruz 8
Puerta de Bisagra 3
Sinagoga de Santa María la Blanca 19
Sinagoga del Tránsito 18
C. del Rio Llano
Puerta de Sol
Bajada de la Antequeruela
C. de Azacanes
C. Gerardo Lobo
C. Venancio González
C. de Núñez de Arce
C. de la Sillria
C. Armas
C. Nueva
Pza. de Zocodover
C. Toledo Ohio
CITY
C. Comercio
Barrio Rey
C. de Cervantes
Alféreces Provisionales
Cta. Carlos V
C. Martin Gamero
Pza. Mayor
C. de Capuchinos
C. Pasquales
Puerta Llana
Pza. San Justo
C. San Justo
Pza. San Lucas
C. de San Lucas
C. del Pozo Amargo
Pza. Don Fernando
C. del Plegadero
San Sebastián
Puente de Azarquiel
(Tagus River)
Puente de Alcántara
Puente Nuevo
Ronda de Juanelo
Ruinas Acqueducto Romano
Río Tajo
FRANCE
PORTUGAL
Madrid
Toledo
SPAIN
Bus Stop
Church
Information
Post Office

By bus

The bus is the quickest and cheapest — and thus probably the most convenient — way to get to Toledo from Madrid. **Galliano Continental,** Estación Sur de Autobuses (☎ **91-527-29-61;** Metro: Méndez Alvaro), buses (4.20€/$5 one-way) leave Madrid for Toledo Monday through Saturday every 30 minutes, beginning at 6:30 a.m. with the last return at 10 p.m. (no bus at 2 p.m.). The trip takes about an hour. Returns to Madrid are also every half-hour, though the first bus is at 5:30 a.m. On Sundays and holidays, the schedule is every half-hour from 8:30 a.m. to midnight.

The Toledo bus station, **Estación de Autobuses,** is next to the river, on Avenida Castilla-La Mancha (☎ **925-21-58-50**). It's about 1km (⅔ of a mile) from the historic center. You can either walk (be warned, it's steep!) or take bus no. 5 or 6.

By train

The train from Madrid, which departs Atocha Station (Metro: Atocha RENFE), takes 75 minutes, slightly longer than the bus. It's also a tad more expensive than the bus, but many visitors to Toledo find it a more relaxing way to travel. In Toledo, the train pulls into a cool, 1917 railway station, with a clock tower and keyhole arches. Several trains per day make the trip; the first leaves at 6:50 a.m. Monday through Friday (8:20 a.m. on weekends and holidays). The first train back to Madrid leaves at 7 a.m. (8:30 a.m. on weekends), the last at 9 p.m. Fare is 8.30€ ($10) one-way.

The **RENFE Train Station** (☎ **925-22-30-99**), on Paseo de la Rosa, is about a 20-minute walk from the Old Quarter. You can also take bus no. 5 or 6. You won't find a permanent taxi stop at the train station. Call ☎ **925-25-50-50** or ☎ 925-22-70-70 if you need a taxi.

Getting oriented

The good news is that Toledo is compact. The bad news is that it's as labyrinthine a place as you're likely to find. Its twisting, turning streets don't even make sense to locals (see "Fast Facts: Toledo," later in this chapter, for a map recommendation). But, it's so loaded with important sights that even if you get lost you'll stumble onto something.

The city is on a hill, and the Tagus River bounds it on three sides. The southwest part of the city is the old **Barrio Sefardí** (Jewish Quarter), where you find the **synagogues, El Greco house and museum,** and the **San Juan de los Reyes Monastery.** The **cathedral** is almost in the dead center of old Toledo. **Alcázar** (the fortress) is high on the hill, just east of the cathedral.

The vista El Greco painted of his city was from the south side of the Tagus River, looking northwest. If you have a car, drive along the

Carretera de Circunvalación (beltway), which provides stunning views of the city and its amazing setting.

Getting around

If you drive to Toledo, take advantage of the public parking at Puerta Vieja de la Bisagra (the Old Bisagra Gateway), at the entrance to the Old City, and ditch your car immediately. Only a couple of hotels, mostly outside the Old City, have parking.

Don't even think about venturing by car into the maddening maze of old Toledo's streets. The only way to make your way around the small historic center is on foot, and virtually everything you want to visit is within the medieval walls. The streets are incredibly steep, though, so make sure you don some comfortable, supportive walking shoes. A day spent walking in Toledo is like a rough day on a stair machine at the gym.

If your legs have had it and you need a taxi to rescue you or whisk you to the train or bus station, call ☎ **925-25-50-50.**

Spending the night

Staying overnight in Toledo is a great idea — there's so much to see, and walking around the tiny, hilly stone streets wears out even the best-conditioned travelers. If you can afford the extra time, pass on a head-spinning one-day tour and see Toledo at your own pace.

Toledo has a smattering of good and affordable hotels, some with gorgeous views and others that really capture the city's special atmosphere. The hotels tend to be small, though, and because Toledo is one of the most popular spots in Spain, you need to make reservations. If you plan to visit anytime between March and September, making phone reservations a month or two in advance is a good idea. The smaller the hotel, the greater the need for early reservations. Be aware that higher room rates are charged for Holy Week and the Corpus Christi festival in early June.

AC Ciudad de Toledo

$$$–$$$$ Across the river south of the city

One of the best hotels in Spain, and the top upscale choice in Toledo, the midsize Ciudad de Toledo took some of the "wow" out of the *parador* down the road when it opened in 1998. It has an equally coveted location, directly across the river from Toledo, and equally brilliant views of the city, but it's brighter, more cheerful, and more luxurious. A member of the AC family, which also includes the ultra swanky Santo Mauro in Madrid, this hotel is model of contemporary luxury and design. The 49 rooms have hip orange and green color schemes with bathrooms done in brightly colored tiles. The very nice restaurant has to-die-for views of Toledo. Room rates are more than fair—and a flat-out bargain if you score one an online *promoción* for as little as 84€ ($101)—for a hotel of this caliber.

See map p. 354. Carretera de Circunvalación 15. On beltway immediately south of Toledo; follow signs to Parador de Toledo. ☎ ***925-28-51-25,*** *for central reservations* ☎ *902-29-22-93. Fax: 925-28-47-00.* www.ac-hoteles.com. *Free parking. Rack rates: 125€–144€ ($150–$173). AE, DC, MC, V.*

Hostal Casa de Cisneros

$$ Old City (near the cathedral)

A delightful small hotel with plenty of style and a great location—if you're not carting around too much luggage—this attractive spot is also a bargain. Inhabiting a structure from the 16th century, it has been restored with taste, but it retains many signature architectural elements, such as brick arches and stone walls. Rooms aren't overly large, but they are handsome and clean, as are the en-suite bathrooms.

See map p. 354. Cardenal Cisneros 12 (at corner of Cárcel del Vicario 1, opposite the cathedral). ☎ ***925-22-88-28.*** *Fax: 925-22-31-73.* www.hostal-casa-de-cisneros.com. *Parking: 6€ ($7.20). Rack rates: 60€–80€ ($72–$96). AE, DC, MC, V.*

Hostal del Cardenal

$$–$$$ Edge of Old City

This relaxed and personal inn feels like an old Toledo home — it's the perfect hotel for the city and is the best bet if you want to stay within walking distance of the Old Quarter. The former residence of an 18th-century cardinal, it's built right into the city's medieval ramparts, just around the bend from the Puerta de Bisagra. It has graceful Moorish gardens with trickling fountains and serene patios. Its twenty-seven antiques-filled rooms are very comfortable, if not lavish. The restaurant (see the review, later in this chapter) has long maintained an excellent reputation for classic Castilian cooking. For the price, this hotel is a steal, but the secret's out. It's so small that it's full most of the year.

See map p. 354. Paseo de Recaredo 24. Just west of Bisagra gate, off Avenida de la Cava. ☎ ***925-22-08-62,*** *reservations* ☎ *925-22-49-00. Fax: 925-22-29-91.* www.hostaldelcardenal.com. *Free parking. Rack rates: 84€–106€ ($105–$133). AE, DC, MC, V.*

Hotel Abad

$$$ Old City (near the Puerta Bisagra)

Just inside the medieval city walls and a short distance from the Puerta Bisagra, this small, modern and affordable hotel, inserted into an early 19th-century home and former blacksmith's workshop, is a fine and comfortable place to stay. Though you can't park right at the hotel, it helps that you can easily drive in and drop off luggage (something that's not always possible at Toledo hotels in the Old Quarter). The hotel retains hand-dewn wood beams and brick walls. Rooms are cheery and well equipped; my favorite are the atticlike spaces on the top floor, though some may complain that they're not well enough soundproofed.

See map p. 354. Real de Arrabal 1. Three blocks south of Puerta Bisagra. ☎ ***925-28-35-00.*** *Fax: 925-28-35-01.* `www.hotelabad.com`. *Parking: 10€ ($12). Rack rates: 100€–125€ ($120–$150). AE, DC, MC, V.*

Hotel Alfonso VI

$$–$$$ Old City (near the Alcázar)

I was ready to write off this old-style Spanish hotel, right across from the Alcázar, until I saw the back rooms that face south. They have small balconies and views that gaze out across Toledo, the river, and the rugged countryside. Even though you're not looking up at the city on the hill (as you do from the *parador* or the Ciudad de Toledo hotels, across the river), the view is still extraordinary. The 83 rooms are a little plain, perhaps (except for the shocking bright green curtains and bedspreads), but the place has an odd, yesteryear character. Wait until you get a load of the kitschy basement bar, done up in full medieval regalia with suits of armor and heavy stone arches. Bring on the grog and gruel! Check for online discounts of up to 40 percent.

See map p. 354. General Moscardó 2. One block south of stairs to Alcázar. ☎ ***925-22-26-00.*** *Fax: 925-21-44-58.* `www.hotelalfonsovi.com`. *Parking: 6€ ($7.20). Rack rates: 130€–180€ ($156–$216). AE, DC, MC, V.*

Hotel Pintor El Greco

$$$ Old City (Jewish Quarter)

Similar in ambience to the Hostal del Cardenal but without the gardens, and named for Toledo's most famous son, this small hotel has a great Toledo feel. A 17th-century noble home and former bakery, it showcases tiles, exposed brick, dark wood, and iron lamps. Rooms around the central courtyard are light and airy. They're immaculately maintained, and have received a slight update since the inn became part of the Sercotel chain. One of the best things about the place is its location in the heart of the old Jewish Quarter. It's close to the El Greco museum and synagogues, and is remarkably peaceful.

See map p. 354. Alamillos del Tránsito 13. One block southeast from Santo Tome Church. ☎ ***925-28-51-91*** *or 902-15-46-45. Fax: 925-21-58-19.* `www.hotel-pintorelgreco.com`. *Parking: Nearby 6€ ($7.20). Rack rates: 110€ ($132). AE, DC, MC, V.*

Parador de Toledo

$$$ Across the river south of the city

This *parador* allows its guests to see Toledo as El Greco did. Overlooking the city, on a hill above the river, the *parador* has regal views. The handsome and fairly spacious rooms look and feel appropriately Castilian, with leather furniture, chests, and heavy, dark wood tables. Once the top place to stay in Toledo, the AC Ciudad de Toledo (see the listing earlier in this section) has displaced it. For relaxing outdoors, though, it can't be beat, and you'll probably spend most of your time (when not traipsing about the city) on the terraces and by the large pool, which is sure to be a hit with children (very few other hotels in the city have one). Most guests just can't get enough of the views (a room with a view is well worth the extra 20€/$24). This is one of the most popular *paradores* in the country, so make your reservations early.

See map p. 354. Cerro del Emperador, s/n. 4km (2 miles) from the center of Toledo; access from Carretera de Circunvalación. ☎ ***925-22-18-50.*** *Fax: 925-22-51-66.* www.parador.es. *Free parking. Rack rates: 140€–150€ ($168–$180). AE, DC, MC, V.*

Dining locally

Asador Adolfo

$$$$ Old City CASTILIAN

Catering to well-to-do locals and discriminating tourists, Asador Adolfo occupies a handsome 15th-century building in the Old Quarter on a little side street not far from the cathedral. Finding it is a bit difficult, just off Calle Hombre de Palo a block north of the cathedral. Dine in one of four quiet dining rooms with elegant place settings and solid beams overhead. The kitchen is creative, pumping out original interpretations of traditional dishes such as *merluza al azafrán* (saffron-flavored hake). Game is a specialty. The wine cellar, though, is the real star. Set in an 11th-century Jewish *cueva,* or basement, with 50,000 bottles and 1,200 wines, it's the best in Toledo. For dessert, everyone raves about the marzipan; if you like the sweet almond paste, you'll love Toledo's (it's lighter than most versions). The service, though, doesn't always match the quality of the food.

See map p. 354. Calle de la Granada 6. One block from cathedral, off Hombre de Palo. ☎ ***925-22-73-21.*** *Reservations required. Main courses: 15€–28€ ($18–$34). Menú del día: 33€ ($40). Tasting menu: 48€ ($58). AE, DC, MC, V. Open: Mon–Sat for lunch and dinner, Sun lunch only. Closed: Last two weeks of July and second week of Jan.*

Casón de los López de Toledo

$$$–$$$$ Old City CASTILIAN/CONTINENTAL

A uniquely handsome restaurant occupying a traditional stone señorial mansion and stuffed with period antiques — many of which are for sale — this is the most sumptuous spot to dine in Toledo. With a vaulted foyer, statuary-laden patio, and Moorish-style ceilings and stucco work, it exudes the flavor of old Toledo. The menu, though, adds fresh and sophisticated contemporary touches to classic Castilian dishes, using excellent, fresh local produce. Try the venison on a bed of spinach and mushrooms or the cod and orange millefeuille. Desserts are equally outstanding.

See map p. 354. Sillería 3 (near Plaza Zocodover). ☎ ***925-25-47-74.*** *Reservations required. Main courses: 14€–24€ ($17–$29). Menú del día: 33€–45€ ($40–$54); tasting menu 51€ ($61). MC, V. Open: Daily for lunch, Mon–Sat dinner.*

El Catavinos

$$ Edge of Old City CASTILIAN/SPANISH

I love this quirky place on the outskirts of Toledo's medieval core, just five minutes from the Bisagra gate. It's not fancy, just a comfortable and relaxing place for a low-key meal away from the hubbub, with an ample choice of wines. Proprietor Luis Martínez is a photographer and hunter of wines; the restaurant's name means wine taster. The bar downstairs is nestled among the wine racks, and the simple dining room upstairs is decorated with Martínez's photographs of Latin America. The menu, a dizzying array of midday and evening fixed-price meals that are excellent deals, is filled with good *comida casera* (home cooking). I've ordered their grilled salmon, which was quite tasty, as was the *solomillo* (sirloin steak) served in a huge portion that came with fries worthy of a Belgian bistro.

See map p. 354. Av. de la Reconquista 10. Just beyond Puerta de Bisagra; ten-minute walk north from Glorieta de la Reconquista, the roundabout on Avenida de la Cava. ☎ ***925-22-22-56.*** *Main courses: 9€–20€ ($11–$24). Menú del día: 12€ ($14). Tasting menu: 24€ ($29). MC, V. Open: Tues–Sun lunch and dinner.*

Hostal del Cardenal

$$–$$$ Edge of Old City CASTILIAN

For many years one of Toledo's most respected eateries, specializing in traditional Castilian cooking, the restaurant at the Hostal del Cardenal is no longer quite so renowned. Some locals report that the kitchen here has become a bit stagnant. Still, you can't go wrong in a setting this fine with such great views and terrific ambience. Attached to the splendid Moorish gardens of the Hostal (see hotel review, earlier in this chapter), the restaurant remains one of the most atmospheric places to dine in the Old City. Oven-baked sea bass, lamb chops, and the local specialties, roast suckling pig and partridge, are well-executed standards. Be sure to take a stroll in the gardens after dinner.

See map p. 354. Paseo Recaredo 24. Just west of Bisagra gate, off Avenida de la Cava. ☎ ***925-22-08-62.*** *Reservations recommended. Main courses: 9€–19€ ($11–$23). Menú del día: 18€ ($22). AE, DC, MC, V. Open: Daily for lunch and dinner.*

La Abadía

$$–$$$ Old City CASTILIAN

I stumbled upon this friendly and nicely designed, slightly upscale restaurant/bar while hunting down the tiny Cristo de la Luz synagogue. La Abadía means The Abbey — appropriate in a city with such a roster of religious monuments. The restaurant serves such solid Castilian fare as *judías con perdiz* (white bean and partridge casserole, a classic Toledo dish), pâtés, and venison. It's also a great place to drop in for tapas; the bar area is often packed with hungry, talkative nibblers. Fittingly, the Abbey serves a handful of Belgian abbey beers for those of you tired of red wine and sherry.

See map p. 354. Plaza de San Nicolás 3. At intersection of Calle de Alfileteros and Núñez de Arce, next to San Nicolás church. ☎ ***925-25-11-40.*** *Reservations recommended.*

Main courses: 12€–18€ ($14–$22). Menú del día: 20€ ($24). MC, V. Open: Tues–Sun lunch and dinner.

La Ermita

$$$ Old City NOUVEAU CASTILIAN

With a spectacular view of Toledo from across the river, this contemporary and upscale, but relaxed, restaurant is where I'd go if I had just one night in Toledo. It has massive picture windows framing the majestic view of the city, and while that is certainly the star of the show, chef Jando Domínguez González's menu doesn't take much of a back seat. He adds a modern touch to traditional Castilian dishes. Starters include a cream of potato soup with clams, shrimp, and salmon roe, and marinated tuna layered with anchovies and piquillo peppers. My wife and I thoroughly enjoyed main courses of monkfish in a clam sauce with green asparagus, and hake with caramelized mushrooms. Carnivores will enjoy classic dishes like oxtail, pig's knuckles, and beef tenderloin. The wine list is fairly priced; check out the Dominio de Valdepusa reds from the local winemaking savant Marqués de Griñon. Though Spaniards eat very late, it's worth arriving early, at sundown — around 9 p.m. in summer — to see the lights begin to twinkle. Later, the cathedral is brilliantly illuminated on the hill.

See map p. 354. Ctra. De Circunvalación, s/n. Across Tagus River. ☎ ***925-25-31-93.*** *Reservations recommended. Main courses: 18€–20€ ($11–$18). AE, MC, V. Open: Tues–Sat lunch and dinner, Sun lunch only.*

La Perdiz

$$ Old City CASTILIAN

A good-looking but unfussy place owned by the same people who run the city's fanciest restaurant, Adolfo, La Perdiz (which means "partridge") is more down-to-earth and comfortable, as well as much less expensive than its upscale relative. In the heart of the Jewish Quarter between the synagogues Tránsito and Santa María la Blanca, its two dining rooms feature exposed brick and crisp white table linens. An excellent starter is the *croquetas de perdiz* (partridge croquettes), a house specialty. Follow that with one of the rice dishes (with shellfish, for example), roast suckling pig, or *albóndigas de bacalao* (cod balls), all solid entrees to fortify you for Toledo's challengingly hilly streets.

See map p. 354. Calle Reyes Católicos 7. Two blocks east of San Juan de Reyes monastery. ☎ ***925-25-29-19.*** *Reservations recommended. Main courses: 15€–19€ ($18–$24). Menú del día: 20€ ($24). MC, V. Open: Tues–Sat lunch and dinner, Sun lunch only. Closed: Third week in Jan, last two weeks of Aug.*

La Tarasca

$$ Old City CASTILIAN

Just a couple of short blocks north of the cathedral, on a busy street lined with jewelry and craft shops, La Tarasca is a good place to duck in for a solid lunch. You can order from the regular menu, but all anyone seems to order is the *menú del día* (fixed-price meal). The décor is merely functional, but it's a little nicer in back, away from the door. It quickly gets crowded with sightseers and locals (there seems to be more of the latter), so try to beat the 2 p.m. lunch rush, especially on weekends. You may start off with a pretty decent paella (a rice, meat, and seafood casserole), and follow it up with *cordonices* (braised game hen) or trout. A glass of wine and dessert (flan or ice cream) is included in the menu.

See map p. 354. Callejón del Fraile, s/n. Off Calle de Comercio, 2 blocks northeast of the cathedral. ☎ ***925-22-43-42.*** *Reservations recommended. Main courses: 8€–16€ ($9.60–$19). Menú del día: 15€ ($18). MC, V. Open: Tues–Sun lunch and dinner.*

Exploring Toledo

In Toledo, separating the must-sees from the can-do-withouts is tough because the distinctions are a bit arbitrary — the city is a fascinating whole with a long roster of complex parts. Really the only way to absorb most of Toledo's great charm is by wandering its narrow, history-suffused streets. Getting too caught up on checking off major sights is probably not the best way to enjoy the city. In any case, seeing everything in a single day is impossible. However, if that's all you have time for, consider only the main stops listed in "The top attractions," later in this chapter. If you can spend the night and at least a second day in Toledo, consider visiting a couple of the locations detailed in the following "More cool things to see and do" section.

Before you set out to conquer Toledo, consult a good map in addition to the one provided here (see "Fast Facts: Toledo," at the end of this chapter, for a recommendation). Toledo is a complicated maze of twisting streets that makes providing good directions nearly impossible. If your map reading fails you, ask a local. Most are more than happy to point you in the right direction.

The best place to start your tour is from the Puerta de Bisagra (where the Tourism Office is located). Pass through the massive gate and enter the twisting maze of Toledo's tiny streets. All the major sights I list are within the Old City.

The top attractions

Catedral de Toledo
Old City

Allow sufficient time to see Toledo's centerpiece, one of the most opulent, jaw-dropping Gothic churches in Spain. The massive asymmetrical structure makes a solid case for Toledo's religious importance in the Middle Ages. Begun in 1226, it wasn't finished until nearly three centuries later, in 1493 (the year after Columbus is credited with discovering America). On the outside, the cathedral is French Gothic; the interior mixes Spanish Gothic with Mudejar, Renaissance, and Plateresque elements. Right in the middle of the cathedral nave is the choir, a splendid example of wood carving on the lower choir stalls and alabaster sculpture on the upper tier. The Alta Mayor (High Altar) is a fabulous, brightly colored polychrome *retablo* (altarpiece) dripping in gold. The kings of Castile are buried here. Walk around the altar and look straight up. Hung from the ambulatory is an almost ridiculously ornate marble sculpture, *Transparente.* A controversial sun roof (it's so incongruous, I don't know what else to call it) was cut to allow sunlight in to illuminate it. Before the opening was carved, the sculpture was almost impossible to see.

The sacristy (to the left of the main altar) holds a treasure trove of artworks, including El Greco's *Expolio (The Denuding of Christ),* as well as works by Titian and Goya. The Sala Capitular, to the right rear of the cathedral, is a mini Alhambra, with intricate Mudéjar (Christian architecture employing Arab motifs and elements) ceilings and stucco doorways. In the Treasury is a wondrous 16th-century *monstrance* — the receptacle used to display communion wafers or bread — that weighs nearly 181kg (400 lbs.) and is nearly 3m (10 ft.) high. Despite the monstrous proportions, the faithful hoist and parade it through the streets of Toledo during the Corpus Christi celebration in June. Plan on spending one to two hours here.

See map p. 354. Arcos de Palacio 2. Just off Plaza del Ayuntamiento. ☎ ***925-22-22-41.*** *Admission: 6 € ($7.20). Open: Mon–Sat 10 a.m.–6:30 p.m., Sun and holidays 2 p.m.–6 p.m. (cathedral closes an hour later in winter).*

Iglesia de Santo Tomé: El Greco's The Burial of Count Orgaz
Old City

The Church of Santo Tomé is a required stop because of a single painting. However, that painting is one of the finest in Spain: El Greco's masterpiece, *The Burial of Count Orgaz.* The painting, created for the space where it still hangs today, is masterful in its color, contrast, and composition. It depicts the miraculous appearance of St. Augustine and St. Stephen at the burial of the Count, a church patron who paid for the construction of Santo Tomé. It's also a self-portrait: El Greco is seventh from the left at the bottom, staring straight ahead. Visitors often cram the small room, so try going the minute it opens in the morning or just after lunch if you want to ponder the work in relative peace. Allow as long as you can stand looking at a stunning work in the company of lots of restless day-trippers — about a half-hour, allowing for the crowd.

See map p. 354. Plaza del Conde 2. One block south of Calle del Angel/Calle de Santo Tomé, in the southwestern part of the city. ☎ ***925-21-60-98.*** *Admission: 1.90€ ($2.30), Wed after 2:30 p.m. free for residents of the E.U. Open: Summer 10 a.m.–6:45 p.m., Nov–Feb 10 a.m.–5:45 p.m.*

Monasterio de San Juan de los Reyes
Jewish Quarter

A Gothic monastery commissioned to commemorate the Spanish victory over Portugal in 1476, this was to have been the burial place of the Catholic Monarchs, Ferdinand and Isabela. (They were eventually buried in the Granada cathedral.) As you may guess, it's suitably grand, a gorgeous and

El Greco: Domenico the Greek

If anyone ever needed a nickname, it was Domenico Theotocopoulous. Spaniards simply called the Greek artist (who didn't adopt Toledo as his hometown until 1577, when he was already 36 years old) El Greco, or The Greek. Toledo made him famous and vice versa. El Greco's *View of Toledo* is a lovely picture of the city on the hill, but the painter is considered one of Spain's greatest for his deeply spiritual portraits of saints and Madonnas, depicted in an otherworldly, elongated fashion.

Contrary to popular legend, El Greco almost surely didn't suffer from astigmatism. The ethereal figures, their forms reaching toward heaven, were a product of the artist's deeply spiritual vision. His portraits were meditative and almost hallucinatory. It's no surprise that his paintings found no favor at Madrid's Royal Court, where realism reigned supreme. However, his adopted city adored him, and El Greco found his place of divine inspiration in its melting pot.

El Greco's supreme artistic achievement, *The Burial of Count Orgaz,* depicted a burial ceremony so important that two saints miraculously appeared at it. But the artist himself met a less ceremonious end: He lies in the Santo Domingo Monastery, underneath a curious little museum run by the nuns there. You can view El Greco's remains by kneeling down and peering through a hole in the floor. The coffin is so small that it looks more like a toolbox.

If you want to see the tomb and the *retablos* (altarpieces) El Greco painted in the monastery, they're at the Convento Santo Domino el Antiguo, Plaza Santo Domingo, s/n (☎ **925-22-29-30**). The hours are Monday to Saturday from 11 a.m. to 1:30 p.m. and 4 to 7 p.m., and Sunday from 4 to 7 p.m. only. Admission is 1.20€ ($1.45).

surprising mix of Gothic and Mudéjar architecture. The fine Gothic cloisters have a superb Moorish-style, wood-carved ceiling, and brilliant stone carving. Peek out over the balcony for a view of some wild gargoyles. The monastery is in the extreme western portion of the city near the Jewish Quarter. An hour here suffices, though the cloisters are a place to linger.

See map p. 354. San Juan de los Reyes 2. Just beyond the point where Calle Reyes Católicos meets Calle del Angel, about 2 blocks west of the Santa María la Blanca synagogue. ☎ ***925-22-38-02.*** *Admission: 1.90€ ($2.40). Open: Daily 10 a.m.–2 p.m. and 3:30–6 p.m., open until 7 p.m. in summer.*

Museo de Santa Cruz

Old City

Built before the era of superstar architects, this museum is as notable for the building itself as for its collection. It was a hospital for orphans and the indigent in the 16th century, so the building seems surprisingly sumptuous with carved wood ceilings and rich marble floors. Better lighting and upkeep wouldn't hurt, but its outstanding early-Renaissance features, including a dramatic, ornamental stairway and Plateresque patio, are impossible to miss. The museum has a number of El Grecos, the most important

Across the river: El Greco's view of Toledo

It's common to feel a little claustrophobic as you navigate Toledo's labyrinthine streets on foot, dodging cars and tour buses. If you have a car, don't miss a drive along the Carretera de Circunvalación, the beltway that runs alongside the Tagus River around the city. Head east toward the Ermita de Nuestra Señora del Valle, a small chapel above the river, the Parador del Toledo, and the Roman Bridge, Puente de Alcántara. The views of the city are dazzling, especially at dusk — you can easily see why El Greco was so enamored of this view of his adopted hometown. A couple of bars and outdoor cafes have sprung up here, though few tourists seem to make the trip. If tourists do venture across the river, most go on up to the terrace at the *parador,* from which the views are equally good (in fact the hill on which the *parador* sits is purportedly the hill from which El Greco painted *View of Toledo*).

If you don't have a car, at least walk out through the San Martín neighborhood, west of the old Jewish Quarter and over the San Martín Bridge (which dates to 1203), and take a look back at Toledo rising on the hill before you. Allow at least an hour (more if you catch the light just right as you gaze at the city).

being *La Asunción de la Virgen* (1613). Originally an altarpiece, this piece is one of the master's final works, painted just months before his death. Extending from ceiling to floor is the battle flag from Lepanto, the landmark 1571 victory over the Moors. Throughout the building's wings, designed in the form of a Greek cross, are excellent 16th-century tapestries, furniture, and decorative arts. You probably need a couple of hours at this fascinating museum.

The Santa Cruz museum is one of the few sights in Toledo that remains open at midday (except Mon). Go at 2 or 3 p.m.; not only is it less crowded, but this way you can squeeze more activities into your day without too much dead time at lunch.

See map p. 354. Calle Miguel de Cervantes 3. One block east of the granite archway on Plaza de Zocodover. ☎ ***925-22-10-36.*** *Free admission. Open: Mon–Sat 10 a.m.–6 p.m. and Sun 10 a.m.–2 p.m.*

Sinagoga del Tránsito (Museo Sefardi)
Jewish Quarter

This 14th-century synagogue, one of the most important examples of Sephardic art and architecture, was one of ten that once existed in Toledo, when one-fifth of the population was Jewish. The exterior is rather nondescript, but inside it's a wealth of elaborate Mudéjar decoration. The two-story interior has a dazzling carved cedarwood ceiling and splendid stucco inscriptions in Hebrew. The upstairs balcony was reserved for women. Within the synagogue is the Sephardic Museum, which displays an interesting collection of tombstones, robes, and books, many dating prior to the expulsion of Spain's Jews in 1492. Allow from a half-hour to an hour.

See map p. 354. Just south of the Casa-Museo de El Greco, near the intersection of Paseo del Tránsito and Calle de San Juan de Dios. ☎ ***925-22-36-65.*** *Admission: 2.40€ ($2.90), free Sat afternoons and Sun. Open: Tues–Sat 10 a.m.–2 p.m. and 4–6 p.m., Sun 10 a.m.–2 p.m.*

More cool things to see and do

Toledo overflows with worthy churches and monuments to draw your attention if you have more than an afternoon or single day in the city.

- **Touring the Alcázar.** Toledo's Alcázar (☎ **925-22-16-73**), or citadel, on the hill is hard to miss, and not a bus tour goes by without stopping at it, but inside it's frankly a bit of a disappointment. Originally built by Carlos V in the 16th century (a conversion of the 13th-century fortress of El Cid, the famed Castilian warrior), it has been destroyed by fire and battle and rebuilt many times — most recently, after the Spanish Civil War. Restored and converted into an army museum, it now looks much as it originally did. Its large Italianate central patio is its most appealing feature, unless you're wowed by unending displays of weapons and uniforms. Note that the Alcázar has been closed as it awaits the installation of the Museo del Ejército (Army Museum), scheduled for 2007. The Alcázar is located at Calle General Moscardó 4. To get there climb the ramp off Cuesta de Carlos V, near Plaza de Zocodover. When it reopens, it is expected to retain its original hours, Tuesday through Sunday from 9:30 a.m. to 2:30 p.m. Admission is 2€ ($2.40), and it's free for E.U. residents on Wednesdays.
- **Getting to know El Greco.** Though the name of this museum, **Casa-Museo de El Greco** (☎ **925-22-44-05**), implies that El Greco actually lived here, he didn't. His actual home was destroyed long ago; this one merely resembles it. Although that sounds like a monumental tourist rip-off, the museum houses a hefty collection of El Greco's paintings, including one of a view of Toledo — but not the famous *View of Toledo,* which belongs to New York's Metropolitan Museum of Art. The museum is located at Calle Samuel Levi 3. It's 1 block south of Calle de Santo Tomé; take Travessía de Santo Tomé. Hours are Tuesday through Saturday from 10 a.m. to 1:45 p.m. and 4 to 6 p.m., and Sunday from 10 a.m. to 1:45 p.m. Admission is 2.40€ ($3), but it's free on Saturday afternoon and Sunday and also free for seniors.
- **Taking in another synagogue.** The 12th-century **Sinagoga de Santa María la Blanca** (☎ **925-22-72-57**), the oldest of ten that once existed in Toledo, is one of only two that remain. (See the Sinagoga del Tránsito review in the attractions section.) A national monument, it has a Christian name because it was taken over by the Catholic Church in 1405. The synagogue has classic horseshoe-shaped arches, similar to those of the landmark Córdoba Mosque (see Chapter 15). The surprising Moorish design is owed to the Muslim craftsmen who were commissioned to build it. The crafty Moors also built the synagogue so that it faces Mecca (luckily, in

the same direction as Jerusalem). The synagogue is at Calle de los Reyes Católicos 4, just down the street from (and east of) the San Juan de los Reyes monastery. It's open daily from 10 a.m. to 6 p.m. In summer it stays open until 7 p.m. Admission is 1.90€ ($2.40).

- **Walking through Puerta de Bisagra, the town gates.** This city has two Bisagra gates. The old gate, built in the 11th and 12th centuries, is the only one that remains of the original Muslim wall around Toledo. Its arch is clearly Moorish in style. The newer, Greco-Roman-style gate, just west of the original one, was completed in 1550. It's much grander and carries the Habsburg coat of arms (at the time, Spain was part of the Holy Roman Empire, ruled by the Habsburgs). The gate (either door no. 1 or door no. 2) is the best place to begin a walking tour of Toledo. Enter at the intersection of Calle del Cardenal Tavera and Avenida de la Cava (the city's north entrance).
- **Admiring a legendary mosque.** The **Mezquita de Cristo de la Luz,** built in the tenth century, is tricky to find but well worth the effort. The Moors built the square brick mosque, one of the oldest surviving in Spain, on the site of a Visigothic church. In fact, some original pillars remain, although molded into Moorish arches. The mosque's name, "Christ of the Light," is attributed to a legend of the military general El Cid, who, on his way into Toledo to seize it from the Moors, knelt in front of the mosque. Later, according to the story, a lamp illuminating a crucifix (said to be left by El Cid) was supposedly uncovered inside a wall of the mosque, where it had been burning for some 300 years. The mosque (☎ **925-25-41-91**) is at Calle del Cristo de la Luz, just inside the walled town from Puerta del Sol, across from Convento de Carmelitas. It's open daily from 10 a.m. to 7 p.m. (6 p.m. in winter); admission is 1.90€ ($2.40).

Shopping for local treasures

Toledo is a mecca for crafts shoppers. The city's distinctive black-and-gold damascene art, nearly as symbolic of Toledo as the Alcázar or the cathedral, is found everywhere within the Old Quarter. The art is an old Moorish practice of inlaying gold (and sometimes copper or silver) against a background of matte black steel. It's the rare tourist who doesn't go home with at least a ring, letter opener, or some other damascene souvenir. (If you're not impressed with the merchandise, the relentless sales pitches you encounter will certainly wear you down.) Damascene items can be handcrafted or machine-made. If it's cheap, it's machine-made; if you're looking for a heftier, better-crafted souvenir, visit one of Toledo's reputable shops that have artisans on the premises.

Toledo has also been known for its swords since the Middle Ages. Although swashbuckling tourists cart them off by the dozens, be warned that airport security considers them weapons. Embroidery from the small provincial towns of Lagartera and Oropesa is featured in many shops; embroidered blouses, napkins, and tablecloths make good gifts.

You may also want to look for local pottery and traditional blue-and-yellow ceramics from Talavera.

Damascene and swords

You can find great hand-forged swords and daggers at **Mariano Zamorano,** Calle Ciudad 19 (☎ **925-22-26-34**), a small factory where the craftsmanship is outstanding. Zamorano ships items pretty much anywhere in the world. **Braojos,** Arco de Palacio 5, and Comercio 44 (no phone), is one of the top places in Toledo for damascene objects and engravings. You won't find cheap machine-made stuff at **Casa Bermejo,** Calle Airosas 5 (☎ **925-22-03-46**). You will, however, find a disciplined team of artisans who, in addition to creating excellent gift items, also crank out ornamental swords and military dress items for West Point and the armies of several European countries. High-quality, hand-crafted damascene jewelry is available at **J.J. Simón Martín de la Fuente,** Calle Samuel Levi 3 (☎ **925-21-69-55**), a small and friendly shop where you can watch an artisan create intricate gold inlaid designs. If your tastes are grander than the key chains, letter openers, rings, and earrings you see everywhere in Toledo, check out **Felipe Suárez,** Paseo de los Canónigos 19 (☎ **925-22-56-15**). It has the entry-level goods, but its damascene artisans also create unique and very pricey art objects.

Marzipan

Pastelerías Santo Tomé is at Calle Santo Tomé 5 and Plaza Zocodover 7 (☎ **925-22-37-63**). Founded in 1856, Santo Tomé exports all over the world. **Casa Telesforo,** Plaza de Zocodover 13 (☎ **925-22-33-79**), is the oldest of the old-time marzipan factories, churning out highly decorative designs in sweet almond paste since 1806. **Pastelería Casado,** Cuesta del Alcázar 11 (☎ **925-22-37-34**), next to Plaza Zocodover, is a traditional Toledan bakery that has been in business since the 1950s. Look for a gift shop at the same address.

Living it up after dark

Toledo, noisy by day, really calms down after the tour buses leave. Early evening is a perfect time to explore the city's crooked streets and plazas. Two blocks west of the Alcázar, at Calle Trastamara 21, is a secluded patio with a trio of restaurants in an open-air patio. The best bar of the bunch is **El Corral de Diego Mesón.** If you're up for more than a walk around town, start near Plaza Zocodover and Calle Alfileritos and drop in on any of these *tascas* for tapas and drinks.

- **La Abadía,** Calle Núñez del Arce 1 (☎ **925-25-07-46**), a stylish bar-restaurant that serves a nice selection of foreign beers.
- **Ludeña,** Corral de Don Diego 10 (☎ **925-22-33-84**), a centrally located and popular tapas spot.
- **La Venta del Alma,** Carretera de Piedrabuena 35 (☎ **925-25-42-45**), housed in an ancient country house on the highway that leads from the *parador,* is popular with an over-30 crowd.

Fast Facts: Toledo

Area Code

Toledo's area code is **925,** which you must dial before every number.

Currency Exchange

ATMs are located around the Plaza Mayor. The Banco de España is on Calle de la Plata near the San Nicolás Church.

Emergencies

For all emergencies, dial ☎ **112.** For medical emergencies, call Ambulancias Cruz Roja, ☎ 925-22-22-22. The municipal hospital emergency number is ☎ **061.** For hospital information, call ☎ 925-26-92-00. For municipal police, ☎ **092.**

Information

The main tourism office is at Puerta de Bisagra, s/n, just outside the city walls (☎ 925-22-08-43; Mon–Fri 9 a.m.–6 p.m., Sat 9 a.m.–7 p.m., and Sun 9 a.m.–3 p.m.)

Police

Call ☎ **092.**

Post Office

Toledo's main post office is on Calle de la Plata 1 (☎ 925-22-36-11).

Part V

Southern Spain: Andalusia

"For tonight's modern reinterpretation of Carmen, those in the front row are kindly requested to wear raincoats."

In this part . . .

When most people close their eyes and dream of Spain, the evocative images of Andalusia probably spring to mind. The south is like an Iberian highlight film with accompanying soundtrack: bullfights in the searing sun, the passionate staccato rhythms of flamenco, and dark-haired beauties with flowers in their hair and polka dots on their twirling dresses. The classic landscape of parched mountains, rolling chestnut hills, and olive groves as far as the eye can see also produces some of Spain's quintessential savory treats: olive oil, gazpacho, sherry, and robust green olives.

Andalusia has so much to see and do that you could spend a lifetime there, not just a vacation. Its scenery includes stunning Moorish monuments, such as Granada's Alhambra and Córdoba's Great Mosque, sun-kissed white villages perched on gorges and mountain tops, the sultry charms of legendary Seville, and Spain's most developed stretch of beaches. Dismissed by some northern Spaniards as lazy hedonists, Andalusians — true, no strangers to crowded tapas joints and noisy bars — are unrepentant in their commitment to enjoying the riches of life in the south.

Chapter 15

Seville and Córdoba

In This Chapter

- Getting around Seville and Córdoba, two legendary Andalusian cities
- Keeping busy with festivals, monuments, museums, and bullfights
- Finding the best places to stay and dine
- Getting out of town: Side trips to Roman and Moorish ruins

The southern region of Andalusia, or Andalucía, is a land of intense summer heat, fiery Gypsy passion, and a sophisticated, if inscrutable, Muslim past. In other words: romantic Spain. In their heyday, the Moors (Arab and Berber conquerors of Spain) dominated almost all of Spain, but their empire took deepest root in the south, the heart of their empire, al-Andalus.

In Córdoba, the Moors built the Great Mosque, or Mezquita — which, along with the Alhambra in Granada (see Chapter 17), ranks as Muslim Spain's supreme achievement and legacy. By the tenth century, Córdoba had become Europe's most advanced and populous city, a capital of high culture and learning. Seville later became Spain's leading light in the 16th-century Golden Age, when riches from outposts in the Americas flowed back through the city via the Guadalquivir River, and great artists like Velázquez, Murillo, and Zurbarán created the flourishing Seville School.

The Old Quarter of each city is a pretty jumble of narrow alleyways lined with tiled portraits of saints and Madonnas, potted plants and bougainvillea, and refreshing interior patios. Seville is unmatched in Spain for ambience: It's the kind of place where the scent of orange trees and the joy of living, not just working, move people to lyrical odes. Córdoba is no longer the great city it once was, but it remains a fascinating, living, historical document. It's known as the city of patios for its flower-bedecked interior spaces, which are celebrated every May. Both cities continue to represent Spain at its most folkloric. Popular religious and secular celebrations are impossibly infectious, and the people are as radiant and nearly as warm as the blinding sun that beats down.

That sun in southern Spain is going to make you sweat: Seville and Córdoba are two of the hottest cities in Europe. Winter, though, is mild, and spring and fall are warm but comfortable. The best time to visit Seville and Córdoba is April and May, when flowers are in bloom and the famous festivals, including Easter Week, possess the locals and transform their cities (although this time is also the hardest to get a hotel room). If you can't make it then, fall and winter aren't bad, because the sun shines year-round. Unless you're a masochist, you're better off avoiding the sizzling summers.

Seville and Córdoba are within easy reach of Madrid, especially with the high-speed AVE train, which gets you to Seville in two-and-a-half hours (Córdoba's a stop along the way, one-and-a-half hours from Madrid).

Major Attractions in Seville and Córdoba

Seville and Córdoba form two of the three bases in Spain's southern triangle of Moorish influence (the other is Granada; see Chapter 17).

Seville

Conquered by the Romans and then the Moors, who ruled the city for more than 500 years, Seville lived a grand Golden Age in the arts during the 16th and 17th centuries, as the gateway to the Americas (and the benefactor of all that loot flowing down its river). Plenty of that history is on view, though the city's greatest attraction is perhaps its easygoing vibe and abundantly gregarious people that make it one of the most charming cities in Spain.

You can get a taste of Seville in just a couple of days, but it's the kind of place that you may want to return to over and over. Seville is well known for the following attractions: the **cathedral,** the world's largest Gothic edifice; **El Alcázar,** the fantastic fortress/royal residence where kings and queens entertained lovers and enemies; **Barrio de Santa Cruz,** the colorful, quintessential Andalusian neighborhood; **Parque de María Luisa** (Maria Luisa Park), a green oasis, lush enough to beat the heat; and Seville's unrivaled **spring festival season** — Easter and April Fair.

Córdoba

You may find it hard to believe that Córdoba was once Europe's most enlightened and populated city. When the rest of the continent sank into the Dark Ages, Muslim Córdoba soared ahead, with libraries, universities, mathematics, and sophisticated architecture and trade. But the city in which Jews and Christians lived alongside the Moors saw its best days long ago. Once a city of one million, the provincial capital today has scarcely 300,000 inhabitants — one of the few cities in the world to suffer so dramatic a population drop without an accompanying natural disaster.

Córdoba's former greatness, though, is instantly revealed when you slip behind the walls of the Great Mosque and are suddenly enveloped by one of the most awe-inspiring scenes in Europe: an unending horizon of overlapped, candy-cane-striped arches. In addition to the **Mezquita**

(Great Mosque) — one of Muslim Spain's great monuments — look for the **La Judería,** the old Jewish Quarter of whitewashed streets, lively bars, and artisans' shops, and Córdoba's spectacular flowered **patios** and May **festivals.**

Seville: City of Festivals

One of the most exuberant cities in Spain, Seville (known as Sevilla in Spanish) stimulates the senses. Boulevards are lined with orange trees, church bells overlap with the clop-clop of horses' hooves, and the smell of fresh flowers permeates small alleys. Seville has inspired artists and musicians like few other cities; from the art of passionate, soul-baring flamenco to operas like *Don Juan, Carmen,* and *The Marriage of Figaro,* Seville has always been a place to sing about.

Spain's fourth-largest city and one of its most sunbaked, Seville never seems in a hurry. *Sevillanos* have earned a reputation, deserved or not, for working less and socializing more than those in any other region in Spain. Locals love few things as much as gathering at bars with loud groups of friends and family for drinks and tapas. As an outsider, you may be inclined to believe that locals spend a good part of the day, and a good portion of their salary, just hanging out. But natives tell you that they simply know how to live better than the workaholics up north.

Perhaps it's that attitude, as well as the languid air of Andalusia, that makes foreigners adore Seville like few places in Spain. Americans are the number one group of tourists in Seville, ranking ahead of Germans, French, and Italians for the past decade. Along with Salamanca (see Chapter 14), Seville is also the most popular place for American college students to spend a semester or full academic year.

Getting there

Seville is accessible by air, train, and bus from all major points in Spain, but in all likelihood you'll cruise into Seville from another part of Andalusia or from Madrid. The easiest way is to glide in on the superfast AVE train, though if you're hopping around Spain by plane, flying into Seville is simple.

By train

Seville's AVE and regular train station is **Santa Justa,** Av. de Kansas City, s/n (☎ **902-24-02-02**), just north of downtown. Major car-rental agencies are all located at Santa Justa, so picking up a car after arriving in Seville by train is a snap. Ticket and information offices for RENFE, Spain's national railway, are located at Calle Zaragoza 29 (☎ **902-24-02-02;** `www.renfe.es`). Buses C1 and C2 go from the rail station to downtown Seville. A taxi costs about 6€ ($7.20).

Seville

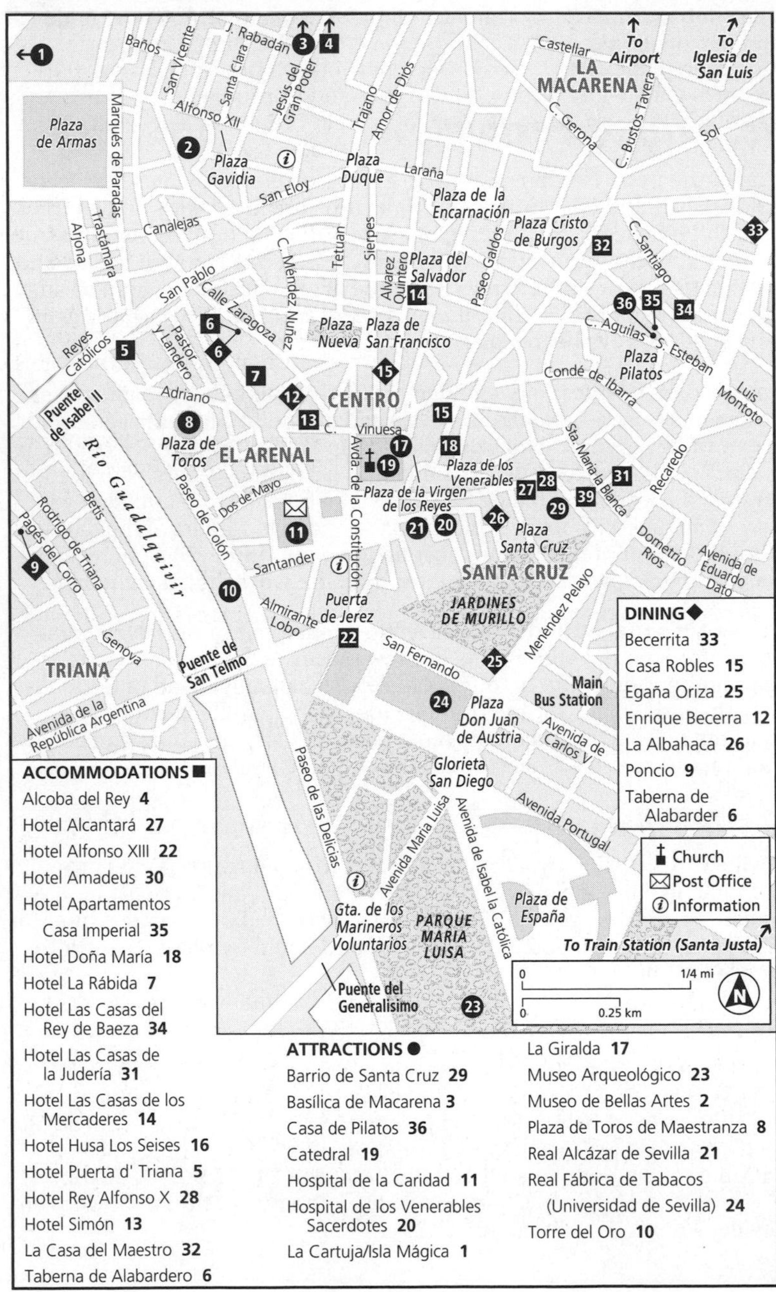

To Airport
To Iglesia de San Luís
LA MACARENA
Castellar
C. Gerona
C. Bustos Tavera
Sol
Baños
J. Rabadán
San Vicente
Santa Clara
Jesús del Gran Poder
Amor de Diós
Trajano
Alfonso XII
Marqués de Paradas
Plaza de Armas
Plaza Gavidia
Plaza Duque
Laraña
San Eloy
Plaza de la Encarnación
Plaza Cristo de Burgos
C. Santiago
Canalejas
Trastámara
Arjona
C. Méndez Nuñez
Tetuan
Sierpes
Alvarez Quintero
Plaza del Salvador
Paseo Galdos
San Pablo
Calle Zaragoza
Pastor y Landero
Reyes Católicos
Plaza Nueva
Plaza de San Francisco
C. Aguilas
S. Esteban
Plaza Pilatos
Condé de Ibarra
Luis Montoto
Adriano
CENTRO
C. Vinuesa
Puente de Isabel II
Plaza de Toros
EL ARENAL
Avda. de la Constitución
Plaza de los Venerables
Plaza de la Virgen de los Reyes
Sta. María la Blanca
Recaredo
Río Guadalquivir
Paseo de Colón
Dos de Mayo
Betis
Rodrigo de Triana
Pagés del Corro
Plaza Santa Cruz
Dometrio Rios
Avenida de Eduardo Dato
Santander
SANTA CRUZ
Almirante Lobo
Puerta de Jerez
JARDINES DE MURILLO
Menéndez Pelayo
Genova
TRIANA
Puente de San Telmo
San Fernando
Main Bus Station
Avenida de la República Argentina
Plaza Don Juan de Austria
Avenida de Carlos V
Glorieta San Diego
Paseo de las Delicias
Avenida Portugal
Avenida María Luisa
Avenida de Isabel la Católica
Plaza de España
Gta. de los Marineros Voluntarios
PARQUE MARIA LUISA
Puente del Generalísimo
To Train Station (Santa Justa)
0 1/4 mi
0 0.25 km
N
Church
Post Office
Information
DINING
Becerrita 33
Casa Robles 15
Egaña Oriza 25
Enrique Becerra 12
La Albahaca 26
Poncio 9
Taberna de Alabarder 6
ACCOMMODATIONS
Alcoba del Rey 4
Hotel Alcantará 27
Hotel Alfonso XIII 22
Hotel Amadeus 30
Hotel Apartamentos Casa Imperial 35
Hotel Doña María 18
Hotel La Rábida 7
Hotel Las Casas del Rey de Baeza 34
Hotel Las Casas de la Judería 31
Hotel Las Casas de los Mercaderes 14
Hotel Husa Los Seises 16
Hotel Puerta d' Triana 5
Hotel Rey Alfonso X 28
Hotel Simón 13
La Casa del Maestro 32
Taberna de Alabardero 6
ATTRACTIONS
Barrio de Santa Cruz 29
Basílica de Macarena 3
Casa de Pilatos 36
Catedral 19
Hospital de la Caridad 11
Hospital de los Venerables Sacerdotes 20
La Cartuja/Isla Mágica 1
La Giralda 17
Museo Arqueológico 23
Museo de Bellas Artes 2
Plaza de Toros de Maestranza 8
Real Alcázar de Sevilla 21
Real Fábrica de Tabacos (Universidad de Sevilla) 24
Torre del Oro 10

Unless you're coming from small towns in Andalusia, where train service is infrequent, I recommend the more comfortable trains over buses, especially in the heat of the south. The fastest and easiest way to get to Seville from either Madrid or Córdoba is the **AVE high-speed train.** It's a little more expensive than slower trains, but oh how it sails. It makes the trip to Seville, with stops in Ciudad Real and Córdoba, in about two-and-a-half hours. The one-way fare from Madrid is 70€ ($84). The trip to/from Córdoba takes about 45 minutes and costs 22€ ($26).

The AVE train from Madrid and Córdoba to Seville flies like a bird (not coincidentally, because that's what *ave* means in Spanish), and although it's the most expensive regular train service in Spain, it's also one of Europe's fastest and most comfortable. Making the trip even more tempting, certain trips and age categories can save you money on the AVE. A round-trip ticket saves you 20 percent; a round-trip ticket for travel on the same day saves you 25 percent. Children ages 4 through 11 get a 40 percent discount, and seniors get 25 percent off.

If you can't catch the AVE, or if you want to save a few euros, hop aboard an **Altaria** train (fast but not lightning fast like the AVE) from Madrid. It takes a little more than three hours and costs 55€ ($66).

By plane

Seville's international airport, the work of the famed architect Rafael Moneo, is **Aeropuerto Internacional San Pablo,** Autopista de San Pablo, s/n (☎ **95-498-82-07**). The national airlines of several European countries fly into Seville, and daily flights arrive on Iberia from Madrid, Barcelona, Bilbao, and Valencia (Air Europa flies to Seville from Barcelona). The airport is 12km (7 miles) north of Seville, on National Highway IV. The **Tourism Information Office** (☎ **95-444-91-28**) is open daily from 9 a.m. to 8 p.m.

From the airport to downtown, you can take an airport bus (☎ **902-21-03-17;** 2.10€/$2.50), a relatively short ride that goes to Alfonso XIII Hotel, on Puerta de Jerez. A taxi from the airport to the zona centro (anywhere near the cathedral) costs about 15€ ($18).

By bus

Seville has two major bus terminals: **Estación Plaza de Armas,** Av. del Cristo de la Expiración, s/n (☎ **95-490-80-40**), for travels throughout Spain (including the province of Huelva); and **Estación Prado de San Sebastián,** Calle Manuel Vázquez Sagastizabal, s/n (☎ **95-441-71-11**), for all other destinations in Andalusia. **Alsina** buses (☎ **95-441-88-11;** `www.alsinagraells.es`) travel to and from the Prado station to Córdoba and Granada. Alsina also makes the trip to Málaga. **Los Amarillos** buses go to Ronda (☎ **95-498-91-84**) from Prado. **Comes** (☎ **95-441-68-58**) buses depart from the Prado station to Cádiz.

For bus schedules and information, call ☎ **95-442-00-11,** or visit www.turismo.sevilla.org/paginas_en/bus.asp.

By car

Spain's big cities aren't great places to deal with wheels, so if you're just traveling to Seville (and Córdoba and Granada), and not planning on touring the surrounding country, you could skip renting a car. Driving to Seville from Madrid, take the N-IV (E-5), which veers right (west) at Bailén and passes through Córdoba. The easy trip is all highway from Madrid, but it takes more than five hours, depending on stops and your willingness to do as the Spaniards do and flout speed limits. The A-92 highway connects Seville with Granada and the Costa del Sol. For roadside assistance, call ☎ **900-12-35-05.**

Orienting yourself in Seville

Seville is divided in two by the Guadalquivir River. The city's historic center, which includes the cathedral, Barrio de Santa Cruz, and just about all the sights you want to see, is on the east side of the river.

Introducing the neighborhoods

Though Seville is a large and complex city, the neighborhoods of interest to visitors are easy to get a handle on. The **Old City** grew up around the city's major monuments, which are among the most important in Andalusia: the Cathedral and Giralda Tower; the Reales Alcázares palace-fortress; and, immediately to its east, the **Barrio de Santa Cruz,** which is the ancient Jewish Quarter. Parque María Luisa, the major green space in the city, is south of here.

The major avenues running through the Old City are Avenida de la Constitución and Calle Sierpes. The ***zona centro,*** or modern center of Seville, proceeds outward from the Old City. The working-class, thoroughly authentic barrio **Triana** is across the Quadalquivir River, as is **La Cartuja,** site of the 1992 World Expo. On the river's banks is the Torre del Oro, a 13th-century cylindrical defense tower and one of Seville's enduring landmarks that was once completely sheathed in glimmering golden tiles (hence the name, meaning Tower of Gold).

Finding information after you arrive

The main **Andalusia Tourism Information Office** is located just down the street from the Cathedral, Av. de la Constitución 21B (☎ 95-422-14-04). You can find others at the **San Pablo Airport** (☎ 95-444-91-28) and **Santa Justa Train Station** (☎ 95-453-76-26). They're open daily from 9 a.m. to 8 p.m. **Municipal tourism offices** are at Plaza de la Concordia, s/n, in front of the Puente de Triana (☎ 902-19-48-97), Plaza de San Francisco 19 (☎ 954-59-52-88), and Paseo de las Delicias 9 (☎ 95-423-44-65).

Getting around Seville

Though Seville is large, the principal areas of interest to most visitors make up a compact, walkable area. The Barrio de Santa Cruz, one of Seville's most enchanting neighborhoods, is almost entirely pedestrian. Almost all the hotels I recommend are within walking distance of the major sights. You really only need public transportation or a taxi to the airport or train station, or in the evening if you want to go over to Triana, across the river, to check out the bars, restaurants, and live music clubs there.

By taxi

Taxis usually line up on Avenida de la Constitución outside the cathedral. You can also hail one anywhere on the street. To call a cab, call **Radio Taxi** (☎ **95-480-00-00**) or **Tele-Taxi Sevilla** (☎ **95-462-22-22**).

By car

If you have time to explore the region, Andalusia is one of the best places in Spain to rent a car and roll through the countryside or along the coast (see Chapter 16). The major agencies in Seville are

- **Avis,** Av. de la Constitución 15 (☎ **95-444-91-22**)
- **Europcar,** Av. Luis de Morales, s/n (☎ **95-425-42-98**)
- **Hertz,** Av. República Argentina 3 (☎ **95-427-88-87**)
- **Thrifty,** Fernando IV 3 (☎ **95-427-81-84**)

By bus

You have little need to take a bus after you've arrived in Seville, although it comes in handy for getting to the train station, **Santa Justa** (see "By train," earlier in this chapter). Bus nos. 32, C-1, and C-2 go between downtown and the train station. For bus information, call ☎ **955-99-92-90.** A single fare on the city buses costs 1€ ($1.20); a "Bonobús" pass good for ten trips costs 5.15€ ($6.20).

Staying in style

Seville is one of the best places to stay in Spain. Several hotels positively drip with local character and offer comparatively reasonable rates (though prices across Seville have steadily crept up in the last few years). All the hotels I recommend here are conveniently located within walking distance of most major sites in the old center of romantic Seville. (Several faceless international hotels are available as well, but for the most part they're removed from what you're going to Seville to see, and so I don't include them.)

If you arrive in town without a reservation, check out **INFHOR,** a private organization that has a kiosk in the Santa Justa train station and that maintains relationships with several dozen hotels in Seville. They'll show you brochures, make suggestions in your price range, and then call and make a reservation for you (at no cost to you; hotels pay a commission).

Note that prices rise significantly (as much as double) during Seville's famous Semana Santa (Holy Week) and Feria de Abril (April Fair) celebrations — basically, two weeks a year (see the "Fiesta time! Seville's popular festivals" box in this chapter). The high end of the rates in the following section reflects those increases (but, because those rates distort the overall picture, I don't base the dollar-sign ratings on those special rates). If you intend on coming to Seville for either celebration, make your reservations very early — as much as a year (that's right, one year) in advance, especially for the choicest spots that I mention in the hotel listings.

The top hotels

Alcoba del Rey

$$$ Zona Centro

A boutique hotel that embraces Andalusia's Moorish past, sometimes right up to the edge of kitsch, this is the place to rest your head if you're fond of the Moroccan teahouse aesthetic. Next door to the Macarena Basilica — a bit removed from some of the major sights in Seville — and a red-and-white colonial facade is an explosion of brilliant Moorish color, textures, and details. The 15 rooms are placed around a lovely central patio and spiral staircase. Bathrooms are stucco and marble, and queen-size beds are of carved wood and have beautiful and bold silk bedding. My favorite rooms are Princesa Wallada, with a delightful painted Moorish ceiling and four balconies, and Beatriz de Suabia, which may have you playing caliph for a night. As a bonus, or perhaps a burden, if you like the furnishings, or even the rugs, everything is available for purchase.

See map p. 376. Bécquer 9. Next to Basilica de La Macarena. ☎ ***954-91-58-00.*** *Fax: 95-491-56-75.* `www.alcobadelrey.com`. *Parking: 15€ ($18). Rack rates: 85€–200€ ($102–$240) double. Holy Week, Easter, and Feria de Abril: 204€–259€ ($245–$311). AE, DC, MC, V.*

Hotel Alfonso XIII

$$$$$ Old City

This Old World classic will break the bank, but if you have a bank to break, it's the place to do it. The finest and most famous hotel in Seville, the historic Alfonso XIII (Alfonso "*treh*-theh") ranks right up there with Madrid's Ritz and Palace — one of Spain's most distinguished and storied hostelries. When Princess Elena got married in Seville a few years back, she and the entire Royal Family stayed here. A beautiful, imposing structure with the city's most prestigious address, it has opulent halls with marble floors, carved wooden ceilings, and Moorish arches and tiles. The 146 rooms are appropriately regal, as are the gardens and magnificent pool, but this indulgent palace isn't for everyone. As the kind of place where the rich and famous drop in and expect to be treated with deference, it seems a bit stilted and snooty to me, but it's undeniably luxurious. The Alfonso XIII is a Westin and Starwood property — perfect for those who've earned a ton of hotel points and want to blow them.

See map p. 376. San Fernando 2. At Puerta de Jerez, junction of Avenida Constitución and San Fernando; near Parque María Luisa. ☎ ***800-325-3535*** *or 888-625-5144 in the United States, in Spain 95-491-70-00. Fax: 95-491-70-99.* `www.hotel-alfonsoxiii.com`. *Parking: 14€ ($17). Rack rates: 534€–566€ ($641–$679) double. Easter and Feria de Abril: 598€–698€ ($718–$838). Weekend rates available. AE, DC, MC, V.*

Hotel Apartamentos Casa Imperial

$$$$–$$$$$ Edge of Old City

Calling this impeccable retreat an aparthotel — a Spanish term that implies cheesy kitchenettes and bad carpeting — seems absurd because nothing is further from the truth. Sure, all rooms have small kitchens and some have small living areas, but this is a refined version, and a great hotel solution for people wanting space and privacy. With four plant-filled, interior patios, brilliantly tiled staircases, small pools and fountains that kids will love, and boldly painted rooms, Casa Imperial is one of a kind. Near the Casa Pilatos, this 15th-century palace (which incredibly belonged to the *butler* of the Marquis of Tarifa) is charming and intimate with great personal attention. As hard as it is to believe that Casa Imperial lies in the middle of bustling Seville, the hotel is perfectly in tune with the city's romanticism. Because the hotel is owned by a joint Spanish and German initiative, the 24 apartments are popular with Germans.

See map p. 376. Calle Imperial 29. One block north of Plaza Pilatos, off San Estéban; northeast of the Cathedral. ☎ ***95-450-03-00.*** *Fax: 95-450-03-30.* `www.casaimperial.com`. *Parking: 18€ ($22). Rack rates: 200€–250€ ($240–$300) double, breakfast buffet included. Holy Week, Easter, and Feria de Abril: 350€ ($420). AE, DC, MC, V.*

Hotel Las Casas de la Judería

$$$ Barrio de Santa Cruz

Secluded at the end of a small alley off the edge of the Santa Cruz neighborhood — the former Jewish enclave, la Judería — this is one of the best value hotels in Spain. But the secret's out. The place is packed year-round, so book a room early. The hotel occupies a 17th-century palace of the Duke of Béja, the patron of Cervantes (the Duke actually owned a series of mansions here). The brightly painted palace — brilliant *sevillano* yellows, whites, and blues — has a series of tranquil interior patios with gurgling fountains. The 57 rooms are impressively appointed, and are all different from one another. They have handsome antique furnishings, and many have four-poster beds and small living rooms. Service is top-notch, although it can get a little hectic at check-in and check-out times. The sister property, **Hotel Las Casas de los Mercaderes,** is very similar in style and a good alternative if this one, among the most popular hotels in Seville, is full.

See map p. 376. Plaza Santa María la Blanca/Callejón de Dos Hermanas 7. Difficult to find; near the church of Santa María la Blanca, on northeast border of Santa Cruz, down a tiny alleyway. ☎ ***95-441-51-50.*** *Fax: 95-442-21-70.* `www.intergrouphoteles.com`. *Parking: 15€ ($18). Rack rates: 135€–168€ ($162–$202) double. Holy Week, Easter, and Feria de Abril: 265€ ($318). AE, DC, MC, V.*

Hotel Las Casas de los Mercaderes

$$$ Zona Centro

Another in a winning family of character-driven Seville hotels in atmospheric palaces, this hotel is a little smaller and only the slightest bit more exclusive than its sister, Las Casas de la Judería. In the city's commercial center, between Plazas San Francisco and El Salvador, it's only minutes away from the cathedral. The 47 rooms in this handsome white mansion with yellow- and blue-trimmed windows are set back from the street on a small courtyard. The rooms are impeccably decorated; many have small balconies overlooking the perfect 18th-century Andalusian patio. Guests are equal parts business travelers and vacationers.

See map p. 376. Calle Alvarez Quintero. Three blocks north of Cathedral, between Plazas El Salvador and San Francisco. ☎ ***95-422-58-58.*** *Fax: 95-422-98-84. Internet:* `www.intergrouphoteles.com`. *Parking: 15€ ($18). Rack rates: 112€–140€ ($134–$168) double. Holy Week, Easter, and Feria de Abril: 230€ ($276). AE, DC, MC, V.*

Hotel Las Casas del Rey de Baeza

$$$ Zona Centro

Recently purchased by the Epoque Hotel group — it was formerly owned by the same people with the other "Casa" hotels in Seville — this luxury boutique hotel has gotten an additional injection of chic style. In a residential neighborhood near the Casa Pilatos (see the review later in this chapter), it's just a tad removed from the tourist hordes but still within walking distance of the cathedral and Santa Cruz district. The 41 spacious and warmly appointed rooms have large, modern, marble bathrooms, and a number of them feature living rooms. Rooms are on three levels around a lovely central courtyard of this 18th-century converted mansion. And if those views aren't enough for you on a warm Seville day, try the ones from the adorable rooftop pool.

See map p. 376. Plaza Cristo de la Redención. Off Calle Santiago, between Corral del Conde and Casa Pilatos. ☎ ***95-456-14-96.*** *Fax: 95-456-14-41.* `www.epoquehotels.com/hospescasasdelrey.html`. *Parking: 15€ ($18). Rack rates: 185€–235€ ($222–$282) double. Holy Week, Easter, and Feria de Abril: 300€ ($360). AE, DC, MC, V.*

Luxury on the outskirts of town

If you're willing to stay outside Seville, and if you're in the mood for true Andalusian luxury, **Hacienda Benazuza** is the place. In Sanlúcar la Major, about 16km (10 miles) from Seville, this sprawling estate was an Arab country house in the tenth century and then a luxurious farmhouse perched on a hill of olive groves. Today it's one of the finest hotels in Spain (with prices to match), a rustic palace with splendidly manicured gardens, Moorish pools and fountains, and palm-tree-lined patios. The elegant guest rooms overflow with Old World style and color. The Michelin two-star gourmet restaurant, La Alquería, is one of the best in the country and a true destination for gastronomes, with spectacularly innovative dishes straight from the unique mind and laboratory of Ferran Adrià of the famous El Bulli restaurant in Cataluña. Even if you don't stay here, a meal, although very expensive (tasting menu: 100€/$120), ranks as perhaps the top dining experience in southern Spain. To get there from Seville, follow the signs for Huelva and go south on the A-49 highway; take exit No. 6.

The hotel is at Virgen de las Nieves, s/n, on a hillside above the little agrarian hamlet of Sanlúcar la Mayor. ☎ **95-570-33-44.** Fax: 95-570-34-10. www.elbullihotel.com. Free parking. Rack rates: 330€nd350€ ($396–$420). Four nights' minimum stay required during Semana Santa and Feria de Abril (412€–433€, or $494–$520). AE, DC, MC, V. Closed August.

La Casa del Maestro
$$$ Zona Centro

A charming house that once belonged to a flamenco guitar legend, this warm and handsome small hotel (with just 12 rooms) opened in 2001; it's one of the best and most intimate options in the city, and one of the best deals, too. It exudes authentic Seville flavor. The rooms, which all carry names like "El Emigrante" and "Gaditanas," are lovingly decorated without being pretentious or frilly. Photographs and objects related to the Maestro's music career and fascination with bullfighting fill the common areas. Although it's some distance from the city's major attractions, the house sits on a tiny pedestrian alleyway and has a beautiful rooftop deck, ideal for relaxing, reading, and having breakfast.

See map p. 376. Almudena 5. Between Alhondiga and Fco. Carrión, near Iglesia de Santa Catalina. ☎ ***95-450-00-07.*** *Fax: 95-450-00-06.* www.lacasadelmaestro.com. *Parking: Nearby 15€ ($18). Rack rates: 100€–116€ ($137–$139) double. Holy Week, Easter, and Feria de Abril: 186€ ($223).AE, DC, MC, V.*

Taberna del Alabardero
$$$ Zona Centro

Consider yourself lucky if you score one of the seven doubles at this exquisite little place. Forget about Easter and April Fair because they're booked at least two years in advance, but as long as you don't plan on scoring a room then, you may luck out. It's a meticulously restored 19th-century mansion that belonged to the poet J. Antonio Cavestany. The hotel features a gorgeous, arcaded central patio, where breakfast and afternoon coffee are served. The rooms, on the third floor of the mansion, are named for places in Spain. They're all top-of-the-line elegant, with rich fabrics, bold flower patterns, and hot tubs, though each is different from the next in configuration and decoration. As you may expect in a place so small, the service is very personal and friendly. If that isn't enough, the restaurant by the same name is one of the city's finest (see the review, below).

See map p. 376. Zaragoza 20. Four blocks northwest of the cathedral, near Maestranza bullfighting ring. ☎ ***95-450-27-21.*** *Fax: 95-456-36-66.* www.tabernadelalabardero.com. *Parking: 15€ ($18). Rack rates: 130€–190€ ($156–$228) double. Holy Week, Easter, and Feria de Abril: 250€ ($300) double. AE, DC, MC, V.*

Seville's runner-up hotels

With the exception of Hotel Doña María and Hotel Los Seises, all the following small hotels represent good bargains.

Hotel Alcántara

$$ **Santa Cruz** A small hotel with modern but plain monochromatic rooms, it isn't as nice as the Amadeus or several others in Santa Cruz, but worth a look if those are full. *See map p. 376. Ximénez de Enciso 28.* ☎ ***95-450-05-95.*** www.hotelalcantara.net.

Hotel Amadeus

$$ **Santa Cruz** This charming, small hotel, in an 18th-century manor house in the heart of Santa Cruz, is relatively new but opts for older-style rooms, which are very nicely decorated (some have touches such as exposed brick walls). It also has a splendid deck with great views. Overall, the Amadeus is a good deal. *See map p. 376. Farnesio 6.* ☎ ***95-450-14-43.*** www.hotelamadeussevilla.com.

Hotel Doña María

$$–$$$ **Old City** This small family hotel is a good alternative if you don't mind frilly bedspreads and curtains; it has a nice terrace with a small pool and dreamy views. It's also right across the plaza from the giant cathedral, at the heart of Seville. Kids can watch the horses line up with their carriages along the plaza. But compared to other small hotels in Seville, it's overpriced. *See map p. 376. Don Remondo 19.* ☎ ***95-422-49-90.*** www.hdmaria.com.

Hotel Husa Los Seises

$$$–$$$$ **Old City** On a small street behind the cathedral, Los Seises (*say*-sehs) has one of Seville's quintessential views. From the rooftop pool, the cathedral tower is just a few hundred yards away. A former 16th-century palace, it has been updated with touches of modernity. Rooms are well-appointed and very large, with foyers and sunken sitting areas. *See*

map p. 376. Segovias 6 (two blocks north of the cathedral, off Placentines). ☎ ***95-422-94-95.*** www.hotellosseises.com.

Hotel La Rábida

$$ Old City This former 19th-century *casa noble* (aristocratic mansion), on a quiet street, is a real find in the inexpensive category. *See map p. 376. Castelar 24 (four blocks west of the cathedral).* ☎ ***95-422-09-60.***

Hotel Rey Alfonso X

$$ Santa Cruz This small, sleek hotel is nicely decorated and well located, right next to the Plaza Santa María la Blanca and the atmospheric Barrio de Santa Cruz. It's a pretty good deal for the location. *See map p. 376. Ximénez de Enciso 35.* ☎ ***95-421-00-70.*** www.reyalfonsox.com.

Hotel Simón

$$ Old City A former 18th-century private mansion, this is Seville's best budget hotel — important if you're bringing the whole family. It has elegant public rooms, a beautiful interior courtyard, and a stately dining room. Rooms are all different from one another and have nice antiques; the place is frequently full. *See map p. 376. García de Vinuesa 19 (two blocks west of the cathedral).* ☎ ***95-422-66-60.*** www.hotelsimonsevilla.com.

Dining out

The natural division in Seville is between restaurants that offer a sit-down dinner and those that are more informal *tapas* (appetizer) joints. At many of the latter, there's no rule against sitting down — if you're lucky enough to score a coveted seat — but it's an entirely different way of assembling a meal. I love snacking my way across Spain, but the joy of eating at bars and restaurant counters and front rooms in Seville is something special. Even the sit-down places have tapas bars in front, so if you arrive at one and it looks dead or too pricey, go with Plan B, tapas.

For more on Spanish dining customs, including mealtimes, costs, and tipping, see Chapter 2.

Eating and drinking like a Sevillano

Fried foods, cold soups, and slightly chilled aperitif wines rule the day in all of Andalusia, but particularly in Seville. The best way to beat the heat is with a cold bowl of gazpacho, a chilled tomato soup. *Pescaíto frito,* deep-fried fish, is served in nearly every bar and restaurant. As in Madrid, the pursuit of tapas and *copas* (all-hours snacking and drinking, respectively) is a local institution, but Andalusians insist that they invented the art of eating tapas. The *tapeo* (tapas crawl) in Seville and Córdoba is a joyous affair like nowhere else in Spain. Andalusian aperitif wines — *jerez* (sherry), from just south of Seville, and *montilla* (mohn-*tee*-yah), a splendid dry wine from Córdoba — are superb.

Enjoying the top restaurants for a sit-down meal

Becerrita
$$$–$$$$ Zona Centro ANDALUSIAN

A classic Seville restaurant with a faithful clientele, this old-style place has the requisite small tapas bar up front and a couple of partitioned, clubby dining rooms. Patrons feasts on *merluza Puerta de Carmona,* hake served with musrooms, Iberian ham, and prawns. If you're not up for being part of the boys' club, sit at the bar and sample some of the imaginative tapas, such as crepes stuffed with foie gras in orange sauce, or white asparagus mousse. Tapas and main dish specials are featured daily. For a special experience try one of the pre-fixe menus, one of which is geared toward wine tasting.

*See map p. 376. Recaredo 9. ☎ **95-441-20-57.** Reservations recommended. Main courses: 14€–27€ ($14–$29). Pre-fixe menus 40€–65€ ($48–$78). AE, DC, MC, V. Open: Mon–Sat lunch and dinner, Sun lunch only. Closed: Last two weeks in Aug.*

Casa Robles
$$$ Zona Centro ANDALUSIAN

Going strong since the 1950s, Casa Robles is as unpretentious and straightforward as its name, which means oak house. Focusing on fresh, top-quality meat, fish, and vegetables, the Robles brothers maintain their place among Seville's traditional, elite restaurants. The family-owned place has an enthusiastic following among locals, and it always seems to be bustling. The fresh fish always looks good; check out *lubina con naranjas* (sea bass with *sevillana* oranges), or hake with clams and Serrano ham.

*See map p. 376. Alvarez Quintero 58. Two blocks north of the cathedral. ☎ **95-456-32-72.** Reservations recommended. Main courses: 12€–20€ ($14–$24). Menú del día: 25€ ($30). Tasting menu: 36€ ($43). AE, DC, MC, V. Open: Daily lunch and dinner.*

Egaña Oriza
$$$$–$$$$$ Zona Centro BASQUE/INTERNATIONAL

If you're only visiting southern Spain and you don't have a chance to sample authentic Basque cooking anywhere else, make a beeline here. And if you've come directly from Bilbao, you may have even more reason to check out Seville's best Basque restaurant, which just happens to be its top-rated dining room. A husband-and-wife team, including the renowned chef José Mari Egaña, operates this swank place, in a building that dates to 1926 and is cater-cornered from the city's most prestigious hotel, the Alfonso XIII. The stylishly decorated restaurant, in a restored mansion just off the Murillo Gardens, is as inspired as the menu. If you get a chance to dine here, start off with *salmorejo* (the thick Cordovan version of gazpacho) with oysters and serrano jam and follow it up with *lubina con crema de patata al azafrán* (silky sea bass with a saffron-potato cream sauce). Savory game and meats, such as duck and wild boar, are given interesting accents, including wild cherries, plums, figs, and apple puree.

See map p. 376. San Fernando 41. At entrance to Murillo Gardens. ☎ ***95-422-72-11.*** *Reservations required. Main courses: 20€–58€ ($24–$35). Menú del día: 48€ ($58). Tasting menu: 60€ ($72). AE, DC, MC, V. Open: Mon–Fri lunch and dinner, Sat dinner only, bar daily 9 a.m. to midnight. Closed: Aug.*

Enrique Becerra

$$$–$$$$ Zona Centro ANDALUSIAN

At this friendly place just around the corner from Plaza Nueva and Seville's cathedral, even first-time visitors are welcomed like members of the regular crew, and it has a slew of regulars. A cozy spot that feels more like a tavern than a restaurant, it has got a hopping tapas bar (with stools!) in front with an impossible-to-choose-from lineup of clams, stuffed mushrooms, and more, and an attractive back dining room with deep yellow walls, dark beams, and leaded glass. If you sit down, you can try crispy codfish with asparagus sauce, or roast lamb covered with honey and stuffed with spinach and pine nuts. The wine cellar is one of Seville's most select.

See map p. 376. Gamazo 2. Three blocks west of the cathedral, off Castelar in El Arenal district. ☎ ***95-421-30-49.*** *Reservations recommended. Main courses: 12€–21€ ($14–$24). Menú del día: 37€–43€ ($44–$52). AE, DC, MC, V. Open: Mon–Sat lunch and dinner.*

La Albahaca

$$$–$$$$ Barrio de Santa Cruz BASQUE/FRENCH

One of the prettiest restaurants on the prettiest square in the prettiest neighborhood in Seville, La Albahaca has a lot going for it. It's in a lovely Andalusian mansion, built in the 1920s, with several dining rooms, a terrace, lots of greenery, and colorful tiles. Because of its location, it gets the upscale tourists, who enjoy the Basque chef's crepes stuffed with mushrooms and foie gras in Port wine sauce, and great salads for starters. You can choose partridge braised in sherry or beef sirloin with foie gras for the main course, among many other options.

See map p. 376. Plaza de Santa Cruz 12. Several blocks east of the cathedral, in heart of Santa Cruz district. ☎ ***95-422-07-14.*** *Reservations recommended. Main courses: 15€–30€ ($17–$36). Menú del día: 24€ ($29). AE, DC, MC, V. Open: Mon–Sat lunch and dinner.*

Poncio

$$$–$$$$ Triana ANDALUSIAN/SPANISH

This distinguished, sedate restaurant is a welcome find. It's on the other side of the river in Triana, where you're more likely to find mass-market fish restaurants and tapas bars. It has a clubby atmosphere, with deep red, earthy walls, black beamed ceilings, red tile floors, and black-framed oil paintings. Service is excellent and the food is prepared in simple, elegant fashion, with such dishes as oxtail cannelloni and *arroz de setas* (similar to mushroom risotto).

See map p. 376. Victoria 8. ☎ ***95-434-00-10.*** *Reservations recommended. Main courses: 13€–24€ ($16–$29). Tasting menu: 45€ ($54). AE, MC, V. Open: Mon–Sat lunch and dinner.*

Taberna del Alabardero

$$$$ Zona Centro SPANISH

If you're lucky enough to secure a coveted room at this tiny hotel (reviewed earlier in this chapter), you can saunter downstairs to dine at one of the city's hottest restaurants. Even if you're not sleeping here, though, you can eat alongside the king, president, and just about everybody else. In a sumptuous 19th-century palace with dark wood, mirrors, and oil paintings, the restaurant boasts five dining rooms (four private, for all those famous folks). The kitchen is the work of the owner, Luis Lezama, who is also a priest, and the head chef, Juan Marcos. The menu is eclectic, offering such delicacies as red fruit soup with mascarpone cheese, Sanlúcar prawn carpaccio, lamb sweetbreads, and tournedos of fresh cod. Every year in February, the restaurant celebrates its utter Spanishness with *semana de arroz* — rice week, which glorifies the art of paella (a casserole of rice, seafood, and meat). Though the restaurant has won a national gastronomy prize and is one of the most ballyhooed restaurants in Seville, I have occasionally felt it a little uninspired and stodgy.

See map p. 376. Zaragoza 20. Four blocks northwest of the cathedral, near Maestranza bullfighting ring. ☎ ***95-450-27-21.*** *Reservations required. Main courses: 20€–30€ ($24–$36). Tasting menu: 39€ ($47). AE, DC, MC, V. Open: Daily lunch and dinner. Closed: Aug.*

Experiencing the best tapas bars

If you've been to other Spanish cities by the time you stroll into Seville (or read the other dining sections of this book), you know that tapas are a fundamental feature of the Spanish dining scene. But in Seville, tapas amount to a joyous popular religion. They aren't as fancy and filling as they are in the Basque Country, but they're hands down the best way to get a handle on Seville. Feasting on tapas is also a great way to get to know the charming, universally friendly Sevillanos who delight in nothing as much as popping into bars — sampling squid, prawns, blood sausage, and cured ham along with a great aperitif wine like a *fino* (dry sherry) — and chatting up bartenders and newly made friends.

I've spent days in Seville without ever so much as sitting down to a proper meal — but I always ate exceedingly well. Sevillanos often set out on *tapeos* just prior to regular mealtimes and continue until midnight or later — basically, until the bars run out. Even breakfast (*tostadas* — toast, with pate or *sobrassada* sausage spread) is just another excuse for hitting tapas bars. Meals at tapas bars generally fall into the inexpensive or moderate range ($–$$).

Hamming it up

Spaniards are wild about ham; *jamón serrano* (cured ham) pretty much qualifies as a national obsession. But Spaniards go absolutely crazy over *pata negra* (sweet cured ham named for its source, the black-hoofed Iberian pig) and especially *jamón de Jabugo.* Jabugo, a tiny town in the mountains of Andalusia, in the province of Huelva, is famed for producing the most delectable cured ham in all Spain. Aficionados of Iberian ham — dry and sliced razor thin — claim that *jamón serrano* is Spain's greatest delicacy. As such, it doesn't come cheap; a *ración* (portion) of thin shavings of the stuff can cost as much as 20€, or $24. Check out **Casa Ruiz,** Francos 59, a tapas bar specializing in its own *pata negra* and other ham products (☎ **95-422-86-24**).

Kids are sure to love this form of eating (all snacking, all the time), though you may have to pick and choose carefully among the tapas (octopus and small fried fish that one eats whole, head and all, may not go over so well).

The best way to dive into a Seville-style *tapeo* (tapas crawl) is to choose a barrio, loosen your belt, and start eating. To wash it all down, ask for a *caña* (*kah*-nyah, draft beer), a *manzanilla* (deliciously dry sherry), or a *vino tinto* or *vino blanco* (red or white wine, respectively). Though tapas bars are all over the city, I suggest only those from three neighborhoods that are particularly ripe for snacking: Triana, Santa Cruz, and Zona Centro.

In Triana

Tourists seldom visit this rambling neighborhood across the Guadalquivir River. Too bad, because they're missing some of Seville's best tapas spots, as locals well know. Check out these great tapas locations.

- **Kiosco de las Flores,** Betis, s/n (☎ **95-433-38-98**), lost its decades-old location wedged into the Triana Bridge; it's now next door to Rio Grande. A rarity, it has outdoor tables with terrific views. Locals fill up on full *raciones* of *jamón de Jabugo* (see the "Hamming it up" box, earlier in this chapter). But the fish is the specialty; try *coquinas* (tiny sautéed clams), baby eels, or shellfish salad.
- **La Albariza,** Betis 6 (☎ **95-433-89-60**), is down the street, the main drag that lines the west side of the river, from Rio Grande. It has a stand-up bar with black wine barrels as tables. The bar area is pure Andalusian casual dining and is much more *auténtico* (authentic) than the restaurant in back. Lean on a barrel and order up *tortillitas de camarones* (yummy, tiny fried shrimp omelets), great, huge pickled olives, and fried *boquerones* (white anchovies).

- **Río Grande,** Betis, s/n (☎ **95-427-83-71**), is a fancy full-scale restaurant with a happening terrace scene overlooking the river. Skip dinner and go for tapas instead — stick to the fish dishes.
- **Sol y Sombra,** Castilla 149–151 (☎ **95-433-39-35**), evokes a *taurino* (bullfighting) culture and serves delightfully earthy tapas. It's a good place for razor-thin cured ham, *puntillitas* (garlicky beef tenderloin), and blood-red Rioja wine. Closed for lunch Mondays and Tuesdays and all of August.

In Santa Cruz

Seville's cool old Jewish Quarter is a favorite of most visitors, and it's a good spot to tapas-hop in the early evening.

- **Bar Giralda,** Mateos Gago 1 (☎ **95-422-74-35**), with old vaults that once formed part of a Moorish bathhouse, is a famous student hangout. Boisterous and hip Sevillanos come for *pastel de puerros y espinacas* (leek and spinach pie) and *pimientos rellenos* (stuffed peppers).
- **Bar Modesto,** Cano y Cueto 3 (☎ **95-441-68-11**), a seafood restaurant, is more ramshackle than modest. Its lively downstairs tapas bar is popular with Sevillanos and tourists alike. The famous dish here is Tío Diego, a stir-fry of cured ham, shrimp, and mushrooms.
- **Casa Román,** Plaza de los Venerables 1 (☎ **95-422-84-83**), is a location that you'll probably pass repeatedly. It's perfect for a meat fix; try the *chorizo* (spicy pork sausage), serrano ham, and other basics, such as a wedge of *tortilla española* (potato and onion omelet).
- **Hostería del Laurel,** Plaza de los Venerables 5 (☎ **95-422-02-95**), also a small, historic hotel (see the box "Did Don Juan win the bet?"), sets tables out in its delightful square. If you've pictured yourself a Don Juan or Carmen, sipping sangria and savoring cured meats, this place is tailor-made.

In Zona Centro (Central Seville)

The central, commercial district of Seville has too many tapas haunts to keep track of. Check out the following, but if you see one with people hanging about the bar and out the door, that's all the information you need to pop in and enjoy.

- **Bodega Extremeña,** San Esteban (☎ **95-441-70-60**), is a dark, atmospheric little place with hanging garlic and hams, near Casa Pilatos. It has a range of cheap tapas, including *morcilla al vino* (blood sausage soaked in sherry) and, for the really adventurous, *orejas en adobo.* (I shouldn't tell you, but that's pig's ears in oregano and vinegar.)

- **Casa Morales,** García de Vinuesa 11 (☎ **95-422-12-42**), just a block back from Avenida de Constitución, is a fantastic old wine bar and tapas joint that dates to 1850, and it looks like it hasn't changed a bit since then. You can get *chorizo* and other snacks to go with your beer or wine, but the best thing to do is to go across the street to **La Isla,** García de Vinuesa 13 (☎ **95-422-83-55**), a fry stand where you can pick up a newspaper full of *pescaíto frito* (tiny fried fish), shrimp, or fish 'n chips (priced by the kilo) to take back to the bar. (Morales is one of the only places I know that doesn't have a problem with BYOT — Bring Your Own Tapas.)
- **Entrecárceles,** Faisanes 1 (no phone), just off Plaza del Salvador, is a tiny nook of a place, but it's hugely atmospheric, with hanging hams, a wooden bar, an old wooden refrigerator, and walls with peeling ochre paint. A tavern since 1894, it looks like a movie set, though it has received a recent renovation. Tapas are written on a chalkboard and on tiles. Try *salmorejo* (the thick Cordovan version of gazpacho) with ham, *pimientos rellenos de carne o bacalao* (peppers stuffed with meat or cod), or *lomo al camembert* (pork loin with Camembert cheese).
- **El Rinconcillo,** Gerona 2 (☎ **95-422-31-83**), may be a little out of your way, but it has been a tavern since 1670, making it the oldest tapas bar in Seville. The name means Little Corner. It has a gorgeous wraparound wooden bar (on which bartenders tally your tab in chalk), walls lined with gorgeous *azulejos* (ceramic tiles), marble-topped tables, and tons of tapas. Popular with the locals, it features a regular cast of characters around the bar. I can still taste the *espinacas con garbanzos* (spinach with chickpeas).

Exploring Seville

You can cover almost everything you want to see in a first or second visit to Seville — everything, in other words, that I outline here — on foot (if you have a car, leave it in the hotel parking area). Seville is loaded with monuments, cathedrals, and other sights, but as important as any of those is the city's special character — its hole-in-the-wall tapas bars overflowing with boisterous patrons, fragrant orange trees, and the unmistakable sounds of flamenco song and dance spilling out into the street. Don't be so intent on seeing the sights that you miss picking up on what makes the city unique. Slow down, like Sevillanos do, and soak up the atmosphere.

Keep in mind as you wander the city that the sun in Andalusia can be scorching, with an average temperature of 32°C (90°F) in summer. I recommend setting out early in the day, so that you aren't rushing around to hit the sights between 11 a.m. and 2 p.m., when the sun is overhead. Bring along a hat or cap and, especially in the summertime, remember to slather on the sunscreen. Also bring bottled water to prevent dehydration, and take frequent breathers — tapas stops are good ways to duck out of the sun — but watch your alcohol intake, because it acts as a dehydrator. Your last defense? Fool-proof deodorant.

Did Don Juan win the bet?

In pop culture, a Don Juan is an irresistible stud, but it wasn't always that way. In the original story, written in the 1600s by Tirso de Molina (a priest who later received the honor of having a Madrid neighborhood and, er, Metro stop named after him), the legendary rogue roams Seville in search of willing — and unwilling — maidens. Don Juan challenges a friend to see who can seduce more women in a calendar year. The rivals meet up one year later to check their scorecards; Don Juan, with six dozen notches on his belt, is declared the winner, but he can't stop there. On a roll, he ups the ante, claiming that in just six days he'll seduce not only his rival's fiancée, but also a nun.

Recall that a priest wrote the story of Don Juan. (Like he's gonna get away with stealing a nun's virtue.) The rapscallion's designs on Sister Doña Inés are the last straw for God, who strikes Don Juan down and condemns him to a sinner's life in hell.

Evidently that struck the 19th-century playwright José Zorilla as much too harsh a penalty, and too dark an ending. In Hollywood fashion, he rewrote the story. In his version, the rivals meet up at Hostería de Laurel in the Barrio de Santa Cruz (where you can go today and test your pick-up lines). Don Juan announces his assault on the holy church, but in the rewrite, he gets the girl (the one in the black habit) and rides off with her to life everlasting. So guess which version lived on? Of course, the one with the scandalous but happy ending.

The top attractions

Barrio de Santa Cruz

The labyrinthine Santa Cruz district, a Jewish ghetto in the Middle Ages, became the fashionable neighborhood of Seville's aristocrats and nobility during the 17th century. The city's most colorful neighborhood, Barrio de Santa Cruz is Seville at its romantic best. Its winding whitewashed alleyways, with names like Gloria (Glory), Vida (Life), and Angeles (Angels), are full of wrought-iron grilles, leafy plazas, and plant- and flower-filled patios. The area remains picturesque despite the hordes of tour-guide-led groups traipsing through speaking all major Indo-European languages. Work your way along the barrio's streets until you find the **Plaza de Santa Cruz,** a pretty square with a Baroque cross at its center. South of the square are the Murillo Gardens, strolling gardens along Menéndez Pelayo. The main attraction within the Santa Cruz district is the **Hospital de los Venerables Sacerdotes** (see review later in this chapter). Allow the better part of a full morning or afternoon in Seville's most picturesque neighborhood.

See map p. 376. Barrio de Santa Cruz begins just east of the Reales Alcázares; walk through the small passageway that appears to be a part of the fortress. You pass through a courtyard, the Patio de Banderas, and a small tunnel, and enter the streets of Santa Cruz — beginning with the Callejón del Agua (Water Alley).

Catedral and La Giralda
Zona Centro/Old City

Seville's massive stone cathedral, built on the site of an ancient mosque, left no doubts about Christian intentions in Andalusia. Begun in 1401 (and, amazingly, finished only a century later), it was intended to make the largest possible statement about Spain's future religious and political rule. Before going in, circle the exterior to get a good look at its rose windows and Gothic flying buttresses. Enter through the **Patio de los Naranjos** (the orange-tree courtyard, a holdover from the old Mosque, where worshippers performed their ablutions before entering to pray). Inside, the cathedral's an impressive sight, with incredible proportions, great art works, and fantastic details in individual chapels. Don't miss the **Capilla Mayor** (Chancel) and its spectacular **Retablo Mayor,** an overwhelming altarpiece (the world's largest) of delicately carved gold leaf depicting the life of Christ. Behind it is the **Capilla Real** (Royal Chapel), with an ornate dome, the tombs of Alfonso X of Castile and his mother, Beatrice (Ferdinand's wife), and a Romanesque Virgin de los Reyes. The patron saint of Seville, this last figure, is removed for the Feast of the Assumption every year and paraded through the streets for her cult of followers. Other highlights include the **Tesoro** (treasury), with works by Goya and Murillo, and the showy 19th-century **Monument to Columbus** — a larger-than-life-size coffin held airborne by the kings of Spain's medieval kingdoms.

About the time the wrecking ball was smashing into the mosque previously on the site of the **Catedral,** the builders reportedly said, "Let us build a cathedral so immense that everyone, on beholding it, will take us for madmen." Those madmen went on to build the largest Gothic building in the world and the third-largest church in Europe (after St. Peter's in Rome and St. Paul's in London). Because of its size, plan on spending a couple of hours getting lost in it (and climbing La Giralda, the tower — see the following review).

La Giralda, the brick minaret that originally stood tall as part of the great mosque on this site, was given gradual makeovers throughout the centuries and incorporated into the cathedral. Your admission ticket to the cathedral allows you to climb the never-ending but, surprisingly, not-all-that-taxing inclined ramp of the belfry/minaret. Horsemen used to ride up the ramp to announce prayers, but you can go up just for the splendid panoramic views, which kids are sure to enjoy. Stay up long enough to hear the bells bong, and take your camera and a map of Seville so you can pick out the tiny neighborhoods and monuments below — the vistas are pretty incredible. The belfry, by the way, is named for its weather vane on top, a statue of faith.

See map p. 376. Plaza del Triunfo/Av. de la Constitución. Corner of Av. de la Constitución and Alemanes. ☎ ***95-5456-33-21.*** `www.catedralsevilla.org`. *Admission: (including visit to Giralda Tower) 7€ ($8.40) adults, 1.50€ ($1.80) students, free for children under 12; free for everyone on Sun. Open: Mon–Sat 11 a.m.–7 p.m., Sun 2:30–6 p.m.*

Real Alcázar de Sevilla
Zona Centro

If you're not going to Granada to see the Alhambra (see Chapter 17), this jaw-dropping royal residence (plain on the outside but spectacular within) is the next best thing. An awesome display of Mudéjar architecture (Christian architecture employing Arab motifs and elements), it's the kind of place you can lose yourself in for hours. A UNESCO World Heritage Site, and one of the oldest royal residences in Europe, it was built by master craftsmen from Granada, and is awash in delicately carved arches, brilliant tiles, and heavenly ceilings. In 1364, Pedro I (also called Pedro the Cruel) ordered its construction on a site previously occupied by a Roman acropolis, a Moorish castle, and the first Moorish fortress in Spain. The palace itself has an amazing history: A long line of monarchs married, gave birth, had affairs, and ruled here; traitors and enemies met untimely ends here; and Columbus and Magellan both came here to beg royal approval for their expeditions.

Perhaps the finest rooms are the **Apartamentos de Carlos V (Apartments of Carlos V),** decked out in gorgeous tapestries and tiles; the **Salón de Embajadores** (Ambassadors' Hall), crowned by a world-class carved cupola of gilded wood; the **Patio de las Doncellas (Patio of the Maidens),** with rich, intricate plasterwork that rivals the Alhambra; and the **Patio de las Muñecas (Patio of the Dolls),** which is small, charming, and spectacularly intricate. Look for two small faces, the dolls of the patio name, supposedly carved into a column (don't worry if you can't find them; I never have). The Moorish gardens are the equal of the sumptuous interiors, and a perfect place to relax amid lush terraces and fountains. You need a couple of hours at least to appreciate the intricacies of the buildings and gardens here.

See map p. 376. Plaza del Triunfo, s/n. Across from the cathedral. ☎ ***95-450-23-23.*** *Admission: 7€ ($8.40) adults, free for students and seniors. Open: Tues–Sat 9:30 a.m.–7 p.m., Sun 9:30 a.m.–5 p.m.*

Royally cruel

Pedro the Cruel, who established his court in Seville, receives much of the credit for creating the **Alcázar,** the gorgeous royal residence (though the structure was considerably expanded and enhanced by later monarchs). But Pedro left his mark in other ways — primarily blood stains. In the **Hall of Justice,** he murdered his brother, Don Fabrique, who conducted a brazen affair with Pedro's wife, Doña Blanca. On a different occasion, King Cruel dispensed with his dinner guest, the Emir of Granada, but not without first pocketing the Moor's fantastic uncut ruby and other priceless jewels. But what goes around comes around: Pedro was eventually assassinated by his own half-brother, Henry the Magnificent.

Hospital de los Venerables Sacerdotes
Barrio de Santa Cruz

While in the Barrio de Santa Cruz, visit the **Hospital for Venerable Priests,** a handsome old structure. It was founded in 1675 as an asylum for priests and is flush with 17th-century Baroque art. The only way to see it, though, is to join a tour that's given in Spanish. The language isn't really the problem; the guide I had was the least inspired, monotone bore I've seen. If you don't understand Spanish, you won't miss anything (the pamphlet in English gives you much more information anyway). The hospital chapel has impressive frescoes by the Seville painter Valdés Leal.

See map p. 376. Plaza de los Venerables 8. Enter neighborhood east of Reales Alcázares; corner of Reinoso and Rueda. ☎ ***95-456-26-96.*** *Admission: 4.75€ ($5.70) adults, 2.40€ ($2.90) students and seniors. Open: Daily 10 a.m.–2 p.m. and 4–8 p.m. Hourly guided visits.*

Museo de Bellas Artes
Zona Centro

This handsome fine-arts museum, a mini-Prado, is almost worth a visit even if you were to skip the art. A painstaking restoration has left this 17th-century former convent in beautiful shape, and its peaceful open-air patios, orange trees, and aged *azulejos* (ceramic tiles) are a great place to view art. The collection is impressive: Many of Spain's greats are here, including works by the 17th-century Seville School's Murillo, Valdés Leal, and Ribera; Velázquez; and Zurbarán. Don't miss **Sala V** (Room 5), a room with frescoed domes and Murillo's terrific angels and saints.

See map p. 376. Plaza del Museo 9. Just off Alfonso XII, 3 long blocks west of Plaza Duque de la Victoria. ☎ ***95-422-07-90.*** *Admission: 1.50€ ($1.80) adults, free for students and members of E.U. Open: Tues 2:30–8 p.m., Wed–Sat 9 a.m.–8 p.m., Sun 9 a.m.–2 p.m.*

More cool things to see and do

Looking for something else to keep you and the kids busy while in Seville? Check out the following ideas.

Cooling off in the shade

When Seville's unrelenting heat begins to barbecue your brain, bolt for (or more likely, stagger to) the park. The lushly shaded gardens of **Parque María Luisa,** designed in the late-19th century along the Guadalquivir River, are the best thing this side of a cold bath. (In the dead of summer, you may be tempted to rip off your clothes and go screaming into the fountain, but don't — the punishing sun beats down on the tiles as if they were the sands of the Sahara.) In spring, the acacia trees and rose bushes are particularly fragrant, and the Arab-style fountains and ponds, punctuated with floating swans, are extremely romantic. Within the park is the **Plaza de España;** a massive semicircular palace with decorative tiles commemorating each province in Spain, it was built for the 1929 Ibero-American Exposition. Though kids are always captivated by this huge structure, it's in a sad state of neglect. (Many of the tiles that I took photos of 15 years ago, on my first visit, are now chipped and faded.) Kids still enjoy rowing boats around the moat, and water still springs from the fountain, but the plaza already seems like a relic.

One of the best ways to visit the park is to hire a horse-drawn carriage (see "Seeing Seville by guided tour," later in this chapter), but if you're walking back to the center of town, take Avenida de María Luisa to San Fernando. On the southwest corner, across from the gardens of the Alcázar, is Seville's university, which inhabits the **Real Fábrica de Tabacos** (Royal Tobacco Factory). This factory is where the Gypsy seductress Carmen, best known as the heroine of Bizet's famous opera set in Seville, rolled cigars along with about 10,000 other Andalusian women. Presumably, they sang and danced all the while. You're welcome to take a stroll through and see the grandeur that came with a 19th-century state tobacco monopoly.

Visiting Casa de Pilatos (Pilate's House)

North of the cathedral, Pilate's House, Plaza de Pilatos 1 (southeast section of the Old City; 4 blocks west of Menéndez Pelayo; ☎ **95-422-52-98**), is a superb, two-story, 15th-century Renaissance palace built by the Marquis of Tarifa. Without doubt one of the finest homes in Seville, it's bursting with grand architectural and artistic treasures: Greek and Roman busts, frescos, handsome painted ceilings, courtyard sculptures, walls plastered with colorful glazed ceramic tiles, and a carved dome Mudéjar ceiling over the staircase. My father's fond of saying "They don't make 'em like they used to," so I brought him here to prove him right. Admission to the ground floor (patio and gardens) is 5€ ($6), to the museum as well 8€ ($9.60); on Tuesdays admission is free from 1 p.m. to 5 p.m. It's open daily from 9 a.m. to 7 p.m.

Picking a side at the bullfights

Plaza de Toros de Maestranza (mah-eh-*strahn*-thah) is one of Spain's oldest, grandest, and most important bullfighting rings — the oldest is a little farther south, in Ronda (see Chapter 16). It's located at Paseo de Cristóbal Colón 12 (intersection of Paseo de Cristóbal Colón and Adriano, across from the river; ☎ **95-422-45-77**). Work started in 1761 and was completed 120 years later. Not round, but oval, the stark white ring seats 14,000 people. As in all Spanish bullrings, you can buy the cheap seats in the *sol* (sun) or the more expensive ones in the *sombra* (shade). You'll understand the price difference after you sit through a bullfight in the intense Seville sun — you'll be virtually dead in the afternoon. Bullfights used to last all day, with 12 *toros* (bulls) meeting their maker and almost as many horses. The steeds that brought in the *picadores* (horsemen who jab the bulls around the neck and shoulders to wear them down) didn't wear protective gear until the 1920s, and many were fatally gored. Today only bulls — six during every bullfight — are slain.

The bullring tour includes a visit to the museum **(Museo Taurino),** which displays various flashy *trajes de luces* (suits of lights) worn by matadors, photos of such bull aficionados as Ernest Hemingway, and paintings of bull lore. You finish the group tour in the chapel, where the bullfighters come to pray to La Macarena, the patron saint of *toreros* (yes, she of the world-famous song and dance number). Admission is 4€ ($4.80); it's open daily from 9:30 a.m. to 2 p.m. and 3 p.m. to 7 p.m. (on bullfight days, it's open 9:30 a.m.–3 p.m. only).

The bullfighting season at la Maestranza begins the first week in April and lasts through October, with fights taking place on various days of the week (check ahead to be sure you're in town on the right day). You can download an advance schedule if you've got a matador of choice (`www.realmaestranza.com`) or pick one up from the tourism office when you arrive in Seville. Tickets are available at the box office or at kiosks set up in major tourist districts in the center.

Discovering La Macarena!

Perhaps you remember the cheesy Spanish pop song "Macarena," which topped the charts all over the world back in the mid-90s. Believe it or not, La Macarena's more than just a participatory dance number. She is one of Seville's most revered Madonnas, a tearful patron saint of bullfighters, a favorite of Gypsies, and a legend when it comes to Holy Thursday's procession. You can see the colonial-looking **Basílica de la Macarena,** Calle Bécquer 1 (Puerta de la Macarena, intersection of Muñoz León and San Luis; ☎ **95-437-01-95**), on the extreme northern ring of the Old City (the fastest way to get here is to take a cab along the outer ring: Colón to Torneo to Resolana Andueza). It's a bit of a hike, but if you're at all fascinated by the cult of Madonna worship that's especially strong in the south of Spain, a visit here is obligatory. You can visit the Macarena museum, with its over-the-top processional floats of Our Lady of Hope (her official name) — one's covered in a forest of candlesticks, another is a shiny golden chariot. If you just want to see the famous crying Virgin Mary, enter the church through the front door with the faithful. Admission to the basilica is free; it costs 3€ ($3.60) to enter the museum. Both are open daily from 9:30 a.m. to 2 p.m. and 5 to 8 p.m.

Traveling into the past, magically

La Cartuja, across the river from Seville's major downtown area, was the site of the 1992 World Expo and a place that Sevillanos hoped would develop into a major tourist attraction. Although the installations languished for a few years after the Expo, they've finally been put to work as a theme park, and one with a 16th-century motif at that. **Isla Mágica** (Magic Island) takes the little ones back in time.

Rides and show themes include the *Amazon, Gateway to the Americas,* and *El Dorado.* The park also has a motion theater with seats that shimmy and shake like the vehicles on the screen you're ostensibly piloting (it's pretty cool and realistic — the kids will love it!). It's located at Pabellón de España, Isla de la Cartuja — across Puente de la Barqueta Bridge; take bus C2 from the city center (☎ **95-902-16-17-16;** www.islamagica.es). Admission for adults, according to season, is 21€ to 24€ ($27–$31) for the whole day or 15€ to 17€ ($19–$22) for the evening only. Admission for children 5 through 12 years old and seniors ranges from 15€ to 17€ ($19–$22) for the whole day, and 11€ to 12€ ($14–$15) for the evening. Children under age 5 enter for free. The park is open March through November daily from 11 a.m. to midnight in summer, with reduced hours in other months.

Going to the hospital — for art's sake

Hospitals are rarely tourist attractions, but hidden within Seville's 17th-century **Hospital de la Santa Caridad** (Hospital of Charity) is a splendid Baroque chapel that is a minimuseum of art. Established to care for the destitute, infirm, and criminal, the hospital — built by a man on whom the legendary character Don Juan was reportedly based — today houses works by the painter Juan de Valdés Leal, including his famous *Postrimerías,* the sculptor Pedro Roldán, and a dozen paintings by native son Bartolomé Murillo, one of the greats of the Seville School. You'll also find a handsome altarpiece by Simón de Pineda. It's located at Temprado 3 (☎ **95-422-32-32**), and is open Monday through Saturday from 9 a.m. to 1:30 p.m. and 3:30 to 7:30 p.m.; Sunday from 9 a.m. to 1 p.m. Admission is 4€ ($4.80).

Fiesta time! Seville's popular festivals

Seville is renowned for its rituals and celebrations during **Semana Santa** (Holy Week), just before Easter, and **Feria de Abril,** the April Fair that erupts two weeks after Easter. During these two weeks, Seville is the most festive and spectacular place in Spain, overflowing with vibrant color. But if you're not in the mood for crowds, packed hotels, inflated prices, and religious ceremonies, plan to be somewhere else.

Semana Santa

Holy Week (the week before Easter) is one big march of processions throughout the city. Assemblies of men carry flower-bedecked, Madonna-topped floats on their shoulders. Penitents in long robes and pointy hoods accompany them — to an American, the uncomfortable visual reference is the KKK (though fortunately, these folks have different things on their minds). Mournful dirge music and candles complete the somber, almost spooky mood. Processions go on all week, but the best days are Holy Thursday and Good Friday. Thursday night is pretty spectacular — parades pass hourly. Don't miss **La Macarena** — not the dance, but the patron saint of bullfighters (see "More cool things to see and do," earlier in this chapter) — or **El Gran Poder.** Macarena returns to her Basilica on Friday around 1 p.m. Pick up schedules of processions, particularly the pamphlet "Sevilla en Semana Santa," from the tourism office.

Feria de Abril

After the somber expressions of faith during Holy Week, Seville explodes during its annual April Fair, a festival of flamenco and *sevillana* dancing, drinking, horse parades, and wonderful costumes. Andalusian women, from little girls to elegant older ladies, are decked out in gay, brightly colored, and often polka-dotted flamenco dresses. Men, atop fine Andalusian horses, look like gentlemen ranchers, with their broad-brimmed hats. The roots of the party are in fact agricultural — it accompanied annual livestock auctions in the mid-19th century. The *alegría* (joy) is contagious, and it lasts all week.

Rocking El Rocío

One of Spain's most spectacular expressions of religious faith is the El Rocío pilgrimage, which takes place at the end of May in the province of Huelva (near Almonte and the Parque Nacional de Doñana), west of Seville. It's like a rowdy religious rave. Accompanied by flutes and tambourines, thousands of the devout travel on foot, on horseback, and in oxen-led carriages to the Almonte marshlands. The faithful, donning their best flamenco duds, take flowers and wax figures to worship at the Our Lady of El Rocío sanctuary. When the float of la Virgen del Rocío — the Virgin of the Dew — passes, mayhem erupts as everyone tries to lay a hand on her and be touched by her saintliness. For more information on this festival, see www.andalucia.com/festival/rocio.htm.

To find out this year's dates for Semana Santa (Easter), Feria de Abril (April Fair), and the El Rocío pilgrimage, contact the tourism office or visit the Web sites www.andalucia.com and www.sevilla.org.

Seeing Seville by guided tour

Sevilla Walking Tour offers complete walking tours of the city, leaving daily at 2:45 p.m. from the Tourist Information Office on Avenida de la Constitución. Tours cost from 9€ to 18€ ($11–$22).

You can choose from two sightseeing bus tours in Seville. **Sevirama** (☎ **95-421-60-52**) has stops at the Torre del Oro, Plaza de España, and Isla Mágica. It's one of those open-top, get-on-and-get-off buses. **Sevilla Tour** offers multilingual tours in buses designed to look like trolley cars (☎ **902-10-10-81**). A ticket is good for 24 hours, and you can pick up the bus at Torre del Oro, Plaza de España, Isla Mágica, and Cartuja (the Expo '92 site).

Among specialty tours are **Cruceros Turísticos Torre del Oro** (river cruises down the Guadalquivir), Paseo Alcalde Marqués del Contadero, s/n, at the Torre del Oro (☎ **95-456-16-92**), and **Toros Tours** (☎ **95-566-42-61**), organized visits to see Spanish bulls and horses outside of the ring.

You can't miss the **horse-drawn carriages** lined up outside Seville's cathedral. They're a very popular way to clip-clop around Seville, and this attractive, romantic city is one of the most enjoyable places in Spain to get off your feet and behind a horse. If you've thought about it in other places such as Córdoba and haven't hopped aboard, Seville is the place to do it, especially if you have your sweetie by your side. Fares are posted and are nonnegotiable (unless you find a rogue driver); they run about 25€ to 30€ ($30–$36) for an hour (and more during the high-demand season, Holy Week, Easter, and the April festivals). Besides the stop in the plaza fronting the cathedral, there are stops in María Luisa Park, Plaza del Triunfo, Plaza Virgin de los Reyes, and Torre del Oro.

Shopping in Seville

Seville's a joy for shopping hounds — as much for the pleasure of strolling the streets as for the typically Andalusian goods that make great gifts.

Best shopping areas

The principal shopping districts are **Barrio de Santa Cruz,** for artisan's shops, antiques, and trinkets, and **Zona Centro** (center, just north of the cathedral tower) — particularly the pedestrian streets **Sierpes** and **Tetuán,** where you can find traditional guitar, ceramics, and flamenco dress shops as well as a wide array or modern clothing stores. The area west of the cathedral, **El Arenal,** is packed with cool little antiques shops, as are **Mateos Gago** and **Rodrigo Caro** in Santa Cruz.

What to look for and where to find it

Look for hand-painted ceramics, old *azulejos* (glazed ceramic tiles), antiques, and, for women who want to play the part of charming *sevillana* seductress, fans, embroidered shawls, and colorful flamenco dresses.

You have to depend on your feet or taxis to get around Seville. Map out where you want to go; if anything looks too far (more than 5 blocks, say), hop in an inexpensive, air-conditioned taxi. And remember that shops are closed for long lunch breaks, often from 1:30 to 5 p.m. If you must shop at midday, head to **El Corte Inglés** department store (on Plaza Duque de la Victoria), which doesn't dare close or turn off the mega-watt air-conditioning.

Antiques

Run by a gregarious *sevillano* family, **Felix e Hijo** (Felix and Son . . . and daughter and in-laws), Av. de la Constitución 20 (☎ **95-422-33-34**), deals in classical archaeological finds: Greek vases, Egyptian masks, and Roman mosaics. Not everything is impossibly expensive and impossible to lug home — you may just find an affordable piece that crystallizes Andalusia's storied past. And if you do find one, Felix also arranges shipping. Mari Carmen, Felix's daughter, runs **Felix,** Av. de la Constitución 26 (☎ **95-421-80-26**), specializing in antique Andalusian posters — of the

April Fair, bullfights, and hard-to-find Deco advertising posters. The old posters of Semana Santa and Feria de Abril are particularly fetching with affordable prices to match.

Baked goods from on high

For pastries from heaven, check out what the nuns are baking. At **Convento de San Leandro,** Plaza de San Ildefonso 1 (☎ **95-422-41-95**), the sisters sell *yemas de San Leandro* (egg yolk candies). You can get all kinds of airy pastries, some made especially for the Christmas holidays, at **Convento de Santa Inés,** Doña María Coronel 5 (☎ **95-422-31-45**), and jams and marmalades at **Convento de Santa Paula,** Santa Paula 11 (☎ **95-442-13-07**). During the month of December, visit the **Palacio Arzobispal** (Archbishop's Palace), Plaza Virgen de los Reyes across from the cathedral (☎ **95-422-48-08**), for a stupendous selection of *dulces navideños* (Christmas sweets).

Books

One of the largest sources of international books is **Vértice,** San Fernando 33 (☎ **95-421-16-54**). Three guesses as to what's sold at **English Bookshop,** Marques de Nervión 70 (☎ **95-465-57-54**). If you need a traveling fix, check out the selection of novels and travel books, which are all in the English language.

Ceramics

El Postigo, Arfe, s/n (☎ **95-421-39-76**), has one of the largest stocks of hand-painted ceramics in Seville with a selection of pottery, planters, and other patio-perfect pieces. You can find good, nontouristy ceramics across the river in Triana; have a look at two shops on Calle Antilliano Campos: **Cerámica Terra** (no. 3) and **Cerámica Rocío** (no. 8). For hand-painted vases, tiles, and plates with historic Andalusian patterns, check out **Martian Ceramics,** Sierpes 74 (☎ **95-421-34-13**). The selection's good, although not out of this world.

Crafts

Artesanía Textil, Sierpes 70 (☎ **95-456-28-40**), is a great place for hand-woven Andalusian blankets, table linens, and shawls. **El Bazar del Barrio** (The Neighborhood Bazaar), Mateos Gago 24 (☎ **95-456-00-89**), a cute shop in the Santa Cruz district, has everything from antique *azulejos* (glazed ceramic tiles) to watercolors of bullfighting scenes. The items are more carefully selected than those you find in souvenir shops.

Department stores

El Corte Inglés, Plaza Duque de la Victoria 10 (☎ **95-422-09-31**), is the megastore that dominates Spain like a fortress on the plains; you can get anything from flamenco dresses, dishes, and vacuum cleaners to shoe polish and CDs of flamenco artists.

Fashion

Zara, Plaza Duque de la Vitoria 1 (☎ **95-421-48-75**), something akin to the Galician incarnation of Banana Republic, has affordable and hip fashions for men, women, and kids. (The menswear Zara is up the street at Calle Tetuán.) One of the hottest names in Spanish fashion is **Victorio & Lucchino,** Sierpes 87 (☎ **95-422-79-51**). The pricey dresses, skirts, and shawls by this Andalusian design couple are Spain's version of Dolce & Gabbana, but more elegant and sophisticated.

Flamenco dresses and fans

You can find cheaper *trajes sevillanos* (flamenco dresses) and shawls in almost any souvenir shop, but you won't find any more exquisite than the hand-embroidered numbers at **Angeles Berral,** Pajaritos 7 (☎ **95-456-31-30**), a small, personalized shop just a few doors down from Casa Pilatos. They're extremely elegant and tasteful (and pricey). **Pilar Vera,** Rivero 2 (☎ **95-422-81-53**), has designed classic flamenco dresses and accessories for women for more than two decades, while generations of Sevillanas have gone to **Perdales,** Cuna 23 (☎ **95-421-37-09**), for the perfect, body-hugging costume to wow 'em at the April festivals (see the sidebar, "Fiesta time! Seville's popular festivals," earlier in this chapter). The outfits aren't cheap (and I have a hard time figuring out when would be the right moment back home to wear one . . .), but if you need a showy number to go with your castanets and fan, this is the place. Don't forget the color-coordinated shoes. **Casa Rubio,** Sierpes 56 (☎ **95-422-68-72**), has a terrific selection of fans, from fancy hand-painted numbers to modern functional items that can keep you cool in the wicked Seville heat.

Flea markets

Los hippies is what locals call these flea-market locations for leather goods, hippie fashions, costume jewelry, and heavenly junk. Wednesday and Thursday it's at Rioja and Plaza Magdalena; Friday and Saturday in Plaza del Duque. On Thursdays, check out "El Jueves," the most traditional market in Seville, on Plaza Feria and Alameda, for antiques, paintings, and furniture.

For the ranch

For more than 20 years, **Arcab,** Paseo de Cristóbal Colón 18 (☎ **95-422-34-64**), has been a sturdy place to get a hand-tooled saddle, riding boots, and other items related to the majestic Andalusian horse (or your regular old Texas steed). For riding saddles, boots, spurs, buckles, blankets, leather pouches, and more, try **San Pablo,** Calle Murillo 9 (☎ **95-422-56-34**). This family-owned place has dealt in equestrian accessories for half a century.

Music

Allegro, Dos de Mayo 37 (☎ **95-421-61-93**), just beside the Teatro de la Maestranza, specializes in classical music. It also has a top-notch selection of Spanish music, including flamenco and zarzuela. You can give a listen before buying. **Sevilla Rock,** on Alfonso XII 1, is the place to come for CDs for your rental car or musical souvenirs of Andalusia. You can find the latest in Spanish pop-flamenco or the deep-throated *cante hondo* stuff (like an anthology of the great singer Camarón de la Isla).

Feeling the rhythm: Seville's nightlife

You don't want to miss the fun on a sultry Seville night. Top choices include the following.

- A rousing professional flamenco *tablao* (performance)
- Outdoor cafes and bars (either near the cathedral or along either side of the river) for people watching, tapas munching, and libation quaffing
- Live, combustible music, with rhythmic hand-claps, cries of *¡olé!* and a palpable sense of community, at clubs where you see locals get down and dirty, performing *sevillanas* (an informal gathering of singing, music, and dancing)

For listings of what's on and what's going down, check out *El Giradillo,* a free publication that contains a detailed monthly list of Seville's nightlife options, exhibitions, and other goings-on (available at tourism offices throughout the city).

Die-hard aficionados of flamenco can plan their visit to Seville to coincide with the annual **Bienal de Flamenco.** During September and the first week of October, the city hosts a daily surfeit of flamenco-related dance, music, and theater. For additional advance information and a program schedule, see `www.bienal-flamenco.org`. Make sure you purchase your tickets in advance (at the Lope de la Vega box office or by calling ☎ **95-459-28-70**), because most shows sell out (and hotels are difficult to come by as well).

Catching a flamenco show

El Arenal, Rodo 7 (☎ **95-421-64-92;** `www.tablaoelarenal.com`), produces one of the best flamenco song and dance shows in Seville. In the back room of a 17th-century building with small tables, the place and performances practically shout passionate Andalusia. Shows are 34€ ($41; dinner and show, 66€/$79); there are two "passes" every night, at 8:30 and 10:30 p.m. El Arenal is located between Dos de Mayo and Varflora, near the bullring and Paseo Colón.

Dressed up like a Seville patio, **El Patio Sevillano,** Paseo de Cristóbal Colón 11 (☎ **95-422-20-68;** `www.elpatiosevillano.com`), popular with large tourist groups, forsakes the intimate, flamenco-focused program for one with exotic costumes and a wide range of Spanish music and dance. Two shows are performed nightly (7:30 and 10 p.m.; 32€/$38). It's near the Maestranza Bullring, on the east side of Guadalquivir River.

Catching flamenco fever

Flamenco fever flows through Seville. If you've been to see a flamenco troupe and want to discover how to stomp your heels dramatically and twirl your arms seductively, maybe a dance class is in order. **Estudio de Baile Mario** offers classes in flamenco, *danza española,* and *sevillanas* Monday through Friday from 11 a.m. to 1:30 p.m. and 6 to 9 p.m. The studio is on Procurador 20 (☎ **95-433-89-14**). **Taller Flamenco** offers four-day music and dance classes in small groups. They're on Siete Revueltas 5 (☎ **95-456-42-34;** `www.tallerflamenco.com`). The **Cristina Herren Flamenco Foundation,** Fabiola 1 (☎ **95-421-70-58;** `www.flamencoheeren.com`), offers intensive, and expensive, dance courses for those who are serious about learning (all levels available).

Los Gallos, Plaza de Santa Cruz 11 (☎ **95-421-69-81;** `www.tablaolosgallos.com`), has been around since 1966 in the heart of the old Jewish Quarter, Barrio de Santa Cruz. It's unapologetically touristy, but the flamenco is pretty authentic, and the place is lively and intimate. Visitors love it, and you may even find a local or two in attendance. There are two shows daily (32€/$38), at 8 and 10:30 p.m. It's 2 blocks south of Ximénez de Enciso, along Santa Teresa.

Concert performances focusing on young flamenco artists and *nuevo flamenco* are held at **Sol Café Cantante,** Sol 5 (☎ **95-422-51-65**), in the old Sala Talía (near Plaza Los Terceros). Shows are Thursday through Saturday at 10 p.m. (12€/$15).

Clapping along to sevillanas

Casa Anselma, Pagés del Corro 49 (no phone), on the west side of the river, rocks with communal singing and camaraderie. Either get here obscenely early to get a table or come around midnight, when it starts to get really steamy — and packed. The garrulous owner, Anselma, is a local institution and quite a singer herself. To get there, take a taxi; Casa Anselma is 4 blocks back from Betis in Triana on the west side of Guadalquivir River.

Along the river, an area packed with bars and great little places for an evening *tapeo* is **Lo Nuestro,** Betis 31-A (☎ **95-472-60-10**), where locals do their thing — sing and dance and drink. To get there, walk across San Telmo Bridge toward the Triana neighborhood; take the first right past the bridge, on the main street facing the river. The bar's about halfway down on the right side.

Making it a night at the opera

Seville's fancy, newish opera house, **Teatro de la Maestranza,** Paseo de Cristóbal Colón 22 (☎ **95-422-33-44;** `www.teatromaestranza.com`), is the place to catch a Seville-inspired production of *Carmen, The Marriage of Figaro,* or *The Barber of Seville.* Also look for jazz concerts and recitals here. The box office is open from 10 a.m. to 2 p.m. and 5 to 8 p.m. As you face the Guadalquivir River, the opera house is halfway between the San Telmo and Isabel II bridges.

Enjoying the theater

On the northern edge of María Luisa Park is this handsome theater, **Teatro Lope de Vega,** Av. de María Luisa, s/n (☎ **95-459-08-53/5**), which brings some of the best productions to Seville — from García Lorca's *The House of Bernarda Alba* to rousing flamenco shows and theater. Productions are in Spanish only (but that doesn't appear to stop large contingents of foreign visitors from attending). It's near the intersection of Menéndez Pelayo, Avenida de Isabel la Católica, and Avenida de Portugal.

Surviving Seville's bar scene

For a full roster of tapas bars, a superb way to spend an evening in Seville, see "Dining in Seville," earlier in this chapter. Plaza del Salvador is always hopping with *jaleo* (commotion). The tiny bars there (**La Antigua Bodeguita** and **Los Soportales**) spill out into the square, where there are rickety little tables and lots of beer-drinking, good-natured, good-looking young people; the scene looks remarkably like a college party.

Abades, Abades 13 (☎ **95-422-56-22**), is a pub in the guise of a converted 19th-century Barrio de Santa Cruz mansion. This is lounge culture at its finest; slip into the rich living room and decadent ambience and enjoy a cocktail with other stylin' folks. To get there, take Mateos Gago east of the cathedral and turn left on Abades. Perched on the banks of the Guadalquivir, **Bar Capote,** Paseo de Cristóbal Colón 11 (☎ **95-421-41-20**), is the place to down a few cocktails in the open air and dance when a *señorita* or *caballero* (gentleman) catches your eye. It's next to the Maestranza Bullring, facing the river.

At **Bar Quitaspesares** (also called Taberna Peregil), Plaza Padre Jerónimo de Córdoba 3 (☎ **95-421-89-66**), proprietor Pepe Peregil is so gregarious it's contagious. His bar is packed with young and old, and a group usually gathers in back with guitars and voices in full swing. Young women often get up and show off their *sevillana* dance moves. Pepe's place is a little removed from the city center near the Church of Santa Catalina. To get there, take Martín Villa (which becomes Laraña) east off of Sierpes, all the way to Plaza Ponce de León, just west of the plaza that the bar is on. Take a taxi there and back; walking is way too far. (Nearer to the center of town is Pepe's son's bar, **La Goleta,** on Mateos Gago 20, in Barrio de Santa Cruz.) **Casa Morales** (García de Vinuesa 11; ☎ **95-422-12-42**) makes a great watering hole as well. It's an evocative mid-19th-century tapas bar, with huge casks of wine and cement floors — the kind of place where the barkeep writes your tab in chalk on the bar top.

Side trips from Seville

A great if rather pricey way to get out of town is to board the **Al Andalus Expreso,** a vintage luxury train whose 12 cars are straight out of the 1920s, and set out for the highlights of Andalusia. Along the way, you pass (in air-conditioned luxury) through the south's spectacular scenery — dry, rugged mountains and rolling olive groves. The Seville-to-Seville round-trip pulls into **Córdoba, Granada** (see Chapter 17), and two of Andalusia's famed *pueblos blancos,* or white towns, **Ronda** and **Jerez** (see Chapter 16). You dine aboard in the luxurious dining car or in fine restaurants (frequently *paradores*). The price includes meals with wine, tours, visits, transfers, and taxes, but traveling in such princely style doesn't come cheap. Prices for six-day, five-night trips range from 2,700€ to 3,800€ ($3,240–$4,560) per person (depending on cabin type) for the Seville round-trip. The train hits the tracks from March to October, skipping the extremely hot months of July and August. Visit the Web site, www.alandalusexpreso.com, or contact your travel agent or **Marketing Ahead,** a Spanish travel specialist in New York, at ☎ **800-223-1356** or 212-686-9213; Fax 212-686-0271; www.marketingahead.com. If a fancy all-inclusive train's not your style, try one of the following recommended side trips.

Itálica: The Roman ruins

Before the Moors and the Visigoths, the Romans ruled Andalusia. The ruins of the Roman city of Itálica, which was founded in 206 B.C., are so close to Seville (10km/6 miles to the northwest) that you can almost walk there. Two of the most famous emperors of the Roman Empire, Trajan and Hadrian, were born in Itálica, and the city was one of the Empire's most important. The main feature is the elliptical amphitheater, which held 25,000 spectators and was the largest the Romans built. The town had about 10,000 inhabitants at its height. Excavations are ongoing, and Roman mosaics continue to be unearthed and transported to the Seville Archaeological Museum. In summer, concerts and dance festivals are held here — an evocative bit of staging.

To get there by car, take Highway N-360 in the direction of Mérida. By bus, take the Santiponce bus that leaves from Calle Marqués de Parada near the Santa Justa rail station. Call ☎ **95-599-73-76** for more information. The site is open April through September, Tuesday through Saturday from 8:30 a.m. to 8:30 p.m., and Sunday from 9 a.m. to 3 p.m.; October through March, Tuesday through Saturday from 9 a.m. to 5:30 p.m., and Sunday from 10 a.m. to 4 p.m. Admission is 1.50€ ($1.80), free for E.U. citizens.

Carmona: A crossroads of cultures

Carmona, a pretty, ancient walled city on a plateau an hour from Seville, has narrow whitewashed streets, a number of handsome, noble Renaissance homes, and a handful of churches and convents. It also has three Moorish fortresses. Carmona's fame rests on its reputation as one of the oldest inhabited places in Spain (Phoenicians and Carthaginians preceded the Romans). It has two landmark gates — the **Puerta de**

Sevilla and **Puerta de Córdoba.** Have a peek at the Gothic **Iglesia de Santa María,** too. But the town's best sight may be the cool **Roman Necropolis (☎ 95-414-08-11;** Tues–Sat 9 a.m.–5 p.m., Sun 10 a.m.–2 p.m.; admission free), where 1,000 former citizens are buried in underground tombs carved out of rock. Look for the impressive *Elephant* and *Seville* tombs. The necropolis is on the outskirts of town and clearly signposted. You can hit it on the way into or out of town.

Carmona is 32km (20 miles) east of Seville. If you're coming into Seville from Córdoba (or, of course, going on to Córdoba from Seville), it's an easy stopover — just follow the signs from the N-V highway.

With its two superb hotels, Carmona is also a great place to overnight. The **Parador Alcázar del Rey Don Pedro,** Alcázar, s/n (**☎ 95-414-10-10;** `www.parador.es`), one of the best in the *parador* system, inhabits a beautiful 14th-century Moorish *alcázar,* or royal residence, and is stunningly evocative of Andalusia's Arab past. It has an Alhambra-style patio, public rooms adorned with tapestries and antiques, an inviting pool, and breathtaking views of the countryside. Rooms are spacious and very handsomely decorated in classic style; a double costs 140€–150€ ($168–$180). A step up from the *parador,* in both luxury and cost, is the superb **Parador de Carmona,** Plaza Lasso 1 (**☎ 95-419-10-00;** `www.casadecarmona.com`), a Relaix and Châteaux property in a 1561 palace, the oldest surviving mansion in Carmona. This sumptuously designed and elegant hotel — which very much looks the part of a Renaissance palace with Mudéjar (Arab-Christian) details and four interior courtyards — is one of the finest in Spain. The rooms are warm, cozy, and luxurious, with beautiful antiques and fabrics, and each evokes a different era of Andalusian history. The massive, over-the-top Suite Azul is fit for a king. The slender pool is very much in character with the region's Moorish architecture, and the restaurant is exquisite — well worth making a reservation at even if you're not staying the night. For this kind of luxury and exclusivity, prices are not at all outrageous: doubles are 90€ to 180€ ($108–$216) and 200€ to 240€ ($240–$288) during Feria de Abril, Easter and Christmas week.

Fast Facts: Seville

Area Code

Seville's area code is **95,** which you must dial before every number.

ATMs/Currency Exchange

You can find banks and ATMs along the main drag in the *centro,* Avenida de la Constitución, just behind the cathedral, and on Plaza Nueva.

Embassies/Consulates

Many Western countries have consulates in Seville: Australia's is at Federico Rubio 14 (☎ 95-422-09-71); Ireland's is at Plaza Santa Cruz 6, Bajos A (☎ 95-421-63-61); and the United States' is at Plaza Nueva 8–8, second floor (☎ 95-421-85-71).

Emergencies

For general emergencies, dial ☎ **112.** For medical emergencies, dial ☎ **061,** or call the Cruz Roja (Red Cross; Avenida de la Cruz Roja) at ☎ 95-422-22-22 or Casa de Socorro (First Aid), Menéndez Pelayo, ☎ 95-441-17-12. To call an ambulance, dial ☎ 95-442-55-65. In case of fire, call ☎ 95-422-00-80. For the police, call ☎ **091.** For roadside assistance, call ☎ 900-12-35-05.

Hospitals

Hospital Virgen del Rocío is on Av. Manuel Siurot, s/n (☎ 95-501-20-00). You can find Hospital Universitario Virgen Macarena at Av. Doctor Fedriani, s/n (☎ 95-500-80-00).

Information

The main Andalusia Tourism Information Office is located just down the street from the cathedral, Av. de la Constitución 1B (☎ 95-422-14-04). You can find others at the San Pablo Airport (☎ 95-444-91-28) and Santa Justa Train Station (☎ 95-453-76-26). They're open daily from 9 a.m. to 8 p.m. Municipal tourism offices are at Plaza de la Concordia, s/n, in front of the Puente de Triana (☎ 902-19-48-97), Plaza de San Francisco 19 (☎ 954-59-52-88), and Paseo de las Delicias 9 (☎ 95-423-44-65). Dial ☎ **010** (8 a.m.–10 p.m.) for general information about the city, including transportation. The information is available in English as well as in other languages.

Internet Access/Cybercafes

Seville, with its throngs of foreign students, has several places where you can surf the Web on good machines. Web surfing generally runs about 2€ to 3€ ($2.50–$3.85) per hour. Check into Seville Internet Center, Almirantazgo 2 (second floor, corner of Avenida de la Constitución; ☎ 95-450-02-75), which is usually packed with study-abroad students. Open from 9 a.m. to 10 p.m. Monday through Friday, and Saturday through Sunday from 10 a.m. to 10 p.m., it's across from the cathedral. Another place to check out is Cyber Olé, an Internet cafe with art exhibitions, San Jancinto 74 (no phone). Work Center, San Fernando 1, at the corner of Avenida de la Constitución (☎ 95-421-20-74), is a 24-hour copy center with about a dozen Internet terminals.

Mail

You can find Seville's main post office at Av. de la Constitución 32 (☎ 95-422-47-60); it's open Monday through Friday 8:30 a.m. to 8:30 p.m. A branch is located at Av. de la Raza 4 (☎ 95-461-56-95).

Maps

The Tourism Office distributes city maps that are sufficient for most visitors. Additionally, you can check with the tourist-oriented shops right around the cathedral.

Police

For a police emergency, call ☎ **091** (national) or ☎ **092** (local). The municipal police station is at Av. de las Delicias 15 (☎ 95-461-54-50). The national police office is located at Av. Blas Infante 2 (☎ 95-428-93-00).

Safety

Locals aren't reticent about issuing safety warnings, which you need to take seriously. Seville has earned an unenviable reputation for having talented thieves who can spot a rental car with helpless tourists at the wheel at more than 100 paces. If you must park your car anywhere other than a guarded hotel parking garage, don't leave anything of value in it — no cameras, no passports, nothing. Seville, still part of the poorest region in Spain, is also one of Spain's biggest tourist draws. Be vigilant in Seville, especially at night. Carry only the amount of money you expect to spend (or don't mind losing) that day, and keep it in your front pocket. Also be very careful around the Santa Cruz district late at night (despite the blistering sun, it's preferable to do your sightseeing there during the day).

Taxis

Contact Radio Taxi (☎ 95-458-00-00), Radio Teléfono Giralda (☎ 95-467-55-55), or Tele-Taxi (☎ 95-462-22-22).

Córdoba: A Glorious Past

Though the Romans founded Córdoba, which became the largest city of their Iberian empire, even greater glories were in store. The Moors captured Córdoba in A.D. 711, and, while the rest of Europe foundered, the city thrived under the North African Muslims. In Córdoba, the Moors built the Mezquita, or Great Mosque, one of the greatest monuments in Spain.

Córdoba was not only the independent caliphate (the office of the caliph, who served as the spiritual head of Islam) of the Moors and the spiritual and intellectual center of Western Islam, but also a place where Muslims, Jews, and Christians lived side-by-side. Córdoba's delightful Barrio de la Judería, the old, whitewashed Jewish Quarter, is testament to the city's multicultural past.

By the tenth century, Córdoba was a city of nearly one million and possessed Europe's greatest libraries (not surprising when you realize that only the Moors knew how to make paper), a superlative university excelling in mathematics and science, and the only paved and lighted streets on the peninsula. The one-time capital also boasted 600 Arab baths, 60,000 noble mansions, 50 hospitals, and 27 schools.

Although Córdoba was instrumental in pulling Europe out of the Dark Ages, the city's preeminence under the Moors didn't last long. The Christian Reconquest captured the city in 1236, and Córdoba never recovered its former glory.

Arriving in Córdoba

You'll most likely roll into Córdoba by road or rail from another point in Andalusia, or from Madrid. Flying isn't an option; Córdoba has an airport, but no commercial routes use it. You have to fly into Granada, Seville, or Málaga, all at least two hours away.

By car

If you go by car, you drive along undulating olive groves, and a car is virtually the only way to see some of the *pueblos blancos* (white towns) efficiently. (See Chapter 16 for more about the *pueblos blancos.*) Driving to Córdoba from Madrid, take the N-IV (E-5), which veers right (west) at Bailén. The toll-free trip takes about three hours. (The same highway continues directly to Seville.)

Córdoba

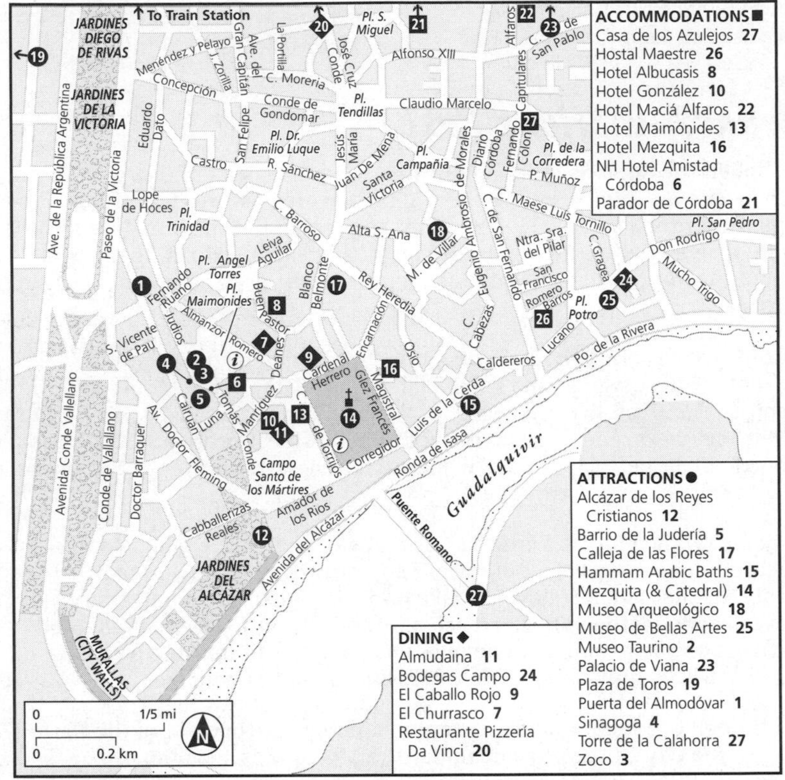

The N-342 highway connects Córdoba with Granada, and the N-331 unites Córdoba with Málaga.

By train

The fastest and least complicated way to get to Córdoba from either Madrid or Seville is definitely the **AVE High-Speed Train.** Though it's the most expensive method of public transportation, I highly recommend it for its efficiency and incredibly smooth ride. From Madrid, the trip takes about one-and-three-quarter hours; from Seville, just under 45 minutes. Fifteen trains travel daily to both destinations. The one-way fare from Madrid is 47€ to 52€ ($60–$67; from Seville, 20€–22€/$26–$28). If you can't catch the AVE, or want to save a few euros, hop on board a **Talgo 200** train (fast but not superfast like the AVE). It takes about two hours and costs 39€to 44€ ($50–$56) from Madrid. Three Talgo trains per day travel between Madrid and Córdoba. Slower regional trains (which go by the names Intercity, Estrecho, García Lorca, and Andalucía Exprés) are cheap, but considerably less comfortable and a waste of valuable time for most travelers.

Córdoba's handsome new train station is northwest of the Old City at Glorieta de las Tres Culturas, s/n, off the Avenida de América (☎ **902-24-02-02**). Bus no. 3 goes directly from outside the train station to the Old Quarter. The **RENFE advance ticket office** is located at Ronda de los Tejares 10 (☎ **957-47-58-84**). For **AVE** train schedules and information, call ☎ **902-24-02-02** or visit www.renfe.es.

By bus

Getting to Córdoba by bus is a simple enough proposition, until you factor in the confusion of local bus stations. Each line has a separate terminal scattered about the city. There are eight terminals in Córdoba; several of them service Madrid (trips take about five hours). The separate terminals can make your trip a bit confusing, especially when the train is so simple. I recommend taking the bus only if you're going to or coming from a small town in which train service isn't available.

The main bus terminal **(Estación Central de Autobuses de Córdoba)** is on Glorieta de las Tres Culturas, s/n (☎ **902-22-92-92**). Buses travel to Seville, Granada, Málaga, and other cities in Andalusia.

Orienting yourself in Córdoba

The provincial capital of Córdoba hugs the banks of the Guadalquivir River, which also flows through Seville, just 129km (80 miles) to the southeast. The Old City, where you find the great Mosque and old Jewish Quarter, is north of the river, across the Roman bridge. Parts of the medieval Arab ramparts still stand on the fringes of the old town. The modern commercial and residential neighborhoods (and the RENFE train station) are north of the Old City, as Córdoba trails off into the foothills of the Sierra Morena Mountains.

Introducing the neighborhoods

Virtually everything you want to see in Córdoba is in or near the ***centro*** (historic center), which is along the river and around the Mezquita (Great Mosque). Immediately northwest of the Mezquita is the **Barrio de la Judería,** the old Jewish Quarter, Córdoba's most enchanting neighborhood.

Finding information after you arrive

There's a tourist information kiosk on the main concourse of the AVE train station. The helpful **Andalusia Provincial Tourism Office** is located at Torrijos 10 (☎ 957-35-51-79; Mon–Fri 9:30 a.m.–7:30 p.m., Sat 10 a.m.–7 p.m. and Sun 10 a.m.–2 p.m.), right next to the Mezquita. **Municipal tourism offices** are located at the Alcázar de los Reyes Cristianos, Campo Santo de los Mártires (☎ 902-20-17-74; Mon–Sun 9:30 a.m.–7:00 p.m.) and Plaza de las Tendillas 5 (☎ 902-20-17-74; daily

10 a.m.–2 p.m. and 4:30–7:30 p.m.), in the modern center of town. There's also a tourist information kiosk on the main concourse of the AVE train station (☎ 902-20-17-74; daily 9:30 a.m.–2 p.m. and 4:30–7:30 p.m.).

Getting around Córdoba

Córdoba's Old City is small and perfect for walking. In fact, many of the streets in this labyrinthine area around the Mezquita are pedestrian only. If you stay at one of the hotels a bit removed from the old center, you'll either need to cover substantial distances by foot or call upon the assistance of taxis and the occasional buses.

By taxi

You find taxi stops on Avenida del Gran Capitán, Calles Cañero, Ciudad Jardín, Arcos de la Frontera, Agustín Moreno, and the Plazas Colón and Tendillas. To order up a cab, call **Radio Taxi** (**☎ 957-76-44-44**). Taxis are inexpensive; unless you take one out to the ruins of Medina Azahara, no trip should cost you more than about 7€ ($8.40).

By car

Wheels are the way to get the most out of your travels in Andalusia, especially if you plan on seeing more than just the three big cities of the south (Córdoba, Seville, and Granada). If you only go to these, and don't plan to do any exploring, I advise against a car, because driving around the cities is difficult and potentially dangerous, with streets originally designed for the horse and buggy.

You can rent a car at one of the major agencies in Córdoba: **Avis,** Plaza de Colón 32 (**☎ 957-40-14-45**); **Europcar,** Rep. Argentina, s/n, and Camino de los Sastres, local 1 (**☎ 957-40-34-80**); and **Hertz,** Av. América, s/n, RENFE Railway station (**☎ 957-40-20-61**).

By bus

You probably won't have much need for buses, unless it's from your hotel or the train station to the Old Quarter. For bus information, call **☎ 957-76-46-76.** Your hotel can also indicate a nearby bus to the major sights in the old town.

Horse for hire?

If you want to clip-clop around the Old Quarter, hire a horse-drawn carriage. You find carriage stops at Campo Santo de los Mártires (next to the Alcázar) and Calle Torrijos (next to the Mezquita). The atmospheric Old Quarter of Córdoba certainly makes the notion appealing, but, on my last visit, most of the horses looked a little anemic. If you're going on to Seville, I think you're better off getting a horse carriage there (if you must choose). The cost in both cities is about 25€ ($30) an hour, though some of the drivers in Córdoba may bargain with you out of high season.

Fiesta! Celebrating in Córdoba

Semana Santa (Holy Week) is intense in Andalusia and is one of the greatest professions of faith in all Spain. Córdoba doesn't exactly take Easter lightly. And forget bunnies, chicks, and chocolate eggs; the worshippers crowding Córdoba's streets are waiting for the passing of 32 colorful ceremonial processions, including floats and penitents. Certain processions, such as María Santísima de la Esperanza (Holy Mary of Hope) and La Virgen de los Dolores (The Virgin of Sorrow) have enthusiastic, cultlike followings. Check with the Tourism Office for a schedule of processions and routes or visit www.guiasemanasanta.com/cordoba/es.

Córdoba is even more famous for its May festivals — if you can get a room (book at least a couple of months in advance), it's by far the best time for a visit to the city. **Las Cruces en Mayo (May Crosses)** marks the beginning of the monthlong celebrations. Crosses are erected in patios and courtyards and decorated with potted plants, flowers, and even shawls. Neighborhood associations, or *peñas,* also set up flamenco stages and small bars nearby — free-flowing wine is about as abundant as flowers in May. Neighborhoods that traditionally sprout May Crosses are **San Agustín, Alcázar Viejo, San Lorenzo,** and **Santa María.**

After the decorated crosses, Córdoba's May party moves to courtyards, when the **Festival de los Patios Cordobeses** — a contest for best patio in Córdoba — takes over about 50 of them across the city. Such exuberant vegetation — red and green pots of roses, carnations, geraniums, jasmine, honeysuckle, and ivy — against the backdrop of stark, whitewashed buildings is a photo op at every turn. Some patios entered in the competition are communal neighborhood efforts, and others belong to palaces or convents. For more information, visit www.patiosdecordoba.net.

Finally, the celebrations reach a crescendo with the **Feria de Mayo (Mayfair),** also called the **Feria de Nuestra Señora de la Salud (Festival of Our Lady of Health).** It's the grand finale, beginning around May 25 and bringing the month's festivities to a rousing close. Feria de Mayo is a smorgasbord of bullfights, flamenco, theater, and *casetas* (stages) set up by neighborhood associations for skits and performances. On generous display is the traditional Cordovan costume, with the *sombrero cordobés* (wide-brimmed hat), Andalusian horses, and, of course, lots of *fino* (fine) wines.

For more information on the best-decorated crosses, the most lavishly verdant patios, and other events, contact the main Tourism Office at ☎ **957-47-12-35** (see "Finding information after you arrive," earlier in this chapter).

Staying in Córdoba

Córdoba gets lots of day-trippers who file into the city to see the Mezquita (Great Mosque) and dash right out of town — which is probably why the hotel scene is somewhat limited. It's a great place for budget travelers, though, with a disproportionate number of good, simple, and inexpensive lodgings near the Mezquita and old Jewish Quarter. At the upper end, choices are considerably slimmer. Prices go up, but not ridiculously so, during high season — April through May across the board, and September through October at some hotels.

Make your reservations far in advance if you want to stay in Córdoba during the popular May festivals.

Casa de los Azulejos
$$–$$$ Old Quarter

A handsome 17th-century colonial house built around a central patio overflowing with plants, this attractive small hotel is full of character and comfort. The eight colorful rooms, which open onto the patio, feature antique doors and lovely Andalusian tile floors (special enough that they're cited in the inn's name). Located a couple of blocks from Córdoba's Roman ruins, the inn contains a cozy library and a genial cantina, called La Guadalupana, which serves a fusion menu of Latin American and Andalusian specialties at lunch and dinner.

See map p. 410. Fernando Colón 5. ☎ ***957-47-00-00.*** *Fax: 957-47-54-96.* `www.casadelosazulejos.com`. *Parking: 12€ ($14). Rack rates: 85€–130€ ($102–$156). AE, DC, MC, V.*

Hostal Maestre
$ East of Centro

A ten-minute walk from the mosque and Jewish Quarter, on two tiny, back-to-back streets overrun with *hostales* and *pensiones* (both informal types of guesthouses), this is the best of the lot. It's a three-in-one establishment — hotel, hostel, and apartments — that hasn't stopped expanding since the mid-1970s. The hotel is the newest of the bunch, dating to 1992. Its 26 rooms are sparse and a bit dull, but they've got the basics: television, air-conditioning, and small bathrooms. The lobby and interior courtyards, with Andalusian tiles and lots of greenery, are more comfortably outfitted than the rooms, so decide how much time you plan to spend in your room. If your answer's "not much," and that's about the amount you want to spend, you'll do fine here. If you've got a family in tow, check out the apartments, which feature one and two bedrooms, small kitchens, and eating areas.

See map p. 410. Romero Barros 4–6. Small street off of San Fernando. ☎ ***957-47-24-10.*** *Fax: 957-47-53-95.* `www.hotelmaestre.com`. *Parking: 9€ ($11). Rack rates: 36€–50€ ($43–$60). MC, V.*

Hotel Albucasis
$$ Old Quarter

A quiet little hotel on an equally quiet little street in the Barrio de la Judería (the Jewish Quarter), the Albucasis does everything in its power to keep its cool in the Andalusian sun. The friendly, family-run hotel has a pretty, plant-filled courtyard, cool marble floors, and green-tiled bathrooms. The 15 air-conditioned rooms (only nine are doubles) are decently sized, with functional, sturdy furnishings. The common areas — a nice breakfast nook, a cozy sitting area, and the inviting patio — are excellent places to relax and share travel tales. Within echo range of the great mosque's bells, the Albucasis is one of the city's best bargains.

See map p. 410. Buen Pastor 11. Three blocks from Mosque, just off Deanes. ☎/Fax: 957-47-86-25. Parking: 13€ ($16). Rack rates: 75€ ($90). MC, V.

Hotel González
$–$$ Old Quarter

A small budget hotel in a restored 16th-century palace, this charmer feels perfectly Andalusian. It's just minutes from the mosque, in the heart of the old Jewish Quarter, which is packed with historic monuments and bustling tourist-oriented shops. Though rooms are simple, they're also delightful, with colorful floor-to-ceiling drapes, antique furnishings, and tile floors (and air conditioning — which is a blessing in steaming Córdoba). The 16 rooms either overlook a pretty square, Plaza Judá Leví, or the hotel's equally pretty interior patio. Original artwork lines the central hall and corridors. The González is easily one of the top bargain places to stay in Córdoba. If you can't get in here, try the owners' other hotel, Hotel Mezquita, with similar facilities and prices (see the listing later in this section).

See map p. 410. Manríquez 3. Off Herreros and Deanes, just west of the mosque. ☎ ***957-47-98-19.*** *Fax: 957-48-61-87. Parking: 12€ ($14). Rack rates: 50€–75€ ($60–$90). AE, DC, MC, V.*

Hotel Maimónides
$$ Old Quarter

If what you care about is location, location, location, you can hardly do better than the Maimónides. Stumble out the front door and you run smack into the Mezquita. And if it's the Mezquita you want to see, request a room with unequaled views of its rooftop (floodlit at night). That's probably enough to justify the price tag for some, but this once-grand hotel isn't up to the standards of the nearby NH Hotel Amistad (see review later in this section). Even though it was fully renovated in 2000, rooms are still unexceptional, and bathrooms aren't exactly spacious. But the unpretentious Maimónides is a comfortable place to stay, and ideally positioned for short walks not only to the mosque but also to the flamenco show down the street, as well as to some of Córdoba's best restaurants in the Jewish Quarter.

See map p. 410. Torrijos 4. Across from west side of mosque. ☎ ***957-47-15-00.*** *Fax: 957-48-38-03.* `www.hotelmaimonides.com`. *Parking: 14€ ($17). Rack rates: 95€ ($114). AE, DC, MC, V.*

Hotel Mezquita
$–$$ Old Quarter

You can't get closer to the mosque unless you were to sneak in and sleep inside. This hotel faces the main entrance of the great Mezquita-Catedral — hard to believe at these bargain prices. Its 21 clean rooms, all with individual air-conditioning units and satellite TV, are well-appointed, especially for the low rates. The antique furnishings, Moorish arches, and bold drapes and bedspreads give the hotel a funky charm. Some rooms have coveted views of the mosque, although others overlook a cool, boldly colored central patio — a good place to hide from the heat of midday (unless you bolt straight for the air-conditioning). Like the Hotel González, which is owned by the same folks, this place has real Andalusian character at bargain prices.

See map p. 410. Plaza Santa Catalina 1. Off M.G. Francés; on east side of the Mosque. ☎ ***957-47-55-85.*** *Fax: 957-47-55-86. Nearby parking: 14€ ($17). Rack rates: 45€–90€ ($54–$108). AE, DC, MC, V.*

NH Hotel Amistad Córdoba

$$$ Old Quarter

Occupying two former 18th-century mansions that face each other across a quiet plaza in the heart of the Jewish Quarter, this five-year-old hotel quickly leapt to the top of the heap, leaving old war horses Meliá Córdoba and Gran Capitán to the package tours. It's easily the choicest place to stay in Córdoba, and pretty fairly priced for the level of comfort it offers. The neoclassical facades give way to a gorgeous central patio with Moorish arches and columns. Furnishings are cleanly modern, focusing on light woods, soft earthy tones, and occasional bright contemporary touches, such as the royal purple chairs in the bar area. An upscale member of the Spanish NH hotel chain, it's next to the bullfighting museum and just a short shuffle from the old synagogue. The entrance, cut right into the old Arab wall, is a nice touch.

See map p. 410. Plaza de Maimónides 3. Off Judíos in Jewish Quarter. ☎ ***957-42-03-35.*** *Fax: 957-42-03-65.* `www.nh-hoteles.es`. *Parking: Nearby 14€ ($17). Rack rates: 140€–153€ ($168–$184). Occasional weekend promotions: 97€ ($116). AE, DC, MC, V.*

Parador de Córdoba (la Arruzafa)

$$$ Outskirts of Córdoba

Córdoba's large and thoroughly modern *parador* (a historic government-run inn) is inconveniently located about 4.8km (3 miles) north of the historic quarter. It's not one of the *parador* system's best efforts — the NH Amistad in the Jewish Quarter (see the preceding review) beats it by a mile. You're best off staying here if Córdoba's heat and tourist hordes get to you; you can get away from it all with a dip in the refreshing pool or a volley on the tennis courts. The gardens are attractive and the panoramic vistas of the city are quite nice. The rooms aren't bad, though they don't rise much above the conventional. Try to get one with a balcony.

See map p. 410. Av. de la Arruzafa 33. About 5km (3 miles) north of city limits, in El Brillante neighborhood. ☎ ***957-27-59-00.*** *Fax: 957-29-04-09.* `www.parador.es`. *Free parking. Rack rates: 125€–135€ ($150–$162). AE, DC, MC, V.*

Dining in Córdoba

Córdoba has a small stable of good Andalusian restaurants, most of them clustered in and around the old Jewish Quarter. However, in contrast to the hotel scene, the city doesn't have too many dependable places for a good, cheap meal. Your best bet is to assemble something informal by tapas grazing; see the section "Setting out on a tapas and tavern crawl," later in this chapter. Casa El Pisto and Taberna Salinas are both perfect for tapas sampling, as are the bars at several of the restaurants listed below.

Almudaina

$$$–$$$$ Old Quarter SPANISH/CONTINENTAL

The top-rated restaurant in Córdoba is also one of its most attractive. Almudaina is in a handsomely restored 16th-century mansion on a pleasing plaza, close to the Mezquita and Alcázar. You can choose from six dining rooms — including a brick-walled and vine-covered, glass-roofed central patio — and elegant side rooms with lush drapes and chandeliers. Edelmiro Jiménez's market-based menu is continually changing, ranging from regional Cordovan dishes to French-inspired entrees. It's really hard to go wrong here; you may start with the excellent eggplant and *champiñones* (mushrooms), or the house foie gras, followed by *lubina* (sea bass) with shrimp and mushrooms. For dessert, the pear and nut mousse sounded great, but I was too stuffed to try it.

See map p. 410. Jardín de los Santos Mártires 1. Across Plaza Campo Santo de los Santos Mártires from the Alcázar. ☎ ***957-47-43-42.*** *Reservations recommended. Main courses: 12€–24€ ($15–$29). Menú del día: 21€ ($25). Tasting menu: 35€ ($42). AE, DC, MC, V. Open: Mon–Sat lunch and dinner, Sun lunch only. Closed: Sun June–Aug.*

Bodegas Campo

$$$ Centro SPANISH/CONTINENTAL

A tavern and bodega since 1908, this restaurant is one of the most inviting in Córdoba. The handsome, warmly rustic environment, decorated with vintage posters of the Córdoba May Festival, is filled with locals day and night. If you arrive early enough, have a drink in the sacristy, a small atmospheric temple in back, past the wall lined by wooden wine vats signed by famous guests. Although wine is clearly an essential, the food is far from an afterthought. The kitchen of Javier Campos concentrates on local and regional dishes; for an appetizer, try the overflowing plate of *pescaditos fritos* (tiny fried fish, eaten whole), or the scrumptious *salmorejo* (a Cordovan version of gazpacho). *Solomillo ibérico* (sirloin steak) is a good choice for the main course, if you've got a big appetite. Oh, and the cellar: It has a fine list of Spanish wine. Some are rather pricy, but the house red is excellent and a bargain.

See map p. 410. Lineros 32. One block in from Paseo de la Ribera along river; 2 blocks east of Plaza del Potro. ☎ ***957-49-75-00.*** *Reservations recommended. Main courses: 14€–20€ ($17–$24). Tasting menu: 37€ ($44). AE, DC, MC, V. Open: Mon–Sat lunch and dinner, Sun lunch only.*

Eating and drinking like a Cordobés

The local cuisine, heavy on garlic and the olive oil in which Andalusia practically swims, concentrates on fried fish and stout meat dishes such as oxtail stew. Don't leave Córdoba without trying *salmorejo* (sahl-moh-*reh*-hoh), a thick, tomato-based soup served cold. It's similar to gazpacho, but more like a puree and more substantial. On a hot day, it can feed you for lunch all by itself. You also find white gazpacho, or *ajoblanco* (ah-hoh-*blahn*-koh), made with olive oil, garlic, and almonds, topped off with grapes. *Rabo de toro* (*rah*-boh deh *toh*-roh, oxtail stew) is a staple in the Córdoba diet, as are *caldereta de cordero* (kahl-deh-*reh*-tah deh cohr-*deh*-roh; lamb) and *cochifrito de la sierra* (koh-chee-*free*-toh deh lah *syeh*-rah; goat or mutton stew). Desserts show ancient Jewish and Moorish influences; try such pastries as *pastel judío* (pah-*stehl* hoo-*dee*-oh; a pastry made with citron preserves), *pestiños* (peh-*stee*-nyohs; honey pancakes), and *buñuelos* (boo-nyoo-*eh*-lohs; fritters). Although Andalusia's the place for *jerez* (heh-*reth;* sherry), try the local variety, *montilla,* an excellent dry and fragrant wine from the wine-producing region Montilla–Moriles. Perfect for tapas, *montilla* comes, like sherry, in several varieties: *finos* (fine and dry); *finos viejos,* also called *amontillados* (aged, fine wines); *olorosos* (aromatic wines); and *olorosos viejos* (aged aromatic wines).

El Caballo Rojo

$$$ Old Quarter ANDALUSIAN/SPANISH

Córdoba's most famous and popular restaurant, El Caballo Rojo (The Red Horse) was a pioneer of Cordovan cooking, reviving ancient Moorish influences. Just yards from the Mezquita, this lively restaurant is one of the top spots to sample some classic Andalusian dishes, such as *salmorejo* (cold, thick Cordovan gazpacho) and *rabo de toro* (oxtail stew), as well as such inventive dishes as almond-and-apple white gazpacho and *rape mudéjar* (monkfish with raisins and pine nuts). The wine cellar is one of the most extensive in the city. The bar downstairs is always noisy with long-time regulars and tourists who've just stumbled in from the mosque. Though that may make you fear for the worst, if you can handle the racket, you'll probably have a fun and even memorable meal here.

See map p. 410. Cardinal Herrero 28. Off Plaza de la Hoguera across from the Mosque. ☎ ***957-47-53-75.*** *Reservations recommended. Main courses: 12€–24€ ($14–$29). Menú del día: 18€ ($22). AE, DC, MC, V. Open: Daily lunch and dinner.*

El Churrasco

$$$ Old Quarter SPANISH

Right in the heart of the historic Judería, this is the place to come — as the name reminds you — for *churrasco,* or juicy grilled meats. If the Cordovan sun has been beating on your head all day and meat sounds like a daunting proposition, start off with *ajoblanco* (white gazpacho) or artichokes in virgin olive oil, and see how your taste buds warm to the idea. If you're not up to charcoal-grilled beef or pork loin, sample any of the tasty fish items, such as *rape a la oliva negra* (monkfish with black olives). The downstairs dining room, with the look of a Moorish courtyard, is more informal than the upstairs rooms. The bar at the entrance is a great place for a sherry or cold beer and tapas, either before or instead of a meal.

See map p. 410. Romero 16. Two blocks west of the Mosque. ☎ ***957-29-08-19.*** *Reservations recommended. Main courses: 13€–25€ ($16–$30). Menú del día: 21€ ($25). AE, DC, MC, V. Open: Daily lunch and dinner. Closed: Aug.*

Exploring Córdoba

Córdoba, though easygoing and enjoyable, can't compare with Seville or Granada: Its history matches or surpasses the past of those other cities, but Córdoba has fewer modern-day attractions. Though the Mezquita is one of the definitive highlights of Spain, a day or day and a half is really all you need to explore the city's major sights. On the other hand, during festival time, you may never want to leave.

Córdoba's municipal museums, including the **Alcázar de los Reyes Cristianos** (Royal Fortress and Gardens), **Museo Taurino** (Bullfighting Museum), and **Julio Romero de Torres Museum** (a collection of the Cordovan painter, on Plaza del Potro), are all free on Fridays.

The top attractions

Mezquita (Great Mosque)
Old Quarter

Córdoba's astonishing Mosque is one of Moorish Spain's greatest achievements, one of Spain's most enduring and treasured monuments, and one of the world's most remarkable mosques. It's brilliant, surprising, and it packs a historical wallop. You'd hardly guess its glory from the mostly plain exterior, though. The Moorish Emir Ab-ar Rahman I ordered it built in A.D. 786 at the height of power of al-Andalus — Muslim Spain. (The Moors controlled all but a small sliver of northern Spain, in the present-day Basque Country). The Mosque was significantly enlarged over the next two centuries (the original mosque makes up only about one-fifth of the present structure), but in the 16th century, part of it was destroyed. In an act of either hubris or revenge, Christians constructed a cathedral smack in the middle of the mosque. This juxtaposition may strike you as an abomination; at the very least, it stands as a fascinating document of Spanish religious and political history.

Enter through the **Patio de los Naranjos** (a large patio of orange trees, where the faithful prayed and cleansed themselves before entering the mosque). Even if you've seen pictures of the interior, the magical forest of candy-cane-striped arches — a seemingly limitless horizon of dazzling harmony — will astound you. More than 850 columns and purely decorative arches of granite, jasper, and marble fill 19 aisles. Notice the capitals, which were rescued in large part from ancient (that is to say, *more* ancient) structures in Córdoba (the mosque was built on the site of a Visigothic basilica). The mosaic tiles and marble that once covered the floors are now sadly gone, as are most of the polychrome ceilings, but the Mosque's grandeur resonates throughout. Wander in a delirious daze, but don't miss the ***mihrab,*** the wonderfully ornate prayer niche in the southeast corner of the mosque. A feast of carved marble, stucco, alabaster, and mosaics, it pointed to Mecca and was the most sacred part of the Mosque. Look up at its magnificent cupola.

The **Capilla Real** (Royal Chapel) and **Capilla Villaviciosa** (Villaviciosa Chapel), the first Christian components of the complex, are Mudéjar (a hybrid of Moorish and Christian architecture) in style and were ordered by Ferdinand III in 1236, as part of the Reconquest. The ostentatious Italianate dome of the **Catedral,** begun in 1253, is a startling contrast to the mesmerizing quiet beauty of the mosque. The cathedral's saving graces are its magnificently carved mahogany choir stalls, which date to 1758 and depict the Old and New Testaments, and its pulpits, also beautiful works of carving.

Unfortunately, you won't get to enjoy the spectacular views of Córdoba and the Sierra from the top of the belfry; it remains closed for restoration, as it has been for years.

In summer, the mosque's interior is heaven on earth, a blessed retreat from the sun (something the Moors surely considered when they designed it in Córdoba). But if you visit Córdoba in winter, even though the sun may shine brilliantly outside and you're decked out comfortably in shorts and sandals, it can get very chilly inside the mosque. As when you go to the movie theater on a blistering day, you're wise to bring a sweater.

See map p. 410. Torrijos 10. One block north of river. ☎ ***957-47-05-12.*** *Admission: 8€ ($9.60) adults, 4€ ($4.80) children ages 10–14, free for children under 10. Open: Winter Mon–Sat 10 a.m.–5:30 p.m., Sun 9 a.m.–10:15 a.m. and 2–6 p.m.; summer Mon–Sat 10 a.m.–7 p.m., Sun 9 a.m.–10:15 a.m. and 2–7 p.m.*

Two for the price of one

You can draw your own conclusions about whether or not it was a heinous crime to insert a cathedral into the middle of the Mezquita, thereby destroying the mosque's perfect symmetry (and about a quarter of its pillars). Before the building of the cathedral, one could see across the forest of pillars, surely a mind-bending optical effect. The cathedral also destroyed the mosque's perfect acoustics. (Even King Carlos V, who gave the okay to build the cathedral, was dismayed upon seeing it. He reportedly exclaimed, "You have destroyed something unique to build something commonplace.")

Ironically, the building of the cathedral may have saved the Mezquita. Of 300 mosques that once existed in Córdoba, the Mezquita is the only one that remains, no doubt in tribute to its Christian church and treasures within, which prevented it from being sacked along with other remnants of Muslim Spain.

Flower power: Calleja de las Flores

Córdoba's Calleja de las Flores (Little Street of Flowers) isn't much more than an alleyway just west of the mosque (off Calles Blanco Belmonte and Victor Bosco), but it's a charming spot: a picture-perfect montage of wrought-iron grilles, potted flowers, and window boxes filled with colorful geraniums. Domestic courtyards, often shared and gardened communal-style by a number of families, also come alive in spring; annual contests crown the best patios in Córdoba. The Tourism Office organizes springtime visits to a number of them; call ☎ **957-49-16-77** for additional information and tour times.

Alcázar de los Reyes Cristianos

Constructed on top of an old Moorish palace, the 14th-century Fortress of the Christian Monarchs, strategically located along the Guadalquivir River, served military and mercantilist purposes. For about eight years during the Reconquest, the Christian monarchs made the Gothic Alcázar their palace, and Christopher Columbus came here to schmooze and lobby the kings for funds to make his maiden voyage to the New World. The extensive gardens, perfect for kids who need to stretch out a bit, are truly regal, with a series of pools, water terraces, fountains, and palm and orange trees that reflect Córdoba's Moorish roots. Within the spare palace quarters (which once served as Inquisition headquarters) are archaeological finds from the area, including Roman mosaics and a sarcophagus from the third century. Below the Mosaics room are steam baths that date to the time of the Moorish caliphate.

The fortress's imposing towers, the **Torre de los Leones (Tower of the Lions)** and **Torre de Homenaje (Homage Tower),** have reopened after restoration. Climb to the top for excellent panoramic views of the Old Quarter of Córdoba.

See map p. 410. Caballerizas Reales, s/n. Between Guadalquivir River and Campo Santo de los Mártires. ☎ ***957-42-01-51.*** *Admission: 4€ ($3.60) adults, 2€ ($240) students; free on Fri for seniors. Open: Mon–Sat 10 a.m.–2 p.m. and 5:30–7:30 p.m., Sun and holidays 9:30 a.m.–2:30 p.m.*

Barrio de La Judería

Córdoba's Jewish Quarter is a fascinating and wonderfully alive area of impossibly narrow and crooked streets, ancient whitewashed houses with cool, colorful interior patios, and historic religious monuments. A stroll through the area is like a history lesson on Moorish Spain. When Córdoba was the largest and most advanced city in Europe in the tenth century, the cobbled streets teemed with silversmiths and craftsmen, and the residents — Jews, Christians, and Moors — all lived as they did in Toledo, in peace. Visit the **Sinagoga (Synagogue)**, built in 1315 and the only Jewish

Pretty on the inside

Andalusian patios serve a very practical purpose — their construction at the center of the house, with cooling ceramic tiles and potted plants and vines, is essential for keeping the house cool. (The labyrinthine design of the Old Quarter, a Moorish innovation featuring houses close together on narrow streets, achieves the same cooling purpose.) But the patios' aesthetic flourishes also reflect a less pragmatic concern. At the heart of the Muslim religion is the notion that beauty is fundamentally internal and should be kept private. Thus, most old Andalusian houses are simple on the outside; decoration is limited to the interior. The same concepts are apparent even in the Moors' greatest monuments; in Córdoba's Great Mosque, notice how severe and unadorned its exterior is, compared to the unrestrained visual beauty concealed inside.

temple in Andalusia that survived the tumult of the Inquisition and expulsion of Jews and Moors. If you're expecting cathedral-like grandeur, its utter simplicity will shock you: Except for the stucco decorations, it's just a tiny, plain box. An important Jewish community once thrived in Spain and built hundreds of synagogues, but the religious fervor of the Inquisition and Expulsion led to most Jews publicly renouncing their faith or, more commonly, fleeing Spain. Only three synagogues remain in Spain: two in Toledo and the modest one in Córdoba.

Across the street from the synagogue, but a world away, is the **Museo Taurino** — the Bullfighting Museum. Housed in a noble 16th-century house, Casa de las Bulas, it displays a replica of the famous bullfighter Manolete's tomb and other *toro* (bull) relics and memorabilia, including bulls' heads and the hide of the bull that gored Manolete to death. Four of Spain's greatest bullfighters, revered throughout the country, came from Córdoba and were known as the "four Caliphs of Córdoba."

Next to the museum is the **Zoco,** the old *souk,* or market area. Today it's again a market vying for your tourist dollars with small shops dealing Córdoba crafts and jewelry. Just up the street from the synagogue is the **Puerta del Almodóvar** — Almodóvar's Gate. Nothing to do with Spain's hippest filmmaker, it's part of the original medieval entrance to the old Jewish Quarter. On the west side of the Judería are the remains of the old Arab city walls.

See map p. 410. La Sinagoga: Calle Judíos. ☎ ***957-20-29-28.*** *Admission: .30€ ($.35), free to E.U. members. Open: Tues–Sat 10 a.m.–2 p.m. and 3:30–5:30 p.m., Sun 10 a.m.–1:30 p.m.*

Museo Taurino: Plaza de Maimónides. ☎ ***957-20-10-56.*** *Admission: 3€ ($3.60) adults, children under 18 free; Fri free. Open: Tues–Sat 10 a.m.–2 p.m. and 5:30–7:30 p.m., Sun 9:30 a.m.–2:30 p.m.*

More cool things to see and do

Do you still have a few extra hours or days in town? If so, check out these other fun activities to do in Córdoba.

- **Peeking in on patios.** Córdoba is known for its splendid patios, but outside of the May patio festival, finding and getting in to see the best ones is sometimes hard. For the best glimpse of aristocratic Córdoba, you have to venture a bit north of the Old Quarter. Tucked away in a busy commercial district, **Palacio de los Marqueses de Viana,** Plaza de Don Gome 2 (5 blocks west of Calle Alfaros, southwest of Plaza de Colón — take bus to Plaza Colón; ☎ **957-49-67-41**), is a sumptuous 16th-century palace, which locals call El Museo de los Patios — The Patio Museum. The mansion has 14 elegant interior patios, as well as halls decorated with rich furnishings, Goya tapestries, carved cedar ceilings, and rare tiles. Admission is 6€ ($7.20; if visiting only the patios, 3€/$3.60). It's open Monday to Friday from 10 a.m. to 1 p.m. and 4 to 6 p.m., Sat 9 a.m. to 2 p.m.; in summer, Monday to Saturday from 9 a.m. to 2 p.m. Closed: first two weeks of June (but you can still visit the patios).
- **Taking a magical history tour.** South of the mosque, at the bend in the Guadalquivir River, are two important works of architecture dating to Córdoba's Roman and Moorish eras, Calahorra Tower and the Roman Bridge. The bridge isn't a quaint Roman artifact but a heavily trafficked thoroughfare with 16 arches. The sad river, all but washed up now, mirrors the city's decline. The Romans used the river as a commercial waterway, and the Moors tapped into its power with waterwheels and mills (still visible from the bridge today). Cross the bridge (notice the shrine to St. Raphael, the archangel of Córdoba, about mid-way, which is usually decorated with flowers and lit candles) to approach the **Torre de la Calahorra,** an imposing tower built in the mid–14th century to guard the entrance to the city. Today it houses an audiovisual museum, **Museo Vivo de Al-Andalus,** Puente Romano, s/n (☎ **957-29-39-29**), with exhibits and a multimedia presentation on the three distinct religions and cultures upon which Córdoba is founded. Although a good opportunity to find out more about Moorish Spain, the museum is probably best if you approach it like an escapist action flick on a hot summer day — a place of refuge. To get there, cross the Roman bridge just south of the mosque. Admission is 4.50€ ($5.75), 3€ ($3.85) seniors and students; the multimedia presentation is an additional 1.20€ ($1.50). The museum is open daily from 10 a.m. to 6 p.m.; in summer months daily from 10 a.m. to 2 p.m. and 4:30 to 8:30 p.m. (Multivisión projection at 11 a.m., and noon, 1, 3, and 4 p.m.)
- **Hanging out in a plaza.** The attractively weathered **Plaza del Potro** is best known for its historic inn, La Posada del Potro (Inn of the Colt), where Miguel de Cervantes, the author of *Don Quixote,* once stayed (the plaza figures into his epic novel). Across the plaza, the **Museo de Bellas Artes de Córdoba** (Fine Arts Museum),

Plaza del Potro 1 (1 block west of Calle San Fernando; a ten-minute walk from the mosque; ☎ **957-47-33-45**), occupies a 15th-century charity hospital and has a small collection of Seville-school painters and Cordovan artists. Admission is 1.50€ ($1.80); free for members of the E.U. The museum is open Wednesday to Saturday from 9 a.m. to 8:30 p.m., Sunday and holidays from 9 a.m. to 2:30 p.m., and Tuesday from 2:30 to 8:30 p.m. A number of outdoor cafes occupy the pedestrian street opposite the plaza and are good places to rest your legs and slurp an iced lemonade.

- **Digging up the past.** Most everything of interest in Córdoba relates to the city's multilayered past, so a good way to explore those layers is to see what's been unearthed at Córdoba's **Museo Arqueológico** (Archaeology Museum), Plaza de Jerónimo Páez 7 (between the Mosque and Plaza del Potro; ☎ **957-47-55-17**). It occupies a handsome Renaissance palace and is a survey of the city's (which is to say, Spain's) history, with Roman, Visigothic, Muslim, Mudéjar, and Renaissance pieces. The diverse collection includes fantastic ceramics, mosaics, sarcophagi, and a terrific bronze stag that came from a fountain at the Medina Azahara palace (see "Side trips from Córdoba: A visit to the ruins of Medina Azahara," later in this chapter). The Moorish decorative arts are particularly well represented. Admission is 1.50€ ($1.80), free for members of the E.U. The museum is open Tuesday, 2:30 to 8:30 p.m., Wednesday to Saturday from 9 a.m. to 8:30 p.m., and Sunday and holidays from 9 a.m. to 2:30 p.m.

Shopping for Cordovan crafts

The Reconquest was 500 years ago, but Córdoba is still known for traditional Moorish crafts, such as handmade gold and silver filigree and embossed leather goods, known worldwide as Cordovan leather. Shops featuring these traditional Cordovan goods, and many more, line the Judería — a bit too thickly for some tastes. A mark — a crowned lion and the name of the city — distinguishes the embossed Cordovan leathers.

If you're in the market for traditional leather goods from Córdoba, be careful of items advertised as embossed or hand-tooled Cordovan leather. Some of the sneakier shops may try to pass off inferior stamped leather from Morocco as the real thing. Unfortunately, the work is generally of

Lots of bull

Toro, Toro, Toro: Córdoba's new Plaza de Toros (bullfighting ring), **Coso de los Califas,** is on the outskirts of town, on Avenida Gran Vía. Most big bullfighting events are in May (usually the last week) to coincide with the city festivals, but look for other scheduled bullfights in this *toros*-crazy town. Call ☎ **957-23-25-07** for information and tickets. Prices range from 5€ ($6.40) to about 75€ ($90).

Arab baths and teahouses

To relive the elegance and sophistication of Al-Andalus, the Moors' dynasty in southern Spain, pop into a *tetería* (teahouse) or the new *baños árabes,* or Turkish-style bathhouse. Though Granada has probably done a better job connecting its Moorish past to the present, Córdoba now has a couple of establishments directed at both locals and visitors that give a taste of Arab traditions. For a phenomenally relaxing couple of hours, don't miss the new **Hammam Arabic Baths** on Corregidor Luis de la Cerda 51 (☎ **957-48-47-46**), which summons a bit of the flavor found at the Mezquita and Alhambra (the latter, in Granada). A series of hot and cold steam pools have been installed under brick arches and tiled walls. The freezing cold pool, in the first room, is only for the hearty. The baths (with or without massage) are every couple of hours, from 10 a.m. to midnight (lasting 90 minutes). Prices for one session range from 20€ to 29€ ($24–$35). Hammam has a teahouse upstairs and occasional belly dance performances, every day in summer beginning at 9 p.m. Reservations are essential. Another teahouse worth stopping into for a hot or cold mint tea or thick *batido* (shake) is **Salon de Té,** Buen Pastor 13 (☎ **957-48-79-84**), a loungelike spot in the heart of the old Jewish Quarter.

lesser quality. Touch and inspect the product, and look for the lion symbol (though that too may be an imposter). After you've seen the real stuff, distinguishing between it and the inferior imposters shouldn't be too hard.

For authentic leather goods, drop by the shop of talented artisan **Carlos López-Obrero.** His shop, specializing in hand-tooled leather and embossed leather products, is on Calleja de las Flores 2 (no phone). **Taller Meryan,** at the same address (☎ **957-47-59-02**), is one of Córdoba's best shops and factories for quality embossed leather products.

For handcrafts of all sorts, particularly jewelry, check out the **Zoco Municipal de Artesanía,** the old *medina* (Middle Eastern market) on Calle Judíos, just behind the bullfighting museum. It's open daily from 10 a.m. to 8:30 p.m. Other shops line the streets Deanes, Romero, and the Plaza Leví and those near the Mezquita.

If you want to buy some local *montilla* (dry sherry), other wines, or Andalusian olive oil, check out the well-stocked **Bodegas Mezquita,** on Corregidor Luis de la Cerda 73 (☎ **957-49-81-17**), just behind the Great Mosque. They let you taste wines and, sometimes, oils and cheese.

Discovering Córdoba's nightlife

You're in one of the legendary cities of Andalusia, the old Moorish kingdom. So what to do at night? Simple. Join the waves of Cordobeses at taverns for tapas and local spirits, and after that, be a tourist: Catch an animated flamenco show. If you're in Córdoba during the annual Guitar Festival (July), you won't want to miss seeing some great picking on the Spanish guitar.

Setting out on a tapas and tavern crawl

A tapas and tavern crawl in Córdoba is virtually irresistible. Here are a few local faves, great places to duck in out of the heat, have a *montilla* (local version of a dry sherry, similar to *manzanilla*), and order a small portion of Serrano ham, chorizo, *aceitunas* (green olives), or *queso* (cheese). These places are very casual and not the type where you need reservations — plus, virtually no one speaks English here. You don't need to call ahead, so I don't list phone numbers here.

Casa El Pisto, or Taberna de San Miguel, Plaza de San Miguel 1, is a charming old tavern, not far from Seville's Roman temple, that has Mudéjar-style tiles, wood beams, and hanging hams and peppers along with hundreds of small framed photos of old bullfighters. If you hit only one bar in town, make it this one. The front bar is always crowded with people knocking back tapas and small glasses of wine or beer; you can continue to stand or wait for a table in the restaurant in back. Near the restored Plaza de la Corredera, **Taberna Salinas,** Tunidores 3, at Espartería is an appealing spot, dating from 1879, for a few tapas and a *montilla.* Choose from the tiny bar at the front or a traditional courtyard sitting area with tables out back. A good option here is the classic Córdoba dish *naranjas "picas" con aceite y bacalao* (strips of cod served with wedges of sweet Andalusian oranges and slices of onion, bathed in virgin olive oil) — as weird as it is wonderful.

Bodega Zoco, Judíos, s/n, is a fantastic underground stone catacomb of a place in the old *medina.* Go down the stairs at the back of the market into the relief of natural refrigeration. The *chorizo al vino* (sausage soaked in *montilla* wine) is a house specialty. Just up the street is **Bodegas Guzman,** Judíos, s/n, an atmospheric spot with wonderful 1920s and '30s posters from the May Festivals at the entrance and a crowd of regulars at the bar. **Bodegas Campo,** Calle de los Lineros 32, is an excellent restaurant (see the listing in the restaurant section of this chapter) with a tiny bar at the entrance, but the real star is the sexy *sacristía* (a tapas temple) at back, past the wine vats. **Mesón Juan Peña,** Dr. Fleming 1, has a terrific wine cellar. The cinematic bar **Pepe el de la Judería** (Pepe of the Jewish Quarter) Romero 1, is a revered institution that has served drinks to generations of Cordovans, and looks the part. Pick up a copy of the owner's book, *Cordobeses Ilustres* (Illustrious Cordovans). But the oldest-tavern-in-Córdoba award goes to **Casa Miguel,** Plaza Cirino 7, serving great tapas since the early 1800s.

Performing arts: Flamenco and more

You're in the heart of Andalusia, and though the local flamenco scene is small, it's still one of the most traditional places in Spain to see flamenco dancing and emotional *cante hondo* (deep song). The place to be is **Tablao Cardenal,** Torrijos 10 (☎ **957-48-31-12**), just across from the

Mezquita. In a pretty open-air square, the group puts on a very respectable flamenco show that doesn't pander to tourists or try to wow them with cheap pyrotechnics. The sparks here are real. There are shows Tuesday through Saturday at 10:30 p.m. The price is 18€ ($22), which includes your first drink. Reserving a spot in advance is wise, because it's popular, and as soon as a large group shows up, you may be out of luck. Try to score a seat as close to the stage as possible. The other locale in town for flamenco music and dance is **Mesón Flamenco La Bulería,** on Pedro López 3 (☎ **957-48-38-39**), near the Plaza de la Corredera. Shows every night at 10:30. Cost is 12€ ($15), including one drink.

On occasion, you can catch flamenco at the **Gran Teatro de Córdoba,** but more often you find opera, classical music, and ballet. It's on Avenida del Gran Capitán (☎ **957-48-02-37**).

Guitarra flamenca: The art of flamenco guitar

Most Spanish guitar greats — such as Paco de Lucía and Tomatito — hail from Andalusia. Spanish classical and flamenco guitar derives — like most everything in southern Spain — from the region's indelible Moorish past. The playing evolved from the sounds of the classical Arab lute. Every July, Córdoba hosts the **Festival Internacional de la Guitarra** (International Guitar Festival), one of its most popular events. If you're here then, it's a great opportunity to see Spanish guitar maestros work their magic on the strings. From classical Spanish guitar to flamenco, you can see some of the fastest hands in the west, performing in great spots in the Old City — the gardens of the Alcázar, the Botanical Gardens, and the Gran Teatro (Grand Theater of Córdoba). For additional information and tickets, call ☎ **957-48-02-37** or visit `www.guitarracordoba.com`. The Spanish Tourism Offices abroad (see the Appendix) usually have their hands on a schedule several weeks in advance, or, as soon as you're in Córdoba, ask for a schedule of performances at the Tourism Office.

Side trips from Córdoba: A visit to the ruins of Medina Azahara

If Córdoba's Great Mosque has whetted your appetite for more remnants of the glorious Moorish domination of Spain, consider a short side trip to the ruins of **Medina Azahara,** or Medinat al-Zahara (☎ **957-32-91-30**). Built in the foothills of the Sierra Morena in A.D. 961 by the Caliph Adb ar Rahman III as a gift to one of his wives (judging by the opulence, she was a favorite), the palace was once a small, stunning city with 400 houses, 300 baths, a mosque, fortress, zoo, and luxurious gardens. Archaeologists believe that the palace was perhaps unrivaled in its opulence with jewel-encrusted pillars, gold fountains, and quicksilver pools. The caliph supposedly had almond trees planted all the way to Córdoba — he liked the visual effect of the trees in bloom, which rolled out a snowy white carpet up to his dream palace. Just seven decades after its laborious construction (which required 10,000 men), the 121-hectare (300-acre) compound was sacked and destroyed by the Almoravids, a group of Berbers with a political beef against the Al Mansur dynasty. The ruins of the grand hall, terraces, and living quarters, unearthed this century, merely suggest the grandeur of the palace-city on the outskirts of Córdoba, but they're worth a visit, even though they're surely not the posthumous record of his rule that ar-Rahman meant to leave. Sections are being painstakingly reconstructed, though, and the Royal Palace doesn't require much imagination.

Medina Azahara is 8km (5 miles) west of Córdoba at Km 5.5. Go by car, taxi or direct bus (☎ **902 201 774;** 5€, or $6). Take Avenida de Medina Azahara and C-431 west from Córdoba to Palma del Río. Admission is 1.50€ ($1.80); free for E.U. citizens. Hours are September 16 to April 30, Tuesday through Saturday from 10 a.m. to 6:30 p.m., and Sunday from 10 a.m. to 2 p.m.; May 2 to September 15, Tuesday through Saturday from 10 a.m. to 8:30 p.m. and Sunday from 10 a.m. to 2 p.m. Closed: January 6, March 25, May 1, August 15, November 1, and December 6 and 25.

Guided visits (in winter, Tues–Fri 4 p.m. and Sat 10:30 a.m.; in summer Tues–Fri and Sat 6 p.m.; 13€, or $17) can be arranged through Córdobavisión by calling ☎ **957-76-02-41.**

Fast Facts: Córdoba

Area Code

Córdoba's area code is **957**, which you must dial before every number.

Currency Exchange

You can find banks and ATMs in the main shopping district in the Old Quarter near the Mezquita and along Avenida Gran Capitán in the modern business section of town (Banco de España, Banco Bilbao Vizcaya, and Banco BNP España are all located almost on top of each other on that street). A *casa de cambio* (exchange house) is Cambio de Divisas, Calle Cardenal Herrero 30 (☎ 957-47-96-99).

Emergencies

For general emergencies, call ☎ **112.** For medical emergencies, dial ☎ **061** or call the Cruz Roja (Red Cross) at ☎ 957-22-22-22. For an ambulance call ☎ 957-29-55-70. In case of fire call ☎ **080.** For a police emergency, call ☎ **091.**

Hospitals

Hospital Reina Sofía is located on Av. Menéndez Pidal, s/n (☎ 957-21-70-00). Hospital Los Morales is on Sierra de Córdoba, s/n (☎ 957-27-56-50).

Information

The Andalusia Provincial Tourism Office is located at Torrijos 10 (☎ 957-35-51-79; Mon–Fri 9:30 a.m. to 6:30 p.m., Sat 10 a.m.–2 p.m. and 4–6 p.m., and Sun 10 a.m.–2 p.m.), right next to the Mezquita. Municipal tourism offices are located at the Alcázar de los Reyes Cristianos, Campo Santo de los Mártires (☎ 902-20-17-74; daily 9:30 a.m.–7 p.m.) and Plaza de las Tendillas, s/n (☎ 902-20-17-74; daily 10 a.m.–1:30 p.m. and 6–9:30 p.m.), in the modern center of town. There's also a tourist information kiosk on the main concourse of the AVE train station (☎ 902-20-17-74; daily 9:30 a.m.–2 p.m. and 5–8 p.m.).

Police

The municipal police station is at Campo Madre de Dios, s/n (☎ 957-23-37-53 or ☎ **092**).

Post Office

Córdoba's main post office is on Cruz Conde 15 (☎ 902-19-71-97).

Safety

Córdoba is a low-key town, but it's also a city that suffers perennially from unemployment and economic hardship. With the large number of tourists that traipse in and out, often along twisting, confusing streets, the city has gained an unfortunate reputation as a place where thieves prey on tourists — though it has always seemed safe to me. Although there's no need to be alarmed, be careful if you venture beyond the Jewish Quarter and the area around the mosque — areas with a noticeable police presence. Some parts west of Calle de San Fernando are uncomfortably deserted and perfect places for thieves-in-waiting. Leave valuables and extra money at the hotel safe, and try to carry things that you don't want to lose on the front of your body.

Chapter 16

Andalusia's Pueblos Blancos

In This Chapter

- Exploring Arcos de la Frontera and nearby towns
- Driving through Andalusia's *pueblos blancos*
- Discovering Ronda — renowned for its gorge and bullfighting
- Taking side trips to the Costa de la Luz and Costa del Sol

Andalusia's *pueblos blancos* — small, whitewashed villages clustered in the rural, mountainous region between Seville and the sea — represent southern Spain at its most mythical. Sprinkled across a dramatic landscape of olive groves and rugged, 1,524m (5,000-ft.) limestone slopes, these dazzling villages are tucked improbably into rocky bluffs. Former defensive strongholds, these villages have a perfect whiteness interrupted only by the ruddy contrast of castle ruins and church bell towers.

The white towns of Andalusia look as though they were entire North African villages uprooted and shipped by boat to the south of Spain. Though the Romans and Visigoths originally settled the region, the Moors built these memorable medieval villages with impenetrable, Arab-style alleyways. Ronda and Arcos de la Frontera are the largest of the so-called white towns, with the best infrastructure for visitors. And they're within easy reach of Andalusia's famous sherry wineries in Jerez, the beaches of the Costa de la Luz, and glitzy, mega-developed Costa del Sol.

Ronda and the other white towns, mostly scattered about the Sierra de Grazalema Nature Reserve, are in the mountainous interior of Spain's southernmost provinces, Cádiz and Málaga. The only things farther south are the Andalusian coastlines and Africa. Because they're mountain towns, the Pueblos Blancos aren't as dreadfully hot as Andalusia's Big Three (Seville, Granada, and Córdoba). Winter is mild, while spring and fall are warm but comfortable. The southern coast is all about sun, getting more than 300 sunny days a year. The best time to visit Ronda and the rest of the white towns is spring (Mar, Apr, and May), when flowers

Andalusia

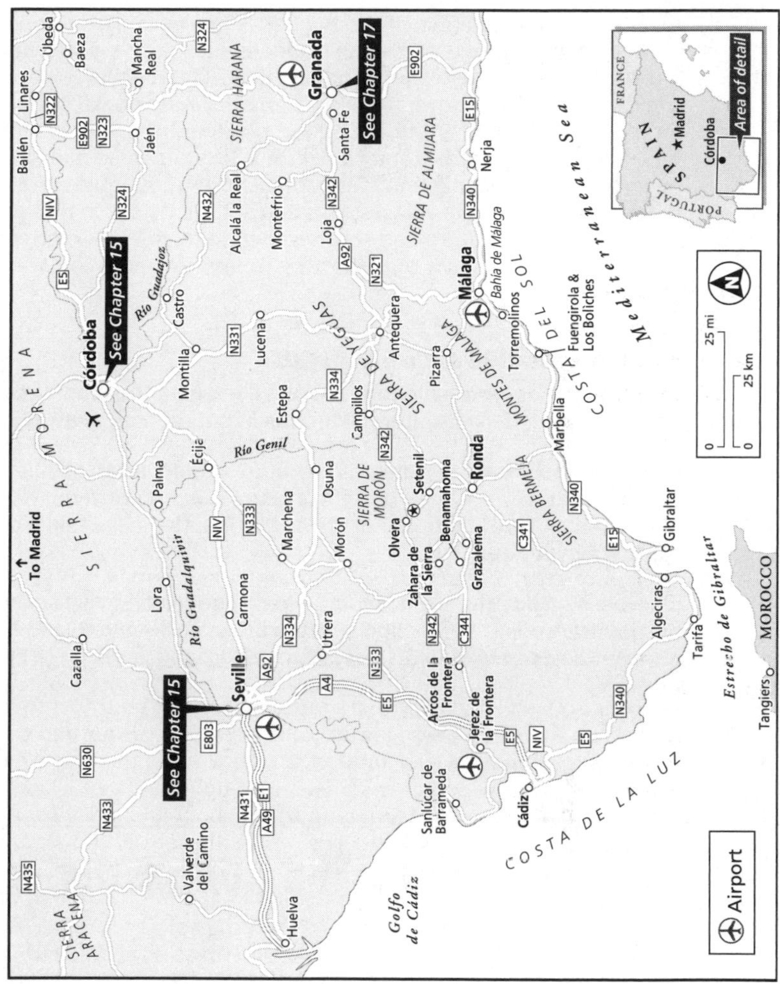

are in bloom across the valleys. If you can't make your trip then, fall is also nice and winter isn't bad, because the sun shines all year. Likewise, the coasts are great year-round, but ridiculously crowded in summer.

The towns in this chapter are ideal for a driving itinerary. Arcos and Ronda are both good bases from which to set out and explore the white towns, so you may want to spend a night or more in either. Most of the small white towns are places to spin through, perhaps have lunch, and then move on.

Arcos: Quiet Inland Beauty

Arcos de la Frontera (usually just called Arcos), perched daringly on a red-rock promontory high above the Guadalete River, the westernmost of the *pueblos blancos,* is also one of the prettiest. The town is so narrow at the top that it squeezes down to a single street. Arcos doesn't offer a whole lot to see — or to do — but it's a good place to base yourself for the first half of a *pueblos blancos* tour. (Jerez de la Frontera also makes a decent base, but I prefer smaller and less congested Arcos.) Arcos serves as a natural gateway to the villages; you can set out by car in the morning and do a loop of the western and southern white towns. Alternatively, it's a short trip to Jerez and a good starting point for travels to Cádiz and the Costa de la Luz.

Getting to and around Arcos

To get to Arcos, you have to drive or take a bus; the closest train destination is Jerez de la Frontera, which is 32km (20 miles) away.

Driving to Arcos is easy, and, as a bonus, scenic. From Seville, take N-IV or A-4 south toward Jerez de la Frontera. Take the turn-off, N-342, east to Arcos. Arcos is 91km (56 miles) from Seville; the drive takes just a bit more than an hour.

Two buses a day (at 8 a.m. and 4:30 p.m.) go from Seville's Santa Justa Station to Arcos (the bus line is **Amarillos: ☎ 95-498-91-84**) for about 5€ ($6). You can also take buses from Cádiz and Jerez de la Frontera.

Arcos is so small and hilly that you must rely on your feet to get you up and down the steep passageways and stairs. To get around the region, from one *pueblo blanco* to another, a rental car is the only practical way.

The secret of the *bull*boards

You may think you're hallucinating at first. As you drive across the rolling landscape of the south, a peculiar image rises on the horizon: a Godzilla-sized black bull. Up close, you quickly realize that the anatomically correct *toro* is a 9m-tall (30-ft.) wood cutout of a bull — it looks like a billboard without a product name and slogan attached. And in fact, that's exactly what it is. Several decades ago, Osborne, the famous winemaker in Jerez, erected "bullboards" across Spain to promote its sherries and brandies. When Spain outlawed all rural billboard advertising, nostalgic Spaniards, who grew up pointing out the bulls on car trips, protested and convinced Parliament to make an exception to the law. The government allowed the Osborne billboards to stand, officially designated National Historic Monuments, as long as they were stripped of all advertising. Today, of course, they're the kind of subliminal product placement a marketer can only dream of.

(Unless, of course, you hate to drive and have oodles of money, in which case you can hire a taxi driver for the day.)

Finding information after you arrive

The **tourist information office** is on the west side of the Plaza del Cabildo (☎ **956-70-22-64**). It has maps and also offers guided tours of town. The tourism office is open Monday to Friday from 9 a.m. to 2 p.m. and 5:30 to 7:30 p.m., Saturday from 10 a.m. to 2 p.m., and Sunday from 10:30 a.m. to 2:30 p.m.

Staying in style

You can find all the hotels listed here, with the exception of Cortijo Fain, in Arcos's *zona monumental* (historic district).

Hacienda El Santiscal

$$

This welcoming hacienda is a lovely country inn. A 15th-century noble house set in the countryside 2km (1.2 miles) outside of Arcos, it is thoroughly Andalusian in character. The 12 inexpensive rooms are handsomely if simply decorated, with rich colors and fabrics. Each is different; some have exposed wood beams, others Mudéjar-style brickwork. The two suites, which are also attractively priced, have either a fireplace and lounge or private terrace. There's a small restaurant serving meals for 25€ ($32) and a small round pool with distant views of olive groves and fields of sunflower and wheat.

Av. El Santiscal 129. ☎ ***956-70-83-13.*** *Fax: 956-70-82-68.* `www.santiscal.com`. *Free parking. Rack rates: 65€–99€ ($78–$120). MC, V.*

El Convento

$$

Tucked into the historic district, down a tiny alleyway behind the *parador* (government-run hotel), this little find typifies the allure of the *pueblos blancos.* Built right into the Las Mercedarias Convent (hence the name), it only has 11 rooms, but they're a good value for the price, and they were recently renovated. The hotel, which has a fine restaurant (which shares the hotel's name and is reviewed later in this chapter) and rooftop terrace, offers great views over the gorge and countryside. Its charm and comfort have placed this hotel in high demand. Make a reservation as soon as you decide to spend the night in Arcos. The restaurant entrance is Marques de Torresoto 7.

Maldonado 2. Take Escribanos from Plaza del Cabildo and turn right on Maldonado. ☎ ***956-70-23-33.*** *Fax: 956-70-41-28.* `www.webdearcos.com/elconvento`. *Parking: 5€ ($6.40). Rack rates: 55€–80€ ($66–$96) double. AE, DC, MC, V.*

Hotel Los Olivos

$$

This two-story, 1912 Andalusian town house with a pretty interior patio was converted into an attractive small hotel. Its 19 rooms are comfortable, with wicker chairs and long, sheer curtains, but you may just want to spend all your time relaxing in the whitewashed patio and airy sitting rooms. Some rooms have splendid views of the olive groves beyond Arcos.

Paseo de Boliches 30. On main road into zona monumental. ☎ ***956-70-08-11.*** *Fax: 956-70-20-18.* losolivosdelc@terra.es. *Parking: 5€ ($6.40). Rack rates: 55€–79€ ($66–$95) double. AE, DC, MC, V.*

La Casa Grande

$$–$$$

The best small option within Arcos, this charmingly rustic, early-18th-century *casa señorial* was converted into an inn a few years ago by a woman from Barcelona. The house is built around a light-filled, glass-enclosed Andalusian patio with marble columns. Its seven warm rooms have original tile floors, stucco walls, and unique decorative touches. The expansive rooftop terrace offers splendid views of Arcos's old town and of the surrounding countryside. Plus homemade breakfasts are a treat.

Maldonado 10. ☎ ***956-70-39-30.*** *Fax: 956-71-70-95.* www.lacasagrande.net. *Free parking nearby. Rack rates: 65€–102€ ($66–$95) double. AE, DC, MC, V.*

Parador de Arcos de la Frontera (Casa del Corregidor)

$$$

You couldn't ask for a more dramatic location. This *parador,* one of the more impressive in the chain, hugs the gorge, unveiling unbelievable views of the valley below that wow adults and kids alike. The building is on the site of the Casa del Corregidor, an 18th-century palace and seat of government. The hotel was given a makeover, and the rooms are modern with a cozy, American Southwest feel. Some of them have small balconies where you can linger and congratulate yourself for sitting on top of the world in southern Spain. The staff is uniformly friendly, which isn't always the case at *paradores.*

Plaza del Cabildo, s/n. Overlooking gorge, next to the castle and Santa María church. ☎ ***956-70-05-00.*** *Fax: 956-70-11-16.* www.parador.es. *Free parking. Rack rates: 125€–135€ ($150–$162). Inquire about discounts for families with children. DC, MC, V.*

Dining out

As with hotels, you can find the restaurants listed here in Arcos's *zona monumental* (historic district). In addition to what's listed in this section, the Parador de Arcos de la Frontera, described in the preceding section, has a handsome dining room serving regional specialties, with a fixed-price menu (lunch or dinner) for 25€ ($32).

Bar Alcaraván
$ TAPAS

If you're not really in the mood for a full sit-down meal, or you've already eaten at the other two main options that I mention in this section, drop into this amiable downstairs bar, which the cheerful owner says offers "the best tapas in town." He doesn't have a lot of competition, but you can assemble a fine meal from the *chorizo* (spicy pork sausage), *champiñones* (sautéed mushrooms), and *estofado de cordero* (lamb stew). The bar occupies tunnels, which may date to the tenth century, that run underneath the town's old Moorish castle (see the following section, "Exploring Arcos").

Nueva, s/n. Just behind castle. No phone. Tapas: 2€–5€ ($2.40–$6). Open: Daily for lunch and dinner. Closed: Sun evenings. No credit cards.

El Convento
$$ ANDALUSIAN

Part of the hotel of the same name (see the review in the hotel section), the restaurant's husband-and-wife team, which also owns the Olivos Hotel, saved the best for their kitchen. The restaurant is absolutely charming, and, though tiny, it has won several national culinary awards. They specialize in local cuisine that they say farmers in the area used to eat, which means game and meat dishes. For starters, try the *abajao* (asparagus soup for two). Main courses include lamb with aromatic herbs and *perdiz en salsa de almendras* (partridge in almond sauce). The wine cellar also has a few nice surprises.

Maldonado 2. Take Escribanos from Plaza del Cabildo and turn right on Maldonado. ☎ ***956-70-32-22.*** *Main courses: 9€–18€ ($11–$22). Open: Daily for lunch and dinner. AE, DC, MC, V.*

Exploring Arcos

Arcos offers precious little to *do,* but the point of being here is to take in the spectacular site of this whitewashed village carved into a crag, and the views down the gorge and over the countryside. The tiny alleys are fun to explore, but you can see the whole place in an hour. You can then plan your tour of the other white towns.

For photo opportunities, head to the **Balcón de Arcos,** an overlook in the Plaza del Cabildo — it literally hangs over the edge of the cliff. The old Moorish castle on the same plaza dates from the tenth century and the Ben Jazrum dynasty; it has been perfectly restored, but is off-limits to visitors (the owners live in it — lucky devils). The 15th-century **Iglesia de Santa María** on the square was built on the site of a mosque in a jumble of styles: Gothic, Mudéjar, Renaissance, and Baroque, with a splendid Plateresque facade. Santa María is open daily from 10 a.m. to 1 p.m. and 4 to 6:30 p.m., with guided visits Tuesday through Saturday at 10:30 a.m. Admission is 2€ ($2.40).

Walk down the main street out of Plaza del Cabildo to the Gothic **Iglesia de San Pedro** (on Calle San Pedro), which has a terrific Renaissance altarpiece, as well as paintings by Zurbarán and Ribera. Another great lookout point nearby for snapping pics is the **Mirador de Abades,** at the end of Calle Abades.

Before leaving Arcos for good, take the south exit from the city (toward Algar), which offers a gorgeous view of the gorge's sheer drop and the town above it.

A side trip to Jerez de la Frontera

Jerez de la Frontera (also called simply Jerez), lodged between the sea and the Sierra de Grazalema Mountains, is the Andalusian capital of wine and horses. It's the home of *jerez* (sherry) and the famous Real Escuela Andaluza del Arte Ecuestre — the Royal Andalusian School of Equestrian Arts. I suggest you visit one or two of Jerez's *bodegas* (wineries) and the horse school on a day's excursion from Arcos. If you're interested in hitting the coast, use the city as a base from which to explore Cádiz and the Costa de la Luz. (I prefer Arcos as a base, however.)

Getting to and around Jerez

Jerez is a straight 97km (60 mile) drive from Seville along N-IV or A-4. The drive takes a bit more than an hour.

Two bus companies offer a total of 11 buses a day (5:30 a.m.–8 p.m.) from Seville's Santa Justa station to Jerez. The lines are **Transportes Comes** (**☎ 95-441-52-01**) and **Linesur** (**☎ 95-498-82-22**). Both charge about 5€ ($6.40) one-way. You can also catch buses from Cádiz and Arcos de la Frontera.

Likewise, you can take train service from Madrid and Seville. Daily high-speed AVE trains from Madrid make the trip in two-and-a-half hours (70€, or $84, one-way). Twenty trains make the trip to Jerez from Seville; the Altaria train, which takes just under an hour, costs 16€ ($18) one-way; the regional Andalucía Exprés train, a better deal, takes an hour and costs 6.25€ ($8) one-way. The **Jerez Estación de Tren** is at Plaza de la Estación (**☎ 956-43-23-19**).

Finding information after you've arrived

The **tourist information office** is on Alameda Cristina 7, just off Porvera Larga 39, and next to Santo Domingo (**☎ 956-33-11-50**). Pick up a tour schedule of *bodegas* and a map plotting their locations. In summer, the tourism office is open Monday to Friday from 9 a.m. to 2 p.m. and 5 to 8 p.m., and Saturday from 9 a.m. to 2 p.m.; in winter it's open Monday to Saturday from 9 a.m. to 3 p.m. and again Saturday from 5 to 7 p.m.

If you wish to spend the night in Jerez, an excellent new option is Hotel Bellas Artes, Plaza del Arroyo 45 (**☎ 956-34-84-30;** `www.hotelbellasartes.com`; 90€, or $108 double). The renovated palace, which has a terrific rooftop terrace, is opposite the cathedral in the historic quarter of town, and the attractively decorated rooms are impeccable.

Checking out some bodegas

Spanish sherry — fortified wine — comes from Jerez. It owes its worldwide popularity to 18th-century British merchants who were searching for alternatives to French wines (which were virtually wiped out by disease). The oh-so-English names of several of the best-known wineries — Sandeman, Harveys, and Williams — reflect the British interest in sherry. A visit to one of the approximately 100 *bodegas* in the area introduces you to the varieties of sherry. At the tourist office, pick up a schedule of *bodegas* that permit visits. The price of the tour includes tastings. Here are some wineries that you may enjoy.

- Pedro **Domecq,** San Ildefonso 3 (☎ **956-15-15-16**), Spain's oldest sherry winery (established in 1730 and called La Mezquita, or the Mosque, for its Moorish-style arches), offers tours Monday through Friday from 9 a.m. to 1 p.m. for 5€ ($6.40), and Saturday and Sunday for 7€ ($8.95). Reserve in advance.
- **González Byass,** Manuel María González (☎ **956-35-70-00;** `www.gonzalezbyass.com`), makes the ubiquitous Tío Pepe (that's the bottle with the *sombrero* on top). Tours at this, the biggest winery and tourist attraction in town, cost 7€ ($8.95) and are available Monday through Saturday from 10 a.m. to 1 p.m. on the hour, as well as at 6 p.m. Reservations required.
- At **Harveys of Bristol,** Arcos 57 (☎ **956-15-10-02**), you can take a tour Monday through Friday at noon. No reservation is necessary.
- **Williams & Humbert Limited,** Nuño de Cañas 1 (☎ **956-34-65-39**), which makes Dry Sack sherry, schedules tours for 5€ ($6.40) from 9 a.m. to 2 p.m., Monday through Friday. Reserve in advance.

Bring on the prancing horses

They prance, they dance, and they *piaffe, courvet,* and *capriole.* If you know what those high-stepping terms mean — or even if you don't — you may enjoy a visit to the **Real Escuela Andaluza del Arte Ecuestre** (Royal Equestrian School). The goal of training is for the horse and rider to commune in perfect synchronicity. You can see the dancing horses of Jerez every Tuesday and Thursday at noon (and mid-July through mid-Oct on Fri at noon as well). Tickets range from 17€ to 23€ ($20–$28), 11€ to 14€ ($13–$17) children under 14 and seniors. On Mondays, Wednesdays, and Fridays, between 10 a.m. and 1 p.m., you can see the training sessions and take a tour of the stables, stocked with beautiful Hispano-Arab horses, and visit the Horse Carriage Museum (tour and admission to museum 6€/$7.70). The school is at Av. Duque de Abrantes 11 (reservations ☎ **956-31-90-08;** `www.realescuela.org`), just north of the old center. Take Porvera north to Ponce, turn right, and go 2 long blocks. The school is on the left side.

¡Salud! Sherry

If you haven't already discovered it, slightly chilled *jerez,* or sherry, is a great accompaniment to tapas, or appetizers. Sherry, fortified wine (with an alcohol volume around 16 to 18 percent), is produced within the sherry triangle of towns in Cádiz province: Jerez de la Frontera, Puerto de Santa María, and Sanlúcar de Barrameda. Sherry runs the gamut from nutty, amber-colored *oloroso* to dark *amontillado* and the cream sherry popular in other countries as a dessert wine (but not in Spain). In my opinion, the best of the bunch in Andalusia are *finos* (very dry) and *manzanilla* (mahn-thah-*nee*-yah), complex and delicate, very dry aperitif wines. Both are made from the palomino grape and are best when served terrifically fresh — so you're in luck if you're in the area. *Manzanilla,* the driest and palest of these fortified wines, has a very slight tangy and salty taste and comes only from the seaside town, Sanlúcar de Barrameda, just up the road from Jerez. Locals drink sherry and *manzanilla* around the clock, not just as aperitifs. They pound them back along with dinner.

A word of caution: If you're driving around Jerez visiting sherry *bodegas,* exercise some restraint when sampling; though they go down easy, remember that these wines are fortified and pack a deceptive punch.

Watching time go by in a museum

If you've seen the horses prance and you're too tipsy on sherry to drive home, pay a visit to Jerez's curious **Museo de los Relojes** (Clock Museum). In the Palacio de Atalaya (Watchtower Palace), more than 300 beautiful French and English timepieces are on display — one of Europe's largest collections — and in working order. Hit the museum at noon for a cool and deafening demonstration of synchronized chiming. You can find the museum, where kids can get a kick out of the peacocks strolling the grounds, just across from the Royal Equestrian School, Cervantes 3 (☎ **956-18-21-00**). Hours are Monday to Saturday from 10 a.m. to 2 p.m. Admission is 2€ ($2.40).

A side trip to Cádiz and the Costa de la Luz

Southern Spain has drawn beach worshippers for decades. If you fear that a trip to the south of Spain is incomplete without some *playa* (beach) and *sol* (sun), check out the western half of the Andalusian coast. You can choose between the relatively tranquil **Costa de la Luz** (Coast of Light) and the self-indulgent, massively developed, and touristy **Costa del Sol** (Coast of the Sun). Attractions at both locations include rough, sandy beaches with strong winds, golf courses galore, and all the nightlife and beautiful people you can handle. The Costa de la Luz (also called the Cádiz coast), is a short distance from Jerez. The Costa del Sol is southeast of Ronda; for more information on it, see "Side trips to Málaga and the Costa del Sol."

Relatively tranquil and unspoiled, the Costa de la Luz extends from Spain's southernmost tip to the Portuguese border, fronting the Bay of Cádiz. If you have limited time, the area of most interest is between Cádiz and Tarifa, a windswept coastline with fine, unpretentious beaches, dunes, the shelter of pine trees, and whitewashed fishing villages. If you want sand and sea, not scene, this area is where to go in the south. A car is the best way to explore the Costa de la Luz.

Despite its history, the large port city of Cádiz — purportedly the oldest inhabited city in the West, founded in 1100 B.C. by the Phoenicians — isn't overly interesting to most visitors at first. Its seaside decay and modern suburbs may be a turnoff for some, but if you come to town looking for a party, you will undoubtedly find it (especially during February's annual Carnaval, the wildest in Spain).

For tourist information, visit the **Oficina de Información Turística** on Av. Ramón de Carranza 11 (☎ **956-24-01-62**). The best beach in the area is lively **La Victoria.** Up the coast (northwest), other recommended beaches are **La Costilla** (in Rota) and **Regia** (in Chipiona). If you want to spend the night in Cádiz, the best place is the **Parador de Cádiz** (formerly Hotel Atlántico), Av. Duque de Nájera 9 (☎ **956-22-69-05;** `www.parador.es`), where doubles run 110€ to 120€ ($132–$144). The large, modern, white construction may not be the most attractive, but it sits right on the coast and has a nice pool. A provincial **tourism office** offering regional information is on Calderón de la Barca 1 (☎ **956-21-13-13**).

Between Cádiz and Tarifa are a couple of modest resorts, **Conil de la Frontera** and **Zahara de los Atunes.** At the southern tip of Spain, Tarifa has the dubious distinction of being the windiest city in Spain — little wonder that it's also the windsurfing capital. From here, Morocco is only about 23km (14 miles) across the Strait of Gibraltar. Morocco was a stronghold of the Moors, and a tenth-century Moorish castle is here. The town still retains a very palpable Arab flavor. Tarifa has an excellent, 5km-long (3-mile) white beach, **Playa de Lances.**

From Jerez de la Frontera, N-443 leads to Cádiz. N-340 leads east along the coast to Tarifa. Trains arrive from Seville (two hours), Jerez (40 minutes), and Córdoba (five hours). The train station (**Plaza de Sevilla;** ☎ **956-25-43-01**) is on Avenida del Puerto, southeast of town. Buses go to Cádiz from all over the south, arriving at two terminals: **Comes,** Plaza de la Hispanidad 1 (☎ **956-22-42-71**), and **Los Amarillos,** Av. Ramón de Carranza 31 (☎ **956-28-58-52**).

Fast Facts: Arcos de la Frontera

Area Code

The area code for Arcos is **956,** which you must dial before every number.

Currency Exchange

You can find both a bank and an ATM around the main plaza on the way into town.

Emergencies

For medical emergencies, call the Cruz Roja (Red Cross), on Corregidores 9; ☎ 956-70-03-55.

Hospitals

Servicio Andaluz de Salud has an outpatient clinic at Calle Calvario, s/n; ☎ 956-70-06-62.

Information

The tourism office (☎ 956-70-22-64) is right on the central square of the old town, Plaza del Cabildo (Cuesta de Belén 1; within the Castle). The staff at the town's *parador* across the plaza is equally helpful.

Police

The police station is at Calle Nueva, s/n (☎ 956-70-16-52).

Post Office

Arcos's main post office is on Paseo de Boliches 24 (☎ 956-70-15-60).

The Pueblos Blancos: A Driving Tour

More than two-dozen whitewashed villages dot the Sierra de Cádiz and the Sierra de Grazalema. The towns — which owe their distinctive look to the Moors, who inhabited this part of Spain for eight centuries — are themselves major attractions. Most have castles and cathedrals perched dramatically above the plains below.

You can easily see all the white villages in under a week, because they're that close together. However, spending a week on the route is probably overkill. In just a day or two, you can visit the four or five most picturesque villages (adding another day to your trip for Ronda). I recommend that you spend a night in Arcos and at least one night in Ronda (covered later in this chapter), hitting the towns in between on one or two day trips. The only practical way to cover more than just Arcos and Ronda is in a car, with rented wheels (you're best off renting in one of the larger cities, such as Seville, Córdoba, or Granada). The region is as scenic as you'll find in Spain. In my last run through, I made many more stops on the side of the road to snap pictures than I did in the actual villages.

If you're a nature lover, you'll appreciate that the Sierra de Grazalema Nature Reserve runs almost the breadth of the route of the *pueblos blancos,* covering an area of more than 125,000 acres. It includes pine and oak forests and an important reserve for griffon vultures.

In Arcos de la Frontera or Ronda, pick up a brochure called a *Guía Práctica* (Practical Guide) to the *pueblos blancos.* It includes a map of the area that's plenty sufficient, and information on the towns that I don't have room to discuss here.

Several routes are available by which you can undertake a tour of the white towns. In this book, I lay out one possibility for exploring the interior of the Cádiz and Malaga provinces: beginning in Arcos and winding up in Ronda. If you want to keep your kilometers down, consider staying in Ronda and doing a circular trip from there because the best of the white towns are closer to Ronda than to Arcos. Feel free to mix and match towns, rearrange the order, or explore some of the smaller places that I can't fully describe here. What you see and the route you take are almost entirely questions of how much time you want to dedicate to seeing the *pueblos blancos.*

The area of the *pueblos blancos* has been inhabited since prehistoric times, by the Iberians, Celts, Romans (in 1 B.C., the Romans founded Arcos de la Frontera and Ronda), Visigoths, and, more recently, the Moors. The Muslims, who dominated Andalusia for 700 years, did the most to shape these villages, as their winding, narrow alleyways, fortresses, and brilliantly whitewashed facades attest. Berber farmers inhabited the villages, with their towns' castles suffering constant attacks from armies during the Christian and Muslim struggles for domination.

In the 20th century, until roads to these mountaintop villages were laid down, the *pueblos blancos* continued as remote agricultural villages. Rugged sorts less savory than farmers took advantage of their strategic locations and inaccessibility. Smugglers, bandits, and even guerrillas fighting for the Andalusian resistance against fascist dictator Francisco Franco took up residence in the *pueblos blancos.*

From Arcos to Benamahoma

Take C-344 west from Arcos toward El Bosque. There you can either veer right and check out the leather-producing, industrial (but still white) town of Ubrique, or, better yet, head to Benamahoma. A sun-kissed, tiny village with stone streets and whitewashed houses (what did you expect?); with wrought-iron balconies, its Arab origins are obvious. Orange and palm trees line the main street. Benamahoma is the kind of place where everybody stares at you, as if they expect you to bring the circus to town. No matter; have a quick look around and check out the white and tile-roofed church next to the tiniest of bullrings. (A little boy told me that the bullring was destroyed "by the bulls" and was no longer in use. I asked him how long ago it happened. "A long time ago," he said. "When I was four, and now I'm seven.")

From Benamahoma to Grazalema

Continue along C-344 west 18km (12 miles) to Grazalema, which is perhaps the fairest of the white towns. Surrounded by craggy, olive-colored mountains on all sides, this immaculate town isn't merely *blanco* (white); it's *blanquísimo* (extraordinarily white). If you approach it on the road from Arcos, you'll circle above it and see unequalled views of its white houses, church steeples, and tile roofs. Spend a little time here, exploring its charming central square, three churches, outdoor cafes (perfect for lunchtime snacks), and wool and ceramic shops. Grazalema offers a couple of full-fledged restaurants, pensions, and even a *discoteca.*

Besides the cafes, for a bite to eat, check out **Casa de las Piedras,** Las Piedras 32 (☎ **956-13-20-14;** www.casadelaspiedras.net), which has excellent home-cooking and cozy rooms (including apartments) to rent for 45€ to 80€ ($54–$96). **Villa Turística de Grazalema,** El Olivar, s/n (☎ **956-13-21-36**), is a relaxing little place with stunning views and pretty nice rooms for 65€ to 75€ ($78–$90). A step up, if you want to spend the night, is **Puerta de la Villa,** Plaza Pequeña 8 (☎ **956-13-23-76;** www.grazhotel.com), a very attractive and exceedingly comfortable small hotel in the center of town with a nice long pool and a restaurant. Doubles here run between 96€ and 120€ ($115–$144).

Hotel El Horcajo (☎ **95-218-40-80;** www.elhorcajo.com) is a working Andalusian farm and country estate and a splendid rural hotel for guests. The place is a real treat and an excellent value; it's well positioned for travels through the *pueblos blancos.* Located within the Sierra de Grazalema Nature Reserve, it features a handsomely decorated 170-year-old main house, rustic accommodations (family suites with lounges are in a converted stable), home-cooking, a large pool, as well as olive trees and gardens. The hotel is 20km (12 miles) northwest of Ronda. (Take the A-376 toward Seville and at Km 106 turn left for Grazalema on A-372; the hotel is signposted at the next intersection.) Doubles are 62€ to 78€ ($74–$94) including breakfast.

To buy the woolen blankets Grazalema is still famous for (though its once-thriving textile industry is nothing like it was), head to **Concha Pérez Coronel's** small shop at Anexo Plaza España 18 (☎ **956-13-21-41**), or **Artesanía Textil de Grazalema,** Carretera de Ronda (☎ **956-13-20-08**), on the road out of town to Ronda.

So much of Andalusia is dry and in perpetual need of rain, but rain frequently bathes the tiny, whitewashed town of Grazalema. In fact, Grazalema has the distinction of having the highest annual rainfall in Spain. If you're here on a sunny day, or if you've been to the rainy northern region of the Basque Country, that annual rainfall statistic seems impossible, but it's true.

From Grazalema to Zahara de la Sierra

The road to Zahara de la Sierra (usually shortened to "Zahara," pronounced "thah-*ah*-rah") from Grazalema (14km/9 miles along CA-531) is a bicyclist's dream and a motorist's nightmare. Passing along the Puerto de las Palomas (Dove's Pass: 1,356m/4,450 ft.), the road winds along the mountain's edge, up one side and down the other, until it reaches a view of a blue-green reservoir stretching out among the olive groves. If the thought of the hair-raising road from Grazalema to Zahara de la Sierra makes, well, your hair raise on end, you can take a longer, less dangerous and ultimately less picturesque route: C-344 East to C-339 North, which leads to Zahara. If you have a steady hand, though, take the spectacular short cut, CA-531. And, as your driving teacher told you, go slowly and try to keep your eyes on the road.

The town of Zahara — stone streets and whitewashed houses (you might notice a trend here) — is wedged into the side of the mountain, with an old tower perched on top, overlooking the water. The Moors founded Zahara de la Sierra, 511 meters (1,676 feet) above sea level, in the eighth century, and today it's a national monument. The main square is a good place to take a break and snack on a couple of tapas and a glass of *manzanilla.* Walk around toward the *mirador* (lookout), past the 18th-century Baroque church, and catch the stone path up the hill, where a ten-minute climb leads you through cacti and almond trees up to a medieval Nasrine castle. The views are sensational. Enter the spooky 13th-century tower **(Torre del Homenaje)** at your own risk — it definitely seems like the kind of place where a hairy hermit will emerge from hiding. You can climb to the second-floor sun terrace (which would make a great place for nude sunbathing).

If you want to crash in Zahara, you can choose from a small hotel, **Arco de la Villa,** Paseo Nazarí, s/n (☎ **956-12-32-30**), which charges 60€ ($72), or two *pensiones* (guesthouses): **Marqués de Zahara,** San Juan 3 (☎ **956-12 30-61**), which charges 42€ ($50), and **Los Tadeos,** Paseo de la Fuente (☎ **956-12-30-86**), whose rates are about 30€ ($36).

From Zahara to Setenil de las Bodegas

Leaving Zahara, you have a choice. You can either continue north to Algodonales or east to El Gastor. Both are nice, as are all these towns, but if you're in a hurry, continue past El Gastor to Setenil de las Bodegas (about 55km/34 miles).

Setenil, as it's known, is one of the most amazing villages in Andalusia — literally crammed into clefts of rock. You need to park the car at one end of the village and get out and walk. Look for Calle Herrería, one of the oldest streets in town. Once lined with blacksmiths' shops, it has houses wedged into the massive rock that forms their roofs. Talk about adapting to your environment. An elderly woman invited me into her small home, which had sloping cave walls that were painted thick white. Barbara García, who got around her *casas cuevas* (cave house — that's literally what they're called in Spanish) on a wheelchair, told me that the house had been in her family for generations. (She thought her grandparents built it, but conceded that it could've been older still.) Setenil's Moorish fortress and twin-towered, 16th-century Gothic church **(Iglesia de la Encarnación)** sit high above the rock and white houses.

The road that leads north out of Setenil leads to a *mirador* and small church; take the turnoff for postcard views of the town and the cave houses below.

The town sports a single *pensión,* in which you can spend the night under the rock ridges: **El Almendral,** Carretera Setenil-Puerto del Monte (☎ **956-13-40-29**), charges just under 40€ ($48).

If you're as delighted as I am by town names that reveal their roots, I have a good one for you. Just outside of Setenil is a tiny settlement, no doubt an agricultural one, called Venta de Leche, which means "milk for sale."

From Setenil to Olvera

The road between Setenil and Olvera (13km/8 miles) is a dreamscape; it winds through olive groves and valleys that suddenly open up and reveal two perfect *pueblos blancos* laid out in the distance. The first is Torre Alhaquime; 4km (2½ miles) beyond it is Olvera, its Moorish tower and neoclassical church glued to the top of the mountain. Olvera, declared a national monument, was a Moorish stronghold and a key part of the Granada Nazari kingdom's defensive lines. You can easily see why raiders had little success storming a settlement perched as high as this one. Head for a small plaza, where the town hall is located, and then park your car and walk up. Next to the castle is **Iglesia de San José,** an unexpectedly large, colonial-looking, pale yellow and brown church (18th-century) with a clock tower. Access to the 12th-century castle is through a door across from the church. Its sign says it's open Tuesday through Thursday and Saturday and Sunday for visits from 9 a.m. to 2 p.m. Townsfolk assured me, though, that you can visit during the morning and afternoon every day but Monday, when it's closed.

Ronda: Perched on a Gorge

Historic Ronda, which clings to a cliff above a narrow 107m (350-ft.) chasm, a dizzying ravine created by the Guadalevín River, is one of the prettiest and most photogenic places in Spain. Whitewashed houses and palatial mansions crowd the edges of the gorge, and an audacious 18th-century bridge spans the drop and connects the Old Quarter with the new expansion, El Mercadillo. Ronda's precipice is spectacular, but as a vista it's got serious competition in the serene valleys and mountain ranges that extend on either side: the Sierra de las Nieves to the east and the Sierra de Grazalema to the west.

Beyond the beauty of its incomparable setting, Ronda is one of the oldest towns in Spain. Its perch was inhabited nearly 3,000 years ago and it was a Celtic, then Roman, and finally Moorish stronghold before Christian forces conquered it in the 13th century. The birthplace of modern bull-fighting, Ronda is home to Spain's oldest and most beautiful bullring and an old-fashioned annual festival to go with it.

Ronda exudes charm at every corner, from its ancient minarets and Arab baths to the oldest bullring in Spain and gorgeous mansions decorated with ornate iron grilles and potted plants. The largest and perhaps most tourist-friendly *pueblo* (it simply has more infrastructure than any of the other white towns), Ronda's the one white town to visit if you don't have time for others. It's a perfect complement to Andalusia's Big Three

(Seville, Granada, and Córdoba); in fact, you'll likely find Ronda one of the highlights of your trip to southern Spain.

Getting there

Ronda is one of the few white towns accessible by means other than a car. You can hop a train from Seville, Córdoba, or Granada, and a bus from Seville, Arcos, and Jerez. If you're really pressed for time, and aren't yet in Andalusia, you can even fly from Madrid or Barcelona — though you have to fly into Málaga, about 100km (62 miles) away, and then catch a bus or train from there.

If you're going to Ronda by car, you can take any number of routes from other spots in Andalusia. Major highways bypass it, though, so you need to get off and take one of the smaller local highways. From Seville, take N-334 Southeast and head south, just after El Arahal, on C-339, which leads directly to Ronda. From Granada, take N-342 West to Olvera, and C-342 South from there. From Málaga, take scenic C-344 directly to Ronda.

Regional trains along the Algeciras-Granada route stop in Ronda. ***Note:*** A number of trains into and out of Ronda make stops and train changes in Bobadilla or Antequera. Ronda's train station, **Estación de FF.CC.,** Av. Alférez Provisional, s/n (☎ **95-287-16-73**), is on the northwestern edge of town next to Avenida de Andalucía. The ticket office for **RENFE,** Spain's national railway system, is at Infantes 20 (☎ **95-287-16-62**).

Buses from Seville, Málaga, Arcos, and Jerez travel to Ronda. **Los Amarillos** (☎ 95-231-59-78) travels to and from Seville and Málaga; **Portillo** (☎ 95-236-01-91) also goes to Málaga. **Transportes Comes** (☎ 95-287-19-92) goes to Arcos, Jerez, and Cadiz. The bus station **(Estación de Autobuses)** is on Plaza Concepción García Redondo 2 (☎ 900-12-35-05), just down Avenida de Andalucía from the train station.

For a **taxi,** call ☎ **95-287-23-16.**

Finding information after you arrive

The regional **tourist information office** is on Plaza de España 1 (☎ **95-287-12-72**), next to the *parador.* It's open Monday to Friday from 9 a.m. to 2 p.m. and 4 to 7 p.m., and Saturday and Sunday from 10 a.m. to 3 p.m. The **municipal tourism office** is located on Plaza de Blas Infante (☎ **95-218-71-19**).

Getting around Ronda

Ronda is so small that using anything other than your own feet is absurd. The areas of greatest interest to visitors are a handful of streets on either side of the gorge. If you're a competent rider, a great way to see the countryside that surrounds Ronda is via horseback (see "Exploring Ronda," later in this chapter).

If you arrive in Ronda without wheels but decide to rent a car in town to explore some of the other white towns, contact **Velasco,** Lorenzo Borrego 11 (☎ **95-287-27-82**). If you need a cab to get to the train or bus station, call **Parada de Taxis** at ☎ **95-287-23-16,** or pick one up in front of the Plaza de Toros (bullring).

Staying in style

Ronda's hotels are conveniently located, with the possible exception of the Reina Victoria, which is farthest from the bridge. High season in Ronda is March to October; low season is November to February. Some hotels charge supplements for local Feria de Pedro Romero and the *corrida goyesca* (first week of September), as well as Easter week in April. (For more on these festivals, see Chapter 3.)

Hotel Don Miguel
$$

The *parador* (reviewed later in this section) isn't the only hotel with a great perch over the gorge. This hotel abuts the back side of the river gorge, which some bedrooms overlook. Rooms are fairly simple, but they're comfortable enough — a decent alternative if you want a dramatic view but don't want to pay the dramatically higher prices at the *parador* across the street. The hotel, which has been around almost 30 years, has recently expanded into one of the *casas antiguas* (old houses) on the same street (with the same views). Definitely get a room overlooking the gorge. The hotel restaurant, with a balcony clinging to the cliff, is quite good (see the review for Don Miguel later in the restaurant section of this chapter).

Plaza de España 4–5. On north side of gorge. ☎ ***95-287-77-22.*** *Fax: 95-287-83-77.* `www.dmiguel.com`*. Parking: 9€ ($11). Rack rates: 85€ ($102). AE, DC, MC, V.*

Hotel La Española
$$$

This simple, good-value small hotel has an excellent location just two minutes from the gorge and Plaza de Toros — although you won't get gorge views. The comfortable rooms are agreeably decorated (for the most part) with either deep-green or ochre walls, and feature piped-in music, minibar, and cheesy antique phones; doubles offer a view of gardens and the distant mountains beyond Ronda. Rooms have full bathrooms (singles, showers only) and air-conditioning. The downstairs restaurant has a nice covered terrace.

José Aparicio 3. On street between bullfighting ring and Plaza de España. ☎ ***95-287-34-88.*** *Fax: 95-287-99-03.* `www.laespanolahotel.com`*. Parking 14€ ($17). Rack rates: 83€–93€ ($100–$112). AE, DC, MC, V.*

Hotel Molino del Arco

$$$–$$$$

About 8km (5 miles) outside of Ronda, in the Serranía de Ronda, this charming *finca,* or 18th-century farmhouse, is a luxury country inn and a real retreat, with pretty gardens, four patios, and an old mill. The small (16-room) inn is relaxing and very tastefully appointed; the rooms are outfitted with elegant antiques. This special little place is worthy of a small splurge if you can afford to spend a few days here; the suites have private terraces and separate living areas, while the Grand Suite is downright Hollywood, with three bedrooms, three bathrooms, two terraces, a patio and its own private pool. There's a very nice small restaurant, with David Fernández at the helm, as well as two (additional) pools.

*Partido de los Frontones, s/n. ☎/Fax **95-211-40-17.** Fax: 95-219-01-17.* `www.hotelmolinodelarco.com`. *Free parking. Rack rates: 120€–240€ ($144–$288). AE, DC, MC, V.*

Hotel Reina Victoria

$$–$$$

This old British-style hotel, opened in 1906 just after the building of the British rail line from Bobadilla to Algeciras, was once the swankest game in town. Today, eclipsed in service and installations by the *parador,* it has a slightly dilapidated feeling, more like a museum than a hotel. The gardens, terraces, and pool, though, are still first-rate. Tour groups and English visitors still appear to enjoy the musty, old-world décor and Nordic look of the place — sloping roofs, high chimneys, and bold green and white paint. But to me, it just seems out of place in this town with such distinct Roman and Moorish roots.

*Jerez 25. In modern part of town, ten-minute walk west of gorge. ☎ **95-287-12-40.** Fax: 95-287-10-75.* `www.husa.es`. *Free parking. Rack rates: 95€–117€ ($114–$140). AE, DC, MC, V.*

Hotel San Gabriel

$$

A small, family-owned-and-operated hotel in a gorgeous 1736 mansion, San Gabriel is my favorite place in Ronda and one of my favorite hotels in Spain. Not only that, but it's among the best deals I have come across in my travels in Spain. The hotel is a labor of love created by a father, his sons, and his daughter. The family worked for 15 years to meticulously select the antiques for every nook and cranny of every welcoming room and complete the painstaking restoration before finally opening it in December 1998. They're so bent on it seeming homelike that they've incorporated "Your House in Ronda" into the name, and individual travelers as well as small families feel equally welcome. Every detail is perfect, cozy, and utterly charming. Located in the artistic and historical center of Ronda, just a five-minute walk east of the gorge, it has Moorish accents, antique-leaded and stained-glass windows, an antique carved central staircase, and even a TV salon with seats salvaged from Ronda's first theater. Each of the 22 rooms is different from the next; my favorites are nos. 4, 9 (a very *suite* deal), and 15, a charming top-floor, bilevel room.

José M. Holgado 19. Just off Armiñán, next to Plaza del Gigante. ☎ ***95-219-03-92.*** *Fax: 95-219-01-17.* `www.hotelsangabriel.com`. *No parking (though usually free street-parking is available). Rack rates: 78€–100€ ($94–$120). AE, DC, MC, V.*

Parador de Ronda

$$$

You can get dizzy staying at Ronda's national *parador.* The hotel is backed right up to the edge of the gorge, next to the stunning bridge that spans its gulf. Built in 1994, the *parador* is modern and extremely comfortable — exactly the reasons some locals have criticized it, for not doing a good enough job assimilating into Ronda's collection of old mansions and whitewashed houses. It's hardly a modern white elephant, though, and most visitors find the *parador* a luxurious, even handsome, place to stay. It's also one of the friendliest *paradores* I've stayed in. Many of the 78 nicely appointed rooms have small balconies. Many also have unrivalled views of the 152m (500-ft.) fall of the gorge and the bridge, which is illuminated at night, or the gorgeous mountainous countryside beyond. Make sure your room is one with a view. Children will appreciate the outdoor pool, as well as the hotel's dramatic location overlooking the gorge.

Plaza de España, s/n. Western side, next to new bridge over gorge. ☎ ***95-287-75-00.*** *Fax: 95-287-81-88.* `www.parador.es`. *Parking: 8€ ($10). Rack rates: 140€–150€ ($168–$180). Inquire about special discounts for families with children. AE, DC, MC, V.*

Dining out

In addition to the in-town restaurants below, the luxury country inn Hotel Molino del Arco (reviewed above), on the outskirts of Ronda, is a perfect place for a romantic dinner. The Parador also has a very good restaurant.

Casa Santa Pola

$$$ **SPANISH/ANDALUSIAN**

A *casa noble* built over the foundations of a ninth-century mosque, this handsome restaurant overlooks the gorge, near the Casa del Rey Moro. Casa Santa Pola is surprisingly elegant, with terra-cotta-colored walls and white tablecloths, but the outdoor tables on the terrace are the most coveted. The menu is varied, though sticking with such basics as *sopa de mariscos* (shellfish soup), *cochinillo* (roast suckling pig), *paella* (rice, seafood, and meat casserole), and the good selection of salads is perhaps the best idea. Behind the beautiful 18th-century front door of Casa Santa Pola is an antiques museum with some extraordinary furnishings.

Santo Domingo 3. Next to Casa del Rey Moro. ☎ ***95-287-92-08.*** *Reservations recommended. Main courses: 17€–24€ ($22–$31). Open: daily for lunch and dinner. AE, DC, MC, V.*

Don Miguel

$$–$$$ ANDALUSIAN/SPANISH

This restaurant, attached to a small hotel by the same name (reviewed earlier in this chapter), has one distinct advantage: location, location, location. Don Miguel's terrace dining area swings out over the river gorge — a spectacular site for a meal. You can also sit in the large indoor dining rooms if the sun's beating down or if it's chilly outside. A great surprise — in a place that may rest on its location — the kitchen is one of Ronda's best. Try the oxtail stew or the partridge casserole.

Plaza de España 2. Right next to the gorge, on the north side. ☎ ***95-287-10-90.*** *Reservations recommended. Main courses: 10€–21€ ($13–$27). Menú del día: 15€ ($18). Open: Mon–Sat lunch and dinner, Sun dinner only. Closed first three weeks of Jan. AE, DC, MC, V.*

Restaurante Pedro Romero

$$ ANDALUSIAN

Ronda has long been considered the cradle of Spanish bullfighting; if you missed seeing a *corrida* (bullfight), you can always come here, just across the street from Spain's oldest Plaza de Toros. Named for a legendary Ronda bullfighter (who is said to have slain nearly 6,000 bulls during his career), the restaurant is all taurine ambience — posters of bullfights, photos of matadors, and, of course, stuffed bulls' heads line the walls. The simple surroundings have quite a bit of charm, touristy though they may seem. Logically, it's a place for meat — *rabo de toro a la Rondeña* (Ronda-style oxtail), lamb, veal, and rabbit. Start off with a house garlic soup.

Virgen de la Paz 18. Next to post office, across from bullring. ☎ ***95-287-11-10.*** *Reservations recommended. Main courses: 9€–21€ ($11–$25). Menú del día: 14€ ($17). Open: Daily for lunch and dinner. AE, DC, MC, V.*

Tragabuches

$$$–$$$$ CREATIVE ANDALUSIAN

The best restaurant in Ronda is a stylish venture that's pretty uptown for this laid-back *pueblo.* The downstairs back dining room (much preferable to the staid front room) has clean white walls and bubblegum-colored tablecloths and seat covers. This is evidently not your typical Spanish *mesón* (inn). The young chef, Daniel García, is as daring as the décor. Dishes are creative, adventurous, and very successfully presented. I had a thick potato soup with salt-cured ham followed by oxtail raviolis with a puree of chestnuts. Also tempting was the sea bass with white beans and blood sausage. The wine cellar has some very well-chosen bottles, especially those under the heading "the great wines of Spain."

José Aparicio 1. Between Plaza de España and Plaza de Toros. ☎ ***95-219-02-91.*** *Reservations recommended. Main courses: 16€–34€ ($19–$41). Tasting menu: 58€ ($70). Open: Daily for lunch and dinner. AE, DC, MC, V.*

Exploring Ronda

Spain's oldest bullfighting ring, **Plaza de Toros de la Real Maestranza de España,** built in 1785, is one of its most storied and most beautiful. Constructed of limestone with double arches and 136 Tuscan columns, it's linked forever in the minds of Spaniards to the legend of Ronda-native Pedro Romero, who is considered the father of modern bullfighting. A different kind of celebrity graced its sands a couple of years back when Ronda's ring was the stage for a *matador* romance music video by Madonna.

Across the Plaza de Toros is the **Museo Taurino** (Bullfighting Museum), one of the better ones in Spain and a big hit with the kids. Its exhibits include bulls' heads, suits of lights worn by Romero and other matadors, and a second floor dedicated to foreigners involved in *toros* — including photographs of Orson Welles, and the paintings and suit of John Fulton, a Philadelphia-born bullfighter and artist who lived most of his life in Seville. Pedro Romero, the 18th-century killer of nearly 6,000 bulls, was the inspiration for Francisco de Goya's remarkable series of etchings on *Tauromaquia.* The first week of September, Ronda hosts a *corrida goyesca,* a festival that recreates the atmosphere of an 18th-century bullfight in honor of Romero. Men and women decked out in fancy dress ride through the streets on horse carriages, and bullfighting aficionados come from all over the world to see classical exhibitions.

Museo Taurino is located at Plaza Teniente Arza, right off of Virgen de la Paz (☎ **95-287-15-39;** `www.rmcr.org`). Admission is 5€ ($6.40); purchase your ticket from the small shop outside. From November through February the museum is open daily from 10 a.m. to 6 p.m.; from March to mid-April, hours are from 10 a.m. to 7 p.m., and mid-April through October, daily from 10 a.m. to 8 p.m.

Ronda's newest museum is the impressive and extremely well laid-out **Museo Lara,** a private collection of arts and antiques housed in the 18th-century Palacio de los Condes de la Conquista. The mansion formerly served as the residence of members of the Spanish Royal Family on visits to Ronda. The museum contains some 5,000 artifacts contained in seven separate collections, including galleries dedicated to clocks, weapons, science, archaeology, knives, bullfighting, and musical instruments. The Lara Museum is located on Calle Armiñán 29, next to the Tajo (☎ **95-287-12-63;** `www.museolara.org`). It's open daily from 10:30 a.m. to 7 p.m. Admission is 2.50€ ($3), students and seniors 2€ ($2.40).

More cool things to see and do

Ronda is more than just a bullfighting town, though bullfighting is the primary attraction. A number of other activities can entertain you while you're here.

Meandering through magnificent mansions

Ronda is the site of several exceptional aristocratic homes open to visitors. **Casa del Marqués de Salvatierra** is a noble Renaissance palace with intricate iron grilles and pre-Columbian figures (sticking their tongues out) adorning its rich Baroque facade. The mansion has remained in the hands of a single family and its descendents since 1475. The original Marquis Salvatierra was a well-traveled *conquistador* who, with orders from the Catholic monarchs, arrived in Ronda to engineer its capture from the Moors. The palace was constructed from a group of 15th-century Arab houses — a gift to the Marquis after the conquest of Ronda. The mansion has wonderful gardens and interior details. The family that owns it still vacations here in the month of August when it's closed to the public. The palace, located at Marqués de Salvatierra, s/n (☎ **95-287-12-06;** admission: 3€, or $3.60), is open from 11 a.m. to 2 p.m. and 4 to 7 p.m.; closed Thursday and Sunday afternoons. You may have to knock at the heavy wooden door and wait for an attendant to answer; small-group tours are only in Spanish. However, check first with the tourism office to be certain of the privately held palace's status; even if it's not open for tours, take a look at its wonderful balcony and carved facade.

Just across the street is **Casa del Rey Moro** (Moorish King's House), an improbably named 18th-century palace with an unusual feature that you have to see to believe. Within the palace is a 14th-century water mine, a secret military structure carved out of the gorge by the Moors. Descend the poorly lit, zigzagging, and damp staircase into the depths until you finally reach the ravine's bottom. Along the way, you pass the former Weapons Room, a secret escape exit, and the Room of Secrets, where the acoustics of the tiny room reportedly protected confidential conversations. It's said that the Moors employed Christian slaves to bring water up from the river. Fortunately, you don't have to do anything more than make the long climb back to the top of the never-ending steps and then emerge to enjoy the sumptuous gardens (designed in 1912) and the terrific views of the gorge and countryside. The palace, located at Cuesta de Santo Domingo 17 (☎ **95-218-72-00**), is open daily from 10 a.m. to 8 p.m. Admission is 4€ ($5.10) for adults, children 2€ ($2.40).

On the other side of the gorge are two more handsome homes with spectacular views to the south of Ronda. They're open daily from 9 a.m. to 6 p.m. The 14th-century **Palacio de Mondragón,** Plaza de Mondragón, s/n (☎ **95-287-84-50**), was built by the Moorish king of Ronda, Abomelic, in 1314 and was later inhabited by the Catholic monarchs Ferdinand and Isabel. In Moorish style, the palace has several interior courtyards adorned with mosaics and beautiful arcaded patios. It also has some of the best views in the city, looking back at the river gorge. The mansion today houses a small Natural History Museum, of less interest than the house itself. The mansion is open Monday to Friday from 9:30 a.m. to 7:30 p.m., and Saturday and Sunday from 10 a.m. to 3 p.m. Admission is

2€ ($2.40); free for children under age 14. Nearby, the **Casa de Don Juan Bosco,** Tenorio 20 (☎ **95-287-16-83**), is most notable for its lovely terrace, with a beautiful fountain and views. Admission for adults is 2€ ($2.40) and for children, 1€ ($1.20).

Soaking up the Moorish past

Ronda's 13th-century **Baños Arabes** (Arab baths), east of Marqués de Salvatierra (☎ **95-287-09-37**), are remarkably well preserved — perhaps the finest surviving example in Spain. From above they don't look like much, and the first chamber is just a series of open-air arches. But the two main chambers, with star-shaped openings that allow light to stream through, and perfect horseshoe arches, are undeniably beautiful. A nearby aqueduct carried water from the point where the two rivers converge. You can reach the baths from the staircase that leads down through the Puerta de Felipe V, just beyond the Casa del Rey Moro and Palacio Salvatierra. They are open Tuesday through Saturday from 9:30 a.m. to 3:30 p.m. Closed Sunday and Monday. Admission for adults is 2€ ($2.40) and for children, 1€ ($1.20); on Sundays admission is free.

Walking on Ronda's wild side

Tajo means "sheer drop," and Ronda's vertiginous ravine certainly is that. The views from the 18th-century **Puente Nuevo,** a spectacular feat of engineering across the gorge, are exhilarating. Inside the so-called New Bridge is a Centro de Interpretación, which offers additional information about the construction of the bridge and a four-minute audiovisual presentation. If you have the time and energy, don't stop at just staring down one side and then the other. A path from the Plaza de Campillo, in the old town, leads down to the bottom of the ravine, through almond trees and pink blossoms, for stunning vistas of the bridge from the bottom up (at sunset, the bridge is bathed in honey-colored light). A less strenuous walk through the Alameda del Tajo (Tajo Promenade), north of the bullring, is nearly as exhilarating. A perch hangs out over the cliff, providing great views.

A walk on the east side of the gorge leads to the 18th-century **Felipe V Gate;** the **Puente Viejo,** the old Roman bridge; and the **Puente Arabe,** the Arab bridge. A walk south from there, past the Arab baths, passes through the old Jewish Quarter and Ronda's ancient ramparts. Look for the Renaissance **Carlos V Gate** and 13th-century **Almocábar Gate,** part of the ancient walls and old entrance to the city.

The countryside beyond Ronda is perfect for more adventurous hikes and even trail-riding on horseback. If you bring boots or very sturdy sneakers, check with the tourism office for information about trails that lead out into the surrounding *serranía* (mountains).

Shopping

Around Plaza del Socorro and Plaza de Abela and the streets Villanueva, Nueva, and Los Remedios are where you can find most of Ronda's shops.

For antiques, check out **El Portón,** Manuel Montero 14 (☎ **95-287-14-69**), and **Muñoz Soto,** San Juan de Dios de Córdoba 34 (☎ **95-287-14-51**). A cool little gift shop, with toys and home items, is **El Pensamiento Ronda,** Calle Espinel 16 (☎ **95-287-21-93**).

Side trips to Málaga and the Costa del Sol

Spain's much-celebrated and sun-drenched southern coast is the focus of many a vacation to Spain — not to mention of retirement dreams, especially among Brits, Germans, and Arabs. Many are surely attracted by the legions of cheap airfares and package deals to Spain's "Sunny Coast." Yet the area pales so dramatically in comparison with the rest of Spain's historic and natural bounty that I can't legitimately recommend it as a top destination. But, if you're the type to camp out on the beach during the day and party it up all night long in the clubs, perhaps even for the duration of your Spanish holiday, you hardly need me either to dissuade you or to validate your decision.

The **Costa del Sol** lives and breathes glitz, and unless you're easily swayed by glamour and ostentatious shows of wealth (and lots, truth be told, of *gente bella,* or beautiful people), I don't recommend spending much time along Spain's overrated "Sun Coast." Though it enjoys more than 300 days of sunshine a year, to me it's the least interesting part of Andalusia. And parts of it are downright grotesque in the crude concrete overdevelopment that has marred the coast.

Bustling **Málaga** (*mah*-lah-gah), the birthplace of Pablo Picasso and Antonio Banderas (now *there's* a pair of Latin lovers), is a pleasant port city that doesn't get too caught up in the resort sheen of the rest of the Costa del Sol. Locals stroll the attractive waterfront promenade, Paseo del Parque, lined by palm trees and jacarandas and bustling with babies and ice-cream vendors. Despite massive development designed to improve the city's standing with tourists, Andalusia's second-biggest city still enjoys a pleasant, tropical feel. The long-awaited **Picasso Museum** is finally drawing plenty of visitors to the revolutionary artist's hometown.

If, despite my cranky objections, you still like the sound of the Costa del Sol (or maybe you just scored a spectacular package deal), the best places to visit are **Marbella** and **Nerja. Torremolinos,** a Mediterranean beach resort (16km/10 miles west of Málaga) known throughout Spain and much of Europe, is a long line of concrete hotel boxes shuttling inexpensive package tours in and out — the epitome of coastal overdevelopment.

Getting to and around Málaga and the Costa del Sol

Málaga is 93km (58 miles) southeast of Ronda. By car, take the interior road C-344 from Ronda (if you want to go along the coast, you have to drop down to San Pedro de Alcántara via C-339 and then head east on N-340). A direct train travels from Madrid in approximately five to six hours. (**Estación de Renfe:** Strachan, s/n; ☎ **902-24-02-02** or

95-236-02-02). By bus, **Los Amarillos** (☎ **95-218-70-61**) and **Portillo** (☎ **95-287-22-62**) both make the trip from Ronda. The **Estación de Autobuses** (☎ **95-235-00-61**) is on Paseo de los Tilos, s/n.

Málaga has an international airport, Av. García Morato, s/n (☎ **95-204-88-84**), 8km (5 miles) southeast of the city; flights from Spanish and European cities arrive at Terminal A; flights from other countries arrive at Terminal B. From the airport into town, take a bus, train, or taxi. From the airport, bus no. 19 runs from 6:30 a.m. to midnight daily (30 minutes to city center; ☎ **95-221-02-95;** 1€, or $1.20). Regular electric trains (1€, or $1.20) from the airport serve the city of Málaga (15 minutes), as well as other Costa del Sol destinations. To many towns in Costa del Sol or the Málaga province, though, taxis are the only direct service. Call **Unitaxi** (☎ 95-235-15-51) if you need a taxi. If you want to rent a car to get around, contact **Avis** (☎ 95-221-66-27), **Budget** (☎ 901-201-12-12), **Europcar** (☎ 95-235-68-12), or **Hertz** (☎ 902-402-405).

Driving to **Marbella** and other points along the Costa del Sol is easy enough, though the main roads are notorious. **Carretera Nacional N-340** is a stretch 100km (62 miles) long, which runs through coastal towns and urban sprawl and has a reputation as one of Spain's most dangerous roads (especially bad is the section west of Marbella). A new **Autopista del Sol** has been built, but its high tolls (8€, or about $10, from end-to-end in high season) have prompted many locals to boycott it. If you take N-340, watch out for pedestrians and drunk drivers. From Ronda, take C-339 south and head east on coastal road N-340. It's a total of 60km (37 miles). From Málaga, head west along N-340 for 67km (42 miles). If you don't want to drive, you can take one of the more than 20 buses per day that travel between Málaga and Marbella.

The regional **tourism information office** in Málaga is located at Pasaje de Chinitas 4 (☎ **95-221-34-45**). If you've flown into Málaga's International Airport, check out the tourism information office for help (☎ **95-204-84-84**).

Málaga: Picasso's home and a place to promenade

By far the biggest attraction in town is the city's very own **Museo Picasso Málaga,** in a 16th-century Renaissance palace, the Palacio de los Condes de Buenavista. It displays more than 200 of the artist's works that were purchased from Picasso's grandson and daughter-in-law, Bernard and Christine Ruiz-Picasso (the widow of Picasso's eldest son, Paul). The museum, which includes works ranging from early portraits, painted in the late 19th century, to late-career works from the 1970s, put the artist's birthplace next in line of importance after Paris and Barcelona in terms of Picasso collections. In the basement is a display of the archeological finds dug up during the restoration of the palace, including remains of a Phoenician wall and tower dating to the seventh century A.D.

The museum, on San Agustín 8 (☎ **95-212-76-00;** `www.museopicassomalaga.org`), is open Tuesday to Thursday from 10 a.m. to 8 p.m.;

Friday and Saturday from 10 a.m. to 9 p.m.; and Sunday and holidays from 10 a.m. to 8 p.m. Admission to the permanent collection is 6€ ($7.20) for adults and 3€ ($3.60) for seniors and students; to the temporary collection, 4.50€ ($5.40) for adults and 2.25€ ($2.70) for seniors and students; combination tickets good for both are 8€/4€ ($9.60/$4.80). You can purchase advance tickets by calling ☎ **901-24-62-46.**

Also in town is Picasso's childhood home, where the great artist was born in 1881 but lived for only three years. The **Casa Natal de Picasso,** Plaza de la Merced 15 (☎ **95-206-02-15**), is home to the Pablo Ruiz Picasso Foundation and has a smattering of Picasso's belongings and photographs, as well as exhibits of contemporary Spanish art. It's open daily from 9:30 a.m. to 8:30 p.m. Admission is 1€ ($1.20), free for seniors and for children under 17.

Málaga shines in summer, when its population swells, and one of the highlights of a visit here is a stroll along the promenade, Paseo del Parque, along which you can stop for ice cream or tapas and fresh seafood. You'll have plenty of company, because the daily (or several times-daily) *paseo* seems to be the city's great pastime. Among the city's more traditional sights is the splendid 11th-century **Alcazaba** (Moorish fortress), Plaza de la Aduana (☎ **95-222-72-30**). Admission to the Alcazaba museum is 1.90€ ($2.30), or 3.15€ ($3.80) joint admission along with **Castillo de Gibralfaro,** on Monte Gibralfaro (☎ **95-222-51-06**), a well-restored 16th-century Moorish fortress with a museum inside. The Alcazaba is open Tuesday through Saturday from 8:30 a.m. to 7 p.m. in winter, and from 9:30 a.m. to 8 p.m. in summer. The ramparts provide excellent views of the city. Near the entrance to the Alcazaba is a **Teatro Romano** (Roman Theater) dating from the first century A.D. and only discovered in 1951. The **Catedral de Málaga,** Calle Molina Lario/Plaza Obispo (☎ **95-221-59-17**), is a peculiar mix of 16th-century architectural styles with a small Museo Catedralicio of religious art. Admission is 3.50€ ($4.20); it's open Monday through Friday from 10 a.m. to 6:45 p.m., and Saturday from 10 a.m. to 5:45 p.m.

The **Museo de Bellas Artes (Fine Arts Museum),** which possesses works by such Andalusian greats as Zurbarán, Ribera, Murillo, and Picasso, is awaiting a new home; in the meantime, some of its collection is being displayed at the **Palacio de la Aduana,** Plaza de la Aduana, s/n (☎ **95-212-85-00**). Admission is free; the palace is open Tuesday through Friday from 3 to 8 p.m., and Saturday and Sunday from 9 a.m. to 3 p.m.

Also worth a visit in Málaga is the **Jardín Botánico-Histórico La Concepción,** Carretera de Las Pedrizas (C. N. 331), Km 166 (☎ **95-225-21-48**), gorgeous, 150-year-old tropical botanical gardens on the outskirts of town. They're open Tuesday to Sunday from 10 a.m. to 7:30 p.m. in summer and from 10 a.m. to 4:30 p.m. in winter. Guided visits cost 3.15€ ($3.80). To get there, take a no. 2 bus from the Alameda or a taxi (about 5€, or $6.40).

The two *paradores* are your best lodging options. In the historical quarter of Málaga, facing the Alcazaba, is the handsome, midsize **Parador de**

Málaga Gibralfaro, Monte Gibralfaro (☎ **95-222-19-02;** www.parador.es). Doubles cost 140€ to 150€ ($168–$180). Located next to the Gibralfaro Castle, it has a top-floor swimming pool and splendid panoramic views of the harbor and coastline. Take the coastal road, Paseo de Reding, which eventually becomes Paseo de Sancha. Turn left onto Camino Nuevo. The other *parador,* 10km (6 miles) from Málaga, is a golfer's delight, wedged between a fine golf course and the Mediterranean. **Parador de Málaga-Golf,** Carretera de Málaga (☎ **95-238-12-55;** www.parador.es). Doubles cost 125€ to 135€ ($150–$162).

For dining, the **Parador de Málaga Gibralfaro** occupies a beautiful spot on Monte Gibralfaro and has a good-value menu (28€/$32) and great views, and **Antonio Martín,** Paseo María Antonio Machado 16 (☎ **95-222-72-98**), along the Malagueta or Paseo Marítimo, is one of Málaga's most traditional (and upscale) seafood restaurants.

Marbella: A stylish resort

The Costa del Sol's most stylish and monied resort, **Marbella** is where the perennially tanned go to lounge on yachts and play golf. As upscale as it is, Marbella still has one of the cheesiest public works I've ever seen: an overpass/welcome gate with huge block letters spelling out MARBELLA above the road into town. Despite that introduction, the red-paved old town with whitewashed alleyways is spotless and pretty enjoyable (even if it's expensive as all get out). Its two invariably packed beaches are **La Fontanilla** and **El Fuerte.**

After you're suitably bronzed, night is the time to shine. Wear white and lots of jewels and head to Marbella's innumerable bars and *discotecas.* If you own a yacht (or if you want to meet someone who does), the right place to go is the port, **Puerto Banús.** The chic places to party late are **Discoteca Olivia Valere** (Carretera Istán, next to the mosque) and **Oh!,** in the **Hotel Don Carlos** (Carretera Cádiz, Km 198.5). If you didn't bring the right duds (and if you didn't pack your very best jewelry, then you didn't, trust me), you can always drop in on one of the relaxed tapas bars in Marbella's Old Quarter.

Marbella's Tourist Information Office is at Glorieta de la Fontanilla, s/n (☎ **95-282-28-18**). Hours are Monday through Friday from 9:30 a.m. to 8 p.m. and Saturday from 9:30 a.m. to 2 p.m. Another tourist office with the same hours is on Plaza de los Naranjos (☎ **95-282-35-50**).

If you want to snob-knob with the fashionable and spend the night in Marbella, pull your fancy rental up to **Marbella Club Hotel,** Boulevard Príncipe Alfonso von Hohenlohe, s/n (☎ **800-448-8355** in the United States, or ☎ 95-282-22-11; www.uk.marbellaclub.com). Doubles go from 250€ to 450€ ($300–$540). The elegant hotel, originally a prince's estate, is a member of the Leading Hotels of the World, with classically decorated, bungalow-style rooms. More affordable is **Hotel El Fuerte,** Av. del Fuerte, s/n (☎ **800-448-8355** in the United States, or 902-34-34-10; www.hotel-elfuerte.es). Doubles cost between 134€ and 217€

($161–$260) with discounts available for online reservations. Built in the 1950s, it's on the beach and surrounded by gardens, with a shaded pool across from a lagoon. Both hotels have deals with local golf courses.

Nerja: A huge prehistoric cave

About 50km (30 miles) east of Málaga, the village of Nerja (*nehr*-hah) has good beaches, an attractive Old Quarter, and a charming seaside promenade. The **Balcón de Europa,** a bell tower surrounded by palm trees, has excellent views of the sea and rocky coastline. But Nerja's biggest attraction is outside town (about a 35-minute drive from Málaga): **La Cueva de Nerja,** a huge cave inhabited 25,000 years ago. Accidentally discovered by a group of kids about 40 years ago, it's full of well-illuminated stalactites and chambers, as well as Paleolithic cave drawings, and is large enough to host a summer festival (July and Aug) of concerts and ballet. The cave, which has been outfitted (some might say cheesily) with lights and music, is in the hills above Nerja, on Carretera de la Cueva, s/n (☎ **95-252-95-20;** `www.cuevadenerja.es`). Hours are daily from 10 a.m. to 2 p.m. and from 4 to 8 p.m. Admission is 6€ ($7.20) for adults, 4.25€ ($5.10) for children ages 6 to 12. Children ages 5 and under are free. Buses depart hourly from Muelle de Heredia in Málaga from 7 a.m. to 8 p.m. Return buses are also hourly until 8:15 p.m. The trip takes about one hour.

One of the best places to stay in Nerja is the **Parador de Nerja,** Almuñecar 8, Playa de Burriana-Tablazo (☎ **95-252-00-50;** `www.parador.es`). Doubles range from 130€ to 140€ ($156–$168). A modern *parador,* it is perched on a cliff and has great views of the sea, coast, and mountains. You can take a lift down to the beach.

Another excellent option, especially for families, is the studio apartments of **Toboso apar-turis,** Paseo Balcón de Europa 4 (☎ **95-252-86-88;** `www.tobosoaparthotel.com`). In the historic center of Nerja, the 30 apartments (many of which have sea views) are modern and nicely equipped. On the premises are indoor and outdoor pools, a gym and a sauna, restaurant, and Irish pub. Studio apartments range from 79€ to 141€ ($96–$169), one-bedroom apartments from 127€ to 193€ ($152–$232).

Casa Luque, Plaza Cavana 2 (☎ **95-2512-10-04**), is a friendly and fancy family-run joint serving traditional Andalusian dishes.

Fast Facts: Ronda

Area Code

Ronda's area code is **95,** which you must dial before every number.

Currency Exchange

You can find banks and ATMs along the town's main drag, Virgen de la Paz. An agency that changes money is Agrotur (Virgen de la Paz, s/n; ☎ 95-287-62-38).

Hospitals

Hospital La Serranía is on Carretera de Burgos, Km 1 (☎ 95-287-15-40). Hospital Ronda is at San Vicente de Paúl, s/n (☎ 95-287-70-40). For an ambulance, call ☎ 95-287-18-75-11 or the Red Cross, ☎ 95-287-14-64.

Information

The main (regional) tourism information office is on Plaza de España 1 (☎ 95-287-12-72), next to the *parador* hotel. It's open Monday through Friday from 9 a.m. to 2 p.m. and 4 to 7 p.m.; Saturday and Sunday from 10 a.m. to 3 p.m. The municipal tourism office is on Plaza de Blas Infante (☎ 95-218-71-19).

Police

The municipal police station is at Plaza Duquesa de Parcent, s/n (☎ **092** or 95-287-13-69). The national police are located at Av. Jaén, s/n (☎ **091** or 95-287-13-70).

Post Office

Ronda's central post office is on Virgen de la Paz 18–20 (☎ 95-287-25-57).

Chapter 17
Granada

In This Chapter

- Getting around Granada
- Choosing a place to stay
- Seeing the Alhambra, the spectacular palace-fortress of the Moors
- Striking out on side trips to caves and the Sierra Nevada

Spain's magical mix of east and west — its shared history of Muslim and Christian culture and conflict — comes into sharpest focus in Granada. The seat of the Nasrid Dynasty and part of al-Andalus (the name given to Muslim Spain), Granada was the last Moorish capital on the Iberian Peninsula, where the Moors ruled for eight centuries. The Moors built the legendary Alhambra, a monumental red palace-fortress and the greatest symbol of Muslim Spain, in the foothills of the snow-capped Sierra Nevada, overlooking a broad, fertile valley. The Alhambra was the Islamic embodiment of an earthly paradise, and its murmuring fountains and regal palaces were testament to the kingdom's power and sophistication.

Ever since the 19th century, when the American author and diplomat Washington Irving happened upon the abandoned Alhambra and reintroduced it to the Western world, most travelers to Spain have put Granada at the top of their must-see list. Indeed, the Alhambra is perhaps the single greatest sight in Spain and one of the most glorious monuments in Europe.

The Moors may have been expelled by Spain's Reconquest in the 15th century, but a lasting Moorish influence remains palpable in Andalusia. Granada's favorite son, Spain's great modern poet Federico García Lorca, was deeply enamored of his native city, its magical setting, and the lingering legends of the Moors. "Only sighs glide/on the waters of Granada," he wrote. As a visitor to the city, you can both wade into its Moorish past and trace García Lorca's life, which ended tragically in Granada during the Spanish Civil War.

The weather in Granada is as dramatic as the Alhambra: It's hotter than blazes in summer and frequently downright cold in winter. Granada sits at an altitude of 671m (2,200 ft.), so nights are much cooler than days. Avoid going to Granada in July and August unless you have a serious masochistic streak. Though it gets blisteringly hot, the Alhambra is still overrun with summer tourists. The best time to visit Granada is spring, followed closely by fall. In winter the snow-topped peaks of the Sierra Nevada beckon skiers. But you won't want to come to Granada between Christmas and New Year's — the Alhambra is closed.

Getting There

Granada is a convenient destination, no matter where you're coming from or how you choose to arrive.

By plane

Granada's Aeropuerto Nacional, or **Armilla airport** (☎ **958-24-52-00**) is 15km (9 miles) south of the city, on Carretera de Málaga, s/n. Daily flights arrive from Madrid, Barcelona, Majorca, Valencia, and the Canary Islands. Armilla isn't a huge or complicated airport, and it does have an easy-to-locate tourism information office as well as an ATM.

An airport bus that costs 3€ ($3.60; ☎ **958-49-01-64**) ferries passengers between the airport and Plaza de Isabel la Católica. It departs only about every two hours. Travel time from the airport to downtown is less than 45 minutes. Taxis, lined up outside the terminals, charge about 18€ ($22) to the center of Granada or 23€ ($28) to the Albaycín district.

By car

National highway N-323 connects Granada to the north, including Madrid, via N-IV/E-5, and the southern coast. From Córdoba, take N-432 and from Seville, A-2.

By train

Express trains (called TALGO) from Madrid to Granada take about six hours. Two trains per day, leaving at 8:10 a.m. and 4:47 p.m. make the trip (31€–35€/$37–42). Trains also arrive from Seville (3 hours; 20€, or $24) as well as from Barcelona, Valencia, Málaga, and Córdoba.

The train station is **Estación de RENFE de Granada** (☎ **958-24-02-02** or 958-27-12-72; `www.renfe.es`); it's at Av. Andaluces, s/n. The ticket office is downtown at Calle de los Reyes Católicos 45 (☎ **958-22-31-19**).

By bus

Granada's main bus terminal for national departures is **Estación de Autobuses de Granada,** located at Carretera de Jaén, s/n (☎ **958-18-54-80**). Six buses per day come in from Seville (the trip takes three-and-a-half hours) and from Córdoba (three hours), and three buses per day arrive from Ronda (three hours). You can also take a bus from Cádiz, Málaga, and Guadix. Contact **Alsina Graells,** Carretera de Jaén, s/n (☎ **958-18-54-80**), for routes and additional information.

Granada

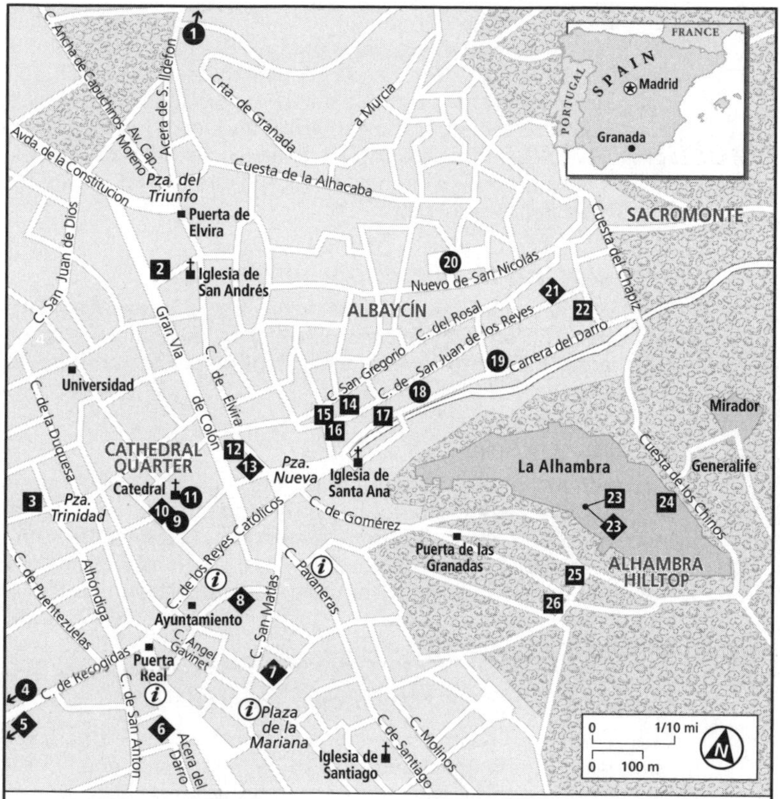

ACCOMMODATIONS ■

AC Palacio de Santa Paula **2**
Alhambra Palace **26**
América **24**
Casa de los Migueletes **14**
Casa Horno del Oro **26**
El Ladrón de Agua **17**
Hotel Carmen de Santa Inés **15**
Hotel Casa Morisca **22**
Hotel Reina Cristina **3**
NH Hotel Inglaterra **12**
Palacio de Santa Inés **16**
Parador Nacional San Francisco **23**
Washington Irving **24**

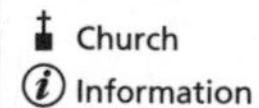

DINING ◆

Alhabaca **7**
Antigua Bodega Castañeda **13**
Chikito **6**
Las Tinajas **5**
Mirador de Morayma **21**
Parador Nacional San Francisco **23**
Real Asador de Castilla **8**
Restaurante Sevilla **10**

ATTRACTIONS ●

Capilla Real **9**
Catedral **11**
El Bañuelo (Arab Baths) **18**
Huerta de San Vicente **14**
Mirador de San Nicolás **20**
Monasterio La Cartuja **1**
Museo Arqueológico **19**

† Church
(i) Information

Orienting Yourself in Granada

Granada seems frightfully congested and not especially appealing on your way in from the web of highways outside the city to Gran Vía de Colón, the city's principal artery. Perpendicular to Gran Vía de Colón is the other main downtown artery, running north-south, Calle de los Reyes Católicos. Near their intersection is the cathedral and most hotels, restaurants, and shops. The Alhambra sits atop a hill, northeast of Plaza Nueva, and the other neighborhood of interest, the Albaycín district, occupies the hill directly facing the Alhambra.

Introducing the neighborhoods

In relatively small Granada, three areas are of interest to visitors. The Alhambra Hilltop and Albaycín districts face each other on opposite hills, and the downtown area, which contains the cathedral and most hotels, is wedged between them.

Alhambra Hilltop

The ancient Nasrid Palace complex sits regally on a hill overlooking Granada. The neighborhood has only a small number of restaurants, but people come here for the **Alhambra** and **Generalife** (the majestic Moorish palace complex and summer retreat), as well as the **Parador Nacional San Francisco,** within the Alhambra grounds. The latter is Spain's most popular *parador* (see the listing in "The top hotels" section later in the chapter).

Cathedral Quarter (Downtown Granada)

The *centro,* or downtown Granada, also called the Cathedral Quarter, is congested but compact and easy to navigate. This neighborhood is the business center of Granada, where you find most hotels, restaurants, and shops. Look for the **Cathedral,** Granada's great Christian monument; the **Royal Chapel,** where the Catholic monarchs are buried; and important sights just beyond downtown: the **La Cartuja Monastery** and poet García Lorca's childhood home, **Huerta de San Vicente.**

Albaycín

The old Arab Quarter, an evocative warren of whitewashed houses and tiny alleyways climbing the hillside, begs you to explore it. This area has few conventional sights, other than the mesmerizing views of the Alhambra and Sierra Nevada mountains, but the whole neighborhood is itself an attraction, an integral part of Granada. Today you can find a growing number of small boutique hotels with great character located here in historic villas. In Albaycín are **El Bañuelo,** ancient Arab baths; the remains of old **Arab walls;** and nearby **Sacromonte,** the old gypsy neighborhood now awash in touristy flamenco caves.

The Moors in Spain, briefly

The Moors crossed into Iberia via the Strait of Gibraltar in A.D. 711 and settled at the base of the Sierra Nevada mountains. After Córdoba — then the Muslim capital — fell in 1031, Granada gained influence and importance among the fragmented Muslim kingdoms. In 1238, Mohammed ben Sasar founded the Nasrid dynasty, and his independent kingdom stretched from Gibraltar to the eastern coast of Spain. After nearly eight centuries of Moorish presence in Spain, King Boabdil, the last ruler of the dynasty, turned over the keys of Granada to the Catholic monarchs, Ferdinand and Isabella. His surrender in 1492 signaled the end of Muslim rule in Iberia and confirmed the Christian Reconquest in Spain.

Finding information after you arrive

Granada has a denser web of **tourism information offices** than just about any city in Spain. Tourism offices are located at the airport; Virgen Blanca 9 (☎ **902-40-50-45**), open Monday through Friday from 9 a.m. to 7 p.m., Saturday from 10 a.m. to 2 p.m., and Sunday from 10 a.m. to 2 p.m.; Real de la Alhambra s/n, near the ticket offices (☎ **958-22-95-75**), open daily from 10 a.m. to 5 p.m.; Santa Ana 2 (☎ **958-57-52-02**), open Monday through Saturday from 9 a.m. to 7 p.m.; and Plaza Mariana Pineda 10 (☎ **958-24-71-28**), open Monday through Friday from 10:30 a.m. to 1:30 p.m. and 4:30 to 7 p.m., and Saturday from 10:30 a.m. to 2 p.m.

Getting around Granada

Granada is relatively compact but quite congested (don't use your car to get around). It's a good walking city if you're confined to the area around Plaza Nueva and the Alhambra and Albaycín districts, but some of the hills may prove challenging. Try the following alternative methods for checking out Granada.

By bus

A hugely convenient way to get around town is the **Alhambrabus** tourist microbus that goes back and forth from the Alhambra to the Albaycín district. The red-and-white minibuses (route nos. 30, 31, and 32), popular with both locals and tourists, run every 10 to 15 minutes between 7 a.m. and 11 p.m. They make multiple stops as they run along the Cuesta de Gomérez between the Alhambra and Plaza Nueva and along the Carretera del Darro and up into the Albaycín district. The one-way fare is .95€ ($1.15).

If you're visiting Granada for a few days, or if you've got friends or family in tow, buy a 9-fare bus ticket (called the "Bono 5.20") for just 5.20€ ($6.25) or a 20-fare ticket for 10€ ($13). You can purchase tickets at *estancos* (tobacco stands — look for the TABACOS sign).

By taxi

To order a taxi, call **Tele Radio Taxi** (☎ **958-28-06-54**) or **Radio-Taxi Granada** (☎ **958-13-23-23**). Few journeys cost more than 8€ ($9.60). You can hail a cab in the street (the little green light on the roof means you can hop in) or pick one up where they line up (usually outside hotels, the Alhambra, and near the minibus stop on Plaza Nueva).

By car

Granada is congested and complicated to drive in; a car isn't necessary in town. However, if you want to explore more of Andalusia, renting some wheels is a good idea. Rental-car companies include **Avis,** Recogidas 31 (☎ 958-25-23-58); **Budget,** Recogidas 35 (☎ 958-25-05-54); **Europcar,** Av. del Sur 2 (☎ 958-29-50-65); and **Hertz,** Luis Braille 7 (☎ 958-25-24-19). Avis, Europcar, and Hertz also have offices at the airport.

On foot

Granada is surprisingly small, but you need to save your feet for the Alhambra and getting around the hilly Albaycín neighborhood. Walking between Albaycín and most of the downtown sights is easy enough, though. Unless you're staying in a hotel that's tucked into the woods near the Alhambra, you need to take a bus or taxi to get there.

Staying in Style

Granada's hotel scene used to encompass the *parador* — the most sought-after reservation in Spain — and everything else. But Granada has added several outstanding and excellent-value small hotels with real Andalusian character to supplement the flagship of the national *parador* network. Many of the boutique hotels are located in the picturesque Albaycín district. Granada is a very popular destination, so make your reservations early — especially in the spring and early summer. Easter week is perennially sold out.

If you want to make sure you get a room either at the **Parador Nacional San Francisco** (☎ **958-22-14-40;** `www.parador.es`) or **América** (☎/Fax **958-22-224-25**) — both within the actual grounds of the Alhambra — book at least three to four months (or more) in advance.

Christmas in Granada with the snow-capped Sierra Nevada mountains in the background may sound romantic, but you'll feel more like the Grinch if you arrive without realizing that the Alhambra, probably Spain's single greatest sight (at the very least it competes neck-and-neck with Madrid's Prado Museum for that honor), closes between December 25 and January 1.

The top hotels

AC Palacio de Santa Paula

$$$–$$$$ Cathedral Quarter

Not far from the Cathedral, housed in the sumptuously converted Jerónimos Convent, this new hotel is perhaps the city's most luxurious. Its location, on one of Granada's busiest thoroughfares, isn't as desirable as either of the top choices on Alhambra hill, but it more than makes up for that shortcoming with easy access to restaurants, shops, and bars, and the beauty of the Mudéjar-style convent. The hotel, a merger of minimalism and historic monument, is built around the stunning, arcaded cloisters, and the excellent El Claustro restaurant is suitably monastic looking. Rooms — each of which is different from the next — are luxurious and well decorated, as is typical of this elite Spanish hotel chain. I especially like those rooms built around the courtyard, with wood-beam ceilings.

See map p. 461. Gran Vía de Colón 33. ☎ ***902-29-22-93.*** *Fax: 917-24-42-63.* `www.ac-hoteles.com`. *Parking: 15€ ($18). Rack rates: 180€–243€ ($216–$292) double. AE, DC, MC, V.*

Alhambra Palace

$$$–$$$$ Alhambra Hill

With a location nearly as privileged as the Alhambra itself, this palatial reddish-pink hotel on the hill envisions itself as the perfect Moorish-style companion to the real Nasrid Palaces just minutes away, and for most visitors to Granada, it is. Built by the Duke of San Pedro de Galatino in 1910, it looks like an Epcot Center version of a Moorish citadel and includes all kinds of neo-Mudéjar touches (splashy tiles, arches, carved plaster walls, wood ceilings, and even a pseudo-minaret). But what it has above all else is a superb location — it's within walking distance of the Alhambra and has priceless views of Granada below. The 122 rooms at the Palace, popular with travelers and business visitors alike, are spacious and impressive without being stuffy. Try to get a room with a small balcony overlooking the city, and ask to see a few rooms if you can, because their size and appeal vary quite a bit.

See map p. 461. Peña Partida 2–4. On southern face of the Alhambra hill; the next-to-last stop on Alhambra minibus leaves you about 180m (600 ft.) from entrance. ☎ ***958-22-14-68.*** *Fax: 958-22-64-04.* `www.h-alhambrapalace.es`. *Free parking. Rack rates: 167€ ($200) double. AE, DC, MC, V.*

América

$$–$$$ Alhambra Hill

Happily, the impossible-to-get-into Parador Nacional San Francisco doesn't have a monopoly on beds inside the Alhambra grounds. And that is the América's calling card. Choose to stay at this charming and homey hotel in a 19th-century Andalusian house, and you'll be just a few paces from the entrance to the Alhambra. The rooms are exceedingly simple, and not terribly spacious, but the house has a lovely plant-filled patio and magnificent gardens all around. Management offers simple, home-cooked meals every day but Sunday. Given its coveted location (for which you pay through the nose at the *parador*), the América is constantly booked. Reserve here at least three to four months in advance.

See map p. 461. Real de la Alhambra 53. Within Alhambra grounds; take Alhambra minibus to edge of grounds, or take a taxi directly to hotel. ☎ ***958-22-74-71.*** *Fax: 958-22-74-70.* www.hotelamericagranada.com. *Parking: 12€ ($14). Rack rates: 125€–145€ ($83–$120) double. Closed: Nov 10–Feb. AE, DC, MC, V.*

Carmen de Santa Inés
$$–$$$ Albaycín

An old Arab *carmen* (villa with a concealed garden), later expanded in the 16th and 17th centuries, was fully renovated and transformed into one of Granada's loveliest hotels in the late 1990s. Carmen de Santa Inés's nine rooms, all different from one another, are replete with handsome antique furnishings, Arab carpets, and wonderful decorative touches; six of the rooms even offer views of the Alhambra (the others overlook the interior patio). Tucked into the tiny streets of the old Arab Quarter, Albaycín, the hotel is as charming as the neighborhood it inhabits. The hosts serve breakfast in the beautiful garden, amid fountains and fruit trees.

See map p. 461. Placeta de Porras 7 (off San Juan de los Reyes). Two short blocks northwest of Carrera del Darro and Iglesia de Santa Ana. ☎ ***958-22-63-80.*** *Fax: 958-22-44-04.* www.carmensantaines.com. *Parking: 12€ ($14). Rack rates: 95€–130€ ($114–156) double. AE, DC, MC, V.*

Casa de los Migueletes
$$$–$$$$ Albaycín

The newest and most luxurious of the crop of interesting boutique hotels in the Muslim quarter of Granada, this 17th-century, three-story mansion, owned and operated by a Norwegian couple, is one of the most sophisticated options in town. On a quiet street near Plaza Santa Ana, it is slightly larger than several inns in the district. Every effort was made to respect the original structure of the house (which was once the headquarters to rural police, known for their armaments called "Migueletes") but the décor does not go in for any kitschy Arab stylings. The 25 rooms have a touch of Scandanavian spareness, though they feature beautiful bathrooms and quality linens, bedding, and furnishings. Superior and deluxe rooms have views either of the courtyard and its fountain or the Alhambra. The hotel has more of a grand museum feel than the cozy inn quality of several of the Albaycín inns that occupy medieval *cármenes,* which will satisfy more demanding guests.

See map p. 461. Calle Benalua 11. Two blocks from Plaza Santa Ana. ☎ ***958-21-07-00.*** *Fax: 958-21-07-02.* www.casamigueletes.com. *Parking 10€ ($12). Rack rates: 129€–199€ ($155–$239) double. AE, DC, MC, V.*

Casa Horno del Oro

$$ Albaycín

This 16th-century house, on a quiet, pedestrian-only street in the heart of the Albaycín district, is one of the newer boutique inns in this picturesque neighborhood. It has a very warm, Mudéjar feel, with ochre-colored walls, Arab-style *azulejos,* or tiles, teahouse-style lanterns, and even a skylight reminiscent of a *hammam* (Arab bath). A plant-filled rooftop deck has splendid views of the Alhambra hilltop. The five rooms are charming and inviting; one even has its own private patio complete with fountain. For the location and level of comfort, and rates under 100€ for a double, the inn is a deal.

See map p. 461. Horno del Oro 6. ☎ ***958-22-32-36.*** *Fax 958-29-42-59.* www.casahornodeloro.com. *Parking: 13€ ($16). Rack rates: 90€–160€ ($132–$192) double. AE, DC, MC, V.*

Hotel Casa Morisca

$$$–$$$$ Albaycín

A gorgeously appointed and romantic 15th-century villa in the Arab quarter, this small luxury inn has catapulted itself to the top of the city's growing roster of intimate places to stay. Rooms have handsome peaked and Moorish-style ceilings and elegant period furnishings. The stylish suite is one long room with a comfortable sitting room and open bedroom at the end, with a remarkable carved polychrome ceiling dating to the 1400s. One room, called Mirador, has splendid views across the rooftops to the Alhambra, and some other rooms open onto the charming garden courtyard. Breakfast is served in an atmospheric, brick-vaulted dining room.

See map p. 461. Cuesta de la Victoria 9. ☎ ***958-22-11-00.*** *Fax: 958-21-57-96.* www.hotelcasamorisca.com. *Free parking. Rack rates: 114€–196€ ($137–$235) double. AE, DC, MC, V.*

Palacio de Santa Inés

$$$ Albaycín

Owned by the same folks who run the terrific Carmen de Santa Inés, this lovingly renovated small palace, recently in complete ruins, is one of Granada's top choices. Dating to the beginning of the 16th century, it was known as the Casa del Padre Eterno (House of the Eternal Father). Today it is a luxurious, five-year-old inn with modern art on the walls, silver chandeliers, a two-story Renaissance courtyard, and thick wood-beamed ceilings. The painstaking renovation restored important frescos on the walls of the patio, painted by a disciple of Rafael. The hotel's six double rooms and seven suites are charmingly decorated, full of interesting antiques. Rooms 3, 6, 7, and 12 offer views of the Alhambra, which is illuminated at night. This hotel is only slightly less intimate than its sister hotel, Carmen de Santa Inés, also located in the attractively labyrinthine Albaycín district. Check online for special off-season offers.

See map p. 461. Cuesta de Santa Inés 9. One short block northwest of Carrera del Darro and Iglesia de Santa Ana. ☎ ***958-22-23-62.*** *Fax: 958-22-24-65.* `www.palaciosantaines.com`. *Parking: 13€ ($16). Rack rates: 110€–160€ ($132–$192) double. AE, DC, MC, V.*

Parador Nacional San Francisco

$$$$$ Alhambra

If you're the sort who plans vacations far in advance, and you're certain of the date you're visiting Granada, you may have a shot at getting a reservation at Spain's most popular and famous *parador.* This hotel is desirable for a good reason: An ancient Moorish palace converted into a convent in the 15th century, the *parador* is lodged within the grounds of the magnificent Alhambra. The serene hilltop gardens, with the snowcapped Sierra Nevada peaks and Albaycín district in the distance, may just be Spain's finest location. The look of the rooms almost doesn't matter, but the good news is that, although they're not over-the-top luxurious, they are decorated in good taste and full of handsome antiques. Do your best to request a room in the old part, as the more modern wing is a bit less appealing. Though it's the most expensive and difficult-to-get-into of all the *paradores,* it is still fairly reasonable, given its unrivaled location. If you're dying to stay within the Alhambra, no doubt a magical experience at night, put down this book and send them an e-mail or fax right away — as long as it's a good three to four months before you'll be arriving in Granada. And if it's not, you can always hope.

See map p. 461. Real de la Alhambra, s/n. Within Alhambra grounds; take Alhambra minibus to edge of grounds or, better yet, taxi directly to hotel. ☎ ***958-22-14-40.*** *Fax: 958-22-22-64.* `www.parador.es`. *Free parking. Rack rates: 250€ ($280) double. AE, DC, MC, V.*

Runner-up hotels

Hotel Reina Cristina

$$–$$$ Cathedral Quarter The family-owned Reina Cristina, is full of charm, history, and warm personal service. The beautiful, plant-filled interior courtyard looks like what it once was: part of a handsome private home, rather than a hotel lobby. Granada's favorite son, the poet and playwright Federico García Lorca, was taken from this hotel by Franco's forces and shot just a couple of miles away. Rooms are simple and aren't overly large, but they're very comfortable. *See map p. 461. Tablas 4. One block west of Plaza Trinidad, southwest of the cathedral.* ☎ ***958-25-32-11.*** *Fax: 958-25-57-28.* `www.hotelreinacristina.com`.

El Ladrón de Agua

$$$ Albaycín Yet another 16th-century mansion in the Albaycín district, this small boutique hotel, inaugurated in 2004 on a narrow street, combines lovely period details, such as a relaxing Renaissance patio and carved-wood ceilings, with a minimalist, modern aesthetic. About half the rooms have views of the Alhambra and, at this inn named for a poem — with lines of poetry stenciled or projected onto walls — guests will find a welcoming library and occasional music, art, and literature programs. *See map p. 461. Carrera del Darro 13.* ☎ ***958-21-50-40.*** *Fax: 958-22-4345.* `www.ladrondeagua.com`.

NH Hotel Inglaterra

$$$ **Cathedral Quarter** Formerly a dilapidated, family-run place in need of a makeover, this hotel on a small but busy street off the city's busiest thoroughfare has been transformed into one of Granada's better hotels. It has 36 very clean and nicely decorated rooms around a brightly colored central courtyard. *See map p. 461. Cetti Meriem 4. Two blocks directly northeast of the cathedral.* ☎ ***958-22-15-58.*** `www.nh-hoteles.es`.

Washington Irving

$$ **Alhambra Hill** If you've just got to be on the hill, near enough to taste the mystique of the Alhambra, but can't get a reservation at the *parador* or América, this hotel is your next best bet. The hotel, in the midst of an extensive renovation, is a comfortable classic, and, even if the rooms leave something to be desired, the staff couldn't be friendlier or more helpful. *See map p. 461. Paseo del Generalife 2 (just outside of Alhambra grounds).* ☎ ***958-22-75-50.*** `www.iberia-hotels.com/granada/washington.htm`.

Dining Out

Despite its enduring popularity on the tourist circuit, Granada doesn't rank as one of the better places in Spain, or even in Andalusia, to eat out. The province as a whole remains pretty unimaginative in terms of dining opportunities, so with a few exceptions, your memories are much more likely to be of the Alhambra than of the local meals. Most places in Granada are simple, no-frills restaurants. Making a meal of tapas (Spanish hors d'oeuvres) is always a reliable choice. Two hotel restaurants stand out: El Claustro at AC Palacio de Santa Paula, in a dramatic dining room carved out of a 1540 convent, and the restaurant at the Parador de Granada, reviewed below.

Tapas grazing is an excellent way to assemble a meal of typical and varied Andalusian tastes; try one of the following joints for an inexpensive and informal meal: **Ajo Blanco,** Palacios 17 (☎ 958-22-81-28); **Casa del Vino,** Monjas del Carmen (☎ 958-22-25-95); **Fogón de Galicia,** Navas 27 (☎ 958-22-68-36); and **Antigua Bodega Castañeda,** Elvira 5 (☎ 958-22-63-62).

Typical dishes in Granada, so close to the Sierra Nevada, Spain's highest mountain range, are hearty. Granada's version of the cold soup gazpacho, *gazpacho granadino,* is usually made with *jamón serrano* (cured ham); *habas con jamón* are small broad beans in olive oil with thin slices of salt cured ham; and *tortilla sacromonte,* perhaps the most famous dish in Granada, is a Spanish *tortilla* (omelet) made not with the usual potatoes and onions, but with calf, pig, or lamb brains. Call me fussy, but that's one tortilla I *won't* taste.

For more on Spanish dining customs, including mealtimes, costs, and tipping, see Chapter 2.

Alhabaca

$$ Cathedral Quarter SPANISH

A simple, tiny establishment — it seats about 20 diners — on a quiet plaza near a number of bars and nightlife, Alhabaca is a bit like a country inn in the big, bad city. It has bare white walls, simple tables with white tablecloths, and the kitchen in full view. Dishes are simple, but well prepared. A good starter is *salmorejo,* the thick, gazpacholike tomato soup from Córdoba. The main course I had, *merluza en salsa de almendras* (hake or white fish in almond sauce), was equally good. For dessert, the *flan de calabaza* (pumpkin flan) is a Spanish version of pumpkin pie.

See map p. 461. Varela 17. Between Varela and San Matías, 5 blocks from Plaza de la Mariana. ☎ ***958-22-49-23.*** *Main courses: 8€–15€ ($9.60–$18). Menú del día: 15€ ($18). AE, MC. Open: Tues–Sat lunch and dinner, Sun lunch only. Closed: Aug.*

Antigua Bodega Castañeda

$ Cathedral Quarter ANDALUSIAN

A lively, cheerful spot just off Plaza Nueva — splitting the distance between the Alhambra and the Albaycín barrio — this long train car of a place, which has been around for about a century, is half inexpensive restaurant, half rollicking tapas bar and bodega. There are only about ten tables, so you'll probably have to wait — or just muscle up to the bar like everyone else. Besides all manner of cheap tapas, sandwiches, and large salads, it specializes in *potajes* — a type of thick stew in clay pots that has probably fortified Spaniards since the time of Columbus. You can choose from six types of *potajes,* including codfish and lentils with *chorizo* (spicy sausage). A great place to stop before making your way up the hill to the Alhambra, Bodega Castañeda is also just a stone's throw from a slew of Moroccan-style tea rooms, where you can grab a fabulous fruit shake for dessert. Night owls will be pleased to know that this joint is open until 1:30 a.m. daily.

See map p. 461. Calle Elvira 5. Just off Plaza Nueva. ☎ ***958-22-63-62.*** *Main courses: 7€–12€ ($8.40–$14). AE, MC, V. Open: Daily lunch and dinner.*

Chikito

$$$ Cathedral Quarter ANDALUSIAN/BASQUE

A classic patronized by local diners and Spanish visitors to Granada (portraits of the most famous line the wall of the lively tapas bar at the entrance), Chikito is cutely named, but serious about food. A little too serious, perhaps. I recommend standing at the bar and downing some excellent tapas rather than sitting in the stuffier dining room. If you do sit down, choose from among *zarzuela de pescado* (seafood stew), breaded and stuffed veal, or oven-baked hake (a white fish similar to cod).

See map p. 461. Plaza del Campillo 9. Between Angel Gavinet and Acera de Darro. ☎ ***958-22-33-64.*** *Reservations recommended. Main courses: 12€–23€ ($14–$28). Menú del dia: 19€ ($23). AE, MC, V. Open: Thurs–Tues lunch and dinner.*

Las Tinajas

$$$ Cathedral Quarter ANDALUSIAN

A delightful Andalusian *mesón* (inn) decorated with original art and lots of plants and flowers, Las Tinajas is the work of José Alvarez, a veteran of the Granada restaurant scene. The tapas bar is a popular and occasionally noisy spot, serving up a delicious variety of hors d'oeuvres. The kitchen consistently elaborates dishes with the freshest possible ingredients, such as *rollitos de lubina rellenos de langostinos y jamón ibérico* (sea bass rolls stuffed with prawns and salt-cured ham). A few items on the menu pay homage to Granada's Muslim past, and the wine cellar is well stocked with Spanish favorites and a few surprises.

See map p. 461. Martínez Campos 17. Just off Recogidas, south of Puerta Real. ☎ ***958-25-43-93.*** *Main courses: 9€–22€ ($11–$26). Menú del dia: 22€–28€ ($26–34). Tasting menu: 32€ ($38). AE, DC, MC, V. Open: Daily lunch and dinner. Closed: Mid-July to mid-August.*

Mirador de Morayma

$$–$$$ Albaycín ANDALUSIAN/SPANISH

A gorgeous, private Renaissance-era home, decorated with what appear to be personal effects, this restaurant is a great chance to experience an authentic Granada *carmen* — an Albaycín villa with stupendous gardens concealed behind high walls. You have to ring at an imposing black door — be patient, it may take awhile for someone to let you inside. Wind your way through the gardens on the way to the restaurant at back; the views of the Alhambra on the hill are nothing short of amazing. (Legend has it that Morayma, the wife of the last Moorish king, Boabdil, was imprisoned here, reduced to gazing at the Alhambra from the opposite hill.) The popular restaurant has several separate dining rooms with idiosyncratic touches (pre-Columbian pieces, a shrine near the bathroom). The traditional menu is diverse and servings are ample; prices are reasonable. Try the *espinacas con almendras* (spinach with almonds) to start, and perhaps the *solomillo de cerdo* (pork sirloin) to follow it up. On Tuesday evenings, you can enjoy a live flamenco performance at 11 p.m.

See map p. 461. Pianista García Carrillo 2. Difficult to find; a few blocks down from and to the left of the Mirador San Nicolás. ☎ ***958-22-82-90.*** *Main courses: 10€–18€ ($12–$22). AE, MC, V. Open: Mon–Sat lunch and dinner.*

Parador Nacional San Francisco

$$$ Alhambra ANDALUSIAN/SPANISH

It's hard as heck to get a room at the *parador,* housed in an illustrious 15th-century convent, and fairly expensive when you do. A good alternative if you've landed somewhere else, is to pop in (well, not exactly pop in — reservations are absolutely necessary) for lunch or dinner to soak up some of the singular Alhambra ambience. The views of the serene rose gardens and the Generalife in the distance are unbeatable. At lunchtime, the attractive garden terrace is open — a great place to dine if you're not here in the middle of a scorching Granada summer. The national *parador* restaurants are generally dependable, if not always exciting, but this may be the very best of the lot. Dine on Antonio Macía Blanco's creative Andalusian specialties such as *rape mozárabe con piñones* (Moorish-style monkfish with pine nuts) or blood sausage lasagna in a sauce of leeks.

See map p. 461. Real de la Alhambra, s/n. Within Alhambra grounds; enter western gate, where you don't have to pay to enter the Alhambra. ☎ ***958-22-14-40.*** *Reservations required. Main courses: 13€–24€ ($16–$29). Menú del día: 25€ ($30). AE, DC, MC, V. Open: Daily lunch and dinner.*

Real Asador de Castilla

$$$ Cathedral Quarter ANDALUSIAN

Welcome, meat lovers, to this authentic Castilian *asador* (barbecue restaurant). Visit this place to get thick ribs, lamb, and roast pig direct from the spit. On a small plaza near the old Ayuntamiento (City Hall), it does big weekend business with local families who huddle around the tapas bar before moving on to more serious pursuits. There's also fresh fish and a series of *guisos caseros* — home-cooked stews thick with vegetables and (mostly) meat.

See map p. 461. Escudo del Carmen 17. Two blocks south of Plaza Isabel la Católica, off San Matías. ☎ ***958-22-29-10.*** *Main courses: 11€–22€ ($13–$26). AE, MC, V. Open: Daily lunch and dinner.*

Restaurante Sevilla

$$–$$$ Cathedral Quarter ANDALUSIAN

A classic in Granada, Restaurante Sevilla, named for that *other* city in Andalusia (see Chapter 15), has been around seemingly forever and is still going strong. The city's best-known restaurant, this two-story place is where the literary and musical elite — including favorite son García Lorca — used to dine back in the early 1930s. Today it's just as popular with Spaniards and the visitors who tramp through town. In summer, the restaurant sets tables in the square next to the Royal Chapel. Andalusian specialties reign. The four dining rooms are charmingly decorated with colorful Moorish-style *azulejos* (tiles). Open your meal with the inevitable gazpacho or *sopa sevillana* (a fish soup), followed perhaps by *cordero a la pastoril* (spicy lamb stew with herbs).

See map p. 461. Oficios 12. Next to Royal Chapel. ☎ ***58-22-12-23.*** *Reservations recommended. Main courses: 12€–24€ ($14–$29). Menú del día: 15€ ($18). AE, DC, MC, V. Open: Daily lunch, Mon–Sat dinner.*

Exploring Granada: The Alhambra and More

No matter how much time you have, make your first stop the Alhambra — unless weather reports call for rain and you've got additional days in Granada. If at all possible, go on a sunny day, when the reflecting pools are brilliant and the views of the Albaycín district and Sierra Nevada are clear. You need at least a half-day — a full four to five hours — to fully explore the Alhambra. In fact, I limit the "Top Attractions" in Granada to just three must-sees; they are crucial to getting a feel for this historic city, and they shouldn't require more than a day and a half to see. Any time left over is a bonus, and you can devote it to the second tier of attractions and things to do.

The top attractions

La Alhambra and Generalife

Alhambra Hill

Gracing a ruddy, wooded hill is southern Spain's spectacular showpiece: the legendary Alhambra fortress and palace complex of the Moors. Though its origins as a fortress date to the ninth century, the present citadel and walled fortifications of the Nasrid dynasty were begun in 1238, and the complex was enlarged throughout the 13th and 14th centuries — as the Moors solidified their hold on southern Spain — with palaces, residences, mosques, spectacular gardens, and a royal summer estate (the Generalife, adjacent to the Alhambra). After Christians captured Granada from the Moors, they added a convent and Renaissance palace to the Alhambra grounds in the 16th century. The entire complex fell into disrepair and, eventually, abandonment over the next hundred years or so, only to be rediscovered in 1829 by the American writer and diplomat Washington Irving. His *Tales of the Alhambra* succeeded in awakening the world's attention and prompting Spanish authorities to restore the palaces and grounds.

The Moors' intentions in constructing the Alhambra were unflinchingly grand: Rulers sought nothing less than to create an earthly paradise. In its

A monumental bargain

A very good deal for anyone intent on making the most of Granada's cultural attractions is the **Bono Turístico Granada,** a combined ticket — in the form of a plastic card that you swipe at the gate of any participating monument — that gets you into the Alhambra, Generalife, Capilla Real, Catedral, and the Cartuja and San Jerónimo monasteries, as well as up to nine free trips on city buses and the tourist microbus and a 24-hour ticket for the Bus Turístico (city tour). The Bono, which is good for a week and costs 23€ ($27) or 25€ ($29) in advance, can be purchased at the Alhambra, Capilla Real, or any Caja Granada bank office. Call ☎ **902-10-00-95** for additional information.

La Alhambra and Generalife

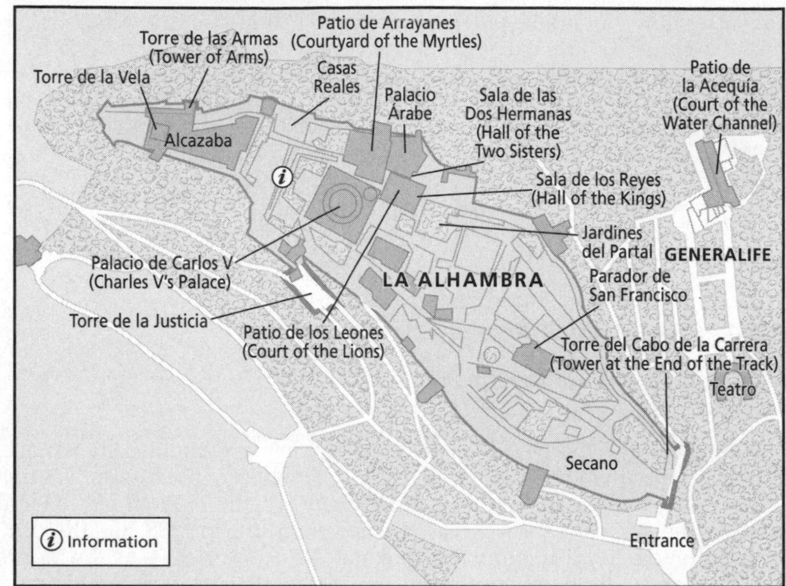

quiet elegance and harmony, its bewitching beauty, and its air of inscrutability and wonder, this sprawling compound, Muslim Spain's greatest achievement, came very close to that ideal.

Your Alhambra ticket (valid for one day only and designated either morning, 8:30 a.m. to 2 p.m., or afternoon, 2 p.m. to close) allows you only a half-hour window of access to the Nasrid Palaces (350 people per half-hour are allowed entrance, and you must enter at the time your ticket specifies, or lose your opportunity to see the finest part of the Alhambra — though you can stay as long as you want after you enter). During peak visitation periods — primarily summer, but also at other vacation times such as Easter — you might not gain admission if you go late in the day. Try to go as early as possible, even though tour groups will be lined up, or try going during the extended lunch hour (2–4 p.m.). Even early in the morning, you may wait a couple of hours or more to enter. You may have some luck late in the day, after large groups have evacuated, but if the day's quota is filled, you'll be denied entrance after 4 p.m.

Enter the Alhambra complex at the end of the Cuesta de Gomérez and stroll along the gardens, where a *medina* (marketplace) once flourished. The first major building is the jarringly self-important 15th-century Renaissance **Palacio de Carlos V** (Palace of Carlos V, a Christian addition to the Alhambra grounds and a stark stylistic contrast). It contains the **Museo de la Alhambra** (a newly redesigned museum devoted to the art of al-Andalus) and a small **Museo de Bellas Artes (Fine Arts Museum).** You

Onward to the Alhambra

The easiest way to get to the Alhambra is to take a taxi or the red-and-white Alhambrabus minibuses that shuttle back and forth between the Albaycín district and the hilltop palace complex (the nearest stop is below the hill, at Plaza Nueva). If you're the energetic sort, however, the steep uphill walk into the luxuriant shade of the woods surrounding the Alhambra is a magnificent way to make your way up. The walk doesn't take more than 20 minutes or so, though I don't recommend it for anyone but the most athletic (you need to save your energy to walk around the large grounds of the Alhambra and Generalife). To walk, follow the signs from Plaza Nueva to Cuesta de Gomérez uphill to Puerta de las Granadas, the first of two gates to the Alhambra. Keep going past the second; the ticket office is on your left (look for all the commotion). Along the way, watch out for thieves masquerading as tour guides.

can either see the Carlos V palace first or save it until after you've seen the palaces of the Moorish kings, which deserve the bulk of your time. If you have time before your appointed hour, visit the **Alcazaba,** the fortress that is the oldest part of the Alhambra, begun in 1238. **Torre de la Campana (Bell Tower),** the highest point of the Alhambra, is where the Catholic monarchs hung their banners after the Reconquest and installed a bell to regulate irrigation times in the fertile valleys below.

Enter the **Palacios Nazaríes (Royal Nasrid Palaces)** through the **Sala del Mexuar,** the main public reception hall, completed in 1365, and pass into the **Cuarto Dorado (Gilded Room)** and its patio, which boasts one of the most splendid facades in the palaces. In the **Palacio de Comares,** built by Yusuf I, you'll come upon the **Patio de Arrayanes (Courtyard of Myrtles),** a beautiful patio with a long, spectacular reflecting pool. Here are some of the palace's most remarkable *azulejos* (glazed ceramic tiles). Behind it is the **Salón de Embajadores (Ambassadors' Hall),** an ornately carved throne room built in the mid-14th century. The dome represents the seven heavens of the Islamic cosmos. Make your way to the magnificent **Palacio de los Leones,** part of the royal family's private quarters and one of the most famous elements of the Alhambra. Built by Mohammed V, the palace is a festival of delicate marble columns with a gurgling fountain at its center where water trickles from the mouths of 12 lions. Here the delicacy of the plasterwork carving reaches new heights. At the back of the patio is the **Sala de los Abencerrajes,** a noble hall with a stunningly rich honeycombed ceiling where the last Moorish king, Boabdil, reputedly beheaded rivals (a legend that purports to explain the reddish, blood-stained color of the pillars). From here, wander around the lions' courtyard and back into the **Apartamentos de Carlos V** — quarters where Washington Irving stayed in the 1820s. His stay in the abandoned Alhambra was the basis for his famous book, *Tales from the Alhambra,* which publicized the great palaces to the world. Exit these parts and find the ruins of the oldest palace in the Alhambra, **El Partal,** with another large reflecting pool and gardens that lead to the Generalife.

The **Generalife** (heh-neh-rah-*lee*-feh), also within the Alhambra's walls, was the country estate of the Nasrid kings. High above the city on 75 lush acres, it sings with murmuring fountains. The 13th-century complex is a series of magically serene courtyards and gently flowing waters, a place to lose yourself, as the swinging sultans and their harems surely did. The **Patio de la Acequía,** a closed Arab garden with a long, narrow pool lined by water jets forming delicate arches, is particularly fetching and photogenic. Don't miss a lovely walk on the footpath, **Escalera del Agua (Water Staircase),** along the upper gardens.

See map p. 474. Real, s/n. Alhambra Hill. ☎ ***958-02-79-00.*** www.alhambra-patronato.es. *To reserve up to one year or as little as one day in advance, call* ***Banco BBV*** ☎ ***902-22-44-60*** *(from outside Spain,* ☎ ***34-91-537-91-78****); you may also purchase advance tickets online at* www.alhambratickets.com. *To get there: red Alhambra–Albaycín minibus from Plaza Nueva. Admission: Comprehensive ticket, including Alhambra and Generalife, morning or afternoon, 10€ ($12) adults; 7€ ($8.40) seniors and students, free for children under 8. Night visits (Nasrid palaces only), 10€ ($12); garden visits only, 5€ ($6). Admission to the Alhambra and Generalife are included in the* ***Bono Turístico Granada*** *(see "A monumental bargain" sidebar earlier in this chapter). Open: Nov–Feb daily 8:30 a.m.–6 p.m., also Fri–Sat 8:30 p.m.–9:30 p.m.; Mar–Oct daily 8:30 a.m.–8 p.m., also Tues–Sat 10–11:30 p.m.*

Museo de Bellas Artes (Fine Arts Museum, within the Carlos V Palace; ☎ ***958-22-48-43****) is open Tues 2:30–6 p.m., Wed–Sat 9 a.m.–6 p.m., and Sun 9 a.m.–2:30 p.m. Admission: 1.50€ ($1.80), free to E.U. members.*

The Museo de la Alhambra (within the Palacio de Carlos V; ☎ ***958-22-75-27****) is open Tues–Sat 9 a.m.–2 p.m. Admission: Free.*

The entire complex is closed Dec25–Jan 1.

Albaycín

Granada's old Arab district, the site of the first Moorish settlement in Granada, is richly evocative of another time, when the city had more mosques than churches. The Albaycín runs along the Darro River and a picturesque street, Carrera del Darro; the whitewashed neighborhood creeps up a steep hillside, full of quick twists and turns and ever-escalating steps, all the while keeping the Alhambra in its viewfinder. The entire district, today as in days past largely a residential neighborhood, has been named a UNESCO Heritage of Mankind site. Lovely discoveries are everywhere — from *cármenes* (Moorish villas with orchards) and quiet plazas to uneven cobblestone paths, tall cypress trees, and *aljibes* (cisterns).

The greatest discovery, though, may be the heart-stopping views from the **Mirador de San Nicolás.** A small plaza in front of the church looks directly across at the Alhambra, perfectly framed against the snow-capped ridges of the Sierra Nevada. A visit is best at sunset, when the Alhambra glows red, or late at night, when it is exquisitely floodlit. You may find yourself returning to this platform, a meeting place for young people and foreign tourists in Granada, time and time again. Take Calle Zafra or Elvira to get there, but plan on getting lost amid the charming and serpentine streets.

Some Alhambra sightseeing tips

An ideal visit to the Alhambra is a thoroughly peaceful experience. With the massive interest in visiting the palace complex, though, serenity can be tough to come by. Visitors are limited to 6,600 per day in order to protect the monument. Here are a few ways to save time and hassles.

- Purchase your ticket, up to one year (and at least one day) in advance, by calling ☎ **902-224-460** (within Spain) or 34-91-537-91-78 (outside Spain); you may also purchase tickets online at `www.alhambratickets.com`. Or get tickets Monday through Friday at the BBV Bank at Plaza Isabel la Católica, at the corner of Reyes Católicos, from 9 a.m. to 2 p.m., or at any branch of BBV in Spain or abroad (London, New York, and so on). I strongly recommend advance purchase of tickets.
- Avoid the early morning if you dislike large groups. Tour groups on whirlwind tours of Andalusia line up to bum-rush the doors at 8 a.m. — get out of their way, because they've got to be in Córdoba by noon!
- Lunchtime is generally a good time to visit — most Europeans take long lunch breaks. (Try to get your timed entrance to the Nasrid Palaces between 2 p.m. and 4 p.m.) Better yet, come during the last hour of the afternoon session (winter 5–6 p.m.; summer 7–8 p.m.). This time is perfect to visit, when the tour groups have moved on and most others still hanging around are tired. Note, however, that during the busiest times of the year, if you wait to get your ticket until late in the afternoon, you risk not getting admitted if the daily maximum is already filled.
- Rent a digital audiophone guide for a detailed explanation of the history of the Alhambra and some of the legends and tales associated with it. The tour is in several languages, including English, and it allows you to go at your own pace, repeating or skipping over passages if you like. It also gives you the great advantage of not having to read when you'd much prefer to look.
- Visit the Alhambra at night — a singular experience. Night is a great time to feel the silence of the floodlit palace and hear the trickling fountains unmarred by groups shouting in French, English, Japanese, German, Italian, and Portuguese. However, you can only visit the Nasrid palaces (not including the Generalife). A nocturnal visit is best as a supplementary visit — when you've already seen it by day and found its beauty intoxicating. As your only visit, you miss too much at night, including the beauty of the reflective pools, the bright tile work, and the views of Albaycín and the Sierra Nevada.

Bring good walking shoes and energy — there's a reason many of the Albaycín's streets begin with the word *cuesta* (slope).

Appropriately enough, this old Moorish neighborhood is again dotted with *teterías* — **Moroccan-style tearooms** with a ton of tea varieties and a bohemian feel — and antiques shops that reflect a *medina* (marketplace) past. The intense Moorish character of the Albaycín is palpable as you climb Calle Elvira. Two streets, Caldería Nueva and Caldería Vieja, teem with teahouses. Atmospheric *teterías* to seek out include **La Casa del Té,** on Caldcrería Vieja 22 (no phone); **Tetería Nazarí,** Caldcrería Vieja 13 (no phone); **Kasbah,** Calderería Nueva 4 (☎ **958-22-79-36**); **Dar Zir-Yab,** Calderería Nueva 11 (☎ **958-22-94-29**); **Tetería Pervane,** Calderería Nueva 24. (☎ **958-22-65-07**); and, one of the newest and nicest, down by the river, **Tetería del Hammam,** Santa Ana 16 (☎ **958-22-99-78**). The best time to go is the late afternoon and early evening, long after siesta hour.

At the bottom of the hill, along the Carretera del Darro at Calle Bañuelo, is **El Bañuelo,** or Arab Baths. One of the oldest Moorish remnants in Granada (built in the 11th century — they predate the Alhambra), the baths are in surprisingly good condition, though they're not as elaborate or as large as those in Ronda (see Chapter 16). The baths (☎ **958-02-78-00**) are open (to take a peek only) Tuesday through Saturday from 10 a.m. to 2 p.m. Admission is free.

Down the street is the **Museo Arqueológico (Archaeology Museum),** in the Casa de Castril, a stately Renaissance mansion. Its exhibits are of interest if you have a great curiosity about Granada's Muslim and Visigothic past, but they may be deadly dull for others.

Museo Arqueológico: *Carrera del Darro 43.* ☎ ***958-22-56-40.*** *Admission: 1.50€ ($1.80), free to E.U. members. Admission is included in the Bono Turístico Granada (see "A monumental bargain" box, earlier in this chapter). Open: Tues 2:30–8 p.m., Wed–Sat 9 a.m–8 p.m., Sun 9 a.m.–2:30 p.m.*

Catedral and Capilla Real

Centro/Cathedral Quarter

Granada's ornate, powerful cathedral was the city's 16th-century Christian answer to the Alhambra, an emphatic statement about the conclusive Reconquest of Spain from the Moors. Leaving little doubt about the succession of power, the Catholic monarchs ordered it placed right in the middle of the Arab *medina* (marketplace). Though it started out Gothic in style, the cathedral wound up Baroque, with five massive naves, thick pillars, and a dramatic altar. In contrast to the airy, delicate, elegant Alhambra left by the Moors, the Christian cathedral is heavy, imposing, and grandiose.

Next door (off Calle Oficios), in the **Capilla Real,** or Royal Chapel, the Gothic marble tombs of the storied Catholic monarchs Ferdinand and Isabella lie behind the flourishes of a black-and-gold grille. When the last Moorish king, Boabdil, surrendered to Christian forces in Granada in 1492, the Catholic monarchs registered their greatest victory and immediately chose Granada for their future burial place. They are interred here along with their daughter Juana la Loca (Joanna the Mad) and her husband, Felipe el Hermoso (Philip the Fair). The chapel museum houses Queen Isabella's crown and Ferdinand's sword, as well as important paintings by Botticelli and others. Allot about an hour at the cathedral and Royal Chapel. On your way out, peek into the **Palacio de la Madraza,** once the

Arab university, directly across from the entrance to the Royal Chapel. Inside is a tiny, but spectacular, *mirhab* (prayer niche).

See map p. 461. Catedral, Gran Vía de Colón 5. Capilla Real, Oficios 3. One block southwest of Gran Vía de Colón. ☎ ***958-22-29-59*** *and 958-22-92-39.* www.capillarealgranada.com. *Admission: Catedral 3€ ($3.60), Capilla Real 3€ ($3.60) adults, 1.50€ ($1.80) seniors, free to children under 10. Admission to both the cathedral and Capilla Real are included in the* ***Bono Turístico Granada*** *(see "A monumental bargain" box, earlier in this chapter). Open: Catedral Mon–Sat 10:30 a.m.–1:30 p.m. and 4–7 p.m., Sun 4–7 p.m.; Capilla Real Apr–Oct Mon–Sat 10:30 a.m.–1 p.m. and 4–7 p.m., Sun 11 a.m.–1 p.m. and 4–7 p.m.; Nov–Mar Mon–Sat 10:30 a.m.–1 p.m. and 3:30–6 p.m., Sun 11 a.m.–1 p.m. and 3:30–6 p.m. Closed: Good Friday, Dec 25, Jan 1 and 2, and the morning of Oct 12.*

More cool things to see and do

Obviously, the Alhambra is the overwhelming reason to visit Granada, but if you have a bit more time, the city affords several other terrific options to get in touch with its complicated Moor and Christian past.

Touring a Baroque monastery

Northwest of downtown is the 16th-century **Monasterio de la Cartuja,** Paseo de la Cartuja, s/n (☎ **958-16-19-32**), which may be even more of a Catholic rejoinder to the city's Arab past than the cathedral is. Bathed in intricate stucco, inlaid marble molding, cedarwood ceilings, wildly painted cupolas, and glittery gold leaf, the Baroque cathedral is anything but subtle. See it after you've already visited the Alhambra; the contrast between the sweet harmony and simplicity of the Nasrid palaces and this ostentatious exercise is startling. The sacristy, with black-and-beige tile floors, mahogany chests, and a spectacle of carved stucco, looks like an optical illusion. To get there, take bus no. 8 or a taxi up Gran Vía de Colón. Hours are Monday through Saturday from 10 a.m. to 1 p.m. and 4 to 6 p.m., and Sunday from 10 a.m. to noon and 4 to 8 p.m. Admission is 3€ ($3.60), but is included in the **Bono Turístico Granada** (see "A monumental bargain" box, earlier in this chapter).

Getting a glimpse of the poet's life

Federico García Lorca (1898–1936), Spain's greatest modern poet and playwright, was born in Granada, and his works bind him eternally to the city and its people. The internationally famous author of such works as *Poet in New York, The House of Bernarda Alba,* and *Blood Wedding,* Lorca was a daring genius whose life was cut short by the Nationalist forces of dictator Francisco Franco. They captured the poet in Granada, took him to a field, and shot him.

Just southwest of downtown, García Lorca's childhood summer home, **Huerta de San Vicente,** Calle de la Virgen Blanca, s/n, is preserved as a museum. It's located within García Lorca Park southwest of downtown, at the end of Recogidas (☎ **958-25-84-66;** www.huertadesanvicente.com). Although the view is now blocked by large apartment buildings, in his youth, Lorca enjoyed unencumbered views of the Alhambra on the hill from here. Adorned with Lorca's art and personal effects — his bedroom and desk, where he wrote *Bodas de Sangre (Blood Wedding),* are almost monastic — it's a fascinating window into the life of one of Spain's greatest and most enigmatic literary figures. The tours are anything but staid house visits — the gentleman who leads the 30-minute walk-through is a Lorca scholar, and he encourages visitors to read from Lorca's works as they wander the house. (A grasp of Spanish helps.)

To get there, you can take a 15-minute walk from Puerta Real down Recogidas; signs indicate a right turn (northwest) to park and Huerta de San Vicente within. Hours are July and August Tuesday through Sunday from 10 a.m. to 2:30 p.m.; October to March 10 a.m. to 12:30 p.m. and 4 to 6:30 p.m.; and April, May, June, and September 10 a.m. to 12:30 p.m. and 5 to 7:30 p.m. Admission is 3€ ($3.60) adults; 1€ ($1.20) students, children under 9, and seniors.

Exploring Sacromonte (while watching your pockets)

The hill called **Sacromonte (Sacred Hill),** northwest of the Albaycín, is famed for its gypsy caves carved out of the earth, touristy flamenco shows, and pickpockets who thrive on visitors to the first two. You can also check out a dilapidated abbey, **Abadía del Sacromonte** (☎ **958-22-14-45**). It's open Tuesday through Sunday from 11 a.m. to 1 p.m. and 4 to 6 p.m. Admission is free. Plenty of people love to wander the streets on the hill, but its residents have earned a reputation for taking advantage of tourists. Therefore, I recommend it with caution, except for fearless travelers; you may want to visit Sacromonte as part of an organized flamenco outing in the evening (ask at your hotel or see "Living It Up after Dark," later in this chapter).

Living the spa life

Maybe your imagination ran wild visiting the ancient Moorish baths or the Alhambra, thinking about the luxurious bathhouse life the sultans must have led. **Hammam Baños Arabes,** Santa Ana 16 (☎ **958-22-99-78;** `www.hammamspain.com/granada`), a Granada spa, does its best to evoke Moorish times with its Arab (Turkish-style) baths. In fact, it has the fountains, colorful, glazed ceramic tiles, and Moorish arches down pat. Clearly, this is not the sauna at your local YMCA. The spa also offers therapeutic massages and a tearoom upstairs. Reservations are required; baths are 16€ ($19) and bathing suits are required.

Shopping the Local Stores

Unsurprisingly, in this town where a Moorish accent remains so pervasive, the best crafts are those inherited from the Arabs, who were superb craftsmen. Look for *fajalauza* (glazed ceramics), wrought-iron objects, leather goods, furniture with inlaid woods, and musical instruments — especially guitars.

Check out two areas first. The **Alcaicería,** right next to the cathedral and Royal Chapel (off Calle Oficios), is the old Arab silk market. Today, it almost entirely showcases goods hawked at tourists, but you can still pick up some interesting Andalusian souvenirs. **The Corral del Carbón,** Mariana Pineda 12 (☎ **958-22-90-63**), an old commercial exchange, is one of the oldest Moorish structures in Granada. Currently it houses a number of artisans' shops. The hours are Monday through Friday from 9 a.m. to 7 p.m., and Saturday and Sunday from 10 a.m. to 2 p.m. You can find similar shops, including most of Granada's antiques stores, in the Albaycín district and particularly along Cuesta de Elvira. Another good street where you can look for crafts, including guitars, is **Cuesta de Gomérez,** leading to Alhambra hill.

For ceramics, check out **Cerámica Fajalauza,** Camino de San Antonio, s/n; or **Céramica Aliatar,** Plaza de Aliatar 18 (☎ **958-27-80-89**). **Artesanía Albaicín,** Calle del Agua 19 (☎ **958-27-90-56**), is one of Albaycín's most dependable places for tooled leather goods. It stocks the obligatory purses and wallets, as well as just about everything else you also find in a Moroccan *medina* (marketplace). **Casa Ferrer,** Cuesta de Gomérez 26 (☎ **958-22-18-32**), is the place for budding flamenco artists to go for authentic, handcrafted Spanish guitars; this family-owned shop has been around for more than a century. If you have the bucks, you can get a fine handmade instrument here (you can also get something more along the lines of a souvenir, for about 250€/$300).

Cava de Puros Eduardo Ruiz, Carretera de la Sierra, near Paseo de la Bomba (☎ **958-22-13-85**), is a smoker's emporium with more than 20,000 Cuban cigars. Granada and its environs have plenty of good puffing places, but remember that you can't bring Cuban cigars back with you into the United States.

Living It Up after Dark

In addition to what I list in this section, Granada usually has a respectable schedule of concert, dance, and theater performances; ask at the tourism office for the current brochure of cultural activities. You can also check out other shows, including pop-flamenco artists and international dance troupes, at the **Palacio de Exposiciones y Congresos,** by the river. For tickets and information, call ☎ **902-40-02-22.**

Flamenco

The Sacromonte barrio is famous, or, more accurately, notorious, for its flamenco *cuevas* — atmospheric, if touristy, live music caves literally carved right out of the hill. Their popularity doesn't alter the fact that they're tourist traps and often nothing more than a well-oiled gypsy con game. You won't see a local anywhere near these places. Their sole purpose is to relieve affluent tourists of their entertainment dollars — by

International song and dance

Granada's big annual music and dance party takes place at unusual theaters, which include some of the city's most wondrous, historic places — the Alhambra, Generalife, Cathedral, Royal Hospital, and San Jerónimo Monastery. The **Festival Internacional de Música y Danza de Granada** (Granada International Festival of Music and Dance) takes place the last week of June and first week of July. Visit the Web site, www.granadafestival.org, for more information. For tickets and reservations, call ☎ **958-22-18-44** or purchase them directly online at www.granadafestival.org/programacompleto.asp or at the festival ticket office in the Corral del Carbón, Calle Mariano Pineda 12.

means both straightforward and shadowy. Don't take cameras or valuables or too much cash, and don't accept or buy any souvenirs or anything beyond what is prepaid on your evening package. Even with those caveats, you can have some fun at the *zambra* shows if you've got a sense of humor and your wits about you.

The shows are pretty interchangeable; most offer package deals that include transportation back and forth to your hotel, one drink, and admission (around 22€–25€/$24–$30; about double that if you include dinner). Granada hotels are well stuffed with Sacromonte fliers, but one to look for is **Zambra de María la Canastera,** Camino del Sacromonte 81 (☎ **958-12-11-83**). This one has a small on-site museum; the hours are Monday through Friday from 4 to 7 p.m., and Saturday and Sunday from noon to 3 p.m. Also look for **Cueva la Rocío,** Camino del Sacromonte 70 (☎ 958-22-71-29); **Cueva la Zingara,** Camino del Sacromonte 71 (☎ 958-22-22-71); **Venta El Gallo,** Barranco de los Negros 5 (☎ 958-22-24-92); and **Cueva los Tarantos,** Camino del Sacromonte 9 (☎ 958-22-45-25). **Casa Juanillo** at Camino del Sacromonte 83 (☎ 958-22-30-94), offers somewhat less touristy, fairly pure flamenco music and decent tapas.

Not in Sacromonte, but downtown, with a restaurant-show and late-night *sevillanas* (informal gatherings of Andalusian dancing and singing), is **El Corral del Príncipe,** Campo del Príncipe 7 (☎ **958-22-80-88;** closed Mon). The nightly 10 p.m. shows at **Jardines Neptuno,** Arabial, s/n (☎ **958-52-25-33**), are probably Granada's best, though they still pale in comparison to what you may see in Madrid, Seville, or Córdoba. Because you'll most likely arrive and leave late, and downtown offers little late-night transportation, I recommend having a taxi take you directly to either of these clubs. If taxis aren't waiting when you emerge, have the clubs call one for you.

Bars and pubs

The Albaycín neighborhood is a lively quarter at night. Check out the picturesque street along the river, Carretera del Darro, where new watering holes continually pop up, complementing interesting old ones. **Bodegas Castañeda,** Cuesta de Elvira 5 (☎ **958-22-22-76**), a hip bar inhabiting old wine cellars, is a great and lively place for tapas and drinks. The bar-restaurant **El Tragaluz,** Nevot 26 (☎ **919-04-70-84**), is a good, relaxed place for talking and occasional theater presentations. Folks with rowdier impulses can pump it up at **Granada-10,** Cárcel Baja 10 (☎ **958-22-40-01**), a cool old restored theater and the city's best *discoteca,* with films and a wide-ranging crowd. It's open until the early-morning hours.

A Side Trip from Granada

From exploring caves to skiing the slopes, if you're hankering to get out of the city, the side trips outlined in this section may be just the ticket.

The Tourism Board of Granada wants you to get out of town. This group is so intent on visitors seeing more of the province than the Alhambra and Albaycín that they'll load you on a bus for free. A tourist bus with an accompanying professional guide carts small groups of visitors (an average of 20) off to destinations outside of the city, such as **Guadix, Alpujarras** (the southern face of the Sierra Nevada), and the **Tropical Coast.** The trips take off in the morning and return to Granada the same day. There's no catch; the only requirement is that you have at least a two-night hotel reservation in Granada (the town). Simply call **Agencia Granavisión** at ☎ **958-13-58-04** and reserve your place.

Guadix: Checking out the cave dwellers

One of Spain's oldest settlements, **Guadix** (*gwah*-deeks) is a place where people still live in caves. The town is perched on a 1,000-foot plateau, and the troglodyte dwellings, called Barrio Santiago, are carved right into the rock — about all you see from the street are a whitewashed front door, a chimney protruding from the ground/ceiling, and a jarring TV antenna. (Cave dwellers want their MTV, too; it looks like every cave is tuned in.) There is an entire neighborhood of *casa cuevas* (cave houses); these oddities (about 2,000 of them) have existed here for half a millennium. On my last visit, I asked an elderly gentleman to show me around his place. He explained that living in a cave was perfect; it was cool in the scorching summer and warm in the mountain winter. If you're shy about asking someone for a peek, visit the **Cueva Museo (Cave Museum)** on Plaza de la Ermita Nueva, opposite the San Miguel church; it does its best to depict how underground people live. It's open Monday through Saturday from 10 a.m. to 2 p.m. and 5 to 7 p.m., and Sunday from 10 a.m. to 2 p.m. Admission is 1.50€ ($1.80).

In town you can also check out a 16th-century cathedral by the same architect who worked on Granada's cathedral. You can visit the Moorish **Alcazaba,** the 11th-century fortress, which is open Monday through Friday from 9 a.m. to 2 p.m. and 4 to 6 p.m. Admission is 1.20€ ($1.50). Or visit the **Mudéjar Iglesia de Santiago** — open Monday through

Saturday from 10 a.m. to 1 p.m. and 4 to 7 p.m., and Saturday from 10 a.m. to 2 p.m. Admission is 1.50€ ($1.80). If you're looking to spend the night or to have a decent meal, check out the rather elegant, turn-of-the-20th-century **Hotel Comercio,** Mira de Amezcua 3 (☎ **958-66-05-00**), which has doubles for 51€ ($61) and a surprisingly good restaurant. For a more unique experience, stay in one of the actual cave dwellings that put Guadix on the map. Some have been converted into aparthotels at **Cuevas Pedro Antonio de Alarcón,** Barriada San Torcuato, s/n (☎ **958-66-49-86;** fax 958-66-17-21; www.andalucia.com/cavehotel/home.htm). Despite the prehistoric look of the caves, which are near the train station and about 1.6km (1 mile) from the cave core of Guadix, the apartments are modernized (if simple) and inexpensive: 57€ to 69€ ($68–$83) for two people. There's even a large pool for the complex.

By car, Guadix is 58km (36 miles) northeast of Granada on N-342. At least six **Autedia** (☎ **958-15-36-36**) buses per day make the one-hour trip to Guadix. The train from Granada takes about an hour (5.25€/$6.30).

Fast Facts: Granada

American Express

Calle Reyes Católicos 31 (☎ 958-22-45-12); open Monday through Friday from 9:30 a.m. to 1:30 p.m. and 4:30 to 7:30 p.m.; Saturday from 10 a.m. to 1 p.m.

Area Code

The area code for telephone numbers within Granada is **958.** You must dial the prefix, even for local numbers.

ATMs/Currency Exchange

Banks and 24-hour ATMs are located on Plaza de Isabel la Católica and Puerta Real.

Emergencies

For general emergencies, call ☎ **112.** For medical emergencies, call ☎ **061.** Call the Red Cross (Cruz Roja) at ☎ 958-22-22-22. For an ambulance, call ☎ 958-28-44-50 or 958-28-20-00.

Hospitals

Hospital Ruiz de Alda is at Av. Constitución 100 (☎ 958-24-11-08); Hospital de San Juan de Dios is on San Juan de Dios, s/n (☎ 958-20-43-00).

Information

Tourism offices are located at the airport, Virgen Blanca 9 (☎ 902-40-50-45), open Monday through Friday from 9 a.m. to 7 p.m., Saturday from 10 a.m. to 2 p.m., and Sunday from10 a.m. to 2 p.m.; Real de la Alhambra s/n, near the ticket offices (☎ 958-22-95-75), open daily from 10 a.m. to 5 p.m.; Santa Ana 2 (☎ 958-57-52-02), open Monday through Saturday from 9 a.m. to 7 p.m.; and Plaza Mariana Pineda 10 (☎ 958-24-71-28), open Monday through Friday from 10:30 a.m. to 1:30 p.m. and 4:30 to 7 p.m., Saturday from 10:30 a.m. to 2 p.m.

Internet Access

Granada has several places where you can check your *correo electrónico* (e-mail). Check out Net, Santa Escolástica (☎ 958-22-69-19), between Campo del Príncipe and Plaza Nueva; open Monday through Saturday from 9 a.m. to 11 p.m. Another place is Navegaweb Café, Calle de los

Reyes Católicos 55 (☎ 95-821-05-28), open Monday through Saturday from 10 a.m. to midnight and Sundays and holidays from noon to midnight. Most places in Granada charge about 2€ ($2.40) an hour. Check with the tourism office before you go, because these places across Spain have a habit of opening and closing at a moment's notice.

Police

For municipal police, dial ☎ **092.** For national police, ☎ **091.** The local police office is at Plaza Carmen 5 (☎ 958-20-94-61).

Post Office

The Central Post Office is located at Puerta Real, s/n (☎ 958-22-48-35). It's open Monday through Friday from 8:30 a.m. to 9 p.m. and Saturday from 8 a.m. to 8 p.m.

Safety

Exercise extreme caution, especially at night, in the Sacromonte district, where the majority of tourist-oriented flamenco clubs are located.

Part VI
The Part of Tens

The 5th Wave — By Rich Tennant

"I think we're close to the village Picasso grew up in."

In this part . . .

I hedge my bets. When people ask me to declare my absolute favorite sight, hotel, restaurant, or cultural experience in Spain — which friends, family, and strangers invariably do — I tend to stammer and stumble. Spain just has so much to offer. So although I started *Spain For Dummies,* 4th Edition, with a personal selection of the best experiences you could reasonably hope to have on a trip to Spain, along with other "best" choices, there really wasn't room to include everything. So I'm taking advantage of these last few pages to throw in a few more. The second list in this part is a collection of curious odds and ends about Spain that are meant to whet your appetite a little more and prompt you to discover for yourself what makes Spain such an intriguing place.

Chapter 18

Top Ten (Other) Can't-Miss Spanish Experiences

In This Chapter

- Dining and drinking in Spain
- Enjoying Spain's festivals and flamenco
- Examining the artistry and history of Spain

In Chapter 1, I give my choices for the very best, or quintessential, Spanish experiences. But in a country as diverse and with as much to offer as Spain, ticking off a top-ten list is much too difficult, so I'm cheating and adding another. These experiences aren't necessarily runners-up; indeed, they're worth seeking out in their own right.

Popping Corks

Oenophiles and casual imbibers alike find that Spanish wines are richly rewarding, not to mention surprisingly affordable. You can enjoy a bounty of red, white, and sparkling wines, as well as unique aperitifs at restaurants across Spain. But for an even greater pleasure, experience local wines in an authentic tavern or tapas joint, where knocking back little glasses of *vino* is a boisterous, popular affair — far from the stuffy atmosphere of wine snobs and rarified cellars. Look for fine vintages from the Rioja, Ribera del Duero, Priorato, Penedès, and Toro wine regions, and sparkling wines from Catalonia called *cava.* Don't forget to sample popular white Albariños from Galicia, and *txakoli* (*cha*-koh-li), a fruity and fizzy white wine drunk in the Basque Country. Have a *fino* or *manzanilla* (dry sherries) in Andalusia. Or blow off all those unfamiliar names and ask for the basic *vino* (*tinto* or *blanco*) *de la casa* — the inexpensive house wine many Spaniards drink. For more details about specific wines and vintages, see the Cheat Sheet at the beginning of this book and Chapter 2.

Braving a Bullfight

El toro, or bull, is a creature of mythic proportions in Spain and a pillar of Spanish popular culture. The bull is central to rituals Spaniards hold dear, such as Pamplona's annual *encierro,* or running of the bulls, and *la corrida,* the bullfight, which has followers every bit as faithful and passionate as soccer does. The life-and-death drama of a bullfight — something aficionados elevate to art and theater rather than mere sport — is a quintessential Spanish experience. But it's not for everyone, or even for most people. It's bloody and it's cruel; death in the afternoon is what you'll go to see, and applaud, when the matador almost inevitably slays the beast. Whether or not you're swayed by such demonstrations of machismo, you're unlikely to forget your first experience of either one. Madrid's Plaza de Toros de las Ventas, Seville, and Ronda are the top three spots to see a *corrida,* with Ronda — home to Spain's oldest bull-fighting ring — being especially evocative. See Chapters 13, 15, and 16.

Feasting on Flamenco

Flamenco dancing is a stunning display of grace and rhythmic fire, and the wail of flamenco *cante hondo* (deep-throated vocals) is a soulful, visceral, people's song unlike any other. You can see a slick and colorful costumed production in any major city in Spain, but the best place to experience authentic flamenco is in a small, dark club in Madrid (Chapter 13), Seville, or Córdoba (Chapter 15 for both), where you'll be among locals as well as tourists and where you can get close enough to see the sweat fly off dancers' arms and feel the hand-clapping and staccato dance steps like a bass drum in your chest.

Making a Gastronomic Pilgrimage to Catalonia or the Basque Country

Spaniards of all stripes love to wine and dine, but nowhere is it such a refined and adventurous art form as it is in northern Spain. The Basque Country has traditionally been the leader of the country's fine dining, but Barcelona and the rest of Catalonia are also now part of Europe's culinary cutting edge. Nothing compares to the culinary artistry of a full-course *menú de degustación* (tasting menu) — a full-throttle dining experience — or a packed bar heaving with *pintxos* (tapas) in the Basque Country. The Basques have developed a level of creativity unmatched in Spain, and their land of Michelin-starred restaurants has represented one of Europe's leading culinary frontiers for more than a decade. Dine in reverence at a celebrated chef's tasting menu in San Sebastián, a city of pilgrimage for gourmands the world over; or behold the magnificence of a Basque *pintxos* crawl in Bilbao. In Barcelona, chic, wildly creative restaurants have sprouted like Catalonia's beloved mushrooms in the Gothic Quarter and in the new port, taking their cues from the celebrated kitchen wizard Ferran Adrià at El Bulli, in Roses on the northern Costa Brava, and from the amazing Roca brothers in Girona. See Chapters 10, 11 and 12.

Succumbing to Moderniste Mayhem

As the 19th century gave way to the 20th century in Barcelona, a creative coterie of architects produced their own take on Art Nouveau, and they produced an incredible number of visionary works of *modernisme.* Antoni Gaudí, Lluís Domènech i Montaner, Josep Puig i Cadafalch, and others changed the face of their native Catalan capital. Getting up close and personal with buildings that still startle today (and make you wonder how they ever got built . . . or almost built), including La Sagrada Familia, La Pedrera, El Palau de la Música Catalana, and the fantastically molded corners of the Manzana de la Discórdia, is a true architectural event. And it appeals to kids and people on whom architecture has never made a big impression before. See Chapter 10.

Disappearing into the Dalí Triangle

Spain's surrealist madman, Salvador Dalí, was one of the art world's biggest superstars of the 20th century. Dalí hailed from rural Catalonia and lived larger than life along the easygoing Costa Brava. A relaxed road trip takes you to the ingeniously oddball museum-cum-theater he designed as his legacy in Figueres, to his idiosyncratic home in Cadaqués, and the bizarro castle he built in true Dalí style for his equally wild Russian wife — and allows you to piece together the home life of a truly revolutionary artist. See Chapter 11.

Partying till You Drop with Madrileños

Spaniards are true creatures of the night, and for plenty of them, a night isn't a true success unless it bleeds into the next day. Perhaps nowhere is the nightlife more exuberant than in Madrid. The capital — where Almodóvar and La Movida got their start — swings like no other city in Spain (or in Europe, for that matter). Its clubs are louder and open later. Whether you're into discos, flamenco clubs, or tapas crawls, you'll find no shortage of people willing to plunge recklessly into the night. As a bonus, when you stumble out of a club with the sun coming up, you can head straight for some chocolate and *churros,* deep-fried munchies that help soak up the alcohol and ward off the hangover. Madrid isn't the only place to go for rollicking nightlife, though. Its perennial rival, Barcelona, runs a very close second, with the waterfront area and atmospheric Gothic Quarter crammed with pulsating bars, pubs, and dance clubs. The stately university town of Salamanca, overrun with Spanish and international students, also really lets its hair down after dark, and its throbbing nightlife is strictly for those who can keep pace. See Chapters 10, 13, and 14.

Appreciating Alternative Views of the Alhambra

Granada's stunning Moorish palace is perhaps the highlight of Spain, and few people dare to miss it on a trip to Andalusia. Although a standard daytime tour with the crowds is memorable, perhaps even more breathtaking is seeing it from another angle. Climb the narrow streets of the old Arab district, Albaycín, and find the Mirador de San Nicolás, which offers a perfect perch from which to view the Alhambra, stunningly framed against the snow-capped ridges of the Sierra Nevada mountains. As the sun goes down, the Alhambra appears lighted from within, glowing an earthy red. Another spectacular way to experience the Alhambra is to visit it at night, when the absence of massive, noisy crowds allows you the privilege of experiencing the palace's softly trickling fountains and silent majesty. See Chapter 17.

Sleeping with History in Spain's Paradores

Ever dreamed of sleeping in a medieval monastery? In Spain, that fantasy can become reality. Many of the country's government-owned *parador* chain of hotels are historic properties housed in ancient castles, convents, and palaces. With thick stone walls and period antiques, you'll get a real taste of Spain's storied history. And although many *paradores* qualify as luxury digs, they're comparatively reasonably priced; most are around 130€ ($156) a night, and they offer great deals for seniors and families. The best *paradores* covered in this book are the Parador Príncipe de Viana in Olite, near Pamplona (see Chapter 12); Parador de Toledo (see Chapter 14); Parador de Carmona in Carmona, near Seville (see Chapter 15); Parador Casa del Corregidor in Arcos de la Frontera (see Chapter 16); Parador de Ronda (see Chapter 16); and Parador Nacional San Francisco, the most sought-after of all the *paradores,* given its incredible location within the grounds of the legendary Alhambra (see Chapter 17). You can even do a *parador*-to-*parador* tour of a region. For more information, see `www.parador.es`.

Going Nuts at a Fútbol Game

Soccer — *fútbol* in Spain — is a near religion. Towns come to complete standstills and nondescript bars are standing-room-only with eager fans watching *el partido* when an important game is on. Seeing a game in person is a classic Spanish experience, but it's fun and pretty relaxed, with plenty of women and children in attendance and, fortunately, very few rowdy hooligan types. Spain's most ballyhooed teams, with the most devoted fans, are F.C. Barça and Real Madrid. Other top teams to check out are Athletic Bilbao, Sevilla, Espanyol, Deportivo La Coruña, and Atlético de Madrid. The season runs from September to June. See Chapters 10 and 13.

Chapter 19

Top Ten (or So) Things You Didn't Know about Spain and Never Thought to Ask

In This Chapter

- Discovering the appeal of fish, wine, and olive oil
- Digging up some tidbits on Picasso, Columbus, and other famous Spaniards
- Figuring out how the Basque people curse (or why they can't)

Maybe it's just a personal quirk, but I often find the odd detail and insider vignette more enlightening, or more telling, than the big picture. If you're looking for more than the standard slide show to enlighten your friends after — or before — your trip to Spain, give these little-known nuggets a whirl.

Olive Oil ¡Olé!

Spain is the world's largest producer of olive oil — a fact that's unlikely to surprise you after you've spent time driving around Andalusia, a land of unending olive groves (see Chapter 16). Andalusia and Catalonia produce so much *aceite de oliva* (olive oil) that the Andalusians sell it to other countries, such as Italy, who in turn bottle it and slyly market it as their own.

More than a Life's Work

Antoni Gaudí, the famed and eccentric Catalan architect who popularized the wildly imaginative, fanciful building style of *modernisme,* dedicated 43 years of his life to building La Sagrada Familia — the legendary, unfinished oddity of a cathedral in Barcelona. During the last ten years of his life, he was consumed by the project's construction and lived hermitlike in a tiny room on the premises until his death, in 1926. (He was run over by a local tram, leaving no blueprints for future architects to use to complete the temple.) At the time, La Sagrada Familia was only about 15 percent completed. After more than 50 years of work, it remains less than half finished. See Chapter 10 for more on Gaudí and the Sagrada Familia.

Calling All Expats in Tight Shorts

The unassuming 2,000-year-old city of Girona is the site of one of Spain's oldest Jewish quarters (El Call), but viewers of the Tour de France, the famously grueling three-week annual bicycle road race, discovered that the Catalan city has another claim to fame: For most of the year, it's home to some pro cyclists, as it was to seven-time champ Lance Armstrong before his retirement. Most of these Lycra-clad folks are Americans who either cycle for Armstrong's former team or for one of the other pro teams that compete in the Tour de France and other European races. Among them were two disgraced American cycling stars: Floyd Landis, who won the 2006 Tour de France but then tested positive for performance-enhancing drugs, and the Olympic gold medalist, Tyler Hamilton, who also tested positive and was banned from the sport. You can often see the riders in their team gear training on the roads around Girona and the Empordá and the foothills of the Pyrenees (followed by team cars and, presumably, their personal doctors). See Chapter 11 for more on Girona and the Empordá countryside.

That's $@#*^!%$ to You, Buster

Euskera, the language spoken by the Basque people of northern Spain, has puzzled anthropologists and linguists for hundreds of years. No one can positively identify its origins. Yet the language is remarkable for another reason: It has no swear words. Even those completely fluent in Euskera have to dip into Spanish when they want to curse their heads off. The Basques themselves have an equally mysterious history. They're one of the oldest ethnic groups in Europe, with a language unrelated to any existing Indo-European tongue, and some theorists believe them to be indigenous Iberians descended from Cro-Magnon man. Others have proposed — not entirely implausibly — that the Basques are the living link to the lost city of Atlantis. See Chapter 12 for more on the Basque region.

Salvador Dalí . . . Bureaucrat?

The surrealist painter-cum-madman Salvador Dalí so loved La Pedrera, Antoni Gaudí's wild apartment house, that he envisioned himself holding public office there. But not just any public office. In his inimitable style, Dalí actually petitioned the Catalan government to create a new "Department of Public Imagination" in the building and to appoint him to oversee it. The government, not surprisingly, rebuffed his proposal. See Chapter 10 for more on La Pedrera, and Chapter 11 for more on Dalí.

Guernica, but Not Forgotten

Pablo Picasso painted his searing black-and-white portrait of war, *Guernica,* in protest of the 1937 Nationalist bombing (carried out by Nazi warplanes) of the small Basque town of that name, during the Spanish Civil War. Picasso refused to allow the painting to be exhibited in Spain until Nationalist dictator Francisco Franco died. *Guernica* remained at New York's Museum of Modern Art, finally making its permanent home in Spain in 1980, after the deaths of both artist and dictator (1973 and 1975, respectively) and the return of democracy to Spain (in 1978). Picasso's masterwork first occupied an annex to the Prado Museum in Madrid; it now has its own gallery in Madrid's Centro de Arte Reina Sofía (see Chapter 13).

Here Lies Columbus — or Does He?

Christopher Columbus's massive coffin sits inside the Seville cathedral, but no one knows whether the great explorer is actually buried there. Disgraced and by no means a hero when he died, his itinerant remains made journeys to Santo Domingo and Havana, before supposedly settling here. See Chapter 15 for more on Seville.

How's That for Heritage?

Spain has more cities designated as UNESCO (United Nations Educational, Scientific, and Cultural Organization) World Heritage Sites than any other country. The eight cities are Segovia, Salamanca, Toledo, Avila (see Chapter 14 for these four), Córdoba (see Chapter 15), Santiago de Compostela, Cáceres, and Cuenca (these last three were left out of this edition for space considerations). In addition to this roster of cities (whose entire old quarters were placed on the list), other World Heritage Sites covered in this book include Granada's Alhambra and Albayzín districts (see Chapter 17); El Escorial in Aranjuez (see Chapter 13); Gaudí's Casa Milá, Parc Guëll, and Palau Guëll, as well as the Palau de la Música and Hospital de Sant Pau, in Barcelona (see Chapter 10); and the cathedral and Reales Alcázares in Seville (see Chapter 15).

That Sounds Fishy to Me

Spain is the world's second largest per-capita consumer of seafood (behind Japan). However, even though Spanish waters produce thousands of tons of seafood each year, it's not nearly enough to feed the Spanish appetite for fish. So Spain, largely through importers in San Sebastián, buys from Norway, France, South Africa, and even South America.

The Original River Walk

Barcelona's famed boulevard, La Rambla, wasn't always a pedestrian-only street — in fact, it wasn't even a street. About 2,000 years ago, when Barcelona was a Roman settlement, the Rambla (the name means riverbed in Arabic) was a mountain stream. In the late 18th century, the stream was gradually filled in; elegant palaces and the city grew up around it.

A Wine Force to Be Reckoned With

The Spanish wine industry has made a lot of noise in the last decade with boutique wineries in Priorat, La Rioja, Ribera del Duero, and fast-rising regions such as Bierzo gaining international recognition. Though Spain still ranks behind France and Italy in terms of wine production and consumption, it has more acreage under vine than any country on earth.

Miss Popularity

Spain isn't hurting for visitors. According to the World Tourism Organization, it ranks second (behind France) in the number of annual visitors — not just in Europe, but worldwide. Spain ranks ahead of and considerably outdraws other perennial frontrunners such as the United States, Italy, and Great Britain on that list. Although Spain's population has hovered around 40 million for decades, it receives more than 50 million visitors annually.

Appendix

Quick Concierge

Fast Facts

American Express

Madrid: Barajas airport, Terminals 1, 2, 4 (☎ 91-393-82-16); Barcelona: Ramblas 74 (☎ 93-342-73-10); Seville: Hotel Inglaterra, Plaza Nueva 7 (☎ 95-421-16-17); Granada: Reyes Católicos 31 (☎ 958-22-45-12).

ATMs

Automated teller machines are widely available throughout Spain. Look for signs that read CAJERO AUTOMATICO or CAJERO 24 HORAS. They dispense currency in euros. You need a four-digit personal identification number (PIN) to withdraw cash in Spain.

Business Hours

Banks are open Monday through Friday from 9 a.m. to 2 p.m. Most offices are open Monday through Friday from 9 a.m. to 2 p.m. and 4 to 7 or 8 p.m. There has been a gradual relaxation of traditional siesta closing hours at midday), but only in the largest cities and tourist destinations — and it's not across the board by any means. Usual shop-opening times are Monday through Saturday from 9:30 a.m. to 1:30 p.m. and 4:30 to 8 p.m. Major shopping malls, department stores, and supermarkets stay open without a break from 10 a.m. to 9 p.m., or in some cases until 10 p.m. On a fixed number of Sundays in the year (approximately 12 in all), the large department stores and supermarkets open to the public. Along the coast, during the high season, shops generally stay open until well after 10 p.m. In restaurants, lunch is usually from 1 to 4 p.m., and dinner from 9 to 11:30 p.m. or midnight.

Credit Cards

The toll-free emergency numbers to call for lost or stolen credit cards in Spain are: American Express ☎ 91-743-70-00; Diners Club ☎ 902-40-11-12; MasterCard ☎ 900-97-12-31; Visa ☎ 900-95-11-25.

Customs

Officially, you're permitted to bring in items for personal use, including a video camera or two still cameras with ten rolls of film for each, as well as a portable radio, CD player, and laptop computer. Sports equipment for personal use (including skis, one bicycle, tennis racquets, and golf clubs) is also allowed. As for booze and tobacco, the maximum allowance per person is 200 cigarettes or 50 cigars or 250 grams of tobacco plus one bottle of wine and one bottle of any other liquor. Don't try to argue that you're bringing in firearms, narcotics, meat, or produce for "personal use" — your excuse won't fly.

Tourists can bring up to 6,010€ ($7,212; including the equivalent in any other form of currency) without declaring the amount in customs. You're required to declare any amount exceeding that total upon arrival or upon leaving Spain.

Drugstores

To find an open *farmacia* (pharmacy) outside of normal business hours, check the list of stores posted on the door of any drugstore. The law requires drugstores to operate on a rotating system of hours so that there's always a drugstore open somewhere, even Sunday at midnight.

Electricity

220 volts AC (50 volts) is common throughout Spain, although some older places may have 110 or 125 volts. Plugs with two round prongs are used in electrical outlets. Carry your adapter with you, and always ask about the voltage at your hotel desk before plugging in any electrical appliance. Traveling with battery-operated equipment is best.

Embassies/Consulates

If you lose your passport, fall seriously ill, get into legal trouble, or have some other serious problem, your embassy or consulate probably has the means to provide assistance.

All embassies are located in Madrid: The United States Embassy, Serrano 75 (☎ 91-587-22-00; Metro: Núñez de Balboa), is open Monday through Friday from 9:30 a.m. to noon and 3 to 5 p.m.

The Canadian Embassy, Núñez de Balboa 35 (☎ 91-423-32-50; Metro: Velázquez), is open Monday through Friday from 9 a.m. to 12:30 p.m.

The Embassy of the United Kingdom, Fernando El Santo 16 (☎ 91-700-82-00; Metro: Colón), is open Monday through Friday from 9 a.m. to 2 p.m. and 3:30 to 6 p.m.

The Republic of Ireland has an embassy at Paseo de la Castellana 46 (☎ 91-436-40-93; Metro: Serrano); it's open Monday through Friday from 10 a.m. to 2 p.m.

The Australian Embassy, Plaza del Descubridor Diego de Ordás 3 (☎ 91-353-66-00; Metro: Cuzco), is open Monday through Thursday from 8:30 a.m. to 1:30 p.m. and 2:30 to 5 p.m., and Friday from 8:30 a.m. to 2 p.m.

Citizens of New Zealand have an embassy at Plaza de la Lealtad 2 (☎ 91-523-02-26; Metro: Banco de España); it's open Monday through Friday from 9 a.m. to 1:30 p.m. and 2:30 to 5:30 p.m.

The South African Embassy is at Claudio Coello 91 (☎ 91-436-37-80; Metro: Serrano), and is open Monday through Friday from 9 a.m. to 1:30 p.m. and 2:30 to 5 p.m.

The following countries have consulates (or honorary consulates) in Barcelona: Australia, Gran Vía Carles III 98, tenth floor (☎ 93-90-90-13); Canada, Calle Elisenda de Pinós 10 (☎ 93-204-27-00); Ireland, Gran Vía Carles III 94, tenth floor (☎ 93-491-50-21); New Zealand, Travessera de Gracia 64 (☎ 93-209-03-99); United Kingdom, Avinguda Diagonal 477 (☎ 93-419-90-44); and the United States, Passeig de la Reina Elisenda 23 (☎ 93-280-22-27).

Emergencies

For general emergencies, dial ☎ **112;** medical emergencies, ☎ **061;** and police emergencies, ☎ **091.** See destination chapters for local fire, police, and ambulance emergency numbers in individual cities.

Health

You don't need any special vaccinations to visit Spain. Although Spain isn't a developing country where you can't drink the water or trust the meat, you should still be prepared by traveling with any prescription medications you need, and above all, drinking plenty of bottled water. Be extremely careful of heat exhaustion, especially in central and southern Spain during the summer.

Information

Tourism information offices (*información turística,* or *turismo*) in every city are identified by a yellow box with a cursive, lowercase "i." See "Where to Find More Information," later in this appendix, for tourist offices abroad; consult individual destination chapters for local information offices. The number to dial for directory information is ☎ **1003,** a service that gives callers information on all national and international codes.

Internet Cafes

In most major Spanish cities you can now find *cafés internet* (or cybercafes) — coffeehouses — or *cabinas internet,* simple storefronts selling Internet access by the hour. Internet cafes and *cabinas* in Spain generally charge 2€ to 3€ ($2.40–$3.60) per hour.

Because new Internet spots are continually popping up and disappearing, your best bet for finding one — other than checking the "Fast Facts" sections in each destination chapter of this book — is to ask at the tourism office in each city. Or, if you want to check online before you go, do so at `www.cybercaptive.com` and `www.netcafes.com`.

Language

The official national language in Spain is Spanish, the third most widely spoken language in the world after Chinese and English. Spanish is spoken in every province of Spain, but local languages, which reasserted themselves with the restoration of democracy in 1975, are the official regional languages in certain autonomous regions. You'll encounter Catalá (Catalan) in Barcelona, Girona, and the rest of Catalonia, and, to a lesser extent, Euskera (Basque) in the Basque Country.

Even if your Spanish is nonexistent, getting by in Spain usually isn't too difficult. People are helpful, and mastering a few key phrases is a snap. The staffs in most hotels and many restaurants and shops speak English. A pocket-sized phrase book is *Spanish Phrases for Dummies* by Susana Wald (Wiley); it has an extensive glossary of both English and Spanish. Also, don't forget *Spanish For Dummies* by Susana Wald (Wiley).

Liquor Laws

The legal drinking age is 18, though it's not uncommon to find obviously underage drinkers at bars and restaurants. Bars, taverns, and cafeterias usually open at 8 a.m., and many serve alcohol until around 1:30 a.m. or considerably later. Generally, you can purchase alcoholic beverages in almost any supermarket.

Mail

Spanish post offices are called *correos* (koh-*ray*-os). In every city you'll find a central post office as well as several branch offices, all identified by yellow-and-white signs with a crown and the words CORREOS Y TELEGRAFOS. Main offices are generally open from 9 a.m. to 8 p.m. Monday through Friday; Saturday from 9 a.m. to 7 p.m.; satellite offices generally have shorter hours (usually Mon–Fri 9 a.m.–2 p.m.; Sat 9 a.m.–1 p.m.). You can purchase stamps at the post office or at *estancos* (eh-*stahn*-kohs, or tobacconist stands — look for the brown-and-yellow sign that reads TABACOS). Rates are divided into four areas of the world, just like telephone calls: the E.U., the rest of Europe, the United States and Canada, and the rest of the world. Airmail letters to the United States and Canada cost .75€ ($.90) up to 20 grams, and letters to Britain or other E.U. countries cost .50€ ($.60) up to 20 grams. Postcards have the same rates as letters. Rates change frequently, so check at the local post office before mailing anything.

Postal service in Spain has greatly improved. Allow about one week for delivery to North America, generally less to the United Kingdom; in some cases, though, letters take two weeks to reach North America. To speed things up, send a letter *urgente* (oor-*hen*-teh, express) or *certificado* (registered).

Maps

For the most part, you'll be fine with the maps in this book and those distributed by the local tourism information offices. If you're driving around Spain, make sure you have a good road map; you can find them at most bookstores and larger newspaper kiosks. To best negotiate the highways and byways of Spain (and for that matter, Portugal), purchase Michelin map no. 990 (for a folding version). Michelin also sells more detailed maps of Spain (nos. 441–446). Most large bookstore chains in the United States (such as Barnes & Noble) stock Michelin maps. Or call Michelin's toll-free order number (☎ 800-423-0485) to order.

Newspapers and Magazines

Most European newspapers are sold on the day of publication and principal European and American magazines are widely available. For Spanish-speakers or those willing to give it a try, the weekly entertainment information magazine *Guía del Ocio* (Leisure Guide) lists bars, restaurants, cinema, theater, and concerts.

Restrooms

In Spain, the restroom is called either a *lavabo, aseo,* or *servicio* (often labeled WC, for water closet). The men's room is usually labeled *caballeros* (or just C), and the women's restroom is labeled *señoras* or *damas* (or just D). The best places for clean, safe public toilets are restaurants and well-lit bars (as a courtesy, order a coffee after using the facilities).

Safety

Violent-crime rates are much lower in Spain than in the United States; although robberies occur, very few of them are by armed attackers. Though terrorism from ETA and to a lesser degree from Islamist groups has received a lot of press, incidents are rare, and, with the exception of the Madrid train bombings in 2004, almost never directed at civilians. The biggest concern for most travelers is pickpockets and thieves breaking into rental cars. If you're careful and take reasonable precautions, you should be able to stay safe and enjoy yourself. Secure valuables in a hidden money bag or belt, and do not leave possessions in open sight in vehicles.

Be especially careful of pickpockets anywhere that's crowded (buses, subways, train stations, street markets). Don't tempt thieves. Leave all your jewelry at home, and don't flash your wallet or valuables. When you aren't using it, keep your camera stowed away in a backpack or other nondescript bag.

In Spain, being physically threatened is rare. If you're accosted, to avoid getting fleeced, just keep moving — and yell a forceful "No!" or "*Socorro*" (soh-*koh*-roh, Help!).

Smoking

Although Spain has earned a reputation as a place where seemingly everyone smokes (in fact, only about one-third of the population does), a new law banning smoking in public places, including on public transportation and in offices, hospitals, and some bars and restaurants, was enacted in early 2006 (similar laws are in effect in Ireland, Italy, and several other European nations). In practice, many Spaniards choose to disregard the law, but smoking is not as prevalent as it was. For now, nonsmoking sections in restaurants are still relatively rare, but expect this to change as Spaniards adapt to the new reality. If you feel strongly about avoiding secondhand smoke, ask establishments if they have a *no fumadores* (nonsmoking) section.

Taxes

A 7 percent value-added sales tax (known in Spain as IVA) is levied on all hotel and restaurant products and services. Visitors are entitled to a reimbursement of the 16 percent IVA tax they pay on most purchases (on a minimum purchase of 90€, or $108). For more information on getting your refund, see Chapter 4.

Telephone

Spain is six hours ahead of Eastern Standard Time. The same dialing instructions apply to sending a fax overseas. From the United States, dial the international access code, **011;** Spain's country code, **34;** the city code, **93** in Barcelona, **91** in Madrid, and so on; and the local number.

The Spanish telecommunications company, Telefónica, is much better today than it was as a state monopoly. Making local, long-distance, and international calls is easy, but tariffs for the last of these remain high — about twice as much from Spain to the United States as the reverse.

To phone home, use these country codes (after dialing the international access code from Spain, **00**):

United States and Canada: **1;** United Kingdom: **44;** Ireland: **353;** Australia: **61;** New Zealand: **64;** South Africa: **27.**

The easiest and most convenient way to place calls is to use phone cards (*tarjetas telefónicas*, tar-*hay*-tahs tel-eh-*phone*-ee-kahs), available in 10€ and 20€ ($12 and $24) denominations. They function like debit cards, and many require you to scratch off a code number and then call a toll-free number before dialing the desired number. Some pay phones accept coins only, but they are fast disappearing (indeed, in large cities you'll be hard pressed to find one). Most accept both phone cards and coins. Phone cards are available at any *estanco* (eh-*stahn*-koh), or tobacconist shop.

Whether you use coins or a phone card, making calls from Spanish pay phones is simple and convenient. You can use *cabinas* (kah-*bee*-nahs; phone booths), identifiable by the big dotted T (for Telefónica) on the side, on virtually every corner and block in cities. I suggest that you pick up a phone card so you don't have to fumble around with coins and keep pumping them into the meter. To make a call, pick up the receiver and wait for the dial tone. The display will say INSERTE MONEDAS O TARJETA, your cue to insert your card or at least .25€ ($.30) in coins.

If you're making a local call, dial the two-digit city code first (even if you're calling the bar across the street, you have to dial the city code, **93** in Barcelona, **91** in Madrid, and so on) and then the seven-digit number — firmly and deliberately. Go too fast, and the numbers may not register. Verify the number you're calling on the display. If you're using coins, a message comes on to warn you that you're running low on phone fuel — an urgent signal to cram some more small coins into the slot. When you're finished with the call, hang up and collect either unused money or your card.

To make a long-distance call within Spain, the procedure is exactly the same because you have to dial the city prefix no matter where you're calling.

To make an international call, dial **00** and wait for the international dial tone. Dial the desired country code, city code, and number. If calling New York, for example, you dial: 00 + 1 (U.S.) + 212 (NY) + 555-5555 (phone number). The number to dial for directory information is ☎ **1003;** for international directory information in Europe, dial ☎ **1008;** for information in the rest of the world, including North America, call ☎ **1005.** An English-speaking operator can furnish callers with information on all national and international codes.

Here are the basic toll-free access numbers you'll need to use your home long-distance calling card for calls while in Spain (make sure you check with your company before going — sometimes the charges are still very expensive). The following numbers will get you to an English-speaking operator: Sprint (☎ 900-99-13); MCI (☎ 900-99-14); AT&T (☎ 900-99-11).

Public telephone offices called *locutorios* are where you can place calls (long-distance and international) with the assistance of a clerk who places the call for you. You have two major advantages when using a *locutorio:* You pay for the call afterwards (although not getting to see how much the call is costing you may not be an advantage), and it's usually infinitely quieter than making a *cabina* call on the street.

Unless it's an emergency, I don't recommend making even a local call from your hotel room. The markup (called a "surcharge") is outlandish — up to several hundred percent. Make a few phone calls over the course of your stay and watch your room bill skyrocket. But whatever you do, don't make an overseas call from your room without a home-country calling card. Even using a calling card, don't be surprised if the hotel tacks on an additional surcharge for making supposedly toll-free connection calls. If they seem ridiculous to you — as much as 1€ ($1.20) per call — don't think twice about arguing the point when it comes time to pay your bill (though you may get nowhere). One thing I've heard about, but never had to deal with myself in Spain, is hotels that block outgoing calls made via other carriers. If you can't get through to one of the access numbers listed previously, ask your hotel if the number is blocked. If it is, tell them you will gladly change hotels — and write every guidebook on the planet to tell them of the hotel's discriminatory policy.

Sending faxes from your hotel can also be ridiculously expensive. Finding an Internet cafe and sending an e-mail if possible is much cheaper.

Time Zone

Spain is one hour ahead of Greenwich Mean Time, or six hours ahead of Eastern Standard Time in the United States. Daylight saving time is in effect from the second Sunday in March to the first Sunday in November.

Tipping

Because a service charge is normally included in hotel and restaurant bills, tipping isn't obligatory. However, it's customary and expected to leave a few coins (about 5 percent of the bill) after service at a bar counter, and 10 percent on restaurant bills. Taxi drivers don't need to be tipped unless one gives you special service. Additional guidelines: Hotel porter, 1€ ($1.20); lavatory attendant, .25€ ($.30); tour guide, 10 percent of the cost of the tour.

Weather Updates

The best source for weather forecasts in Spain, assuming you don't have access to the Internet, is the local newspaper. You need to familiarize yourself with centigrade temperatures, however. The best Web site to consult is The Weather Channel (www.weather.com), which allows you to plug in any Spanish city destination and get a five-day forecast.

Toll-Free Numbers and Web Sites

Major North American carriers

Air Canada
☎ 888-247-2262
www.aircanada.ca

American Airlines
☎ 800-433-7300
www.americanair.com

Continental Airlines
☎ 800-525-0280
www.continental.com

Delta Airlines
☎ 800-221-1212
www.delta.com

Northwest Airlines
☎ 800-225-2525
www.nwa.com

United
☎ 800-241-6522
www.united.com

U.S. Airways
☎ 800-428-4322
www.usairways.com

European carriers

Ireland

Aer Lingus
☎ 800-474-7424 in the United States
☎ 020-8899-4747 in the United Kingdom
☎ 0645-737-747 in London
☎ 01-886-8888 in Ireland
☎ 02-9321-9123 in Australia
☎ 09-379-4455 in New Zealand
www.aerlingus.com

Spain

Air Europa
☎ 888-238-7672 in the United States
☎ 087-02-401-501 in the United Kingdom
www.aireuropa.com

Iberia
☎ 800-772-4642 in the United States
☎ 800-363-4534 in Canada
☎ 0845-601-2854 in the United Kingdom
☎ 02-9283-3660 in Australia
☎ 09-379-3076 in New Zealand
☎ 902-400-500 in Spain
www.iberia.com

Spanair
☎ 888-545-5757 in the United States
www.spanair.com

United Kingdom

British Airways
☎ 800-247-9297 in the United States and Canada
☎ 0345-222-111 or
☎ 0845-77-333-77 in the United Kingdom
☎ 02-9258-3300 in Australia
www.britishairways.com

Virgin Atlantic Airways
☎ 800-862-8621 in the United States and Canada

☎ 0293-747-747 in the United Kingdom
☎ 02-9352-6199 in Australia
www.virgin-atlantic.com

Major car rental agencies

Avis
☎ 800-331-1212 in the continental United States
☎ 800-TRY-AVIS in Canada
www.avis.com

Budget
☎ 800-527-0700
www.budget.com

Dollar
☎ 800-800-4000
www.dollar.com

Hertz
☎ 800-654-3131
www.hertz.com

National
☎ 800-CAR-RENT
www.nationalcar.com

Car rental agencies specializing in Europe (and Spain)

Auto Europe
☎ 888-223-5555
www.autoeurope.com

Europe by Car
☎ 800-223-1516
☎ 800-252-9401 in California
☎ 212-581-3040 in New York City
www.europebycar.com

Kemwel Holiday Auto (KHA)
☎ 800-678-0678
www.kemwel.com

Where to Find More Information

You can get tons of information about all things Spanish, large and small, from the Internet, tourism offices, and travel agents. Remember, though, that almost all of those outfits have a clear financial interest in luring you to their deal or their part of the world, so it's not impartial information.

Getting the official line

The Tourist Offices of Spain, with outposts in several countries, are good places to start. They put out monthly newsletters and have stockrooms full of brochures put out by every regional government and tour organizers, including information on the national *paradores* (a government-operated chain of hotels usually in historic buildings — palaces, former monasteries, and the like). They also have reams of information on Spanish culture and customs, and they operate useful Web sites, www.okspain.org and www.spain.info, with links to all sorts of travel information. You can also get maps of most major Spanish cities and all regions from them.

For the Tourist Office of Spain, from which you can request a standard package with introductory information about Spain, contact:

- **United States:** Chicago: Tourist Office of Spain, 845 North Michigan Ave., Suite 915-E Chicago, IL 60611 (☎ **312-642-1992**). Los Angeles: Tourist Office of Spain, 8383 Wilshire Blvd., Suite 956, Beverly Hills, CA 90211 (☎ **213-658-7188**). Miami: Tourist Office of Spain, 1395 Brickell Ave., Suite 1130, Miami, FL 33129 (☎ **305-358-1992**). New York: Tourist Office of Spain, 666 Fifth Ave., 35th floor, New York, NY 10103 (☎ **212-265-8822**). For all offices in the United States, the relevant Web site is www.okspain.org.
- **United Kingdom:** Spanish National Tourist Office, 22–23 Manchester Square, London W1M 5AP (☎ **207-486-8077;** www.tourspain.co.uk). For tourist information, e-mail info.londres@tourspain.es, and to request a brochure, call ☎ **09063-64-06-30.**
- **Canada:** Tourist Office of Spain, 2 Bloor Street West, Suite 3402, Toronto, Ontario M4W 3E2 (☎ **416-961-3131;** www.tourspain.toronto.on.ca).

The U.S. Department of State offers a consular information sheet on Spain with a summary of safety, medical, driving, and general travel information taken from official Department of State reports. Check its Web site at http://travel.state.gov-travel_warnings.html, or contact the State Department at Overseas Citizens Services, U.S. Department of State, Room 2201 Sea Street, NW, Washington, D.C. 20520 (☎ **202-647-5225**).

Surfing the Web

I've compiled some of the best online resources to Spain (see below). In addition to these, I provide you with other, more specific sites (including hotel Web sites) throughout the book.

The best Web sites to start with are those run by Spain's Department of Tourism and its National Tourist Offices abroad. Turespaña's Web site, www.tourspain.es, is the next best thing to the book you're holding in your hands. Go to the site and click on leisure travel, adventure travel, or business travel. Its News feature has Spain news from around the world, including from London (Londres, with news relevant to U.K. travelers) and the U.S. The A–Z feature has good listings on things like "Accommodations" and "Sun and Beaches," and features a helpful "Temperature Converter" (just plug a Celsius temp in and it comes out in Fahrenheit degrees).

The U.S. Tourist Offices of Spain operate a Web site, www.okspain.org. It has detailed "Before You Go" information (including U.S. air departures).

Logging on to regional sites

For detailed information about Barcelona, try www.bcn.es, www.barcelonaturisme.com, and www.barcelona-on-line.es. You can find information about the Costa Brava and the city of Girona, as well as other parts of Catalonia, at www.cbrava.es and www.catalunya turisme.com. For the Basque Country, try www.paisvascoturismo.net, www.paisvasco.net, or www.euskadi.net. Information on the city of Bilbao is at www.bilbao.net, and the other important Basque city, San Sebastián, at www.donostia.org and www.sansebastianturismo.com. For Pamplona and the rest of Navarra, the address is www.cfnavarra.es. You can find specific information about Pamplona at www.pamplona.net.

Madrid's site, www.munimadrid.es, has been improved and is now available in English. Other sites worth a look are www.descubremadrid.com and www.madrid.org/turismo. The smaller cities in Castile also have their own sites: www.avilaturismo.net, www.segovianet.com, www.infosegovia.com, www.salamanca.es, and www.guiatoledo.com. Andalusia, the region in the south of Spain, has a main site, www.andalucia.org, as well as official sites for individual cities. Information about Seville is at www.sevilla.org and www.turismosevilla.org, Córdoba at www.turiscordoba.es, Ronda at www.ronda.net, Granada at www.turismodegranada.org and www.granada.org.

Some of Spain's greatest hits also have their own Web sites. Pamplona's Running of the Bulls festival tramples the Web at www.sanfermin.com.

Locating hotel and train information

To look into a selection of Spanish hotels, check out the Web sites www.interhotel.com and www.hotelsearch.com. For the Spanish national *parador* system, visit www.parador.es.

For train information, call the 24-hour RENFE information and reservation number, ☎ **902-24-02-02** or visit www.renfe.es.

Index

• A •

• B •

• C •

• F •

• G •

• H •

• N •

• O •

• P •

• R •

• U •

• V •

• W •

• X •

• Z •

Notes